Writing Logically, Thinking Critically with Readings

"Our _real_ first line of defense, wouldn't you agree, is our capacity to reason."

Writing Logically, Thinking Critically with Readings

Sheila Cooper
Rosemary Patton

Longman

New York   San Francisco   Boston
London   Toronto   Sydney   Tokyo   Singapore   Madrid
Mexico City   Munich   Paris   Cape Town   Hong Kong   Montreal

Acquisitions Editor: Lynn M. Huddon
Marketing Manager: Carlise Paulson
Supplements Editor: Donna Campion
Production Manager: Mark Naccarelli
Project Coordination, Text Design, and Electronic Page Makeup: Nesbitt Graphics, Inc.
Cover Designer/Manager: Nancy Danahy
Cover Image: *Ocean Park No. 54,* 1972 by Richard Diebenkorn (American, 1922–1993), oil on
canvas. Gift of the friends of Gerald Nordland. Photo Source: Ben Blackwell. San Francisco
Museum of Art.
Photo Researcher: PhotoSearch, Inc.
Print Buyer: Al Dorsey
Printer and Binder: The Maple-Vail Book Manufacturing Group
Cover Printer: Coral Graphic Services, Inc.

For permission to use copyrighted material, grateful acknowledgment is made to the copyright
holders on pages 725–730, which are hereby made part of this copyright page.

Library of Congress Cataloging-in-Publication Data

Cooper, Sheila
  Writing logically, thinking critically: with readings / Sheila Cooper, Rosemary Patton.
    p. cm.
  Includes bibliographical references and index.
  ISBN 0-321-03803-7
    1. English language—Rhetoric. 2. Critical thinking. 3. Academic writing. 4. College
  readers. 5. Logic. I. Patton, Rosemary. II. Title.

PE1408.C5486 2000
808'.0427—dc21   00-059713

Please visit our website at http://www.ablongman.com/cooper

ISBN 0-321-03803-7

12345678910—MA—03 02 01 00

He who will not reason, is a bigot; he who cannot, is a fool; and he who dares not, is a slave.

—LORD BYRON

A mind that is stretched to a new idea never returns to its original dimension.

—OLIVER WENDELL HOLMES

The vital habits of democracy: the ability to follow an argument, grasp the point of view of another, expand the boundaries of understanding, debate the alternative purposes that might be pursued.

—JOHN DEWEY

DETAILED CONTENTS

CHAPTER 3

CHAPTER 8

CHAPTER 9

PREFACE

Writing and thinking are interdependent skills, each illuminating the other. By adding five sections of readings to the nine chapters that make up the rhetoric, we expand the equation. Reading critically about important issues promotes critical thought and provides a basis for successful written argument. Writing, reading, and thinking are inextricably linked. *Writing Logically, Thinking Critically with Readings* explores and exploits this triad.

Chapters 1 through 9 cover the same material as found in *Writing Logically, Thinking Critically* Third Edition, a more concise text designed for a course devoted to writing and critical thinking with an emphasis on argumentation. With the addition of readings addressing a broad spectrum of timely current issues, *Writing Logically, Thinking Critically with Readings* offers springboards for discussion and subjects for writing assignments and thus provides a more complete text.

Throughout the readings you will find topics for both discussion and writing, with periodic references back to Chapters 1–9 when appropriate. And many of the writing assignments in these first nine chapters can draw on material presented in the readings, especially assignments for written argument in Chapter 4.

The Rhetoric

Chapters 1 through 5, while always keeping critical thinking and critical reading in focus, emphasize writing. Chapter 1, Thinking and Writing—A Critical Connection, introduces the importance of writing persuasively and thinking critically, the role of audience and purpose, and strategies for a successful writing process. In Chapter 2, Inference—Critical Thought, we explore distinctions among inference, fact, and judgment and how they apply to writing and critical reading. Chapter 3, The Structure of Argument, straddles issues of critical thinking and writing logically with a study of how arguments are structured and thus organized. Chapter 4, Written Argument, gives a thorough introduction to written argument with step-by-step methods for selecting a topic, writing a thesis, presenting evidence, and considering all sides of an issue. In Chapter 5, The Language of Argument—Definition, we discuss the nature of language and present definition as it relates to written argument.

Chapter 6, Fallacious Arguments, and Chapter 7, Deductive and Inductive Argument, provide an introduction to informal logic as it applies to reading, thinking, and writing. In Chapter 8, The Language of Argument—Style, we address questions of form and style at the sentence and paragraph level, necessary tools for revising and polishing drafts. You may want to refer to Chapter 8 throughout the course.

Chapter 9, Research and Documentation, covers strategies for developing and researching a topic and documenting sources with emphasis on electronic resources, particularly the Internet. The chapter concludes with a sample research paper, documented in MLA style. While this chapter is not intended to replace the many useful handbooks on the subject, it does serve as a quick reference.

The Readings

The numerous readings in this text will provide you with the material from which to arrive at your own conclusions on significant issues. You will use this material, as well as independent research where appropriate, to construct reasonable arguments of your own. We ask you to join the conversation on critical issues confronting society and affecting us as individuals— freedom of speech and censorship, the ethics of biotechnology, sexual harassment, and relationships between men and women, cyber-dating and same-sex marriage. The various points of view expressed here will inform you and allow you to arrive at your own conclusions. An uninformed opinion, one without substantive support, is without value. These readings will give you that substance so that the conclusions you reach are based on critical reading and thoughtful consideration of an issue in all its complexity.

These readings include many voices in many forms—essays, speeches, editorials, Supreme Court opinions, government reports, Internet postings, excerpts from books, letters to the editor, poems, short stories and a play. This diversity of voice and form reflects the diversity of audience and purpose the writers are addressing. Consideration of one's audience and purpose is a critical step in any writing task, one we discuss in Chapters 1 and 3.

Chapter 14 is a departure from the first four chapters of Part Two in that it focuses not on any issue but on the medium with which we debate the issues: language. Because we are immersed in language—speaking it, hearing it, reading it—it is natural that we take it for granted, not realizing that in and of itself, language is a fascinating subject, both a reflection and a creator of thought and culture. In this chapter we ask you to become aware of language as a subject and to become more skillful in using it, topics we introduce in Chapters 5 and 8.

Throughout the readings, you will find many helpful references to Chapters 1 through 9. These chapters complement the readings, providing you with the skills you will need to write successful arguments. In particular, refer to Chapter 4, Written Argument, and Chapter 9, Research and Documentation, for constructing arguments and researching a topic. Chapter 5 will help you to achieve precision in the use of language, while Chapter 8 offers specific tools for creating graceful and logical sentences and for revising essays. Chapter 2, Inference—Critical Thought, will aid you in critical reading, as it points out the difference between opinion and fact. Chapter 6, Fallacious Arguments, will also contribute to your ability to read critically as it describes the most common fallacies to look for in the arguments of others.

Pedagogy

We include a number of collaborative activities to encourage an interactive approach to learning. Most of the writing assignments, exercises, and discussion topics can, in fact, be approached collaboratively and are designed to invite a broad range of responses that should cover the demands of writing across a diverse curriculum.

We expect instructors to change the sequence of chapters to suit the particular needs of a given class and to select from the broad range of readings, a collection more extensive than any class could cover in one semester or quarter. We have tried to choose lively materials that you will enjoy reading, although there is no denying that some of the selections are quite challenging. We trust that meeting this challenge to read, to write, to join the conversation will prove worthwhile.

An Instructor's Manual is available for teachers who are using *Writing Logically, Thinking Critically with Readings.*

Acknowledgments

As always, we owe many debts of gratitude. We continue to be grateful to our students. They have helped us test, shape, and reflect upon the material, and, with their enthusiasm and their questions, inspired us to grow with them in the rewarding enterprise of writing logically, reading and thinking critically. We are also indebted to those instructors who have commented on our book and helped us improve it: John Bird, Winthrop University; Donna Dunbar-Odom, Texas A&M–Commerce; Mary A. Fortner, Lincoln Land Community College; Julia Galbus, University of Southern Indiana; Toni Glover, University of Texas at Dallas; Chris Grooms, Collin County Community College; Susan Hoyne, Centralia College; Stephen E. Hudson, Portland Community College; Richard Jenseth, St. Lawrence University; Mariann Maris, University of Wisconsin-Milwaukee; Joan Naake, Montgomery College; James Papworth, Ricks College; Rachela Permenter, Slippery Rock University; Catherine S. Quick, University of Texas–Pan American; William E. Sheidley, University of Southern Colorado; Kim Stallings, University of North Carolina at Charlotte; Diane Wahto, Butler County Community College; Annette Wyandotte, Indiana University Southeast; Sally B. Young, University of Tennessee at Chattanooga.

Sheila Cooper
Rosemary Patton

The Rhetoric

CHAPTER 1

Thinking and Writing— A Critical Connection

It is doubtful whether a man [or woman?] ever brings his faculties to bear with their full force on a subject until he writes upon it.

—CICERO

For more than 2000 years, thinkers and writers have commented on the close relationship between thinking and writing. It would hardly seem debatable that to write well we need to think clearly. And the evidence is strong for concluding that writing about ideas can help to clarify them. Taking this notion a step further, many would argue that the act of writing can create ideas, can lead writers to discover what they think. Language, according to many scholars, can give birth to thought, and written language provides a way to refine our thoughts since, unlike speech, it can be manipulated until it accurately reflects our thinking.

Thinking Made Visible

Consider writing then as thinking made visible, as thinking in slow motion, a process whereby we can inspect and reflect on what we are thinking about. As novelist E. M. Forster put it, "How can I tell what I think till I see what I've said?" Roger Traynor, a former Chief Justice of the California Supreme Court, agreed when he spoke of writing and the law:

> I have not found a better test for the solution of a case than in its articulation in writing, which is *thinking at its hardest.*

Discourse doesn't simply convey thought; it also forges it. Language is a two-way street, both expressing and generating ideas.

Writing and thinking, when taken seriously, are not easy—a reality that led painter and critic Sir Joshua Reynolds to comment, "There is no expedient to which we will not resort to avoid the real labor of thinking." And many writers have groaned over the pain of writing. New York writer Fran Lebowitz takes an extreme position on the subject: "Writing is torture. It is very hard work. It's not coal mining, but it's work."

After visiting the Galapagos Islands in the 1830s, evolutionist Charles Darwin wrote to his sister from his ship, the *Beagle*, about the special challenge of reasoning on paper, the kind of writing we emphasize in this book.

> I am just now beginning to discover the difficulty of expressing one's ideas on paper. As long as it consists solely of description it is pretty easy; but where reasoning comes into play, to make a proper connection, a clearness and a moderate fluency, is to me a difficulty of which I had no idea.

The Power of Writing Persuasively

But, while writing and thinking may be difficult, mastery and success in both can be well worth the effort. We live in an increasingly complex society where clear writing is often essential. If we are not able to articulate a request, a complaint, or an endorsement in precise, forceful language, we may find ourselves settling for less than we need or deserve or giving to others the right to impose their decisions on us. If we can't write a persuasive application, the job or graduate school position may go to someone else. Linguist Robin Lakoff, in her book, *Talking Power: The Politics of Language*, puts it this way:

> In a meritocracy such as ours, we believe that those who best demonstrate the ability to think and persuade should have the lion's share of power. Articulateness according to the rules goes a long way; and its possessors are assumed to possess intelligence and virtue as inseparable concomitants. People who say things right, who plead their cases well, will be listened to and their suggestions acted upon. They will make the money, win the offices, find love, get all the goodies their society has to give.

CARTOON REPRINTED BY PERMISSION OF THE DETROIT FREE PRESS.

Our Multicultural Society

It should be noted, however, that in a multicultural society such as ours, there are those who question our singular admiration for persuasive rhetoric, who look to less confrontational means of exploring issues and resolving differences. Seen through the eyes of a Japanese visitor, Yoshimi Ishikawa, who came here at age 18 and spent two years working and observing, the United States is a surprisingly violent nation. In his book, *Strawberry Road,* he claims that "the violent impression that America makes on foreigners is a result not just of its high crime rate but also of the one-sided nature of conversation here." But he too concludes that "the power to persuade and be eloquent are weapons one needs to survive in America." Whether a virtue or a weapon, the power of persuasion is seen as an asset in America today. As you will discover in *Writing Logically, Thinking Critically with Readings,* we are inclined to share both Lakoff's and Ishikawa's views and recognize that if we are to embrace the multiplicity of views represented in our culture we must avoid dogmatic, one-sided advocacy.

Critical Thinking

If, as we maintain, there is a strong relationship between thinking clearly and writing well—if one skill strengthens the other—then integrating the two as a course of study makes sense. But what do we mean by "thinking clearly"? Poets and engineers, marketing experts and philosophers would find any number of differing applications for such a broad term. For our purposes, we have found it helpful to narrow our focus and concentrate on the phrase **critical thinking.** This term has assumed a central position in both academic and public life and is variously defined today.

EXERCISE 1A

Defining Critical Thinking

Before you read further in this chapter, put this book aside, take a piece of paper, and write a few sentences discussing what you think the phrase *critical thinking* means. If you do this in class, you may want to compare notes with other students.

Critical Thinking as Self-Defense

In most contexts today the term **critical** means censorious or faultfinding, but it comes to us from the Greek *kriticos* and Latin *criticus*, meaning able to discern or separate. It is this sense of critical that we have in mind—discerning or discriminating thought characterized by careful analysis and judgment. As student Denise Selleck described it: "Thinking critically is the ability to understand a concept fully, taking in different sides of an issue or idea while not being swayed by the propaganda or other fraudulent methods used to promote it." She recognizes the importance of an open mind and the element of self-defense implicit in critical thinking.

As society and the kinds of work it demands have changed over the past few decades, so has the need for particular job skills. Today, in the information age, people have to know how to think, to think critically and creatively, if they are going to succeed. There are no certainties. We are surrounded by facts, all of which are open to interpretation. Such interpretation requires complex critical thought. And if our democracy is to endure, we all have a moral responsibility to engage in deliberate, critical thinking. How else can we make informed decisions about political candidates and issues?

In his novel, *I Married a Communist*, Philip Roth describes a memorable high school English teacher who taught his students the liberating power of critical thinking. "Cri-ti-cal thinking," Mr. Ringold said, using his knuckles to rap out each of the syllables on his desk top—"there is the ultimate subversion." Critical thinking was his route to opening up young minds and making them strong, by demanding that they question the world around them and recognize the power critical thinking could give them.

Advertising and the media, with which we are confronted every day, require careful critical scrutiny if we are to protect ourselves from false claims, questionable judgments, and confusing or deceptive argument. The cigarette industry, for example, has been particularly persistent in its efforts to entice potential smokers. In the early 1990s, the Philip Morris Company ran what were called by *Newsweek* the "smokeless cigarette" ads, a series showing celebrated public figures endorsing the Bill of Rights, part of the U.S. Constitution. Nowhere did the actual product—cigarettes—appear, either in print or image. These ads were designed for people like you—literate adults. The creators of such ads expected you to apply limited critical thinking at one level—to make the necessary connections—but to suspend such thinking at a crucial point in their seduction.

More recently, the manufacturers of Camel cigarettes had significant success promoting their product among teenagers when they draped billboards and filled their magazine ads with a lively animal character they named Joe Camel. He always looked cheerful, even cool. In the interest of juvenile health, Joe Camel was outlawed in 1998 but not before he had worked his insidious magic on many young people.

As advertising invades ever-increasing corners of our lives, we can be hard-pressed to distinguish information from promotion. Names of public buildings reflect their corporate sponsors. The new baseball stadium in one city was named PacBell Park for Pacific Bell, and you can probably name others in your community. When we go to the movies, we can't tell which is a preview, which an ad for some unrelated product. School textbooks carry advertising as companies reach for young minds. The Public Broadcasting Service, which used to be the one source of advertising-free television, now carries as much advertising as some of its commercial rivals. Television infomercials push new products even as they masquerade as objective information. And our computers, when connected to the Internet, bombard us with an ever-increasing array of products and services for sale.

Even news reporting in reputable newspapers requires intelligent evaluation. Two different papers reporting on a Supreme Court decision illustrate how a message can vary according to the way an editor construes the story. Here's how *The New York Times* opened its article on one of Chief Justice Rehnquist's opinions:

High Court Upholds Buffer Zone of 15 Feet at Abortion Clinics

BY LINDA GREENHOUSE

Washington, Feb. 19—The Supreme Court today upheld a lower court's order keeping demonstrators at least 15 feet away from the doorways and driveways of clinics in upstate New York that were the targets of blockages and boisterous protests in the early 1990s. The decision reaffirmed the Court's broadly protective approach toward maintaining access for patients entering abortion clinics. . . .

On the same date, the *San Francisco Chronicle*, relying on the *Los Angeles Times,* reported:

Abortion Foes Entitled to Confront Patients
Supreme Court Says It's Free Speech

BY DAVID G. SAVAGE
Los Angeles Times

Washington—Abortion protesters have a free-speech right to confront pregnant women on the sidewalks outside clinics and to urge them vehemently
not to go ahead with the procedure, the Supreme Court ruled yesterday.

The 8–1 decision calls into doubt a wave of new city ordinances and
judges' orders that have barred persistent protesters from confronting and
harassing doctors, nurses and patients outside clinics. . . .

The Supreme Court opinion was long and contained a number of different
judgments on various parts of the case. The two papers chose to emphasize
very different features with startlingly different effects. Later in each article, the other issues emerged, but who can tell how far a reader will go in
the morning paper? Headlines and lead paragraphs can be misleading or
emphasize only one element in a complex story.

We cannot be vigilant enough in our efforts to defend ourselves from
those who would deliberately manipulate us for personal gain or those who
may innocently be choosing and packaging our news for us.

> **READINGS:** For examples of advertising, see the ad for
> "The People vs. Larry Flynt" on page 271 and "Symbol-
> ism in Advertising" on page 713.

EXERCISE 1B

Scrutinizing the Media

1. What connection do you think the Philip Morris Company wanted
   you to make between the Bill of Rights and smoking their cigarettes?

2. Explain why an animal like Joe Camel might be so effective in selling cigarettes. If you are not familiar with this cartoon character,
   look back at magazines from the mid 1990s to find a picture of the
   famous animal.

3. Find an up-to-date example of an advertisement in print media that
   seduces the reader by indirect means and explain the methods the
   advertiser uses.

4. What conclusions might you draw about the writers who presented
   the two differing slants on the abortion clinic rulings quoted above?

5. Look for a single news story that is reported in different ways. You may
   watch several TV news broadcasts on the same evening and note dif-

ferences in emphasis. Network news programs may differ from those on cable television or Public Broadcasting Service. Summarize the story and describe how different sources presented the same facts.

An Open Mind—Examining Your Worldview

Another definition of critical thinking that also captures the spirit we hope to foster in this book comes from Richard Paul of Sonoma State University: "the disposition to think clearly and accurately in order to be fair." Like the earlier definition by student Denise Selleck, Paul's suggests the importance of developing an open mind, of listening attentively to the views of others.

It is, however, equally important to be aware of where our views come from. Cultures, subgroups within those cultures, and families within these groups tend to share what is called a **worldview,** a set of assumptions about the world and the behavior of people in it. Without acknowledging that we hold such views, we may harbor prejudices about groups that cloud our thinking and restrict fair judgment. Many of these attitudes grow from the contexts of our lives that we take for granted—the opinions of parents and friends, our ethnic and religious backgrounds. Questioning our personal worldview can be one of the most challenging steps in our growth as critical thinkers.

Where does the weakness in Jennifer's defense lie?

Profile of a Critical Thinker

If we examine the implications of Denise Selleck and Richard Paul's definitions, we can begin to formulate a profile of how a critical thinker might behave. Critical thinkers question their own beliefs and the sources of these beliefs as well as the beliefs of others. They also formulate well-reasoned arguments to support their beliefs, recognize the possibility of change in their beliefs, and express their beliefs in clear, coherent language. As a consequence, critical thinkers stand a better chance of being both fair and reliable in the conclusions they reach and the actions they take and will find themselves better protected from those who seek to take advantage of them.

Sometimes a successful critical thinker must be able to hold two or more opposing views on an issue at once. For example, raising tuition at your college could be the only way to ensure current levels of instruction. Paradoxically, doing so could mean that you and other students would be unable to stay in school. Reconciling such conflicts, thinking through the issues to discover alternatives, can represent a difficult but important accomplishment of critical thinking.

EXERCISE 1C

Your Own Worldview

Try a little self-analysis. Rate yourself according to the following checklist to discover how closely your critical thinking conforms to Paul's definition:

> Do you automatically dismiss positions opposed to your own?
>
> Do you take your own beliefs for granted without recognizing the need for support?
>
> Do you deny that your beliefs could change?
>
> Do you accept public information without question?
>
> Do you recognize that some assumptions based on your worldview need to be critically evaluated?

After you have rated yourself, compare notes with a small group of your classmates and, with their help, start to create a description of your own worldview. This will not be an easy task, but don't be discouraged or feel threatened. Putting such views into writing or even formulating what you think can be a challenge. There is no right or wrong answer here: just a critical exploration of your thoughts discussed with your peers.

This exercise may take the form of discussion or note taking and list making or a short written report of your findings.

Reason, Intuition, and Imagination

The heart has its reasons which reason knows nothing of.

—BLAISE PASCAL

Critical thinking can involve more than logical analysis. The creative imagination adds another dimension. We don't see sharp lines drawn between reason and imagination or rational analysis and intuition but rather an interplay between them. Intuition, imagination, and creativity as well as logic are ways of knowing. Our theory of critical thinking welcomes originality, encourages personal opinion, and considers paradox and ambiguity to be central to thinking and writing well, reflecting the world as we know it. The great French philosopher, Blaise Pascal, quoted above, declared that there were two extravagances: "to exclude reason and to admit only reason." Contemporary biologist Richard Dawkins, supporting this view, claims that scientists must also be poets and thinks that poets are well served by a knowledge of science. Poet John Ciardi found reason inadequate for explaining the natural world:

> Who could believe an ant in theory.
> A giraffe in blueprint?
> Ten thousand doctors of what's possible
> Could reason half the jungle out of being

Sometimes a **metaphor** (a figure of speech that imaginatively implies a comparison between one object and another) can carry, through images and associations, an understanding beyond what explicit reasoning can convey. Writer Zora Neale Hurston, in her autobiography, *Dust Tracks on a Road*, remembers the persuasive power of a mentor's argument for honesty: "Truth is a letter from courage." The image contributes to the point she is making.

Audience and Purpose

A major distinction between writing outside the classroom and writing for a class lies in the audience to whom we write, what novelist and essayist Virginia Woolf referred to as "the face beneath the page." Job-related writing tasks, for example, include a designated audience and a real purpose. An employee may write to a superior requesting a raise or to another company proposing a cooperative venture. Readers of a newspaper often express their opinions in persuasive letters to the editor, and many a college student has depended on familiarity with the audience and careful manipulation of circumstance to explain a poor grade to parents. But in a class, students are asked to write papers for the teacher to critique and grade, usually with no specified purpose beyond successfully completing an assignment. Teachers cannot remove themselves from the role of ultimate audience, but for most of the major writing assignments in this text we have suggested an additional audience to lend some authenticity to each project.

Although different academic disciplines require variations in format, all good writing of an explanatory or persuasive nature is built on a balance between three essential elements: knowledge of the subject or argument, an identified audience, and a clearly defined purpose. The task of thinking through an argument, the audience, and the purpose for the writing introduces a significant critical thinking component to an assignment. Only when you take a conscious rhetorical stance toward your writing, can you have an appropriate voice and give power to what you write. The goal for you, therefore, is to define your subject or argument, identify your audience, determine your purpose in writing to this particular audience, and thus establish a tone that fits the writing task. You will be aiming for a balance between you, the writer, and the audience you are hoping to inform or persuade.

For example, suppose you have found that the college preparation provided by your high school was clearly inadequate. You have decided to take steps to remedy the situation. You will have to write letters to several different people explaining your concerns, citing supporting examples, and suggesting possible solutions. You know the issues and your purpose is clear: explaining a problem and calling for action. But the tone of your letters will vary according to your audience. The language you choose and the emphasis of your argument will be different when you direct your argument to a classmate for support; to your high school principal and teachers expressing your concerns; and to local, state, and national political representatives asking for help in the improvement of secondary education. For more on the relationship between writer and audience, see the section on *Rogerian Strategy* in Chapter 4.

WRITING ASSIGNMENT 1

Considering Your Audience

Choose any public issue that disturbs you—be it small or large, campus, community, or cosmic—and write *two* short papers (one-and-a-half to two pages *each*) expressing your concern.

1. In the first version, direct your writing to someone connected to, perhaps responsible for, the problem you are concerned about. Your purpose here is to communicate your concern or displeasure and possibly persuade the person responsible to take appropriate action.

2. In the second version, address an individual who is in no way connected to the problem you are disturbed about. Your purpose here is to explain the situation and to inform your reader of something he may know nothing about and is not necessarily in a position to change.

Label the two papers at the top (*1*) and (*2*) and clearly identify each audience.

> **READINGS:** For another opportunity to consider audience, see "A Mother's Name" on page 640 and the assignment which follows.

Writing as a Process

Where do you begin when faced with a writing assignment? Many students turn to the five-paragraph essay format—introduction, three supporting paragraphs, and conclusion—and choose material that will fit easily into this preconceived mold. Writers rely on this formula because they fear that without it they will produce an incoherent essay. They assume that if they follow it, their writing will at least be organized. Even inexperienced writers must learn to let go of this "safety net" because although it may save them from anxiety and a disorganized essay, it can also determine the content of the essay; if an idea does not fit easily into the mold, the writer must discard it. This rigid structure prevents writers from exploring their topic, from following thoughts that may lead to interesting insights, and from allowing the material, the content, to find the shape that best suits it.

The most common misconception that student writers have is that a good writer is one who sits at his desk and produces in one sitting a polished, mechanically correct, cohesive piece of writing. If students are unable to do this, they conclude that they cannot write and approach all writing tasks with dread and apprehension. As a first step toward improving their writing, students must discard this myth and replace it with a realistic picture of how writers write. Hemingway, in Paris in the 1920s writing his first collection of short stories, *In Our Time*, spent whole mornings on single paragraphs. French novelist Gustave Flaubert, who wrote *Madame Bovary*, would spend a day finding *le mot juste*, the right word. While no one expects students, whose goal it is to produce a competent essay or report rather than a literary masterpiece, to spend this kind of time on their writing, students must realize that writing is a complex intellectual act, that it involves many separate tasks, and that the mind is simply not able to handle all of these tasks at once. It is unrealistic to expect that it should.

As writer Henry Miller saw it, "Writing, like life itself, is a voyage of discovery." Let's look at the distinct tasks involved in the act of writing a paper, in this voyage of discovery:

Generating ideas

Focusing a topic

Establishing a thesis

Organizing the essay

Organizing paragraphs

Providing transitions between sentences and paragraphs

Polishing sentences for fluency

Choosing appropriate diction (word choice)

Correcting grammar, usage, spelling, and punctuation

Each of these tasks could, of course, be broken down further. What is the solution to this problem, this mental overload that writing forces on us? The answer is that it must be done in stages.

Writing is a process that breaks down into roughly three stages—creating, shaping, and correcting. A common error students make is to focus their energy on what should be the last stage (correcting) at the beginning, when the focus should be on the creative stage of the writing process. The effect of this misplaced attention is to inhibit creative thinking. It is essential that the writer give ample time to the first stage, to generating ideas, to following impulsive thoughts even if they may initially appear unrelated or irrelevant. At this stage a writer must allow himself to experience confusion, to be comfortable with chaos; he must learn to trust the writing process, to realize that out of this chaos a logical train of thought will gradually emerge. Most important of all, writers must learn to suspend all criticism as they explore their topic and their thinking.

Strategies for Generating Ideas

Two concrete methods for beginning this exploration of your topic are brainstorming and freewriting, one or both of which you may already be familiar with.

To **brainstorm,** simply put the topic of the writing assignment at the top of a blank piece of paper or your screen. Then jot down words or phrases that come to mind as you think about this topic—as many words as possible even if you are not sure they relate directly to the topic. After brainstorming, look at your list: Circle ideas that you want to develop, draw lines through those that are decidedly unrelated or uninteresting, and draw arrows or make lists of ideas that are connected to one another. At this point you should be able to go to the next stage, organizing your essay either by writing an outline or simply by listing main points that you want to develop into paragraphs. Brainstorming is particularly effective with two or more people.

In **freewriting,** you begin by writing your topic on a blank sheet, but instead of jotting down words and phrases, you write continuously, using sentences. These sentences do not have to be mechanically correct, nor do they have to be connected. The only rule of freewriting is that you may not stop writing; you may not put down your pen or leave the keyboard for a set length of time. After freewriting for five to ten minutes if writing by hand, or longer if using a computer, read over your freewriting, circling ideas that you find interesting or insightful. Now you may do another freewriting on the idea or ideas you have circled, or you may try to formulate a thesis or list ideas you want to develop.

Both of these methods have two things in common. They are relatively painless ways to begin the writing process, and they allow you to circumvent your own worst enemy, your self-criticism, the voice that says, "That's not right," "That's not what I mean," "This doesn't make sense." Critical evaluation of your writing is necessary but inappropriate and self-defeating if you are critical at the beginning. In addition, freewriting may offer surprising access to ideas you never knew you had.

EXERCISE 1D

Generating Ideas

1. Choose an issue that is currently causing concern on your campus or in your community. Following the process discussed above, brainstorm as many ideas as possible on this topic. If others in your class agree on a shared topic, brainstorm together in groups of three or four, with one person acting as scribe or note-taker. After ten or fifteen minutes, go through your list of ideas and put them into some form of organized sequence that could later help give shape to a paper on the issue. Remember that you may have to discard some details that don't seem relevant. None of your points will be adequately developed yet.

2. As an alternative to brainstorming or as a follow-up, take a separate sheet of paper and freewrite for ten minutes on the issue. Then, in

preparation for a paper, read over your writing and circle or under-line ideas that would contribute to an essay.

These steps are offered here as practice for Writing Assignment 1. We suggest you try them on assignments throughout this text. If, in this exercise, you have identified a different topic but one that interests you, keep these preliminary steps. They may fit a longer paper later.

The First Draft

After exploring your topic in this way and examining your data if you have done research, you will have a sense of what you want to say and will be ready for a first draft. If your paper requires research, consult Chapter 9, "Research and Documentation," both before you start the process and again later when you are ready for the "polishing" stage discussed below.

Successful writer Anne Lamott, in her book about writing, *Bird by Bird: Some Instructions on Writing and Life*, discusses the role of first drafts. Her advice grew out of her own experience as a writer and from writing classes she has taught. The title refers to a family story in which her brother, when 10 years old, was overwhelmed by a school report on birds that had been assigned three months earlier and was now due. Their father, a professional writer, put his arm around his almost weeping son and counseled, "Bird by bird, buddy. Just take it bird by bird." Good advice for writing and for life. See if you can start treating your first drafts as what Lamott calls "the child's draft" in the excerpt from her book which follows.

> Now, practically even better news than that of short assignments is the idea of shitty first drafts. All good writers write them. This is how they end up with good second drafts and terrific third drafts. People tend to look at successful writers, writers who are getting their books published and maybe even doing well financially, and think that they sit down at their desks every morning feeling like a million dollars, feeling great about who they are and how much talent they have and what a great story they have to tell; that they take in a few deep breaths, push back their sleeves, roll their necks a few times to get all the cricks out, and dive in, typing fully formed passages as fast as a court reporter. But this is just the fantasy of the uninitiated. I know some very great writers, writers you love who write beautifully and have made a great deal of money, and not *one* of them sits down routinely feeling wildly enthusiastic and confident. Not one of them writes elegant first drafts. All right, one of them does, but we do not like her very much. We do not think that she has a rich inner life or that God likes her or can even stand her. (Although when I mentioned this to my priest friend Tom, he said you can safely assume you've created God in your own image when it turns out that God hates all the same people you do.)

Very few writers really know what they are doing until they've done it. Nor do they go about their business feeling dewy and thrilled. They do not type a few stiff warm-up sentences and then find themselves bounding along like huskies across the snow. One writer I know tells me that he sits down every morning and says to himself nicely, "It's not like you don't have a choice, because you do—you can either type or kill yourself." We all often feel like we are pulling teeth, even those writers whose prose ends up being the most natural and fluid. The right words and sentences just do not come pouring out like ticker tape most of the time. Now, Muriel Spark is said to have felt that she was taking dictation from God every morning—sitting there, one supposes, plugged into a Dictaphone, typing away, humming. But this is a very hostile and aggressive position. One might hope for bad things to rain down on a person like this.

For me and most of the other writers I know, writing is not rapturous. In fact, the only way I can get anything written at all is to write really, really shitty first drafts.

The first draft is the child's draft, where you let it all pour out and then let it romp all over the place, knowing that no one is going to see it and that you can shape it later. You just let this childlike part of you channel whatever voices and visions come through and onto the page. If one of the characters wants to say, "Well, so what, Mr. Poopy Pants?," you let her. No one is going to see it. If the kid wants to get into really sentimental, weepy, emotional territory, you let him. Just get it all down on paper, because there may be something great in those six crazy pages that you would never have gotten to by more rational, grown-up means. There may be something in the very last line of the very last paragraph on page six that you just love, that is so beautiful or wild that you now know what you're supposed to be writing about, more or less, or in what direction you might go—but there was no way to get to this without first getting through the first five and a half pages.

The Time to Be Critical

In agreement with Anne Lamott, teacher and writer Donald Murray, in an essay on revision entitled "The Maker's Eye," points out a key difference between student writers and professional writers:

> When students complete a first draft, they consider the job of writing done— and their teachers too often agree. When professional writers complete a first draft, they usually feel that they are at the start of the writing process. When a draft is completed, the job of writing can begin.

The time to be critical arrives when you have a complete draft. Now is the time to read with a critical mind, trusting your instinct that if a word, a sentence, or a passage seems unclear or awkward to you, your reader will most likely stumble over the same word, sentence, or passage. You are ready to reshape your first draft, adding and deleting ideas, refining your thesis, polishing sentences for fluency, and finally writing another draft. Writer

Zora Neale Hurston described the process as "rubbing your paragraphs with a soft cloth."

Hurston didn't have the advantage of a word processor with which to move words, sentences, and paragraphs around freely. Sometimes the writing of the first draft will tell you when you need to do a little more research, expand your explanation of a point, or check some of your facts to be sure of your evidence. Computers make it relatively easy to revise your work and make repeated drafts.

Finally, you will be ready to check your spelling (in the dictionary or with a computer spell check) and your punctuation (in an English handbook; to date, computer grammar checks have been disappointing) and to read your essay aloud to yourself or to a friend, always ready to write another draft if it becomes necessary.

Every stage in the writing process is important, and each must be given its due. To slight one is to limit the success of the final product. There are exceptions of course. Some writers are able to compress some of these steps, to generate and organize ideas before ever putting pen to paper. But for most of us, successful writing results from an extended writing process that is continually recursive.

A caution: The danger in the way we have described the writing process is that we make it seem as though it progresses in three neat steps, that it proceeds in a linear fashion from prewriting to writing to rewriting and correction. In fact, this process is messy. You may be editing the final draft when you decide to add a completely new paragraph, an idea that didn't exist in any of the previous drafts. Nevertheless, if you realize that writing involves many separate tasks, that it is chaotic and unpredictable, you will not be defeated before you begin by criticizing yourself for having to do what all writers do—struggle to find your way, to express your thoughts so that you and your reader understand them.

In the following poem, Richard Wilbur describes this struggle.

THE WRITER

In her room at the prow of the house
Where light breaks, and the windows are tossed with linden,
My daughter is writing a story.

I pause in the stairwell, hearing
From her shut door a commotion of typewriter-keys
Like a chain hauled over a gunwale.

Young as she is, the stuff
Of her life is a great cargo, and some of it heavy:
I wish her a lucky passage.

But now it is she who pauses,
As if to reject my thought and its easy figure.
A stillness greatens, in which

The whole house seems to be thinking,
And then she is at it again with a bunched clamor
Of strokes, and again is silent.

I remember the dazed starling
Which was trapped in that very room, two years ago;
How we stole in, lifted a sash

And retreated, not to affright it;
And how for a helpless hour, through the crack of the door,
We watched the sleek, wild, dark

And iridescent creature
Batter against the brilliance, drop like a glove
To the hard floor, or the desk-top,

And wait then, humped and bloody,
For the wits to try it again; and how our spirits
Rose when, suddenly sure,

It lifted off from a chair-back,
Beating a smooth course for the right window
And clearing the sill of the world

It is always a matter, my darling,
Of life or death, as I had forgotten. I wish
What I wished you before, but harder.

EXERCISE 1E

Understanding Metaphor

Consider this poem for a few minutes. To what two things does Wilbur compare the writing process? What do these metaphors say about his view of the writing process? Identify and explain a metaphor that describes your own writing process.

As pointed out on page 9, metaphors can provide a vivid means of probing and revealing ideas. The creative thinking we do when we compare one thing to another can lead to new understanding. When we think creatively about our writing process, we are likely to *see* our writing in fresh and instructive ways.

> **READINGS:** For further discussion of metaphor, read "Metaphor, Simile, Personification" on page 694, "Concepts We Live By" on page 696, and "Fighting for Our Lives" on page 698.

"I was on the cutting edge. I pushed the envelope. I did the heavy lifting. I was the rainmaker. Then I ran out of metaphors."

One Writer's Process

Let us add to Lamott's suggestions and Wilbur's poem a description of the writing process that produced this section of Chapter 1.

Day 1:

I spent two hours at the computer writing on the topic, "writing as a process." During this freewriting, my goal was to say everything I could think of on this subject that was important for students to know. Most of the paragraphs were focused on one point, but there were no transitions between sentences and paragraphs, and most of the sentences were only an approximation of the ideas I was trying to express. As I typed, I jotted down ideas which I wanted to include but which at the moment were interrupting the idea I was currently working on. I gave no thought to punctuation or spelling. Getting ideas on paper was my top priority.

Day 2:
I printed a copy of the three pages of freewriting I had done the previous day and spent three hours revising: eliminating, adding, and moving passages; providing transitions; and rephrasing most of the sentences.

Day 3:
I spent one hour polishing my sentences but made no major additions or deletions in the content.

Day 4:
I spent one last hour on a final review of my sentences, revising only a few of them. I checked my spelling with the help of a computer program, which indeed turned up several misspellings.

As you can see, it took a total of seven hours to write three single-spaced, typed pages that will take most readers ten minutes to read. And still I was not finished. The next step was to give this draft to my coauthor, who made further revisions. In Chapter 8, you will find an entire Writing Assignment devoted to revising one of the essays you considered finished. As Donald Murray notes in his essay on revision, "Most readers underestimate the amount of rewriting it usually takes to produce spontaneous reading." But we can take heart from novelist Kurt Vonnegut: "This is what I find most encouraging about the writing trades: They allow mediocre people who are patient and industrious to revise their stupidity, to edit themselves into something like intelligence."

WRITING ASSIGNMENT 2

Your Writing Process

Write an essay in which you discuss your writing experiences and yourself as a writer. Describe in some detail your writing process, what you consider your strengths and weaknesses as a writer, and conclude with your thoughts about the value of writing well.

Audience

Your primary audience for this assignment is your instructor, but you will also be an audience as you write your way to an understanding of yourself as a writer.

Purpose

To inform your instructor about your writing experiences and to gain insight into your individual writing process.

He or She?

You will notice that in our references to a writer or a student in this text, we alternate between female and male designations. This reflects not arbitrary choice but one of the ways writers today resolve the problem posed by the lack of a gender-neutral pronoun for the third person singular. This deficiency in our language reflects more than a simple inconvenience. The way we use language—the choices we make, the emphasis we place—suggests a broad range of personal and community attitudes, a worldview, conscious and subliminal. A world described only in terms of masculine references assumes a world dominated by men. It is not surprising that as women began to share the public worlds of business, politics, medicine, art, and sport, the universal *he, him, his,* without the balance of *she, her, hers,* presented a bruising contradiction and a linguistic dilemma for writers and public speakers. Women were no longer willing to seem invisible.

Attempts to invent a new singular pronoun comparable to the helpful plural "they" to solve this problem have so far failed. In the meantime we are left with a number of choices. We must choose carefully on the basis of audience, purpose, circumstance, context, and, ultimately, personal inclination, all the time recognizing the implications of our choice.

Often we can use a plural noun to which the all-purpose plural pronouns—they, their, them—refer:

> *Writers* need to be aware of *their* audience when choosing language.

But when the noun we are referring to is singular, we have various choices:

> *Each* writer must consider the audience when revising *his or her* [*his/her*] paper.
>
> First, *he or she* [*she/he, s/he*] must decide how much background information the particular audience will need.
>
> First, *he* must decide how much background information the particular audience will need. [This represents the traditional use of "he" as a referent for both males and females.]

"You'll just love the way he handles."

First, *she* must decide how much background information the particular audience will need. [This choice redresses centuries of exclusion.]

Or we can sometimes drop the pronoun:

Each writer must consider the audience when revising a paper. [A simplification of " . . . when revising his/her paper."]

Many readers object to the awkwardness that multiple pronouns create in the flow of a sentence. But others are offended by the implicit sexism of relying exclusively on the third person masculine pronoun [*he, him, his*].

The crucial point is to be sensitive to the audience and aware of the power of language, while at the same time observing conventions of written English as closely as possible.

> **READINGS:** For more on the connection between language and identity, see "What's in a Name" on page 621.

What You Can Expect from This Book

More Than One Approach

We explore a variety of strategies for expanding both writing and thinking skills, emphasizing the symbiotic relationship between them. We propose no formulas, no quick solutions. Rather, we view the development of each as a process that can take different turns for different people according to the occasion for writing. Reflecting our views on this diversity, the writing assignments throughout this book aim to avoid rigid adherence to form. Contrary to the advice of many writing texts, assignments in real life are not limited to prescribed numbers of paragraphs or a required sequence of parts. Essays or reports, whether explanatory or persuasive, should be designed to communicate a writer's ideas in such a way that the writer's purpose is clear and logical and satisfies the needs of a particular audience or discipline.

Collaboration

With your instructor, you can work out collaborative approaches to many exercises and writing assignments. You will find that the more opportunities you have to work with classmates, the clearer your thinking is likely to become, and the more likely it will be that the assignments reflect the writing and problem solving you will encounter in all academic disciplines and in the working world. Writing in the workplace more often than not requires collaboration with others. (This text, written by two authors, represents an example of such a collaboration.)

Sharpening Sentence Skills

Throughout many of the chapters, you will find practice in sentence-building skills, simple review for some of you, new strategies for others. Ideas tend to travel in sentences, and the greater the fluency of your sentences, the better equipped you will be to express complex reasoning in cohesive, logical prose. This is not a handbook of grammar and usage, but rather a carefully sequenced selection of rhetorical strategies selected to complement particular topics and issues. The logical relationships between ideas in a sentence and techniques for creating coherence come in Chapters 3 and 4. More on coherence and sentence development with appositives, verbal modifiers, and parallel structure comes in Chapter 8, as do other refinements of style such as sentence focus with concrete subjects and active verbs. These sentence skills may also be addressed on an individual basis as the need arises, not necessarily in the sequence given.

Enjoying the Challenge of Thinking and Writing

In his poem *The Four Quartets,* T. S. Eliot writes of the "intolerable wrestle / With words and meaning." But before you conclude that this whole enterprise is to be a bleak struggle, let us assure you that our goal is quite the contrary. Systematic thinking can be an exciting adventure. Polishing your prose to convey your ideas precisely and logically can be enormously satisfying. Writer Isaac Asimov expresses such an outlook well:

> Thinking is the activity I love best, and writing to me is simply thinking through my fingers.

Our expectations are broad and flexible. What we ask is that you reflect on your ideas, support your opinions, and practice writing about them with care. We hope to foster fair and independent thinking, a capacity for empathy, and the ability to advocate your own ideas logically and fluently.

KEY TERMS

brainstorming   unrestrained, spontaneous generation of ideas

critical thinking   discerning or discriminating thought characterized by fairness, openmindedness

freewriting   unrestrained, spontaneous, continuous generation of complete sentences for a set length of time

metaphor   figure of speech that imaginatively implies a comparison between one object and another

worldview   a set of assumptions about the world and the behavior of people in it

CHAPTER 2

Inference—Critical Thought

THE FAR SIDE   By GARY LARSON

© 1981 FarWorks, Inc. All Rights Reserved

Question

What do you infer from this cartoon?

Answer

As the evidence suggests, someone, we don't know who, jumped on his or her pogo stick and out the window of a very tall apartment building, meeting a gruesome fate. Though we do not see this unfortunate event, we see the opened box labeled "POGO STICK" and the marks of the stick on the floor leading to the broken window. On the basis of these observations, we infer what must have happened. But it is important to note, however, that we do not see an individual on a pogo stick jumping through a window; instead, we see evidence indicating that this is the case. We make an inference.

What Is an Inference?

An inference is a conclusion about the unknown made on the basis of the known. We see a car beside us on the freeway with several new and old dents; we infer that the driver must be a bad one. A close friend hasn't called in several weeks and doesn't return our calls when we leave messages; we infer that she is angry with us. Much of our thinking, whether about casual observations or personal relationships, involves making inferences. Indeed, entire careers are based on the ability to make logical inferences. In *Snow Falling on Cedars,* a contemporary novel by David Guterson, a coroner describes his job.

> It's my job to infer. Look, if a night watchman is struck over the head with a crowbar during the course of a robbery, the wounds you're going to see in his head will look like they were made with a crowbar. If they were made by a ball-peen hammer you can see that, too—a ball-peen leaves behind a crescent-shaped injury, a crowbar leaves, well, linear wounds with V-shaped ends. You get hit with a pistol butt, that's one thing; somebody hits you with a bottle, that's another. You fall off a motorcycle at 40 miles an hour and hit your head on gravel, the gravel will leave behind patterned abrasions that don't look like anything else. So yes, I infer from the deceased's wound that something narrow and flat caused his injury. To infer—it's what coroners do.

How Reliable Is an Inference?

The reliability of inferences covers an enormous range. Some inferences are credible, but inferences based on minimal evidence or on evidence that may support many different interpretations should be treated with skepticism. In fact, the strength of an inference can be tested by the number of different explanations we can draw from the same set of facts. The greater the number of possible interpretations, the less reliable the inference.

In the cartoon, given the marks made by the pogo stick and the broken window, we cannot arrive at any other inference but that the person on the pogo stick went out the window. But the inferences drawn in the other two cases are not as reliable. The driver of the dented car may not be the owner: She may have borrowed the car from a friend, or she may own the car but have recently bought it "as is." Our friend may not have called us for a number of reasons: a heavy work schedule, three term papers, a family crisis. She may not have received our messages. These alternate explanations weaken the reliability of the original inferences. Clearly, the more evidence we have to support our inferences and the fewer interpretations possible, the more we can trust their accuracy.

THE LANGUAGE OF INFERENCE

The verbs to infer and to imply are often confused, but they can be readily distinguished.

 to imply: To suggest, indicate indirectly, hint, intimate; what a writer, speaker, action, or object conveys.

 to infer: To arrive at a conclusion by reasoning from facts or evidence; what a reader, listener, or observer determines or concludes.

 A writer, speaker, action, or object implies something, and readers, listeners, or observers infer what that something is. A final distinction: Only *people* can make inferences; *anything* can imply meaning.

I infer from what yo imply

EXERCISE 2A

Interpreting a Cartoon

Quickly determine the message the following cartoon implies. What inferences do you draw from the evidence given? After writing a short response, compare your interpretation with those of others in the class. Are they the same?

What Is a Fact?

We make inferences based on our own observations or on the observations of others as they are presented to us through speech or print. These observations often consist of **facts, information that can be verified.** Marks on the floor lead to a broken window. We see dents in the car. You have not spoken to your friend in several weeks. "A crowbar leaves linear wounds with V-shaped ends." Our own observations attest to the truth of these claims. But often we are dependent on others' observations about people, places, and events that we cannot directly observe. Take, for example, the claim that the last Americans left Vietnam in 1975. Few of us observed this action firsthand, but those who did reported it, and we trust the veracity of their reports. Books, newspapers, magazines, and television programs are filled with reports—facts—giving us information about the world that we are unable to gain from direct observation. If we doubt the truth of these claims, we usually can turn to other sources to verify or discredit them.

Facts come in a vast array of forms—statistics, names, events—and are distinguished by their ability to be verified. Confusion tends to grow less from the facts themselves than from the inferences we make based on a given set of facts. It is important, however, to think critically about our sources, including our own observations, in order to understand possible biases. Eyewitness reports and individual experiences, your own or those of others, can serve as valuable factual evidence. Whether or not evidence is accepted depends on how your audience views you as a witness or on their evaluation of a cited witness and the circumstances under which the report was made. The celebrated Japanese movie, *Roshomon,* in which four witnesses give different reports of the same crime, and numerous other tales, such as Lawrence Durrell's Alexandria Quartet or Ford Maddox Ford's *The Good Soldier,* illustrate how perceptions of the same event can vary.

Facts and Journalism

In "The Facts of Media Life," writer Max Frankel comments on the growing number of journalists, some of them well known, who have forgotten that verifiable facts are the foundation of good journalism.

The Facts of Media Life

In journalism, the highest truth is truth. Period.

The roster of fallen journalists grows apace: Stephen Glass, Mike Barnicle, Patricia Smith, James Hirsch, a whole team of CNN investigators. But the year's toll is proof not that many reporters often lie; it bespeaks a heroic battle by the news media to preserve the meaning of fact and the sanctity of quotation marks. Reporters have been losing their jobs for committing fiction, a crime that is no crime at all in too many other media venues, notably film and television docudramas.

While news teams root out the tellers of tall tales, the rest of our culture argues that a good yarn justifies cutting corners, imagining dialogue, inventing characters and otherwise torturing truth.

Barnicle was rightly fired by *The Boston Globe* for spinning sob stories around characters nowhere to be found. But he simply labored in the style of Truman Capote, who gained fame and wealth for the inventive conjecture and made-up conversations of "In Cold Blood," his "nonfiction novel." Glass and Smith were sacked for composing too-good-to-be-true plots. But Geoffrey Rush won an Academy Award for "Shine," his false depiction of David Helfgott as a pianist improbably driven mad by an abusive father reenacting Nazi brutalities.

The CNN producers were fired for believing too passionately that they had unearthed a wartime atrocity by American troops. But no one was punished for the atrocious slander committed by an MGM team in a movie called "Hoodlum," which showed Thomas E. Dewey, the three-term Governor of New York and Republican nominee for President in 1944 and 1948, taking bribes from mobsters whom in truth he had prosecuted fearlessly, at great personal risk.

Hirsch's unforgivable offense was to print a lie, albeit an inconsequential one: that *The New York Times* had no comment about the Barnicle affair. (It had commented that *The Globe,* its subsidiary, was editorially "autonomous.") But Random House sells "Midnight in the Garden of Good and Evil" as "all true" (and *The Times* has for nearly four years listed it as a "nonfiction" best seller) even though John Berendt, the author, acknowledges "rounding the corners" and inventing dialogue "to make a better narrative."

As for television, it routinely appropriates the personas of celebrities and crudely distorts their words, thoughts and features. Just the other night, I watched imposters trying to steal my treasured images of John and Robert Kennedy and Frank Sinatra, Sammy Davis Jr. and the rest of the Rat Pack.

What's wrong with a little mendacity—so goes the theory—to give a tale velocity?

It is unforgivably wrong to give fanciful stories the luster of fact, or to use facts to let fictions parade as truths. The authors of hybrid "factions" and "nonfiction novels" claim poetic license to distort and invent so as to serve a "higher truth" than—sneer—"mere journalism." But why then won't they create fictional names and characters and pursue their higher truths in imaginary plots? Why usurp the label of history while rejecting its disciplines?

The answer is that fiction and fact live in radically different emotional worlds and the fabricators greedily want the best of both. Fiction thrills by analogy, by the reader's knowledge that unreal plots can illuminate the deepest truths. Nonfiction excites by experience, by extending a reader's knowledge and understanding of reality. Why should not writers, editors, producers and publishers pretend, like carnival barkers, that fictions are facts? Because a reader who is lured into the House of Facts, poor sap, has paid to experience facts.

I have learned from Prof. Ben Yagoda that when Capote first submitted "In Cold Blood" to *The New Yorker* in 1965, its editor, William Shawn, re-peatedly questioned the book's authenticity with a marginal note: "How know? d[iscuss]/w/author." Whatever the discussion, Capote escaped with his conjectures and fraudulent quotation marks. Though famous also for its fiction, Shawn's *New Yorker* pretended that Capote had satisfied their vaunted fact checkers.

Shawn was not called to account until 1984, when another of his writ-ers, Alastair Reid, was discovered to have for many years routinely invented Spanish taverns and characters because, he said, "if one wants to write about Spain, the facts won't get you anywhere." Shawn defended the false-hoods with the fatuous remark that their author was "a man of utter in-tegrity, and that's all I have to know." Watch out, Tina Brown, late of *The New Yorker:* the filmworthy manuscripts you seek for your new Disney mag-azine will encourage the maulers of fact to drown you in falsehoods.

Happily, journalism's infantry slogs on, struggling to distinguish fact from fiction. It wants to preserve the thrills of reality and believes that read-ers deserve the honesty implicit in Frank McCourt's refusal to put quotation marks around the reconstructed dialogue in his memoir of an Irish child-hood, "Angela's Ashes."

It is a noble but uphill struggle. Admired intellectuals like Joyce Carol Oates have scoffed at the distinction, observing that all language tends by its nature to distort experience and that writing, being an art, "means arti-fice." But see how much she, too, values separating fact from fiction: Oates defeats her own defense of artifice with the supporting observation that Thoreau compressed two years into one in "Walden" and "lived a historical life very different from the . . . monastic life he presents in his book." How could she ever know in a world without fact?

Facts, unlike literature, do not promise truth. They only record what has been seen and heard somehow, by someone, subject to all the frailties and biases of their observers and interpreters. Yet they must be defended, particularly in a society that values freedom, because by definition, facts can be challenged, tested, cross-examined. Wrong facts and the truths derived from them are always correctable—with more facts. Fictional facts are forever counterfeit.

EXERCISE 2B

Questions for Discussion

1. What does Frankel mean by "the sanctity of quotations marks?"
2. Why did author Frank McCourt refuse to put quotation marks around the dialogue in his childhood memoir, *Angela's Ashes?*
3. What is Frankel's explanation for this outbreak of dishonesty among journalists?
4. Why is the phrase "nonfiction novel" an oxymoron (a figure of speech in which contradictory ideas are combined)?

What Is a Judgment?

When we infer that the individual on the pogo stick took one jump too many, we laugh but are unlikely to express approval or disapproval of the event. On the other hand, when we infer that the woman in the car in front of us is a poor driver, we express disapproval of her driving skills; we make a **judgment,** in this case a statement of disapproval. Or, when we infer from a friend's volunteer work with the homeless that she is an admirable person, we express our approval, i.e., make a favorable judgment. **A judgment is also an inference, but although many inferences are free of positive or negative connotation, such as "I think it's going to rain," a judgment always expresses the writer's or speaker's approval or disapproval.** In an attempt to mitigate disapproval of his client's behavior, one of Bill Clinton's lawyers asked that special prosecutor Ken Starr in his then not-yet-released report, refrain from interpreting facts: "Nothing . . . authorizes your office to prepare a 'report' to the House that purports to summarize and analyze evidence." In other words, he was asking Starr to make no inferences or express any judgments (though many would say the facts spoke for themselves).

Certain judgments are taken for granted, become part of a culture's shared belief system, and are unlikely to be challenged under most circumstances. For example, most of us would accept the following statements: "Taking the property of others is wrong" or "People who physically abuse children should be punished." But many judgments are not universally accepted without considerable well-reasoned support or may be rejected regardless of additional support and cogent reasoning. Frequently, a judgment is further complicated by potentially ambiguous language and even punctuation. Take for example the highly controversial wording of the Second Amendment to the Constitution:

Amendment II
A well-regulated militia, being necessary to the security of a free State, the right of the people to keep and bear arms, shall not be infringed.

Those in favor of gun control interpret this to mean that only "a well-regulated militia," not every individual, is guaranteed the right to bear arms. "Well-regulated" implies an official militia, not a private one free of government regulations. But those against gun control believe that the Second Amendment guarantees "the people," meaning all individuals, the right to bear arms.

To merit the right to be heard on this volatile issue, a person must provide considerable factual evidence and cogent reasoning.

THE FAR SIDE   By GARY LARSON

9-17   © 1985 Universal Press Syndicate

"Oh, what a cute little Siamese. ... Is he friendly?"

Failure to draw logical inferences can sometimes be dangerous.

EXERCISE 2C

Distinguishing Between Facts, Inferences, and Judgments

Determine whether the following statements are facts (reports), inferences, or judgments and explain your reasoning. Note that some may include more than one, and some may be open to interpretation.

> *Example:* I heard on the morning news that the city subway system has ground to a halt this morning; many students will arrive late for class.

"I heard on the morning news that the city subway system has ground to a halt this morning": *fact.* I did hear it and the information can be verified.

"Many students will arrive late for class": *inference.* This is a conclusion drawn from the information about the breakdown of the subway.

1. Material on the Internet should not be censored by government or any other organization.
2. For sale: lovely three-bedroom house in forest setting, easy commute, a bargain at $325,000. ~Judgement~
3. Forty-one percent of Californians who die are cremated—almost twice the national average of 21 percent. *Fact*
4. Arnold has a drinking problem. *Judgement*
5. John Updike, reviewing Tom Wolfe's *A Man in Full*, concludes that the novel "amounts to entertainment, not literature." *Fact*
6. After I took Richard Simmons' Vitamin Pills, the boss gave me a raise. Those pills sure did the trick.
7. Commuter—one who spends his life
   In riding to and from his wife;   *Judgement*
   A man who shaves and takes a train
   And then rides back to shave again.
   —E. B. WHITE

EXERCISE 2D

Drawing Logical Inferences

Draw inferences from the following statistics and evaluate the relative reliability of your inferences.

N U M B E R S

$725 million Total fines the Justice Department levied on two of the world's largest drug companies for fixing vitamin prices

$1.4 billion Other antitrust fines collected by Justice since 1997

$95 million Annual budget for Justice's antitrust division

- -

$28.5 million Box-office receipts on the opening day of *Star Wars: Episode I*

$300 million Estimated cost to the economy of people's skipping work to see the movie

- -

77% Proportion of parents surveyed who say they would like to use a V-chip to block TV programs, if they had one

2 Number of nationwide electronics chain stores that stopped selling V-chip decoder boxes, for lack of interest

- -

3% Teenage girls in Fiji with eating disorders in 1995, before TV arrived

15% Fijian girls with eating disorders three years after the islands got TV

Sources: Washington Post, CNN, AP, L.A. Times, Kaiser Foundation

EXERCISE 2E

Solving Riddles

Use your inferential skills to solve these riddles by English poet John Cotton.

1.
Insubstantial I can fill lives,
Cathedrals, worlds.
I can haunt islands,

*Raise passions
Or calm the madness of kings.
I've even fed the affectionate.* music
*I can't be touched or seen,
But I can be noted.*

2.
*We are a crystal zoo,
Wielders of fortunes,* stars
*The top of our professions.
Like hard silver nails
Hammered into the dark
We make charts for mariners.*

3.
I reveal your secrets. mirror
*I am your morning enemy,
Though I give reassurance of presence.
I can be magic,
or the judge in beauty contests.
Count Dracula has no use for me.
When you leave
I am left to my own reflections.*

4.
*My tensions and pressures
Are precise if transitory.* bubble
*Iridescent, I can float
And catch small rainbows.
Beauties luxuriate in me.
I can inhabit ovens
Or sparkle in bottles.
I am filled with that
Which surrounds me.*

5.
*Containing nothing
I can bind people forever,* ring
*Or just hold a finger.
Without end or beginning*

I go on to appear in fields,
Ensnare enemies,
Or in anothere guise
Carry in the air
Messages from tower to tower.

6.
Silent I invade cities,
Blur edges, confuse travelers,   fog
My thumb smudging the light.
I drift from rivers
To loiter in the early morning fields,
Until Constable Sun
Moves me on.

—JOHN COTTON, *TIMES LITERARY SUPPLEMENT*

Now apply the same skills to these two poems by Sylvia Plath (1933–1963).
What does each describe?

7.
I am silver and exact. I have no preconceptions.
Whatever I see I swallow immediately   mirror
Just as it is, unmisted by love or dislike.
I am not cruel, only truthful—
The eye of a little god, four-cornered.
Most of the time I mediate on the opposite wall.
It is pink, with speckles. I have looked at it so long
I think it is a part of my heart. But it flickers.
Faces and darkness separate us over and over.

Now I am a lake. A woman bends over me,
Searching my reaches for what she really is.
Then she turns to those liars, the candles or the moon.
I see her back, and reflect it faithfully.
She rewards me with tears and an agitation of hands.
I am important to her. She comes and goes.
Each morning it is her face that replaces the darkness.
In me she has drowned a young girl, and in me an old woman
Rises toward her day after day, like a terrible fish.

8.
I'm a riddle in nine syllables,
An elephant, a ponderous house,
A melon strolling on two tendrils.
O red fruit, ivory, fine timbers.
This loaf's big with its yeasty rising.
Money's new-minted in this fat purse.
I'm a means, a stage, a cow in calf.
I've eaten a bag of green apples,
Boarded the train there's no getting off.

Pregnant
Woman

> **READINGS:** For two more poems on which to practice your inference skills, see "Marriage" on page 607 and "The Marriage" on page 607.

APPLICATION TO WRITING

Achieving a Balance Between Inference and Facts

We need to distinguish inferences, facts, and judgments from one another to evaluate as fairly as possible the events in our world. Whether these events are personal or global, we need to be able to distinguish between facts, verifiable information that we can rely on, and inferences and judgments, which may or may not be reliable.

We also need to evaluate the reliability of our own inferences. Are there other interpretations of the facts? Have we considered all other possible interpretations? Do we need more information before drawing a conclusion? These are useful thinking skills that we need to practice, but how do these skills relate to writing? To answer that question, read the following paragraph and distinguish between statements of fact and inference.

> A white player's life in the National Basketball Association is a reverse-image experience all but unique in American culture. Although fewer than 13 percent of United States citizens are African-American, about 80 percent of the N.B.A.'s players are. Of the 357 players on N.B.A. rosters, 290 were African-American, including several of mixed descent. Every one of the league's 20 leading scorers was black, and all but 2 of its leading rebounders. Not one N.B.A. team has as many whites as blacks.
>
> —ADAPTED FROM "THE LONELINESS OF BEING WHITE" BY BRUCE SCHOENFELD

This paragraph contains one inference while the remaining statements are factual, capable of verification. Notice that the facts support and convince us of the inference.

INFERENCE	FACTS
A white player's life in the National Basketball Association is a reverse-image experience all but unique in American culture.	Although fewer than 13 percent of United States citizens are African-American, about 80 percent of the N.B.A.'s players are.

Of the 357 players on N.B.A. rosters, 290 were African-American, including several of mixed descent.

Every one of the league's 20 leading scorers was black, and all but 2 of its 20 leading rebounders.

Not one N.B.A. team has as many whites as blacks.

Facts Only

> Now, what I want is Facts. Teach these boys and girls nothing but Facts. Facts alone are wanted in life. Plant nothing else, and root out everything else. You can only form the minds of reasoning animals upon Facts: nothing else will ever be of any service to them. This is the principle on which I bring up my own children, and this is the principle on which I bring up these children. Stick to Facts, sir!

So says Thomas Gradgrind in Charles Dickens' novel *Hard Times,* an indictment against Victorian industrial society. Dickens knew that facts alone do not make for a good education nor for good writing. Expository writing frequently consists of a blend of inference and fact with the one supporting the other. If you were to write a paper consisting only of facts, it would be of no interest to the reader because reading facts that lead nowhere, that fail to support a conclusion, is like reading the telephone book. Jeff Jarvis, a book reviewer for *The New York Times Book Review,* comments on the dangers of this kind of writing:

Objectivity, in some quarters, means just the facts, ma'am—names, dates, and quotations dumped from a notebook onto the page. But facts alone, without perspective, do not tell a story. Facts alone, without a conclusion to hold them together, seem unglued. Facts alone force writers to use awkward transitions, unbending formats or simple chronologies to fend off disorganization.

A facts-only approach can also have serious consequences in our schools' textbooks. A recent report on public education cites such facts-only textbooks as one of the causes of students' lack of interest and poor achievement.

> Elementary school children are stuck with insipid books that "belabor what is obvious" even to first graders. At the high school level, history—or "social studies"—texts are crammed with facts but omit human motivations or any sense of what events really meant.

Keep the danger of a facts-only approach in mind when you are assigned a research paper. Do not assume that teachers are looking exclusively for well-documented facts; they also want to see what you make of the data, what conclusions you draw, what criticisms and recommendations you offer. Do not fall into the trap of one eager young college freshman, Charles Renfrew, who, proud of his photographic memory, expected high praise from a distinguished philosophy professor for a paper on Descartes. He suffered disappointment but learned a lasting lesson when he read the comment: "Too much Descartes, not enough Renfrew." A photographic memory for factual information can be an asset, but your own inferences and judgments fully explained are also important.

Selecting Facts

Equally important when considering the facts you use in your papers is your selection of which facts to include and which to omit. When we omit relevant facts, we may be reflecting personal, political, or cultural biases and in the process distorting "reality." The omission of certain facts from accounts of historical events can have serious consequences, in small ways and large. Audre Lorde in her book, *Zami: A New Spelling of My Name*, illustrates this point eloquently.

> I had spent four years at Hunter High School, with the most academically advanced and intellectually accurate education available for "preparing young women for college and career." I had been taught by some of the most highly considered historians in the country. Yet, I had never once heard the name mentioned of the first man to fall in the American revolution [Crispus Attucks], nor even been told that he was a Negro. What did that mean about the history I had learned?

Lorde is illustrating what others in recent decades have noted. For example, *Harvey Wasserman's History of the United States* and Frances Fitzgerald's *America Revised: History Schoolbooks in the Twentieth Century* explore the ways in which historians, through a systematic selection process, have distorted history. (Some would say Wasserman also distorts history in his efforts to right past wrongs.)

Inferences Only

It is possible to err in another direction as well; a paper consisting only of inferences and judgments would bore and antagonize readers as they search for the basis of our claims, the facts to support our opinions. If our writing is to be logical, convincing, and interesting, we must draw inferences and support them with relevant facts.

Reading Critically

Finally, distinguishing between facts, inferences, and judgments and evaluating their reliability allow us to analyze information, to read critically as writers, as consumers, as voters. Whether it is an article we find on the Internet, an auto salesperson, or a political candidate, we need to be able to separate facts from judgments and to ask that the judgments offered be supported by the facts. If we read or listen without these distinctions in mind, we are susceptible to false claims and invalid arguments, often with serious consequences for us as individuals and for society as a whole.

WRITING ASSIGNMENT 3

Analyzing a Recent Inference

Write a paragraph or two about a recent inference you've made. Include what facts the inference was based on and why you made it. Discuss with your classmates whether the inference was logical given the facts that led to it, whether others might have made a different inference from the same data, and why they might have done so.

Audience

Yourself and other members of the class.

Purpose

To think critically about your own thinking.

WRITING ASSIGNMENT 4

Reconstructing the Lost Tribe

> *Every language is also a special way of looking at the world and interpreting experience. Concealed in the structure of language are a whole set of unconscious assumptions about the world and the life in it.*
>
> —CLYDE KLUCKHOHN

With the above quotation in mind, imagine that a previously unknown civilization has been discovered and that linguistic anthropologists, after observing the civilization for a while, have delineated the following characteristics about the society's language:

Three words for terrain, designating "absolutely flat," "rolling," and "slightly hilly."

No word for ocean.

Dozens of terms for grains, including eight for wheat alone.

Several words for children, some of which translate as "wise small one," "innocent leader," and "little stargazer."

Seven terms to describe the stages of life up to puberty, only one term to describe life from puberty to death.

The word for sex translates as "to plant a wise one."

Terms for woman are synonymous with "wife and mother."

Terms for man are synonymous with "husband and father."

Twenty words for book.

No words for violent conflict or war.

Nine words for artist.

Terms for praise translate as "peacemaker" and "conciliator."

Words designating cow, pig, calf, and sheep but no terms for beef, pork, veal, leather, or mutton.

Several words for precipitation, most translating as "rain," only one meaning "snow."

Several words for leader but all are plural.

Four words meaning theater.

The Topic

Write an essay in which you characterize the society that uses this language.

As you analyze the characteristics of the language, you will be reconstructing a culture. Obviously, because the data are limited, you will have to make a few educated guesses and qualify conclusions carefully. ("Perhaps," "possibly," "one might conclude," "the evidence suggests," and similar hedges will be useful.)

The Approach

Examine and group the data; look for patterns.

Draw inferences, depending only on the data given.

Cite evidence to support these inferences—be sure to base all your conclusions on the linguistic evidence provided. Do not draw inferences that you don't support with specific examples. Be sure to use all the data. Explain your line of reasoning—how and why the data lead to the inferences you have made.

Don't simply write a narration or description based on the information. A narrative or story will only imply the conclusions you have arrived at from examining the data. This can be enjoyable to write and entertaining to read and certainly requires critical thinking, as does all good fiction. But your purpose here is to explain why you have made the inferences you have and to back up your inferences with facts drawn from the language list.

Consider giving a name to this tribe to help focus your sentences.

Audience and Purpose

You have a wide range of possibilities here; we leave the choice to you. Your paper may assume the form of a report, scholarly or simply informative, directed to any audience you choose. It may be a letter to a personal friend or fictional colleague. It may be a traditional essay for an audience unfamiliar with the assignment, explaining what the language tells us about the people who use or used it. What is crucial for success is that you, as the reporter-writer, assume that *you have not seen this tribe and have no first-hand evidence of it. You will also assume that your reader does not have a copy of this assignment;* it is up to you to cite all the specific evidence (the terms given in the list) to justify your inferences.

> **READINGS:** Before writing your essay, read "Chinese Relations" on page 676 for a fuller understanding of the relationship between language and culture.

Making Inferences—Writing About Fiction

Many students are intimidated by assignments that require them to write about a poem, play, short story, or novel. What can they say about a piece of literature? Isn't there a right answer known to the author and the teacher but not to them?

Fiction is implicit. Writers of fiction—through character, plot, setting, theme, point of view, symbolism, irony, and imagery—imply meaning. Fiction is oblique. The work implies meaning; you infer what that meaning is. As you can see, interpreting literature requires critical thinking; it requires you to make inferences about the meaning of the work and to support these inferences with details from it as you have done with cartoons, statistics, and poems earlier in this chapter.

Reading is the making of meaning and the meaning we make depends on who we are—our sex, age, ethnicity, culture, and experience all influence our reading. Given the multiple interpretations possible, there is not a single right answer but only well-supported inferences that add up to a logical interpretation.

A final point: A critical essay is not a continuation of class discussion but a formal piece of writing that can stand on its own apart from the class. To accomplish this, you may think of your audience as one who is not familiar with the work you are writing about. This does not require you to retell every detail of the piece, but it ensures that you include the relevant details, the facts, on which your inferences are based rather than assume your reader knows them.

The next three assignments will give you ample opportunity to practice the skill of reading closely and thinking critically while making and supporting inferences about literature. The three stories, all quite short, on which the assignments are based are arranged in order of difficulty, so regardless of the one or more assignments chosen by your instructor, you may want to read all three stories and see how you do.

EXERCISE 2F

Making Inferences About Fiction

Read "The Story of an Hour" by Kate Chopin [1850–1904] and answer the following question: Does Louise die "of joy" as her doctors suggest? Support your answer, your inference, with facts from the story.

The Story of an Hour

Knowing that Mrs. Mallard was afflicted with a heart trouble, great care was taken to break to her as gently as possible the news of her husband's death.

It was her sister Josephine who told her, in broken sentences; veiled hints that revealed in half concealing. Her husband's friend Richards was there, too, near her. It was he who had been in the newspaper office when intelligence of the railroad disaster was received, with Brently Mallard's name leading the list of "killed." He had only taken the time to assure himself of its truth by a second telegram, and had hastened to forestall any less careful, less tender friend in bearing the sad message.

She did not hear the story as many other women have heard the same, with a paralyzed inability to accept its significance. She wept at once, with sudden, wild abandonment, in her sister's arms. When the storm of grief had spent itself she went away to her room alone. She would have no one follow her.

There stood, facing the open window, a comfortable, roomy armchair. Into this she sank, pressed down by a physical exhaustion that haunted her body and seemed to reach into her soul.

She could see in the open square before her house the tops of trees that were all aquiver with the new spring life. The delicious breath of rain was in the air. In the street below a peddler was crying his wares. The notes of a distant song which some one was singing reached her faintly, and countless sparrows were twittering in the eaves.

There were patches of blue sky showing here and there through the clouds that had met and piled one above the other in the west facing her window.

She sat with her head thrown back upon the cushion of the chair, quite motionless, except when a sob came up into her throat and shook her, as a child who has cried herself to sleep continues to sob in its dreams.

She was young, with a fair, calm face, whose lines bespoke repression and even a certain strength. But now there was a dull stare in her eyes, whose gaze was fixed away off yonder on one of those patches of blue sky. It was not a glance of reflection, but rather indicated a suspension of intelligent thought.

There was something coming to her and she was waiting for it, fearfully. What was it? She did not know; it was too subtle and elusive to name. But she felt it, creeping out of the sky, reaching toward her through the sounds, the scents, the color that filled the air.

Now her bosom rose and fell tumultuously. She was beginning to recognize this thing that was approaching to possess her, and she was striving to beat it back with her will—as powerless as her two white slender hands would have been.

When she abandoned herself a little whispered word escaped her slightly parted lips. She said it over and over under her breath: "free, free,

free!" The vacant stare and the look of terror that had followed it went from her eyes. They stayed keen and bright. Her pulses beat fast, and the coursing blood warmed and relaxed every inch of her body.

She did not stop to ask if it were or were not a monstrous joy that held her. A clear and exalted perception enabled her to dismiss the suggestion as trivial.

She knew that she would weep again when she saw the kind, tender hands folded in death; the face that had never looked save with love upon her, fixed and gray and dead. But she saw beyond that bitter moment a long procession of years to come that would belong to her absolutely. And she opened and spread her arms out to them in welcome.

There would be no one to live for her during those coming years; she would live for herself. There would be no powerful will bending hers in that blind persistence with which men and women believe they have a right to impose a private will upon a fellow-creature. A kind intention or a cruel intention made the act seem no less a crime as she looked upon it in that brief moment of illumination.

And yet she had loved him—sometimes. Often she had not. What did it matter! What could love, the unsolved mystery, count for in face of this possession of self-assertion which she suddenly recognized as the strongest impulse of her being!

"Free! Body and soul free!" she kept whispering.

Josephine was kneeling before the closed door with her lips to the keyhole, imploring for admission. "Louise, open the door! I beg; open the door—you will make yourself ill. What are you doing, Louise? For heaven's sake open the door."

"Go away. I am not making myself ill." No; she was drinking in a very elixir of life through that open window.

Her fancy was running riot along those days ahead of her. Spring days, and summer days, and all sorts of days that would be her own. She breathed a quick prayer that life might be long. It was only yesterday she had thought with a shudder that life might be long.

She rose at length and opened the door to her sister's importunities. There was a feverish triumph in her eyes, and she carried herself unwittingly like a goddess of Victory. She clasped her sister's waist, and together they descended the stairs. Richards stood waiting for them at the bottom.

Some one was opening the front door with a latchkey. It was Brently Mallard who entered, a little travel-stained, composedly carrying his gripsack and umbrella. He had been far from the scene of the accident, and did not even know there had been one. He stood amazed at Josephine's piercing cry; at Richards' quick motion to screen him from the view of his wife.

But Richards was too late.

When the doctors came they said she had died of heart disease—of joy that kills.

WRITING ASSIGNMENT 5

Interpreting Fiction

Read the short story, "Hostess," by Donald Mangum, and write an essay based on the inferences you make about the narrator. Include the facts on which these inferences are based and an explanation of why you made such inferences.

Audience

Someone who has not read the story.

Purpose

To characterize the hostess—what kind of woman is she?

Hostess

My husband was promoted to crew chief, and with the raise we moved into a double-wide, just up the drive. Half the park came to the house-warming. Well, Meg drank herself to tears and holed up on the toilet, poor thing. "Meg? Hon?" I said from the hall. "You going to live?" She groaned something. It was seeing R.L. with that tramp down in 18 that made her do this to herself. Now there was a whole line of beer drinkers doing the rain dance out in the hall, this being a single-bath unit. I was the hostess, and I had to do something. "Sweetheart," I said, knocking. "I'm going to put you a bowl on the floor in the utility room." The rest of the trailer was carpeted.

Dale, my husband, was in the kitchen with an egg in his hand, squeezing it for all he was worth. Veins stuck out everywhere on his arm. Paul and Eric were laughing. "What's going on in here?" I said.

Dale stopped squeezing and breathed. "I got to admit," he said, "I never knew that about eggs." I could have kicked him when he handed Paul five dollars. I found the bowl I was after, plus a blanket, and took care of Meg.

Then Hank and Boyce almost got into a fight over a remark Hank made about somebody named Linda. They had already squared off outside when it came out that Hank was talking about a Linda *Stillman,* when Boyce thought he meant a Linda *Faye.* Well, by that time everybody was ready for something, so the guys agreed to arm-wrestle. Hank won, but only because Boyce started laughing when Kathy Sueanne sat in Jason's supper and Jason got madder than Kathy Sueanne did because there wasn't any more potato salad left.

You won't believe who showed up then. R.L.! Said he was looking for Meg. "You think she wants to see you, R.L.?" I said. "After what you did to her with that trash Elaine?" So he said he'd only kissed Elaine a couple of times. "Or not even that," he said. "She was the one kissed *me.*"

"You know what you can kiss," I said. He stood there looking like some dog you'd just hauled off and kicked for no good reason. "Well, come on," I said, taking him by the shirt. I led him to the utility room to show him the condition he'd driven his darling to. I'm here to say, when R.L. saw that precious thing curled up in front of the hot-water heater he sank to his knees in shame. I just closed the door.

Back in the den, there was this Australian kangaroo giving birth on the television. The little baby kangaroo, which looked sort of like an anchovy with legs, had just made it out of its mama and was crawling around look-ing for her pouch. The man on the show said it had about ten minutes to get in there and find a teat or it would die. He said a lot of them don't make it. I got so wrought up watching that trembly little fellow that I started cheering him on. So did everyone else. Well, to everyone's relief, the little thing made it. Then Gus wanted to know why everyone over there always called each other Mike. Nobody had any idea.

Eric ate a whole bunch of dried cat food before figuring out what it was and that somebody had put it in the party dish as a joke. He tried to act like it didn't bother him, but he didn't stay too long after that. Melinda went out to her car for cigarettes, and a yellow jacket stung her behind the knee, so when she came in howling, Rod slapped this wad of chewing tobacco on the spot to draw out the poison, which made her howl even louder, till I washed it off and applied meat tenderizer and let her go lie in the guest bed for awhile.

That's when something strange happened. The phone started ringing, and I ran back to get it in Dale's and my bedroom, which was the closest to quiet in the trailer. I answered and just got this hollow sound at first, like you get with a bad connection over long-distance.

There was a mumble, then a woman's voice said, "She's gone." I didn't recognize the voice, but I was sure what "gone" meant by the way she said it. It meant someone had died. Then she said—and she almost screamed it—"Someone should have been here. Why weren't you and Clarence here?"

Now, I don't know a soul in this world named Clarence, and this was clearly a case of the wrong number. "Ma'am," I said as gently as I knew how.

"You'll have to talk louder," she said. "I can hardly hear you."

I curled my hand around my lips and the mouthpiece and said, "Ma'am, you have dialled the wrong number."

"Oh, God, I'm sorry," she said. "Oh dear God." And here is the strange thing. The woman did not hang up. She just kept saying, "Dear God" and crying.

I sat there listening to that woman and to all the happy noise coming from everywhere in the trailer and through the window from outside, and when she finally brought it down to a sniffle I said, "Honey, who was it that passed away?"

"My sister," she said. "My sister, Beatrice." And it was like saying the name started her to sobbing again.

"And none of your people are there?" I said.

"Just me," she said.

"Sweetheart, you listen to me," I said, trying to close the window for more quiet. Sweet Christ, I thought. Dear sweet Christ in Heaven. "Are you listening, angel? You should not be alone right now. You understand what I'm telling you?" I said, "Now, I am right here."

—DONALD MANGUM

WRITING ASSIGNMENT 6

Analyzing Fiction

One critic said of Ernest Hemingway (1899–1961) that his writing is like an iceberg—nine-tenths of it is beneath the surface. A writer having difficulty adapting one of Hemingway's novels for the screen complained that the novelist wrote in the white spaces between the lines. Hemingway's elliptical style stems, in part, from his frequent use of the objective point of view. A writer employing this point of view is like a video camera that only records what it sees and hears: It cannot comment or interpret or enter a character's mind. This point of view demands that the reader make inferences about the characters' behavior and motivations. Hemingway's "Hills Like White Elephants" is just such a story. After reading the story and answering the questions that follow it, write an essay about the conflict at the heart of this story.

Audience

Someone unfamiliar with the story.

Purpose

To infer the meaning of the story.

Hills Like White Elephants
ERNEST HEMINGWAY

The hills across the valley of the Ebro were long and white. On this side there was no shade and no trees and the station was between two lines of rails in the sun. Close against the side of the station there was the warm shadow of the building and a curtain, made of strings of bamboo beads, hung across the open door into the bar, to keep out flies. The American and the girl with him sat at a table in the shade, outside the building. It was very hot and the express from Barcelona would come in forty minutes. It stopped at this junction for two minutes and went on to Madrid.

"What should we drink?" the girl asked. She had taken off her hat and put it on the table.

"It's pretty hot," the man said.

"Let's drink beer."

"Dos cervezas," the man said into the curtain.

"Big ones?" a woman asked from the doorway.

"Yes. Two big ones."

The woman brought two glasses of beer and two felt pads. She put the felt pads and the beer glasses on the table and looked at the man and the girl. The girl was looking off at the line of hills. They were white in the sun and the country was brown and dray.

"They look like white elephants," she said.

"I've never seen one," the man drank his beer.

"No, you wouldn't have."

"I might have," the man said. "Just because you say I wouldn't have doesn't prove anything."

The girl looks at the bead curtain. "They've painted something on it," she said. "What does it say?

"Anis del Toro. It's a drink."

"Could we try it?"

The man called "Listen" through the curtain. The woman came out from the bar.

"Four reales."

"We want two Anis del Toro."

"With water?"

"Do you want it with water?"

"I don't know," the girl said. "Is it good with water?"

"It's all right."

"You want them with water?" asked the woman.

"Yes, with water."

"It tastes like licorice," the girl said and put the glass down.

"That's the way with everything."

"Yes," said the girl. "Everything tastes of licorice. Especially all the things you've waited so long for, like absinthe."

"Oh, cut it out."

"You started it," the girl said. "I was being amused. I was having a fine time."

"Well, let's try and have a fine time."

"All right. I was trying. I said the mountains looked like white elephants. Wasn't that bright?"

"That was bright."

"I wanted to try this new drink. That's all we do, isn't it—look at things and try new drinks?"

"I guess so."

The girl looked across at the hills.

"They're lovely hills," she said. "They don't really look like white elephants. I just meant the coloring of their skin through the trees."

"Should we have another drink?"

"All right."

The warm wind blew the bead curtain against the table.

"The beer's nice and cool," the man said.

"It's lovely," the girl said.

"It's really an awfully simple operation, Jig," the man said. "It's not really an operation at all."

The girl looked at the ground the table legs rested on.

"I know you wouldn't mind it, Jig. It's really not anything. It's just to let the air in."

The girl did not say anything.

"I'll go with you and I'll stay with you all the time. They just let the air in and then it's all perfectly natural."

"Then what will we do afterward?"

"We'll be fine afterward. Just like we were before."

"What makes you think so?"

"That's the only thing that bothers us. It's the only thing that's made us unhappy."

The girl looked at the bead curtain, put her hand out and took hold of two of the strings of beads.

"And you think then we'll be all right and be happy."

"I know we will. You don't have to be afraid. I've known lots of people that have done it."

"So have I," said the girl. "And afterward they were all so happy."

"Well," the man said, "if you don't want to you don't have to. I wouldn't have you do it if you didn't want to. But I know it's perfectly simple."

"And you really want to?"

"I think it's the best thing to do. But I don't want you to do it if you don't really want to."

"And if I do it you'll be happy and things will be like they were and you'll love me?"

"I love you now. You know I love you."

"I know. But if I do it, then it will be nice again if I say things are like white elephants, and you'll like it?"

"I'll love it. I love it now but I just can't think about it. You know how I get when I worry."

"If I do it you won't ever worry?"

"I won't worry about that because it's perfectly simple."

"Then I'll do it. Because I don't care about me."

"What do you mean?"

"I don't care about me."

"Well, I care about you."

"Oh, yes. But I don't care about me. And I'll do it and then everything will be fine."

"I don't want you to do it if you feel that way."

The girl stood up and walked to the end of the station. Across, on the other side, were fields of grain and trees along the banks of the Ebro. Far away, beyond the river, were mountains. The shadow of a cloud moved across the field of grain and she saw the river through the trees.

"And we could have all this," she said. "And we could have everything and every day we make it more impossible."

"What did you say?"

"I said we could have everything."

"We can have everything."

"No, we can't."

"We can have the whole world."

"No, we can't."

"We can go everywhere."

"No, we can't. It isn't ours any more."

"It's ours."

"No, it isn't. And once they take it away, you never get it back."

"But they haven't taken it away."

"We'll wait and see."

"Come on back in the shade," he said. "You mustn't feel that way."

"I don't feel any way," the girl said. "I just know things."

"I don't want you to do anything that you don't want to do——"

"Nor that isn't good for me," she said. "I know. Could we have another beer?"

"All right. But you've got to realize——"

"I realize," the girl said. "Can't we maybe stop talking?"

They sat down at the table and the girl looked across at the hills on the dry side of the valley and the man looked at her and at the table.

"You've got to realize," he said, "that I don't want you to do it if you don't want to. I'm perfectly willing to go through with it if it means anything to you."

"Doesn't it mean anything to you? We could get along."

"Of course it does. But I don't want anybody but you. I don't want any one else. And I know it's perfectly simple."

"Yes, you know it's perfectly simple."

"It's all right for you to say that, but I do know it."

"Would you do something for me now?"

"I'd do anything for you."

"Would you please please please please please please please stop talking?"

He did not say anything but looked at the bags against the wall of the station. There were labels on them from all the hotels where they had spent nights.

"But I don't want you to," he said, "I don't care anything about it."

"I'll scream," the girl said.

The woman came out through the curtains with two glasses of beer and put them down on the damp felt pads. "The train comes in five minutes," she said.

"What did she say?" asked the girl.

"That the train is coming in five minutes."

The girl smiled brightly at the woman, to thank her.

"I'd better take the bags over to the other side of the station," the man said. She smiled at him.

"All right. Then come back and we'll finish the beer."

He picked up the two heavy bags and carried them around the station to the other tracks. He looked up the tracks but could not see the train. Coming back, he walked through the barroom, where people waiting for the train were drinking. He drank an Anis at the bar and looked at the people. They were all waiting reasonably for the train. He went out through the bead curtain. She was sitting at the table and smiled at him.

"Do you feel better?" he asked.

"I feel fine," she said. "There's nothing wrong with me. I feel fine."

EXERCISE 2G

Questions for Discussion

1. What is "the awfully simple operation" the man refers to? How does he feel about it? How does Jig feel about it? Is the man sincere in everything he says?

2. Why do you think Hemingway gave the woman a name but not the man?

3. What do you know about their life together? What is the relevance of the woman's comments about absinthe?

4. What is the significance of Jig comparing the hills across the valley to white elephants? Why does Hemingway use that comparison for his title?

5. How is the conflict between the couple resolved?

READINGS: For a greater challenge to your inference skills, see "What Does the Falcon Owe?" a short story in the form of a police report on page 615.

EXERCISE 2H

Analyzing a Film

As a final exercise in making and supporting inferences, rent the 1999 John Sayles film, *Limbo*. The conclusion of the movie is open to interpretation; members of the audience are left to decide for themselves if the three individuals stranded on the island are rescued or murdered. What do you think? Write a short paper explaining your answer, citing as evidence specific details from the movie.

SUMMARY

In order to interpret the world around us and write effectively about it, we need to be able to distinguish facts, inferences, and judgments from one another and to evaluate the reliability of our inferences.

In written exposition and argument, and in the interpretation of literature, it is important to achieve a balance between fact and inference, to support our inferences with facts and reasoning.

KEY TERMS

- **Facts**   information that can be verified.
- **Inference**   a conclusion about something we don't know based on what we do know.
- **Judgment**   an inference that expresses either approval or disapproval.

CHAPTER 3

The Structure of Argument

You always hurt the one you love!

When we offer our own views on an issue we are expressing an **opinion.** We all have them. We all should have them. But we should also recognize the difference between voicing an opinion and developing an argument. Someone might insist that using animals for medical research is wrong; a research physician might respond that this attitude is misguided. Both are expressing opinions. If they both stick to their guns but refuse to elaborate their positions, then each may simply dismiss the opponent's statement as "mere opinion," as nothing more than an emotional reaction. If, on the other hand, they start to offer reasons in support of their opinions, then they have moved the discussion to an argument. The critic might add that animals suffer pain in much the same way that humans do, and thus experiments inflict cruel suffering on the animals. The physician might respond that modern techniques have greatly reduced animal suffering and that such experiments are necessary for medical breakthroughs. They are now offering support for their opinions. Don't be afraid of your opinions. Just be prepared to defend them with good reasoning. Think of opinions as starting points for arguments.

In logic, an **argument** is not a fight but a rational piece of discourse, written or spoken, which attempts to persuade the reader or listener to believe something. For instance, we can attempt to persuade others to believe that cutting old timber will harm the environment or that a vote for a particular candidate will ensure a better city government. Though many arguments are concerned with political issues, arguments are not limited to such topics. We can argue about books, movies, restaurants, and cars, as well as about abstractions found in philosophical issues, to name just a few of the possibilities. Whenever we want to convince someone else of the "rightness" of our position by offering reasons for that position, we are presenting an argument.

Premises and Conclusions

The structure of all arguments, no matter what the subject, consists of two components: **premises** and **conclusions.** The **conclusion** is the key assertion that the other assertions support. These other assertions are the **premises,** reasons that support the conclusion.* For example:

> Because the poor spend proportionately more of their income on gambling than higher income groups and because gambling sends a "something for nothing" message that erodes the work ethic, government should take steps to contain and curtail the spread of gambling.

In this example, the conclusion—that government should take steps to contain and curtail the spread of gambling—is supported by two premises: that the poor spend proportionately more of their income on gambling than higher income groups and that gambling sends a message that erodes the work ethic. For a group of assertions to be an argument, the passage must contain both these elements—a conclusion and at least one premise.

Look at the following letter to the editor of a news magazine:

> I was horrified to read "Corporate Mind Control" and learn that some companies are training employees in New Age thinking, which is a blend of the occult, Eastern religions, and a smattering of Christianity. What they're dealing with is dangerous—Krone Training will be disastrous to the company and the employee.

---

*Throughout this book, we use the term premise in its contemporary, general sense, meaning a claim (or statement) that leads to a conclusion. We do not restrict its meaning to the classical definition—either one of the two propositions of a syllogism from which the conclusion is drawn. See syllogisms in Chapter 7.

This writer thinks that she has written an argument against Krone Training, but her letter consists of a conclusion only, which is in essence that Krone Training is not a good idea. Because she fails to include any premises in support of her conclusion, she fails to present an argument and fails to convince anyone who did not already share her belief that Krone Training is "dangerous" and "disastrous." A conclusion repeated in different words may look like an argument but shouldn't deceive a careful reader. (See Chapter 6 for more on fallacious, or deceptive, arguments.) Can you formulate a premise that would transform the letter into an argument?

Distinguishing Between Premises and Conclusions

In order to evaluate the strength of an argument, we need to understand its structure, to distinguish between its premises and conclusion. **Joining words**—conjunctions and transitional words and phrases—indicate logical relationships between ideas and therefore often help us to make this distinction. Notice the radical change in meaning that results from the reversal of two clauses joined by the conjunction "because":

> *I didn't drink because I had problems. I had problems because I drank.*
> —BARNABY CONRAD

The use of joining words in argument is especially important because they indicate which assertions are being offered as premises and which are offered as conclusions. For example:

> Our government's decision to apply a similar tariff on luxury Japanese cars sold here was a just one *because* Japan imposed a prohibitive tariff on the sale of new American cars in their country.

> Japan imposed a prohibitive tariff on the sale of new American cars in their country, *so* our government's decision to apply a similar tariff on luxury Japanese cars sold here was a just one.

In the first example, "because" indicates a premise, a reason in support of the conclusion that the decision to impose a tariff on Japanese cars was a just one. In the second example, "so" indicates the conclusion. Both statements present essentially the same argument; the difference between the two sentences is rhetorical—a matter of style, not substance.

note

"Because" and "since" frequently introduce premises whereas "so," "therefore," "thus," "hence," and "consequently" often introduce conclusions.

conclusion because *premise*

premise therefore *conclusion*

Note: "and" as well as "but" often connects premises.

Standard Form

With the help of joining words and transitional phrases, we can analyze the structure of an argument and then put it into **standard form.** An argument in standard form is an argument reduced to its essence: its premises and conclusion. In other words, it is an outline of the argument. In the previous argument on gambling, each premise is indicated by the "because" that introduces it, the conclusion then following from these two premises. In standard form, the argument looks like this:

Premise 1 The poor spend proportionately more of their income on gambling than higher income groups.

Premise 2 Gambling sends a "something for nothing" message that erodes the work ethic.

∴ Government should take steps to contain and curtail the spread of gambling.

Note: ∴ is a symbol in logic meaning "therefore."

Read this argument about college grading policies taken from a *New York Times* editorial by Clifford Adelman, a senior research analyst with the Department of Education.

If there are 50 ways to leave your lover, there are almost as many ways to walk away from a college course without penalty. What are prospective employers to make of the following "grades" that I have seen on transcripts: W, WP, WI, WX, WM, WW, K, L, Q, X and Z. What does "Z" mean? "The student 'zeed out,'" one registrar told me. At another institution, I was told that it stood for "zapped." Despite the zap, I was informed, there was no penalty.

But there is a penalty. The time students lose by withdrawing is time they must recoup. All they have done is increase the cost of school to themselves, their families and, if at a public institution, to taxpayers.

This increasing volume of withdrawals and repeats does not bode well for students' future behavior in the workplace, where repeating tasks is costly. Many employers agree that work habits and time-management skills are as important as the knowledge new employees bring. It wouldn't take much for schools to change their grading policies so that students would have to finish what they start.

Though this argument is three paragraphs long, in standard form it can be reduced to four sentences:

Premise 1 The time students lose by withdrawing is time they must recoup.

Premise 2 They increase the cost of school to themselves, their families and, if at a public institution, to taxpayers.

Premise 3 Work habits and time-management skills are as important as the knowledge new employees bring.

∴ Schools should change their grading policies so that students would have to finish what they start.

The first paragraph provides the reader with necessary background information because the writer can't assume that his readers will know the specifics of current college grading policies. The second paragraph contains two of his three premises while the final paragraph contains his third premise (and development of that premise) and his conclusion.

The conclusion of this argument—that schools should change their grading policy—is an inference, a judgment. Indeed, all conclusions are inferences. If they were facts we would not need to supply premises to support them; we would simply verify them by checking the source. In this argument, the first two premises are factual and the third is an inference, one which, on the basis of experience, most of us would be inclined to accept.

Examine the argument.

Baseball fans have long argued that the city should build a downtown baseball stadium. If the city doesn't build a new stadium the team may leave, and a major city deserves a major league team. Furthermore, downtown's summer weather is superior to the freezing wind of the present site, and public transportation to downtown would make the park more accessible.

In this example, four separate premises are offered for the conclusion.

Premise 1 If the city doesn't build a new stadium, the team may leave.

Premise 2 A major city deserves a major league team.

Premise 3 Downtown's summer weather is superior to the freezing wind of the present site.

Premise 4 Public transportation to downtown would make the park more accessible.

∴ The city should build a downtown baseball stadium.

> **READINGS:** For an example of an argument in which premises are laid out clearly point by point, see "Fahrenheit 451.2: Is Cyberspace Burning?" on page 300.

EXERCISE 3A

Reducing Simple Arguments to Standard Form

Put each of the following arguments into standard form by first circling the joining words and transitional phrases, then identifying the conclusion, and finally identifying the premises. List the premises, numbering each separate statement, and write the conclusion using the symbol ∴. Leave out the joining words and phrases, because standard form identifies premises and conclusions, but write each premise and the conclusion as a complete sentence.

Example: All politicians make promises they can't keep, and Jerry is nothing if not a politician. He will, therefore, make promises he can't keep.

1. All politicians make promises they can't keep.
2. Jerry is a politician.
   ∴ He will make promises he can't keep.

1. Because technical jobs are increasing more rapidly than other jobs, American high schools need to collaborate with industry in apprenticeship programs for those students who do not plan to attend college.

2. Because school vouchers would undermine public schools, permit discrimination, and transfer taxpayer money to those who need it least, private school parents, voters should not pass such legislation.

3. The student union building is ugly and uncomfortable. The preponderance of cement makes the building appear cold and gray both inside and out. Many of the rooms lack windows, so that one is left staring at the cement wall. The chairs are generally cheap and uncomfortable, while the poor lighting makes studying difficult, and the terrible acoustics make conversations almost impossible.

4. Abortion raises important moral questions, for abortion involves both a woman's right to privacy and the question of when life begins, and anything that involves personal rights and the onset of life raises serious moral questions.

5. Many biologists and gynecologists argue that life does not begin at conception. And the Supreme Court ruled in 1973 that to restrict a woman's right to have an abortion violates her right to privacy. These two facts lead us to believe that abortion should remain a woman's choice.

6. Capital punishment is not justified since with capital punishment, an innocent person might be executed, and no practice that might kill innocent people is justified.

7. Because some killers are beyond rehabilitation, society should have the right to execute those convicted of first-degree murder. More uniform implementation of the death penalty may serve as a deterrent, and victims' families are entitled to appropriate vengeance. Furthermore, the costs of maintaining a prisoner for life are too great, and no state guarantees that life imprisonment means no parole.

8. In his celebrated work *On Liberty*, a defense of freedom of speech, John Stuart Mill argues that "power can be rightfully exercised over any member of a civilized community" only to "prevent harm to others." Because he maintains that no opinion, no matter how disagreeable, can inflict harm, it follows that we don't have the right to suppress opinion.

9. Despite the controversy, we didn't need the movie rating NC–17 as we did not need the X rating before it. The R rating already protects children, and any further restriction of choice violates our freedom of expression guaranteed under the First Amendment. And as critics have pointed out, several R-rated films are more sexually explicit than some rated NC–17, making the distinction between the two ratings unclear as well as unnecessary.

10. S. Frederick Starr, former president of Oberlin College, argues in a controversial *New York Times* column that colleges and universities should explore the possibility of a three-year baccalaureate. He claims that "higher education, private and public, is too expensive," with costs having risen 4.4 percent faster than inflation over a decade. He believes that a three-year degree would automatically reduce the cost to families and taxpayers by one-quarter and would provide several concrete educational benefits as well.

EXERCISE 3B

Reducing an Editorial to Standard Form

Put the argument presented in the following editorial into standard form.

Solves Surplus Problem

To the Editor:

At last, someone else—Elizabeth Joseph (Op-Ed, May 23)—has put into words what I have been silently thinking for some time: Polygamy makes good sense.

Ms. Joseph writes from the perspective of a wife. I write from the perspective of a divorced working mother. How much more advantageous it would be for me to be part of a household such as Ms. Joseph describes, rather than to be juggling my many roles alone.

Nurit Karlin

If polygamy were legal, the problem—and I see it as a problem—of the surplus of extra women would disappear rapidly. No matter how many polemics there may be in favor of the free and single life-style, a divorced woman can feel extra in today's society, more so if she has children, which can isolate her from a full social life. How much easier to share the burdens—and the jobs.

When more women can rediscover the joys of sisterhood and co-wifehood (which are as old as the Bible), and overcome residual jealousy as a response to this type of situation, I think our society will have advanced considerably.

FRIEDA BRODSKY
BROOKLYN, NEW YORK

EXERCISE 3C

Creating a Political Handout

The following handout urges Californians to vote "no" on Proposition 174. This proposition (like other school voucher initiatives) would require the state to give parents vouchers to apply to their children's tuition if they choose private schools over public. This issue is currently being debated at the national level as well. As you will recognize, the content of this hand-

CARTOON COURTESY OF NURIT KARLIN/NYT PICTURES

out is essentially an argument in standard form: premises in support of a conclusion. Each premise is then developed and supported by a sentence or two.

After evaluating the effectiveness of this handout, create one of your own in support of or in opposition to a current political issue or campus issue. If the topic you choose is a ballot issue, refer to the Voter's Guide in your area for help in identifying the major premises. Pay special attention as well to the format and visual appeal of your document. Your computer program may allow you to add graphics to your design.

Five <u>Good</u> Reasons
to Oppose
the Vouchers Initiative

It provides no accountability.

- Though they would receive taxpayer dollars, the private and religious schools would be wholly unaccountable to the taxpayers—or to anyone other than their owners. Anyone who could recruit just 25 youngsters could open a "school." It would not need to be accredited, to hire credentialed teachers, or to meet the curriculum, health, and safety standards governing the public schools.

It undermines 'neighborhood' schools, making large tax hikes likely.

- The initiative would strip our public schools of 10 percent of their funding—even if not one student transferred to a private or religious school—to give vouchers to students currently in non-public schools. Either the public schools would be devastated—or hefty tax increases would be needed . . . not to improve education in the public schools, but to pay for subsidizing private, religious, and cult schools.

It permits discrimination.

- Private and religious schools could refuse admission to youngsters because of their religion, gender, I.Q., family income or ability to pay, disability, or any of dozens of other factors. In fact, they wouldn't even have to state a reason for rejecting a child.

It transfers taxpayer money to the rich.

- Rich parents already paying $7,000 to $9,000 or more in private school tuition would now gain $2,600 from the vouchers—a form of "Robin Hood in reverse."

It abandons public school students.

- The children left behind, in the public schools, would sit in classrooms that were even more crowded—and that had even less money, per student, for textbooks, science equipment, and other materials and supplies.

Vote No on Prop. 174

California Teachers Association/NEA • 1705 Murchison Drive • Burlingame, CA 94010

Ambiguous Argument Structure

Sometimes, the precise direction of an argument seems ambiguous; what is offered as conclusion and what is meant as supporting premise can be unclear. In such cases, it is important to look for what is most reasonable to believe, to give *the benefit of the doubt.* Try each assertion as the conclusion and see if the premises provide logical support for it, beginning with what seems most likely to be the intended conclusion.

Closely allied with the benefit of the doubt is the ancient methodologic principle known as **Occam's razor.** Named for William of Occam, the most influential philosopher of 14th-century Europe (immortalized a few years ago as William of Baskerville in Umberto Eco's novel, *The Name of the Rose*), this principle advocates economy in argument. As William of Occam put it, "What can be done with fewer assumptions is done in vain with more." In other words, the simplest line of reasoning is usually the best. Newspaper columnist Jon Carroll invoked Occam's razor when commenting on the O.J. Simpson trial: "I am not a juror; I am not required to maintain the presumption of innocence. I used Occam's razor, a tool that has served me well before. The simplest explanation is usually the true one; if a wife is killed, look to the husband."

Convoluted arguments, often those that sound the most impressive, can be difficult to unravel and rarely advance good reasoning. The ultimate question, however, when constructing an argument is always: What is enough? In the words of Toni Morrison, in her novel *Beloved,* "Everything depends on knowing how much, and good is knowing when to stop." But in most cases, our readers require more detailed support than we, as the advocates of a position, are likely to think necessary.

Argument and Explanation—Distinctions

As you elaborate support for premises in written argument, you often rely on explanation—of terminology, of background, of your reasoning—but you must not lose sight of your purpose, which is to persuade your reader of the wisdom of your position.

An **argument** is an attempt to establish a basis for belief, for the acceptability of your conclusion. In argument, you present reasons for your conclusion in order to convince someone of your point of view.

In **explanation,** on the other hand, you are clarifying why something has happened or why you hold a given opinion. Look at these examples:

> I'm convinced he committed the crime because his fingerprints were
> on the murder weapon.

We are given a reason for believing that he committed the crime. We have
an argument.

> He committed the crime because he needed money.

We are given a reason why he committed the crime. We have an explanation.

What about these? Which illustrates argument, which explanation?

> Don't go to that market because it's closed for renovation.
>
> Don't go to that market because the prices are higher than anywhere
> else and the checkout lines are slow.

This distinction between explanation and argument may play a crucial role
in your understanding of specific writing assignments and save you wasted
effort on a false start. Is the instructor asking for an explanation, information on a particular subject or is he asking you to write an argument, to
take and support a position? A written argument naturally includes explanation, information, but this material serves the purpose of convincing
your reader of your point of view, which will be expressed in your thesis—
the conclusion of your argument—and supported by premises. The following exercise should help to clarify further this important distinction.

EXERCISE 3D

Distinguishing Arguments from Explanations

The following two essays were both featured in the editorial section of *The
New York Times;* one presents an argument whereas the other offers an explanation. Read them both carefully and decide which is which. Explain
your answer with references to specific passages in both editorials.

A Threat to Student Privacy

The Orleans Parish School Board in Louisiana has ill-advisedly joined other
educational institutions in considering broad student testing for drug
abuse. The board is reviewing a program that would require random testing of all students involved in athletics and extracurricular activities, with
voluntary testing for the rest of the student body.

The program was recommended to the board by the Orleans Parish
District Attorney's office. Some board members have expressed concern
over potential legal issues, as well they should. Testing on this scale clearly

endangers students' Fourth Amendment rights, which guard against searches without probable cause. The District Attorney's office is also encouraging the use of hair tests, as opposed to more conventional urine sampling. But the reliability of hair tests has yet to be firmly established, and until it is, such tests should not be used. A false positive reading could have drastic effects on a child's life.

The public schools seem to have been inspired partly by the schoolwide drug testing in some private schools. But a key factor is the Supreme Court's 1995 decision upholding testing of student athletes. Justice Antonin Scalia's majority opinion argued that athletes were a distinct community because they had joined their teams on a voluntary basis and already had a "reduced expectation for privacy" in the locker-room atmosphere. He further argued that because school administrators served in loco parentis, students could not expect to enjoy the same privacy right as adults.

In a soundly reasoned dissent, Justice Sandra Day O'Connor argued that even random tests for athletes could be considered "blanket searches of mostly innocent students." She said that "suspicion based testing," invoking probable cause, would more effectively guard privacy rights. Nevertheless, the Scalia argument prevailed, raising fears among civil libertarians that it would someday open the door to schoolwide testing in public schools. In a subsequent case, the Seventh Circuit Court of Appeals ruled that an Indiana high school could require students involved in extracurricular activities to submit to random drug testing.

As for the tests themselves, there is general agreement that hair retains evidence of drug use for a longer period than urine. But scientists have raised questions, including whether the tests have a racial bias. False positives occur more frequently among minorities than among whites.

In many ways, students form a captive and vulnerable population. Justice O'Connor called the random testing of athletes a "mass, suspicionless search regime." Tests that applied to every student from the French club to the debate team would be an even broader threat to personal privacy. The Orleans board would be better advised to emulate school districts in Florida, New Jersey and Washington, which have chosen instead to build comprehensive drug education programs and trust between school administrators and students.

Women on the Soccer Field
Brazil Averts Its Eyes
By LARRY ROHTER

RIO DE JANEIRO

Across the United States right now, the Women's World Cup of soccer is the sports event of high summer, attracting stupendous crowds and frenzies of attention usually not seen there for any kind of soccer, or any women's sport, let alone both. Today Brazil meets the United States in the semifinals, but you would hardly know it from the coverage here in Rio.

While Sissi and Kátia (Brazilian soccer players use only one name) are heading toward their confrontation with Mia Hamm and Julie Foudy, Brazilian sports pages are focused almost entirely on the prospects of their men's soccer team winning the Copa America and the reasons why its coach, Wanderley Luxemburgo, left the top goal scorers Romário and Edmundo off the squad.

Soccer may be the king of sports here, but only the men's version of the game seems to wear the crown. Not one of this year's matches of the Brazilian national women's team has been televised live, sponsors have shied away from any association with the team, and hard-core fans who can recite the entire roster of the 1950 men's World Cup squad are hardpressed to name even one of the current World Cup women.

"Unfortunately, women's soccer still doesn't have a chance in Brazil," Armando Nogueira, one of the country's leading sports commentators, said when asked about the lack of interest here. "The best woman player in

"Jason, I'd like to let you play, but soccer is a girls' game."

Brazil will never be as popular as the worst male player, and the main reason is that women have been idolized as delicate objects of desire, incapable of playing a physical-contact, body-to-body sport."

Renata Cordeiro, 29, is one of Brazil's new female sportscasters, working for the SporTV cable channel as a soccer specialist. She recalls that when she was a teen-ager, her best friend asked that soccer be added to their school's physical education curriculum. "Absolutely not," was the answer that came back. "Soccer is not an appropriate activity for girls."

Such attitudes can be encountered all over Latin America, where the passion for soccer is exceeded only by the deeply ingrained machismo that governs the social roles of daily life. And everything is accentuated in Brazil, which has won four men's World Cups, more than any other country. Since the days of Pelé, it has prided itself on grooming the world's best players and playing the most inventive and flashy version of the game.

"In Brazil, soccer has a strong gender demarcation that makes it a masculine domain par excellence," said Roberto da Matta, a prominent anthropologist and sociologist. "It is a sport that contains all of the various elements that are traditionally used to define masculinity: conflict, physical confrontation, guts, dominance, control and endurance."

> **READINGS:** To see further examples of the distinction between explanation and argument, note differences between articles in "The Story of Dolly the Sheep and Her Aftermath" starting on page 343, and those in "The Debate" starting on page 356.

APPLICATION TO WRITING

Argument Structure, Logical Essay Organization, and Revision

When we put arguments into standard form, we ask critical questions: Is this assertion the conclusion, the focus of the argument? Or is it a premise supporting the conclusion? Or does it support another premise? Asking and answering questions such as these sharpens our analytical skills and enables us to read more critically. But analyzing argument structure also has specific application to writing.

Standard form can provide an outline of the argument, an excellent aid in essay organization, one you can use either to plan your essay or to revise it. Such an outline states the thesis of the essay—the conclusion of the argument—and each premise signals a new point to be developed.

If you have thought out your argument carefully before you start writing, you will find that putting it in standard form can lead to a good working outline from which to proceed. Or you may find that you can impose standard form on your argument only when you have done some writing. (Remember writing's power to actually generate ideas.) This kind of outlining is particularly helpful in the revision stage of your paper.

After writing a rough first draft of your argument, if time permits, put it away for a few hours. When you return to it, approach it as if you were not the writer but a reader. Set aside concerns of style, coherence, and mechanics; focus exclusively on the bones of the argument—the conclusion and the premises that support it. Write this skeleton of your draft in standard form. Now you are in an ideal position to evaluate the foundation of your argument—before proceeding to matters of development (well-supported premises), coherence, style, and mechanics. If the structure of your argument has problems—for example, information you initially saw as serving as a premise in your first draft, you now see does not directly support the conclusion—the time has come to repair any cracks you find in the foundation of your argument. This solid foundation makes the rest of the writing process less difficult and ultimately more successful.

Summaries

One way to explore an argument and reveal the important premises leading to a conclusion is to write a summary. Educator Mike Rose sees summarizing as an essential writing skill: "I [can't] imagine a more crucial skill than summarizing; we can't manage information, make crisp connections, or rebut arguments without it. The great syntheses and refutations are built on it."

Summaries come in many lengths, from one sentence to complete pages, depending on the purpose of the summary and the length of the piece to be summarized. Note, for example, the brief summaries at the conclusion of each chapter in this text.

A good summary is both complete and concise. To meet these conflicting goals, you must convey the essence of the whole piece without copying whole passages verbatim or emphasizing inappropriate features of the argument. Background information, detailed premise support, and narrative illustrations are usually omitted from summaries. Paraphrases of ideas— the author's meaning expressed in your own words—rather than direct quotations, except for a critically important phrase or two, are preferred. A summary should also be objective, excluding inferences and opinions. These are reserved for argument analysis.

Strategies for Writing a Summary

Read the piece you want to summarize carefully, identify the question at issue, and mark off the conclusion and important premises. A short summary sentence written in the margin beside each important premise and the conclusion(s) can be helpful. Now you are ready to write a first draft based on this outline. To ensure a smoothly written, coherent summary, in your second draft provide appropriate conjunctions and transitional phrases to join sentences and connect ideas (look ahead in this chapter for joining strategies). To ensure the conciseness that a summary demands, eliminate all "deadwood" from your sentences.

> SUMMARIES SHOULD BE OBJECTIVE, CONCISE, COMPLETE, COHERENT, AND WRITTEN IN YOUR OWN WORDS.

WRITING ASSIGNMENT 7

Constructing a Summary and Response

A. Read the following newspaper essay carefully, identify the question at issue, and sort out the various arguments offered.

B. Identify the conclusion of the argument written by Harvard Law School professor Laurence Tribe and supply the key premises in its support. Standard form can help you here.

C. Now write a summary of the article (approximately 150–200 words). You may want to compare summaries with classmates.

D. Having read the article critically and organized your interpretation in writing, write a letter to the editor of the newspaper in which you express your opinion of Tribe's article and your position on the issues he raises. Discuss the premises he presents, and if you think of others not mentioned in the article, include them. Letters to newspapers, like summaries, are usually compressed, so you will need to be economical and selective with words here, limiting yourself to between 300 and 400 words.

Audience

Readers of the daily newspaper who will need the key points of the original argument before they move on to your response.

Purpose

To present an insightful analysis of a complex argument in order to illuminate the issue for your readers.

Second Thoughts on Cloning

LAURENCE H. TRIBE

Some years ago, long before human cloning became a near-term prospect, I was among those who urged that human cloning be assessed not simply in terms of concrete costs and benefits, but in terms of what the technology might do to the very meaning of human reproduction, child rearing and individuality. I leaned toward prohibition as the safest course.

Today, with the prospect of a renewed push for sweeping prohibition rather than mere regulation, I am inclined to say, "Not so fast."

When scientists announced in February that they had created a clone of an adult sheep—a genetically identical copy named Dolly, created in the laboratory from a single cell of the "parent"—ethicists, theologians and others passionately debated the pros and cons of trying to clone a human being.

People spoke of the plight of infertile couples: the grief of someone who has lost a child whose biological "rebirth" might offer solace; the prospect of using cloning to generate donors for tissues and organs; the possibility of creating genetically enhanced clones with a particular talent or a resistance to some dread disease.

But others saw a nightmarish and decidedly unnatural perversion of human reproduction. California enacted a ban on human cloning, and the President's National Bioethics Advisory Commission recommended making the ban nationwide.

That initial debate has cooled, however, and many in the scientific field now seem to be wondering what all the fuss was about.

They are asking whether human cloning isn't just an incremental step beyond what we are already doing with artificial insemination, in vitro fertilization, fertility enhancing drugs and genetic manipulation. That casual attitude is sure to give way before long to yet another wave of prohibitionist outrage—a wave that I no longer feel comfortable riding.

I certainly don't subscribe to the view that whatever technology permits us to do we ought to do. Nor do I subscribe to the view that the Constitution necessarily guarantees every individual the right to reproduce through whatever means become technically possible.

Rather, my concern is that the very decision to use the law to condemn, and then outlaw, patterns of human reproduction—especially by invoking vague notions of what is "natural"—is at least as dangerous as the technologies such a decision might be used to control.

Human cloning has been condemned by some of its most articulate detractors as the ultimate embodiment of the sexual revolution, severing sex from the creation of babies and treating gender and sexuality as socially constructed.

But to ban cloning as the technological apotheosis of what some see as culturally distressing trends may, in the end, lend credence to strikingly similar objections to surrogate motherhood or gay marriage and gay adoption.

Equally scary, when appeals to the natural, or to the divinely ordained, lead to the criminalization of some method for creating human babies, we must come to terms with the inevitable: the prohibition will not be airtight.

Just as was true of bans on abortion and on sex outside marriage, bans on human cloning are bound to be hard to enforce. And that, in turn, requires us to think in terms of a class of potential outcasts—people whose very existence society will have chosen to label as a misfortune and, in essence, to condemn.

One need only think of the long struggle to overcome the stigma of "illegitimacy" for the children of unmarried parents. How much worse might be the plight of being judged morally incomplete by virtue of one's man-made origin?

There are some black markets (in narcotic drugs, for instance) that may be worth risking when the evils of legalization would be even worse. But when the contraband we are talking of creating takes the form of human beings, the stakes become enormous.

There are few evils as grave as that of creating a caste system, one in which an entire category of persons, while perhaps not labeled untouchable, is marginalized as not fully human.

And even if one could enforce a ban on cloning or at least insure that clones would not be a marginalized caste, the social costs of prohibition could still be high. For the arguments supporting an ironclad prohibition of cloning are most likely to rest on, and reinforce, the notion that it is unnatural and intrinsically wrong to sever the conventional links between heterosexual unions sanctified by tradition and the creation and upbringing of new life.

The entrenchment of that notion cannot be a welcome thing for lesbians, gay men and perhaps others with unconventional ways of linking erotic attachment, romantic commitment, genetic replication, gestational mothering and the joys and responsibilities of child rearing.

And, from the perspective of the wider community, straight no less than gay, a society that bans acts of human creation for no better reason than that their particular form defies nature and tradition is a society that risks cutting itself off from vital experimentation, thus losing a significant part of its capacity to grow. If human cloning is to be banned, then, the reasons had better be far more compelling than any thus far advanced.

Logical Relationships Between Ideas— Joining Words

Joining words and transitional phrases are especially important in written argument because the strength of an argument is in part dependent on the clarity of the relationships between the premises and the conclusion. But their use and importance is not limited to argument. In a recent murder trial, the jury stopped its deliberations, asking the judge to clarify his instructions. "The questions dealt with subtle discrepancies between the jury instructions and other information given to the six-man, six-woman panel—for example, whether the word 'and' or the word 'or' was intended in several instances."

Whether we are analyzing jury instructions, describing our Aunt Frances, or telling of our narrow escape from an avalanche, these words are essential to conveying a logical sequence of thought. If logical connections are missing, the reader cannot follow the line of reasoning and either stops reading or supplies his own connections, which may not be the ones intended.

As an example of the kind of "choppy" or disjointed writing that results from the omission of logical connections, look at the following excerpt from former President Bill Clinton's Inaugural Address.

> (1) When our Founders boldly declared America's independence to the world and our purpose to the Almighty, they knew that America to endure would have to change. (2) Not change for change's sake but change to preserve America's ideals—life, liberty, the pursuit of happiness. (3) Though we march to the music of our time, our mission is timeless. (4) Each generation of Americans must define what it means to be an American.

Although sentence 1 relates to sentence 2, sentences 3 and 4 fail to relate to these first two sentences or to each other. The result: a correct but incoherent paragraph. Joining words may not "fix" this paragraph—incoherence is sometimes the result of problems in organization that can't be remedied by the mere addition of joining words. But their use promotes coherence, showing your reader the logical connections between your ideas.

Joining words fall into three categories: coordinating conjunctions, subordinating conjunctions, and transition words.

Note that, while the list of coordinating conjunctions is complete, the other two lists are partial, featuring only the most commonly used words from both categories.

JOINING CHART

Logical relationship	Coordinating conjunctions	Subordinating conjunctions	Major transitions
Addition	and		also, moreover
Contrast and Concession	but yet	while whereas although though even though	however on the other hand
Cause	for	because since as	
Result Effect	so and so	so that in that in order that	therefore thus hence consequently
Condition		if unless provided that	

Note book (handwritten marginal note)

I love foreign films, *but* I have difficulty with subtitles.

I love foreign films *although* I have difficulty with subtitles.

I love foreign films; *however,* I have difficulty with subtitles.

Many of these words mean almost the same thing; they express the same logical connections between the ideas they join. For example, "but," "although," and "however" all express contrast, so we can join the following two ideas with any one of the three, and arrive at a similar, if not identical, meaning.

Choice of Joining Words

So what determines our choice? Notice that the two sentences joined by "but" and "although" are less formal in tone than the sentences joined by "however." We often find transition words such as "however," "moreover," "hence," and "consequently" in formal documents—legal briefs and contracts. In less formal writing, these words can be distracting, so the best writers use them sparingly. Try an "And" or a "But" instead of "Moreover" or "However" to open a sentence and save the transition words for major transitions.

On those occasions when we use transition words, it can often be effective for fluency to embed them within the clause rather than begin with them. For example:

Zoe loves foreign films and rarely sees American made movies; *however*, her roommate prefers American gangster films. ["However" begins the clause.]

Zoe loves foreign films and rarely sees American made movies; her roommate, *however*, prefers American gangster films. ["However" is embedded within the clause.]

A REVIEW: PUNCTUATION OF JOINING WORDS

Coordinating conjunctions—put a comma before the conjunction when it joins two independent clauses unless the clauses are short.

> The homeless are creating and living in unsanitary conditions all over America, so cities must provide housing for them.

Subordinating conjunctions—introductory subordinate clauses [clauses that begin with a subordinating conjunction] are usually followed by a comma.   *phrase that needs help*

> *Although* the homeless are creating and living in unsanitary conditions all over America, cities are not providing needed housing.

When a subordinate clause follows the main clause, the comma is usually omitted.

> Cities are not providing needed housing *even though* the homeless are creating and living in unsanitary conditions all over America.

Transition words—transitional words and phrases, because they do not join sentences but only connect ideas, should be preceded by a semicolon or a period when they come between two clauses.

> The homeless are creating and living in unsanitary conditions all over America; *therefore,* cities must provide adequate housing for them.

If, in the preceding example, a comma rather than a semicolon preceded "therefore," many readers would consider it a run-together sentence or comma splice.

When a transition word is embedded within a clause, it is usually set off with commas.

> The homeless are creating and living in unsanitary conditions all over America; cities, *therefore,* must provide adequate housing for them.

formal / writing

EXERCISE 3E

Joining Sentences for Logic and Fluency

Make this disjointed argument cohesive and logical by joining sentences with appropriate joining words. You don't need to change the sequence of sentences.

> Obstetricians perform too many Cesareans. They can schedule deliveries for their own convenience. They can avoid sleepless nights and canceled parties. They resort to Cesareans in any difficult delivery to protect themselves against malpractice suits. Cesareans involve larger fees and hospital bills than normal deliveries. Cesarean patients spend about twice as many days in the hospital as other mothers.

> The National Institutes of Health confirmed that doctors were performing many unnecessary Cesarean sections. They suggested ways to reduce their use. The recommendation was widely publicized. The obstetricians apparently failed to take note. In the 1980s, the operation was performed in 16.5 percent of United States' births. In the 1990s, 24.7 percent of the births were Cesareans.

Revising for Coherence

Joining words are one important tool available to writers to promote coherence—a logical flow—in their writing. Sentence focus, a consistent sentence subject that reflects the rhetorical subject (see Chapter 8, The Language of Argument—Style), is another. But since coherence comes from content as well as style, no textbook could specify every conceivable option available to writers. So a writer, when revising a draft, must keep his audience in mind, never forgetting to take his reader with him as he moves from sentence to sentence and paragraph to paragraph. The writer must be conscious of the separateness that exists between himself and his reader. The reader's only access to the mind of the writer is through the words on the page; the reader has no other access to the writer's thoughts.

Hidden Assumptions in Argument

Even when arguments appear to be well supported with premises, and where necessary, logical relationships are signaled with joining words, many real life arguments come to us incomplete, depending on **hidden assumptions,** unstated premises and conclusions. Sometimes a missing premise or conclusion is so obvious that we don't even recognize that it is unstated.

The burglar had dark hair, so Tracey certainly wasn't the burglar.
[Missing premise: Tracey does not have dark hair.]

Ken is lazy and lazy people don't last long around here. [Missing conclusion: Ken won't last long around here.]

Since I've sworn to put up with my tired VW until I can afford a BMW,
I must resign myself to the bug for a while longer. [Missing premise:
I can't afford a BMW now.]

Filling in the omitted assumptions here would seem unnecessarily
pedantic or even insulting to our intelligence.

Literature, by its nature elliptical, depends on the reader to make
plausible assumptions:

> Yon Cassius has a lean and hungry look; such men are dangerous.
>
> —SHAKESPEARE, *JULIUS CAESAR*

Shakespeare assumes his audience will automatically make the connection—Cassius is a dangerous man. But not all missing assumptions are
as obvious or as acceptable. At the heart of critical thinking lies the ability
to discern what a writer or speaker leaves **implicit**—unsaid—between the
lines of what he has made **explicit**—what he has clearly stated.

Dear Abby's readers took her to task for a response she made to a man
who complained that because he shared an apartment with a man, people
thought he was gay. Abigail Van Buren called this rumor an "ugly accusation." The implicit assumption here is that homosexuality is ugly, an assumption many of her readers—both gay and straight—objected to. One
reader asked, "If someone thought this man was Jewish, Catholic or
African American—would you call that an 'ugly accusation?'" Van Buren
apologized.

Law professor Patricia J. Williams, in *The Alchemy of Race and Rights*,
examines the implicit assumptions that led to the death of a young black
man in New York in the late 1980s. In this incident, three young black men
left their stalled car in Queens and walked to Howard Beach looking for
help, where they were surrounded by eight white teenagers who taunted
them with racial epithets and chased them for approximately three miles,
beating them severely along the way. One of the black men died, struck by
a car as he tried to flee across a highway; another suffered permanent
blindness in one eye.

During the course of the resultant trial, the community of Howard
Beach supported the white teenagers, asking "What were they [the three
black teenagers] doing here in the first place?" Examining this question,
Williams finds six underlying assumptions:

Everyone who lives here is white.

No black could live here.

No one here has a black friend.

No white would employ a black here.

No black is permitted to shop here.

No black is ever up to any good.

These assumptions reveal the racism that led the white teenagers to behave as they did and the community to defend their brutality.

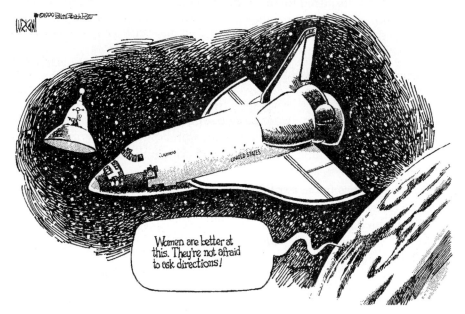

What unstated assumption does this cartoon depend on?

Dangers of Hidden Assumptions

Examine this seemingly straightforward argument:

John is Lisa's father, so clearly he is obligated to support her.

What's missing here? All fathers are obligated to support their daughters (or their children). But would everyone find this premise acceptable under all conditions? Probably not. What about the age factor? What about special circumstances: Lisa's mother has ample means while John is penniless and terminally ill? Or Lisa was legally adopted by another family, John being her birth father?

The danger with such incomplete arguments lies in more than one direction. A writer may leave his readers to supply their own assumptions, which may or may not coincide with those of the writer. If the issue is controversial, the risks of distorting an argument increase. Or, writers may deliberately conceal assumptions to hide an unsound, often misleading argument. Watch for these in advertising and politics. If you are on the alert for such deceptions, you are better able to evaluate what you read and hear and thus protect your own interests.

An example of a misleading argument:

> Echoing the arguments of the National Physicians for Social Responsibility and some public school districts, the Board of Education of a prominent Archdiocese refused to participate in a federal civil defense program that taught ways of preparing for nuclear war. They objected to instructions for teachers and students which recommended that "if there should be a nuclear flash, especially if you feel the warmth from it, take cover instantly in the best place you can find. If no cover is available, simply lie down on the ground and curl up." Their objections were leveled not at the specific suggestions but at the underlying unstated assumption: that nuclear war is survivable. In the words of the Board: "To teach children that nuclear war is a survivable disaster is to teach them that nuclear war is an acceptable political or moral option."

Hidden Assumptions and Standard Form

To help sort out the stated and unstated assertions in an argument, it can be illuminating to write out the argument in standard form. This means including the important hidden assumptions so the complete argument is before you and putting brackets around these assumptions to distinguish them from stated premises and conclusions.

Examples:

1. Harold is a politician so he's looking out for himself.
   a. [All politicians look out for themselves.]
   b. Harold is a politician.
      ∴ Harold is looking out for himself.
2. Products made from natural ingredients promote good health, so you should buy Brand X breads.
   a. Products made from natural ingredients promote good health.
   b. [Brand X breads are made from natural ingredients.]
      ∴ You should buy Brand X breads.
3. Products made from natural ingredients promote good health, and Brand X breads are made from natural ingredients.
   a. Products made from natural ingredients promote good health.
   b. Brand X breads are made from natural ingredients.
      ∴ [You should buy Brand X breads.]

EXERCISE 3F

Identifying Hidden Assumptions

A. The following arguments are missing either a premise or a conclusion. Put them into standard form, adding the implicit premise or conclusion; then place brackets around the missing assumptions you have inserted. A word to the wise: As with all argument analysis, find the conclusion first and then look for what is offered in its support.

1. Maggie is a musician, so she won't understand the business end of the partnership.
2. Those who exercise regularly increase their chances of living into old age, so we can expect to see Anna around for a very long time.
3. I never see Loretta without a book; she must be highly intelligent.
4. "Most professional athletes don't have a college degree, and so have no idea how to handle the big salaries suddenly dumped in their laps." (Harry Edwards, college professor and financial consultant for professional athletes)
5. "I start with the assumption that all human beings sin. So all I'll say is that I've led a human life." (former Senate Majority Leader Newt Gingrich in response to reporters' questions concerning an extramarital relationship)
6. Having become so central a part of our culture, television cannot be without its redeeming features.
7. **CONVICTED:** U.S. Petty Officer 3/c **Mitchell T. Garraway, Jr.,** of premeditated murder in the stabbing of a superior officer. The military court must now decide his sentence; its options include the death penalty. The last execution carried out by the Navy took place in 1849. (*Newsweek*)
8. From a letter to *The Sacramento Bee* after an article reporting that a nursing mother had been evicted from a downtown department store cafeteria (thanks to Perry Weddle of Sacramento State University for this one):

   It was inhumane to deny this woman the right to nurse her baby in the cafeteria because she was simply performing a natural bodily function. (Where will this argument take you once you supply the suppressed assumption?)

B. The following article appeared in the news section of several major newspapers. Read it carefully and supply the hidden assumption it seems to be leading us to. Why would the writer choose to make this assumption implicit?

Robert Redford's Daughter Rescued

SALT LAKE CITY—Shauna Redford, daughter of actor Robert Redford, was rescued when her car plunged into a river, authorities said yesterday.

They said Redford was wearing a seatbelt and suffered only minor injuries in the accident Friday. Redford, 23, of Boulder, was rescued from her partially submerged auto by three other motorists, who saw her vehicle crash through a guardrail into the Jordan River, eight miles south of Salt Lake City.

The Utah Highway Patrol said the three rescuers released Redford's seatbelt, pulled her from the car and carried her to the riverbank.

She was held at a hospital overnight for observation and released.

Last summer, Sidney Wells, 22, a Colorado University student who had dated Shauna Redford, was shot and killed in Boulder. Police said the killing may have been drug related.

C. The Republican National Committee, referring to the then newly elected Democratic Speaker of the House, issued a three-page memorandum titled "Tom Foley: Out of the Liberal Closet." The memo went on to compare Foley's voting record with that of Representative Barney Frank, Democrat, of Massachusetts, openly homosexual, who was described in the memo as "the ultra-liberal representative from Massachusetts."

What **innuendo** (an indirect derogatory remark that is implicit rather than explicit) is the Republican National Committee making about former speaker of the house, Tom Foley?

D. Find one advertisement or political cartoon in print journalism that clearly depends for its message on one or more unstated assumptions. Clip or photocopy the ad, write out the principal argument including the missing assertions, and bring it to class to discuss with classmates.

> **READINGS:** For additional exercises concerning hidden assumptions, see the following selections: "Three Cartoons from the Archives of *The New Yorker* Magazine" on page 454, Topic #2; "The Trouble with Sex" on page 464, Topic #3; "Sexual Separatism" on page 491, Topic #3.

Hidden Assumptions and Audience Awareness

As stated above, politicians and advertisers may deliberately suppress assumptions in order to manipulate the public. We will assume that we, as careful writers, do not share this goal and would not deliberately leave important assumptions unstated. At the same time, we don't want to bore our readers by spelling out unnecessary details. How do we determine what material to include, what to leave out?

George Lakoff and Mark Johnson, in their book *Metaphors We Live By*, point out that meaning is often dependent on context. They offer the following sentence as an example.

We need new sources of energy.

This assertion means one thing to a group of oil executives and quite another to an environmental group. The executives may assume the writer is referring to more offshore drilling, whereas the environmentalists may think the writer is referring to greater development of solar or other alternate sources of energy.

As writers, we must consider our audience carefully and understand the purpose for which we are writing. We make choices about which assumptions must be made explicit according to our knowledge of the reader. Are we writing for an audience predisposed to agree with us, or one that is opposed to our point of view? Are we writing for readers who are knowledgeable about the subject or ignorant? The answers to these questions help us to determine what material to include and what to omit.

A reviewer of the book *Murderers and Other Friends* criticizes the author, British writer John Mortimer, for making too many assumptions about his audience:

> Mortimer doesn't for a moment seem to believe that his new book will be read by anyone but old friends. He assumes we know Horace Rumpole and She Who Must Be Obeyed and that we've seen the television adaptations he has written of Evelyn Waugh's novel "Brideshead Revisited" and his own "Summer's Lease." He knows that we know about his father, the blind divorce lawyer, and the play he wrote about him, just as we know about his own years as a Queen's Counsel defending colorful riffraff in the Old Bailey. In short, he assumes we have not only read his autobiography but also have been paying close attention to "Mystery!" and "Masterpiece Theater."

You may find it helpful to have a friend, one who is unfamiliar with your topic, read a draft of your paper. Such a reader may help you spot assumptions that need clarification.

EXERCISE 3G

Identifying Your Reader

A common feature of many publications today is a section called "Personals." *The Nation* and *The New York Review of Books* (both probably in your library) and many local periodicals, including some campus papers, carry "Personals." What follows are four such ads, two from women who advertised in *Focus,* a public television magazine, and two from men who advertised in *The Daily Californian,* the University of California at Berkeley student newspaper. Form four groups and choose one of the following ads to analyze and respond to together.

From *The Daily Californian*

> **MALE UCB student,** 25, 6′1″, interested in music, religion, literature, psychedelics, nature etc. seeks Lithuanian woman with beautiful soul—witty, pretty, intellectual, virtuous—for fun, friendship, maybe more.
>
> **ENGLISH/MUSIC major,** 25, would like to meet witty, intellectual, attractive female (pref. math/physics/other science major) for concerts, foreign films & after dinner activities.

From *Focus*

> **Sensual Blue-eyed Blonde,** successful entrepreneur, 30, 5′4″, who is attractive, well traveled, well read, and has a great sense of humor, seeks a spiritual, self aware single white male, 30–45, 5′10″ or taller, who is worldly but grounded, successful but sensitive, healthy but not fanatical and open to pursuing a long-term commitment. Note and photo appreciated.
>
> **Pretty Woman, International** travel, Ivy education, health career, would like to meet professional man, 35–50, for tennis, dancing, bear hugs and possible first-time family. Photo appreciated.

Your aim is to understand the writer of the ad, who will then become the audience for your response. Read the ad of your choice carefully. What kind of person is the writer? What can you infer about his or her character, personality, and values? What does the publication he or she chose to advertise in reveal about the writer? Read between the lines: What hidden assumptions are buried there?

After completing your analysis, as a group write a brief response informed by your knowledge of the writer of the ad. If time permits, reading these responses to the class might be entertaining.

WRITING ASSIGNMENT 8

A Letter of Application

Now, turn to the classified ads in any newspaper, select a job, and write a letter of application (a one-page cover letter). You need to consider your audience carefully in order to create a profile of your reader and a response that will appeal to him. Instead of a job in the classifieds, you may prefer to select an internship or a job on campus for this application.

Audience

A person who will be evaluating you for a position you particularly want.

Purpose

To present yourself as a desirable and qualified applicant for the position.

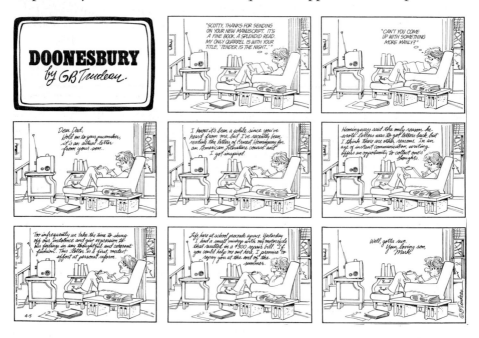

This writer has certainly considered his audience very carefully.

SUMMARY

In logic, the word argument has a special meaning, referring to rational discourse composed of premises and a conclusion rather than to a fight. It is useful to be able to recognize premises and conclusions in order to fully understand what an argument is proposing. Expressing arguments in standard form is a helpful strategy for understanding arguments.

Understanding the structure of arguments can be useful to writers when considering the organization of their written arguments.

The logical connections between assertions in argument can be signaled by conjunctions and traditional phrases to promote a logical flow of prose and ideas.

Arguments are frequently presented with some of the premises or the conclusion implied rather than stated. Sometimes such hidden assumptions are obvious, but in some instances they can be misleading and need to be made explicit. Recognizing hidden assumptions in argument is an important part of critical thinking.

KEY TERMS

Argument   a rational piece of discourse, written or spoken, which attempts to persuade the reader or listener to believe something; composed of at least one premise in support of a conclusion.

Conclusion   the key assertion in an argument, the statement which the other assertions support; the point one hopes to make when presenting an argument.

Explanation   an attempt to clarify why something has happened or why you hold a given opinion.

Explicit   clearly stated, distinctly expressed.

Hidden assumptions   missing, unstated premises and conclusions in arguments; assertions that are necessary to recognize in order to fully understand an argument.

Implicit   suggested so as to be understood but not plainly expressed.

Innuendo   an indirect remark or reference, usually implying something derogatory.

Joining words   words or phrases that indicate, or signal, the logical relationship between assertions in an argument. "Therefore" and its synonyms signal a conclusion; "because" and its synonyms signal a premise.

Occam's razor   a principle of argument that advocates ecomony, maintaining that the simplest line of reasoning is usually the best.

Opinion   a provisional judgment or belief, requiring proof or support; a first step in developing an argument.

Premise   a reason that supports the conclusion in an argument.

Standard form   an argument reduced to its essence, its principal premises and conclusion listed in simple outline form, with premises numbered and conclusion stated at the end.

CHAPTER 4

Written Argument

If the cultivation of understanding consists in one thing more than in another, it is surely in learning the grounds of one's own opinions.

—JOHN STUART MILL

In the previous chapter, we focused on the structure of argument, distinguishing between premises and conclusions and reducing arguments to these two basic components. But how do we begin to write an argument?

Focusing Your Topic

A first critical step is to focus and refine the topic. At one time or another, we have all been part of heated political discussions between friends or family members. Grandfather states that taxes are too high under the current administration. Cousin Susan points out that corporations do not pay their fair share, while Dad shouts that the government funds too many social programs and allows too large a number of immigrants to enter the country. These discussions are often discursive and unsatisfying because they are not focused on one clear and precise **question at issue.**

For an argument to be successful, one person does not necessarily have to defeat another; one point of view does not have to be proven superior to another. An argument can also be considered successful if it opens a line of communication between people and allows them to consider—with respect—points of view other than their own. But, if an argument is to establish such a worthwhile exchange, it must focus first on a single issue and then on a particular question at issue.

The Issue

An **issue** is any topic of concern and controversy. Not all topics are issues since many topics are not controversial. Pet care, for instance, is a topic but not an issue; laboratory testing of animals, on the other hand, is an issue. In the hypothetical family discussion above, four issues are raised: taxes, the current administration, immigration, and government-funded social programs. No wonder such a discussion is fragmented and deteriorates into people shouting unsupported claims at one another.

Where and how do you find appropriate topics? In your work or personal life you might need to write an argument that has a real-world purpose. Why product X is superior to all other brands and how using it will turn a customer's business around. Why you are the most qualified applicant for the job. For your classes, you are often assigned topics. But sometimes in a writing class you are asked to select a topic of interest to you, and then you are on your own. Newspapers, in your community and on your campus, can suggest issues, as can news broadcasts. The Internet has opened up a vast new world of information from which you might select a topic once you have identified a broad category that interests you. Although it can be useful to choose a subject that you know something about, particularly if you want to take a strong stand right away, don't be afraid of exploring new areas. In a freshman history class some years ago, one of us was handed the unknown name *Leon Trotsky.* That required paper led to a whole new world of knowledge: Russia, the Soviet Union, the Russian Revolution, and communism. Your writing assignments can be a way of opening new worlds.

The Question at Issue

Whether you choose you own issue or are assigned one, the next step is to select one **question at issue**—a particular aspect of the issue under consideration. Affirmative action, for instance, is an issue that contains many distinct questions at issue.

Should affirmative action play a role in university admissions?

Should affirmative action play a role in the work place?

Should affirmative action play a role in government contracts?

Has affirmative action led to discrimination against white males?

Should affirmative action based on gender be separated from affirmative action based on ethnic origin?

A writer who does not focus on one and only one question at issue risks producing a disorganized essay, one that is difficult to follow because the readers will not be sure they understand the point the writer is arguing. Writing on the issue of how affirmative action has benefitted women, one student kept drifting away from that question at issue to another: Should affirmative action play a role in university admissions? Since both her questions at issue were part of the **same issue,** affirmative action, and hence related, she was unaware that her paper was going in two different directions. The result was a disorganized, disjointed essay.

The following diagram illustrates that a single issue may contain any number of separate and distinct questions as issue. Your task as a writer is to isolate a particular question at issue and stay focused on it.

AFFIRMATIVE ACTION

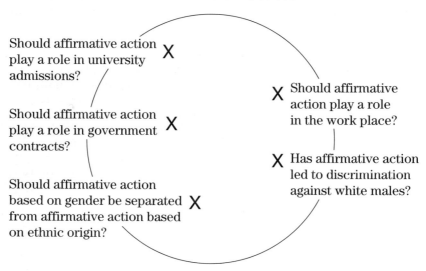

Should affirmative action X play a role in university admissions?

Should affirmative action X play a role in government contracts?

Should affirmative action based on gender be separated X from affirmative action based on ethnic origin?

X Should affirmative action play a role in the work place?

X Has affirmative action led to discrimination against white males?

The Thesis

The final step in establishing the focus of an essay is determining the **thesis.** Although the issue and question at issue state, respectively, the subject and focus of the paper, they are neutral statements; they do not reveal the writer's opinion nor should they. To encourage objective analysis, the question at issue should be expressed in neutral rather than biased or emotionally charged language. The **thesis,** however, states the writer's position, her response to the question at issue, the *conclusion* of her argument, the primary claim she is making. Your thesis takes central stage in both the final paper you write and the thinking you do as you conduct your research and prepare drafts. It controls the evidence you gather and clarifies the stand you want to take.

Suppose you want to write a paper about affirmative action and narrow the issue to a more focused question at issue:

Should affirmative action play a role in university admissions?

You might start with a sentence that states the topic:

> Affirmative action in university admissions has become a controversial subject.

Yes, your reader would say. You're right on target with the topic, but what about the assertive edge? Where is your opinion? What have you to prove in such a statement? Not much. Not many people would argue that affirmative action is a controversial issue. You need to move on to an assertion of something you want to prove in your paper, a statement that lays out the grounds for an argument.

Perhaps you want to convince your university that affirmative action is necessary on your campus.

> Affirmative action has played an important role in bringing minorities into our university and thus into society as a whole. Our country is not ready to abandon the significant gains it has made under affirmative action guidelines for university admissions.

You have set up reasonable expectations for what you need to develop and support your point: convincing evidence of the "important role" affirmative action has played, further evidence of why "our country is not ready to abandon" these gains, and elaboration of the term "significant." (See *Definition* in Chapter 5.)

Or, you may want to join others who have argued that affirmative action in admissions must stop.

> Because affirmative action in university admissions has created more problems than it has solved, the time has come to end special admissions for minorities.

Here you need to provide detailed examples of problems created by affirmative action and show how affirmative action is responsible for such problems. You also need to recognize any advantages that have come from affirmative action and balance them with the problems you identify.

With either of these thesis statements, your reader will know the point you are advocating in your paper and the purpose behind your choice of question at issue. Just as important, you will have pinned down your ideas so that you have a road map to guide you as you search for and sift through the evidence necessary for supporting your position.

Sometimes when we begin exploring a topic for a paper, we may not know our position. We may need to learn more about the question at issue through research before arriving at a conclusion. If, however, our question at issue is clear and precise, we can proceed without a definite thesis or with only a tentative one since the writing process itself will help us to arrive at one. (Refer to Chapter 1.)

We don't necessarily have to arrive at a completely yes or no response to the question at issue. For example, if the question at issue is whether or not school administrators should have the right to censor student newspapers, our response may not be an unequivocal yes or no but a qualified response:

> School administrators should not have the right to censor student newspapers unless an article is libelous.

After completing the necessary research and examining various points of view, we may still be unable to reach a final conclusion. In this case, the thesis of the paper may be an evaluation of these different points of view with a tentative stand based on the unfolding of future events.

Keep in mind that arguments don't always have to be adversarial. Often you will find yourself taking a tentative position, researching the issue, and finally arbitrating a conclusion, settling for a consensus. This option can be more challenging to write on successfully but often reflects reality since careful examination of issues frequently reveals that both sides have reasonable arguments. Your thesis for this kind of paper also requires careful thought and should reflect the compromise position you have chosen. Take, for example, the conflict in Yugoslavia. Your thesis might run something like this:

> When they were able to return to their ravaged country, Kosova Albanians maintained that atrocities committed against them by Serbs required retribution. Although much of the world understood their bitterness, international peacekeepers were morally obligated to protect the Serbs just as they had tried to defend the Kosovas.

Your paper would have to explore the degree of atrocity carried out by both sides and then show why peace would be best served by protecting Serbs as well as Kosovas. You would not be taking an adversarial position on either side yet would be mounting an argument for a complex solution to a perplexing issue. In Writing Assignment 11 on page 118, we ask you to try such an approach.

In essays by professional writers, the thesis is sometimes indirectly stated; it may be implicit rather than explicit. For instance, writer Sheila Koran argues in an essay that gay and lesbian couples should have the same legal spousal rights as married couples. She never directly states this thesis as she describes the life she lives with her mate, a life like any other family's, but the point is clearly made; the reader is never confused about the purpose of the essay. In general, the more experienced the writer, the more she is able to write a focused essay without an explicit thesis. But for the most part, writer and reader are best served by a clearly defined thesis.

In summary, you should take the following steps as you prepare your topic:

> Select an **issue** that is debatable, an issue on which you can argue more than one position.

Narrow that issue to a focused **question at issue.**
Write a "working" **thesis** that makes an assertion about this question at issue; your thesis states your opinion on the question at issue.

Two Kinds of Thesis Statements

Another option we have when writing a thesis is to decide whether or not it should be "complete" or "open." An open thesis states the writer's opinion but not the reasons for her opinion. A complete thesis includes both the writer's opinion and all of the reasons or premises that support this conclusion. For example:

> An "open" thesis:
>> Access to the Internet should be controlled.
> A "complete" thesis:
>> Because children need protection from pornography, our right to pri-
>> vacy is threatened, and "intellectual property" can be too easily
>> pirated, access to the Internet should be controlled.
> A compromise:
>> Access to the Internet raises serious moral, legal, and even constitu-
>> tional questions, the nature of which suggests that such access should
>> be controlled.

Which thesis statement is preferable? It is a matter of choice, the writer's choice. Some writers fear that the complete thesis will not capture the reader's interest, believing that if all the reasons for the conclusion are given in the thesis, the reader's curiosity will not be aroused. On the other hand, a writer may prefer the greater clarity of the "complete" thesis, for herself and her readers. In any case, even if a writer chooses the open the-sis approach, at some point in the process she should be just as clear about the reasons for her position as the writer who chooses the complete thesis.

As a general guideline to assist you in deciding the most suitable thesis approach to take, consider the complexity of the topic, the length of the paper, the needs of your audience, and the purpose of your project. In a long paper on a complex topic, the reader may welcome the clarity of the complete thesis or at least a modified one, but in a short essay on a simple topic, the complete thesis is probably not necessary and may sound too mechanical.

A thesis is not necessarily restricted to one sentence. In fact, it's not unusual for a complete thesis to require a paragraph. As your work pro-gresses and new ideas change your thinking on your topic, you may need to revise your thesis. You may also find yourself refining the language of your thesis during the final editing process. But a well thought out and clearly expressed thesis guides writer and reader, keeping both focused on the question at issue and on the position the writer has taken.

EXERCISE 4A

Identifying the Issue, Question at Issue, and Thesis

Complete the following sets by supplying the missing element.

1. *Issue:*

    Question at Issue: Should universities put a cap on fee increases?
    Thesis: To ensure an economically diverse student population, universities should put a cap on fee increases.

2. *Issue:* First Amendment rights to free speech and the Internet

    Question at Issue:
    Thesis: Because the safety of children using the Internet is a growing concern to parents and educators, some restrictions on free speech are necessary and inevitable.

3. *Issue:* Private militias

    Question at Issue: Should the government have the right to control the public speech of private militias?
    Thesis:

4. For the following example, supply two examples of a thesis: (1) An open thesis and (2) a complete thesis.

    Issue: Gambling on the Internet
    Question at Issue: Should gambling on the Internet be available and unrestricted?

> **READINGS:** See "Fertility for Sale" on page 421 for an example of a broad topic narrowed to a specific question at issue. Each writer in the piece responds to the question in a different way. Can you state the conclusion or thesis of each mini-argument?

Shaping a Written Argument—Rhetorical Strategies

What do we mean by *rhetorical?* The term **rhetoric** has various shades of meaning, but the following definition adapted from the Greek philosopher Aristotle provides the most useful approach for our purposes: "The art of using language to good effect, to prove, to convince, to persuade."

And thus to argue. The structure of written argument as we know it to-day dates back to the orations of Greeks and Romans. The following features of classical argument, modified by contemporary rhetoric, can serve us well as long as we recognize that they are options, not requisite components. We write to communicate, not to fit a formula or fulfill a set of narrow expectations.

The Introduction

How you begin your argument depends on the issue, the audience, and your own style. The key question is: How much can you expect your readers to know about your question at issue? If your subject has received a great deal of recent media attention, you probably do not need to supply much background. If, on the other hand, your subject is obscure or technical, then you will probably have to give your readers the necessary background information—the history of the case or the specific circumstances that give rise to the present problem—so that they can understand the argument to follow.

If not much background is required, you may want to begin your essay with a relevant narrative, either actual or fictional, which illustrates your question at issue. For example, if your subject is euthanasia, you may want to describe a day in the life of a terminally ill patient. Such a scene captures the reader's interest—not a necessity but sometimes a valuable rhetorical strategy. A relevant quotation can also provide an interesting way into your argument. Or you may choose to open with an opposing view and build your argument on a refutation of what is often the prevailing wisdom on an issue.

No matter what approach you choose, you have considerable flexibility. Your introduction may be a single paragraph or run to three or four paragraphs depending on the strategies you choose and the amount of background required. Usually, you will state your thesis (your position, your opinion) somewhere in the introductory paragraphs so that your reader is clear about the purpose of the essay.

For a variety of introductory strategies, examine the three sample essays in 4E, page 106. The author of "Alternative Sentencing" starts with the broad issue of crime, moves to problems associated with sentencing, offers a short concession, and states the thesis, all in the first paragraph. The author of "Rap Takes a Bum Rap" includes an analogy and a statement of what Rap is not before stating his thesis. Journalist Cynthia Tucker presents her position on affirmative action in university admissions in the form of two questions, a more indirect approach than the two previous essays but nonetheless clear.

The Development of Your Argument

Once again, the possibilities, although not infinite, are numerous. You need to present as many strong premises in support of your position as necessary. These in turn have to be elaborated, explained, and defended with as much specific detail, example, and illustration as you can provide. You may draw on personal experience, research, and respected authorities to support your position. Called, in classical rhetoric, the *confirmation* of your position, this support should be connected explicitly to your thesis unless the logical ties are self-evident. As the Greek philosopher and rhetorician Plato said in the *Phaedrus,* "What is stated outright will be clearer than what is not."

Sometimes one premise requires a whole paragraph or more. Others may need only a few sentences and can be effectively grouped with additional premises. Audience and purpose as well as your topic play a role in your choices. Here are two examples of paragraphs lifted from the middle of student essays, one that develops a single premise in some detail, another that groups a series of premises together in one paragraph.

A Single Premise Paragraph

Since the NCAA (National Collegiate Athletic Association) policy of random drug testing was begun some years ago, public debate on this issue has increased, and the idea of drug testing for college athletes has been challenged for a variety of reasons. The strongest argument against drug testing of college athletes is that it is unconstitutional. An athlete should be entitled to the same constitutional rights as other citizens, and drug testing violates both the Fourth Amendment's provisions against unreasonable search and seizure, and the Fifth Amendment's provision of the right to refuse to furnish potentially incriminating evidence about one's self.* As various forms of drug testing were subjected to legal challenges, the courts needed to rule that drug testing is, indeed, unconstitutional. *Time* magazine reported that ". . . a number of judges have already ruled that mass testing violates workers' constitutional rights to privacy and protection from self-incrimination," and quoted Federal Judge Robert Collins, who called a U.S. Customs Service drug testing program "unreasonable and wholly unconstitutional." In the late 1980s, the Appellate Division of the New York State Supreme Court ruled that probationary teachers in a Long Island school district could not be compelled to submit to urinalysis because the tests would be an unconstitutional invasion of privacy (Kaufman 19). In the case of Simone LeVant, the Stanford diver who has so far been the only athlete to challenge the NCAA drug tests in court, *The New York Times* reported that Judge Peter G. Stone of the Santa Clara county Superior Court agreed with the athlete and her attorney that mandatory urine tests were an obtrusive, unreasonable, and unconstitutional invasion of privacy.

---

*Given the length of this paragraph, some writers might choose to divide it in two, starting a new paragraph here where the examples begin. Paragraphing, while certainly not arbitrary, can be flexible and should serve the needs of the reader as well as the logic of the argument.

A Multipremise Paragraph

Although it is a controversial proposition, legalizing drugs has many advantages. First of all, it will free the now overburdened legal system to do its job dispensing justice. Cases will be processed with greater speed because the system won't be overwhelmed with drug cases. With the legalization of drugs, violent drug-related crimes will decrease. As a result, prisons will be less crowded, which in turn will allow serious offenders to serve longer terms. Legalizing drugs will free law enforcement officials to combat other serious crimes more effectively. With the money saved from law enforcement and legal procedures, a more effective campaign of educating the public on the maladies of drugs can be mounted, and more money will be available for the rehabilitation of drug addicts. Finally, by legalizing drugs, we can slow down the spread of AIDS among IV drug users, who will be able to get clean needles and not have to share with other drug addicts, many of whom are infected with the AIDS virus. The positive results of legalizing drugs definitely outweigh the negative consequences.

In the second paragraph, the writer has only just begun with such a summary approach to a broad subject. Each individual premise will have to be given specific support in subsequent paragraphs.

How Many Premises Should an Argument Have?

It would seem that the greater the number of premises, the stronger the argument, but this quest for quantity should not be at the expense of quality; in other words, weak or questionable premises should not be included just to increase the number of premises. It's possible to have a strong argument with only one or two premises if those premises are extremely convincing and are developed in detail.

The Conclusion

We have no simple rule of thumb here other than to suggest you conclude your essay rather than simply stop. If your paper is long and complex, you need to help your reader by briefly summarizing where you have been and what you propose. If you present only a tentative or partial thesis in the introduction, then you need to be sure that your final position is clear in the conclusion. If you think that further investigation is still needed before you can arrive at a responsible "conclusion" on the issue, then recommend what direction you think such investigation should take. If, as a result of your argument, you have definite recommendations for action, your conclusion can carry such suggestions.

You and your readers should feel satisfied at the close of your paper. This does not mean that every paper needs a long and redundant formulaic conclusion. Once again, we refer you to the sample essays in Exercise 4E for models.

And so your argument assumes its shape. Commenting on effective rhetoric, Plato, quoting Socrates, summed it up in his *Phaedrus:*

> Every discourse, like a living creature, should be so put together that it has its own body and lacks neither head nor feet, middle nor extremities, all composed in such a way that they suit both each other and the whole.

READINGS: For examples of well-crafted introductions and conclusions, see "Politics of Biology" on page 404, "Eggs for Sale" on page 421, "The Trouble with Sex" on page 464, "The Quare Gene" on page 684.

A Dialectical Approach to Argument

Effective argument is more than the straightforward presentation of a thesis, premises, and their support. Most issues worth arguing today are complex, with evidence sometimes contradictory or ambiguous. Arguments on such issues should reflect a flexible mind, one capable of thinking dialectically. From this term's various meanings, we can extract a definition of **dialectic** appropriate for written argument: a process of examining an issue by looking at it from opposing points of view; or, to elaborate a little: a method of argument that systematically weighs contradictory ideas with a view to resolution of their contradictions.

It is this interplay of conflict among seeming opposites that can help us arrive at some form of "truth" or resolution. The German writer Goethe said that what we agree with leaves us inactive, but contradiction makes us productive. The world is full of contradictions. Those trained in dialectical thinking are better equipped to handle such contradictions. Through logical disputation we test and explore our ideas as we search for a viable position. As philosopher Georg Hegel saw it, the dialectic is a *process* of change whereby an idea, a *thesis,* is transformed into its opposite, *antithesis.* The combination of the two is then resolved in a form of truth, *synthesis.* Aristotle described this final common ground as *stasis.*

The English philosopher John Stuart Mill was trained by his father to argue both sides of every question and was taught that you had no right to a belief unless you understood the arguments for its opposite.

Eleanor Roosevelt advised women in politics to "argue the other side with a friend until you have found the answer to every point which might be brought up against you." We would second her advice.

And cognitive psychologist Piaget maintained that one mark of a maturing mind is the ability to take another's point of view and thus be capable of considering two conflicting views on the same issue.

A book reviewer takes Camille Paglia and her book *Sex, Art, and American Culture* to task for not having this capability:

> . . . she is constitutionally incapable of splitting a difference. She is one of the least dialectical minds that ever claimed to be critical. Her style is a style of pure assertion. It has no philosophical shading or depth.

Dialectical thinking moves us to a richer form of argument in which the process of interweaving premises and counterarguments leads us to a new, stronger position on the issue.

Addressing Counterarguments

To take this dialectical approach to argument, you as a writer must pay careful attention to opposing views, acknowledging within your paper important **counterarguments** and thus those members of your audience who might hold them.

But, one might ask, why aid and abet the opposition by calling attention to their arguments? For a number of good reasons, such strategies can actually strengthen your own position.

- By *anticipating* your opponent's reasoning, you can often disarm the opposition. The "I recognize that . . ." approach can be very effective, showing the writer's knowledge of the opposition's viewpoint.
- You can make your own position stronger when you state and then *refute* opposing premises by demonstrating their weakness or falseness. You must handle refutation tactfully, however, if you hope to convince those opposed to your position. If you treat them with contempt, as though they are shortsighted and thickheaded for holding the position they do, you only alienate them and defeat your own purpose, which is to have your views heard.
- By addressing counterarguments to your position, you also appear more reasonable, more fair. You are seen not as narrow-minded, dogmatic, or unheedful of others' views, but as broad-minded and aware of complexity and so ultimately as more intelligent, reliable, and thus credible.
- And when you *acknowledge* the possibility of merit in some of your opponents' reasoning, you have taken the ultimate step in establishing yourself as a "generous" thinker. Arguments are rarely truly one-sided, no matter how strong your convictions. When you can *concede* a point, you move closer to a middle ground, opening a line of communication and thus increasing your chances of winning your final point.
- You may even discover weaknesses and contradictions in your own thinking as you sort through the reasoning of your opponents. It is not easy to abandon cherished beliefs, but clear thinkers often must.

How Much Counterargument?

How much counterargument should writers include in their papers? There is no precise answer. If the writer has strong refutations for every one of the opposition's premises, then she may want to address all these counterarguments. If, on the other hand, a writer thinks the premises she has to support her conclusion are stronger than her refutation of the opposition, she may want to include only a minimum of counterargument. In any case, a writer cannot ignore the most compelling opposing premises even if they provide the greatest challenge to the writer's own view.

For a paper on limiting gun ownership, one would have to address the fact that many Americans believe the Second Amendment to the Constitution guarantees the right to own guns, and acknowledge that, in the eyes of some, hunting rifles should form a category separate from assault weapons or small handguns. And in a paper in favor of euthanasia, the writer would have to deal with the widely held belief that euthanasia is a form of murder or suicide. Precisely how the writer would present these counterarguments would depend on the evidence she presents and the precise position on the issue she decides to take. Once again, this is where the wording of the thesis is important.

Refutation and Concession

As you can see from this discussion, there is more than one way to address counterarguments. But address them you must, since to present a contradictory position and then leave it alone would confuse your reader. Here are two possible responses.

1. **Refutation:** Present a counterargument and then explain why this position is false, misleading, irrelevant, or weak; discredit it in some well-reasoned way.

   From a student essay in support of a law sanctioning active euthansia:

   Some say death and suffering are in keeping with God's universal plan for humanity. Functioning to educate, to prepare people for the painless eternity of heaven, the dying process, no matter how long or how agonizing, has both spiritual and moral purpose. **To believe this argument though, one must believe there is life after death and many do not. So why can't people live and die in accordance with their own value system? Let both the religious and secular have some control of their own destiny; give those who choose to die that alternative, while honoring the belief of those who do not.** [emphasis added]

2. **Concession:** Recognize the merit of a counterargument and so
   concede that point or (as in our example below) a feature of it. If,
   for example, you are arguing in favor of euthanasia and want to refute the counterargument that euthanasia is a form of murder, you
   might begin this way:

   Although I also believe that life is sacred and murder is wrong, I
   don't think that ending the life of a brain-dead patient is equivalent to
   murder since in the true sense of the word "life," this patient is not
   living.

Visually, the relationship between counterargument and refutation and
concession looks something like this:

Counterargument

Refutation   Concession

Rogerian Strategy

For a deeper appreciation of concession, we turn to the psychology of
communication, particularly the work of Carl R. Rogers, a psychotherapist
and communication theorist. Carl Rogers recognized that people tend to
establish barriers and to grow more rigid in their beliefs when threatened
and are thus less open to alternatives. If we view argument, whether spoken or written, not as a hostile contest between adversaries but as a dialogue, as an open exchange of ideas directed toward mutual understanding, we may find a more responsive audience and thus have greater
success with changing people's opinions. If we are genuinely concerned
with communicating our ideas to others, we must cultivate the audience to
whom we direct these ideas. To achieve this end, we must develop *empathy*—the ability, in Rogers' words, "to see the expressed idea and attitude
from the other person's point of view, to sense how it feels to him, to
achieve his frame of reference in regard to the thing he is talking about." It
is through empathy that we can most successfully understand another's position and so concede appropriate points, often gaining rather than losing
ground in the process.

Take, for example, the issue of the death penalty. If a writer can understand why someone believes the death penalty serves as a deterrent and
can acknowledge that understanding, a reader who favors the death
penalty will be more inclined to consider the writer's arguments opposing
the death penalty. The reader will feel less threatened as the writer reduces the gap between them and replaces hostile judgment with "mutual

communication," helping a defensive opponent to see alternatives to her beliefs. Such a commitment can, as Rogers points out, carry risks. As a writer begins to "really understand" another person's point of view, she runs "the risk of being changed" herself. This spirit of conciliation and co-operation can sometimes be painful. But the gain in understanding can pay off handsomely as rigidity and defensiveness evolve into problem solving.

A British politician turned to Rogerian strategy when Iran and Britain were in a political crisis over the publication of Salmon Rushdie's *The Satanic Verses*, a novel which offended Moslems to such a degree that the then ruler of Iran, the Ayatollah Khomeini, called on Moslems around the world to kill Rushdie, sending the author into hiding for 10 years. The British government, while providing the author with continuous police protection, tried to temper Iran's fury. Britain's foreign secretary, Sir Geoffrey Howe, in a BBC radio broadcast meant to be heard by Iran, delivered the following message:

> We do understand that the book itself has been found deeply offensive by people of the Moslem faith. We can understand why it has been criticized. It is a book that is offensive in many other ways as well. We are not upholding the right of freedom to speak because we agree with the book. The book is extremely rude about us. It compares Britain with Hitler's Germany. We don't like that any more than people of the Moslem faith like the attacks on their faith.

He concluded with his belief that no matter how offensive its content, "nothing in the book could justify a threat to the life of the author." His comments were meant to forge a bond of empathy between the British and the Iranians—both groups, both governments were criticized by Rushdie—so of course, the British understand the anger of the Iranians. Through this mutual understanding, the foreign secretary hoped to persuade Iran to withdraw its demand that Rushdie be assassinated. We wish we could claim success for Rogerian strategy in this instance, but in fact, it was not until the Ayatollah Khomeini died, that the death sentence was lifted from Rushdie's head.

The Rogerian approach is not entirely new. Well over two thousand years ago, Aristotle spoke of an essential triad in argument, *logos, ethos,* and *pathos:*

logos the argument itself (derived from the Greek, meaning both "word" and "reason")

ethos the disposition of the writer (speaker) to present herself well

pathos empathy with the audience

In this chapter we have already addressed *logos* when discussing the elements of mounting a successful written argument. In Chapter 1 and in this

MACHLIS

> **READINGS:** Notice the skillful use of a dialectical approach in the following selections: "Human Cloning and the Challenge of Regulation" on page 372, "Second Thoughts on Cloning" on page 71, and "Politics of Biology" on page 404.

chapter, we discuss the ways you, the writer, must think about how you present yourself to your audience—the *ethos*. And *pathos* is precisely what Carl Rogers means when he talks of cultivating the audience, making them sympathetic to your point of view.

Aristotle saw the essential bond between writer and reader that leads to meaningful communication. To write convincing argument, you, the writer, must present yourself as a reasonable, sympathetic person at the same time that you convey respect for your readers. Both Carl Rogers and Aristotle suggest that effective argument depends not only on a well-informed writer but also on a writer who is acutely aware of her audience and well disposed toward them. The same holds true for public speaking.

The alternatives for organizing Rogerian concessions within an essay are the same as those discussed above under refutation and concession and as illustrated in the sample essays in Exercise 4E.

Can you identify the Rogerian strategy in this cartoon?

*"He says his ballads sing of the brotherhood of man, with due
regard for the stabilizing influence of the nobility."*

When There Is No Other Side

What makes an issue worth arguing? While there are no fast rules, issues
inappropriate for argument fall into three general categories. Some positions are simply too offensive to the majority of writers or readers. Arguments advocating racial bigotry or denial of the Holocaust, for example,
fall into this category. Others are so personal or so self-evident that they
don't lend themselves to intelligent debate. Take for example the following
claims:

Chocolate ice cream is far superior to strawberry.

or

Free, quality education should be provided for all children in America.

Neither proposition lends itself to the kind of exploration we have been discussing in this chapter, in the first instance because it concerns a personal and insignificant preference, and in the second because no one could in all seriousness argue against such a proposition.

FOR AN EFFECTIVE ARGUMENT

express your thesis clearly
support your own position as thoroughly as possible
present relevant opposing views
provide appropriate concessions and refutations
develop empathy with your audience

Application to Writing

Logical Joining of Contrasting and Concessive Ideas

To express contrast and concession, so necessary for effective written argument, you need to manipulate your sentences to create a coherent flow of ideas and to convey logical relationships. We introduced principles of logical joining with the discussion of conjunctions in Chapter 3 and continue that discussion here.

EXERCISE 4B

Expressing Contrast and Concession

Below are three different attitudes on smoking in the workplace. Read the passages carefully, examine the logical relationship between ideas, then state the position of each writer and explain how you reached your decision.

1. The battle rages on. Whereas some contend that smoking, as a direct threat to health, should be banned in the workplace, others maintain that forbidding smoking is too extreme a measure. Medical evidence demonstrates that cigarette smoke is harmful to nonsmoking bystanders as well as to smokers, but smokers argue that

their emotional health is at stake. They point out that such discrimination threatens their constitutional civil rights, whereas executives and nonsmoking employees claim that medical costs from health problems and time lost from work justify such restrictions of personal choice.

2. Although most people recognize that smoking is a direct threat to health, making nonsmoking a condition of employment constitutes a new form of discrimination.

3. While banning smoking on the job can create serious personnel problems for a company, current medical evidence strongly supports those who insist on a completely smoke-free work environment.

As you have no doubt noticed, it is through the different choices of joining words that these writers established their slant on the issue here. Let's review these distinctions:

Coordinating Conjunctions	Subordinating Conjunctions	Major Transitions
contrast:	contrast & concession:	contrast & concession:
but	while	however
yet	whereas	on the other hand
	although	
	though	

The Concessive Sentence

The degree to which subordinating conjunctions express concession can vary according to the content of the sentence. In sentence 3 above, the writer recognizes the merit of a counterargument. But in some cases you may simply acknowledge your opponent's position without really conceding it, as in the following example:

Although smokers defend their constitutional rights, the health of a nonsmoker should come first.

EXERCISE 4C

Making Rhetorical Choices

Try joining the following pair of sentences in three different ways: from the perspective of a film buff, a responsible student, and someone genuinely uncommitted.

1. I desperately want to see the latest Star Wars movie.

2. I know I need to work on my report due next week in my economics class.

More on Coherence

While you can manipulate ideas with grammatical word choice to signal relationships at the sentence level, you also need to develop rhetorical patterns of coherence throughout your paper. The form of your paper can take many shapes, but you want the whole to be held together by an almost invisible glue. Your thesis should guide you as you build paragraphs and create a thread that weaves its way from opening sentence to conclusion, each paragraph relating back to the thesis. The result will be a unified whole. Every sentence should follow from the sentence before it; each paragraph must follow logically from the one preceding it. As a writer, you take your reader's hand, never letting that reader stray from the flow of your argument. If you were to cut your paper into individual paragraphs, shake them up, and throw them in the air, a stranger should have no difficulty putting them together in the original order. The same is true of sentences within a paragraph.

To accomplish this logical flow from sentence to sentence, you will arrange points in a logical sequence, select joining conjunctions and major transitions carefully, and repeat or echo key words to keep your reader focused on your train of thought. Pronouns, those words that refer back to nouns (his, him, hers, her, they, this, that, these), can help relate one sentence to another, as can synonyms for nouns when repetition begins to sound monotonous. For more on keeping ideas connected within a paragraph, see Sentence Focus—Techniques for Sharpening the Flow of Ideas and Parallel Structure in Chapter 8.

To develop coherence between paragraphs within the essay, be sure that each paragraph connects to and makes a point about your thesis; follows a logical, clearly organized sequence; and creates a link to the one preceding it. The first sentence of a paragraph can pick up a phrase or idea expressed in the last sentence of the paragraph before it. A transitional word may signal the logical relationship, as discussed previously under joining words. Or the opening sentence might echo the thesis and so keep the main idea moving forward. All writers from time to time are tempted to include a graphic but unrelated example or an irrelevant line of reasoning, especially if time is short and material is thin. To be sure that your paper conveys a unified, coherent argument, one that "sticks" together and keeps your reader's attention, depend on details that clearly support major points and connect ideas logically.

A caution: Coherence devices should not be heavy-handed or too obvious. Remember to go lightly on the major transitions. It is the logical progression of your ideas that is important, not the deployment of conjunctions alone.

EXERCISE 4D

Identifying Coherence Strategies

It is difficult to create artificial coherence strategies without a context. But, as you revise your papers, you can look back at the suggestions given here. To illustrate some of these strategies in action, we ask you to select one of the essays that follows in Exercise 4E and identify the ways in which the writer has achieved coherence, both between sentences and between paragraphs. Explain the precise way in which each example works to create these links. ₁₀

Sample Essays

To help you see some of the rhetorical features of effective written argument in action, we have selected three examples for you to examine closely. The first two are by students; the third is by a professional journalist. Note that all three address topics that could be relevant to you as a college student. Academic arguments don't always have to consider global topics such as world trade, euthanasia, or the death penalty.

EXERCISE 4E

Identifying Rhetorical Features of Argument

In the first essay, we identify the elements of written argument presented in this chapter. In the second and third essays, we ask you to do the same.

> thesis
> premises
> counterarguments
> concessions and refutations used to address the counterarguments
> Rogerian strategy

This model of a student essay, used in our classes to illustrate effective written argument, shows one way to organize, support, and advocate a position on a pressing problem.

Alternative Sentencing

Thesis

As the newspapers confirm daily, Americans are worried about crime. Often responding emotionally to the many reports of crime we read and see on TV, people want to throw into prison everyone convicted of a crime. But our prisons are overcrowded and costly to run. In addition they are now producing more repeat offenders than reformed citizens. To begin to deal with this problem, we need to explore new solutions. First we should distinguish between violent and non-violent criminals. Then we could find alternative sentences for the non-violent ones. Instead of automatically choosing a jail sentence, a number of judges have begun to order non-violent offenders to perform a set number of hours of community service tailored to the criminal and the crime committed. While this solution has its critics, I believe the advantages of alternative sentencing outweigh any negative risks. We should support this innovative response to the pressing problem of rising crime.

Prisons are not only dangerously overcrowded, but prison programs are completely insufficient to rehabilitate criminals or to help them re-enter society as productive citizens. The number of repeat offenders tells us this. Most prisons are depressing places of despair, which instill anger and resentment in the prisoner. Taken from family and friends, deprived of normal relationships and privacy, caged under the most humiliating circumstances, often threatened and raped by other inmates, the prisoner is constantly reminded of his misdeed. We shouldn't be surprised that when these prisoners are released, they have become hostile, bitter, depressed people who lack the motivation to become useful citizens.

With the option of alternative sentencing, judges will be able to devise sentences that, while punishing the offender, also benefit the community. For example, instead of sending a drug dealer to prison, where he can continue to sell drugs, a judge might order him to work 200 hours in a drug crisis center, a place where he would be forced to help the very people he had been hurting and where he would have to face the misery of the addict and thus have the chance of becoming less inclined to push drugs. One such sentence, which a judge gave to an offender who had killed a man while driving drunk, illustrates how the community can benefit from an alternative sentence. The driver was allowed to continue working so that his family wouldn't have to go on welfare, thus saving the taxpayers money. Still, the offender had to live at the county jail and pay for his room and board there. And for one year he was ordered to work 200 hours in a hospital trauma center and to spend 200 hours on the lecture circuit describing the catastrophic results of his actions. Sentences like this one benefit everyone involved and help us realize how conventional sentencing can sometimes be worthless.

But what about the drug-dealers, shop-lifters, embezzlers who decide they need not fear prison? With no threat of prison, won't they receive the wrong message and feel that their crimes are insignificant? Surprisingly, al-

Refutation

ternative sentences can deter crime better than conventional sentences. *The New York Times* reported the interesting case of Morris Cage, an apartment building owner in the Bronx, who was fined and ordered to pay $198,000 in civil penalties to correct code violations in one of his buildings. He was also sentenced to serve 22 days in an apartment in that decrepit building, forced to live alongside tenants who daily endured leaking pipes, falling plaster, little heat and less water. Tenants greeted Mr. Cage with a banner: "Welcome, You Rodent." The judge also ordered Cage to develop a housing plan and to spend 20 hours a week for five years carrying it out. That was 5,000 hours of community service. Such sentences will catch the attention of other slum landlords, who will want to avoid similar sentences which deprive them of their freedom and force them to confront the horrible problems they have created.

Premise

Statistics also shed light on the advantages of alternative sentencing. According to *The Baltimore Sun,* in 1997 the state of Maryland had, after only three years, reduced the chance of an offender committing a new crime by 50 percent and "saved the state from having to construct a new prison." The report came from Maryland's Correctional Options Program which was seen as "a national model by the U.S. Department of Justice." Programs include "home detention, which requires offenders to wear electronic ankle bracelets, drug abuse treatment, and military-style boot camps to rehabilitate convicts and return them to society." Intensive supervision is included, ensuring "that offenders stay off drugs and go to work instead of being kept in prison."

"'The bottom line behind all these programs is, who do you want in prison?' said Leonard A. Sipes, Jr., a spokesman for the Department of Public Safety and Correctional Services. 'Do you want the rapist? Do you want the armed robber? Or do you want the shoplifter? The program was designed to save prison beds for violent offenders,' Sipes said. 'And the findings have been nothing short of outstanding.'" Although the options program was relatively new at the time of the report, results so far certainly support alternative sentencing.

Premise

Further bolstering the arguments for such sentencing, Bob Pendergrass, an alternative sentencing advocate for the 5th Judicial District public defender's office in New Mexico, "estimates that he has saved the state of New Mexico more than $18 million."

Refutation Concession

"At first, the alternative program met a lot of resistance," he conceded. Ten years earlier, public sentiment was running against alternative programs because people were afraid criminals would be set loose to commit new crimes. But Pendergrass recognized that locking up non-violent offenders was not the answer; it only taught them to be better criminals (*Roswell Daily Record*).

"'It's not about letting them out. It's about providing them what they need so they don't recycle,' Pendergrass said."

Concession (Rogerian)

Counter-argument

Refutation

Some may question Pendergrass's financial claims, thinking that the kinds of specialized intervention required to make alternative programs work would be very costly. While it is true that effective alternatives come at a high price, it is also true that the costs of incarceration are even higher. According to the Maryland report cited above, "the program costs $4,100 for each inmate, compared with $18,000 per inmate in prison." Add to that difference the cost of a new prison with its high operating expenses and we can see that the state would have had to earmark enormous sums for prisons beyond what they already must spend.

Concession (Rogerian)

Counter-argument

Refutation

But even if innovative sentencing works in some cases, how can we be assured that judges aren't being given too much flexibility in devising sentences? This too is a valid concern, but if our judges are well trained in alternative sentencing, if strict guidelines are set up for them, and if they work closely with the criminal reform specialists—criminologists, rehabilitation experts, psychologists, and directors of alternative services programs—most judges will be able to give fair and appropriate sentences. After evaluating each case by interviewing the persons involved, deciding whether the offender is criminally oriented and whether he or she has a good chance of rehabilitation, and then determining which type of program would be the most appropriate, the experts can advise the judge.

Rogerian

While crime remains a terrible problem in our society, we must find ways of dealing more effectively with the less dangerous criminals and, at the same time, better serve those who need to be incarcerated. We can deal effectively with violent criminals only if we have room for them in our prisons. I recognize that no one proposal can solve a problem so complex. But one way to remove the hardened criminal from our streets is to keep non-violent offenders out of the prisons so that we have more space for those who truly belong there. And, with some states forced to transfer money from their education budgets to prison construction, we might wonder why every judge in every state doesn't take a closer look at sentence reform.

Works Cited

"Bronx Apartment Owner Cited." *The New York Times* 17 March. 1994.

Penn, Ivan. "Alternative Sentencing." *The Baltimore Sun* 21 Oct. 1997. 21 Jan. 1999
<http://library.northernlight.com/pn19990630030073894.html?cb=o&dx=10048&sc=odoc>.

Sanner, Tammy. "Alternative Sentencing Advocate Retiring." *Roswell Daily Record* 3 March. 1998. 25 Jan. 1999
<http://www.roswell-record.com/news1326.html>.

In the following essay, student John Herschend defends popular music.

Rap Takes a Bum Rap

Even the president and vice president have gotten into the act, posturing about Ice-T's "Cop Killer" (as if boycotting Time Warner would reduce the national debt).

—SHERLEY ANNE WILLIAMS

Since its birth, Rap music has taken the blame for many of the problems plaguing America's inner cities—violence, drugs, AIDS, you name it. But Rap music cannot take the blame for these problems any more than, say, soap operas can shoulder the blame for infidelity in America. Rap is an art form, a medium which expresses, enrages and educates like most other art forms. As Guru says in the introduction to his album *Jazzmataz,* Rap is "musical, cultural expression based on reality." It does not cause problems but, instead, expresses them just as some movies, television shows and other forms of music do. However, unlike most of the mindless violence depicted in today's popular movies—*True Lies, Killing Zoe, Pulp Fiction*—Rap is a constructive outlet which brings attention to our country's problems in a creative, innovative and sometimes positive fashion.

In fact, the roots of rap are based in creativity and innovation. With its humble beginnings in the black ghettoes as filler between songs at parties, Rap has become a multi-million dollar business and one of the most established forms of new music in the past decade. The original idea was simple: two turntables and a microphone. The DJ, in command of the turntables, manipulates the records in order to form a beat or provide snippets of musical accompaniment. The "MC" then "busts out" in a fit of rhyme based stories, usually about the DJ's ability to "spin" or the MC's ability to "rap." However, as rap became more and more popular, the rappers began focusing their attention on the larger issues of life in the ghetto—violence, drugs, and oppression—forming two separate branches of Rap.

The first, and currently the most popular, is known as "gangsta" rap, a rough mix of extreme violence and heavy rhythms, sounding something like broken glass on an inner city basketball court. The second, which is quickly gaining momentum, is known as hip-hop, a jazz based, dance mix which is much more complex and layered than gangster. The music of hip-hop evokes the feel of a smoky, Soho jazz club in the 1950s while the words relate stories of ghetto life in the 1990s. The message of hip-hop is upbeat, oftentimes offering solutions or alternatives to the problems rather than focusing solely on them. Although gangsta and hip-hop differ in their style and message, both forms are important for their ability to educate and to offer a creative outlet.

Rap's ability to educate its listeners is an often overlooked but crucial element of the music. Several groups envision the music as their way to speak directly to kids. Groups such as the Bay Area's Disposable Heroes of Hiphoprisy believe that they, as Rap artists, are the only role models the children may have and therefore work to fill their music with thoughts on politics, environmentalism and other social issues in hopes of raising the consciousness of their listeners. Many of their songs are like quick morality plays. For instance, on the Disposable Heroes' latest album, *Hypocrisy Is the Greatest Luxury,* they have a song entitled "The Language of Violence" about a boy who goes to jail for killing another boy. In the song, the killer is caught and sent to jail where he is raped by the inmates. Michael Franti, the lyricist of the group, writes, "He had never questioned his own sexuality but this group of men didn't hesitate their reality, with an awful powerful show-erful an hour full of violence." In the end, the song takes a more philosoph-ical vein and asks: "is this a tale of rough justice in a land where there's no justice at all. Who is really the victim? Or are we all the cause, and victim of it all." Franti's aim is to get the kids who might commit acts of violence to think not only of the immediate physical consequences of their actions, but of the larger picture of violence and victimization. He says that "death is the silence in this circle of violence." The same is true of other rap artists such as the Digable Planets, The Pharcyde and Guru. These groups fill their albums with a smoky coolness of life on the streets and the choices available to the kids. They tell stories of street life with a more positive and hopeful edge, working to expand the vision of the listener, to help them see beyond the ghetto. Their music doesn't seek to exploit or cause violence but rather paint a picture of reality and offer alternatives.

But not all Rap music offers such positive alternatives. A good portion of Rap, particularly gangsta, offers little or no alternatives. It simply paints a picture of a bleak world where the gun is king. And it is here where Rap foes focus their efforts and here where I would agree with them. They say that Rap glamorizes the violence on the streets. They say that kids look to these groups as heroes and follow their lyrics as a zealot Christian might follow the Bible. In fact, a recent *Newsweek* article entitled *A Gangster Wake-Up Call* questions whether kids will "change their attitudes about money, sex, and violence now that gangster rap appears to be doing a drive-by on itself?" In essence, the article is assuming that Rap is the only place that kids get these ideas. The article is about the death (due to AIDS) of Eazy-E, one of the first major Rap stars, and the jailing of three other Rap superstars because of their violent ways. It seems that the Rap foes are making an important point: Rap stars live the life they sing about. But all this is presupposing the fact that the listeners of Rap are motivated by the lyrics to take action in the streets. In fact, it completely bypasses the notion that violence has existed in our streets before Rap and that the musicians, particularly the ones indi-cated in the *Newsweek* article, are victims of these streets.

Rather than say that Rap lyrics are a cause of street violence, I would like to offer the idea that violence is the cause of Rap lyrics, and that our so-ciety seems to have a double standard when it comes to judging the vio-lence of Rap music versus the violence of popular cinema and television. If we are to isolate Rap for its violence what, then, do we make of movies like

Killing Zoe, Pulp Fiction, Reservoir Dogs or *The Bad Lieutenant.* Or while we're on the subject, how about such popular TV shows as *Cops, Rescue 911* and *Real Stories of the California Highway Patrol?* It seems that violence is an obsession with Americans and still we don't indict these shows as being the cause of it. They are accepted and even called "artistic," and works of genius. For instance, in "Vox Populi," an article which appeared in *The Atlantic* magazine, Francis Davis credits Quentin Tarantino for his subtle handling of an extremely violent scene in *Reservoir Dogs.* In the scene, a captive cop is bound to a chair while Mr. Blonde, played by Michael Madsen, dances around with a razor in his hand, eventually cutting off the cop's ear and dousing him in gasoline. Davis is impressed with the scene because it takes our emotions for a ride. He writes about the scene, saying that Madsen

> does a series of graceful little dance steps to Stealers Wheel's "Stuck in the Middle with You," and closes in on his defenseless, screaming captive. "Was that as good for you as it was for me?" Madsen asks the cop afterward. . . . Madsen might also be asking those of us who sat through the scene without averting our eyes.

Davis feels that this form of violence is more acceptable because it is complex and plays with the audience's emotions. Conversely, Rap artist Ice-T was forced, due to heavy protest from police organizations, to remove the song *Cop Killer* from an album with the same name. The police groups, who felt that the album encouraged kids to kill police officers, won their argument and Ice-T had to pull the song and change the name of the album. Interestingly enough, Tarantino did not meet the same criticism and was praised by many for his "genius" in handling the violence of the police scene. A double standard? To say that one form of violence is better or more acceptable than another is ridiculous. The hard edges of gangsta Rap are no different than Tarantino's violence. By stating that the violence of movies and TV shows does not cause acts of aggression while at the same time indicting Rap music as a reason for aggression, we set an absurd double standard.

Rap music is violent because it reflects the real life struggles of life on the inner city streets. And although this is not an appealing vision for many, it is still a telling story, one that deserves attention. Of course many songs are often blown out of proportion, but the kernel of struggle is still discernible. When groups sing about drive-bys, drugs and beer drinking, it's because the singers grew up with these realities. These are not imaginary issues that are drummed up to sell records; they are the incidents of real life for many kids in America. Rap music is a window to real life, an expression of frustration and a way for Americans to understand what is going on in our streets. This is not to validate the violence, but to say that the expression is a positive release for both listener and singer, something that should not be so readily ignored and dismissed.

We look to expression—music, literature, cinema—as a way of release. Indeed, it is powerful; it can change hearts and minds. But expression is ultimately a product of experience. It is an interpretation of life and all the emotions that go along with it—fear, love, anger, happiness—feelings as old as our ability to express them. Rap, as a member of this community, cannot and should not be singled out as the cause of violence. It is an expression of life in our inner cities, a vision that is sometimes hopeful and sometimes violent but always based in reality. And if we listen without prejudice, we might begin to hear the words behind the violence. We might even be able to begin focusing on the real factors of ghetto life rather than constantly blaming the messenger for the delivery of bad news.

Works Cited

Davis, Francis. "Vox Populi." *Constellations: A Contextual Reader for Writers.* 2nd ed. Ed. John Schilb, Elizabeth Flynn & John Clifford. New York: HarperCollins, 1995: 603–610.

Marriott, Michel. "A Ganster Wake-Up Call." *Newsweek* 10 Apr. 1995: 74–76.

Atlanta Constitution editor Cynthia Tucker, in her weekly column "As I See It," addresses the grave concerns many people have about the abandonment of affirmative action in several states and the threat in others. Note how effectively she summons arguments to support her points and how skillfully she keeps her opponents with her by acknowledging their views.

A Case for Affirmative Action

Why are many Americans—white Americans, mostly—so upset about college admissions programs that take race into account for a handful of students whose test scores are slightly below standards? Why are programs that boost the chances of black and brown students so controversial, while similar programs that benefit white students go without notice?

For example, the country's premier colleges and universities have long reserved places for the lesser-achieving children of their well-heeled graduates and donors. At the University of Georgia, family connections are one of the dozen or so factors—along with race—used to assess about 20 percent of its applicants who don't quite meet academic standards. In other words, a kid whose test scores and grades are not quite good enough may get into Georgia anyway if his mom or dad is a graduate.

That practice allows weaker students—most of them white—to be admitted at the expense of better students. Yet no one bemoans it as an assault on the vaunted "meritocracy."

College admissions also grant athletic "preferences," a device that happens to benefit many kids—black, white, and brown—who otherwise could not get near their chosen college. For some reason, a black kid with low SATs who can score touchdowns and generate a lot of money for the university is not nearly as offensive as a black kid with low scores who just wants an education.

To be fair, some criticism of college admissions efforts is legitimate. Awarding scholarships based on race makes no sense, since they would often end up giving financial aid to the black upper-middle-class but not to the white poor. Besides that, poorly run affirmative-action programs, such as the contracting set-aside program run by the city of Atlanta, tend to generate resentments that splash over onto better-run and more necessary programs.

But much criticism of affirmative action in college admissions is based on myth, misunderstanding and—how shall I say this?—simple bigotry. Affirmative-action programs exist only in 25 percent to 40 percent of the nation's institutions of higher learning; the other 60 percent to 75 percent accept all applicants. So the controversy centers around the nation's most prestigious institutions.

Admission to those elite colleges is highly competitive, because a diploma from Harvard or Emory nearly guarantees a financially rewarding career. Rejected white applicants, looking for an explanation for their failure, often believe they were unfairly supplanted by an unqualified minority student.

Consider, however, an analogy used by Thomas Kane of the Brookings Institution, likening affirmative action in colleges to the handicapped parking space:

"Eliminating the reserved space would have only a minuscule effect on parking options for non-disabled drivers. But the sight of the open space will frustrate many passing motorists who are looking for a space. Many are likely to believe that they would now be parked if the space were not reserved."

Scaling back affirmative action would cripple the prospects for black participation in this nation's economic, political and social elite. William Bowen, former president of Princeton University, and Derek Bok, former president of Harvard University, recently conducted a landmark study of affirmative action at 28 elite institutions, including Atlanta's Emory University. They found that black graduates of those colleges go on to earn advanced degrees—medicine, law, MBAs—at slightly higher rates than their white counterparts, and also become more active in civic affairs.

Because America proffers advancement through education, programs to enhance educational opportunities for students of color remain critical—perhaps more important than any other form of affirmative action. Since my grandfathers would not have been admitted to white universities, it does not seem unreasonable to create a form of "legacy" for their descendants.

Four Approaches to Writing Arguments

The next four writing assignments all focus on argument. Writing Assignment 9 serves as preparation for Writing Assignment 10. Writing Assignment 11 presents a more complex and thus more challenging approach to an issue. Assignment 12 focuses on working collaboratively with classmates on complex issues chosen by the class.

WRITING ASSIGNMENT 9

Arguing Both Sides of an Issue

The Topic

Below is a list of proposals advocating a position on a social issue. Choose *one* and write two arguments, one defending and one refuting the proposal. For each argument, convey clearly the position you are taking by writing a short thesis (the conclusion of your argument) at the top of the page. For each position, provide relevant reasons (premises) that are, to the best of your knowledge, accurate. You will have two separate papers with a paragraph for each reason. Although each paragraph should be written coherently with fluent sentences, you don't, at this stage, need to provide logical transitions between paragraphs for a coherent whole. And you need not provide an introduction or conclusion. All this will come later in Writing Assignment 10.

Make your selection with care, for you will be spending considerable time on this one issue.

1. Free speech may have to be limited in order to protect children from pornography on the Internet.
2. If economics is not a factor, the mother of a young child or children is still justified in choosing to work outside the home.
3. School administrators should be permitted to censor student Web sites.
4. Online gambling should be prohibited by federal law.
5. Nationwide standardized tests throughout elementary and secondary school have a negative effect on education.
6. The genetic engineering of plants used for food poses a danger to consumers.
7. Basic Education requirements at my college place an unnecessary burden on students.

8. The use of car phones while a driver is in motion should be prohibited.

9. All medical research on animals should be forbidden by law.

If another issue interests you more—for instance, a campus topic or a controversy in your neighborhood—you may write on it. Be sure the issue is one worth arguing from both sides and can be expressed as a proposal similar to those above. You may, of course, change any of the given topics to suit your own purpose.

Audience

A wide range of your peers: those who would agree with you, those who would disagree, and those who have not, as yet, formed any opinion

Purpose

To present both sides of a controversial issue so you and your readers are forced to consider alternatives to one position

> **READINGS:** Most of the readings in Part Two offer potential topics for Writing Assignments 9, 10, 11, and 12.

WRITING ASSIGNMENT 10

Taking a Stand

The Topic

In this essay, take a stand on the issue you debated in Writing Assignment 9, constructing as persuasive an argument as possible.

Your thesis may express a strong position either for or against the proposition you addressed in the previous assignment or may be qualified as appropriate to reflect your view of the issue. (See the discussion of the thesis earlier in this chapter.)

To support your position fully, draw on the premises you presented in Writing Assignment 9, discarding reasoning that seems weak or irrelevant, adding reasons where you find gaps in your earlier paper. Strengthen your argument with as much available data as you think necessary to make your case. As you expand your argument, you will probably need to consult outside sources—newspapers, magazines, books, and individual authorities—for supporting information. Be sure to cite all references. For guidelines, consult Chapter 9, Research and Documentation.

To address opposing views, select the most important premises from your list of arguments on the other side of your position and briefly address them, acknowledging, conceding, and refuting in the manner best suited to your stand on the issue. Do not elaborate the opposing views in the same way you have your own premises.

For help in organizing your paper, refer once again to the sample essays in Exercise 4E.

Important: To complete the assignment, include the following attachments written out on a separate page:

Your issue, question at issue, and thesis

Your principal argument set out in standard form (see Chapter 3)

Peer Editing

If your instructor can find the time, you will find it useful to edit a first complete draft with classmates. Bring photocopies of your paper to class and exchange papers with one or more students, asking questions and noting strengths and weaknesses on each others' drafts.

Audience

The same as for Writing Assignment 9

Purpose

To present a convincing, balanced, fair argument for your position on a controversial argument in order to persuade your readers to adopt your point of view

---

A CHECKLIST OF ESSENTIAL COMPONENTS FOR ASSIGNMENT 10

A clear thesis to guide you as a writer and prepare your reader

Support for this thesis—plenty of well-reasoned premises supported with examples, explanation, and analysis

Counterarguments with appropriate concessions and refutations

Sentences logically joined for contrast and concession, cause and effect, and coherence

---

WRITING ASSIGNMENT 11

Exploring an Argument in Depth

Not all issues lend themselves to a pro or con, yes or no argument. In Writing Assignment 9, you argued two opposing positions on the same question at issue, and then in Writing Assignment 10, took a position on that issue. For this paper, address an issue in more of its complexity, considering arguments from as many sides as possible and coming to a conclusion that seems reasonable in light of your in-depth exploration. Such topics often present paradoxes in which two contradictory claims may both merit approval. In such a conclusion, you may incline to one position or another or may settle for explaining and clarifying the issues without going so far as to make a definitive decision.

The Topic

Choose a current controversial issue of interest to you, one that suggests more than a simple pro and con approach. Because you will/present a number of viewpoints, you must make sure your readers know which point of view you are expressing at any given point in the paper. Clear and logical transitions between points will help you accomplish this (note discussion of joining words in Chapter 3 and contrast and concession earlier in this chapter), as will smooth attributions of quotations and references to the ideas of others (see Chapter 9).

Be prepared to face a degree of chaos as you sort out the different perspectives. Don't be afraid of the inevitable confusion that a more complex issue often produces. It is through such a thinking and writing process that critical thinking takes place.

Once again, you may want to edit a draft with classmates.

Audience

The same as for Assignments 9 and 10

Purpose

To clarify your audience's understanding of a complex controversial issue

---

A CHECKLIST FOR WRITING ASSIGNMENT 11

An introduction that presents the question at issue with appropriate background, acknowledges its complexity, and suggests your thesis even though you may not be taking a clear stand either pro or con

A detailed discussion of arguments for as many positions as possible

Refutations and concessions as appropriate for a thoughtful examination of alternatives

Your personal recommendation on the issue, based on an evaluation in which you weigh the strengths and weaknesses of the positions you have presented, a synthesis of them, a call for further investigation, or a summary of possible alternatives.

WRITING ASSIGNMENT 12

Collaborating on a Complex Issue

Here we offer an alternative approach to writing the kind of argument presented in Assignment 11. Rather than preparing your paper on your own, you will be working with a group of classmates. Once out in the world, writing for business, politics, for many jobs, you will find that much of the writing you do is collaborative.

The Topic

Each member of the class will submit two or three controversial issues. From this list, the class will select four or five topics around which research groups will form on the basis of preference. You should end up with groups of five or six students.

Here are the guidelines for working with classmates to construct a written argument:

1. The topic research groups will meet in class to narrow the issue to a specific question at issue.
2. Students will conduct research to find at least one relevant article each that addresses the question at issue. They will make copies for

members of the group. Because these articles are to represent the various positions on the question at issue, members of the group must confer to ensure that the articles together reflect the diverse points of view.

3. Students will reduce the central argument of their own articles to standard form (see Chapter 3).

4. Each group will meet as often as necessary, in class and out as time permits, to share and discuss these materials. Members of each group will also have an opportunity to discuss the organization and development of their papers.

5. The class will choose whether students complete these papers on their own or whether they work together as a group to compose one final product as a fully collaborative effort.

6. Each group may want to select the best paper to read to the class, or in the case of collaborative papers, there may be time to hear them all.

Audience

The same as for Writing Assignments 9, 10, and 11

Purpose

To present different perspectives on an issue and to engage or persuade an audience through collaborative effort

SUMMARY

Convincing arguments usually contain an introduction to the topic, a thesis stated or clearly implied, well-supported premises, acknowledgment of opposing views, and a conclusion. Successful written argument depends on a dialectical approach in which writers address both their own position and opposing views.

A well-written argument requires joining sentences for logic and fluency and developing coherent links to express relationships.

Collaboration on the production of a written argument can be helpful and reflects the process often used in the working world.

KEY TERMS

Concession   a statement that grants the opposing view.

Counterargument   an opposing view in an argument.

Dialectic   a method of argument that systematically weighs contradictory ideas with a view to resolution of their contradictions.

Issue   any topic of concern and controversy.

Question at issue   a particular aspect of the issue under consideration.

Refutation   an explanation of why a position is false or weak.

Rhetoric   the art of using language to good effect, to prove, to convince, to persuade.

Rogerian strategy   an explicit effort to see ideas from an opponent's point of view; the cultivation of empathy with the opposition; a concept derived from the research of psychologist Carl Rogers.

Thesis   a statement of a writer's position; in argument, a response to the question at issue, the conclusion of the central argument in an essay.

CHAPTER 5

The Language of Argument— Definition

"When I use a word," Humpty Dumpty said in rather a scornful tone, "it means just what I choose it to mean—neither more nor less."
— LEWIS CARROLL, *ALICE THROUGH THE LOOKING GLASS*

In Chapter 4, we discuss how to construct written arguments that explore an issue in depth, weigh evidence, and address opposing views. Now we'd like to concentrate on the precise use of language, on paying close attention to how we choose our words, and thus on how we make our meaning precise and clear to others. As Francis Bacon put it four hundred years ago, "Men imagine that their minds have the command of language, but it often happens that language bears rule over their minds." Language itself, he suggests, can shape—even control—our thoughts. Poet W. H. Auden agrees: "Language is the mother, not the handmaiden, of thought; words will tell you things you never thought or felt before." While scholars today disagree about the possibility of thought without language, it remains enormously important that we know the meaning of the words we use and that when we write, our readers, to the degree possible, share our understanding of words. To achieve this clarity in our writing, we must, when necessary, define our terms.

Logical Definition

Cicero, the Roman orator, claimed that every discourse should begin with a definition in order to make clear what the subject under consideration is. French philosopher Voltaire wrote, "If you would argue with me, first define your terms."

Ellen Willis, writing in *Rolling Stone*, admonishes us, "Find out who controls the definitions, and you have a pretty good clue who controls everything else." Toni Morrison, in her novel, *Beloved*, illustrates the brutal oppression of slavery with the story of the slave Sixo. When the school teacher accused him of stealing the shoat (a piece of pork), Sixo claimed he wasn't *stealing* but *improving his property*. The teacher beat Sixo "to show him that definitions belonged to the definers—not the defined."

For a close look at the importance of definition in today's world, let's examine the following sentences:

1. Was Bill Clinton an effective president?
2. Does money mean success?
3. Is the violence portrayed in today's movies obscene?
4. Is television addictive?
5. Is alcoholism an illness?
6. Should we encourage entrepreneurs?

Remembering our discussion in Chapter 4, you will note that each sentence is a question at issue. Examine these questions more closely and you will notice that each contains at least one key term that is open to interpretation. For example, what does it mean to be an "effective" president? If you were to write a paper based on this question at issue, you would first have to define "effective," to list the criteria for such a presidency before applying them to Bill Clinton.

You need to define, to stipulate, to pin down precise meaning for terms such as these. To supply useful definitions, where do you begin? A good dictionary is the best *initial* source. Following the tradition of classical rhetoric laid down by Plato and Aristotle, first place the term in its general *class* and then narrow the definition by determining the **distinguishing characteristics,** the ways in which it differs from other terms in the same class.

Such a rigorous process is hardly necessary for a concrete term such as "fork," which belongs to the class of eating utensils and is distinguished from other members of its class, other eating utensils, by its shape, a handle at one end with two or more pointed prongs at the other. But abstract terms such as "success" and "obscene" must be carefully defined.

A definition of key terms in questions two and three above would look like this:

Term	Class	Distinguishing Characteristics
Success	(is) a favorable result	(which) implies economic and social achievement in one's chosen professional field.
Obscene	(is) a negative quality	(which) offends prevailing notions of modesty or decency.

Note that the distinguishing characteristics are still subject to interpretation, to individual assessment. Another writer could define success in terms of personal relationships or contributions to the community rather than professional achievement. And, of course, stipulating the precise meaning of "obscene" is a task that has long bedeviled our courts and has continued to do so with cases such as the violence in rap lyrics and the on-going controversy over censorship of the Internet.

John White is my idea of an intellectual. He buys Playboy magazine, cuts out the interviews and hangs them all over his bedroom.

EXERCISE 5A

Defining Key Terms

For the remaining three questions at issue above (4–6), identify terms that require clarification and stipulate a definition. Place each term first in its general class and then narrow your definition with distinguishing charac-teristics as we have done. You may find it interesting to compare your def-initions with those of classmates.

CARTOON REPRINTED BY PERMISSION OF THE DETROIT FREE PRESS.

Definition and the Social Sciences

In a study on child abuse and health, which we cite in Chapter 7, the researchers first had to define child abuse before they could determine its effect on women's health. They separated child abuse into three categories—emotional, physical, and sexual. Then they defined each category.

> *emotional abuse:* repeated rejection or serious physical threats from parents, tension in the home more than 25 percent of the time, and frequent violent fighting among parents.
>
> *physical abuse:* strong blows from an adult or forced eating of caustic substances; firm slaps were excluded.
>
> *sexual abuse:* any nonvoluntary sexual activity with a person at least five years older.

Researchers interviewed 700 women from a private gynecological practice and tabulated their responses according to these categories. Without clear-cut definitions to guide them, social scientists would be left with subjective impressions rather than quantifiable results.

Definition and Perception

Our definitions can reveal how we see people—as individuals and collectively. In his book *Days of Obligation,* writer Richard Rodriguez points out that American feminists have appropriated the word *macho* "to name their American antithesis," a man who is "boorish" and "counterdomestic." But in Mexican Spanish, he tells us that *"Machismo* is more akin to the Latin *gravitas.* The male is serious. The male provides. The Mexican male never abandons those who depend upon him." As this example illustrates, when different cultures share languages, shifts in meaning often occur, reflecting cultural bias.

Feminist Gloria Steinem points out our culture's sexual bias in its traditional definitions of the following terms, definitions that have played crucial roles in determining how women and men view themselves and others.

> *work:* something men do, go to; as distinguished from housework and childcare, which is what women do
>
> *art*: what white men produce
>
> *crafts:* what women and ethnic minorities do

We can hope that these definitions are changing. And indeed, we have historical precedent for scientific definitions shifting to conform to new ways of thinking. In the nineteenth century, alcoholism was defined as criminal behavior. When the term was redefined as an illness after World War I, considerable progress in treatment became possible.

Conversely, when the American Psychological Association recently stopped classifying homosexuality as an illness, the homosexual community was understandably gratified by the revision of a definition it found unjust and damaging to its members.

Writer Katie Roiphe, author of *The Morning After: Sex, Fear, and Feminism on Campus,* inspired angry responses when she claimed that the definition of date rape had gone too far. "It's creating stereotypes of men as predatory beasts and women as delicate vessels. It's destructive. When you use rape to mean so many things, the word itself loses its meaning."

Language evolves over time. It's a natural process. But when expanded meaning results in loss of precision, we do well to examine the causes and effects of the revised meaning.

Language: An Abstract System of Symbols

As you have noticed from the preceding discussion, abstract words can present particular difficulties when it comes to stipulating precise meaning. But language itself, whether it refers to an abstract concept or a concrete object, is an abstract system of symbols. The word is not the thing itself, but a *symbol* or *signifier* used to represent the thing we refer to, which is the *signified.* For example, the word "cat" is a symbol or signifier for the animal itself, the signified.

"Cat"	
THE SYMBOL or SIGNIFIER (the word)	THE SIGNIFIED (the thing being referred to)

But meaning is made only when the signified is processed through the mind of someone using or receiving the words. This process serves as an endlessly destabilizing force. Whenever a speaker, writer, listener, or reader encounters a word, a lifetime of associations renders the word, and thus the image it conjures up, distinct for each individual.

> **READINGS:** Thomas Lux expresses this same idea in his poem "The Voice You Hear When You Read Silently" on page 657 as does Sven Birkerts in "The Shadow Life of Reading" on page 661.

As literary theorist Stanley Fish points out, meaning is dependent not only on the individual but also on the context, situation, and interpretive community. To illustrate this point, let's look at the word "host." It means one thing if we are at a party, something different if we're discussing parasites with a biologist, and something else entirely if we are at church. Hence, the context or situation determines our understanding of "host."

If, however, you are not a member of a religion that practices the ritual of communion or are not conversant with parasitology, then you may understand the meaning of "host" *only* as the giver of a party. You are not part of the interpretive community, in this case a religious community or a scientific discipline, which understands "host" as a consecrated wafer, a religious symbol, or as an organism on which another lives.

As you can see, language remains perpetually contingent and thus, as a means of communication, slippery. Even when the signified is *concrete,* individual experience and perception will always deny the word complete stability; the range of possible images will still be vast. Take the word "table." Nothing of the essence of table is part of the word "table." Although most words in English (or any modern language) have roots and a history in older languages, the assignation of a particular meaning to a given term remains essentially arbitrary. While all English speakers share a *general* understanding of the word "table," each user or receiver of this word, without having considerably more detail, will create a different picture.

If the symbolic representation of a *concrete,* visible object such as a table is as unstable as our discussion suggests, think how much more problematic *abstract* terms must be. Were we to substitute the abstraction "freedom" for the concrete "table," the range of interpretations would be considerably more diverse and much more challenging to convey to others. Visual pictures, which arise when concrete objects are signaled, don't come to mind as readily when we refer to abstractions, a distinction that required us to define the abstract terms in the questions at issue above and led Shakespeare to explain why poets give "to airy nothing a local habitation and a name."

Semanticist S. I. Hayakawa discusses the idea of an abstraction ladder in which language starts on the ground, so to speak, with an object available to our sense of perception, and moves up to concepts abstracted from, derived from, the concrete source—for example, from a specific cow to livestock to farm assets to assets. He stresses that our powers of abstraction are indispensable. "The ability to climb to higher and higher levels of abstraction is a distinctively human trait without which none of our philosophical or scientific insights would be possible." But he cautions against staying at too high a level of abstraction.

> The kind of "thinking" we must be extremely wary of is that which *never* leaves the higher verbal levels of abstraction, the kind that never points *down* the abstraction ladder to lower levels of abstraction and from there to the extensional world:
> "What do you mean by *democracy?*"
> "Democracy means the preservation of human *rights.*"
> "What do you mean by *rights?*"
> "By rights I mean those privileges God grants to all of us—I mean man's inherent privileges."
> "Such as?"
> "Liberty, for example."
> "What do you mean by *liberty?*"
> "Religious and political freedom."

"And what does that mean?"
"Religious and political freedom is what we enjoy under a democracy."

The writer never moves down to the essential lower levels on the abstraction ladder, and a discourse consisting only of abstractions, devoid of concrete details and examples, is necessarily vague, often difficult for the reader to understand and, in this definition of democracy, circular.

The Importance of Specificity

To avoid the confusion that unclarified abstractions can generate, Hayakawa suggests pointing down "to extensional levels wherever necessary; in writing and speaking, this means giving *specific examples* of what we are talking about," grounding our arguments in experience.

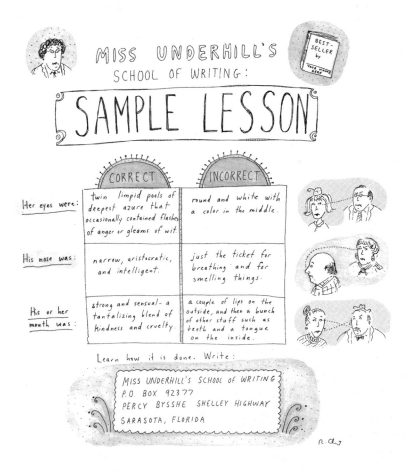

Compare the empty, circular definition of democracy Hayakawa quotes above with the concrete illustrations that illuminate E. B. White's celebrated World War II definition of the same term.

> July 3, 1943
> We received a letter from the Writers' War Board the other day asking for a statement on "The Meaning of Democracy." It presumably is our duty to comply with such a request, and it is certainly our pleasure. Surely the Board knows what democracy is. It is the line that forms on the right. It is the don't in don't shove. It is the hole in the stuffed shirt through which the sawdust slowly trickles; it is the dent in the high hat. Democracy is the recurrent suspicion that more than half of the people are right more than half of the time. It is the feeling of privacy in the voting booths, the feeling of communion in the libraries, the feeling of vitality everywhere. Democracy is a letter to the Editor. Democracy is the score at the beginning of the ninth. It is an idea that hasn't been disproved yet, a song the words of which have not gone bad. It's the mustard on the hot dog and the cream in the rationed coffee. Democracy is a request from a War Board, in the middle of a morning in the middle of a war, wanting to know what democracy is.

Such specificity is what writer Annie Dillard values when she says, "This is what life is all about: salamanders, fiddle tunes, you and me and things . . . the fizz into particulars" (*Teaching a Stone to Talk*). And what novelist Vladimir Nabokov prizes when he asks us to "Caress the details, the divine details" (*Lectures on Literature*).

> **READINGS:** For an example of an essay filled with specific details, see "He and I" on page 608.

The Manipulation of Language

Sometimes abstractions are used, consciously or unconsciously, to confuse, distort, conceal, or evade, in short, to manipulate others—a practice Hemingway comments on in *A Farewell to Arms*, his World War I novel.

> I was always embarrassed by the words sacred, glorious, and sacrifice and the expression in vain. We had heard them, sometimes standing in the rain almost out of earshot, so that only the shouted words came through, and had read them, on proclamations that were slapped up by billposters or other proclamations, now for a long time, and I had seen nothing sacred, and the things that were glorious had no glory and the sacrifices were like the stockyards at Chicago if nothing was done with the meat except to bury it. There were many words that you could not stand to hear and finally only the names of places had dignity. Certain numbers were the same way and certain dates and these with the names of the places were all you could say and have them mean any-

thing. Abstract words such as glory, honor, courage, or hallow were obscene beside the concrete names of villages, the numbers of roads, the names of rivers, the numbers of regiments and the dates.

Hemingway eloquently indicates the power of concrete nouns to generate precise meaning readily visualized.

Closer to home, during debates on the complex environmental issue of preserving wetlands, then-President George Bush declared that "All existing wetlands, no matter how small, should be preserved." But when pressured by real estate, oil, and mining interests to open protected wetlands to development and exploration, Bush expediently redefined the word, a definition that left at least 10 million acres of wet lands unprotected. Such examples lend fresh meaning to our opening claims of power for those who control the definitions.

In the 1940s, British writer George Orwell addressed the political significance of language in his celebrated essay, "Politics and the English Language," claiming that "political speech and writing are largely the defense of the indefensible. . . . Defenceless villages are bombarded from the air, the inhabitants driven out into the countryside, the cattle machine-gunned, the huts set on fire with incendiary bullets: this is called pacification." In his novel *1984*, he satirizes the official use of deceptive language, coining, among other terms, the words "doublethink" and "newspeak."

We continue to have had our own share of befuddling language, dubbed psychobabble, spacespeak, doublespeak, gobbledygook. Euphemisms, indirect, less expressive words or phrases for sensitive ideas, are sometimes justified as a means of sparing feelings: Someone passed away rather than died, or a large woman is referred to as mature in size. And the specialized lingo of a particular discipline may be necessary even though it appears as needless jargon to a lay person.

We must be particularly wary of language that deliberately camouflages precise meaning. When opposition to building the controversial MX missiles grew heated, the proponents began to call the missiles "peacemakers." Such an example reminds us of our claim, earlier in this chapter, that those who hold the power want to control the definitions.

EXERCISE 5B

Beware the Euphemism

1. Below is a list of paired terms or phrases. For each, briefly explain how the language of the second phrase dulls the meaning, and thus the reality, of the initial term, and discuss why you think such eu-

phemistic language crept in. For some of these terms, you may need to do a little research in order to fully understand the meaning.

foreign   /   offshore
taxes   /   revenue enhancement
civilian losses /   collateral damage
cloning   /   "somatic cell nuclear transfer"

"'Born in conservation,' if you don't mind.
'Captivity' has negative connotations."

2. From newspapers, magazines, television, or the Internet find a current example of usage that you think represents a manipulative euphemism. Advertising is often a good source of deceptive language.

WRITING ASSIGNMENT 13

Composing an Extended Definition of an Abstract Term

Step 1

Choose a word from the list of abstract terms below, think about its implications for a few minutes, and then start writing a definition that captures
its meaning and significance for you. (If an abstract term other than one of
those on the list comes to mind and interests you, substitute it, but clear it
with your instructor first.) Using a freewriting approach (see Chapter 1),
keep going for about 20 minutes. If time and your instructor permit, do
this in class; you will find the combination of spontaneity and structure imposed by writing during class to be an aid to composing. You can't get up to
make a phone call or clean the refrigerator.

education	addiction
originality	defeat
machismo	courage
maturity	leisure
creativity	progress
cult	trend
gossip	art
pornography	political correctness
imagination	character
sexual harassment	marriage
soul	generosity
intelligence	heroism

Volunteers can enlighten (and entertain) the class by reading these
drafts aloud.

Step 2

With more time for reflection and revision, take the spontaneous draft you
have written and, in a page or two, expand and edit your definition. In the
process of defining your term, analyze and clarify what it means to you, arriving at, or at least implying, a significant point.

You may want to argue a point, to use the term you are defining as a
springboard for a complete written argument. With this option, your paper
would grow into one of persuasion. As the discussion in this chapter has
emphasized, you must include specific detail to animate your abstraction.

THE LOCKHORNS

"IT'S NOT GOSSIP....IT'S ORAL HISTORY!"

If, for example, you have selected the phrase *burn out*, then, after clarifying what you mean by the term, you might decide to argue that the pressure and stress of life in today's society leads to *burn out* with serious consequences for both the individual and society as a whole, and then possibly suggest solutions.

> **READINGS:** If you have chosen one of the following terms, note useful articles in Part Two. For *pornography*, see Chapter 10; for *sexual harassment*, see Chapter 12; for *marriage*, see "Leave Marriage Alone" on page 649.

If time permits, multiple definitions of the same term can be read to the class for comparison and discussion.

Here are some possible strategies for writing an extended definition; do not feel compelled to use them all.

- stipulate your precise meaning (see logical definition above), but don't include a dictionary definition unless you plan to use it or disagree with it
- provide examples of the term
- explain the function or purpose of the term
- explore etymology (origin and history of a word). The most fruitful source for such explorations is *The Oxford English Dictionary*, a multivolume work available in most college libraries, and a dictionary well worth your acquaintance. Use the history of a term to help make a point.

- examine the connotations of the term
- discuss what it is not (Use this sparingly.)
- draw analogies (Here you will want to be precise; be sure the analogy really fits.)

A few cautions

- define or illustrate more complex words with more familiar ones
- stick to one sense of the word unless you clarify an intended distinction
- avoid circularity

Look ahead to Chapter 8, The Language of Argument—Style, for helpful sentence hints:

appositives for inserting short definitions, identifications, and concrete examples into your sentences

clear *"focus"*—appropriate sentence subjects and active verbs

parallel structure to organize and balance points and give emphasis

Audience
The instructor and other members of the class

Purpose
To make an abstraction concrete or to establish the focal point of an argument

---

Extended definitions: Student examples Several of our students have contributed their efforts on this topic. Here is a sampling.

Two different approaches to the same term

Radical

The word "radical" has been defined in *The Oxford-English Dictionary* as "going to the root or origin, touching or acting upon what is essential and fundamental." Thus, a radical reform is said to be a fundamental, "thorough reform." In a political sense, an advocate of "radical reform" was described as "one who holds the most advanced views of political reform on democratic lines, and thus belongs to the extreme section of the Liberal party." While this may have been a commonly accepted usage of the term in England at the time, the word "radical" has drifted away from its original specific meaning to a rather vague term for anyone who appears to be trying to disrupt the status quo.

In the late 1800s and early 1900s, socialists, Communists, and anarchists alike were popularly categorized by the general American public with the term "radical." With the controversy surrounding the political goals of these different activists, "a radical" was at the very least a controversial figure. More often than not, the word "radical" brought to mind some sort of disruptive character, a nonspecific image of an extremist, most probably from the far left. On the political spectrum the "radical" is still viewed as an individual on the extreme left, opposite the "right" or "conservative" parties. "Conservatives" holding radically different views and goals are not normally termed "radicals"; they are merely part of the "ultraright."

The term "radical" today is used less as a description of political intent and more as a critique of overall manner and appearance. While many of the "radicals" in the 1960s did indeed advocate numerous political reforms, the general public was more impressed by their personal character and style of advocacy. It is not surprising that when asked to define "a radical," most individuals conjure up a vague image of some young person wearing ragged clothes and long hair. It is a pity that in this society, where progressive change is so essential, the term "radical" has been imbued with so much negativity, so many connotations which really have nothing to do with political reform.

Radical

A radical is an algebraic symbol which tells a person to carry out a certain mathematical operation. The end result of this operation will tell a person the root or origin of a number or problem.

Recently, while in Los Angeles, I overheard someone describe a car as radical. I immediately thought to myself, something is wrong here. Radicals do not have engines. They may contain a number, like 32, underneath their top line, but never a stock Chevy 302 engine. It simply would not fit. When I asked this person why he called the car a radical, he replied, "Because the car is different and unusual." Once again, I thought to myself, he has made a mistake. Radicals are quite common. In fact, they are an essential part of most algebraic theories. I had to infer that this man knew nothing about algebra. If he did, he would have realized that radicals are not different or unusual at all, and would not have called the car one.

While I was in New York this past summer, I happened to see a group of people carrying signs of protest in front of the United Nations Building. As I watched them, a man came over to me, pointed at the group and muttered, "Radicals." I thought to myself, man are you ever wrong. Radicals do not carry signs saying, "Feed the Poor." They may carry a number, like 2, in their top right hand corner, but this number only means to find the root of a problem. It does not mean, "Feed the Poor."

These two events show that there is a great deal of misunderstanding throughout the country in regards to what a radical is. At their simplest level, radicals tell us to find the root of a problem. At their most complex level, they tell us the same thing.

A student's definition in which the approach reflects the word itself:

Fun

What's fun? In the black community fun means trippin'.[1] For example, the fellas pitchin' pennies, shootin' dice, playin' three-card molly[2] on the back of the bus, or playin' stick ball in the streets from the time they are five until they are 25. Little girls and big girls playin' Double Dutch,[3] jumpin' ropes and singin' to the rhythm of their feet. Blastin' the ghetto box to the latest beat and watching the brothuhs break. Bustin' open the fire hydrants on a hot day in order to cool off by runnin' through the water. Listenin' to the dudes standing on the street corner rappin' to a sistuh as she strolls down the street. "Hey, Mamma, what it is! You sho' is lookin' mighty fine today! How 'bout slidin' by my pad for a bit?" Gettin' happy in church and callin' out, "Lordy, Lordy! Lordy have mercy! Yes, Lord! Help me Lord!" Helpin' Mamma wash the collard greens and sweet potatoes, stirrin' the corn bread and slicin' the fatback[4] for Sunday supper after church. The whole family sittin' on the stoop in the evening listenin' to grandmamma tell stories 'bout the ol' days while fussin' about the young folk. All of this comes down to trippin', enjoying one's self, and havin' fun in the hood.[5]

Stipulating Personal Meaning

Through the centuries, people have been defining what they consider themselves to be, using the term "man" in a number of inventive ways.

---

[1]trippin'—enjoying yourself

[2]three-card molly—a card game involving three different-colored cards

[3]Double Dutch—a jump rope game involving two ropes swung in opposite directions. The jumping technique involves intricate rhythm and style and is often accompanied by a song or a chant recited by a child.

[4]fatback—discarded meat in the back of a butcher shop

[5]hood—the African-American community or neighborhood

Plato

First, he put man in the class "biped" and differentiated him from others in the class by describing him as "a featherless biped." When his rival, Diogenes, produced a plucked chicken, Plato had to add "having broad nails" as a further distinguishing characteristic.

Shakespeare

"What a piece of work is a man! How noble in reason! how infinite in faculty! in form, in moving, how express and admirable! in action how like an angel! in apprehension how like a god! the beauty of the world! the paragon of animals! And yet, to me what is this quintessence of dust? Man delights not me; no, nor woman neither." (*Hamlet,* II.ii. 316)

Ambrose Bierce

"An animal so lost in rapturous contemplation of what he thinks he is as to overlook what he indubitably ought to be. His chief occupation is extermination of other animals and his own species, which, however, multiplies with such insistent rapidity as to infest the whole habitable earth and Canada." (*Devil's Dictionary*)

Inventing New Words to Fill a Need

Contemporary American writer Alice Walker sought to rectify some of the linguistic imbalance in gender representation when she coined the term *womanist* for her collection of nonfiction, *In Search of Our Mothers' Gardens: Womanist Prose.* Why, we might ask, did she need to invent such a word? We can assume that she experienced a condition for which there was no term, so she created one. To stipulate the meaning of her neologism (a newly coined word or phrase), she opens the book with a series of definitions. What inference can you make from her decision to coin such a word and define it as she does?

Womanist:
1. From womanish. (Opp. of "girlish," i.e., frivolous, irresponsible not serious.) A black feminist or feminist of color. From the black folk expression of mothers to female children, "You acting womanish," i.e., like a woman. Usually referring to outrageous, audacious, courageous or *willful* behavior. Wanting to know more and in greater depth than is considered "good" for one. Interested in grown-up doings. Acting grown up. Being grown up. Interchangeable with another black folk

expression: "You trying to be grown." Responsible. In charge. *Serious.*

2. Also: A woman who loves other women, sexually and/or nonsexually. Appreciates and prefers women's culture, women's emotional flexibility (values tears as natural counter-balance of laughter), and women's strength. Sometimes loves individual men, sexually and/or nonsexually. Committed to survival and wholeness of entire people, male *and* female. Not a separatist, except periodically, for health. Traditionally universalist, as in: "Mama, why are we brown, pink, and yellow, and our cousins are white, beige, and black?" Ans.: Well, you know the colored race is just like a flower garden, with every color flower represented." Traditionally capable, as in: "Mama, I'm walking to Canada and I'm taking you and a bunch of other slaves with me." Reply: "It wouldn't be the first time."

3. Loves music. Loves dance. Loves the moon. *Loves* the Spirit. Loves love and food and roundness. Loves struggle. *Loves* the Folk. Loves herself. *Regardless.*

4. Womanist is to feminist as purple to lavender.

Writer and performer Rich Hall created the word *sniglet* for "any word that doesn't appear in the dictionary, but should." Two examples from his collection:

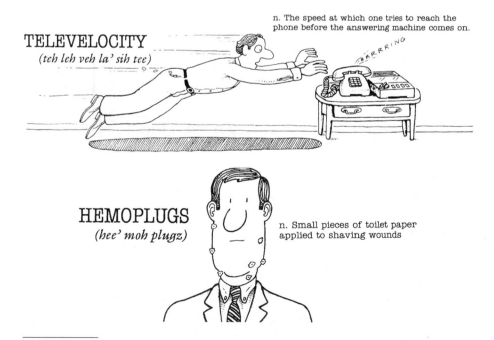

TELEVELOCITY
(teh leh veh la' sih tee)

n. The speed at which one tries to reach the phone before the answering machine comes on.

BRRRRING

HEMOPLUGS
(hee' moh plugz)

n. Small pieces of toilet paper applied to shaving wounds

WRITING ASSIGNMENT 14

Creating a New Word

Now it's your turn to create a new word. Give the word an extended definition so that those in your class can see how to use it and why our culture needs such an addition to the language. Here, again, you have an opportunity to develop an argument, using your new word as a springboard.

Audience

The instructor and other members of the class

Purpose

To identify a meaning in need of a name

SUMMARY

Words at a high level of abstraction such as "success" and "obscene" must be defined.

Definitions can affect how people view themselves and others, "addiction" being one example of many such terms.

Language is an abstract system of symbols.

The assignation of a particular meaning to a given term remains essentially arbitrary.

Meaning is dependent to a large degree on the individual, the context, and the interpretative community.

Political systems and advertising often manipulate abstract language for their own purposes.

The power to abstract is what makes us human. Specific, concrete details are what flesh out our ideas so our readers can grasp, visualize, and retain meaning.

Rather than contradictory, these two imperatives—the abstract and the concrete—are best seen as complementary in both our writing and our thinking.

KEY TERM

Distinguishing characteristics   in logical definition, the ways in which a term differs from other terms in the same class.

CHAPTER 6

Fallacious Arguments

So convenient a thing it is to be a reasonable creature, since it enables one to find or make a reason for everything one has a mind to do.
—BENJAMIN FRANKLIN

What Is a Fallacious Argument?

To answer this question, look carefully at two short arguments.

Short people do not make good presidents.

The democratic candidate is short.

Therefore, the democratic candidate will not be a good president.

Senator Smith was expelled from college for cheating on an exam.

His wife divorced him because of his numerous affairs.

Therefore, he is a man without honor, a politician who cannot be trusted, and we should not support his National Health Bill.

Which of these two arguments is more persuasive? Technically, the line of reasoning in the first argument is logical because the two premises lead inescapably to the conclusion. There is nothing fallacious in the *form* of this argument. The difficulty lies in the first premise; it is an absurd claim and an unacceptable premise. This argument is not persuasive and would convince no one. (Look ahead to Chapter 7, Deductive and Inductive Arguments, for a detailed explanation of form and acceptability of premises.)

But what about the second argument? Would you be in favor of a National Health Bill created by such a man? Some might find it persuasive, believing that such a man could not propose worthwhile legislation. But because nothing in the premises indicates flaws in the bill—only flaws in the man—the conclusion is not logically supported. The bill may be worthwhile despite the nature of the man who proposes it. This then is a fallacious argument, an argument that is persuasive but does not logically support its conclusion.

141

Because fallacious arguments are both appealing and abundant, we as critical readers and writers must guard against them. The first step in this defense is to familiarize ourselves with the most common fallacies. Fallacious reasoning may be intentional, as is sometimes the case with unscrupulous merchandisers and politicians, or it may be an innocent mistake resulting from fuzzy thinking or unexamined bias. In any case, if we are familiar with fallacies we can avoid them in our own thinking and writing. We can also spot them in the arguments of others, a skill that makes us wiser consumers and citizens.

There are many fallacies, a number of which tend to overlap. Our intention here is not to overwhelm you with an exhaustive list of fallacies and a complex classification scheme. Instead, we offer a list of the more common fallacies, presented in alphabetical order for easy reference.

Appeal to Authority

The opinion of an authority can support an argument only when it reflects his special area of expertise; the authority must be an expert on the subject being argued, as is the case in the following examples:

> The Surgeon General warns that smoking is injurious to health.
>
> Vladimir Horowitz, the internationally acclaimed pianist, preferred the Steinway piano.
>
> Studies conducted by *The New York Times*, the *Los Angeles Times*, and the ABC Network suggest that increasing numbers of viewers object to TV violence.

But, if the appeal is to an authority who is not appropriate, the appeal is fallacious, as is the case in the following example:

> Abortion to save the life of a mother is an irrelevant issue because a former surgeon general, a well-known pediatric surgeon, claimed that in all his years of surgical practice he had never seen a case in which such a dilemma had arisen.

The problem here is that a pediatric surgeon is not an appropriate authority on an issue involving obstetrics, a different medical specialty.

Fallacious appeals to authority are bountiful in advertising, which employs well-known actors and athletes to sell us everything from banking services to automobiles to coffee. Since many of these celebrities have no specialized knowledge—no authority—on the particular service or product they are promoting, they are not credible sources. Some may remember an actor known for his role as a TV doctor who endorsed a painkiller on television commercials.

Appeals to authority also appear in the form of snob appeal or appeal to the authority of the select few. The following advertisement for a resort hotel illustrates this fallacy, which appeals to people's desire for prestige and exclusivity:

> Palmilla's not for everyone. The best never is.

Keep in mind that fallacious appeals to authority should not cause us to doubt all authorities but rather should encourage us to distinguish between reliable and unreliable sources. In constructing your own arguments, be prepared to cite, explain, and, if necessary, defend your sources when relying on authority.

THE FAR SIDE   By GARY LARSON

"Why, yes . . . we do have two children who won't eat their vegetables."

Parents often rely on appeals to fear to persuade their children.

Appeal to Fear

An appeal to fear attempts to convince by implicitly threatening the audience. Its efforts to persuade are based on emotion rather than reason. An ad for a business college uses this approach.

> Will there be a *job* waiting when *you* leave college?

This ad attempts to frighten students by implying that unless they attend this business college, they will be unable to get a job after attending a four-year traditional college.

Senator Jesse Helms of North Carolina raised millions in campaign funds by sending voters a letter that contained the following warning:

> Your tax dollars are being used to pay for grade school classes that teach our children that **CANNIBALISM, WIFE-SWAPPING** and the **MURDER** of infants and the elderly are acceptable behavior.

Appeal to Pity

An appeal to pity attempts to win our sympathy in order to convince us of the conclusion. Like an appeal to fear, it appeals to our emotions rather than our intellect. Some students use this approach when arguing for a particular grade.

> Professor Hall, I must get an A in your course. If you don't give me an A, I won't be able to go to law school.

As we know, a student's work in a course—papers, exams, participation—determines the final grade. The consequences of a grade, no matter how dire they may be, should have no effect in determining that grade.

Emotion may play a part in argument, but its role must be secondary, a backdrop to logical reasoning. In fact, effective arguments often begin with frightening statistics—"If nothing is done about the Greenhouse Effect, the earth's temperature will increase 10 degrees by the year 2010 with disastrous consequences for our environment." Or they may begin with an emotional illustration. For example, an argument for mandatory fencing around all private swimming pools may open with a description of a mother caring for a child who is brain damaged as a result of almost drowning in a private pool. Either of these introductions will capture the emotions and interest of the audience, but they should be followed by facts, appropriate appeals to authority, and logical reasoning.

Begging the Question

When a person begs the question, he offers no actual support for his conclusion while appearing to do so. Instead, he may argue in a circle, just restating, as a premise, his conclusion in different words.

Students like rock music because it is the most enjoyable music around.

The writer is simply stating that students find rock music enjoyable because it is enjoyable. He begs the question. "They like it" means the same as "They find it enjoyable."

Or, take a couple of classics:

Parallel lines will never meet because they are parallel.

. . . your noble son is mad.
Mad call I it, for to define true madness,
What is't but to be nothing else but mad?

—Polonius to Queen Gertrude in *Hamlet,* II.ii

[We can discern something of Polonius' character from the manner of his argument.]

"You know what I like about power? It's so damn empowering."

Some such fallacious arguments beg the question not by restating the conclusion but by supporting the conclusion with assumptions (stated or hidden) that are as much in need of proof as the conclusion. A familiar example is frequently offered by those opposed to rent control who argue that rent controls should be removed because such decontrol could result in a significant rise in housing construction and thus relieve the shortage of affordable rental units. A letter to the editor points out the weakness.

> Editor: In your editorial concerning the housing crisis, you rely on one of the oldest rhetorical tricks of accepting as a given that which you could not possibly prove, that is, "There can be little question that removal of rent controls would result in a boom in apartment house construction. . . ." If rent control is such an important factor, construction should have been booming in the '70s before rent control laws existed in our state. It wasn't. . . .

Before we can accept the conclusion, the "truth" of the premise—that construction of new housing will increase if rent control laws are abolished—must be established.

We can also encounter question begging (avoiding the issue) in the form of an actual question, **a loaded question.**

> An example: Have you started paying your fair share of taxes yet?

First, the questioner would have to establish what he means by "fair share" and then establish that the person to whom he addressed the question had not been paying it.

In some arguments, just a single word—reactionary, negligent, warmonger, deadbeat—can beg the question. Be on the alert for such prejudicial language.

Equivocation

Equivocation is the shifting of the meaning of a given term within a single argument. This fallacy stems from the often ambiguous nature of language. A term may be ambiguous because it has more than one meaning; for instance, the word "affair" may mean a party, a controversial incident, or an extramarital relationship. Look at this example:

> We are told by the government that to discriminate against a person in employment or housing is wrong and punishable by law. But we must discriminate when we hire an individual (Does he have the necessary experience?) or rent an apartment (Does he have sufficient income?). Discrimination is a necessary part of making such decisions.

The word "discriminate" is the culprit. In the first sentence, "discriminate" refers to prejudice, to denying an individual employment or housing because of his or her race, sex, or religion. In the second sentence, "discriminate" refers to making careful distinctions between applicants on the basis of relevant issues.

Often equivocation is used to manipulate the language for rhetorical effect and positive associations, especially in advertising. A color film company refers to its product as "The Color of America," a slogan that is superimposed over images of African-American and Asian-American families. Hence, color refers to color film and to race, a clear case of equivocation.

**"Tonto, when I said put silver on the table,
I meant knives, forks, spoons."**

Tonto annoys the Lone Ranger when he equivocates, mistaking the horse
Silver for tableware.

In writing our own arguments, we can avoid equivocation by defining all ambiguous terms and being consistent in our use of them. (See Chapter 5 for definition strategies.)

False Analogy

One creative way to mount an argument can be through analogy. An argument by analogy compares two or more things, alike in certain respects, and suggests that since they share certain characteristics, they probably share other characteristics as well. A doctor argues effectively for drug therapy over psychotherapy as the best treatment for schizophrenia or severe depression by comparing the brain to the heart. "The brain is an organ, like the heart, and like that organ, can malfunction as a result of biochemical imbalances."

But in a **false analogy,** one compares two things in which the key features are different. A mountain climber offers this analogy to minimize the danger of his sport:

> I don't want to die falling off a rock. . . . But you can kill yourself falling in the bathtub, too.
>
> —JOHN BACHAR

He is comparing two extremely dissimilar acts: climbing a mountain and taking a bath, one a sport, the other a daily routine. And while it is possible to kill oneself slipping in the bathtub, if we were to compare the number of deaths in proportion to the number of bathers and the number of mountain climbers, we would surely find a higher incidence of deaths in mountain climbing than in bathing. To construct a more convincing analogy, the mountain climber should compare the risk in mountain climbing with that in another high-risk sport such as race-car driving.

A "Dear Abby" reader writes in response to Abby's recommendation that young people use contraceptives for premarital sex, "We know that premarital sex is wrong, just as we know shoplifting is wrong." Dear Abby's reply points out the fallaciousness of this comparison.

> One of the most powerful urges inborn in the human animal is the sex drive. Nature intended it to ensure perpetuation of our species. It is not comparable with the temptation to swipe a candy bar or a T-shirt.

In debating whether or not it is appropriate for Miss America beauty contestants to have plastic surgery, those in favor of allowing such surgery compare it with other practices women use to improve their appearance such as makeup and hair color. *The Boston Globe* columnist Ellen Goodman points out that this analogy is false since cosmetics are superficial while cosmetic surgery, such as breast implants, is physically invasive. She then offers a more accurate analogy—cosmetic surgery for beauty contestants is like steroids for athletes—each gives an unfair advantage to contestants involved in a competition.

Reasoning by analogy is appealing because it is vivid and accessible. But we must not accept analogies without careful examination. We must

*"For all his brilliance, we're going to have to replace Trewell. He
never quite seems able to reduce his ideas to football analogies."*

ask if the two things being compared are similar in ways that are significant
to the point being made. Pay particular attention to advertising that relies
on analogies to sell its products, sometimes effectively, sometimes approaching the absurd.

> **READINGS:** For examples of arguments that rely on
> analogy to make their point, read "Getting Off Easy in
> Tobacco Land" on page 707, and "In Defense of Abor-
> tion" on page 709.

False Cause

The fallacy of **false cause** is also called post hoc reasoning, from the
Latin *post hoc, ergo propter hoc,* which means "after this, therefore because of this." As this translation indicates, the fallacy of false cause assumes a cause–effect relationship between two events because one pre-
cedes another. It claims a causal relationship solely on the basis of a
chronological relationship. Mark Twain uses this relationship for humorous effect.

I joined the Confederacy for two weeks. Then I deserted. The Confederacy fell.

We know, as Twain did, that his desertion did nothing to end the Civil War, but this fallacy is not always so obvious. Look at the following example:

Governor Robinson took office in 1998.

In 1999, the state suffered a severe recession.

Therefore, Governor Robinson should not be re-elected.

(Hidden assumption: The governor caused the recession.)

Elected officials are often credited with the success or blamed for the failure of the economy. But in fact, anything as complex as the economy is affected by numerous factors such as inflation, environmental changes, the laws of supply and demand, just to name a few. Elected officials may indeed affect the economy but are unlikely to be the sole cause of its success or failure.

In a letter to *The New York Times Book Review*, a doctor takes exception with a book in which the author claims that his nephew's autism resulted from brain damage due to a vaccination.

> To the Editor:
> There will always be people who are convinced that because the signs of mental retardation or a seizure disorder or autism first became evident after an immunization, then certainly the immunization caused their problems; millions of dollars have been awarded in damages because some such people served on juries.
> For those people of reason who remember that **post hoc, ergo propter hoc** is a logical fallacy and not a standard of proof, let me state categorically that careful review of the literature confirms that a DPT shot might result in a fever or a sore leg or an irritable child. But it will not cause retardation, it will not precipitate epilepsy, and it never has and never will lead to autism.
> DIANE LIND FENSTER, M.D.
> GREEN BAY, WIS.

Some have argued that the atomic bombs we dropped in Hiroshima and Nagasaki caused Japan to surrender at the end of World War II. Others argue that this is a case of post hoc reasoning, that other factors such as Russia's threat to enter the war against Japan caused Japan to surrender, so that the killing of 110,000 Japanese, many of them women and children, was unnecessary.

Determining the cause of all but the simplest events is extremely difficult. Post hoc reasoning is appealing because it offers simple explanations for complex events.

False Dilemma

A **false dilemma** presents two and only two alternatives for consideration when other possibilities exist. For this reason, a false dilemma is often referred to as either/or reasoning.

> Either you are in favor of recalling the mayor, or you are a supporter of his political platform.

We are presented with only two positions when in fact we may hold neither. We may want the mayor to continue in office because we believe him to be a strong administrator, but we may object to his proposal to encourage big business by lowering the business tax.

In his essay, "Love One, Hate the Other," movie critic Mick LaSalle rails against what he calls "false polarities." He offers the following examples: Lennon or McCartney, Monroe or Bardot, Hemingway or Fitzgerald, Freud or Jung. He calls them false "because, in each case, two elements are arbitrarily set apart as opposites when they are not opposite at all, and the idea is that we must choose between the two when there's no legitimate need to do that."

Narrowing to two choices is a strategy designed to forestall clear thinking and force a quick decision. This kind of reasoning can be seductive because it reduces the often difficult decisions and judgments we must make by narrowing complex problems and issues to two simple options.

Columnist Anna Quindlen comments on how this either/or reasoning shaped the public's opinion and the trial of Erik and Lyle Menendez, two brothers accused of murdering their parents for financial gain.

> . . . the question has become: venal rich kids or tormented victims? Which are the Menendez brothers? Few seem to consider a third possibility: maybe both. . . . Lyle and Erik [are] either tormented, abused child-men or cold-blooded climbers in Porsches. Not both. Never both.
>   The ultimate either-or decision belongs to the jurors in the Menendez case. But perhaps they will consider things that we overlook when we are turning public tragedy into social mythology: sometimes bad things happen to bad people, that it is possible to be both victim and victimizer. Life is so messy that the temptation to straighten it up is very strong. And the result's always illusory.

Columnist Ellen Goodman offers an example of one young critical thinker who refused to accept the limits of either–or thinking.

> Remember the story of Heinz, the man whose wife was dying for lack of medicine or the funds to buy it? Children are asked to decide whether it's OK for Heinz to steal the drugs. On the one hand it's wrong to break the law, on the other, it's wrong to let the woman die.

What I remember most about the Heinz dilemma is the response of an 11-year-old little girl named Amy, as described in Carol Gilligan's book, *In a Different Voice.* Amy didn't think that Heinz should steal the drugs because if he did he might end up in jail—and what would happen next time his wife needed the pills? Nor did Amy think she should die.

This 11-year-old refused to choose from column A or column B. She thought they should "talk it out," get a loan, or find another way out of the dilemma. Traditional moralists thought Amy was "illogical." But the truth was that she took the long, wide moral view—six steps down the road, up a side road and back to the main road. Amy stepped outside the multiple-choice questionnaire.

"Damn it, Eddie! If you don't believe in nuclear war and you don't believe in conventional war, what the hell kind of war do you believe in?"

What alternative has the speaker completely overlooked?

> READINGS: For analysis of false dilemma in the nature versus nurture debate, see "Politics of Biology" on page 404.

Hasty Generalization

A **hasty generalization** is a conclusion based on a sample that is too small or in some other way unrepresentative of the larger population.

> Students in Professor Hall's eight o'clock freshman composition class are often late. There's no doubt that people are right when they claim today's college students are irresponsible and unreliable.

In this case the sample is both unrepresentative and too small; unrepresentative because we would expect an eight o'clock class to have more late students than classes offered later in the day, and too small because one section can't represent an entire freshman class.

It is impossible to avoid making generalizations, nor should we try to. But we must examine the basis for our generalizations to determine their reliability (see Chapter 7).

One way to avoid this fallacy is to qualify your generalizations with words such as "many" or "some." Most of us would accept the claim that "some women are bad drivers" but would reject and even be offended by the claim that "women are bad drivers."

Personal Attack

Often called by its Latin name, *ad hominem* ("against the man"), the fallacy of **personal attack** substitutes for a reasoned evaluation of an argument an attack against the person presenting the argument. By discrediting the source, often in an abusive or irrelevant way, a person can disguise the absence of a substantive position.

> Because she is extremely wealthy and owns two luxurious homes, our mayor, Carolyn Quinn, cannot properly represent the people of this city.

But does a person's economic status necessarily rule out understanding of those in different circumstances?

A few years ago, conservative John H. Bunzel wrote a controversial book, *Challenge to American Schools.* In it he attacked the National Education Association for criticizing some reform ideas he admired—merit pay and standardized tests. He focused on their "leftist" politics rather than examining the reasons for their opposition.

When Rachel Carson's *Silent Spring*, a seminal work on the health hazards of insecticides and pesticides, was published in 1962, a leading scientist (male), questioned her concern for future generations because she was a spinster who had no children. He attacked her personally, not her argument that certain commonly used chemicals caused cancer.

Those given to Latin names like to label a particular kind of personal attack as *tu quoque*—"you also." In this instance, a person and thus his arguments are discredited because his own behavior does not strictly conform to the position he holds. We've all heard about the parent who drinks too much but admonishes his child about the dangers of drinking.

Antigun-control groups were delighted when Carl Rowan, a prominent Washington columnist and a staunch advocate of gun control, used an unregistered pistol to wound a young man who broke into his backyard. But Rowan's failure to follow his own beliefs does not necessarily make his argument for gun control a weak one.

BIZARRO *Piraro*

> Thank you for sharing your feelings so honestly, Dean, but the first thing you must realize is that as a MAN, your perceptions are hopelessly inaccurate.

Poisoning the Well

A person **poisons the well** when he makes an assertion that precludes or discourages an open discussion of the issue. This assertion will intimidate the listener, who fears that any resistance on his part will lead to a personal disagreement rather than a critical discussion.

> Every patriotic American supports legislation condemning the desecration of the flag.

The listener must now prove his patriotism rather than express his doubts about the legislation, and the speaker avoids having to defend his conclusion with relevant premises.

Slippery Slope

We know the **slippery slope** fallacy by other names too: the domino theory, the ripple effect. One thing leads to another. People often claim that an action should be avoided because it will inevitably lead to a series of extremely undesirable consequences. Sometimes such a chain reaction is probable, but often it can be exaggerated for effect.

Writer Wendy Kaminer, reviewing *Under Fire: The NRA and the Battle for Gun Control,* presents one group's position on gun control:

> What seems like reasonable restrictions on guns with no legitimate civilian purpose (assault rifles, for example) will lead inevitably to total prohibition of gun ownership that ends in virtual slavery at the hands of a totalitarian regime.

The argument here is that if we allow the government to take one step—the banning of assault weapons—the next step will be the banning of all guns—and the final step, loss of all freedom for all citizens.

In this argument, the downward slope is more precipitous than the evidence warrants, leading to an erroneous conclusion and, tragically, to private militias and the Oklahoma City bombing.

Look, if you give them a nuclear freeze, the next thing you know they'll want to outlaw war altogether.

If only all slippery slopes led to such a desirable outcome.

Special Pleading

When an argument contains the fallacy of **special pleading,** it judges and labels the same act differently depending on the person or group who performs the act. It is the application of a double standard.

When Shannon Faulkner, the first woman ever admitted, dropped out of The Citadel, a military college in South Carolina, the other cadets cheered as she departed the campus and the media covered her departure in great detail. What neither the jeering male cadets nor the media paid any attention to were the 34 other first-year students, all men, who also dropped out. Shannon Faulkner and her classmates made the same decision, but she was subjected to ridicule and close media scrutiny while her 34 male classmates were not; a double standard was applied.

Sometimes a double standard can be applied subtly through the manipulative use of language. A well-known defense lawyer, while discussing legal strategies on television, stated that he "prepares" his witnesses while the prosecution "coaches" theirs. "Prepares" suggests professional legal preparation for the courtroom whereas "coaches" suggests that a witness is encouraged to say what the lawyer tells her to whether it is true or not. Both lawyers are working with their clients before trial, but the lawyer's subtle use of language casts a negative slant on opposing counsel.

> **READINGS:** In "Feminism's Double Standard," "High Court's Mixed Decisions," and "Sexual Harassment and Double Standards," the authors accuse feminism and the U.S. Supreme Court of applying a double standard, in other words, of committing the fallacy of special pleading. Read their arguments to see if their accusations are justified in Chapter 12, Sexual Harassment.

Straw Man

In a **straw man** argument, a person creates and then attacks a distorted version of the opposition's argument.

> The democratic candidate wants the federal government to house everyone, feed everyone, care for everyone's children, and provide medical care for everyone. And he's going to take 50 percent of every dime you make to do it.

This argument overlooks the candidate's proposal to reduce defense spending to meet his goals. Hence, this is an unfair presentation of the opposing view, but one that could be extremely effective in discouraging votes for the democratic candidate. And this is the purpose of a straw man argument: to frighten supporters away from the opponent's camp and into one's own.

Columnist Ellen Goodman comments on this strategy in an essay titled "The Straw Feminist."

> The straw man has been a useful creature throughout history. Whenever people argued, he could be pulled together quickly out of the nearest available haystack, and set up as an opponent. The beauty of the straw man was that he was easily defeated. The straw man was also useful as a scarecrow. The arguments attributed to him were not only flimsy, they were frightening.

So I wasn't surprised when the straw feminist was sighted burning her bra at a "Miss America" pageant. The fact that there never was a bra-burning was irrelevant. Feminists became bra-burners. Not to mention man-haters.

The straw feminist wanted to drive all women out of their happy homes and into the workforce. The straw feminist had an abortion as casually as she had a tooth pulled. The straw feminist was hostile to family life and wanted children warehoused in government-run day and night care. At times, the straw feminist was painted slightly pinko by the anti-Communists or rather lavender by the anti-lesbians. But it was generally agreed upon that she was a castrating—well, you fill in the blank.

This creature was most helpful for discrediting real feminists but also handy for scaring supporters away.

A caution: German philosopher Arthur Schopenhauer [1788–1860] pointed out that "It would be a very good thing if every trick could receive some short and obviously appropriate name, so that when a man used this or that particular trick, he could at once be reproved for it." Fallacies provide us with those short and appropriate names for tricks or errors in reasoning, but we must not assume that all such errors can be labeled. Whenever we find fault with a particular line of reasoning, we should not hesitate to articulate that fault, whether or not we have a label for it. On the other hand, we must be careful not to see fallacies everywhere, perhaps even where they don't exist. We must *read critically,* informed by our knowledge of fallacies; at the same time we should avoid tedious witch hunts on the charitable assumption that most arguments are offered in good faith.

EXERCISE 6A

Identifying Fallacies

Identify by name the fallacies in each of the following arguments and justify your responses. You may want to turn to the end of the chapter for a chart of the fallacies.

Competition and collaboration: An interesting approach to this exercise combines competition and cooperation. The class is divided into two teams who compete in identifying the fallacies, with team members cooperating on responses.

---

1. "You say 'Why do I think [America is] in danger?' and I say look at the record. Seven years of the Truman–Acheson Administration and what's happened? Six hundred million people lost to the Communists, and a war in Korea in which we have lost 117,000 American casualties." (From Richard Nixon's Checkers Speech, September 23, 1952)

2. "Students should not be allowed any grace whatsoever on late assignments. Before you know it, they will no longer complete their work at all. If they don't do their assignments, they will be ignorant. If the students who are being educated are ignorant, then all of America will become more ignorant." (Thanks to a former student)

3. America: Love it or leave it.

4. You can't expect insight and credibility from the recent book *The Feminist Challenge* because its author David Bouchier is, obviously, a man.

5. Politicians can't be trusted because they lack integrity.

6. Closing the gay baths to prevent the spread of AIDS is like closing bars to prevent the spread of alcoholism.

7. How long must we allow our courts to go on coddling criminals?

8. "I'm firm. You are stubborn. He's pig-headed." (philosopher Bertrand Russell)

9. Anyone who truly cares about preserving the American way of life will vote Republican this fall.

10. "Why is it okay for people to choose the best house, the best schools, the best surgeon, the best car, but not try to have the best baby possible?" (A father's defense of the Nobel Prize winners' sperm bank)

11. Socrates, during his trial in 399 B.C.: "My friend, I am a man, and like other men, a creature of flesh and blood, and not of wood or stone, as Homer says; and I have a family, yes, and sons, O Athenians, three in number, one almost a man, and two others who are still young; and yet I will not bring any of them hither in order to petition you for an acquittal." (Plato, the "Apology")

12. "All Latins are volatile people." (Senator Jesse Helms, on Mexican protests against Senate Foreign Affairs subcommittee hearings on corruption south of the border)

13. Mark R. Hughes, owner of Herbalife International, was questioned by a Senate subcommittee about the safety of the controversial diet products marketed by his company. Referring to a panel of three nutrition and weight-control authorities, Hughes asked: "If they're such experts, then why are they fat?"

14. During these same hearings, Senator William Roth, R-Delaware, the Senate subcommittee chairman, reminded Hughes of criticism by some physicians that Herbalife fails to recommend that consumers seek guidance from doctors about their diets. "Do you be-

lieve it's safe to use your products without consulting a doctor?" Roth asked. "Sure," replied Hughes, 29. "Everybody needs good, sound, basic nutrition. We all know that."

15. When the Supreme Court ruled that school officials need not obtain search warrants or find "probable cause" while conducting reasonable searches of students, they violated freedoms guaranteed under the Bill of Rights. If you allow a teacher to look for a knife or drugs, you'll soon have strip searches and next, torture.

16. Since I walked under that ladder yesterday, I've lost my wallet and received a speeding ticket. False cause

17. Sometimes, the *best* is not for everyone. (an ad for a "Parisian boutique") Snob appeal

18. "I'm being denied the right to own a semiautomatic firearm simply because someone doesn't like the way it looks. If you look at all the different automobiles out there, the majority of them travel on regular roads. So how do you explain the dune buggies or off-road vehicles? They're different, but you don't hear anybody saying, 'Why does anyone need to have a dune buggy or an off-road vehicle? What's wrong with your regular run-of-the-mill traditional automobile?' It's all a matter of personal preference." (Marion Hammer, president of the National Rifle Association, in *George* magazine)

19. We are going to have to ease up on environmental protection legislation or see the costs overwhelm us.

20. Any rational person will accept that a fetus is a human being.

21. "Editor—Is anyone really surprised that students' grades haven't improved when all they do is listen to rock 'n' roll? Rock lyrics don't ever develop into anything cohesive and the music never expands itself like real music does. All it does is just sit there and make a lot of very loud noise that goes boom, boom, boom, boom, boom that blots off the mind completely. How can a mind ever expand when that's all it ever takes in? It all started about 35 years ago with bubble-gum rock and then went into heavy metal and grades have been going down steadily ever since." (Bob Grimes in a Letter to the Editor, *San Francisco Chronicle*)

22. Heat Wave Blamed For Record Temperatures Across U.S. (a Grass Valley *Union* headline)

23. The erosion of traditional male leadership has led to an increase in divorce because men no longer possess leadership roles.

24. "**Dear Ann Landers**: I have been a nudist for 36 years and am firmly convinced that if everyone would accept the concept of nudism, there would be no more wars, no crime and no greed, and we would live together in perfect harmony as God intended us to. Anyone who reads the Bible knows that all the trouble started when Eve ate that apple and put on the fig leaf." (*San Francisco Examiner*)

25. Now, all young men, a warning take,
    And shun the poisoned bowl; (alcohol)
    'Twill lead you down to hell's dark gate,
    And ruin your own soul.
    (ANONYMOUS, FROM CARL SANDBURG, ED., *THE AMERICAN SONGBAG*)

26. While our diplomats in France were gathering intelligence, their diplomats in Washington were practicing espionage.

27. I recently read about a homeless man with a burst appendix who was turned away from a hospital emergency room to die in the street. It's obvious that hospitals don't care about people, only money.

28. Do the vastly inflated salaries paid to professional athletes lead them into drug abuse?

29. The Nuclear Freeze movement was misguided and dangerous from the beginning, dependent as it was on "unilateral" disarmament. (A common argument of the movement's opponents. Those supporting the Nuclear Freeze movement actually proposed "bilateral" disarmament.)

30. Haemon: So, father, pause, and put aside your anger.
    I think, for what my young opinion's worth,
    That, good as it is to have infallible wisdom,
    Since this is rarely found, the next best thing
    Is to be willing to listen to wise advice.
    Creon: Indeed! Am I to take lessons at my time of life
    From a fellow of his age?
    (SOPHOCLES, *ANTIGONE*)

31. S & W vegetables are the best because they use only premium quality. *Snob appeal)*

32. "We would not tolerate a proposal that states that because teenage drug use is a given we should make drugs more easily available." (Archbishop John R. Quinn in response to a National Research Council's recommendation that contraceptives and abortion be made readily available to teenagers.)

33. Reading test scores in public schools have declined dramatically. This decline was caused by the radical changes in teaching strategies introduced in the 1960s.

34. The rates of teen pregnancy, youth violence, and drug use have increased rapidly in the years since school prayer was banned. The evidence is clear: We must bring prayer back to the classroom.

35. "Just as instructors could prune sentences for poor grammar, so the principal was entitled to find certain articles inappropriate for publication—in this situation because they might reveal the identity of pregnant students and because references to sexual activity were deemed improper for young students to see."

36. "Editor: Now that it has been definitely established that nonsmokers have the right to tell smokers not to pollute their air, it follows that people who don't own cars have the right to tell car owners not to drive. Right?" (Jim Hodge, *San Francisco Chronicle*)

37. The Black Panthers—Were they criminals or freedom fighters? (From a televison ad promoting a documentary on the radical group from the 1970's) *Special pleading*

38. We must either give up some of our constitutional liberties to ensure that the government can protect us against terrorism or we will again fall prey to terrorists. *False Dilemma*

39. "I give so much pleasure to so many people. Why can't I get some pleasure for myself?" Comedian John Belushi to his doctor in justification of his drug use.

EXERCISE 6B

Analyzing a Short Argument

The following letter is not a genuine letter to the editor but a critical thinking test devised by educators. Test yourself by writing a critique of this deliberately flawed argument. It contains at least seven errors in reasoning, some of them fallacies that you have studied in this chapter, some of them weaknesses that can be identified and described but not labeled.

230 Sycamore Street
Moorburg
April 10

Dear Editor:
    Overnight parking on all streets in Moorburg should be eliminated. To achieve this goal, parking should be prohibited from 2 a.m. to 6 a.m. There are a number of reasons why an intelligent citizen should agree.
    For one thing, to park overnight is to have a garage in the streets. Now it is illegal for anyone to have a garage in the city streets. Clearly then it should be against the law to park overnight in the streets.

False cause

Three important streets, Lincoln Avenue, Marquand Avenue, and West Main Street are very narrow. With cars parked on the streets, there really isn't room for the heavy traffic that passes over them in the afternoon rush hour. When driving home in the afternoon after work, it takes me thirty-five minutes to make a trip that takes ten minutes during the uncrowded time. If there were no cars parked on the side of these streets, they could handle considerably more traffic.

Traffic on some streets is also bad in the morning when factory workers are on their way to the 6 a.m. shift. If there were no cars parked on these streets between 2 a.m. and 6 a.m., then there would be more room for this traffic.

Furthermore there can be no doubt that, in general, overnight parking on the streets is undesirable. It is definitely bad and should be opposed.

If parking is prohibited from 2 a.m. to 6 a.m., then accidents between parked and moving vehicles will be nearly eliminated during this period. All intelligent citizens would regard the near elimination of accidents in any period as highly desirable. So we should be in favor of prohibiting parking from 2 a.m. to 6 a.m.

Last month the Chief of Police, Burgess Jones, ran an experiment which proves that parking should be prohibited from 2 a.m. to 6 a.m. On one of our busiest streets, Marquand Avenue, he placed experimental signs for one day. The signs prohibited parking from 2 a.m. to 6 a.m. During the four-hour period there was *not one accident* on Marquand. Everyone knows, of course, that there have been over four hundred accidents on Marquand during the past year.

The opponents of my suggestions have said that conditions are safe enough now. These people don't know what "safe" really means. *Conditions are not safe if there's even the slightest possible chance for an accident.* That's what "safe" means. So conditions are not safe the way they are now.

Finally let me point out that the director of the National Traffic Safety Council, Kenneth O. Taylor, has strongly recommended that overnight street parking be prevented on busy streets in cities the size of Moorburg. The National Association of Police Chiefs has made the same recommendation. Both suggest that prohibiting parking from 2 a.m. to 6 a.m. is the best way to prevent overnight parking.

I invite those who disagree as well as those who agree with me to react to my letter through the editor of this paper. Let's get this issue out in the open.

Sincerely,

Robert R. Raywift

WRITING ASSIGNMENT 15

Analyzing an Extended Argument

From the following collection of editorials, choose one (or find one in a newspaper or periodical) on which to write an essay evaluating the argument. We suggest the following process for approaching this paper:

Analyze each paragraph of your chosen editorial in order. Compose a list of the fallacies you find in each paragraph—give names of fallacies or identify weaknesses in reasoning (not all weaknesses can be precisely named) and illustrate with specific examples from the editorial. Avoid the trap of being too picky; you won't necessarily find significant fallacies in every paragraph.

During this paragraph-by-paragraph analysis, keep the argument's conclusion in mind and ask yourself if the author provides adequate support for it.

Next, review your paragraph-by-paragraph analysis to determine the two or three major problems in the argument. Then group and condense your list of faults or fallacies and, in a coherently written essay organized around these two or three principal categories of weaknesses, present your evaluation of the argument. For example, if you find more than one instance of personal attack, devote one of your paragraphs to this fallacy and cite all the examples you find to support your claim. Follow the same procedure for other weaknesses. Identify each specific example you cite either by paraphrase or direct quotation, imagining as you write that the reader is not familiar with the editorial you are critiquing.

Audience

College-age readers who have not read the editorial and who are not familiar with all of the fallacies listed in the text

Purpose

To illustrate to a less critical reader that published arguments written by established professionals are not necessarily free of fallacious reasoning

On Date Rape

Dating is a very recent phenomenon in world history. Throughout history, women have been chaperoned. As late as 1964, when I arrived in college, we had strict rules. We had to be in the dorm under lock and key by 11 o'clock. My generation was the one that broke these rules. We said, "We want freedom—no more double standard!" When I went to stay at a male friend's apartment in New York, my aunts flew into a frenzy: "You can't do that, it's dangerous!" But I said, "No, we're not going to be like that anymore." Still, we understood in the '60s that we were taking a risk.

Today these young women want the freedoms that we won, but they don't want to acknowledge the risk. That's the problem. The minute you go out with a man, the minute you go to a bar to have a drink, there is a risk. You have to accept the fact that part of the sizzle of sex comes from the danger of sex. You can be overpowered.

So it is women's personal responsibility to be aware of the dangers of the world. But these young feminists today are deluded. They come from a protected, white, middle-class world, and they expect everything to be safe. Notice it's not black or Hispanic women who are making a fuss about this—they come from cultures that are fully sexual and they are fully realistic about sex. But these other women are sexually repressed girls, coming out of pampered homes, and when they arrive at these colleges and suddenly hit male lust, they go, "Oh, no!"

These girls say, "Well, I should be able to get drunk at a fraternity party and go upstairs to a guy's room without anything happening." And I say, "Oh, really? And when you drive your car to New York City, do you leave your keys on the hood?" My point is that if your car is stolen after you do something like that, yes, the police should pursue the thief and he should be punished. But at the same time, the police—and I—have the right to say to you, "You stupid idiot, what the hell were you thinking?"

I mean, wake up to reality. This is male sex. Guess what, it's hot. Male sex is hot. There's an attraction between the sexes that we're not totally in control of. The idea that we can regulate it by passing campus grievance committee rules is madness. My kind of feminism stresses personal responsibility. I've never been raped, but I've been very vigilant—I'm constantly reading the signals. If I ever got into a dating situation where I was overpowered and raped, I would say, "Oh well, I misread the signals." But I don't think I would ever press charges.

The girl in the Kennedy rape case is an idiot. You go back to the Kennedy compound late at night and you're surprised at what happens? She's the one who should be charged—with ignorance. Because everyone knows that Kennedy is spelled S-E-X. Give me a break, this is not rape. And it's going to erode the real outrage that we should feel about actual rape. This is just over-privileged people saying they want the world to be a bowl of cherries. Guess what? It's not and it never will be.

—CAMILLE PAGLIA, HUMANITIES PROFESSOR AND CULTURAL CRITIC,
SAN FRANCISCO EXAMINER

> **READINGS:** For more of Paglia's view on relationships between men and women, see "A Call for Lustiness" on page 493.

Boxing, Doctors—Round Two

Before I went on vacation a few weeks ago, I wrote a column criticizing the American Medical Association for its call to abolish boxing. As you might have expected, I have received letters from doctors telling me I'm misinformed and scientifically naive. One doctor even said I must have had terrible experiences with doctors to have written what I wrote.

That just shows how arrogant doctors are. It never would occur to them that I might have a defensible position. If I disagree with them, it's because I'm ignorant.

Doctors are used to being right. We come into their offices sick and generally not knowing what's wrong with us. We are in awe of their expertise and afraid for our well-being. We have a tendency to act like children in front of them. "If you can only make me well, Doc, I will love you for life." Doctors, who start out as regular human beings, come to expect us to worship them. They thrive on the power that comes from having knowledge about life and death.

Which brings us to their misguided stand against boxing. Doctors are offended by injuries in boxing, although they don't seem as mortified by the people who die skiing or bike riding or swimming every year. You rarely hear a peep out of them about the many injuries football players sustain—that includes kids in the peewee leagues and high school. Why the outrage over boxing?

Because many doctors are social snobs. They see people from ethnic minorities punching each other in a ring and they reach the conclusion that these poor, dumb blacks and Latinos must be protected from themselves because they don't know any better. The AMA is acting like a glorified SPCA, arrogantly trying to prevent cruelty to animals. They would never dare preach this way to football players, because most of them went to college. Nor would they come out against skiing, because many doctors love to ski.

Boxers know the risks of taking a right cross to the jaw better than doctors, and they take up the sport with a full understanding of its risks. A man should have the right to take a risk. Doctors may want to save us from adventure, but there still is honor in freely choosing to put yourself on the line. Risk is why race-car drivers speed around treacherous tracks. Danger is why mountain climbers continue to explore the mystery of Mount Everest. Yet doctors do not come out against auto racing or mountain climbing.

One physician wrote a letter to the Sporting Green saying the AMA's position against boxing is based on medical evidence. As I read the letter's twisted logic, I wondered if the AMA causes brain damage in doctors. "Skiing, bicycle riding and swimming kill more people each year (than boxing)," he writes. "Obviously, far more people engage in those activities than enter a boxing ring."

Does his position make sense to you? We should eliminate boxing, the sport with fewer negative consequences, but allow the real killer sports to survive. Amazing. If this doctor were really concerned with medical evidence, as he claims, he would attack all dangerous sports, not just boxing.

But he doesn't. The truth is, boxing offends the delicate sensibilities of doctors. They don't like the idea that two men *intentionally* try to hurt each other. They feel more comfortable when injuries are a byproduct of a sport—although ask any batter who has been beaned by a fastball if his broken skull was an innocent byproduct.

In other words, doctors are making a moral judgment, not a medical judgment, about which sports are acceptable. Every joker is entitled to ethical opinions, but doctors have no more expertise than you or I when it comes to right and wrong. If preaching excites them, let them become priests.

What if the AMA is successful in getting boxing banned? Will the sport disappear? No way. As long as man is man, he will want to see two guys of equal weight and ability solve their elemental little problem in a ring. If the sport becomes illegal, it will drift off to barges and back alleys, where men will fight in secret without proper supervision. And then you will see deaths and maiming like you never saw before.

Whom will the AMA blame then?

—LOWELL COHN, A SPORTSWRITER
SAN FRANCISCO CHRONICLE

Guns Save Lives

The data from the 1990 Harvard Medical Practice Study suggest that 150,000 Americans die every year from doctors' negligence—compared with 38,000 gun deaths annually. Why are doctors not declared a public health menace? Because they save many more lives than they take. And so it is with guns.

Every year, good Americans use guns about 2.5 million times to protect themselves and their families, which means 65 lives are protected by guns for every life lost to a gun. For every 101 California tragedy, many others are averted.

An unsurprising 1 percent of America's 240 million guns are used for protection annually. The U.S. Bureau of Justice Statistics has repeatedly shown that guns are the most effective means of self-protection. If guns are as dangerous for self-defense as the alarmists claim, why does their leading researcher, Dr. Arthur Kellermann, want his wife to have a gun for defense?

Physicians who advocate gun prohibition have promoted confiscatory taxation and fees on guns, ammunition, and gun owners, in hopes that those taxes will be funneled into their research and their emergency rooms. To strengthen their case, they ignore the lives protected by guns and exaggerate the medical costs, claiming $20 billion per year in costs from gun violence.

In fact, the cost of medical care for gun violence is about $1.5 billion per year, less than 0.2 percent of our $800 billion annual health care costs. So advocates of gun prohibition routinely include estimates of "lost lifetime earnings," assuming gang bangers, drug dealers and rapists to be as productive as teachers and factory workers.

Even the virulently anti-self defense New England Journal of Medicine and Journal of Trauma have published studies showing that three-fourths of gun homicide "victims" are drug dealers or their customers. On the street, they cost society an average of $400,000 per criminal per year. In prison, they cost an average of $30,000 per criminal per year and, some cold-hearted analysts have noted, in the ground, they hurt no one and cost us nothing.

Cost-benefit analysis is necessarily hardhearted and, though it may be repugnant to consider, the gun deaths of those predators may be a savings to society on the order of $5.5 billion annually, more than three times the medical "costs" of guns.

—EDGAR A. SUTTER, NATIONAL CHAIRMAN OF DOCTORS FOR INTEGRITY IN
RESEARCH AND PUBLIC POLICY

KEY TERMS

Term	Description	Example
Fallacious argument	Persuasive but does not logically support its conclusion.	Senator Smith was expelled from college for cheating on an exam. His wife divorced him because of his numerous affairs. Therefore, he is a man without honor, a politician who cannot be trusted, and we should not support his National Health Bill.
Appeal to authority (2 forms)	1. Appeals to an authority who is not an expert on the issue under discussion.	Abortion to save the mother is irrelevant because a pediatric surgeon has never seen a case in which such a dilemma has risen.
Snob appeal	2. Appeals to people's desire for prestige and exclusivity.	Pamilla's not for everyone. The best never is.
Appeal to fear	Implicitly threatens the audience.	Will there be a *job* waiting when *you* leave college?
Appeal to pity	Attempts to win sympathy.	Professor Hall, I must get an A in your course. If you don't give me an A, I won't be able to go to law school.
Begging the question	1. Offers no actual support; may restate as a premise the conclusion in different words.	Students like rock music because it is the most enjoyable music around.
Loaded question	2. Asks a question that contains an assumption that must be proven.	Have you started to pay your fair share of taxes yet?
Question-begging epithet	3. Uses a single word to assert a claim that must be proven.	Reactionary, negligent, warmonger, deadbeat.

Equivocation	Shifts the meaning of a term within a single argument.	We are told that to discriminate in employment or housing is punishable by law. But we must discriminate when we hire an individual or rent an apartment.
False analogy	Compares two or more things that are not in essence similar and suggests that since they share certain characteristics, they share others as well.	I don't want to die falling off a rock. But you can kill yourself falling in the bathtub too.
False cause [Latin name: *post hoc, ergo propter hoc*]	Claims a causal relationship between events solely on the basis of a chronological relationship.	I joined the Confederacy for two weeks. Then I deserted. The Confederacy fell.
False dilemma	Presents two and only two alternatives for consideration when other possibilities exist.	Either you are in favor of recalling the mayor, or you are a supporter of her political platform.
Hasty generalization	Generalizes from a sample that is too small or in some other way unrepresentative of the target population.	Students in Professor Hall's eight o'clock freshman composition class are often late. Today's college students are irresponsible and unreliable.
Personal attack [Latin name: *ad hominem*]	**1.** Attacks the person representing the argument rather than the argument itself.	Because she is extremely wealthy, our mayor cannot properly represent this city.
Tu quoque ("you also")	**2.** Discredits an argument because the behavior of the person proposing it does not conform to the position he's supporting.	A teenager to his father: Don't tell me not to drink. You drink all the time.
Poisoning the well	Makes an assertion which will intimidate the audience and therefore discourage an open discussion.	Every patriotic American supports legislation condemning the desecration of the flag.

Slippery slope	Claims that an action should be avoided because it will lead to a series of extremely undesirable consequences.	What seems like reasonable restrictions on guns with no legitimate civilian purpose will lead inevitably to total prohibition of gun ownership that ends in virtual slavery at the hands of a totalitarian regime.
Special pleading	Judges and labels the same act differently depending on the person or group who performs the act.	The supplying of weapons to Central America by the Russians was an act of aggression. Our military aid to the region, however, helped the Freedom Fighters in their quest for peace.
Straw man	Creates and then attacks a distorted version of the opposition's argument.	The democratic candidate wants the federal government to house everyone, feed everyone, care for everyone's children, and provide medical care for everyone. And he's going to take 50 percent of every dime you make to do it.

CHAPTER 7

Deductive and Inductive Argument

There is a tradition of opposition between adherents of induction and deduction. In my view, it would be just as sensible for the two ends of a worm to quarrel.

—ALFRED NORTH WHITEHEAD

Sometimes arguments are classified as inductive or deductive. Induction and deduction are modes of reasoning, particular ways of arriving at an inference. Different logicians tend to make different distinctions between deductive and inductive reasoning, with some going so far as to declare, as Whitehead did, that such a distinction is spurious. But classifications, if carefully made, help us to understand abstract concepts, and scientists and humanists alike often refer to patterns of reasoning as deductive or inductive. This classification also helps us to distinguish between conclusions we must accept and those we should question, a valuable skill for both reading critically and writing logically.

Key Distinctions

The key distinctions between deduction and induction are generally seen as falling into two categories.

Necessity Versus Probability

In a **deductive argument,** the conclusion will follow by *necessity* from the premises if the method of reasoning is valid, as in this familiar bit of classical wisdom:

1. All men (updated—people) are mortal.
2. Socrates is a man (person).
   ∴ Socrates is mortal.

Deduction
All can be proven

170

Diff
1)ded - rock solved conclusion
2) General to particular
DEDUCTIVE AND INDUCTIVE ARGUMENT   **171**

In an **inductive argument,** the conclusion can only follow with some degree of *probability* (from the unlikely to the highly probable). British philosopher Bertrand Russell made the point implicitly but emphatically in *The Problems of Philosophy:* "The man who has fed the chicken every day throughout its life at last wrings its neck instead." The chicken reasons thus—

1. He has fed me today.
2. He has fed me this next day.
3. He has fed me this day too.
4. He has fed me yet another day, etc.
   ∴ He will feed me tomorrow.

The poor chicken has made a prediction, and a reasonable one, based on its past experience.

A related distinction here becomes clear. The premises of a deductive argument contain all the information needed for the conclusion, whereas the conclusion of an inductive argument goes beyond the premises. For this reason, some prefer the certainty of deduction to the probability of induction. Italian writer Italo Calvino describes such a person in his novel, *Mr. Palomar:*

> To construct a model—as Mr. Palomar was aware—you have to start with something; that is, you have to have principles, from which, by deduction, you develop your own line of reasoning. The principles—also known as axioms or postulates—are not something you select; you have them already, because if you did not have them, you could not even begin thinking. So Mr. Palomar also had some, but since he was neither a mathematician nor a logician, he did not bother to define them. Deduction, in any case, was one of his favorite activities, because he could devote himself to it in silence and alone, without special equipment, at any place and moment, seated in his armchair or strolling. Induction, on the contrary, was something he did not really trust, perhaps because he thought his experiences vague and incomplete. The construction of a model, therefore, was for him a miracle of equilibrium between principles (left in shadow) and experience (elusive), but the result should be more substantial than either.

Ambrose Peré, an Italian Renaissance physician, revealed his distrust of induction when he defined inductive diagnosis as "the rapid means to the wrong conclusion." One assumes that he would have argued for the value of a few well-learned principles behind one's observations.

From General to Specific, Specific to General

In a **deductive** argument, the inference usually moves from a generalization to a particular, specific instance or example that fits that generalization. Two examples:

1. All students who complete this course successfully will fulfill the critical thinking requirement.
2. Jane has completed this course successfully.
   ∴ Jane has fulfilled the critical thinking requirement.

1. Children born on a Saturday will "work hard for a living."
2. Nick was born on a Saturday.
   ∴ Nick will work hard for his living.

You may not believe this folk wisdom, especially if you were born on a Saturday, but the line of reasoning is still deductive.

In an ***inductive*** argument, the inference usually moves from a series of specific instances to a generalization.

1. Droughts have been more frequent in some areas.
2. Skin cancers related to ultraviolet rays have been increasing.
3. The tree line is moving north about 40 meters a year.
4. Polar ice has been melting more rapidly than in the past.
5. Oceans have been rising at measurable annual rates around the globe.
   ∴ The early stages of the dreaded "Greenhouse Effect" are upon us.

*"Gentlemen, it's time we gave some serious thought
to the effects of global warming."*

Sometimes in inductive reasoning, we begin with a hypothesis, an unproved theory or proposition, and gather the data to support it. For instance, when Jonas Salk thought his vaccine would cure polio, he first had to test it inductively by administering it to a broad sample before concluding that the vaccine prevented polio.

The Relationship Between Induction and Deduction

In Exercise 7B we ask you to distinguish between inductive and deductive reasoning, but in reality the two are inextricable. Consider the source for the generalizations upon which deductions are based. In some cases they seem to be the laws of nature (or of God if one is religiously inclined), but more often than not we arrive at these generalizations by means of repeated observations. Throughout history, people have observed their own mortality, so we can now take that generalization—all people are mortal—as a given from which we can deduce conclusions about individual people. Induction has, in this case, led to a trusted generalization that in turn allows us a "necessary," or deductive, inference.

Humorists have sometimes turned these concepts on their heads. Here's Woody Allen reflecting on deduction: "All men are Socrates." And Lewis Carroll, in "The Hunting of the Snark," on induction: "What I tell you three times is true."

In a more serious approach, Robert Pirsig, in his philosophical novel, *Zen and the Art of Motorcycle Maintenance*, attempts to explain deduction, induction, and the relationships between them in language we can all understand. These terms were never intended to be the exclusive domain of academics but, rather, descriptive of the ways in which we all think every day.

Note how the following excerpt from Pirsig's novel explains both the differences between induction and deduction and their dependence on one another.

Mechanics' Logic

Two kinds of logic are used (in motorcycle maintenance), inductive and deductive. (Inductive inferences start with observations of the machine and arrive at general conclusions. For example, if the cycle goes over a bump and the engine misfires, and then goes over another bump and the engine misfires, and then goes over another bump and the engine misfires, and then goes over a long smooth stretch of road and there is no misfiring, and then goes over a fourth bump and the engine misfires again, one can logically conclude that the misfiring is caused by the bumps. That is induction: reasoning from particular experiences to general truths.

Deductive inferences do the reverse. They start with general knowledge and predict a specific observation. For example, if, from reading the hierarchy of facts about the machine, the mechanic knows the horn of the cycle is powered exclusively by electricity from the battery, then he can logically infer that if the battery is dead the horn will not work. That is deduction.

Solution of problems too complicated for common sense to solve is achieved by long strings of mixed inductive and deductive inferences that weave back and forth between the observed machine and the mental hierarchy of the machine found in the manuals. The correct program for this interweaving is formalized as scientific method.

Actually I've never seen a cycle-maintenance problem complex enough really to require full-scale formal scientific method. Repair problems are not that hard. When I think of formal scientific method an image sometimes comes to mind of an enormous juggernaut, a huge bulldozer—slow, tedious, lumbering, laborious, but invincible. It takes twice as long, five times as long, maybe a dozen times as long as informal mechanic's techniques, but you know in the end you're going to *get* it. There's no fault isolation problem in motorcycle maintenance that can stand up to it. When you've hit a really tough one, tried everything, racked your brain and nothing works, and you know that this time Nature has really decided to be difficult, you say, "Okay, Nature, that's the end of the *nice* guy," and you crank up the formal scientific method.

For this you keep a lab notebook. Everything gets written down, formally, so that you know at all times where you are, where you've been, where you're going and where you want to get. In scientific work and electronics technology this is necessary because otherwise the problems get so complex you get lost in them and confused and forget what you know and what you don't know and have to give up. In cycle maintenance things are not that involved, but when confusion starts it's a good idea to hold it down by making everything formal and exact. Sometimes just the act of writing down the problems straightens out your head as to what they really are.

The logical statements entered into the notebook are broken down into six categories: (1) statement of the problem, (2) hypotheses as to the cause of the problem, (3) experiments designed to test each hypothesis, (4) predicted results of the experiments, (5) observed results of the experiments and (6) conclusions from the results of the experiments. This is not different from the formal arrangement of many college and high-school lab notebooks but the purpose here is no longer just busy-work. The purpose now is precise guidance of thoughts that will fail if they are not accurate.

The real purpose of scientific method is to make sure Nature hasn't misled you into thinking you know something you don't actually know. There's not a mechanic or scientist or technician alive who hasn't suffered from that one so much that he's not instinctively on guard. That's the main reason why so much scientific and mechanical information sounds so dull and so cautious. If you get careless or go romanticizing scientific information, giving it a flourish here and there, Nature will soon make a complete fool out of you. It does it often enough anyway even when you don't give it opportunities. One must be extremely careful and rigidly logical when dealing with Nature: one logical slip and an entire scientific edifice comes tumbling down. One false deduction about the machine and you can get hung up indefinitely.

In Part One of formal scientific method, which is the statement of the problem, the main skill is in stating absolutely no more than you are positive you know. It is much better to enter a statement "Solve Problem: Why doesn't cycle work?" which sounds dumb but is correct, than it is to enter a statement "Solve Problem: What is wrong with the electrical system?" when you don't absolutely *know* the trouble is *in* the electrical system. What you should state is "Solve Problem: What is wrong with cycle?" and *then* state as the first entry of Part Two: "Hypothesis Number One: The trouble is in the electrical system." You think of as many hypotheses as you can, then you design experiments to test them to see which are true and which are false.

This careful approach to the beginning questions keeps you from taking a major wrong turn which might cause you weeks of extra work or can even hang you up completely. Scientific questions often have a surface appearance of dumbness for this reason. They are asked in order to prevent dumb mistakes later on.

Part Three, that part of formal scientific method called experimentation, is sometimes thought of by romantics as all of science itself because that's the only part with much visual surface. They see lots of test tubes and bizarre equipment and people running around making discoveries. They do not see the experiment as part of a larger intellectual process and so they often confuse experiments with demonstrations, which look the same. A man conducting a gee-whiz science show with fifty thousand dollars' worth of Frankenstein equipment is not doing anything scientific if he knows beforehand what the results of his efforts are going to be. A motorcycle mechanic, on the other hand, who honks the horn to see if the battery works is informally conducting a true scientific experiment. He is testing a hypothesis by putting the question to Nature. The TV scientist who mutters sadly, "The experiment is a failure; we have failed to achieve what we had hoped for," is suffering mainly from a bad scriptwriter. An experiment is never a failure solely because it fails to achieve predicted results. An experiment is a failure only when it also fails adequately to test the hypothesis in question, when the data it produces don't prove anything one way or another.

Skill at this point consists of using experiments that test only the hypothesis in question, nothing less, nothing more. If the horn honks, and the mechanic concludes that the whole electrical system is working, he is in deep trouble. He has reached an illogical conclusion. The honking horn only tells him that the battery and horn are working. To design an experiment properly he has to think very rigidly in terms of what directly causes what. This you know from the hierarchy. The horn doesn't make the cycle go. Neither does the battery, except in a very indirect way. The point at which the electrical system *directly* causes the engine to fire is at the spark plugs, and if you don't test here, at the output of the electrical system, you will never really know whether the failure is electrical or not.

To test properly the mechanic removes the plug and lays it against the engine so that the base around the plug is electrically grounded, kicks the starter lever and watches the spark-plug gap for a blue spark. If there isn't any he can conclude one of two things: (a) there is an electrical failure or (b) his experiment is sloppy. If he is experienced he will try it a few more times, checking connections, trying every way he can think of to get that plug to fire. Then, if he can't get it to fire, he finally concludes that *a* is correct, there's an electrical failure, and the experiment is over. He has proved that his hypothesis is correct.

In the final category, conclusions, skill comes in stating no more than the experiment has proved. It hasn't proved that when he fixes the electrical system the motorcycle will start. There may be other things wrong. But he does know that the motorcycle isn't going to run until the electrical system is working and he sets up the next formal question: "Solve problem: what is wrong with the electrical system?"

He then sets up hypotheses for these and tests them. By asking the right questions and choosing the right tests and drawing the right conclusions the mechanic works his way down the echelons of the motorcycle hierarchy until he has found the exact specific cause or causes of the engine failure, and then he changes them so that they no longer cause the failure.

An untrained observer will see only physical labor and often get the idea that physical labor is mainly what the mechanic does. Actually the physical labor is the smallest and easiest part of what the mechanic does. By far the greatest part of his work is careful observation and precise thinking. That is why mechanics sometimes seem so taciturn and withdrawn when performing tests. They don't like it when you talk to them because they are concentrating on mental images, hierarchies, and not really looking at you or the physical motorcycle at all. They are using the experiment as part of the program to expand their hierarchy of knowledge of the faulty motorcycle and compare it to the correct hierarchy in their mind. They are looking at underlying form.

EXERCISE 7A

Analyzing Pirsig

1. According to Pirsig, what is the most important part of the mechanic's work?
2. How does Pirsig define induction and deduction?
3. Which method of reasoning—induction or deduction—does the scientific method rely on?
4. Return to the statement by mathematician and philosopher Alfred North Whitehead (1861–1947), which begins this chapter, and explain its meaning.

EXERCISE 7B

Distinguishing Inductive from Deductive Reasoning

A. Read the following passages carefully and determine which are based on deductive reasoning and which on inductive. Briefly explain your answers.

1. Marie must be out of town. She hasn't answered her phone in a week, nor has she returned the messages that I have left on her answering machine. When I drove by her house last night, I noted that the lights inside and out were off.

2. Cat lovers do not care for dogs, and since Colette had numerous cats all of her life, I assume she did not care for dogs.

3. According to polls taken prior to the national convention, the candidate I support held a substantial lead in the presidential race. I am now confident that he will win in November.

4. Every Frenchman is devoted to his glass of *vin rouge*. Philippe is a Frenchman so he too must be devoted to that glass of red wine.

5. Bill Clinton lied to the American people about his relationship with a White House intern. Richard Nixon lied about Watergate. Lyndon Johnson lied about the Gulf of Tonkin and the Viet Nam War. I'll let you draw your own conclusions.

6. As an expert testified on the MacNeil/Lehrer News Hour following the *Challenger* space shuttle disaster, the solid rocket booster had proved safe in over 200 successful launchings of both space shuttles and Titan missiles. It was reasonable to conclude that the same rocket booster would function properly on the *Challenger* mission.

7. Students educated in the past three decades are not as well informed as were students attending universities prior to the mid 1960s. And since our rising generation of leaders has been educated in the past three decades, they must not be as well informed as those leaders who preceded them.

8. When people are confident and cheerful, they are generally inclined to spend more freely. With this in mind, we have designed these ads to project a feeling of cheerful confidence that should encourage viewers to spend more freely on your product. [Ad agency pitch to a potential client.]

B. Arthur Conan Doyle would often tell this story about his first American lecture tour in 1894. A cabby, dropping him off, asked for a ticket to that night's lecture instead of a fare.

"How on earth did you recognize me?" Doyle asked.

The cabman replied: "If you will excuse me, your coat lapels are badly twisted downward, where they have been grasped by the pertinacious New York reporters. Your hair has the Quakerish cut of a Philadelphia barber, and your hat, battered at the brim in front, shows where you have tightly grasped it, in the struggle to stand your ground at a Chicago literary luncheon. Your right shoe has a large block of Buffalo mud just under the instep; the odor of a Utica cigar hangs about your clothing. . . . And, of course, the labels on your case give a full account of your recent travels—just below the brass plaque reading 'Conan Doyle.'"

We can safely infer that the creator of Sherlock Holmes had a sense of humor. Is our inference arrived at inductively or deductively?

Deductive Reasoning

Class Logic

Having established the differences between deductive and inductive reasoning, we can now examine each in greater detail. Underlying both forms of reasoning is an understanding of class logic. In fact, good reasoning in general often depends on seeing relationships between classes.

A **class** in logic is all of the individual things—persons, objects, events, ideas—that share a determinate property, a common feature. What is that determinate property? Anything under the sun. A class may consist of any quality or combination of qualities that the classifier assigns to it. A class may be vast, such as a class containing everything in the universe, or it may be small, containing only one member, such as Uncle Fred's last girlfriend. Making classes and assigning members to those classes is an essential part of everyday reasoning—it's how we order our experience. Indeed, each word in the language serves as a class by which we categorize and communicate experience. We can then take these words in any combination to create the categories or classes that serve our purpose.

A recent article in *The Journal of the American Medical Association,* for example, features a piece titled "Risk of Sexually Transmitted Diseases Among Adolescent Crack Users in Oakland and San Francisco." This title, which identifies one class (and the subject of the article), was created by combining seven classes: the class of things involving risk, the class of things that are sexually transmitted, the class of disease, the class of adolescents, the class of crack users, the class of persons living in Oakland, and the class of persons living in San Francisco.

Relationships Between Classes

There are three possible relationships between classes: **inclusion, exclusion,** and **overlap.**

INCLUSION   One class is included in another if every member of one class is a member of the other class. Using letters, we can symbolize this relationship as all As are Bs. Using circle diagrams, also called Euler diagrams after Leonhard Euler, an 18th-century mathematician, we can illustrate a relationship of inclusion this way:

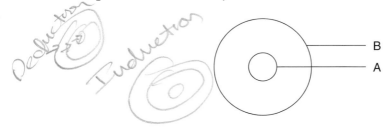

For example, the class of professional basketball players is included in the class of professional athletes because all professional basketball players are also professional athletes. The following diagram illustrates this relationship.

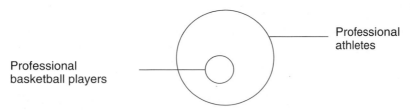

EXCLUSION   One class excludes another if they share no members, that is, if no As are Bs. Such a relationship exists between handguns and rifles.

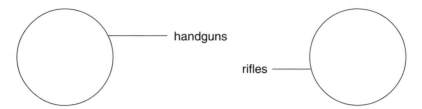

OVERLAP   One class overlaps with another if both have at least one member in common—if at least one A is also a B—for example, students at this university and students who like classical music.

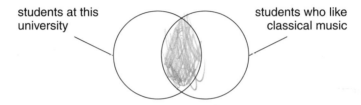

The way our public institutions classify relationships between groups of people can have a significant impact on their lives. The federal department of Housing and Urban Development (HUD) is authorized to allocate housing funds to individuals with disabilities. People with AIDS argued that they were entitled to such funds, but HUD, until recently, had denied them any such subsidy. Clearly, HUD saw the relationship between disabilities and AIDS as one of exclusion, whereas those with AIDS saw their relationship to those with disabilities as one of inclusion, a relationship they were, over time, able to convince HUD of.

EXERCISE 7C

Identifying Relationships Between Classes

Using circle diagrams, illustrate the relationships between the following pairs of classes.

1. cantaloupes and watermelons
2. judges and lawyers
3. Saabs and convertibles
4. mollusks and amphibians

5. cosmetics and hairspray

6. the homeless and the mentally ill

7. euthanasia and suicide

Now create your own classes.

1. Identify two classes, one of which is inclusive of the other.

2. Identify two classes that are exclusive of one another.

3. Identify two classes that overlap one another.

Class Logic and the Syllogism

Both inductive and deductive reasoning often depend on supporting a conclusion on the basis of relationships between classes. Let's look first at deduction. Deductive arguments usually involve more than two classes; in fact, the simplest form of deductive argument involves three classes. Remember this famous argument?

All people are mortal.

Socrates is a person.

∴ Socrates is mortal.

The three classes are "people," "mortality," and "Socrates." We can use circle diagrams to illustrate the relationship between these three classes. The first premise asserts that the class of people is included in the class of mortality. The second premise asserts that the class of Socrates is included in the class of people; and thus the conclusion can claim that Socrates is included in the class of mortality.

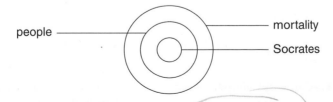

people ——————————— mortality

Socrates

This type of argument is called a **categorical syllogism**—a deductive argument composed of three classes; such an argument has two premises and one conclusion derived from the two premises.

THE SUBJECT AND THE PREDICATE   To help identify the three classes of a categorical syllogism, you may want to identify the subject and predicate of each premise. Categorical propositions, and indeed all English sentences, can be broken down into two parts—the **subject** and **predicate.** These terms are shared by both grammar and logic and mean the same thing in both disciplines. The subject is that part of the sentence about which something is being asserted, and the predicate includes everything being asserted about the subject. In the first premise above, "all people" is the subject and "are mortal" is the predicate; in the second premise, "Socrates" is the subject and "is a person" is the predicate. The subject identifies one class; the predicate, the other.

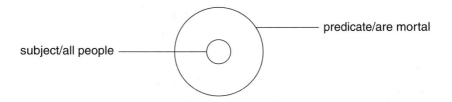

Note: If the premise stated "people are mortal" rather than "all people are mortal," the meaning would be the same because, if a class is not quantified in some way—some, many, few, one—it is assumed that the assertion refers to the entire class.

TRUTH, VALIDITY, AND SOUNDNESS   If the conclusion follows of necessity, inescapably, from the premises, as it does in the syllogism about Socrates, then it is a **valid** argument.

We frequently use the term "valid" in everyday language. For example, we say, "That's a valid point." But in logic validity has this very precise meaning: The conclusion follows of necessity from the premises, the form of the argument is correct, the line of reasoning conforms to the rules of logic. When we learn to evaluate the validity of a deductive argument, we can see what it means for a conclusion to follow inescapably from the premises.

Validity, however, is not the only requirement for a successful deductive argument; the premises must also be "**true**" or "**acceptable**." Logicians use the term true, appropriate when a proposition can be evaluated by absolute or mathematical standards. But proof must often fall short of what can be claimed as true, an absolute term too imposing, even intimidating, for many assertions that we would nonetheless be inclined to accept. In most of our arguments, we must settle for what is reasonable to believe, what has been adequately supported and explained. Oliver Wendell Holmes, Supreme

Court Justice 1902–1932, skirted the issue when he said, "What is true is what I can't help believing." We prefer the term "acceptable" to "true." As Tom Bridges of Montclair State University puts it, "The goal of inquiry is not objective truth, but reasonable belief, *pistis*—the state of being persuaded." Here lies the goal of written argument, not to assert a universal, irrevocable truth, but to establish a reasonable, acceptable position.

An important point here is that to evaluate an argument successfully, we must begin by evaluating the premises, one by one, rather than moving in on the conclusion first. The conclusion will only be as acceptable as the sum of its premises.

To summarize, two requirements must be met for us to accept the conclusion of a deductive argument:

1. The structure of the argument must be *valid*—that is, the conclusion must follow of necessity from the premises.

2. The premises must be *acceptable* (true).

A deductive argument whose premises are acceptable and whose structure is valid is a **sound** argument—a successful deductive argument. Put another way, if the argument is valid and the premises are acceptable, then the conclusion cannot be false. Keep in mind that the terms validity and soundness can refer only to the argument as a whole. In contrast, individual statements can only be described as acceptable or unacceptable (true or false). In logic, we don't describe an argument as being true or a premise as valid.

Some examples of sound and unsound arguments:

1. A sound argument—the premises are acceptable and the structure valid.

   Drift-net fishing kills dolphins.
   Mermaid Tuna uses drift nets.
   ∴ Mermaid Tuna kills dolphins.

2. An unsound argument—one of the premises (in this example the first one) is false or not acceptable, even though the structure is valid.

   All Latins are volatile.
   Jesse is a Latin.
   ∴ Jesse is volatile.

3. An unsound argument—the premises are acceptable but the structure is invalid.

   All athletes are people.
   All football players are people.
   ∴ All football players are athletes.

Note that in example 3, all the statements are acceptable, both the premises and the conclusion, but because the structure of the argument is invalid—the premises do not lead inescapably to the conclusion—the argument is unsound. Sketch this argument with circle diagrams to illustrate the principle.

Unreliable syllogisms turn up as accident and as humorous intent in a variety of places. Writer and critic Donald Newlove once claimed that, because he fell asleep while reading Harold Brodkey's *Runaway Soul*, which he also did his first time through literary classics *Moby Dick* and *Ulysses*, *Runaway Soul* must also be a great work of literature. Writer Ian Frazier found the following graffiti on a library table at Columbia University:

David Bowie is supreme.

God is supreme.

∴ David Bowie is God.

GUILT BY ASSOCIATION   Let's look at another example of an invalid argument with acceptable premises.

Drug dealers wear electronic pagers.

Doctors wear electronic pagers.

∴ Doctors are drug dealers.

All of us would reject this ridiculous argument, but this pattern of reasoning, erroneous as it is, is fairly common. One famous example took place in 1950 when communism was referred to as the "red menace," and Senator Joseph McCarthy and the House Un-American Activities Committee were beginning their witch hunt against anyone who had ever had an association, no matter how slight or distant, with communism. It was in this climate of national paranoia that Republican Richard Nixon, running against Democrat Helen Gahagen Douglas for a California senate seat, presented the following argument, allowing the voters to draw their own conclusions:

Communists favor measures x, y, and z.

My opponent, Helen Gahagen Douglas, favors these same measures.

∴ [Helen Gahagen Douglas is a Communist.]

This kind of reasoning, based on guilt by association, is faulty (but often effective—Douglas lost the election) because it assumes that if two classes share one quality, they share all qualities. Such reasoning is a source of much racism and sexism; it assumes that if two people are of the same sex or race, they share not only that characteristic but an entire set of characteristics as well. But a simple diagram can illustrate where the logic fails.

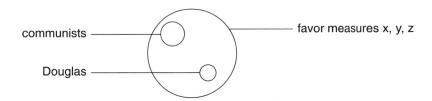

MORE ON SYLLOGISMS   Before you examine some syllogisms on your own, we need to look once again at exclusion, overlap, and inclusion. Examine the following example and use circle diagrams to illustrate the relationship between each of the classes to determine the validity of the reasoning.

> All Alice's friends are Libertarians.
>
> Deborah is not a Libertarian.
>
> ∴ Deborah is not a friend of Alice.

Were you able to illustrate by exclusion that this is a valid argument? Can you do the same for this one?

> None of Alice's friends are Libertarians.
>
> Deborah is not a friend of Alice.
>
> ∴ Deborah is not a Libertarian.

Can you illustrate why this reasoning is not reliable, why the argument is invalid?

So far we have been dealing with what we call a **universal proposition,** an assertion that refers to all members of a designated class. What happens when we qualify a premise with "some" and then have what logicians call a **particular proposition?** Let's look at an example.

> All gamblers are optimists.
>
> Some of my friends are gamblers.
>
> ∴ Some of my friends are optimists.

A diagram illustrates that because the conclusion is qualified, it can follow from one qualified, or "particular," premise. Although it's possible for some friends to fall outside the class of gamblers and thus, perhaps, outside the class of optimists, the second premise guarantees that some (at least two) of my friends are included in the class of gamblers.

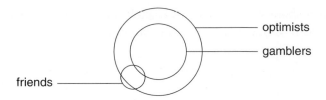

This argument is valid. But if the first premise also says "*Some* gamblers are optimists," you can't necessarily claim that even one friend has to be an optimist. Use a diagram to show the possibility that even the qualified conclusion could be false. When making claims in your written arguments, examine carefully how you use qualifiers and how you state conclusions based on qualified premises. Just because *some* politicians are dishonest, it doesn't necessarily follow that the mayor is dishonest.

EXERCISE 7D

Determining the Validity of Categorical Syllogisms

Use Euler diagrams to determine the validity of the following categorical syllogisms.

Example

1. Stealing is a criminal act.
2. Shoplifting is stealing.
   ∴ Shoplifting is a criminal act.

VALID Inclusion

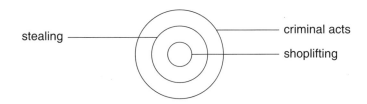

1. Liberals want to ban offshore drilling.
   Conservationists want to ban offshore drilling.
   ∴ Conservationists are liberals.

2. A cautious pilot wouldn't drink before a flight.
   Maxine is a cautious pilot.
   ∴ Maxine wouldn't drink before a flight.

3. All Jose's parrots understand Spanish.
   Pepe is his favorite parrot.
   ∴ Pepe understands Spanish.

4. Gauguin's paintings of Tahiti have brilliant and unrealistic colors.
   "Starry Night" has brilliant and unrealistic colors.
   ∴ "Starry Night" is a Gauguin painting of Tahiti.

5. Young men with shaven heads and swastikas tattooed on their arms
   are racists.
   John is a young man who doesn't shave his head or have a swastika
   tattooed on his arm.
   ∴ John is not a racist.

6. Nations that do not respect human rights shouldn't receive favored
   nation status.
   Tiananmen Square demonstrated China's complete lack of respect
   for the rights of its citizens.
   ∴ China doesn't deserve its favored nation status.

7. Every pediatrician knows that each child develops at his own rate.
   Dr. Haskell knows that each child develops at his own rate.
   ∴ Dr. Haskell is a pediatrician.

8. Some artists are completely self-absorbed.
   Frida Kahlo was an artist.
   ∴ Frida Kahlo was completely self-absorbed.

9. Members of the Christian Coalition believe in family values.
   Carlos and Maria believe in family values.
   ∴ Carlos and Maria are members of the Christian coalition.

10. Killing the innocent is morally wrong.
    Modern warfare always involves killing the innocent.
    ∴ Modern warfare is always morally wrong.

Create three categorical syllogisms of your own—one valid but unsound,
one invalid, and one sound.

EXERCISE 7E

Evaluating Deductive Arguments in Everyday Language

Determine whether the following arguments are sound or unsound. For
each argument follow these steps: First, reduce each one to a categorical
syllogism (supplying any unstated premises or conclusions—see hidden assumptions in Chapter 3); then use circle diagrams to determine validity;
and finally, discuss the truth or acceptability of each premise.

1. Plagiarism is wrong, and paraphrasing the words of others without proper acknowledgment is the same as plagiarism, so paraphrasing the words of others without proper acknowledgment is wrong.

2. Mafia member Joe Bonano was guilty of criminal activities because he claimed the Fifth Amendment in the course of his trial. The Fifth Amendment, you will recall, is the privilege of a witness not to testify on the grounds that the evidence called for might be incriminating. One may choose not to testify against oneself, but there is a risk attached to this privilege. For we cannot avoid the fact that people who take the Fifth Amendment have something to hide—their guilt. In the case of Joe Bonano, that something to hide was his criminal activities.

A Note on Deduction and Written Argument

While understanding the logic of valid syllogisms represents a valuable component of critical thinking, arguments as they appear in written discourse seldom take such a restricted shape. A clear grasp of deductive reasoning, however, is important for ensuring that the conclusions you reach from a given set of premises follow logically. Skeptical opponents of your position may be on the lookout for flawed deductions. Remember, for example, that just because two people, or two circumstances, share one set of common properties, it does not necessarily follow that they share other ideas or qualities. Attempts to smear political candidates often rely on this kind of fallacious reasoning. The case of Richard Nixon and Helen Gahagen Douglas cited above illustrates this point. Advertising, too, may lead us to draw a conclusion based on similar tricks of false association. Why else are beautiful models on hand when the product is an automobile, a vacuum cleaner, a carpet?

> READINGS: To see syllogistic reasoning as part of a written argument, refer to "In Defense of Abortion" on page 709.

Inductive Reasoning

The fundamental distinction between deductive and inductive reasoning lies in the relative certainty with which we can accept a conclusion. The certainty guaranteed when a deductive argument is validly reasoned from acceptable premises cannot be assumed in an inductive argument, no matter how carefully one supports the inference. The terms most appropriate for inductive arguments then are strong and weak, reliable or unreliable rather than valid and invalid.

Some logicians prefer the categories deductive and nondeductive to deductive and inductive, given the varied forms arguments can take when they don't conform to the rigorous rules of inference required for deduction.

Generalization

Determining cause and effect, formulating hypotheses, drawing analogies, and arriving at statistical generalizations are examples of nondeductive reasoning, or as we have chosen to call it, inductive reasoning. In this section, we concentrate on the statistical generalization. **Statistical generalizations** are best characterized as predictions, as claims about the distribution of a **projected property** in a given group or population, the **target population.** From the distribution of such a property in *part* of the target population, the **sample,** we infer a proposition, a conclusion that is either strong or weak depending on how carefully we conduct our survey. We make a prediction, an inference, about the unknown on the basis of the known; on the basis of our observations of the sample, we make a

THAT'S LIFE *Mike Twohy*

© 1999 Mike Twohy. Dist. by Washington Post Writers Group.

"Spin through and see if anything's targeted at us tonight."

generalization about all of the population, including that part we have not observed closely.

> Suppose we want to determine whether New York taxpayers will support a tax designated specifically for building shelters for the homeless. Here the **projected property** would be the willingness to support this particular tax (what we want to find out). The **target population** would be New York taxpayers. The **sample** would be that portion of New York taxpayers polled. From their answers, we would draw a conclusion, make a generalization about New York taxpayers in general: unanimous support, strong support, marginal support, little support, no support—whatever their answers warrant. But no matter how precise the numbers from the sample, we cannot predict with absolute certainty what the entire population of New York taxpayers will actually do. When we make an inference from some to all, the conclusion always remains logically doubtful to some degree.

Let's look at another example.

> For several years now, scientists and health officials have alerted the public to the increased risk of skin cancer as the thinning of the ozone layer allows more of the harmful ultraviolet rays to penetrate the atmosphere. Imagine that the student health center at your school wanted to find out if students were aware of this danger and were protecting themselves from it. In this case, the **projected property** would be taking preventive measures to protect oneself from the sun. The **target population** would be all the students attending your school, and the **sample** would be the number of students polled. Once again, any conclusions reached by the health center on the basis of its survey would be tentative rather than certain, with the certainty increasing in proportion to the size of the sample—the greater the number of students polled, the more reliable is the conclusion, assuming the sample is representative as well.

The Direction of Inductive Reasoning

The direction of inductive reasoning can vary. We may start by noting specific instances and from them make general inferences, or we may begin with a general idea and seek specific examples or data to support it. The following example moves from specific cases to a generalization.

> Observing a sudden increase in the number of measles cases in several communities, public health officials in the 1990s inferred that too many infants were going unvaccinated.

Even here you may notice that our ability to think both deductively and inductively has a way of intertwining the two modes of thought, but the structure of this argument is still inductive, the conclusion being probable rather than guaranteed.

Often we start with a tentative generalization, a possible conclusion called a **hypothesis,** an assertion we are interested in proving.

> Rousel Uclaf, the French manufacturers of a revolutionary new pill to prevent pregnancy and avoid abortion, hoped to prove that it was both effective and safe. To do so, they had to conduct elaborate studies with varied groups of women over time. Until they had gathered such statistical support in a sample population, their claim that it was effective and safe was only a hypothesis, not a reliable conclusion. But once they had tested their product, RU 486, on 40,000 women in several European countries and found only two "incidents" of pregnancies and no apparent harm, they were ready to claim that RU 486 is reasonably safe and statistically effective.

Even here, the conclusion remains inductive—it is a highly probable conclusion but not a necessary one as it would be in deduction. Unfortunately, there are examples of such inductive reasoning leading to false (and disastrous) conclusions. Approved for use in Europe, the drug thalidomide, given to pregnant women for nausea in the 1960s, caused many children to be born with grave deformities. And the Dalkon Shield, an intrauterine birth control device of the 1970s, although tested before being made available, caused sterility in many of its users.

Testing Inductive Generalizations

With inductive arguments, we accept a conclusion with varying degrees of probability and must be willing to live with at least a fraction of uncertainty. But the question always remains, how much uncertainty is acceptable?

CRITERIA FOR EVALUATING STATISTICAL GENERALIZATIONS   *How* we infer our conclusions, the way in which we conduct our surveys, is crucial to determining the strength of an inductive argument. Whether we are constructing our own arguments or evaluating those of others, we need to be discriminating. Many of our decisions on political, economic, sociological, even personal issues depend on inductive reasoning. Scarcely a day goes by without an inductive study or poll reaching the news sections of daily papers or the evening news on TV: surveys show the president's popularity is rising or falling, Americans favor socialized medicine, one in five non-government workers is employed at firms with drug testing programs. A few principles for evaluating such generalizations can help us all examine the conclusions with the critical perspective necessary for our self-defense.

In order to accept a conclusion as warranted or reliable, we need to control or interpret the conditions of the supporting survey.

Two features of the sample are essential:

1. The **size** must be adequate. The proportion of those in the sample must be sufficient to reflect the total size of the target population. Statisticians have developed complex formulas for determining adequate size proportionate to a given population, but for our general purposes common sense and a little well-reasoned practice will serve. The Gallup Organization polls 2,500 to 3,000 to determine how 80 million will vote in a presidential election and allows for only a 3 percent margin of error. This suggests that the size of a survey can often be smaller than we might initially assume.

2. The sample must be **representative.** It must represent the target population in at least two different ways.

   a. The sample must be selected *randomly* from the target population.

   b. It must also be *spread* across the population so that all significant differences within the population are represented. Such a contrived approach might seem contradictory to a random sample, but some conscious manipulation is often necessary to assure a sample that is genuinely typical of the target population.

Examine the following diagram to see these principles illustrated.

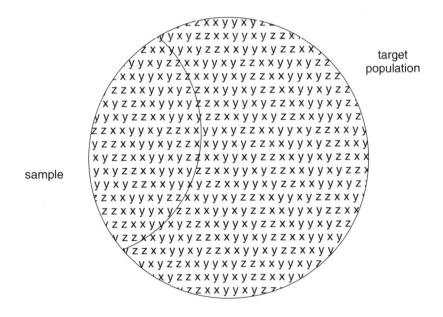

As you can see, we are back to classes (see Class Logic above). The sample is a subclass included in the larger class of the target population. As we make inferences, we move from a conclusion about the smaller class, the sample, to a conclusion about the larger class, the target population.

> *If they remove all the fools from Congress, it wouldn't be a representative Congress.*
>
> —Political commentator Molly Ivins

Let's evaluate the reasoning in the following argument:

A visitor of modest means from a midwestern city comes to San Francisco for five days and is instructed by her friends to assess the prices of San Francisco's restaurants; some of them are considering a trip there in the near future. Our tourist, let's call her Martha, picks up a guidebook and takes the first five restaurants listed in the book: Masas, Campton Place, Postrio, the Ritz Carlton, and Aqua, all of which are located downtown. Verging on bankruptcy, poor Martha returns home with the report that restaurants in San Francisco are staggeringly expensive. For a resident of San Francisco, the error in her conclusion and the flaw in the reasoning that led to her false conclusion are easy to spot—she has inadvertently chosen five of the most expensive restaurants in the city. Before selecting her restaurants, she should have examined her guidebook carefully to be sure that her survey of restaurants was, to some degree, representative. The book clearly began with a list of the major splurges and that was as far as Martha went.

With only five days, she was necessarily limited when it came to the *size* of her sample, and thus she would have to place a strong qualifier on any conclusions she drew. But, with a little care, she could have aimed for a more *random* sample by investigating different sections of her guidebook, referring to more than one guide, and visiting various geographical areas of San Francisco. Such a sampling would also have helped her arrive at examples spread more effectively over different types of cuisines. A visitor intent on savoring the best fare regardless of cost would have done well following Martha's approach, but one interested in the prices was doomed to a distorted picture.

Can you identify the projected property, the target population, the sample, and the conclusion for this inductive argument?

HASTY GENERALIZATIONS When, like Martha, we leap to an unwarranted conclusion, we commit the common logical fallacy of hasty generalization. If, for example, after one semester at a university as a student having had two professors who failed to return work, often missed class, or arrived late, you concluded that the university had a rotten faculty, you would be guilty of hasty generalization. The sample is clearly too small to warrant such a conclusion. For further discussion of this familiar fallacy, see Chapter 6.

Garfield ® by Jim Davis

Garfield doubts his conclusion when he discovers three counterexamples.

COUNTEREXAMPLES

With any generalization supported by specific examples, one counterexample can discredit, or "embarrass," the conclusion. Warranted conclusions must be consistent with the data used in their support, and where necessary, qualified appropriately—"most," "some," "usually," "occasionally," "in most cases."

Thinking Critically About Surveys and Statistics

Because surveys and statistics suggest an authority they may not warrant, we must read them critically rather than accept them without question. Statistics should contribute to reasoning, not serve as a substitute for it.

Time magazine ran a recent cover story on the high cost of a college degree entitled "How Colleges Are Gouging You," by Erik Larson. In his article Larson accused colleges of protecting their endowment funds while charging whatever the traffic will bear for tuition. The piece elicited this angry response.

> To generalize the situation at the University of Pennsylvania and other Ivy League schools and apply it to major universities across the board is like using the cost of a Lexus to discuss the price of an average family van. In the real world of most institutions, faculty members do not average earnings of $121,000 a year; they are lucky to make $40,000. And they are teaching larger classes with fewer resources and support staff and reduced budgets for essential expenses. Unfortunately, Larson's diatribe will probably be used by state legislatures as justification to cut budgets of many public institutions.
> —JOHN BRUNCH, ASSISTANT PROFESSOR
> DEPARTMENT OF MANAGEMENT
> KANSAS STATE UNIVERSITY, MANHATTAN, KANSAS

This professor from a public university is rightfully concerned that a generalization based on a study of private universities will be applied to public universities (which often do not have endowment funds), with the consequence of fewer resources for him and his students.

In 1948 Alfred C. Kinsey published *The Kinsey Report,* one of the first surveys on the sexual mores of Americans. Kinsey concluded among other things that 10 percent of the population was homosexual. James H. Jones, who wrote a recent biography of Kinsey, points out that the sample on which this conclusion was based was not representative of all Americans.

> Kinsey did a great deal of interviewing in prisons, where the incidence of homo-sexuality was higher than in the general population. More damaging still to the reliability of his sample was his practice of seeking out individuals on the basis of their sexual tastes and behavior. In compiling his sample of the American population, Kinsey targeted gay people, becoming the first scientist to study in depth the nascent gay communities in large urban areas and elsewhere. In city after city he tapped into gay networks, using the contacts he made with gay subjects to generate introductions to their partners, lovers and friends. This practice enabled Kinsey to collect a large number of gay histories, but, in con-junction with his prison interviews, it also skewed his data in the direction of overestimating the percentage of gay people in the American population.

Bad science is made worse by the media's reporting of all surveys in abbreviated and often sensational ways. Even when a study is carefully done by a reputable institution, the press will often reduce the results to the most attention-getting headline. The media reported that heavy coffee drinkers had two to three times the risk of heart disease on the basis of a study done at Johns Hopkins University that used many subjects over several years. But a careful reading of the study from beginning to end revealed that its authors didn't ask participants about their diet, smoking habits, and exercise levels, mitigating factors in any study of heart disease. The report concluded that there was "a need for further investigation" into the dangers of caffeine, a conclusion the media failed to report. All that one could safely conclude from the Johns Hopkins study is a **correlation** between heavy caffeine use and heart disease, not **causation.** The distinction between correlation and causation is an important one. There is a correlation between home ownership and car accidents. If you are a home owner, you're more likely to own a car, so you're more likely to be in a car accident, but that doesn't mean that home ownership causes car accidents.

Note also subtle slants in the emphasis the media give to statistics. In the same issue of a major daily newspaper, the summary caption on page one stated that, "A new poll finds that 1 in 5 Californians still resent Japan for the attack on Pearl Harbor," while the inside story was headed, "50 years after attack on Pearl Harbor, only 1 in 5 is still resentful, poll shows." What are the different implications of these two captions?

Consider the Source

When evaluating a survey and its conclusions, we must consider the source of the survey—who conducted the survey and who paid for it—to determine if there is a conflict of interest or a hidden agenda. A recent study of silicone breast implants concluded that there was no link between rup-

tured implants and connective tissue disease. Lawyer and consumer advocate Mary Alexander criticizes this study not only for the limited size of its sample and its failure to allow for the 8.5 years of latency between implantation and silicone disease, but also for two of its authors who "admitted on the threat of perjury that they were paid consultants of breast implant manufacturers." Furthermore, Dow Corning, the world's largest silicone breast implant manufacturer, had donated $5 million to one of the hospitals involved in the study. Such a study is riddled with conflict of interest. It is not in the best interest of those who benefit directly from Dow Corning to find fault with the company's product.

One of the most respected medical publications, *The New England Journal of Medicine,* has been found guilty of violating its conflict-of-interest policy. In 1989, the journal included an article that played down the risks from exposure to asbestos but failed to inform its readers that the authors had past ties to producers of asbestos. In 1996, the journal ran an editorial claiming that the benefits of diet drugs outweighed the risks but failed to note that the two authors had been paid consultants for firms that made or marketed one of the diet drugs under discussion. In 1997, the journal featured a negative review of a book connecting environmental chemicals and various cancers, a review written by the medical director of a large chemical company.

CRITICAL READING OF SURVEYS

1. Is the sample representative of the target population? Is it large enough?

2. Does the media's report on the survey seem fair and reasonable?

3. Does the survey establish causation or correlation?

4. Who wrote or published or called your attention to the survey? Are they impartial or do they have a hidden agenda or conflict of interest? Is the survey cited in advertising or in another context in which the motive is to sell you something?

EXERCISE 7F

Evaluating Inductive Reasoning

In the following studies, identify the conclusion, the projected property, the target population, and the sample. Then, drawing on the principles of reliable inductive generalizations, evaluate their reliability.

1. The quality control inspector at Sweet and Sour Yogurt removes and tests one container out of approximately every thousand (about one every 15 minutes) and finds it safe for consumption. She then guarantees as safe all the containers filled that day.

2. In her book *Women and Love,* Shere Hite claims that a large percentage of American women are unhappy in their marriages and feel that men don't listen to them. She felt confident in her conclusions after mailing out 100,000 questionnaires to women's political, professional, and religious organizations and having 4 percent of the questionnaires returned.

3. Setting out to document her theory on the prevalence of racism on television, a sociologist examines 40 episodes from the new fall prime-time situation comedies and finds that 36 of them contain racist stereotypes. She concludes that 90 percent of television drama is racist.

4. On November 1, to consolidate his frequent flier miles, businessman Eric Nichols decided to select one domestic airline from his two favorites. He planned to base his decision on each airline's reliability. From November through April he made 20 evenly spaced trips on United, experiencing two cancellations, nine delayed departures, and eight late arrivals. From May through October, he flew American Airlines 22 times, but improved his record with only one cancellation, seven delays, and five late arrivals. Without further consideration, he chose American as the more reliable of the two.

5. The French Ministry of Social Affairs reported that three well-known research physicians at the Laennec Hospital in Paris had observed "dramatic biological improvements" in a group of patients with AIDS. The physicians reported a "dramatic" slowing of acquired immune deficiency syndrome in one of the six patients and a complete halt in the disease's progress in another after only five days of treatment with a compound called cyclosporine. (Hint: The conclusion is implicit.)

6. A recent study by the University of Medicine and Dentistry of New Jersey concluded that "women who were abused [physically, emotionally, or sexually] as children have more health problems and require more hospital care than women who were not abused." Seven hundred women from a private gynecological practice were interviewed. Mostly white, middle class with college degrees, they ranged in age from 16 to 76.

EXERCISE 7G

Finding Weaknesses in Inductive Arguments

In the following article, a critic points out weaknesses in an inductive argument. Analyze the original inductive study, then the critic's response, and summarize your findings according to these steps:

1. Identify the projected property, the target population, the sample, and the conclusion.

2. Explain the weaknesses as discussed by the critic and conclude with discussion of your own opinion. Do you support the critic or the researchers who first presented the conclusions?

Dispute Over Claims of Ibuprofen Dangers
—United Press International

Washington

Federal officials and makers of ibuprofen medicines yesterday disputed the conclusions of medical researchers who claim that a 12-patient study indicates that over-the-counter doses of the pain killer may cause kidney failure in high-risk people.

In a study published in the Annals of Internal Medicine, doctors from Johns Hopkins University medical school in Baltimore looked at the effects of ibuprofen and two other types of nonsteroidal, anti-inflammatory drugs in 12 women with chronic kidney problems but no obvious symptoms. Three of the patients developed complications.

But Food and Drug Administration spokeswoman Bonnie Aikman said yesterday that consumers have no cause for alarm about taking over-the-counter ibuprofen, as long as they read the label telling them to contact a doctor if they experience any unusual symptoms. That advice will be highlighted on ibuprofen labels starting in June, Aikman added.

The patients in the study were given the prescription-level dose of ibuprofen—2,400 milligrams a day—two times the maximum daily dose recommended for over-the-counter versions of the drug. Eight days into an 11-day course of treatment, three of the patients were judged to have severe enough kidney impairment that researchers stopped giving them the drug. When researchers later tried giving them lower doses of ibuprofen, 1,200 milligrams per day—or the top over-the-counter dose, two of the three patients again developed evidence of acute kidney failure.

Ibuprofen was recommended to patients by doctors nearly 50 million times in 1987, according to the National Disease and Therapeutic Index. An estimated 100 million people have used the nonprescription drug since it was introduced in 1984.

T. R. Reid, a spokesman for the Upjohn Co. of Kalamazoo, Mich., maker of Motrin, a prescription ibuprofen medication, and Motrin IB, the over-the-counter version, called the conclusions of the Johns Hopkins study "warped."

Reid noted the study only looked at 12 patients, and all patients were predisposed to kidney failure. But his major objection was that its authors extended the findings about prescription ibuprofen to over-the-counter ibuprofen.

Other common over-the-counter products containing ibuprofen are Nuprin, made by Bristol-Myers Squibb Co. of New York, and Advil, made by Whitehall Laboratories Inc. of New York.

"We do not believe the findings of this study apply to the safety of nonprescription ibuprofen in the general population," Whitehall said in a statement.

Reid said labels on prescription Motrin already inform doctors there is a slim risk—1 percent or less—of kidney complications from prolonged use of the drug.

In addition, the Upjohn Company said labels on nonprescription ibuprofen tell people with serious medical conditions, such as poor kidney function, to consult with their doctors before starting any new over-the-counter medication.

EXERCISE 7H

Collecting Generalizations

Humorist James Thurber, celebrated for his long association with *The New Yorker* magazine, had fun exploiting our tendency to overgeneralize in his essay, "What a Lovely Generalization." Many of his examples are absurd, but some suggest the dangers that can spring from such patterns of thought. For those interested in collecting generalizations, he suggests listening "in particular to women, whose average generalization is from three to five times as broad as a man's." Was he sexist or making a not-so-funny joke? He listed many others from his collection, labelling some "true," some "untrue," others "debatable," "libellous," "ridiculous," and so on. Some examples from his collection: "Women don't sleep very well," "There are no pianos in Japan," "Doctors don't know what they're doing," "Gamblers hate women," "Cops off duty always shoot somebody," "Intellectual women dress funny." And so his collection ran, brimming with hasty generalizations.

Your task is to collect two "lovely generalizations" from the world around you, comment on the accuracy, absurdity, and dangers of each and discuss the implications of your generalizations for those who seem to be the target.

WRITING ASSIGNMENT 16

Questioning Generalizations

Add the two generalizations you chose for Exercise 7H "Collecting Generalizations" to the following list of generalizations and choose one to write a paper in support of, or in opposition to. This list could be even longer and more diverse if your instructor collects the entire classes' generalizations and makes them available to you.

1. Women are better dancers than men.
2. Men are better athletes than women.
3. Everyone is capable of being creative.
4. Nice guys finish last.
5. Appearances can be deceiving.
6. The purpose of a college degree is to prepare an individual for a career.
7. A college graduate will get a higher paying job than a high school graduate.
8. A woman will never be elected president of the United States.
9. All people are created equal.
10. War is a necessary evil.

Audience

A reader who is not strongly invested in the proposition one way or another but who is interested in hearing your point of view

Purpose

To cast a critical eye on a generalization that people tend to accept without question

WRITING ASSIGNMENT 17

Conducting a Survey: A Collaborative Project

Conduct a survey at your school to determine something of significance about the student body and then write a report in which you state either a question or a hypothesis, describe the survey, and speculate on the results. (Apologies to statisticians for the oversimplification of a very complex task.)

The class as a whole can brainstorm possible questions to ask the student body, the target population. What do students think about the current administration on campus or in Washington? Our nation's involvement in foreign wars? Or a host of other political issues. How many students take a full academic load and work part-time as well? There are many possibilities.

Choose five or six topics from these many possibilities and divide into groups around them. These groups will then create a survey—a questionnaire appropriate to the topic they are researching—and a strategy for distributing it to a representative sample.

The next step is to collect, tabulate, and discuss the data. Either each student can then write her own report or the group can write a single report, assigning a section to each member of the group.

The report will contain the following:

1. A description of the survey

   What questions did you ask?
   When and where did you ask them?

2. A description of the sample

   Whom did you ask?
   How many did you ask?

3. Evaluation of the survey

   Was the sample large enough?
   Was it representative?
   Were your questions unbiased?
   What could you do to make it better?

4. Analysis of the results

   How does it compare with what you expected the results to be before you began gathering the data?
   What do you imagine are the causes that led to these results?
   What are the implications of the results?

Audience

Your campus community—students, faculty, and staff

Purpose

To inform your campus community about its student members

> **READINGS:** For additional survey topics, see the following articles and assignments: "From His Dorm Room," Topic #4, page 318; Bioethics—Concluding Topics, #3, page 448; "Man Handling," and the topic that follows, page 495; "Maiden Names," Topic #6, page 629.

Application to Writing

Deduction, Induction, and Organizational Patterns

Textbooks about writing frequently describe organizational patterns for essays as being strictly deductive or inductive. It is true that a written argument may start with a broad generalization offered as a given upon which applications to more specific circumstances may be built. Such a shape does resemble one definition of deduction—a generalization applied to a particular instance or example. A paper that assumes the majority of mothers are working outside the home today could then go on to argue for a particular course of action to address problems surrounding the trend of both parents working outside the home. A deductive paper tends to greater formality, a construction based on defined principles that sets out to prove a stated conclusion.

Often a collection of specific data—empirical observations including personal experience, examples from research, and statistics—can add up to a generalization in the conclusion and thus appear to reflect the inductive process. A survey of urban households, for example, could, with careful analysis, lead to a conclusion about trends in family eating habits. Inductive writing, reflecting its open-ended character, is often looser than its more rigid counterpart.

Legal scholar Patricia J. Williams expresses it this way in describing her personal approach to writing about legal issues:

> Legal writing presumes a methodology that is highly stylized, precedential, and based on deductive reasoning. Most scholarship in law is rather like the "old math": static, stable, formal—rationalism walled against chaos. My writing is an intentional departure from that. I use a model of inductive empiricism, borrowed from—and parodying—systems analysis, in order to enliven thought about complex social problems.

She goes on to explain that she is "trying to create a genre of legal writing to fill the gaps of traditional legal scholarship" by writing "in a way that . . . forces the reader to participate in the construction of meaning."

Ultimately, as Pirsig emphasizes in "Mechanics' Logic," it takes an interplay of the two thinking methods to reflect accurately how we arrive at our conclusions. The writer of the paper on family eating habits would be likely to start speculating on why trends in family meals have changed and possibly on what impact such changes would have on society. Such an approach would not be described as inductive, but, in fact, represents a combination of inductive and deductive reasoning.

Our ability to distinguish between inductive and deductive reasoning enables us to see if a conclusion absolutely follows from the evidence or if it is one possibility among others. Understanding our reasoning and the reasoning of others in these terms increases our ability to both think critically and write logically.

SUMMARY

Inductive and deductive reasoning are distinct from one another in two ways.

1. In a deductive argument, the conclusion follows by necessity from the premises if the method of reasoning is valid. In an inductive argument, the conclusion can only follow with some degree of probability.

2. In a deductive argument, the inference moves from a generalization to a particular instance or example that fits that generalization. In an inductive argument, the inference usually moves from a series of specific instances to a generalization.

Induction and deduction are interdependent; it takes an interplay of the two thinking methods to arrive at our conclusions.

There are three possible relationships between classes: inclusion, exclusion, and overlap.

Both inductive and deductive reasoning often depend on supporting a conclusion on the basis of relationships between classes.

For a categorical argument to be sound, the structure of the argument must be valid and the premises acceptable.

The statistical generalization, based as it is on an inductive leap from some to all, is never as certain as a conclusion drawn from sound deductive reasoning.

The direction of inductive reasoning can vary. We may note specific instances and from them make general inferences, or we may begin with a general idea and seek specific examples or data to support it.

For a statistical generalization to be reliable, the sample must be adequate in size and representative of the target population.

With any generalization supported by specific examples, one counterexample can discredit the conclusion.

KEY TERMS

Categorical syllogism   a deductive argument composed of three classes; the argument has two premises and one conclusion derived from the two premises.

Class   in logic all of the individual things—persons, objects, events, ideas—that share a determinate property.

Deduction   a pattern of reasoning in which the conclusion follows of necessity from the premises if the reasoning is valid.

Exclusion   a relationship between classes in which classes share no members.

Hypothesis   a tentative generalization, a possible conclusion, an assertion we are interested in proving.

Inclusion   a relationship between classes in which every member of one class is a member of another class.

Induction   a pattern of reasoning in which the conclusion follows only with some degree of probability.

Overlap   a relationship between classes in which classes share at least one member.

Particular proposition   refers to some members of a designated class.

Predicate   includes everything being asserted about the subject.

Projected property   what is to be determined about the target population.

Sample   the surveyed members of the target population.

Soundness   describes a deductive argument whose premises are acceptable and whose structure is valid.

Statistical generalization   a prediction about the distribution of a particular feature in a given group.

Subject   that part of the sentence about which something is being asserted.

Target population   the group about which the conclusion will be drawn.

Universal proposition   refers to all members of a designated class.

Validity   the conclusion follows of necessity from the premises; the form of the argument is correct.

CHAPTER 8

The Language of Argument— Style

Style is the dress of thought.

—SAMUEL WESLEY

Some may dismiss style as ornament, as the decorative frills of writing, or as something limited to matters of correct grammar and usage. A wiser definition of style would encompass more: choices of diction and word order that aim to strengthen our ideas and render them more precisely. An effective style chosen with your audience, your purpose, even your personal integrity in mind, can capture your reader's attention and possibly win the day for your argument. Style certainly includes a carefully proofread, grammatically correct final draft, but it also means well-crafted sentences that carry meaning gracefully to your readers, contributing to clear communication.

Sentence Length

How many times have you heard, "Keep it short, write short sentences?" Too many, probably. To be clear, direct, and concise, you do not always have to fall back on repetitive short sentences. As the discussion of logical joining in Chapters 3 and 4 and of appositives, parallel structures, and verbal modifiers to follow in this chapter suggests, you can extend the flow of your ideas and insert necessary information by expanding your repertoire of sentence structures.

Appositives—A Strategy for Defining and Identifying Terms Within the Sentence

As we illustrate in Chapter 5, abstract terms need defining so that our readers understand what we mean. One might agree in theory but question in practice how a writer defines terms without derailing the organization of the paper or paragraph. Often, the answer is to use **appositives**— noun phrases placed beside nouns to elaborate on their meaning (note the appositive here).

Here is Joan Didion, contemporary American essayist and noted stylist, giving us a vivid picture of the Los Angeles climate:

> In fact the climate is characterized by infrequent but violent extremes: *two periods of torrential subtropical rains* which continue for weeks and wash out the hills and send subdivisions sliding down toward the sea; *about twenty scattered days a year of the Santa Ana,* which, with its incendiary dryness, invariably means fire.

Didion has added details and combined ideas into one sentence by using appositives. In each case, the appositive (italics) modifies the noun "extremes," explains or defines what the extremes are, all within one sentence.

Appositives usually follow the nouns they modify, but some writers introduce a sentence with an appositive:

> *An expression of frustrated rage,* gangsta rap tries to be outrageous in order to provoke strong reactions.

The phrase, "an expression of frustrated rage" modifies "gangsta rap." Such additions allow a writer to include essential information or background details that may not warrant separate sentences. And as you pile up ideas, you can expand meaning even as you remain economical in sentence length. A series of appositional phrases often replaces a series of separate sentences expressing the same ideas. The effect is streamlined thought in fluent prose, as the following examples in Exercise 8A illustrate.

EXERCISE 8A

Recognizing Appositives

In the three passages that follow, identify the appositives and the nouns they modify by underlining the appositives and circling the nouns.

1. A descriptive passage with examples

> The Evertons are introduced to a second national peculiarity, one they will soon recognize on the streets of Ibarra and in towns and cities beyond. It is something they will see everywhere—a disregard for danger, a companionship with death. By the end of a year they will know it well: the antic bravado, the fatal games, the coffin shop beside the cantina, the sugar skulls on the frosted cake.
>
> —HARRIET DOERR, STONES FOR IBARRA

2. Identification

Cotton Mather was an exception, one who so fully accepted and magnified the outlook of his locality that he has entered folklore as the archetypal Puritan, not only a villainous figure in the pages of Hawthorne, William Carlos Williams and Robert Lowell, but an object of parody even to his fellow townsmen in 18th-century Boston.

—LARZER ZIFF, THE NEW YORK TIMES BOOK REVIEW

3. Definition

As Baranczak points out, Milosz [Nobel Prize–winning poet] rejects symbols in favor of metonymy and synecdoche, those figures of speech which represent a whole by a thing allied to it or by a part of it.

—HELEN VENDLER IN THE NEW YORKER

Appositives and Argument

In arguments, appositives can be helpful, allowing you to expand and emphasize ideas and to show opposing points of view in the same sentence, as illustrated in the following example.

Unilateral disarmament, a policy that was considered dangerous and impractical by many, but one that was vigorously promoted by a number of hardline strategists, would require only one side to reduce its arms.

Two views on disarmament are juxtaposed in one strong sentence.

Punctuation of Appositives

Punctuation choices are simple and logical. In most cases, the appositive phrase is set off from the noun it modifies with commas. If you want greater emphasis, you can do as Harriet Doerr did and use a dash: "It is something they will see everywhere—a disregard for danger, a companionship with death."

Or choose a colon (appropriate only when the appositive ends a sentence) for an even sharper break as Joan Didion did:

In fact the climate is characterized by infrequent but violent extremes: two periods of torrential subtropical rains which continue for weeks and wash out the hills and send subdivisions sliding down toward the sea; about twenty scattered days a year of the Santa Ana, which, with its incendiary dryness, invariably means fire.

This passage also illustrates the way in which Didion varies punctuation to control all the information in this long sentence, providing logical markers for the reader: The colon sets off the appositive series; the semicolon marks the major division in the series, separating these points from the lesser pauses marked by commas.

For the vast array of punctuation rules and conventions in English, refer to a handbook. But as a start, think of punctuation as organizing patterns of thought and guiding the reader through the meaning of sentences. It is in this role that punctuation provides a vital service.

EXERCISE 8B

Creating Appositives

Most of you already use appositives to some extent in your writing whether you recognize them or not. But a little conscious practice may expand your knowledge of this useful device.

A. Combine the following sets of sentences by reducing one or more sentences to appositives. You may find more than one way to combine them.

> Example:
>
> Unilateral disarmament was considered dangerous and impractical. It was a policy that would require only one side to reduce its arms.
>
> becomes
>
> Unilateral disarmament, *a policy* that would require only one side to reduce its arms, was considered dangerous and impractical.
>
> or
>
> Unilateral disarmament, *a policy* that was *considered dangerous and* impractical, would require only one side to reduce its arms.

1. New York has long been the destination of America's adventurous young. It is a city of danger and opportunity.

2. Punk was a return to the roots of rock 'n' roll. It was a revolt against the predictability of disco.

3. People have very different ideas about the meaning of poverty. It is a condition that to some suggests insufficient income, to others laziness, and to still others a state of unwarranted discomfort.

4. Writing ability can have far-reaching effects on a college graduate's future accomplishments. Writing ability is the capacity to generate and organize relevant ideas, compose coherent sentences, choose precise diction, control mechanics.

5. They regarded the dictator with a mixture of fear and awe. These feelings were not conducive to an attitude of respect and trust toward their government.

6. According to the lieutenant's testimony during his court-martial, he was simply following orders as any military man is trained to do. These orders came from his commanding officers.

7. When the Soviets sent troops into Vilnius, Vytautas Landsbergis isolated himself and members of his government in a fortified parliament building. Vilnius is the capital of Lithuania and Landsbergis was the Lithuanian president.

8. Lisa read only spare modern novels. She liked ones with quirky characters, subtle structure, and ambiguous turns in plot, if they had plots at all.

9. Over time, psychiatrists have expanded the definition of the term "addiction." It is a word whose meaning has undergone revision to cover a broader range of compulsive behaviors. These compulsions now include sex, television viewing, designer clothes, shopping, computers. These extend to a whole spectrum of dependencies.

10. Concrete has spread over wider and wider areas of the American landscape. It has covered not just the weed patches, deserted lots, and infertile acres but whole pastures, hillsides, and portions of the sea and sky.

B. Finally, write a sentence about your major, your job, or another interest, being sure to include a related technical term. Then add an appositive that defines or illustrates the term.

C. Read the following passage:

James R. Johnson, general manager of the city zoo and a noted authority on reptiles and amphibians, died shortly after his morning run on Thursday, June 25. He was 47.

Mr. Johnson's body was found in his home, on Marsh Lane, a landmark craftsman house constructed by Johnson and his wife Marie out of unusual woods gathered all over the United States. Zoo staffers Jeffrey Kelley and Susan McMillan became concerned when Johnson failed to show up at the zoo and went to his house to investigate. James Kincaid, a spokesman for the zoo, notified authorities yesterday morning.

Mr. Johnson, manager of the zoo since 1992 and an expert on reptiles and amphibians since earning a PhD from Johns Hopkins University in 1980, was an avid runner and noted collector of books and manuscripts relating to his field. He was also well known for his personal collection of iguanas and rare lizards—particularly those found in Mexico, a favorite travel destination.

The coroner, Jacob Feinstein, reported that Johnson died suddenly of a cerebral hemorrhage. He was alone in the house at the time of his death.

Johnson is survived by his wife, Marie Coleman Johnson, daughter of Marvin Coleman, the district attorney from 1970 to 1998; his parents, Laura and Daniel Johnson of St. Louis; and three children: Beverly, Anna, and Robert, all residing at home. Funeral arrangements are pending.

Using this as a model, write an obituary for either a public figure or a fictional character you make up as you go along. Feel free to embroider upon the life of the person you choose for this assignment. Write as many appositives as you can think of and underline each of them. You will find it helpful to first identify the appositives in the passage above.

You may choose to do this exercise in small groups in class.

Parallelism

In previous chapters we have discussed strategies for increasing the coherent flow of ideas in your writing. **Parallel structures** used to organize items in a sentence, and even ideas in a paragraph, can contribute another element to coherence. The emphasis you achieve by harnessing your points into balanced grammatical structures increases the force of your written arguments.

The Structure of Parallelism

Parallel structure is simply a repetition of like grammatical units—a list of items if you will—often joined by conjunctions.

Look at the following two sentences:

I came, I saw, I conquered.
They plan to visit Rio, Madrid, and Bangkok.

Though different in content, they are similar in form: They both illustrate parallel structure. As stated above, parallel structure is simply repetition, usually of the same grammatical structures used in the same way, sometimes of the same word or phrase, often joined by the conjunctions *and, but, or, yet.*

Parallelism is a useful rhetorical device, providing a powerful means of emphasizing relationships by organizing ideas into predictable patterns. We hear a repetition and expect the pattern to continue. Read the two sentences above. Listen to the "ring" of the first sentence and the aid to attention and memory such a rhetorical device provides. Then note the logical organization and its contribution to meaning in the second sentence; the grammatical grouping underscores the implicit relationships between these cities: historical cities of diverse beauty, international centers representing distinct cultures, and interesting travel destinations for some, home for others.

When our expectations are thwarted, we may falter briefly in our reading or even lose the thread of the writer's thought. In most cases, our ear tells us when a series is wandering off the track, but sometimes it can be helpful to check the grammatical structure. Here is a strategy for examining your own sentences.

Think of parallel structures as lists, in the preceding case, a list of cities to visit. We can illustrate this list and the need for it to conform to the principles of parallelism by placing parallel lines at the beginning of the list:

> They plan to visit // Rio, Madrid, and Bangkok.

The conjunction "and" joins three proper nouns acting as direct objects of the verb "plan to visit."

We can do the same thing to more complicated sentences taken from writer Joan Didion's essay on Alcatraz, "Rock of Ages."

> It is not an unpleasant place to be, out there on Alcatraz with only // the *flowers* and the *wind* and a bell *buoy* moaning and the *tide* surging through the Golden Gate. . . . [a list of nouns as direct objects of the preposition "with"]
>
> Once a week the Harts take their boat to San Francisco to // *pick up* their mail and *shop* at the big Safeway in the Marina. . . . [a list of two infinitive phrases]
>
> Mr. Scott, whose interest in penology dates from the day his office acquired Alcatraz as a potential property, // *talked about* // *escapes* and *security routines* and *pointed out* the beach where Ma Barker's son Doc was killed trying to escape. [This sentence contains two lists, one within the other—two verbs for the subject "Mr. Scott"; and two nouns acting as direct objects of "talked about."]

Now read the next sentence (aloud if possible) and hear how the loss of expected balance or harmony offends the ear.

> When I should be studying, I will, instead, waste time by watching television or daydream.

The two verbs are not in the same form and are therefore not parallel. They can be made parallel by simply changing "daydream" to "daydreaming."

While it is important to listen for grammatical parallel structures in a series, English can be somewhat flexible when it comes to parallelism. For example, few readers would object to this sentence:

> The bus system is economical, but it is crowded, uncomfortable, and may not be depended on.

Here the third element, a phrase with a verb, does not conform to the grammatical structure of the first two, both adjectives, yet it is neither confusing nor harsh in its rhythm. All three elements serve as complements to *bus system*. We could easily revise the ending to read "undependable," but some writers might prefer the original. Careful writers make such decisions judiciously, generally preferring to maintain the grammatical and rhetorical integrity of a parallel series.

Before doing Exercise 8C, note the rhetorical effects of parallel structure on the following passage taken from *The Road from Coorain*, an autobiography by Jill Ker Conway, the first woman president of Smith College. Use our system of notation to mark off the different series or lists.

> Those night train journeys had their own mystery because of the clicking of the rails, the shafts of light pouring through the shutters of the sleeping compartment as we passed stations, and the slamming of doors when the train stopped to take on passengers. In the morning there was the odd sight of green landscape, trees, grass, banks of streams—an entirely different palette of colors, as though during the night we had journeyed to another country. Usually I slept soundly, registering the unaccustomed sounds and images only faintly. This time I lay awake and listened, opened the shutters and scanned unknown platforms, and wondered about the future.

This passage has several parallel lists. Did you find them all?

EXERCISE 8C

Supplying Parallel Elements

Complete these sentences with a parallel element.

1. Writing a good paper is a task that demands // hard work, patience, and . . .
2. She // rushed home, threw her assorted debris into a closet, and . . .
3. Fewer Americans are saving these days // not because they don't think it's wise to save, but . . .
4. The first lady is a woman who // has an open mind but . . .
5. The first lady is a woman who has // an open mind and . . .

In the following sentences, identify the misfits—the element of the sentence that is not parallel—and revise the sentence so that all the elements of the list are parallel. Putting slashes where each series starts will help you see where the sentence goes off track.

6. Many influences shape a child's development: family, church, peer groups, economic, social, and school.

7. Michelle lives in a neighborhood where knife wounds, killings, and people are raped are as common as the sun rising in the morning.

8. He helped to wash the car and with cleaning out the garage.

9. Free inquiry in the search for truth sometimes necessitates the abandonment of law and order but which always demands freedom of expression.

10. Pineapple juice is my favorite because it is a good source of energy, it isn't artificially sweetened, and because of its low cost.

11. The president launched a campaign against drunk driving and promoting the use of seat belts.

Now write three of your own sentences—one with three or more verbs sharing the same subject, one with three or more adjectives, and one with three or more nouns. Use as your subject a topic you are currently writing on for this or another class.

Logic of the Parallel Series

The items in a list, however, must not only be **grammatically** similar but also relate **logically** to one another. Sometimes faulty parallelism offends not only our ear but also our reason.

> People who have "book smarts" usually work in places like // *libraries* or *assistants* to attorneys.

Though the writer has joined two nouns (grammatically compatible elements, both nouns), an assistant of any kind cannot be a "place." He has lost control of the sentence because he has forgotten where the list begins. There is more than one way to fix this sentence, to make it logical and balanced. How would you correct it?

To understand further what we mean, look at the following sentence.

> We will have to look at the language used in the text for sexism, racism, and bias.

The list in this sentence is "sexism, racism, and bias." The list is *grammatically* parallel because all three words in the list are nouns, but not *logically* parallel since sexism, racism, and bias are presented as three separate and distinct categories when in fact sexism and racism are particular forms of bias; they are included in what we can call the class or group of *bias*, not separate from it. One way to correct this faulty logic would be to replace *bias* with *other forms of bias* and thus illustrate the logical and actual relationship that exists between the three terms.

EXERCISE 8D

Editing the Illogical Series

Revise the following sentences for logical parallel structure.

1. In their attempt to excel, our employees often work extra hours and work through many lunch hours.
2. I have seen city ordinances that do not allow smoking in restaurants popping up all over the place: in offices, in buildings.
3. I asked Linda if she had any materialistic aspirations such as living in a mansion, having a nice car, or being extremely wealthy.
4. The customers at the bank where I work are wealthy depositors, checking account holders, cooperative individuals, and those who are thoughtlessly rude to me.
5. For the most part, he is handsome, active, and well dressed, usually in expensive clothes or a suit and tie.

Emphasizing Ideas with Parallelism

As we mentioned above, parallelism can be a powerful rhetorical device. Beyond the sentence, parallelism can provide emphasis and organize major ideas in paragraphs, particularly in argument. Pamela Reynolds, an editor at the *The Boston Globe*, focuses her reader's attention on the pain and horror of a race riot in Los Angeles by closing an editorial with emphatic parallelism. In both paragraphs she relies on parallel structure at both the sentence and paragraph levels.

Read the following passage aloud for full effect and then mark examples of parallelism, both within sentences and running through the paragraphs.

> At least half a dozen other stores within walking distance of my parents' home had disappeared in smoke and flames as well. The beauty supply store was gone. The liquor store was trashed and looted. My father sighed. Life wouldn't get any easier with fewer stores, fewer banks, fewer businesses in the area. I was sad that things like this were happening.
>
> I was sad that a community would turn on itself, and destroy the banks, stores, supermarkets that are already so scarce in black neighborhoods. I was

sad that innocent motorists had been bludgeoned on national television. I was sad that I, in Boston, couldn't protect my family, who had protected me while I was growing up in Los Angeles. I was sad because I never thought I would ever identify with the kind of bleak anger and dark frustration that drives a riot.

> **READINGS:** For an example of an essay that uses parallel structure effectively, see "He and I" on page 608.

Sentence Focus—Techniques for Sharpening the Flow of Ideas

He draweth out the thread of his verbosity finer than the staple of his argument.

—SHAKESPEARE, *LOVE'S LABORS LOST*

We are all familiar with the confusion and obfuscation of much official prose today—political, bureaucratic, academic. Some of this muddled language may be deliberate, to conceal meaning, as we discuss above. But often it is inadvertent, a result of writers surrendering to the abstractness of language, of fuzzy language overwhelming complex ideas. We refer to such writing as "unfocused," in much the same way that fuzzy, confused thought is often unfocused. It may help you to understand our discussion of sentence **focus** to think in terms of focusing a camera. When you take a picture, you select and concentrate on a given image—you focus your camera to sharpen that image. An unfocused photograph is blurred. In much the same way, unfocused writing may be easy to write, but it is usually difficult to read.

The New Yorker magazine found this example of unfocused writing:

> Agreement on the overall objective of decision usefulness was a prerequisite to the establishment of a conceptual framework. Now, at least, we know where we are headed. (The Week in Review, newsletter of Deloitte Haskins & Sells)

After this, do we know where they are going?

Compare the following memo from the Internal Revenue Service and a possible revision.

> Advice has been requested concerning tax deductions for research expenses, including traveling expenses, incurred by college and university professors. (original)

> College and university professors have requested advice about tax deductions for their research expenses, including traveling expenses. (possible revision)

Which version is clearer, easier to read? We assume that the majority of readers will prefer the second. What are the differences? The possible revision is shorter by two words. But is this the only distinction? Make your evaluation before reading on.

Calvin and Hobbes

by Bill Watterson

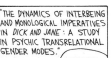

Concrete Subjects

Look at the grammatical subjects in the two sentences on page 216—"advice" in the first, "professors" in the second—and notice what kinds of nouns they are. One is an *abstract noun,* the other a *concrete noun.* Because the sentence subject tends to reflect what a passage is about, the subject is where the *focus* of a sentence usually sits. A concrete noun is capable of producing a visual picture and thus can also *focus* a reader's attention more closely. When that concrete noun is a person or people, readers can visualize an action and so more readily follow the precise progression of ideas in a sentence. Hence, "professors" as the subject of the second sentence is preferable to the "advice" of the original. The reader can see the "professor" but not the abstraction "advice."

Active and Passive Verbs

Now look at the verbs. In the original sentence on tax deduction, the verb is "has been requested" while in the revision the verb is "has requested." The first is **passive voice,** the second, **active voice.** The basic distinction is that

> with a passive verb, the subject is acted upon; the subject is not doing anything in the sentence—it is passive.

"Advice" is being requested, not, obviously, doing the requesting.

When the verb is active, its subject is performing the action of the sentence,

and thus the reader can see a subject doing something. The "professors" are doing the requesting.

We must wade through the original IRS memo to understand the point, whereas in the possible revision we see from the beginning that professors are requesting advice, people are doing something. A possible confusion about who is doing the requesting is made clear. Bureaucrats, often writing about vague or abstract subjects in which they have little invested interest or feeling, can easily fall into the passive verb trap. They are rarely the ones actually *doing* anything they are writing about. Don't let your academic writing succumb to this danger.

Sentences written in the passive are easy to spot because they always follow a grammatical pattern:

subject + a form of the verb "to be" (am, is, are, was, were) + the past participle of the verb (usually with an *-ed* ending) + an expressed or implied "by" phrase, which contains the agent of the verb.

(subject)	(to be)	(past participle)	(optional by phrase)
Mistakes	were	made	(by the chief of staff)

The following two sentences say essentially the same thing, but note how the change in the form of the sentence shifts the emphasis from the concrete subject, "J. Robert Oppenheimer," to the abstract, "elemental danger."

Active J. Robert Oppenheimer, one of the creators of the atom bomb, *felt* the elemental danger loosed on the earth.
Passive The elemental danger loosed on the earth *was felt* by J. Robert Oppenheimer, one of the creators of the atom bomb.

Which version do you prefer? Why?

Passive Verbs and Evasion

A less honorable use of the passive, however, one politicians have a tendency to rely on, is, to evade responsibility. William Safire in his *New York Times* column, "On Language," comments on this predilection, focusing on a former White House chief of staff, John Sununu, who, when asked at a press conference about the use of government funds for personal expenses, replied, "Obviously, some mistakes were made."

Safire notes that "The passive voice acknowledges the errors, but it avoids the blame entirely. . . . When deniability is impossible, dissociation is the way, and the [passive voice] allows the actor to separate himself from the act."

When the Passive Is Appropriate

Aiming for direct, assertive prose, careful writers usually prefer active verbs. But, on occasion, when one wants to emphasize someone or something not performing the action in a sentence, the passive is useful. Scientists and social scientists, for example, must often focus on the content of their research rather than on themselves as researchers. Under such circumstances, the passive serves a useful purpose.

> This research *was undertaken* with a grant from the National Science Foundation.
> rather than
> I *undertook* this research with a grant from the National Science Foundation.

In this case, the **focus,** the emphasis, of the sentence falls on *research* rather than on *I*. Thus *research should* be the grammatical sentence subject.

Not surprisingly, however, when you rely on concrete nouns as your sentence subject, you stand a better chance of automatically using an active verb. Concrete subjects, as we point out above, can *do* something whereas abstract nouns usually cannot.

More Ways to Sharpen Focus

Beyond the issues of concrete subjects and active verbs, we can note four additional features to be alert for when considering sharp focus:

1. **The logical progression of focus:**
   Central to good paragraph focus is the logical progression of ideas within a paragraph. Read the following paragraph closely to see how research physician and writer Lewis Thomas maintains consistent sentence subjects, emphasizing the topic of the paragraph—how we relate to the concept of death. Note how the grammatical subjects provide a coherent line of reasoning even though at the heart of the passage lies an abstract idea.

   We continue to share with our remotest ancestors the most tangled and evasive attitudes about death, despite the great distance **we** have come in understanding some of the profound aspects of biology. **We** have as much distaste for talking about personal death as for thinking about it; it is an indelicacy, like talking in mixed company about venereal disease or abortion in the old days. **Death** on a grand scale does not bother us in the same special way; **we** can sit around a dinner table and discuss war, involving 60 million volatilized human deaths, as though **we** were talking about bad weather; **we** can watch abrupt bloody death every day, in color, on films and television, without blinking back a tear. But when the numbers of dead are very small, and very close, **we** begin to think in scurrying circles. At the very center of the problem is the naked cold **deadness** of one's own self, the only reality in nature of which **we** can have absolute certainty, and **it** is unquestionable, unthinkable. **We** may be even less willing to face the issue at first hand than our predecessors because of a secret new hope that maybe **it** will go away. **We** like to think, hiding the thought, that with all the marvelous ways in which *we* seem now to lead nature around by the nose, perhaps *we* can avoid the central problem if **we** just become, next year, say, a bit smarter.

2. **The expletive "there is":**
The expletive "there is" ("there are," "there were") is useful when a writer means that something exists:

There are several reasons for recycling.

There is every reason to believe that a third political party will grow stronger in the future.

But when you can use a concrete noun paired with a more vigorous verb, the prose is tighter. If you are unconvinced on the "there" issue, read the following paragraph from an essay written for Writing Assignment 4 (Chapter 2).

Children and the ability to have them are equally important to the society of the Small People. *There is* only one word for sex in their language and it translates as "to plant a wise one." To me this implies the final product is more important than the act of "planting a wise one." *There is* also a great emphasis put on childhood. *There are* seven terms used to describe stages of life from birth to puberty. *There is* only one word describing life after puberty.

This paragraph conveys the existence of the terms but very little additional reasoning. Poor focus is combined with choppy prose and needless passive verbs. Note how easy it is to avoid vigorous, active prose once you let the "there disease" take over. Let's fix the focus in three of these sentences.

Original
There is also a great emphasis put on childhood. There are seven terms used to describe stages of life from birth to puberty. There is only one word describing life after childhood. (original)

Revision
They clearly emphasize childhood, using seven terms to describe stages of life from birth to puberty, with only one word describing life after childhood. (revision)

The revision is tighter and reveals the logical relationship between each point. When the sentences stood isolated with their "theres," that logic was less obvious.

3. **Over use of "to be"**
Beware of the verb "to be" (am, is, are, was, were). It is, of course, an important verb, but again, it states existence (being) only, and

you often want your prose to be more expressive than that. Here's another reason to use passive verbs sparingly; they always, by definition, contain a form of the verb "to be." The same applies to "there are" sentences.

4. **Dangling modifiers**
   Experienced writers often turn verbs into **verbal modifiers** (participles such as running, buying, avoiding). Such transformations increase sentence fluency and combine ideas to express logical relationships. Look at the examples below.

   two choppy sentences
   She *thought* critically about the issue. She *recognized* that her opponents had a good argument.

   one revision
   Thinking critically about the issue, she recognized that her opponents had a good argument.

   another option
   She thought critically about the issue, *recognizing* that her opponents had a good argument.

   Such modifiers can enhance the fluency of your prose, but you need to be cautious about their logic. When you use a verbal as a modifier, the person or object serving as the sentence subject must usually also work logically as the agent of the modifier.

In the two revisions above, "she" is logical as the agent of "thinking" or "recognizing" as well as the grammatical subject of the actual verb in each variant of the sentence.

When the logical agent is missing from the sentence, the verbal modifier is said to dangle, hence the term **dangling modifier.** One newspaper columnist, a stickler for sound sentence structure, was disgusted with himself when he fell into the dangling modifier trap:

"Having used up all his frequent-flier miles to Paris to woo and win her, Attorney Joe Freitas and Douce Francois . . ."

Had he looked back, he would have noticed that it wasn't logical for both of them to have used his frequent flier miles in this context, and Douce was unlikely to have been wooing herself. As he wrote in a future correction, "right there I should have stopped and started over."

EXERCISE 8E

Repairing Dangling Modifiers

Many an experienced writer has lost track of the logic in her sentence. Identify the illogical dangling modifiers in these examples from published writers and recommend a remedy.

1. While writing today's piece, Gerald Nachman's column was lost in the computer. (Did his column write itself?)

2. After passing around pictures of Christopher, the couple's conversation returned to the latest Star Wars movie. (Can a conversation pass pictures around?)

3. Walking up the staircase to Joyce Carol Oates' office in the Creative Arts building, through the halls that smell of artists' paint, past the neat rows of studios and classrooms, the blood-stained story of her most recent book, "Angel of Light," seems a tale told on another planet. (Did her blood-stained story walk up the staircase?)

4. Speaking as an old friend, there has been a disturbing tendency in statements emanating from Beijing to question the good faith of our President on the issue of Taiwan. (Do you see how the "there" construction has led the "old friend" astray? Did a disturbing tendency speak as an old friend?)

Revising for sharp sentence and paragraph focus helps to maintain the clear, direct expression you and your readers demand, no matter what your academic or professional discipline. Keep in mind, however, that revising is often most effective as a late stage in the writing process. We may expect a first draft to have several poorly focused sentences and paragraphs. Look back at Chapter 1 to refresh your memory on the writing process.

EXERCISE 8F

Sharpening Sentence Focus for Clear Expression and Fluent Style

A. Revise the following sentences for good focus, combining where appropriate for a smooth, logical flow of ideas. Look back at the discussion of active and passive verbs, overuse of "there" and verb "to be" constructions. Think in terms of assertive sentences, ones that use strong verbs and say directly who is doing what.

Example: It was while I was waiting in the registration line that the realization came to me of how complicated a university is.

revision

While I was waiting in the registration line, I came to realize (or I realized) how complicated a university is.

1. Fear of brutality from customers is a concern many prostitutes have.

2. When it is seen that a criminal act is being committed, a call should be placed to the police.

3. A strike is used when employees want things their employers are unwilling to provide.

4. The leaders have determined that the spiritual initiate has no need of worldly things, so only minimum wages are paid.

5. There is a much bigger emphasis placed on the role of the individual in this generation than in our parents' generation.

6. Teenagers are easily influenced by TV. Specific violent acts have been committed by teenagers after such acts have been shown on prime time.

7. The people of this tribe are literate, given that they have twenty terms for "book." There also may be several kinds of artwork they create, since they have nine words for "artist."

8. Having developed a complex social order, cultural patterns have been shown by the people of this tribe. These patterns are reflected in their arts and their theater.

B. Now try your hand at revising this student paragraph with the same strategies in mind. Note how difficult it is to follow the writer's reasoning in this poorly focused paragraph.

There are many ways to be a bad teacher. There are mistakes made by bad teachers that come in a variety of forms. Assignments are given unclearly so that when papers are graded it isn't known what students are graded on or what the grade means. Grading by the ineffective teacher is according to arbitrary standards, so students think their grades are unfair. There are problems with explanations given by bad teachers and understanding is hard to arrive at. This disorganization can be seen by students when the poor teacher fails to bring all materials to class. There are many explanations given, but the dissatisfaction of students is clearly not done away with. In such cases it is not clear who is responsible for a bad grade—the student or the teacher.

Wrap-up on writing style

1. Use parallel structure to increase coherence, organize lists, and emphasize relationships.

2. Focus your thoughts and your writing on precisely what you want to say. When logically possible, use concrete, consistent subjects. As you develop ideas through a paragraph, your sentence subjects develop and change, reflecting the new information introduced in the previous sentence.

3. Unless you have compelling reasons for preferring the passive voice, choose active verbs that allow for more direct, vigorous expression of your ideas.

4. Unless you intend to express the existence of something, avoid the over-used, empty phrases "there are" and "it is" and in the process look for more vigorous verbs.

5. To increase the flow of ideas, expand your sentence repertoire with appositives and verbal modifiers.

Caution: **Do not think about these writing strategies until you have completed a first draft. Content and organization must come first; then you can turn your attention to coherent, graceful sentences and the final proof read for spelling and other mechanical details.**

Revision

Throughout the text, we have discussed ways to both write and rewrite your papers. You may want to review Chapter 1 for the sections on audience and purpose and the writing process. In particular, the section on writing first drafts provides essential material when it comes to revising your papers. Assignments in Chapter 4 also offer ways in which longer written arguments can be written in stages, allowing you to separate the steps toward a successful finished paper. The sample essays in that chapter may help you think about the organization of your own papers. We offer suggestions for revising at the sentence level in several places throughout the text, particularly in this chapter, where we illustrate how you can polish for coherence, style, and fluency. In Chapter 9, you will find suggestions for selecting and researching your topic.

As a final step, you always need to proofread carefully for mechanical errors—typographical and spelling errors, omitted words—as well as for appropriate verb tenses, subject/verb agreement, and pronoun reference. After reading through your final draft with close attention to detail, try reading it aloud, slowly, perhaps to a critical friend or classmate. Reading pages in reverse order can help you find small technical mistakes easily overlooked when you read straight through for meaning.

WRITING ASSIGNMENT 18

Revising an Essay

Choose one of the assignments you completed earlier and revise it in light of material covered in this chapter particularly and in the book in general, and in response to suggestions from your instructor or possibly your classmates. As you reread your work, consider whether you have changed your mind about the issues and whether you have discovered new material relevant to your topic. You may also want to look back to Chapter 6 to see if your arguments contain any logical fallacies and to Chapter 7 for reminders on logical thinking. Consider your word choice carefully in light of Chapter 5, The Language of Argument: Definition, and review the "Wrap-up on writing style" above for a refresher on polishing your prose. Read your own prose just as critically as you did the stories in Chapter 2 or in any other important academic work.

Going back to a paper after time has elapsed can give you a useful new perspective. Whichever assignment you choose, these skills and the passage of time will help you strengthen the draft you choose to work on.

SUMMARY

Style as well as correctness is an essential part of effective written argument.

Parallelism is a useful rhetorical device, providing a powerful means of emphasizing relationships by organizing ideas into predictable patterns.

For a vigorous and concise writing style, writers prefer concrete subjects and active verbs and use "there is" only to express existence.

Combining and expanding sentences with appositives and verbal modifiers increase the logical flow of ideas.

Revising a manuscript plays an important role in strengthening any writer's prose.

KEY TERMS

Active voice   a sentence construction in which the subject performs the action of the sentence. Example: The Supreme Court ruled on the constitutionality of the 1991 civil rights legislation.

Appositives   noun phrases placed beside nouns to elaborate on their meaning; useful for describing, identifying, and defining.

Dangling modifier   a verbal modifier that lacks a logical agent in the clause it modifies. Example: *Before resorting to violence,* all other means of resolution must be thoroughly investigated.

Focus   concrete, consistent sentence subjects that reflect the rhetorical subject of the writing.

Parallel structure   a repetition of like grammatical units, often joined by the conjunctions and, but, yet.

Passive voice   a sentence construction in which the subject is acted upon, not doing anything in the sentence. Example: The constitutionality of the 1991 civil rights legislation was ruled on by the Supreme Court.

Verbal modifier   participles—verb forms usually ending in -*ing*—used as sentence modifiers. Example: *Before resorting to violence,* we must thoroughly investigate all other means of resolution.

CHAPTER 9

Research and Documentation

Research

Think First

Before you rush to the library or your computer, topic in hand, to begin your research, consider the two important preliminary steps.

A. **First Step, the Topic:** In some instances your instructor may select your topic for you or assign a general subject area from a reader. Or, you may develop a topic of your own, either from a subject in which you are already interested or from a library search. Databases in your library or keyword searches on the Internet may prove helpful as you look for ideas. For example, let's say you are interested in Japan. You might start with a keyword search on the search engine, *Infoseek* (**<www.Infoseek.com>**) and, following their directions for "Tips/Quick reference," search for ideas by narrowing the scope: *Japan* and *"Samurai tradition"* or *Japan* and *"Mitsubishi production."* (For additional discussion of researching your topic on the Internet, see below under "How to Conduct Your Research" and the subheading "The Internet.") Your topic must be sufficiently narrow and focused, no matter where it comes from. Once you think you know your topic, you need to narrow it to a clear **question at issue** (see Chapter 4), a process that will help you to focus your research efforts. With only a general topic to guide you, you might become lost in an avalanche of material, taking voluminous notes, conducting fruitless computer searches, most of which would have no application to your final paper.

Look at the difference in scope between an issue and a related question at issue:

Issue: Protection of the environment
Question at issue: Should the environment be protected at the expense of jobs?
Or, even more refined
Question at issue: Should spotted owl habitat be protected at the expense of jobs in the lumber industry?

Imagine what it would be like to research the issue, and then imagine what it would be like to research one of the questions at issue. Which would be easier?

Sometimes you need to do further investigating in the library or on the Internet before you are able to arrive at a question at issue, just as you might have done when first deciding on a broader topic. Or you may be led to revise your question at issue as your research leads you in unexpected directions. But a well-focused question at issue is essential for ensuring that you know where you are going with your paper and what further research you need to do. Narrowing the focus of your research pays substantial dividends in time, energy, and the ultimate success of your paper, although it is also important to keep an open mind as you explore multiple sources in depth.

After you have narrowed your topic to a question at issue and done some research, you will be ready to take a stand on the question, your research providing the basis for your position. Expressing your opinion on the question at issue will help you craft a thesis. You may argue for or against a position or you may want to qualify it without taking a particular stance. No matter where you stand, you will eventually need to express the primary conclusion you have reached in a **thesis statement,** one or two sentences clearly stating the position you will argue in your paper. This thesis may be tentative, subject to revisions as you continue to explore your topic, but as your drafts begin to take shape you will need a thesis to help organize your ideas and guide you to a finished written argument.

As you prepare a research paper, you will find it useful to review strategies discussed under "Writing as a Process" in Chapter 1 and suggestions for narrowing an issue, writing a thesis, and shaping an argument in Chapter 4. If you have studied journalism, you are familiar with the useful questions Who? What? When? Where? Why? How? that journalists use to probe a topic.

It is often a good idea to check your topic and the question at issue with your instructor before you start off on an unproductive tangent. Try talking to others, inside and outside of class, and when possible, pursue a subject that relates to your own interests. But don't be afraid of exploring an issue that's new to you. That's how you expand your knowledge.

As a preliminary step, after you have established your question at issue, you may want to write a short **proposal or abstract** (for placement in your paper, see below). Doing so gives you a chance to express in writing just what your topic is, why you are exploring it, who your audience is (see "Audience and Purpose" in Chapter 1), and, when you are ready, what position you expect to take.

B. **Second Step, the Argument.** As well as establishing a question at issue at the outset of your research, you should construct an argument both for and against the question at issue. This argument will consist of premises in their roughest form—not developed, not supported, not yet refined. Such a framework or working outline will serve as a guide as you develop your paper.

You will already have some knowledge based on your experience, your reading, or your Internet searches. This knowledge may be general but it will be sufficient to enable you to construct a preliminary argument (see Assignment 9, Chapter 4).

The two advantages to this approach are as follows:

1. You are not overwhelmed by the opinions of experts, feeling as if they have left you nothing to say.

2. Your research has a focused, precise purpose as you look for support for your premises, discovering in the process gaps in your reasoning and counterarguments that had not occurred to you.

Don't be surprised if you find yourself changing direction as you gather more information. This stage can sometimes seem chaotic, but the process of exploring available material on your topic is essential to learning as you write. Research and writing about what you know and what you uncover will not only provide unexpected opportunities for discovering new material on your topic but may also lead you to take a different position. This is the point at which you may need to revise your question at issue and your working thesis. In the process, you will write a more convincing paper and also expand your own outlook. Being able to look at an issue from another perspective represents an important step in refining **critical thinking.**

How to Conduct Your Research

What follows is a condensed summary of strategies, sources, and documentation conventions necessary for writing a successful research paper. If you have not been assigned an additional guide to research you may find it useful to select one of the many excellent little books currently available. *The Essential Guide to Writing Research Papers* (Lester), and *Researching Online* (edited by Munger), are short and easy to use. *The Little, Brown Handbook*, available in both complete and compact editions, and *S F Writer* offer more in-depth guidance. The list will have changed by the time this book is published. The Modern Language Association (MLA) publishes helpful guides to conducting research and documenting sources: *The MLA Handbook for Writers of Research Papers* and *The MLA Style Manual and Guide to Scholarly Publishing*, the second designed for more advanced research needs. The **MLA** Web site: **<www.mla.org/>** keeps the technical details of documenting electronic sources up to date under the heading, *MLA Style*. Their handbooks can be ordered through this Web site. The American Psychological Association (**APA**), preferred in the social sciences, also publishes research information on the Web. Their home page does not offer documentation support, but currently two additional sites do: **<www.lib.ricks.edu/inet_apa.html>** provides excellent information on documentation of electronic sites. **<http://humanities.byu.edu/linguistics/Henrichsen/APA/APA01.html>** offers thorough coverage of the APA approach to documenting sources and gives a broad range of examples. The APA also produces the *Publication Manual of the American Psychological Association*. Be warned that these sites have a way of disappearing as others emerge, so no list can be definitive. In addition, you may want to consult your instructor for specific research guidelines and investigate whether your campus offers courses in using the Internet. Your **reference librarians** are a valuable asset in suggesting useful bound indexes and online sources. We suggest you establish a working relationship with such a librarian as a guide to the many resources available in both print and electronic sources.

Reading Strategies

If you are limiting your research to a collection of preselected articles in an assigned reader, some of the work will have already been done for you. If, however, you are going farther afield and must survey a number of books, articles, and Web sites, you will have to use some methods of reading for main points without including every word. For example, learn to select **relevant** material by checking the table of contents, subtitles, abstracts of longer articles, topic sentences of paragraphs, and opening and concluding paragraphs. With a book, read the introduction and preface to be sure the book is what you think it is. Where possible, try to determine whether the author is a **credible source.** If you find one book or article useful, be alert for references to additional sources and bibliographies mentioned there.

Essential to your research in books and journals or in electronic sources is **critical judgment.** As you read, **think critically** about the author, the point of view, the quality of the argument, the date a piece was written, and the possible relevance of this date.

From the outset, start taking notes that highlight the important points. Small cards work well, because you can shuffle the sequence when you start writing the paper. Be careful to write down the complete bibliographical material you'll need later when you provide the necessary documentation of your sources. Formats for this follow. For a more in-depth treatment of the technicalities of attribution, consult one of the books mentioned above. With the proliferation of electronic sources, the mechanics of documenting sources has grown ever more complex.

When gathering material from sources, either quote exactly, paraphrase what an author says, or summarize the passage.

Direct quotation: A word-for-word transcription of what an author says, requiring quotation marks.

Paraphrase: A restatement of an idea in language that retains the meaning but changes the exact wording. Such references require documentation but not quotation marks.

Summary: A short restatement of the main points in a passage, an article, or a book. See "Summaries," Chapter 3. When summarizing the works of others, you need to document the source.

Printed Sources

Although a vast amount of information is now available on the computer, if you are looking up material dated before the last ten years, you need to be familiar with some of the print indexes available in your library. Of particular use: The *Readers' Guide to Periodical Literature* (your library may have this on a CD-Rom database) lists articles from a broad range of general magazines. You can find articles on more specific subject areas in, for example, the *Humanities Index, Social Science Index, Business Periodicals Index, Biological and Agricultural Index, Education Index, Applied Science and Technology Index.* For even more specialized searches, you could try sources such as the *Music Index* or *Philosopher's Index.* Newspapers such as *The Washington Post, The New York Times, The Wall Street Journal, The Los Angeles Times, The Chicago Tribune,* and possibly your own local newspaper are indexed for back issues not available on the Web. For biographical information on specific individuals, you will find a number of biographical resources on your library shelves. Ask a librarian to point you in their direction. When you are searching for a specific essay published in a larger collection, you can turn to the *Essay and General Literature Index*. With time and experience in your library, you will find many more useful sources of data.

The government publishes a vast number of pamphlets and other documents important for research purposes. More and more of these are becoming available on the Web, but once again, you may need to consult your reference librarian. The *Monthly Catalog of US Government Publications* and the *Congressional Record* are two useful sources. In some cases you may need to order a particular document directly from the Government Printing Office, Washington, DC, 20402.

Once you have located a specific citation for an article, you will be able to find the text on either microfilm or microfiche in your library, except for very early editions, which may still be bound. Your library will have an alphabetized list of publications available on your campus and identify the format.

The Internet is a seductive source of research information, but because of limitations discussed below, you will be wise to include books and journals, the traditional print media, as a solid basis for much of your research.

The Internet

The Internet and the World Wide Web, which attempts to gather up and organize the material on the Internet, have revolutionized research in the last ten years. Electronic resources vary from library to library, but most offer databases that list recent newspapers, magazines, journals, and speeches, in some cases providing texts of articles in full. Some of these databases can be accessed from your home computer; for others you must go to your library. Although some, such as Lexis-Nexis (law, newspapers, and business), may charge for their services, others are free to students, some free to all users. To access databases offered through your campus library from home, you need a modem attached to your computer, a telephone line connection, and software provided by your university. For direct Internet connection on your own computer, all you need is the modem with telephone connection and an Internet server, often offered through your college or university.

Electronic searches can be confusing—think of the Internet as a vast unindexed encyclopedia. Or, as someone said: Everybody is connected but nobody is in charge. The seemingly random nature of information on the Internet makes it difficult to find precisely what you want. The metaphors imbedded in the terms "Internet" and "Web" say a lot about the shape of this field of virtual knowledge—an endless sea of netting or webbing, every corner filled with facts and ideas waiting to be found, constantly ebbing and flowing, never stable or complete. Once again, we urge you to consult your research librarian or instructor for directions to specific sources.

The Internet has introduced an entirely new vocabulary, as you already know. Once you have the necessary equipment, you need three different levels of access for maximum information:

> An **Internet server** or **provider.** Technology is rapidly expanding, but your university, telephone company, cable company, and such commercial organizations as AOL, JUNO, and others link users to the Internet.
>
> Commercial **browsers,** such as Netscape Navigator or Microsoft Internet Explorer, take you to the World Wide Web.
>
> A constantly multiplying list of **search engines** helps you narrow your searches.

As new companies emerge and Internet use is refined, the character and names of these steps to successful interaction with the Internet will keep changing, with some trusted sites suddenly disappearing.

SEARCHING THE INTERNET   Material for your research paper may be scattered all over the Internet. Your best way to reach the Internet is through the World Wide Web, using one of the commercial browsers. Organizing the immense amount of random knowledge available, a growing number of **search engines** operate on the Web to help you find what you need. If you are still looking for a topic, you can begin with a **subject search.** Once you have settled on your topic and narrowed it to a specific question at issue, you will be ready to refine your search. First, you will want to experiment with **keywords,** which you type in as you try different search engines (see examples below). While you may be lucky if your keyword is precise enough, many such searches give you so many responses that you don't know where to begin. Usually, those that seem most relevant appear at the top of the list, but often the initial list is too long to be useful. To be more successful, you need to **refine your searches,** providing clusters of words rather than single terms. For example: *First Amendment* and *the Internet* rather than just the *First Amendment.* Most search engines now use techniques known as **Boolean** for phrase searches, but each search engine depends on variations of the method. You need to check the "Help" menus to find specific suggestions for what many call "advanced search." Here, for a start, are a few common Boolean search devices shared by most resources.

> Some search engines ask that you group more than one word as a single term by putting double quotation marks around the words; for example, *"nature versus nurture," "Dolly the sheep."* Proper names, *Abraham Lincoln* for example, do not need the quotations.
>
> The word *AND* indicates that you want all the terms to appear in your search; for example, *selling AND embryos.*

The word *NOT* indicates that you want to exclude irrelevant words; for example, *embryos NOT "adoption of."*

The word *OR* can widen your search to two or more terms; for example, *"indecent speech" OR "pornographic speech" OR "Cyberporn."*

On some databases, you group words in a phrase by placing parentheses around the words: *(embryos and selling)* not *adoption.*

On the search engine Yahoo!, for example, you can limit your search to the titles of articles: *t: harassment,* means the term must appear in a document's title only.

Proximity operators can also help in some instances: *adj.* (adjacent)*, near, before, followed by.* Such terms can help limit the number of hits—the listing of sites you specify—to a manageable number.

Many sites have highlighted **links** that can connect you to related sites, some useful, others false leads. Links usually appear in blue and are underlined. Most of you are familiar by now with the feature called either a **bookmark** or a **favorite place** by which you can store a useful site in your own list. Given how tricky it sometimes can be to arrive at such a site, it makes sense to "save" it for future reference, especially if you are going to need the Web address for documenting your research.

Every year new **search engines** appear, helping to supply some form of order to the chaos of information on the Web. Each one has its own special features, so you should refer to the *hints* and *help* and *advanced search techniques* each provides. Here are a few from what is growing constantly into a long list:

Yahoo! http://www.yahoo.com/
> Very comprehensive in its coverage. Popular for casual browsing and for research. Subject directory and news sources are excellent.

Google http://www.google.com
> A recent, highly rated addition to the search engine list. A fast, clean homepage with no advertising and thoughtful searches make this site particularly easy to use.

Infoseek http://www.Infoseek.com/
> Large subject directory and list of services including travel information and maps. Foreign language available. Provides good documentation information.

Magellan Internet Guide http://www.mckinley.com/
> Annotated subject directory on opening page is helpful. Useful for magazine searches. Many peer-reviewed sites.

Excite http://www.excite.com/
> Broad reach but can be complicated to use. Provides a relevancy rating to the left of each result.

Northern Light http://www.northernlight.com
  An excellent choice for serious research. Provides free article synopses, full texts for a fee.

HotBot http://www.hotbot.com/
  Highly rated for fast, comprehensive searches.

AltaVista http://www.altavista.digital.com/
  Useful for information about careers, entertainment, finance, health, news, travel.

Livelink Pinstripe http://pinstripe.opentext.com/
  Designed for business users.

Lycos http://www.lycos.com/
  Another business site. Larger database than Livelink. Foreign languages available. Material is stored in directory form.

"Go ask your search engine."

These are just an introduction. For long lists of additional search engines, you could consult **Best Search Engines** at **http://kresch.com/ search/search.htm** or **Beaucoup** at **http://beaucoup.com/,** which lists search engines by category. For special subject areas such as medicine or scientific research, you need to consult your librarian. To find specific journals through a search engine, you can search by subject, such as *native american culture journals,* which should produce a list of relevant journals. Some search engines are more helpful than others for this type of search.

An early academic browser was **Gopher** at **gopher://veronica.psi. net:2347/7-tl.** This is helpful for methodical academic searches that move down from general lists to more and more specific levels.

For access to newsgroups that provide broad coverage of current events and allow you to participate in discussions, try **Usenet,** reached by keyword or, for a complete index of newsgroups, go to **http://www.liszt. com/news/.** Keep in mind that the reliability of Usenet sources varies enormously. No one is reviewing them in an orderly way. In addition to a wide range of newspapers, you can find even greater variety through the major news services, Associated Press and Reuters.

Sometimes you can print the results of your search or save them, either to a directory on your own computer or to a floppy disk, which may reduce the number of note cards you use in keeping track of your research before you actually write your paper. You should be particularly careful about saving information found in newsgroups. Such sites change rapidly and may not be reachable the next day. Always remember to make a note of the **Web address,** called a **URL** (Uniform Resource Locators), and the **date you used the site** (retrieval date) along with other data such as name of site, author, title of article (if relevant), and date of posting if available. As you will have noticed, Web addresses are divided into complex sequences of letters, numbers, and punctuation marks.

http://www.mla.org/main__stl.htm
protocol   server   domain type   file name

Thinking Critically About the Material

It is easy to be overwhelmed by the volume of documents you find on the Internet. Part of your job as a researcher is to determine the **relevance** of sources. Does a given source relate directly to the question at issue to which you have narrowed a broader topic? Do you see how the material is going to fit into the paper you plan to write? For example, if you are going to write a paper on the environmental impact of acid rain on the forests of Pennsylvania, you will not want to do in-depth research on the environmental impact of smog on redwood forests, even though the two topics are related. Another issue is the level at which an article is written. Is it written at a level you can fully understand without being too simplistic? Although you may need technical data, you also want to be able to interpret it for your audience.

Evaluating Web Sites—A Warning

Now for the **cautions.** Unlike journals that are subject to peer review, magazines that are closely edited even if they have a particular bias, and books that undergo a lengthy editing process, the Internet provides open season for anyone who wants to post material on a Web site. The Web is only as good as the people who put material on it, sometimes excellent, sometimes uninformed, sometimes deliberately deceptive. In many cases, articles come from reputable sources, and sites provide information you can trust, but in plenty of instances, a reference from a reliable site can send you to something completely unreliable, or a search will turn up an undependable list of documents. No matter which search engine you use, you need to keep in mind that each one creates its own database without impartial, outside review or evaluation. And economic interests often play a role in the selection a search engine may feature. You must constantly be on guard against the potentially unreliable, often muddled information lurking everywhere. You don't want your paper to be as bewildering as the Web so often seems. Nowhere are your **critical reading skills** more urgently needed than in discriminating among sites on the Web.

Sprinkled throughout are pornographic sites that come up on your screen without your having knowingly asked for them. In 1999, controversy surrounded the Web address, www.wallstreet.com. One could assume that such an address would lead to some centralized site in the heart of New York's financial district. But, in fact, it was a small financial domain, run privately, which decided to sell its address, worth considerable money. One of the would-be buyers was a pornographer hoping to cash in on unsuspecting visitors to the site. The same is true of sites spewing hate speech. **Chat rooms** are particularly dubious as authoritative or trustworthy sources. They may be engaging, even productive for generating ideas, but it is impossible to verify information gleaned from such sources. The same skepticism is necessary when you use e-mail as a source. Names are easy to forge and no one is out there in cyberspace monitoring who is posting what. Keep in mind that accessing pornographic sites on campus computers can be a serious offense.

So, what do you do? How can you know if information on a site is **reliable?**

- Use reputable search engines (see above), although they don't always screen out questionable sources and can be linked to sites over which they have no control. Because search engines can sometimes be self-serving or unintentionally limiting, try more than one to avoid omissions or hidden biases. Try to compare some Internet findings with those available in more familiar print sources.

- Rely particulary on the "edu," "org," and "gov" domains, other than search engines, and know what each of these domain types signifies: *edu* stands for an educational institution like your college; *org* means a nonprofit organization; *gov* means a government site. Note that *.com* indicates a commercial site with all the perils to be found in self-serving commercial ventures.

- Try to find out something about the author or at least about the publication in which an article appears. Are you aware of any particular bias attached to a given source? For example, the weekly political journal, *The Nation,* is known to give a very liberal, if not sometimes a radical, view. *The National Review,* on the other hand, is recognized for its conservative perspective.

- Ask yourself, have you searched out opinions on both sides of the issue?

- Does the author reason well according to some of the principles discussed in *Writing Logically?* Does the author support assertions with strong evidence and address opposing views? (See "A Dialectical Approach to Argument," Chapter 4.)

- Be alert for inflammatory language and be prepared to qualify or explain sources that sound didactic and heavily one-sided.

- You will also want to note the date of an Internet posting. Often information has become out of date but looks current at first glance.

- Ultimately, you will begin to develop a critical sense of what looks reliable, what dubious.

All this is not to say that developing a sense of what is reliable in books, magazines, and journals isn't still important. Remaining alert to seriously slanted material, no matter what the source, is an extremely important feature of research.

Finding Your Own Data

Keep in mind that you can, and often should, conduct your own research in the field. You may want to survey a group of people, conduct an experiment, especially if you are working in the sciences, or interview people who can provide information for your paper or project. (For how to set up a survey, see Writing Assignment 17, Conducting a Survey: A Collaborative Project, in Chapter 7.) In addition to face-to-face interviews (still the best option), you can also interview someone over the phone; by e-mail (electronic mail sent over the Internet); in chat rooms, discussion groups, or newsgroups online (note caution above); or by various more complex synchronous communication arrangements over the Internet, by which you can communicate with individuals simultaneously. Your campus probably has a computer center where you can receive help in learning about these online sources and activities if you are not already familiar with them.

Documentation

What Information Should Be Documented?

1. All direct quotations.
2. All indirect quotations in which you summarize the thoughts of others without quoting them directly. For example:

   Semanticist S. I. Hayakawa notes that although poetry and advertising seem unrelated, they actually share many characteristics (162).

3. All facts and statistics that are not common knowledge. If we were to state that many modern marriages end in divorce, documentation would not be necessary because the assertion reflects common knowledge. But if we state that one out of six women in this country has been raped, we must provide documentation; our readers would want to know the source of this exact conclusion to evaluate for themselves its reliability. When you cite numbers and percentages, your readers may be skeptical. Careful documentation of your sources contributes authority and thus strengthens your claims.

The key issue here is that you correctly attribute all the ideas and information you gather from outside sources. Plagiarizing the work of others is an extremely serious offense that can have grievous consequences. Once you have completed your research, remember that the paper is going to be yours, written in your own words, interpreting the information you have gathered, and expressing the opinions you have developed during the course of your research.

Incorporating the Ideas of Others into Your Own Writing

If you want your paper to read smoothly, you must take care to integrate direct quotations and paraphrases of other people's ideas into the grammatical flow of your sentences. Don't just "drop" them with a thud into a paragraph. Rely, rather, on a ready supply of introductory or signal phrases with which to slide them in gracefully, for example, "As Freud discovered," "Justice O'Connor notes," and "according to *The New York Times*."

Sometimes, to make a quotation fit in smoothly with your own writing, you must add a word or words. Such additions are placed in brackets. For example:

> Carson McCullers sets a strangely luminous night scene:
>
> There was a party at the banquet table in the center, and green-white August moths had found their way in from the night and fluttered about the clear candle flames.
>
> She seems to make a point of the "green-white August moths [that] had found their way in from the night. . . ."

As well as introducing quotations and paraphrases smoothly into the syntax of your sentence, you must also pay attention to semantics. Don't assume that the relevance of the quotation is self-evident. Make its relationship to your reasoning explicit. Is it an example? An appeal to authority? Premise support? A counterargument? Whatever the case, the purpose of the quotation—how it relates to the point you are making—should be made explicit.

Punctuation and Format of Quotations

Periods and commas are placed *inside* quotation marks unless the quotation is followed by a parenthetical citation, in which case the period follows the citation.

> "Writing, like life itself, is a voyage of discovery," said Henry Miller, author of *Tropic of Cancer*.

> "Thinking is the activity I love best, and writing to me is simply thinking through my fingers."
>
> —ISAAC ASIMOV

> "The true relationship between a leader and his people is often revealed through small, spontaneous gestures" (Friedman 106).

Colons and semicolons go outside quotation marks.

> Read Tamar Lewin's essay, "Schools Challenge Students' Internet Talk"; we'll discuss it at our next class meeting.

Use single quotation marks [' '] for quotations within quotations.

> "In coping with the violence of their city, Beirutis also seemed to disprove Hobbes's prediction that life in the 'state of nature' would be 'solitary.'"
>
> THOMAS FRIEDMAN, *FROM BEIRUT TO JERUSALEM*

If the prose quotation is more than four lines long, it should be indented, about 10 spaces for MLA, 5 for APA, and double spaced as in the rest of the text. No quotation marks are necessary.

Omitting Words from a Direct Quotation

Sometimes we don't want to include all of a quotation, but just certain sections of it that apply to the point we are making. In this case, we may eliminate a part or parts of the quotation by the use of *ellipsis* dots: three spaced periods that indicate the intentional omission of words. If the *ellipsis* concludes a sentence, add a final period.

1. Something left out at the beginning:
   " . . . a diploma from Harvard or Emory nearly guarantees a financially rewarding career," says columnist Cynthia Tucker of *The Atlanta Constitution.*

2. Something left out in the middle:
   Explaining the desperation of a writer, William Faulkner once said, "Everything goes by the board: honor, pride, decency . . . to get the book written. If a writer has to rob his mother, he will not hesitate; the 'Ode on a Grecian Urn' is worth any number of old ladies."

3. Something left out at the end:
   As Henry Lewis Gates says, "The features of the Black dialect of English have long been studied and found to be not an incorrect or slovenly form of Standard English but a completely grammatical and internally consistent version of the language. . . ."

How Should Information Be Documented?

Although each discipline has its preferred style of documentation, four standard styles prevail. The Modern Language Association **(MLA),** documented in the *MLA Handbook for Writers of Research Papers* and mentioned above, is the choice in English, foreign languages, and some other humanities. The American Psychological Association **(APA),** documented in the *Publication Manual of the American Psychological Association,* is preferred by psychology and other social sciences. History, art history, and philosophy tend to follow *The Chicago Manual of Style.* The sciences, including the health sciences, and mathematics rely on a system created by the Council of Science Editors (CSE) (formerly, the Council of Biology Editors, CBE), documented in *Scientific Style and Format: The CBE Manual for Authors, Editors, and Publishers. The Chicago Manual of Style* and the CBE use raised numerals in the text to refer to either footnotes or endnotes. The MLA and the APA have evolved a system of parenthetical references—author and page number cited in the text of the paper—with a list of cited works or electronic sources and all relevant publishing information at the end of the paper. Chances are, you will be following MLA style. If writing for a class that requires one of the other forms, consult your instructor about the preferred documentation.

In most cases, more important than the fine details of documentation is a sensible consistency. The major concern is that you provide accurate information from the sources you have used and insert that information into your paper in a reasonably standard way. We illustrate examples from the MLA style, offer the basic distinctions of the APA system, and introduce electronic documentation.

The MLA Style of Documentation for Printed Sources

When referring to a cited work, MLA style generally uses the present tense ("Gloria Feldt shows.") This is a distinction from the APA style.

CITATIONS WITHIN YOUR TEXT   In many cases, you can slide a reference into the text of your paper without disturbing the flow of your ideas. Introduce the material being cited with a signal phrase, usually the author's name, and use a parenthetical citation stating the page number of the sentence. Readers can then turn to the list of works cited at the end of the paper to discover the title and publishing information, which are listed under the author's or authors' last name.

1. A book by one author

   S. I. Hayakawa points out that advertising and poetry are alike in that "they both strive to give meaning to the data of everyday experience" (162).

   When the author is not identified in the text—when there is no signal phrase—the author is identified in a parenthetical citation.

   Consumers want to identify with the happy, attractive people featured in advertisements (Hayakawa 164).

   Note that there is no punctuation between the author's name and the page reference.

2. A magazine article
   Once again, you may identify the work and/or author in a signal phrase, placing the page number in a parenthetical citation.

> In "Reinventing Baltimore," author Tony Hiss tells us, "A city [Baltimore] that was almost two-thirds white in 1960 is now almost three-fifths black" (41).

Or, in the absence of a signal phrase, you may identify both the author and page number in a parenthetical citation.

> Baltimore, "almost two-thirds white in 1960 is now almost three-fifths black" (Hiss 41).

3. More than one author

When the source is a book or a magazine with two or more authors, list all the last names in either the text or the parenthetical citation. If there are more than three authors, you may list all their last names (within reason) or cite one last name followed by *et al* and the page number. If an author has more than one work cited, you need to provide a shortened version of each title in the text reference, relying on the concluding list of works cited for the full title.

Sometimes you will be quoting a writer who is cited by another author you are reading. If you are unable to find the original source yourself, acknowledge both sources: original author in the body of your text, followed by (qtd. in Hiss 68). Note that MLA now suggests abbreviations in their parenthetical references.

Here is an example of multiple authors quoted from an essay from a collection:

> The authors reason that "since gene selection is not limited to cloning, what we have to say about the demand for cloning may well have implications for other reproductive technologies" (Eric A. Posner and Richard A. Posner, "The Demand for Human Cloning," qtd. in Nussbaum and Sunstein 235).

Place your parenthetical citations close to the material quoted or referred to, sliding them in at the end of grammatical units in the sentence and thus making them as unobtrusive as possible.

> Consumers want to identify with the happy, attractive people featured in advertisements (Hayakawa 164), and thus you will find that advertising models are forever young, healthy, and slender.

The idea in the first part of the sentence belongs to Hayakawa, the comment in the second half reflects the idea of the student writing the paper.

Although disciplines that follow the *Chicago Manual of Style* may still use traditional numbered footnotes at the bottom of the page or the end of a paper, this is rare in literature or the social sciences.

List of Works Cited: MLA

This list, to be titled "Works Cited," will be the final page of your paper and include all of the works cited in it, documented according to the examples that follow:

1. The information comes in three units—author, title, and publishing information—each separated by a period.
2. List, in alphabetical order, the authors by last name, with first names following. If more than one author, all *additional* authors are listed first name then last.
3. Capitalize the first word of a book's title and proper nouns.
4. For the publisher, write place or publication, colon, name of publisher, and date. Dates now follow the European form, day, month, year. Example: 29 April, 1999.
5. Where there is an editor, write *Ed.* and the editor's name before the title of the book, after the article or chapter taken from it.
6. Indent the second line five spaces under the first.

1. **Book by one author**

   Hayakawa, S. I. *Language in Thought and Action.* Orlando: Harcourt Brace Jovanovich, 1990.

   You can find the publishing information on the reverse side of the title page of the book.

2. **Excerpt from a collection or anthology**

   Posner, Eric A. and Richard A. Posner. "The Demand for Human Cloning." *Clones and Clones: Facts and Fantasies about Human Cloning.* Ed. Martha C. Nussbaum and Cass R. Sunstein. New York: Norton, 1998. 233–261.

3. **Magazine article**

   Toufexis, Anastasia. "Seeking the Roots of Violence." *Time* 19 April, 1993: 53.

4. **Professional or academic journal article**—(same format as for a magazine article)

   Reiss, David. "Genetic Influence on Family Systems: Implications for Development." *Journal of Marriage and the Family* August 1995: 547.

5. **More than one author**

   Use the last then first name of the initial author followed by additional authors' names in reverse order—first name then last.

   Specter, Michael, and Gina Kolata. "After Decades and Many Missteps, Cloning Success." *The New York Times* 3 March 1997: A1.

When a magazine article is unsigned, list the title of the article first, alphabetized by the first letter of the article, followed by the title of the magazine, appropriate dates, and the page number.

If an entry refers to an editorial or letter to the editor, cite the author, or if no author, title, followed by either "Editorial" or "Letter" set off by periods.

The APA Style of Documentation for Printed Sources

Because this book is intended primarily for classes in the humanities, we concentrate on MLA style, but for quick reference we include an introduction to the fundamentals of APA documentation.

CITATIONS WITHIN YOUR TEXT

1. **Book by one author**
   Introduce the quotation using the author's name followed by the date of publication in parentheses. Place the page reference in parentheses at the end of the passage.
   Semanticist S. I. Hayakawa (1990) points out that advertising and poetry are alike in that "they both strive to give meaning to the data of everyday experience" (p. 162).

2. **Paraphrase**
   If paraphrasing rather than quoting directly, include the author's name in a signal phrase followed by the publication date in parentheses, similar to the example above. Or, if the author is not identified in a signal phrase, place his or her name and the publication data in parentheses at the end of the sentence. Note that a page number is not required for a paraphrase.

3. **Magazine article**
   For a quotation taken from a magazine article, follow the same format required for a book by one author.
   According to Toufexis (1993), the roots of violence are complex and diffuse.

LIST OF WORKS CITED: APA   In APA style, the alphabetical list of works cited is entitled "References" and conforms to the following guidelines (you will note several distinctions between APA and MLA):

1. List the authors by last names, and use initials instead of first names.
2. Capitalize only the first word of a book's title and proper names.

3. When more than one author, separate their names with a comma and the symbol &.
4. Place publication date in parentheses after the author's name.
5. Omit quotation marks around title of an article.
6. Where there is an editor, place the name before the title of the book, write (Ed.) followed by a comma and the book's title, the pages in parentheses, location, and name of publisher.

1. **Book by one author**

   Hayakawa, S. I. (1990). *Language in thought and action.* Orlando: Harcourt Brace Jovanovich.

2. **Book by more than one author**

   Nelkin, D. & Lindee, S. (1996). The DNA mystique: The gene as a cultural icon. In P. Brown (Ed), *Perspectives in medical sociology* (pp. 415–433). New York: Waveland.

3. **For a magazine article**

   Hiss, T. (1991, April 29). Annals of place: reinventing Baltimore. *The New Yorker,* pp. 40–73.

Electronic Sources

Precise information about author, date, and other source details is not always consistent on the Internet, but the Modern Language Association (**MLA**) and the American Psychological Association (**APA**) have established guidelines for documenting online sites. Web sites for these updates change, as we've said before, but at time of printing the following addresses for documenting electronic sources, introduced earlier in the chapter, can help. For MLA, try **<www.mla.org>**; for APA, **<www.lib.ricks.edu/inet_apa.html>**, or for more complete research help, **<http://humanities.byu.edu/linguistics/Henrichsen/APA/APA01. html>**. If you have difficulty with these sites, consult your instructor. You will also find expanded coverage of documentation of electronic sources in *The MLA Handbook for Writers of Research Papers, The MLA Style Manual and Guide to Scholarly Publishing,* and the APA's *Publication Manual.* If your paper is intended for the sciences or social sciences, you should consult your instructor about preferred electronic documentation. When you are not able to find all the information desirable for complete documentation of electronic sources, provide as much as possible. The point is to provide easy Web access to your readers, acknowledging that address and sites change and information available on a given date may not be accessible later.

Under most circumstances, you need the following information from an Internet site:

1. Author (if one is named)
2. Name of the specific page(s), usually in quotation marks
3. Name of the main page, usually underlined or in italics. Sometimes this and the previous citation are the same.
4. Date of the page or the last update
5. URL in angle brackets
6. Date of access (preferably given in parentheses after the URL so as not to be confused with the date of the Internet page)

CITATION WITHIN YOUR TEXT   You may refer your reader directly to a Web site without including it in your list of works cited. The form follows the same guidelines for printed sources listed above, reflecting either MLA or APA style as appropriate.

> For a complete legal brief prepared by the National Legal Center, visit the Web site, <www.filteringfacts.org/ >.

LIST OF WORKS CITED: MLA   The author or first of several authors' last names come first with additional authors listed first names first, in the same form they appeared under List of Works Cited (MLA) (see above under MLA). Next comes the title in quotation marks, and then the **source and date** of publication or posting. This material is followed by the **date you accessed the site** and then the Web address or **URL** (Uniform Resource Locator). It is particularly important to make a note of the address before leaving the site because, if you wanted to recheck your documentation, you need that address. When a line break occurs in the middle of an address (some can be astonishingly long), make the break immediately following a punctuation mark, not between letters or numbers. Another way of safeguarding your own retrieval of material is to use the bookmarking or "favorite places" storage on your Internet server (see above), but that may not include the electronic address and could be unavailable when you try to return to it. Printing a hard copy from the Internet can also be helpful, especially if you want to quote a substantial passage. Again, list the documentation information; printed pages often omit it.

1. **Source directly from the Web**

> Beeson, Ann, Chris Hansen, and Barry Steinhardt. "Fahrenheit 451.2: Is Cyberspace Burning? How Rating and Blocking Proposals May Torch Free Speech on the Internet." ACLU Whitepaper 16 Jul. 1997. <http://www.aclu.org/ issues/cyber/ burning.html> (26 Aug. 1997).

2. **Article from the World Wide Web that has also been published in print magazines**

Include that source before the electronic address.

Morton, Oliver. "Overcoming Yuk." *Wired* Jan. 1998. <http://www.wired.com/wired/ 6.01/Morton.html> (20 Mar. 1998).

Wilmut, I, A. E. Schniek, J. McWhir, A. J. Kind, and K. H. S. Campbell. "Viable Offspring Derived from Fetal and Adult Mammalian Cells." *Nature* 27 Feb. 1997. <http://www.nature.com/Nature2/serve?SID=90209795&CAT=NATGEN&PG=sheep/sheep3.html> (19 Jul. 1997).

3. **Article in a newspaper or from a newswire**

Wade, Nicholas. "The Genome's Combative Entrepreneur." *The New York Times* 18 May 1999. <http://www.nytimes.com/library/national/science/051899sci-genome-venter-html/> (19 May 1998).

LIST OF WORKS CITED: APA   Here is an example of an article from the Web to show distinctions between MLA and APA.

Inada, K. (1995). "A buddhist response to the nature of human rights." *Journal of Buddhist Ethics 2*, 55–66. http://www.cac.psu;edu/jbel/twocont.html (visited 1996, July 23)

Sources on CD-ROM   Cite author, title, magazine or journal if applicable, and specific disk publication information.

Information received through e-mail (electronic mail)   Give the name of the writer, describe the transmission with name of receiver, and give the date the e-mail was sent.

Todd, Alexandra. E-mail re status of the human genome project sent to the authors, Cooper and Patton. 2 June 1998.

Formatting Your Paper

When you prepare the final draft of your paper, some matters of format will vary according to whether you are following MLA or APA guidelines. But in general, you should double space, have margins of at least 1" all around, and for APA allow 1 1/2" on the left. Beginning with the title page, number each page. If you are including an abstract, place it on a separate, introductory page.

For MLA, you have a choice of using a title page for your title, name, class name, and number, and date **or** of placing identifying material at the top left of page one with the title centered below it, immediately above the opening paragraph. In general, you will omit section headings within the paper unless called for in a technical subject.

For APA, put identifying material and title on a title page and place your name and a short version of the title at the top right-hand margin of every page. Scientific disciplines tend to be more demanding on specifics of format than the humanities, so when writing papers that require the APA style, consult your instructor about details of format.

Placement of Quotations

If a quotation runs over four typed lines of text, set it off with a five-space indent and continue to double space. You may choose to set off shorter quotations for clarity or emphasis. Drop the quotation marks when you indent. (This advice for quotations holds for almost any category of student paper or published article.)

Verb Tenses

Verb tenses in English are complex, but when writing in the humanities, it is customary to use the present tense when referring to matters discussed in the writings of others. This is a convention and not all disciplines follow it. Trusting your ear and depending on common sense will usually serve you well.

> An example of the *present tense* used in a paper about a book: "In *Zen and the Art of Motorcycle Maintenance,* Robert Pirsig *breaks down* the steps of motorcycle repair into logical components."

> An example of the *past tense* to express a contrast in time: "Richard Epstein, in his essay 'A Rush to Caution,' *warned* against a quick ban on all cloning, but today he might approve of cloning under some circumstances."

Sample Research Paper

"Antibiotics in Food Animals Can Be Hazardous to Your Health," the sample research paper which follows, illustrates The Modern Language Association (MLA) style of documentation and also reflects some of the features of successful written argument presented in Chapters 1 through 9. Grasso states her thesis in the introductory cover page and then works to support it in her paper. (See discussion of the thesis earlier in this chapter and also in Chapter 4.) Because the subject is technical, Grasso has extended her introduction to provide sufficient background explanation. In documenting her sources, she has used initials rather than first names for authors, a preference of science writing. MLA style prefers first and last names. Whether a citation refers to an author, an article, or a government agency, she provides a brief reference in parenthesis within the text rather than numbered footnotes or endnotes used in other reference styles. Most important, in the tradition of sound argumentation, she presents compelling evidence to support her position and also acknowledges, and then concedes or refutes, opposing views.

The essay was published in the winter 1999–2000 issue of *Vertices*, the Duke University Journal of Science and Technology, a publication devoted to work of undergraduates.

Introducing the paper is an outline of the issue, question at issue, and thesis. These topics are discussed in Chapter 4 and assigned in Writing Assignment 9.

Antibiotics in Food Animals Can Be
Hazardous to Your Health

Paola Grasso

Issue: Effects on human health of using
                              antibiotics in food animals

Question at Issue: Does the use of antibiotics in
                              food animals increase the risk
                              of resistance to antibiotics
                              in humans?

Thesis: Antibiotic use in beef and
                              poultry can harm consumers by
                              increasing drug resistance levels
                              in bacterial populations. To help
                              control emerging drug resistance,
                              consumers should support stricter
                              federal regulations of
                              antibiotics in food animals.

Grasso 1

Paola Grasso

28 November 1999

Antibiotics in Food Animals Can
Be Hazardous to Your Health

Antibiotic use in beef and poultry can harm consumers by increasing drug resistance levels in bacterial populations. To help control emerging drug resistance, consumers should support stricter federal regulations of antibiotics in food animals.

Outbreaks of food-borne bacterial diseases are common. The yearly cost of food-borne diseases in the United States is between 7.7 and 23 billion dollars. Every year in the United States, about 6.5 to 33 million people suffer from a food-borne disease; about 9,000 of these people die. Young children and elderly are especially at risk for complications. Food-borne diseases may trigger chronic illness, such as hemolytic uremic syndrome, Guillain-Barré syndrome, and reactive arthritis (U.S. FDA "Food and Drug") and can be contracted from eating food animals that are contaminated with disease-causing bacteria and have been improperly raised, shipped, slaughtered, or marketed.

Grasso 2

The most common disease-causing bacteria from food animals are *Salmonella enteritidis*, *Campylobacter jejuni* and *Escherichia coli* (US GAO "Antimicrobial Resistance"). *Salmonella* is the leading cause of bacterial gastroenteritis, but can also cause blood infection and enteric fever (Curtis et al.). Symptoms include nausea, vomiting, abdominal cramps, diarrhea, fever, and headache (U.S. FDA "Food-borne").

Recognizing the problem, the U.S. government has taken steps to reduce the prevalence of food borne disease. Since 1996, the Centers for Disease Control and Prevention (CDC) has monitored the food-borne illness through the Food-borne Diseases Active Surveillance Network. In 1998, the U.S. Department of Agriculture (USDA) introduced the Pathogen Reduction and Hazard Analysis and Critical Control Points rule ("Incidence of Food-borne Illnesses"). This rule calls for increased hygiene in American meat and poultry processing plants to reduce bacterial contamination; however, this rule does not address the use of antibiotics in food animals and thus does not help prevent the development of drug resistance.

Over a hundred million antibacterial drug prescriptions are distributed by physicians in the

Grasso 3

United States every year (U.S. GAO "Antimicrobial").
In 1954, the United States produced two million pounds
of antibiotics; this year over 50 million pounds of
antibiotics were produced (CDC "Antibiotic
Resistance"). First introduced in the 1940s, and
heralded as miracle drugs, antibiotics attack specific
pathogens (disease-causing agents). It is possible,
however, for bacteria to develop resistance against a
specific drug's attack.

Scientists have identified increasing drug
resistance as a current trend in pathogen evolution.
"We're facing a serious global problem with
[antibiotic] resistance now," Director Hughes of the
CDC National Center for Infectious Diseases comments.
"It affects virtually all of the pathogens we
previously considered easily treatable." Emerging
multiple drug resistance in human pathogens is
extremely worrisome. Without effective antibiotic
weapons, we are defenseless against bacterial
pathogens. Federal agencies are, we must acknowledge,
taking action to monitor drug resistance and
understand its development. For example, up until
1992, the CDC allocated $55,000 yearly to antibiotic
resistance surveillance. This year, the figure was

$2 million, and $14 is planned for the year 2000 (CDC "Antibiotic Resistance").

Multiple types of studies (ecological, cross-sectional, case-control, and longitudinal) and temporal trends in antibiotic use and resistance demonstrate that antibiotic use leads to resistance (Schwartz 212). Bacterial pathogens evolve drug resistance through the evolutionary mechanism of natural selection. Bacteria with advantageous traits are selected for survival. A drug applied to kill bacteria acts as a selective pressure which only allows bacteria that can resist the drug to survive. The surviving bacteria, carrying the drug resistance trait, become the dominant strain as further selective pressure is applied; however, this drug resistance trait can decrease fitness by detracting from the energy used for other cellular processes. In the absence of the drug's selective pressure, the drug resistance trait is disadvantageous.

Mathematical models have been constructed to represent the population genetics of antibiotic resistance. They show that the drug resistance trait in bacterial populations will persist despite the cost of fitness as long as antibiotic treatment continues

Grasso 5

to be applied (Levin et al.). Thus, the best way to control and prevent antibacterial resistance is to reduce selective pressures by limiting antibacterial use as much as possible.

Accordingly, national intervention programs strive to minimize antibiotic use. For example, the national campaign to promote judicious antibiotic use aims to decrease unnecessary antimicrobial use and reduce the spread of resistance (Schwartz 213). In the United States, however, this has been limited thus far because antibiotics in agriculture have been overlooked. Intervention measures have focused on preventing antibiotic resistance by limiting physician prescriptions and increasing patient compliance. While these are certainly appropriate goals, it is also important to curtail antibiotics in food animals.

The United States has approved numerous antibiotics for use in the beef and poultry industry. Antibiotics have been approved for use in food animals for three different reasons: to treat a specific disease, to prevent the disease from spreading in the flock, and to promote growth by increasing the amount of food absorbed (U.S. GAO, "Food Safety"). The majority of drugs approved for use in food animals are also approved for humans; some of these are even approved for growth promotion. Although studies have linked decreasing antibiotic effectiveness in humans with giving antibiotics to food animals for disease treatment and prevention (Threlfall, Rowe, and Ward), such practice has not been controversial because the need for veterinary medicine is generally recognized.

On the other hand, the approval of antibiotics for growth promotion is extremely controversial. The agricultural industry claims that antibiotic growth promotion provides a great economic benefit and the medical risks are unfounded. Most scientific experts agree, however, that if the antibiotics are also used therapeutically in humans, giving antibiotics to animals for growth promotion is an unnecessary risk.

In 1997, the World Health Organization recommended eliminating all antibiotic growth promotion (Alliance for Prudent Use). In 1998, the 15 members of the European Union responded by banning four growth promoters (tylosin, spiramycin, bacitracin, and virginiamycin) because they are structurally similar to human antibiotic treatments (Wegener et al. 331). The United Kingdom banned penicillin and tetracycline for growth promotion in

Grasso 7

the 1970s; soon other European countries followed, and Sweden banned all antibiotics for growth promotion in 1986 (U.S. GAO "Food Safety").

The United States has increased awareness of the link between antibiotics in agriculture and increasing drug resistance in human pathogens; the only steps taken thus far, however, have been research-oriented. The Food and Drug Administration's (FDA) Center for Veterinary Medicine has organized three public health meetings on antimicrobial resistance (Food and Drug Administration's Center). These meetings consist of a general public meeting (Oct. 1999), a workshop about risk assessment and the establishment of resistance threshold (Dec. 1999), and a discussion on the design of pre-approval studies and the extent to which models can predict the rate of resistance development (Feb. 2000). It is not the first time the FDA has considered the medical impacts of antibiotics in food animals. In 1978, the FDA "proposed withdrawing approval of penicillin and tetracycline for other [reasons] than disease treatments in animals." At the same time, however, the National Academy of Sciences responded that "the postulated hazards to human health were neither proven nor disproven" (U.S. GAO "Food Safety"). Although researchers continue to investigate the link between antibiotics in agriculture and increasing antibiotic resistance, the regulations have yet to be tightened.

Stricter regulations have been advocated by other organizations as well. The Alliance for the Prudent Use of Antibiotics (APUA) is a non-profit international organization founded in 1981 which advocates appropriate antibiotic use through research and education programs (Alliance for Prudent Use). The APUA recommends that the FDA implement regulations to reduce the use of antibiotics in agriculture. Specifically, it encourages the FDA to (1) eliminate the use of antibiotics in growth promotion of food animals; (2) monitor resistance levels in animals; (3) prohibit the use of antibiotics that increase drug resistance above a determined level. The APUA recommends that the FDA curtail non-therapeutic use of antibiotics in animals to reserve the drugs' effectiveness for disease treatment.

Programs in which the FDA regulates antibiotics do exist. The FDA evaluates domestically produced and imported food for antibacterial residues to enforce Environmental Protection Agency tolerance levels.

In addition, the National Antimicrobial Resistance Monitoring System-Enteric Bacteria program was started in 1996 by the FDA, the CDC, and the Department of Agriculture. They monitor drug resistance levels in *Salmonella, Campylobacter,* and *E. coli* isolated from people and in *Salmonella* isolated from animals. Beginning in 1998, the program also began monitoring drug resistance levels in *Campylobacter* and *E. coli* that had been isolated from animals (U.S. GAO "Food Safety").

Monitoring drug resistance levels will help identify increasing drug resistance levels in food-borne human pathogens. These data are expected to provide enough evidence of the human health hazards posed by antibiotic use in food animals to support establishing stricter FDA regulations; however, there is currently no federal regulation that requires companies to eliminate antibiotic growth promotion. Consumers should support stricter regulations that minimize the use of antibiotics in food animals.

Grasso 10

Works Cited

Alliance for the Prudent Use of Antibiotics. 10 Oct.
    1999 <http://www.healthsci.tufts.edu/apua>.

Centers for Disease Control and Prevention (CDC).
    "Antibiotic Resistance: A New Threat to You and
    Your Family's Health." 12 Apr. 1999. 22 Oct.
    1999 <http://www.cdc.gov/ncidod/dbmd/
    antibioticresistance>.

Curtis R., MacLeod, D.L., Galan, J.E., Kelly, S.M.
    "Colonization and Invasion of the Intestinal
    Tract by Salmonella." *Biology of Salmonella*. Ed.
    F. Cabello et al. New York: Plenum Press, 1993.

Food and Drug Administration's Center for Veterinary
    Medicine. 3 Nov. 1999 <http://www.fda.gov/cvm/
    fda/mappgs/antitoc.html>.

"Incidence of Food-borne Illnesses: Preliminary Data
    from the Food-borne Diseases Active Surveillance
    Network." Food Net—United States 1998. 10 Oct.
    1999 <http://www.cdc.gov/epo/mmwr/preview/
    mmwrhtml/00056654.htm>.

Levin, B.R. et al. "Population Genetics of Antibiotic
    Resistance." Clinical Infectious Diseases 24.2:
    S9-16.

Grasso 11

Schwartz, B. "Preventing the Spread of Antimicrobial
    Resistance among Bacterial Respiratory Pathogens
    in Industrialized Countries: The Case for
    Judicial Antimicrobial Use." <u>Clinical Infectious
    Diseases</u> 28.2 (1999): 211-13.

Threlfall E.J., Rowe B., Ward L.R. "Changing Trends in
    Antibiotic Resistance in Salmonella Isolated
    from Humans in England and Wales." <u>Biology of
    Salmonella.</u> Ed. F. Cabello et al. New York:
    Plenum Press, 1993.

U.S. FDA, Center for Food Safety and Applied
    Nutrition. <u>Food-borne Pathogenic Microorganisms
    and Natural Toxins Handbook, The Bad Bug Book.</u>
    1997.

U.S. FDA, Center for Food Safety and Applied Nutrition.
    <u>Food and Drug Safety Progress Review</u> 26 Sep.
    1995. 28 Oct. 1999 <http://vm.cfsan.fda.gov/mow/
    hp2knat.html>.

U.S. General Accounting Office. <u>Antimicrobial
    Resistance: Data to Assess Public Health Threat
    from Resistant Bacteria Are Limited</u>. Washington:
    GAO/RCED, 1999. 99-132.

Grasso 12

United States General Accounting Office. <u>Food Safety:</u>
<u>The Agricultural Use of Antibiotics and Its</u>
<u>Implications for Human Health</u>. Washington:
GAO/RCED, 1999. 99-174.

Wegener et al. "Use of Antimicrobial Growth Promoters
in Food Animals and Enterococcus faecium
Resistance to Therapeutic Antimicrobial Drugs in
Europe." <u>Emerging Infectious Diseases</u> 5.3
(1999): 329-35.

In Conclusion

This chapter contains a great deal of detailed information that we don't expect you to memorize. Before each paper that requires research, we suggest you look over the chapter to refresh your memory on the basic principles of generating ideas for a research project, finding material, and documenting sources. Once you have gathered your information and are ready to start writing, use the chapter as a reference, consulting Web sites and research handbooks for more complete technical support.

"You've taught me how to think."

PART TWO

The Readings

CHAPTER 10

The First Amendment— Freedom of Speech and Censorship

As Americans we assume that we have the right to think and say what we like without government control. The framers of our Constitution insisted on that freedom over two hundred years ago when they wrote the First Amendment, incorporated into the Constitution as part of the Bill of Rights.

> Congress shall make no law respecting an establishment of religion, or prohibiting the free exercise thereof, or **abridging the freedom of speech or of the press,** or the right of the people peaceably to assemble, and to petition the Government for a redress of grievances.

Sometimes the rights of one person will collide with the rights of another, and thus the need to curtail some forms of speech soon became apparent. The freedom of others is impinged upon if you shout fire in a crowded theater when no fire exists. Verbal threats cannot be tolerated on airliners. Individuals must be protected from slanderous falsehoods uttered in public. But, in fact, most utterances, spoken and written, are still protected by the Bill of Rights. As Jim Lehrer said on his PBS *News Hour,* "When press freedom goes, all other freedoms are at increased risk and will likely go too."

But would journalist Lehrer extend his "freedoms" to what some call pornography, to what many find damaging to children, to what even more would agree are dangerous examples of hate speech? All these issues center around how far individuals may push the right to free speech. When famed movie producer Oliver Stone and director Milos Forman released their controversial film, *The People vs. Larry Flynt,* they ran head on into questions of pornography and First Amendment rights. Then, more crucially, the Supreme Court addressed the complex question of controlling "indecent" material on the Internet. At the same time, the world was confronted with a rising tide of hate speech on the Internet, argued by many to be protected by that same Amendment.

269

Such controversies are not new. Over the centuries different generations have defined and redefined what is considered publicly indecent. The librettos of Mozart's comic opera, *Cosi Fan Tutti* and the all-time opera hit *Carmen* were both censored in the nineteenth century. Today, they are considered high art, deemed appropriate cultural experiences for high school students. Thomas Hardy's novel, *Jude the Obscure,* also assigned in some schools, was once classified as indecent because Jude, the hero, marries his cousin. After it was censored, Hardy stopped writing. Explicit sex in James Joyce's *Ulysses* and in *Lady Chatterly's Lover* by D. H. Lawrence kept them out of American bookshops for more than half a century. More recently, Allen Ginsberg's *Howl*—celebrating erotic homosexuality, and *Naked Lunch,* William Burroughs's account of his drug-addicted obsessions, were both condemned when first published. Today, they are widely available in bookstores. On the other hand, some would be shocked today by Boccaccio's fourteenth century Italian classic, *The Decameron,* the sixteenth century works of Rabelais, or in the eighteenth century, the poetry of Lord Rochester and the most celebrated of erotic novels, *Fanny Hill.* No one censors these revered works today. You might be interested in looking them up in your library.

Deciding where we stand on the vast topic of what is pornography, what is indecent speech in general, what rights individuals have to defame or threaten others is confusing. But once we isolate issues of free speech to a given context, we can come closer to sorting out what we believe.

In this text, we do not address all areas where free speech comes up against a perceived need to protect us from unpleasant or potentially damaging material. We don't, for example, address the controversy surrounding rock lyrics, violence on television, or government funding of art deemed offensive by some. A controversial film, indecent speech on the Internet, and hate speech on the Internet provide three examples of contexts in which opposing rights are contested.

As you read the following selections, you will need to focus your *critical attention* on the issue itself and on the position each writer takes. When you answer the questions and write papers in response to assigned topics, you will be applying your *critical thinking* to your own arguments.

The First Amendment: Protected or Exploited?

The storm that surrounded the release of the film, *The People vs. Larry Flynt,* illustrates the long reach of the First Amendment. The movie tells the story of Larry Flynt, controversial publisher of *Hustler* magazine, and of his legal battles over free speech and censorship. The following collection of articles illustrates the nature of the controversy. While the movie it-self quickly dropped from view, the issues surrounding it are always with us, creating conflict. At the time, some saw the film as honoring the First Amendment, others saw it as honoring pornographer Larry Flynt. Both sides carried on this debate in the press and over the airwaves.

The Critics Express Their Views on *The People vs. Larry Flynt*

As excerpts from the following advertisement show, critics from major newspapers around the country applauded the film.

Some people have attacked the film THE PEOPLE VS. LARRY FLYNT. They call it dishonest and guilty of whitewashing the ugly truth about Larry Flynt and Hustler magazine.

Columbia Pictures and Phoenix Pictures would like you to read the following excerpts from our country's most distinguished journalists and publications.

<u>YOU DECIDE.</u>

NEWSWEEK

David Ansen

". . . this Milos Forman film is both provocation and anomaly.

Flynt was no angel, and the film never pretends otherwise. But he is as American as RC Cola and a Moon Pie. In 'The People vs. Larry Flynt,' comedy and tragedy frolic together with surprising abandon as Forman confronts the gaudy excesses of a life out of control. . . .

Forman doesn't glorify this intransigent, abrasive man, but he has mounted a rousing and persuasive case for the defense."

THE NEW YORK TIMES

Frank Rich

"'The People vs. Larry Flynt' deserves a huge adult audience because it is the most timely and patriotic movie of the year. This film is an eloquent antidote to anyone who would jawbone the First Amendment to clean up the grotesque excesses of our culture. . . ."

MIAMI HERALD

Rene Rodriguez

". . . It's not the porn that interests Forman. For a movie about a self-proclaimed 'pervert,' 'The People vs. Larry Flynt' is downright discreet. What Forman does is use Flynt's story to examine our obsessions with sex, religion and morality—and the eternal battle among the three. 'The People vs. Larry Flynt' doesn't make a case for pornography; it argues for diversity, for the right to choose, for basic American principles under attack by those who would protect us from ourselves."

THE NEW YORK TIMES

Janet Maslin

"Milos Forman's film describes the Hustler publisher and his many liberties, civil and otherwise. Above all the film emerges as an object lesson in open-mindedness, winning a reluctant respect for its main character's right to crude self-expression just as Mr. Flynt has won his days in court. . . ."

THE BOSTON GLOBE

Jay Carr

"Raucously entertaining and wickedly provocative, 'The People vs. Larry Flynt' reminds us—as few films of this decade have—that social satire is still capable of giving off sparks in a Hollywood increasingly given to corporate pieties in a culture falling all over itself in a rush to the middle of the road."

LOS ANGELES TIMES

Kenneth Turan

"'The People vs. Larry Flynt' is not interested in glorifying Larry Flynt, quite the opposite. It rather delights in showing how this crass and cold-eyed hustler, a man of wildy contradictory and often offensive urges and impulses, ended up, to his own great surprise as much as anyone's, doing something significant for society."

THE WALL STREET JOURNAL

Joe Morgenstern

". . . Who would have thought that Milos Forman and his writers, Scott Alexander and Larry Karaszewsky, could make a hugely entertaining film about a scummy, self-promoting smut peddler and his punked-out druggy wife? Yet they did. They found a shrewd pretext—the publisher of Hustler magazine as a poster boy for the First Amendment—and ran with it all the way to the Supreme Court. . . . "

THE NEW YORK OBSERVER

Rex Reed

"A few words of praise and endorsement for 'The People vs. Larry Flynt,' a powerful, challenging film about a detestable subject (the sordid life of the smut-peddling publisher of Hustler magazine) and a detestable premise (in Amercia, you can get away with anything as long as you hide behind the First Amendment) that is so well written (by Scott Alexander and Larry Karaszewski) and directed (by Milos Forman), the overall effect hits you between the eyes like a stun gun. . . . Nobody seems to like him, including Flynt himself, but you do go away reluctantly agreeing with his nutty demand that in this country, like it or not, "a pig has the same rights as a President."

TOPIC FOR DISCUSSION AND WRITING

Do you find something disingenuous, deliberately misleading, about the invitation in this ad: "YOU DECIDE"? Explain. (For a brief discussion of advertising and critical thinking, see Chapter 1, Critical Thinking as Self-Defense.)

Three Columnists Express Their Views on *The People vs. Larry Flynt*

Newspaper columnists Gloria Steinem, Ellen Goodman, and Oliver North took issue with the film and much of the glowing reaction to it. Interestingly, Goodman and Steinem are usually associated with issues concerning women's rights and other liberal causes. They would rarely be on the same side of an argument as Oliver North, former military officer and supporter of traditional Christian family values. North in particular addresses the Supreme Court ruling in which Larry Flynt successfully defended himself against charges of defamation brought by Jerry Falwell, a leader of the Christian right. Falwell claimed that he'd been libeled by what Flynt called a satire in his notorious magazine, *Hustler,* and argued for censorship. That case played a central role in the movie. Flynt continues to challenge the outer limits of free speech, openly courting the indictment he received for an adult bookstore in downtown Cincinnati in 1998. And he cheerfully revealed sexually compromising stories about congressmen during the impeachment trial of President Clinton in 1999.

Larry Flynt Is No Hero

Gloria Steinem

Larry Flynt the Movie is even more cynical than Larry Flynt the Man. "The People vs. Larry Flynt" claims that the creator of Hustler magazine is a champion of the First Amendment, deserving our respect. That isn't true.

Let's be clear: A pornographer is not a hero, no more than a publisher of Ku Klux Klan books or a Nazi on the Internet, no matter what constitutional protection they secure. And Flynt didn't secure much.

In this film, produced by Oliver Stone and directed by Milos Forman, Hustler is depicted as tacky at worst, and maybe even honest for showing full nudity. What's left out are the magazine's images of women being beaten, tortured and raped, women subject to degradations from bestiality to sexual slavery.

Filmgoers don't see such Hustler features as "Dirty Pool," which in January 1983 depicted a woman being gang-raped on a pool table.

Nor do you see such typical Hustler photo stories as a naked woman in handcuffs who is shaved, raped and apparently killed by guards in a concentration-camp-like setting. You won't meet "Chester the Molester," the famous Hustler cartoon character who sexually stalks girls. (The cartoonist, Dwaine Tinsley, was convicted in 1990 of sexually molesting his daughter.)

On the contrary, the Hollywood version of Larry Flynt, played by the charming Woody Harrelson, is opposed to violence. At an anti-censorship rally, he stands against a backdrop of beautiful images of nude women that are intercut with scenes of Hiroshima, marching Nazis and the My Lai massacre. "Which is more obscene," the Flynt character asks, "sex or war?" Viewers who know Hustler's real content might ask, "Why can't Larry Flynt tell the difference?"

Flynt's daughter Tonya, 31, is so alarmed by this film's dishonesty that she joined women who picketed its opening in San Francisco. She also publicly accused Flynt of having sexually abused her when she was a child, a charge he vehemently denies and attributes to her "mental problems."

"I'm upset about this film because it supports my dad's argument that pornography does no harm," she has said. "If you want to see a victim of pornography, just look at me."

Unlike his film character, the real Flynt is hardly an unwavering advocate of free speech. Indeed, other feminists and I have been attacked in Hustler for using our First Amendment rights to protest pornography.

My question is, would men be portrayed as inviting, deserving and even enjoying their own pain and degradation, as women are in Flynt's life work? Suppose Flynt specialized in such images as a young black man trussed up like a deer and tied to the luggage rack of a white hunter's car. Or a nude white man being fed into a meat grinder.

Would Oliver Stone—who rarely lets powerful men emerge unscathed—bowdlerize and flatter that kind of man too? Would Woody Harrelson, who supports animal rights and protests logging, pose happily next to that Larry Flynt? Would Milos Forman defend that film by citing his memories of censorship under the Nazis?

The truth is, if Flynt had published the same cruel images even of animals, this movie would never have been made. Fortunately, each of us has the First Amendment right to protest.

Larry Flynt's Big Makeover

Ellen Goodman

I have long regarded Larry Flynt as the curse of the First Amendment. He's the catch that comes with the freedom of speech. The asterisk on the Constitution.

You want the freedom to say whatever you want? Fine, but you can't shut up the smutmeister. Nevertheless, there is one thing that Larry Flynt is not. My hero.

That brings us directly to "The People vs. Larry Flynt," a film that opened with the most fawning reviews. This movie has morphed a curse into a hero with greater ease than it transformed Flynt into Woody Harrelson.

Director Milos Forman has fulfilled Flynt's last fantasy: "I would love to be remembered for something meaningful." This biopic cleans up Flynt's act to fit producer Oliver Stone's description of the pornographer as someone "in the rapscallion tradition of Mark Twain's Huckleberry Finn."

The cleanup takes place magically by making women disappear. The love story of Larry and Althea edits down Flynt's relationships with other women and edits out his effects on all women. This movie about a pornographer is virtually devoid of questions surrounding pornography.

We do see Flynt at some drugged-out moments. But the average viewer can leave the darkened theater without knowing that Flynt had five wives, two of whom he trashed for promiscuity, without knowing that he had, and neglected five children, one of whom he refers to as a "lying little whacko."

But if "The People vs. Larry Flynt" is now the text for the debate about free speech, tell it like it is. Anyone leaving the theater should be handed a copy of

Hustler before they go off for their espresso and erudite conversations about Courtney Love's performance.

This is what's in the current Hustler:

Enough ads for phone sex to constitute a porn yellow pages.

Dozens of centers of centerfolds.

Women having sex with each other with large plastic male organs strapped on.

A feature called "How to Know if Your Girlfriend Is a Dog."

Enough racist cartoons to "balance" an article against neo-Nazis.

And don't leave out Nataly's sexual fantasy about occupying armies. "She knows that her only hope for survival is complete submission to their will—a price she is prepared to pay."

This is the porn that reduces a woman to the sum of her sexual parts. The real porn that is degrading, desensitizing and arguably dangerous.

In the film, Larry says, "If the First Amendment can protect even a scumbag like me, then it will protect all of you, because I am the worst." But the irony is that the filmmakers don't present "the worst." It's as if they didn't trust the answer to the question they ask the public: "You may not like what he does, but are you prepared to give up his right to do it?" They don't show what he does.

For my own part, I accept the curse that comes with the First Amendment. When the Falwell case went to court, I wrote a friend-of-the-Flynt brief in this column. But I continue to regard him as an enemy. Those of us who are free speech absolutists believe absolutely that you fight speech with more speech. I don't truck with censors. But spare me those in Hollywood who turn the scumbag into the star.

A Great Hustle for Porn King

Oliver North

"The People vs. Larry Flynt" opened in theaters recently, amid heaping praise from film critics.

In Newsweek, the movie about the life of Hustler magazine publisher Larry Flynt is called "brave" and "spectacularly entertaining," with the title character dubbed as "American as RC Cola and Moon Pie." USA Today echoed the sentiments, calling the Oliver Stone-produced and Milos Forman-directed movie "a civics lesson that will still be regaling film enthusiasts four decades hence."

Asked by Larry King what he thought of the movie, Flynt glowingly replied, "I was very happy with it." And why shouldn't he be? It's not every day a drug-abusing panderer of pornography is depicted on the silver screen as the man who saved the Constitution.

The movie centers around Flynt's legal battles to make America safe for smut. Challenging local obscenity statutes in Cincinnati and rural Georgia, Flynt's quest for the right to make millions while selling X-rated magazines culminates in his Supreme Court faceoff with Jerry Falwell.

"The People vs. Larry Flynt" casts Woody Harrelson as the hard-living porn tycoon. The multimillionaire Flynt is portrayed as an underdog crusader for free speech unmercifully persecuted by (you guessed it) the Religious Right.

Not surprisingly, the film treats those who oppose pornography—especially those motivated by religious beliefs—as more dangerous than Flynt, the supposedly mischievous, yet lovable, capitalist.

Religious figures in the film are depicted as mindless dupes at best—at worst, as hypocritical zealots threatening the liberties of ordinary Americans. It seems that whenever those who oppose the widespread proliferation of pornography speak, their sole purpose is to set up Flynt or his lawyer for an eloquent soliloquy on the virtues of free speech.

Presumably at movie's end, we are all to be grateful that Flynt wins his Supreme Court case and makes it permissible to publish liquor-ad parodies depicting Jerry Falwell losing his virginity to his mother in an outhouse. Not exactly what the Founding Fathers had in mind when they penned the First Amendment.

In the delusional world of Oliver Stone, Flynt may very well be a champion of the First Amendment. For those of us not consumed by paranoid conspiracies, however, the character portrayed in the film is a bizarre inversion of the real life of Larry Flynt.

Tonya Flynt, whom her father lovingly describes as a "lying little wacko whom I don't even know," claims that the man lionized in the Stone/Forman film abused and molested her when she was a child. When she planned to write a book about her horrid experiences, Ms. Flynt states that her father twice threatened to kill her. Some civil libertarian!

Freedom of speech protects Flynt's "right" to peddle layouts of nude women made up as 5-year-olds but apparently stops short of allowing his daughter to write an unflattering book about him. Somehow, these inconvenient realities never made it into the movie.

Somehow, members of the film industry and those who critique their products in the Fourth Estate seem to think that the more someone pushes the boundaries of taste in our culture, the more that person should be seen as a "defender of civil liberties." But Jerry Falwell had it right when he so adeptly observed, "Larry didn't save the First Amendment. The First Amendment saved him."

TOPICS FOR DISCUSSION AND WRITING

1. Briefly summarize the principle arguments presented by Gloria Steinem, Ellen Goodman, and Oliver North against the film *The People vs. Larry Flynt*, emphasizing where their arguments differ. (See Summaries in Chapter 3.)

2. Ellen Goodman is torn by conflicting issues in her reaction to Larry Flynt and the movie about him. What is her conflict, why did she submit a "friend-of-the Flynt brief" in her column, and where do you stand on the two sides she explores?

3. Oliver North quotes Jerry Falwell: "Larry didn't save the First Amendment. The First Amendment saved him." What do North and Falwell mean by this claim?

4. North refers to the "boundaries of taste." Write a paper in which you discuss whether or not *The People vs. Larry Flynt* violated good taste. Where do you consider the boundaries of taste should be set? (The movie should be available in your local video store or campus media center.)

Four Supporters of *The People vs. Larry Flynt* Defend Their Motives

Those connected with making the movie were outspoken in its support.

An Unseemly Man

Larry Flynt with Kenneth Ross

The producer, Oliver Stone, the director, Milos Forman, the star of the movie, Woody Harrelson, and Al Goldstein, the publisher of another pornographic magazine, defend the film in the forward to Flynt's autobiography, which came out at the same time as the movie.

Larry Flynt has lived a life of classic highs and lows that few men in our age will ever come close to experiencing. I suppose he is the late twentieth-century version of Horatio Alger pursuing the Amercian Dream, but with the perverse twist of building his empire from pornography. And like most men who succeed based on fierce determination and moral ambiguity, he draws judgments as extreme as the highs and lows he has lived. For this reason I find him personally to be more in the rapscallion tradition of Mark Twain's Huckleberry Finn—the country boy, misunderstood by so many, trying to figure it all out, rafting down the American psyche of a country gone wacko. Larry, by some standards, is a First Amendment hero and defender of the Constitution; he is also an exploiter of women and a one-man wrecking crew on "community standards." Does he fight the dirty fight for us, or does he care only about a buck, as the head of a sleazy media empire that hides behind a cause? Therein lies the reason Larry Flynt is fascinating. When you actually step inside his life, as we tried to do in our movie, you navigate a minefield of contradictions.

On one hand, Larry Flynt was raised dirt poor in a one-room shack in Kentucky. On the other, he knows what it is to have more money than he could ever spend. He has had sex both with a chicken and with some of the world's most beautiful women. He has been a fervent born-again Christian and a reckless atheist. He has lived a pagan, orgiastic lifestyle, but he has also had to contend with being paralyzed in the prime of his life. He has been railroaded and jailed

by the justice system, but he has also had his most noble triumph in the halls of the Supreme Court, in one of the finest hours of recent Amercian legal history. He is someone desperately trying to obtain a certain respect, but he is also hopelessly tethered by his crude roots and the derivation of his wealth. And finally, while he has known the great power of running an empire, he has also known the hopelessness of watching the true love of his life suffer from AIDS and eventually die of a drug overdose.

From my personal experience with Larry Flynt, I get the sense of someone still a little stunned by everything that has happened to him; someone still looking back, in the last act of his life, at the good and the bad, with a strange recognition of the painful wisdom his experiences have given him. He's had his fair share of life—poverty, jail, drug addiction, and a partly successful assassination attempt—and he's also had great joy. I'm not sure where he stands on it all, because life, for people who live passionately, tends in the end to be an overwhelmingly vast and neutral canvas that renders no final decision, no sense of win or lose. I sometimes even get the feeling that if Larry could rewind his life and edit it like a home movie, there is a bitter wisdom within that would not allow him to change anything.

Is Larry Flynt a hero? Not in the classic cinematic sense. Hardly. But is there not another definition of heroism? I think of Ron Kovic, who lived in the same era and wrote *Born on the Fourth of July,* which I adapted into a movie. Kovic came to understand, in the end, that the definition of a hero is a shifting one, and very often where we end up has very little resemblance to where we started.

Screenwriters Larry Karaszewski and Scott Alexander, and our director, Milos Forman, have very much grappled with the question of who Larry Flynt really is. The answer, I believe, as with many of us, lies in the contradictions—and so to judge him by community standards or conformism, or small thinking, is to face a hopeless conundrum. He has helped us all as Amercians by scapegoating himself, and as we know, those people who speak the loudest in any age are often the most condemned—until history, on its own eccentric path, discovers them years later. As you look into Larry Flynt's life, look at it, if nothing else, as an examination of the extremes of the human experience; try to empathize as a fellow traveler with his suffering and his triumph. And there, I believe, you will discover the real relevance of his story.

> —Oliver Stone
> Producer, *The People vs. Larry Flynt*
> Santa Monica, California

I am definitely one of those old-fashioned, small-town people who was conditioned, in my childhood in Czechoslovakia, to think that pornography is bad, and—I am afraid—I shall never be able to shake off this notion.

So the only reason I consented to read a script about Larry Flynt was as a courtesy to Oliver Stone, who figured as producer on the project. After I had turned the last page, to my shock and in contravention of my childhood conditioning, I knew I wanted—and had—to make this film.

Twice in my life I have had the misfortune to live in societies where freedom of expression was totally suppressed, and where open discourse was an illegal act: first under the Nazis, and then the Communists. I have seen the devastating effect these repressive measures had on the quality of life. Boredom ruled everyone except those in power and those who were marching to the gallows.

I think it significant that both these regimes started with crusades against those they classified as perverts: pornographers, homosexuals, Jews, and blacks. As time went by, the list grew longer and longer, until one day it included Shakespeare, Jesus Christ, Mark Twain, and William Faulkner; and finally, any plumber, teacher, or housewife who did not conform to the official ideology. Perverts all.

I must admit that I have never bought *Hustler* magazine, and I believe I never will. But as long as I live, I will always admire Larry Flynt: his life, his courage, and his tenacity. Less surprisingly, the Supreme Court of the United States is and will always be my hero.

> —Milos Forman
> Director, *The People vs. Larry Flynt*
> New York, New York

I remember Bryan Lourd giving me a script called *The People vs. Larry Flynt,* and telling me that the great Milos Forman was interested in having me play the title role. Before I read it, I asked *the* question, the one I have heard asked many times since: "Why would anyone want to make a movie about him?" Bryan said, "Woody, it's Milos Forman. Read it." So I read it and liked it, but wasn't at all satisfied. I was living near Cincinnati when his trial was going on, and shared the opinion of most everyone else in my church-influenced environment: Larry Flynt was a scumbag! Why does he deserve a movie? Then I watched a documentary about him and was struck by his sense of humor and charisma. But most of all, I was struck by what he was saying: If the First Amendment did not protect him, it did not protect anyone. Is it possible that the First Amendment freedoms we enjoy today exist only through the considerable efforts of a lowly pornographer? The more I learned about Larry's life, the more intrigued I became.

When I went to meet Larry in his offices in Beverly Hills, I was nervous. I didn't know what to expect. I had heard he was not terribly coherent because of prescription drug use, and of course, he had been confined to a wheelchair for nearly twenty years. What had paralysis done to this man who drew so much of his vitality from the waist down? While waiting outside his office, I was surprised by the way everything was decorated. The place had a very conservative, expensive, almost Victorian flavor to it. Quite a contrast to the humble beginnings of a man who grew up in the hills of Kentucky "so far back in the hollow we had to pipe in sunshine." In fact, one of the things that I found intriguing about Larry was the fact that both of us were poor white trash who somehow got a leg up in the world. When I was summoned and walked in, I found him on the other side of an enormous office, behind a huge desk, seated in a gold wheelchair. He greeted me in his slow, raspy eastern Kentucky drawl, which I would subsequently spend many hours trying to duplicate.

I asked Larry many questions, getting increasingly personal as the interview progressed, and began to realize why this man deserved to have a movie made about his life. The reasons go well beyond his passionate defense of freedom of the press. Larry is human, and it is always refreshing to discover the humanity in someone we have demonized. Larry is as vulnerable as anyone I've ever met because of the unfettered way he expresses himself. How often do you say exactly what you feel without censoring yourself, and without worrying about what others might think? Larry does not censor himself, and rightfully believes our government shouldn't do so, either. Granted, his outspoken honesty has gotten him into a lot of trouble. He has spent millions in the last twenty years defending himself in court. But he loves to stir things up and to jolt people out of their lethargy.

Well, I can't wait to read the book you're holding, but I will also be very interested to see the chapters not yet written. I don't know what drives this man, but when you have finished his autobiography, you might believe with me that there is plenty of fight left in him. You haven't heard the last of Larry Flynt.

—Woody Harrelson
Actor, *The People vs. Larry Flynt*
Los Angeles, California

Larry Flynt is a monster and a madman. He is a monster to those who hate freedom and madman in pursuit of his own freedom.

I first met Larry a quarter century ago, when the sexual landscape was quite different than it is today. The American libido was still firmly chained in its backyard, hidden from company as if it were a cretinous child. People were still coy talking about sex in public. Abuse, incest, and rape were dirty little secrets, which "propriety" helped keep hidden.

"Good poets borrow, great poets steal," said T. S. Eliot. By this measure, Larry Flynt is a great poet. He freely admits he stole part of *Hustler's* format from my magazine, *Screw*. He went on to steal my defense lawyers and one of my best editors. But that is all to Larry's credit. He is the most determined bulldog I've ever known.

Larry has made a success of virtually everything he has attempted, and he has done it with integrity and consistency. He absolutely refuses to permit anyone to censor any word or thought; more important, he refuses to censor himself.

Larry Flynt is my role model. His extraordinary Supreme Court victory in the Jerry Falwell satire case set one of the most important legal precedents of the twentieth century. He is always there to remind us not to take sex too seriously.

I salute Larry Flynt as a publishing genius and as a sexual warrior. With this book and with the film *The People vs. Larry Flynt*, maybe, finally, possibly, this brilliant man will get the recognition he deserves.

—Al Goldstein
Publisher, *Screw* Magazine
New York, New York

TOPICS FOR DISCUSSION AND WRITING

1. Briefly summarize the principle arguments presented by the four who defend the movie: Oliver Stone, Milos Forman, Woody Harrelson, and Al Goldstein (See Summaries in Chapter 3.)

2. How does Harrelson support his decision to play the lead in Forman's movie?

3. In his essay, Al Goldstein, publisher of his own pornography magazine, makes a reference to poet T. S. Eliot. Do you find anything wrong with his equation centered on "good" and "great" poets? Explain. (See False Analogy in Chapter 6 and Analogy in Chapter 14.) Do you find other weaknesses of a more general nature in Goldstein's reasoning?

4. Goldstein is enthusiastic in his praise of Larry Flynt, his strongest competitor. Why do you think Goldstein publicly applauds Flynt?

5. Goldstein refers to Larry Flynt's "extraordinary Supreme Court victory in the Jerry Falwell satire case." Write a paper in which you discuss your own reaction to the Court's decision. For this, you will have to go to the library or the Internet and research the Court's written opinions. This case found many people torn between their distaste for smearing an individual and their concern for preserving First Amendment rights.

An Address to the National Press Club

Milos Forman

Speaking before a large forum of reporters, director Milos Forman justifies his commitment to the film and the First Amendment.

Thank you very much for giving me the opportunity to address this distinguished gathering. . . .

I recently directed a film called *The People vs. Larry Flynt.* It is being called "the most controversial movie of the year." But this controversy, stimulating though it may be, is based on a false premise. And I thank you for giving me the opportunity to speak to you about this.

I know that everything, even the most innocuous and silly joke, can be subject to distorted political interpretation. I will never forget the chill we felt—I was living then in communist-dominated Czechoslovakia with the Soviet Army still on its soil—when we heard about a comedian who told a joke in a pub about a Czech citizen who came to a police station to complain that "three Swiss soldiers stole my Russian watch." The policeman looked at him quizzically and said: "I think you meant to say that three Russian soldiers stole your Swiss watch." To which the man replied quickly: "You said it! Not me!"

The comedian was sentenced for this joke to three years in a concentration camp.

I know that pornography is a more sensitive subject than petty theft but still, to accuse my R-rated film, as a few have, for not being sufficiently dirty to deserve the NC–17 rating strikes me as odd. But I forgive them. They are not obliged to be so familiar with my work to have noticed that dirty pictures are not my metier.

I have no argument with those who find some of the contents of *Hustler* objectionable. I myself find some of its stuff objectionable. I had never bought *Hustler* in my life. When I was preparing this film and had to go through endless amount of *Hustlers,* I cringed. Men as well as women are often portrayed on its pages with brutish vulgarity. Sexual and otherwise.

But surely to equate—as one of my film's critics does—a printed page, however tasteless, with the Nazi slaughter, a slaughter that deprived a sizable portion of the earth's population of their lives is, to say the least, intemperate. The critics of my film know that it is not possible to legislate taste, therefore they argue that pornography results in acts of violence.

Well, I don't know whether studies have proved this assertion. I do know, however, that a study of human social history will unarguably disclose that one of our most noble emotions—love—has prompted more damage, more violence, more suicides, even more murders than can ever be ascribed to pornography.

Should we blame *Romeo and Juliet* or *West Side Story* every time an unhappy lover loses control and does something damaging because of the unbearable pain of love in his or her heart? Should we call on Hollywood to stop making these kinds of movies?

I did not want to make pornography the focus of this talk. It is a digression. I did so because the same few critics are trying to convince the public that the goals and themes of my film are identical to those of *Hustler*.

Nothing can be further from the truth.

My film is not, and never was intended to be, about pornography, pro or con. Its writers did not conceive it that way nor did I.

That's why the film's climax is the case Larry Flynt and his lawyers brought before the Supreme Court. And this case itself is not about pornography.

The case is about our right to satirize, to be irreverent in newspaper columns, in political cartoons, in books and theatres and movies.

There has been a concerted attempt to trivialize this victory for the First Amendment, to sneer at it as insignificant.

I am not a civil rights specialist but I believe that this victory is not only not trivial, it is vital.

I would hate to think of the voices that might be silenced or in jails had the Supreme Court ruled differently.

And I am not ashamed to say that this film for me is a love letter to the Supreme Court of the United States.

As to the objections to Larry Flynt as protagonist: I hardly think the First Amendment would have been put to the test by somebody who, on occasion, used a few profane words. I understand that irony and ambiguity can make some people feel uneasy but I am drawn to both. And for good reason: comfortable certainties in human behavior are rarely worth exploring and, moreover, they are boring. I am a filmmaker, so you do understand that I am not averse to entertaining the audience. Or myself. In truth, I think it essential. Especially when you are trying to get across ideas that I believe are more important than just a car chase.

The ambiguities in Mr. Flynt's actions certainly engaged my interest.

And still do.

Was he a sincere, tenacious battler for freedom of expression or is he a cynical smut peddler who used his constitutional rights to ensure that he would be able to sell more dirty pages?

Is it possible that he is both?

And if he is, is he more one than the other? Which? Was Oscar Schindler, the German industrialist who aided Jews, a humane saver of lives or a Nazi, an exploiter who used slave labor for notably profitable results? Which? Or both?

These issues, and many others, will, I hope, make us think. But is thinking about such matters—even if we are using the pornographer as a protagonist of our story—so dangerous that it could destroy the moral fiber of our society?

Some insist that it will do just that. If this is the case, we have a serious problem on our hands. Including rethinking the wisdom of our Founding Fathers.

The argument that they would be shocked to see what's published today on the pages of *Hustler* doesn't really persuade me that we should turn the clock back. I don't buy that.

First: I am convinced that the English and European politicians of the seventeenth century would have been absolutely alarmed by some of the ideas of our Founding Fathers.

Second: I doubt that they were so ignorant as not to be familiar with Boccaccio or Rabelais or the etchings of the period which would make Larry Flynt blush. Which is probably exaggeration.

Not every country has the guts to rise to its best when challenged by its worst. In this century alone, the countries of Goethe, Schiller, Beethoven, Mozart, Freud, when challenged by the Nazis—they buckled.

The countries of Pushkin, Dostoevsky, Tchaikovsky, Chopin, Kafka, Dvorak, when challenged by the communists, they buckled.

Does anybody believe that Hitler or Stalin could have survived if they had not muzzled the free press? If people could have read, heard and discussed the atrocities committed daily by these regimes?

I doubt that.

And it was always the pornography that was their first target.

Understandably. Who would object to cleaning up smut? As a matter of fact, the majority usually welcomes such high moral purpose. But how surprised this same majority was, once they realized that the official definition of smut no longer included only pornographers, prostitutes and homosexuals. The Nazis quickly added Jews, Blacks, Slavs. The Communists expanded the list to include Christians, Moslems, the capitalists and all of western culture. Finally both regimes commonly labeled anybody who didn't agree with the official regulations and taste as criminal enemies of the state.

To regain their lost freedoms was not cheap for these people. Millions paid for it with their lives.

Maybe I am oversensitive about these issues because of my life experience but I really believe that it is a sign of ignorance or over-security to think that our freedoms are a permanent gift, without daily obligations, that nothing will happen to us if we bend our Constitution a little to satisfy a particular group or ideology.

The problem is that even in the most civilized societies the demagogues are always in wait, ready and testing. They are indefatigable and we will never entirely prevail over them. And that is OK.

But if we stop resisting them, they will prevail over us. And that is not OK.

If you open the door to censorship just a little, it never stays open just a little and the draft that follows is always more than chilling.

That's why the real hero of my film is not a person but the Supreme Court of the United States.

Our country is the strongest country in the world not because it is the biggest or the most populous. Our country is the strongest because it is the freest. And if my film disturbs some people because they must digest its points through an uncomfortable character, then, I am sorry, I have turn to a voice from the seventeenth century: John Milton of *Paradise Lost* fame writes in his "Areopagitika about the freedom of the press" something like this: if a stomach is unable to distinguish healthy food from a bad one, then it is the stomach who is sick.

TOPICS FOR DISCUSSION AND WRITING

1. In both the forward to Flynt's autobiography and in his speech, how does Forman defend his decision to make a movie about Larry Flynt?

2. In the middle of his speech to the National Press Club, Forman talks about *irony* and *ambiguity*. What does he mean by these two terms and what is the point he's making by contrasting them to "comfortable certainties"? Do you prefer "certainties" or "ambiguities" in your own life? Explain.

3. In the same speech, Forman describes the progressive erosion of freedoms under the Nazis and Communists in Europe. Is his argument an example of *slippery slope* or is he providing justifiable examples in support of his position? (See Slippery Slope in Chapter 6.)

4. Why is the National Press Club a "safe" audience for Forman to present his argument? How might he have presented a similar argument to a less "safe" audience? Can you suggest such an audience, one less inclined to think favorably of Forman's position?

5. Write an extended definition of *pornography*. (Follow the sequence suggested in Writing Assignment 13 in Chapter 5.)

Controlling Offensive Speech on the Internet

The Communications Decency Act

In 1996, Congress passed and the President signed into law the Communications Decency Act (the CDA) to protect children from "indecent" and "patently offensive" material on the Internet. The act made it a crime to knowingly send or display "indecent" material over the Internet. On June 26, 1997, the Supreme Court declared the Act unconstitutional on the grounds that it violated protections of free speech under the First Amendment. (For the precise wording of the First Amendment, see the introduction to this chapter.) From the beginning, opposition to the Act had been strong, and thus the Court's decision in the case of *Reno* (Attorney General Janet Reno, on behalf of the United States Justice Department) *v. The American Civil Liberties Union* (the principal plaintiff in the case) came as no surprise. Soon after the enactment of the CDA, the Federal District

Court in Philadelphia struck it down. The Supreme Court affirmed their decision in its June 26, 1997 ruling.

Making a distinction between "indecent" and "obscene," the Supreme Court did not consider the issue of obscenity, which is already covered by other statutes and therefore was not addressed in the CDA. This act was attempting to add "indecent" to material regulated by statute. The Columbia Encyclopedia attempts to clarify the legal meaning of "obscenity":

> **obscenity,** in law, anything that tends to corrupt public morals by its indecency. The words *obscenity* and *obscene* are not, however, technical legal terms and are not susceptible of exact definition, since the moral concepts that the terms connote vary from time to time and also from place to place. The meaning may also vary according to the context in which it is used, although usually it relates to sexual impurity. In the 1950s the U.S. Supreme Court began to relax rules prohibiting the possession, sale, and distribution of obscene material, often called pornography, but in 1973 that trend was reversed. The court ruled that material that appealed to prurient interest in sex and that did not have serious literary, artistic, political, or scientific value could be banned as obscene. It ruled that a national definition of obscenity was not necessary and, therefore, that communities could develop local standards within the court's guidelines. The decision on whether material falls within a definition of obscene is usually made by a jury.

The Random House Unabridged Dictionary defines **indecency** as "the quality or condition of being indecent; impropriety or immodesty; obscenity or indelicacy." Thus we see that the line between "obscene" and "indecent" remains problematic as the controversies discussed in this chapter attest. (See discussions of Definition in Chapter 5.)

Opinion of the Supreme Court

In reaching their decision, the Supreme Court Justices sympathized with the goal of protecting children, but put First Amendment protections first. Whenever the Court reaches its decision on each case, one or more justices write the opinion or opinions of the Court, often setting important precedents for future legal cases. In this case, Justice John Paul Stevens wrote the opinion for the majority.

> At issue is the constitutionality of two statutory provisions enacted to protect minors from "indecent" and "patently offensive" communications on the Internet. Notwithstanding the legitimacy and importance of the congressional goal of protecting children from harmful materials, we agree with the three-judge panel District Court that the statute abridges "the freedom of speech" protected by the First Amendment. . . .

Stevens's first concern lay with the vagueness of the language, "indecent" and "patently offensive." Would a "serious discussion about birth control practices, homosexuality, . . . or the consequences of prison rape . . . violate the Communications Decency Act"?

He went on to write,

> It is true that we have repeatedly recognized the governmental interest in protecting children from harmful materials. But that interest does not justify an unnecessarily broad suppression of speech addressed to adults. . . .
>
> In arguing that the CDA does not so diminish adult communication, the Government [Congress and the President, who had passed and signed the bill] relies on the incorrect factual premise that prohibiting a transmission whenever it is known that one of its recipients is a minor would not interfere with adult-to-adult communication. The findings of the District Court make clear that this premise is untenable. Given the size of the potential audience for most messages, in the absence of a viable age verification process, the sender must be charged with knowing that one or more minors will likely view it. Knowledge that, for instance, one or more members of a 100 person chat group will be minors and therefore that it would be a crime to send the group an indecent message would surely burden communication among adults. The District Court found that at the time of trial existing technology did not include any effective method for a sender to prevent minors from obtaining access to its communications on the Internet without also denying access to adults. . . .
>
> Under the CDA, a parent allowing her 17-year-old to use the family computer to obtain information on the Internet that she, in her parental judgment, deems appropriate could face a lengthy prison term. Similarly, a parent who sent his 17-year-old college freshman information on birth control via e-mail could be incarcerated even though neither he, his child, nor anyone in their home community, found the material "indecent" or "patently offensive," if the college town's community thought otherwise. . . .
>
> . . . The Government [arguing in *support* of the Communications Decency Act] asserts that, in addition to its interest in protecting children, its "equally significant" interest in fostering the growth of the Internet provides an independent basis for upholding the constitutionality of the CDA. The Government apparently assumes that the unregulated availability of "indecent" and "patently offensive" material on the Internet is driving countless citizens away from the medium because of the risk of exposing themselves or their children to harmful material.
>
> We find this argument singularly unpersuasive. The dramatic expansion of this new marketplace of ideas contradicts the factual basis of this contention. The record demonstrates that the growth of the Internet [which Justice Stevens referred to as the "town crier" of the modern age] has been and continues to be phenomenal. As a matter of constitutional tradition, in the absence of evidence to the contrary, we presume that government regulation of the content of speech is more likely to interfere with the free exchange of ideas than to encourage it. The interest in encouraging freedom of expression in a democratic society outweighs any theoretical but unproven benefit of censorship. . . .

Justice Sandra Day O'Connor wrote a dissenting opinion in which she generally concurred with the majority but disagreed on some points. She used the word "zones" to describe particular physical places where minors have traditionally been denied access without interfering with adult access—pornography in adult bookstores and adult dance shows, for example.

She identifies

> a world with two characteristics that make it possible to create "adult zones": geography and identity. A minor can see an adult dance show only if he enters an establishment that provides such entertainment. And should he attempt to do so, the minor will not be able to conceal completely his identity (or, consequently, his age). Thus, the twin characteristics of geography and identity enable the establishment's proprietor to prevent children from entering the establishment, but to let adults inside.

She, acknowledges, however, that

> the electronic world is fundamentally different. . . . Cyberspace allows speakers and listeners to mask their identities. Cyberspace undeniably reflects some form of geography; chat rooms and Web sites, for example exist at fixed "locations" on the Internet. Since users can transmit and receive messages on the Internet without revealing anything about their identities or ages, however, it is not currently possible to exclude persons from accessing certain messages on the basis of their identity.

In spite of these differences between "physical" places and cyberspace in limiting access only to those under 18, O'Connor found that

> the "indecency transmission" provision [of the CDA] makes it a crime to transmit knowingly an indecent message to a person the sender knows is under 18 years of age. The "specific person" provision proscribes the same conduct, although it does not as explicitly require the sender to know that the intended recipient of his indecent message is a minor. . . . So construed, both provisions are constitutional as applied to a conversation involving only an adult and one or more minors e.g., when an adult speaker sends an e-mail knowing the addressee is a minor, or when an adult and minor converse by themselves or with other minors in a chat room. . . . Restricting what the adult may say to the minors in no way restricts the adult's ability to communicate with other adults. He is not prevented from speaking indecently to other adults in a chat room (because there are no other adults participating in the conversation) and he remains free to send indecent e-mails to other adults. The relevant universe contains only one adult, and the adult in that universe has the power to refrain from using indecent speech and consequently to keep all such speech within the room in an "adult zone."

O'Connor's point, with which Chief Justice William H. Renhquist concurred, seems to be that specific provisions of the Communications Decency Act did not have to infringe "on adult speech in *all* situations." They acknowledged the serious problem of children's easy access to "indecent" material on the Internet, and thus wanted to go on record in support of some features of the law, although they ultimately joined the rest of the court in rejecting the CDA.

TOPICS FOR DISCUSSION AND WRITING

1. Write a short summary of Justice Stevens's reasoning in overturning the Communications Decency Act. (See Summaries in Chapter 3.)

2. Justice Stevens, near the beginning of his argument above, mentions difficulty with the vagueness of the term "indecent." Write your own definition of the term so that it could be used to clarify material labeled "indecent" for children on the Internet. For distinctions between "indecent" and "obscene," look back at the Columbia Encyclopedia's definition of "obscene." (See also Language: An Abstract System of Symbols in Chapter 5.)

3. In your own words explain what Sandra Day O'Connor, in her dissenting position, means by "zones." She talks about them both in terms of the real world and the world of Cyberspace. Do you find her analogy here useful for her argument? (See discussions of analogy in False Analogy in Chapter 6 and Analogy in Chapter 14.)

Unshackling Net Speech

Joshua Quittner

In the following article, *Time* magazine columnist Joshua Quittner explains the Supreme Court decision and also discusses alternatives to protecting children from indecent material such as software browsers that can filter inappropriate material and industry-designed rating systems.

One of the key ideas behind the Internet was to build a computer network that could withstand a nuclear holocaust. Last week the Net proved its resilience in the face of another sort of attack. The Communications Decency Act, signed into law by President Clinton last year, was designed to protect children by prohibiting "indecent" speech or images from being sent through cyberspace. But even before Congress passed the legislation, free speech advocates were blasting it as an unacceptable infringement on the First Amendment.

Now the Supreme Court has agreed that the CDA is precisely that. The court, while disagreeing about some issues in the case, unanimously concluded that reducing online communication to a safe-for-kids standard is unconstitutional. "The interest in encouraging freedom of expression in a democratic society," wrote Justice John Paul Stevens, " outweighs any theoretical but unproven benefit of censorship."

It was a decisive—though not unexpected—victory for civil libertarians. Opponents of the CDA, led by the American Civil Liberties Union and the American

Library Association as well as dozens of other plaintiffs, including Planned Parenthood and Human Rights Watch, had argued that the statute was so vaguely worded and ill defined that discussions in online chat rooms about abortion or contraception could have attracted the vice squad. Says Ira Glasser, executive director of the A.C.L.U.: "It would have criminalized all sorts of speech that would never have been criminalized before."

And that, said the court, could have crippled the Internet, which now has some 50 million users. Indeed, wrote Stevens in his 15-page opinion, the CDA threatened "to torch a large segment of the Internet community." Clearly the Justices, like many newbies before them, were swept up in the global reach and boundless potential of the medium. "Any person with a phone line can become a town crier with a voice that resonates farther than it could from any soapbox," Stevens observed.

Minutes after the ruling was handed down, the court could have seen that phenomenon in action. At the click of a mouse, the text of the opinion was piped across the Net and plastered on computer sites from New York City to Australia. A laptop computer in New York was used to "Netcast" the audio portion of an A.C.L.U. press conference to all corners of the earth. Chat rooms and message boards were choked with Net folk weighing in about what it all meant. Computer jocks even ventured forth into the sunlight for real-time, non-virtual victory parties. "Let today be the first day of a new American Revolution—a Digital American Revolution!" said Mike Godwin, attorney for the Electronic Frontier Foundation, addressing a crowd of revelers in San Francisco.

CDA proponents were every bit as vociferous in defeat as their counterparts were in victory. Members of the anti-porn group Enough Is Enough, led by former Gary Hart co-scandalist Donna Rice Hughes, demonstrated outside the Supreme Court with signs that read HONK IF YOU HATE PORN and CHILD MOLESTERS ARE LOOKING FOR VICTIMS ON THE INTERNET. Legislators seized the moment as well. "Parents are going to have to realize that a computer without any restrictions to children is just as dangerous to their minds and development as a triple-X store," said retiring Indiana Senator Dan Coats, co-author of the CDA. "The court has ignored the clear will of the Executive Branch and the Congress and the clear will of the American people."

In fact, though, the court did not rule that government cannot regulate the Internet. Nor did it alter the long-standing legal prohibition against obscenity, which remains unprotected speech, both on and off the Net. It simply said that the CDA as written was fatally flawed because in trying to protect children it would also keep adults from getting material they have legal right to see. That gives CDA forces hope that they'll be able to revisit the issue. "The opinion gives us a good road map to what the courts will allow," says Bob Flores, senior counsel of the National Law Center for Children and Families. Vows Don Hodel, the recently installed president of the Christian Coalition: "We won't accept this as the last word."

Nor, evidently, will the President. The White House began backing away from its support of the clearly doomed CDA months ago. But Administration officials have recently come at the problem from a new angle. They propose to fight technology with technology. This week President Clinton will convene a meeting of Internet providers, family groups and others during which he'll propose to protect kids from indecency with a software fix.

While the details have yet to be worked out, White House staff members hope to talk Website operators into a kind of universal rating system. Combining it with software browsers used to access much of the Net, parents could in theory set their own comfort level and filter out the naughty bits. "If we are to make the Internet a powerful resource for learning, we must give parents and teachers the tools they need to make the Internet safe for children," Clinton said last week. "With the right technology and rating systems, we can help ensure that our children don't end up in the redlight districts of cyberspace."

Good luck. Software filters and online ratings systems have been around since before the CDA was born, and they've always been beset with problems. Recently, for instance, when Microsoft began backing a ratings standard known as RSACI and started including the filter as part of its browser, Internet Explorer, the company quickly found that the "solution" could keep large numbers of viewers away from its news site, MSNBC. Microsoft quietly removed the rating. The problem should have been foreseen. News, after all, frequently covers violent, adult-oriented subjects, which puts many news stories into the same verboten range as porn. While RSACI officials have proposed offering a news exemption, it's hard to see how that could work. Readers of the sex-oriented newspaper *Screw,* for instance, might well consider it just as newsworthy as the *New York Times.*

Still, the First Amendment notwithstanding, many Americans feel that parents have a legitimate right to protect their kids from inappropriate material. "You can't connect every high school in America to the Net unless there's some way to ensure that kids won't see what they're not supposed to," says Lawrence Lessig, a Harvard Law School professor and author of an essay, "Reading the Constitution in Cyberspace," that was cited repeatedly by Justice O'Connor in a minority opinion. "It can't be the case that Congress has no power to regulate here."

It can be the case, however, that Congress's power is largely symbolic. Even if the government figures out a constitutional way to impose limited censorship online, these rules can apply only within the U.S.—and the Internet is international. If parents want to control what their children see, they'll probably have to resort to an old-fashioned, low-tech solution: they'll have to supervise their kid's time online.

TOPICS FOR DISCUSSION AND WRITING

1. What kind of discussions—ones that many insist constitute important features of the Internet—would have been at risk had The Communications Decency Act been upheld?

2. What particular problem does the Internet pose when American legislators, on their own, try to regulate it?

3. Given the complexities of monitoring the Internet, technical as well as legal, what does Quittner suggest is the only real answer to controlling children's exposure to inappropriate material? Do you think this is a reasonable expectation?

A Free Web Benefits Public Health

Gloria Feldt

As Joshua Quittner pointed out in the article above, organizations around the world were quick to post their reactions to the Supreme Court Decision on the Internet. Planned Parenthood, one of the plaintiffs in the case against the CDA, was one such group. They saw the decision as a victory for public health.

Today's Supreme Court decision overturning the Communications Decency Act is a victory for freedom in cyberspace and for the public health. It means that the national Planned Parenthood Web site, www.ppfa.org/ppfa, can remain online, and uncensored.

A crucial aspect of today's ruling is that it allows people to continue to use the Internet as a private information and referral source for reproductive health needs. People wanting to learn in private, for instance, how to put on a condom have been able to do so via the Internet by visiting the national Planned Parenthood home page. And thanks to today's Supreme Court ruling, that kind of information will stay available to Americans and to the global on-line community. People as far away as Russia, Swaziland, and Cambodia have e-mailed to thank us because they found needed birth control information on our Web site.

More than 80 years ago, Planned Parenthood's founder, Margaret Sanger, was jailed on obscenity charges for providing birth control information. Today, the rates of HIV infection and unintended pregnancy should make it unthinkable to censor reproductive health information, whether in a clinic, a bookstore, on the Internet, or in a school library or classroom. But many people, including many lawmakers, remain attached to the myth that keeping young people in the dark about their own bodies and about sexual health will keep them innocent and safe. So generations after Margaret Sanger, the struggle against censorship continues, accompanied by false rhetoric about protecting families.

Planned Parenthood believes knowledge will protect young people more effectively than censorship. We have produced a new video kit, "Talking About Sex," to help parents talk to pre-teens and young teens about puberty, sex, and their own family's values. As for the issue of supervising Web browsing by young people, we feel today's Supreme Court ruling leaves that responsibility where it should be—in the hands of families, not the government.

TOPICS FOR DISCUSSION AND WRITING

1. What, according to Gloria Feldt, is the "public health" victory resulting from the Supreme Court's decision on the CDA? Do you share Feldt's position?

2. Research other positions taken by Planned Parenthood to develop a profile of this organization, which has played such a prominent role in issues surrounding reproductive rights.

Letters to the Editor

Even prior to the Court decision, citizens were writing letters to newspapers expressing their concerns. One letter writer suggested that, under specific terms of the CDA, if he were to use the Internet to send a high school student an analysis of Molly Bloom's soliloquy in James Joyce's celebrated novel, *Ulysses,* he could be sentenced to two years in prison and fined up to $250,000. In the letters below, two readers of the *New York Times* disagree on the issue.

INTERNET NEEDS DECENCY RULE TO SHIELD YOUNG

To the Editor:

Kristen Farron (letter, March 23), in arguing against the Government's setting up decency rules for the Internet, says "it is the parents' responsibility to watch their children, not the Government's."

Would Ms. Farron abolish laws forbidding the sale of cigarettes and alcohol to minors because "it's the parents' responsibility to watch their children"? Because it is impossible for parents constantly to monitor their children, especially as their children get older, sometimes the community, and government, must serve in loco parentis.

Ms. Farron is also afraid that she will not have access to the material she needs for school work. Like Ms. Farron, I am a high school student. I recently used the Internet to complete a science project on muscular dystrophy, and the Internet was indeed an invaluable tool. But I cannot imagine a school project that would require material that the Government would term indecent.

As wonderful as the Internet is, it is not sacred. There is no reason that the laws that govern the distribution of other "indecent" material to children in the form of magazines and videos should not apply to the Internet as well.

Sara Butler
New York, March 25, 1997

GOVERNMENT SHOULDN'T RULE ON INTERNET CONTENT

To the Editor:

Sara Butler (letter, March 28) makes a crucial error in her defense of the Internet indecency legislation: indecency is not the same as obscenity. While Ms. Butler is unable to imagine a project that would require material the Government would term indecent, I can think of several.

A report on the transmission of AIDS through sexual intercourse or one on abortion might contain material that could be termed "indecent" under more than one set of community standards. In fact, a paper discussing J. D. Salinger's "Catcher in the Rye" might well violate such standards. A paper detailing Holocaust atrocities might also be affected by this legislation.

Contrary to Ms. Butler's assumptions, and those of many other individuals throughout the country who have seen no reason to oppose this law, indecency refers not only to pornography but also to any sexually or otherwise explicit material, without regard to artistic or social merit.

Additionally, laws already governing distribution of pornography to minors can and have been applied to cases involving the Internet. No new legislation is needed to accomplish this.

> Jon Lasser
> Baltimore, March 28, 1997

TOPIC FOR DISCUSSION AND WRITING

After reading the Supreme Court Decision on the Communications Decency Act and the reactions to it, write your own reply to one of the letters to the editor or compose your own letter on the issue to your local or campus newspaper or post your letter on the Internet and report on responses you receive. (See Hidden Assumptions—Audience Awareness in Chapter 3.)

Ongoing Efforts to Limit Pornography

The Problem: "Cybersmut"

Many who vigorously opposed the Communications Decency Act and applauded the Supreme Court decision on First Amendment grounds remain concerned about the amount of "cybersmut" on the Internet. While lawmakers in all branches of government have been debating the issue of indecency and censorship to be found there, "indecent speech" and "display" in cyberspace have grown into what some estimate to be a billion dollar industry. Each fall, while the major Comdex computer trade show is spread out over Las Vegas, two or three thousand strong, a smaller but lively show is giving them competition. AdultDex, the trade association for the x-rated computer industry, draws a big crowd and represents the most lucrative of all online businesses, raking in more than $1 billion a year. As one person put it, "Comdex is the classroom, AdultDex is recess."

According to a National Public Radio business report addressing sex on the Internet, entrepreneurs can net over a million dollars a year selling a wide variety of sexual activities through credit card billing on their relatively low-overhead Web sites. With such huge profits to be made and the nation's seemingly insatiable appetite for sexually explicit titillation, we cannot be surprised to learn of this growth industry.

A Father, a Friend, a Seller of Cyberporn

Seth Schiesel

Internet entrepreneur Joe Warshowsky makes no apologies for his business, even as he proclaims some regrets. While Web site operators like Warshowsky claim they screen out underage customers, pornographic images are easily available at many sites. Anyone can end up in a chat room inappropriate for children. For example, when we were researching sexual harassment, innocent searches led to potentially pornographic chat rooms, and anyone can encounter "accidents by design." Unscrupulous pornographers have been known to name their sites with very slight spelling corruptions of terms such as Microsoft or a seemingly safe "Whitehouse."

Joe Warshowsky used to help teen-age gang members. Until about two years ago, he spent his days, and some nights, at a publicly financed group home in Rockford, III., encouraging Latin Kings and Vice Lords to "challenge their values, make them think a little differently, that there's a different way to solving problems than shooting someone."

A 47-year-old father of six, Mr. Warshowsky is in a different line of work these days. He runs a lucrative live pornography site on the World Wide Web called Videofantasy.com, where young women disrobe and pose for digital voyeurs who pay the service $5.95 a minute.

"I miss it terribly," Mr. Warshowsky said in an interview on Friday, speaking of his old job. "I loved working with kids. Kids like me for some reason. They find it easy to talk to me: I think because I'm not a judgmental individual."

The Communications Decency Act of 1996, which the Supreme Court struck down on Thursday on First Amendment grounds, was meant to keep the work of people like Mr. Warshowsky away from children. Pornography has become one of the Internet's main growth engines, sowing the computer network with millions of explicit images and rich opportunities for technology-savvy entrepreneurs while provoking widespread parental consternation.

The act, which never went into effect because of a stay issued by a lower court, prescribed penalties of up to $250,000 in fines and two years in prison for those who displayed indecent material accessible to minors on line.

Not that Mr. Warshowsky was worried. Few minors can afford to spend $6 a minute for anything, and Video Fantasy verifies the age of each of its 20,000 customers by calling them over a normal telephone line, Mr. Warshowsky said.

"You can't access anything of an adult nature until you're registered as part of our data base," he said. "You can't just click on pictures and see pornographic stuff."

A cursory visit to Video Fantasy's Web site supported Mr. Warshowsky's claim. The site's public areas might earn a PG-13 rating from the Motion Picture Association.

TOPICS FOR DISCUSSION AND WRITING

1. Selling sex on the Internet raises many moral issues including possible exploitation of those who actually perform on line. Discuss what you think about such activities and whether a person is morally justified in making money in this way, either as a performer or as the individual who runs an "adult entertainment" site. If you were offered a lucrative job creating or maintaining one such profitable pornographic Web site on the Net, would you be tempted to take it?

2. See if you can find accounts of others who make large profits running "adult entertainment sites." Check statistics to see if the industry has grown since 1998.

The Controversy: Limiting Access to Selected Sites

Who determines what is "obscene," what is "indecent," what is "art," what is educational material, what is appropriate for children, what is protected speech? As these questions continue to confound both sides in the dispute, Congress has made repeated efforts to reintroduce government controls. Bills cracking down on pedophiles on the Internet passed without a whisper of opposition, but then laws controlling pedophilia already exist. In 1998, Senator Dan Coats, hoping to circumvent objections raised against the Communications Decency Act (see above), introduced the Child Online Protection Act (COPA), requiring Web sites "harmful to minors" to put up barriers preventing access by those 17 and under. COPA sought to prohibit children's access to "harmful" material by penalizing commercial purveyors of such content if they provided easy access. In 1999, Federal Judge Lowell A. Reed of the District Court in Philadelphia struck it down, fearing it "could result in the censoring of constitutionally protected speech." Another bill sponsored by Senator John McCain would require schools and libraries, whose Internet connections are federally funded, to use filters for "indecent speech." Many individuals, schools, and libraries have already turned to blocking software to filter inappropriate material, but government mandates of any kind, even parental control, continue to prove controversial. Congress, in response to public demand, will continue to introduce restrictive legislation; the court will continue to review such laws.

In addition to concerns about pornography, the debate carries over into what students may *post* as well as read online, as the story about Aaron Smith's troubles with his Chihuahua Web site reveals (see below). And as the number of hate sites promoting virulent racism and homophobia grows, so do worries about how to address the issue within the limits of the First Amendment.

The Technology

With so much talk about blocking software at the heart of current debate, we need a rudimentary understanding of how such software works. PICS, the Platform for Internet Content Selection, is a technology standard created by the World Wide Web Consortium, a nonprofit alliance of Internet developers, in reaction to the threat of the Communications Decency Act. Their primary concern has been with *government* controls and so they have been addressing ways in which the industry itself could offer choices. Not a rating system itself, PICS is a technical set of Web-oriented protocols, designed to give parents and content providers an easy means to filter what they think inappropriate for children.

A Tool That Filters the Web, for Better or Worse

A Diagram

A number of organizations, using PICS technology, have designed blocking software to reflect their particular worldview. For example: Catholic Telecom Inc. represents Catholic values; CYBERsitter is vigilantly anti-pornography, pro-family; Net Nanny is rated by a wide variety of evaluators including parents, employees, and others; Net Shepherd has rated a much larger number of sites than any of the competition and tends to be general in its outlook. Some services provide their own selective ratings, others gather information from users and outside volunteers. The number of rating services is growing each year, allowing viewers to filter what comes in and also what a child can send out. Without such a filter, children can indiscriminately give names and credit card numbers to any site that asks, as well as find unsuitable material online. The flow chart that follows illustrates how Web filters work.

A Tool That Filters the Web, for Better or Worse

The World Wide Web Consortium has endorsed a technical standard for filtering electronic information on the Web, called PICS. The new standard is being cheered as a tool for concerned parents, but at the same time it is being attacked by civil libertarians as a means of censorship.

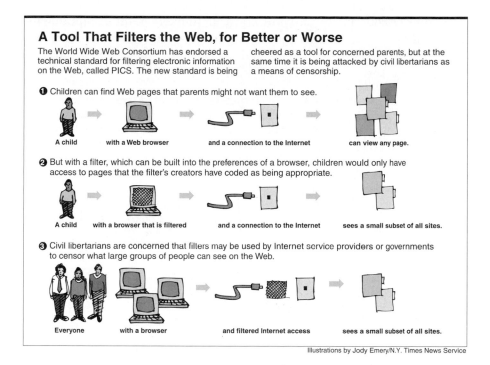

❶ Children can find Web pages that parents might not want them to see.

A child   with a Web browser   and a connection to the Internet   can view any page.

❷ But with a filter, which can be built into the preferences of a browser, children would only have access to pages that the filter's creators have coded as being appropriate.

A child   with a browser that is filtered   and a connection to the Internet   sees a small subset of all sites.

❸ Civil libertarians are concerned that filters may be used by Internet service providers or governments to censor what large groups of people can see on the Web.

Everyone   with a browser   and filtered Internet access   sees a small subset of all sites.

Illustrations by Jody Emery/N.Y. Times News Service

TOPICS FOR DISCUSSION AND WRITING

1. In your own words, write a paragraph explaining filtering software that blocks designated Web sites.

2. How effective do you find Internet rating systems and filters? Do ratings for movies and TV programs work? Would young people be more attracted to Web sites tagged as containing "indecent" material? From your own experience, do most parents depend on such systems?

Who Should Make the Decisions?

Opinion continues to be divided on how and if to control access to information on the Internet, a question not limited to the United States. Reflecting the worldwide scope of the Internet, the Bertelsmann Foundation, a German policy research organization, in cooperation with American First Amendment experts, published a lengthy Memorandum on Self-Regulation of the Internet, hoping to create an international rating and filtering system. Their aim has been to avoid government regulation by urging the Internet industry to create its own avenues of choice. But even such optional programs come under fire from civil libertarians and free speech advocates always on the lookout for threats of censorship.

Esther Dyson, one of the most powerful thinkers in the computing industry and usually an ardent defender of free speech on the Internet, sees a difference between individuals and government. In her book, *Release 2.0,* she expresses concerns about

> zealous free-speech advocates who forget that freedom of speech includes the right to be selective about content—as long as that choice is not imposed on others. One organization called Peacefire has raised objections not only to the selection of sites CYBERsitter has seen fit to block, but to CYBERsitter's insistence on keeping its list of blocked sites encrypted so that users . . . can't easily find out what's blocked. . . .
>
> What organizations like Peacefire seem to forget is that the issue here is not that there should be no content control, but that there should be no content control *imposed by government.* As long as people are free to choose CYBERsitter or avoid it, this is not censorship, but optional filtering. [Peacefire and its founder Bennett Haselton—see "From His Dorm Room," on page 318—can be found at www.peacefire.org]

But others like Virginia State Legislator Robert Marshal, writing for the Family Research Council in Washington D.C. (see his essay on page 310), express grave concerns about using the free speech argument as a screen to protect pornography on the Internet.

The American public remains confused about this avalanche of new issues. Ken Dautrich, who conducted an elaborate poll on Americans' attitude to the First Amendment and issues that depend on it, was concerned about a slide from sensible censoring of pornography to limitations on other freedoms. Commenting on inconsistencies he found in people's opinions, he said he was encouraged that people do understand the "slippery slope" concept. According to his study:

> Nearly 9 in 10 agree that once any restriction is placed on a freedom, it becomes much easier to place further restrictions.

And yet people are willing to ignore the peril, he said, "particularly when sexually explicit and/or offensive material is at stake." (For more on the fallacy of "slippery slope," see Slippery Slope in Chapter 6 and Topic for Discussion and Writing #3 on page 286).

Fahrenheit 451.2: Is Cyberspace Burning? How Rating and Blocking Proposals May Torch Free Speech on the Internet

After the Communications Decency Act was overturned, the American Civil Liberties Union (the principal plaintiff in the Supreme Court case which overturned the CDA), found reason for concern about additional censorship through the use of filters. In response to White House proclamations applauding ongoing efforts to limit children's access to inappropriate Internet sites, the ACLU issued a position paper, "Fahrenheit 451.2: Is Cyberspace Burning? How Rating and Blocking Proposals May Torch Free Speech on the Internet" which they circulated on the Internet. A selection from this paper follows. For decades, the American Civil Liberties Union has been on the front lines in defense of free speech and civil liberties of the individual. Despite its usually liberal profile, it has provided legal support for a wide range of causes including not only the free speech of journalists, but also the right of Nazis to parade in Skokie, Illinois, an action that earned them considerable criticism from their traditional supporters.

EXECUTIVE SUMMARY

In the landmark case *Reno v. ACLU,* the Supreme Court overturned the Communications Decency Act, declaring that the Internet deserves the same high level of free speech protection afforded to books and other printed matter.

But today, all that we have achieved may now be lost, if not in the bright flames of censorship then in the dense smoke of the many ratings and blocking schemes promoted by some of the very people who fought for freedom.

The ACLU and others in the cyber-liberties community were genuinely alarmed by the tenor of a recent White House summit meeting on Internet censorship at which industry leaders pledged to create a variety of schemes to regulate and block controversial online speech.

But it was not any one proposal or announcement that caused our alarm; rather, it was the failure to examine the longer-term implications for the Internet of rating and blocking schemes.

The White House meeting was clearly the first step away from the principle that protection of the electronic word is analogous to protection of the printed word. Despite the Supreme Court's strong rejection of a broadcast analogy for the Internet, government and industry leaders alike are now inching toward the dangerous and incorrect position that the Internet is like television, and should be rated and censored accordingly.

Is Cyberspace burning? Not yet, perhaps. But where there's smoke, there's fire.

"Any content-based regulation of the Internet, no matter how benign the purpose, could burn the global village to roast the pig."
—U.S. Supreme Court majority decision, *Reno v. ACLU* (June 26, 1997)

INTRODUCTION

In his chilling (and prescient) novel about censorship, "Fahrenheit 451," author Ray Bradbury describes a futuristic society where books are outlawed. Fahrenheit 451 is, of course, the temperature at which books burn.

In Bradbury's novel—and in the physical world—people censor the printed word by burning books. But in the virtual world, one can just as easily censor controversial speech by banishing it to the farthest corners of cyberspace using rating and blocking programs. Today, will Fahrenheit, version 451.2—a new kind of virtual censorship—be the temperature at which cyberspace goes up in smoke?

The first flames of Internet censorship appeared two years ago, with the introduction of the Federal Communications Decency Act (CDA), outlawing "indecent" online speech. But in the landmark case *Reno v. ACLU,* the Supreme Court overturned the CDA, declaring that the Internet is entitled to the highest level of free speech protection. In other words, the Court said that online speech deserved the protection afforded to books and other printed matter.

Today, all that we have achieved may now be lost, if not in the bright flames of censorship then in the dense smoke of the many ratings and blocking schemes promoted by some of the very people who fought for freedom. And in the end, we may find that the censors have indeed succeeded in "burning down the house to roast the pig." . . .

SIX REASONS WHY SELF-RATING SCHEMES ARE WRONG FOR THE INTERNET

To begin with, the notion that citizens should "self-rate" their speech is contrary to the entire history of free speech in America. A proposal that we rate our online speech is no less offensive to the First Amendment than a proposal that publishers of books and magazines rate each and every article or story, or a proposal that everyone engaged in a street corner conversation rate his or her comments. But that is exactly what will happen to books, magazines, and any kind of speech that appears online under a self-rating scheme.

In order to illustrate the very practical consequences of these schemes, consider the following six reasons, and their accompanying examples, illustrating why the ACLU is against self-rating:

Reason #1: Self-Rating Schemes Will Cause Controversial Speech To Be Censored

Kiyoshi Kuromiya, founder and sole operator of Critical Path AIDS Project, has a web site that includes safer sex information written in street language with explicit diagrams, in order to reach the widest possible audience. Kuromiya doesn't want to apply the rating "crude" or "explicit" to his speech, but if he doesn't, his site will be blocked as an unrated site. If he does rate, his speech will be lumped in with "pornography" and blocked from view. Under either choice, Kuromiya has been effectively blocked from reaching a large portion of his intended audience—teenage Internet users—as well as adults.

As this example shows, the consequences of rating are far from neutral. The ratings themselves are all pejorative by definition, and they result in certain speech being blocked.

The White House has compared Internet ratings to "food labels"—but that analogy is simply wrong. Food labels provide objective, scientifically verifiable information to help the consumer make choices about what to buy, e.g. the percentage of fat in a food product like milk. Internet ratings are subjective value judgments that result in certain speech being blocked to many viewers. Further, food labels are placed on products that are readily available to consumers—

unlike Internet labels, which would place certain kinds of speech out of reach of Internet users.

What is most critical to this issue is that speech like Kuromiya's is entitled to the highest degree of Constitutional protection. This is why ratings requirements have never been imposed on those who speak via the printed word. Kuromiya could distribute the same material in print form on any street corner or in any bookstore without worrying about having to rate it. In fact, a number of Supreme Court cases have established that the First Amendment does not allow government to compel speakers to say something they don't want to say—and that includes pejorative ratings. There is simply no justification for treating the Internet any differently.

Reason #2: Self-Rating Is Burdensome, Unwieldy, and Costly

Art on the Net is a large, non-profit web site that hosts online "studios" where hundreds of artists display their work. The vast majority of the artwork has no sexual content, although there's an occasional Rubenesque painting. The ratings systems don't make sense when applied to art. Yet Art on the Net would still have to review and apply a rating to the more than 26,000 pages on its site, which would require time and staff that they just don't have. Or, they would have to require the artists themselves to self-rate, an option they find objectionable. If they decline to rate, they will be blocked as an unrated site even though most Internet users would hardly object to the art reaching minors, let alone adults.

As the Supreme Court noted in *Reno v. ACLU,* one of the virtues of the Internet is that it provides "relatively unlimited, low-cost capacity for communication of all kinds." In striking down the CDA, the Court held that imposing age-verification costs on Internet speakers would be "prohibitively expensive for noncommercial—as well as some commercial—speakers." Similarly, the burdensome requirement of self-rating thousands of pages of information would effectively shut most noncommercial speakers out of the Internet marketplace.

The technology of embedding the rating is also far from trivial. In a winning ACLU case that challenged a New York state online censorship statute, *ALA v. Pataki,* one long-time Internet expert testified that he tried to embed an RSACi label in his online newsletter site but finally gave up after several hours.

In addition, the ratings systems are simply unequipped to deal with the diversity of content now available on the Internet. There is perhaps nothing as subjective as a viewer's reaction to art. As history has shown again and again, one woman's masterpiece is another woman's pornography. How can ratings such as "explicit" or "crude" be used to categorize art? Even ratings systems that try to take artistic value into account will be inherently subjective, especially when applied by artists themselves, who will naturally consider their own work to have merit.

The variety of news-related sites on the Web will be equally difficult to rate. Should explicit war footage be labeled "violent" and blocked from view to teenagers? If a long news article has one curse word, is the curse word rated individually, or is the entire story rated and then blocked?

Even those who propose that "legitimate" news organizations should not be required to rate their sites stumble over the question of who will decide what is legitimate news.

Reason #3: Conversation Can't Be Rated

You are in a chat room or a discussion group—one of the thousands of conversational areas of the Net. A victim of sexual abuse has posted a plea for help, and you want to respond. You've heard about a variety of ratings systems, but you've never used one. You read the RSACi web page, but you can't figure out how to rate the discussion of sex and violence in your response. Aware of the penalties for mis-labeling, you decide not to send your message after all. The burdens of self-rating really hit home when applied to the vibrant, conversational areas of the Internet. Most Internet users don't run web pages, but millions of people around the world send messages, short and long, every day, to chat rooms, news groups and mailing lists. A rating requirement for these areas of the Internet would be analogous to requiring all of us to rate our telephone or streetcorner or dinner party or water cooler conversations.

The only other way to rate these areas of cyberspace would be to rate entire chatrooms or news groups rather than individual messages. But most discussion groups aren't controlled by a specific person, so who would be responsible for rating them? In addition, discussion groups that contain some objectionable material would likely also have a wide variety of speech totally appropriate and valuable for minors—but the entire forum would be blocked from view for everyone.

Reason #4: Self-Rating Will Create "Fortress America" on the Internet

You are a native of Papua, New Guinea, and as an anthropologist you have published several papers about your native culture. You create a web site and post electronic versions of your papers, in order to share them with colleagues and other interested people around the world. You haven't heard about the move in America to rate Internet content. You don't know it, but since your site is un-rated none of your colleagues in America will be able to access it.

People from all corners of the globe—people who might otherwise never connect because of their vast geographical differences—can now communicate on the Internet both easily and cheaply. One of the most dangerous aspects of ratings systems is their potential to build borders around American- and foreign-created speech. It is important to remember that today, nearly half of all Internet speech originates from outside the United States.

Even if powerful American industry leaders coerced other countries into adopting American ratings systems, how would these ratings make any sense to a New Guinean? Imagine that one of the anthropology papers explicitly describes a ritual in which teenage boys engage in self-mutilation as part of a rite of passage in achieving manhood. Would you look at it through the eyes of an

American and rate it "torture," or would you rate it "appropriate for minors" for the New Guinea audience?

Reason #5: Self-Ratings Will Only Encourage, Not Prevent, Government Regulation

The webmaster for Betty's Smut Shack, a web site that sells sexually explicit photos, learns that many people won't get to his site if he either rates his site "sexually explicit" or fails to rate at all. He rates his entire web site "okay for minors." A powerful Congressman from the Midwest learns that the site is now available to minors. He is outraged, and quickly introduces a bill imposing criminal penalties for mis-rated sites.

Without a penalty system for mis-rating, the entire concept of a self-ratings system breaks down. The Supreme Court that decided *Reno v. ACLU* would probably agree that the statute theorized above would violate the First Amendment, but as we saw with the CDA, that won't necessarily prevent lawmakers from passing it.

In fact, as noted earlier, a senator from Washington state—home of Industry giant Microsoft, among others—has already proposed a law that creates criminal penalties for mis-rating. Not to be outdone, the filtering software company Safe Surf has proposed the introduction of a virtually identical federal law, including a provision that allows parents to sue speakers for damages if they "negligently" mis-rate their speech.

The example above shows that, despite all good intentions, the application of ratings systems is likely to lead to heavy-handed government censorship. Moreover, the targets of that censorship are likely to be just the sort of relatively powerless and controversial speakers, like the groups Critical Path AIDS Project, Stop Prisoner Rape, Planned Parenthood, Human Rights Watch, and the various gay and lesbian organizations we represented in *Reno v. ACLU*.

Reason #6: Self-Ratings Schemes Will Turn the Internet into a Homogenized Medium Dominated by Commercial Speakers

Huge entertainment conglomerates, such as the Disney Corporation or Time Warner, consult their platoons of lawyers who advise that their web sites must be rated to reach the widest possible audience. They then hire and train staff to rate all of their web pages. Everybody in the world will have access to their speech.

There is no question that there may be some speakers on the Internet for whom the ratings systems will impose only minimal burdens; the large, powerful corporate speakers with the money to hire legal counsel and staff to apply the necessary ratings. The commercial side of the Net continues to grow, but so far the democratic nature of the Internet has put commercial speakers on equal footing with all of the other non-commercial and individual speakers.

Today, it is just as easy to find the Critical Path AIDS web site as it is to find the Disney site. Both speakers are able to reach a worldwide audience. But mandatory Internet self-rating could easily turn the most participatory communications medium the world has yet seen into a bland, homogenized, medium dominated by powerful American corporate speakers. . . .

CONCLUSION

The ACLU has always favored providing Internet users, especially parents, with more information. We welcomed, for example, the American Library Association's announcement at the White House summit of The Librarian's Guide to Cyberspace for Parents and Kids, a "comprehensive brochure and Web site combining Internet terminology, safety tips, site selection advice and more than 50 of the most educational and entertaining sites available for children on the Internet."

In *Reno v. ACLU*, we noted that Federal and state governments are already vigorously enforcing existing obscenity, child pornography, and child solicitation laws on the Internet. In addition, Internet users must affirmatively seek out speech on the Internet; no one is caught by surprise.

In fact, many speakers on the Net provide preliminary information about the nature of their speech. The ACLU's site on America Online, for example, has a message on its home page announcing that the site is a "free speech zone." Many sites offering commercial transactions on the Net contain warnings concerning the security of Net information. Sites containing sexually explicit material often begin with a statement describing the adult nature of the material. Chat rooms and newsgroups have names that describe the subject being discussed. Even individual e-mail messages contain a subject line.

The preliminary information available on the Internet has several important components that distinguish it from all the ratings systems discussed above: (1) it is created and provided by the speaker; (2) it helps the user decide whether to read any further; (3) speakers who choose not to provide such information are not penalized; (4) it does not result in the automatic blocking of speech by an entity other than the speaker or reader before the speech has ever been viewed. Thus, the very nature of the Internet reveals why more speech is always a better solution than censorship for dealing with speech that someone may find objectionable.

It is not too late for the Internet community to slowly and carefully examine these proposals and to reject those that will transform the Internet from a true marketplace of ideas into just another mainstream, lifeless medium with content no more exciting or diverse than that of television.

Civil libertarians, human rights organizations, librarians and Internet users, speakers and providers all joined together to defeat the CDA. We achieved a stunning victory, establishing a legal framework that affords the Internet the highest constitutional protection. We put a quick end to a fire that was all but visible and threatening. The fire next time may be more difficult to detect—and extinguish.

TOPICS FOR DISCUSSION AND WRITING

1. Read the six reasons offered by the ACLU in "Fahrenheit 451.2" and state each in one or two clear sentences. (See Premises and Conclusions in Chapter 3.) Which reason do you find most compelling? Which the least compelling? Why?

2. Identify the analogies the ACLU uses in presenting its argument and comment on their effectiveness. (See False Analogy in Chapter 6 and Analogy in Chapter 14.)

3. Under Reason 4, the ACLU suggests that American controls will inhibit useful Web activity in other parts of the world. What particular feature of controls will be most troubling for people in foreign countries wanting to post material to be read in the United States? Do you think making distinctions between what the United States filters and what other countries do poses a problem? If so, what would you recommend?

Sex, Kids, and the Public Library

Marilyn Gell Mason

The question of whether or not to filter material in public and school libraries has been particularly troubling. In a 1998 lawsuit closely watched by public libraries across the nation, a group of citizens in Loudoun County, Virginia, charged that the system for filtering obscene material (X-Stop), installed in their library, presented an unconstitutional form of government censorship. Later in the year, the courts ruled against the library, finding that screening out Internet sites possibly harmful to minors violated constitutional rights of free speech. In 1999, a federal judge upheld this decision, but appeals were immediately considered as other libraries across the country watched. Writing in *American Libraries,* Marilyn Mason, the director of the Cleveland (Ohio) Public Library, addresses the problem public libraries are facing as they juggle differing community opinions on how to handle the burgeoning Internet.

"Sex at the library. News at eleven." Television, talk shows, and newspapers are shouting the message in community after community across the country from Orange County to Boston, from Oklahoma City to Medina, Ohio, from Houston to New York.

They say that public libraries are no longer safe havens for children. They say that ALA has libraries peddling pornography. They say that librarians are unresponsive to the public's concern. They say that something must be done.

The problem is a knotty one. How does a library provide free and open access to the 34 million sites now available worldwide through the Internet without inflaming parents and others in the community concerned about children viewing pictures that most believe are pornographic? It is one thing to fight the Communications Decency Act in court for its obvious legal failings and quite another to confront a room full of enraged parents and elected officials armed with pictures printed off the Internet in a public library.

The legal aspects of pornography on the Internet are outside the purview of this article. I believe that the current position of ALA in its suit challenging the Communications Decency Act is appropriate. What I fear, however, is that we may win in court and lose in the court of public opinion. The very real issues arising from pornography on the Internet are not going to be resolved by the courts; they are going to be resolved by public libraries and public library users. How they are resolved will determine whether public libraries continue to be the most respected (perhaps the *only* respected) public institution in the country.

In spite of the official ALA position outlined in the Library Bill of Rights and its interpretation on electronic information (*AL,* Mar. 1996, insert) that there should be free and open access to all library materials for everyone, regardless of age, including material on the Internet, libraries across the country are experimenting with some mechanism for limiting children's access, at least to the seamier sites. Some are using the technological solution of filtering software; others have sought legal sanction by requiring parental approval for children to use the Internet; still others rely on behavioral responses such as making the computer screen public, making the computer screen private, or asking users to desist when viewing offensive images.

The problem with all of the solutions currently available is that none of them work all that well, and many of them are creating additional, unanticipated problems. Current filtering software screens out some material we want left in and leaves in material we want screened out, and suggests to the public that the problem is solved when it is not. Even so, and whatever the official position of ALA on this subject, there is no question in my mind that were filtering software available that reliably filtered out the "adults only" sites without screening out information on sexually transmitted diseases and breast cancer, libraries would leap at the chance to install it.

As for the parental-approval approach, it doesn't take children without their parents' permission long to borrow someone else's card. And having to monitor screens may put library staff in an awkward position.

In the absence of a technological silver bullet, we are struggling to solve a radically new problem with old paradigms. With the Internet we are now offering the public material we have not, and in some instance would not, select. What does censorship mean in this context? What is our real responsibility to children? What is the purpose of the public library—from the public's point of view?

Intellectual freedom is a bedrock issue for libraries. Most of us at one time or another have been called upon to defend a selection decision and are proud of our ability to defend the retention of Judy Blume, J. D. Salinger, or Salman

Rushdie. Some of us make and defend more-controversial purchases, like Madonna's *Sex*. Most libraries make these decisions and defend them on the basis of a well-thought-out, carefully crafted selection policy. Our selection policies and the library profession's strong defense of intellectual freedom are grounded in our conviction that libraries serve individuals not groups, and that our communities have a wide spectrum of social, political, and religious belief. Moreover, access to a broad spectrum of ideas is fundamental to a democracy.

Nevertheless, there has always been material that most libraries don't buy. (Much of what can be found in an adult bookstore falls into this category.) When we make these judgments we call it selection. When we choose to exclude material we call it censorship. Evidence suggests that the distinction lacks meaning in an electronic environment.

Consider the following: Public Library A decides to handle the furor over a child's access to pornographic material by selecting several hundred sites out of the 34 million available as appropriate to children and making those, and only those, available in its children's room. Public Library B decides to install filtering software that blocks access to several thousand questionable sites. Which library is providing better access to more information? The one that selects or the one that censors? Is it any less valid to "select out" material than it is to "select in" material?

Many have argued that selection is cost-driven, that no library can afford to buy everything and selection policies codify priorities. Many claim that there is no marginal cost involved in providing access to everything on the Internet because once a library is wired there is no separate charge for each site accessed. Yet consider the following: A representative of one large urban library that has recently installed banks of computers privately acknowledges that at any given time as many as half of the public-access PCs are being used to view pornography. Is this the library's purpose in installing the computer system? Can we say that access is free? What about costs for hardware, software, and space? The cost for the material itself is only a small part of the total costs.

Purists argue that if we "select out" some material we are opening the door for would-be censors to impose even greater constraints on our collections. This argument sounds very much like the "domino theory," a diplomatic posture that has become obsolete in our post—Cold War era. In truth, many feel that by casting our protective net wide enough to cover material that would be illegal in many communities we are losing our credibility in defending other selection decisions.

UNRESOLVED ISSUES

The issues here are far from being resolved. The ACLU is threatening to sue libraries for use of blocking software, for asking library users to remove offending images from screens, for failure to provide private viewing places, for almost anything that doesn't ensure full access to everything by everyone. Some library users have asked if public viewing of pornography constitutes a new form of sexual harassment. Some political jurisdictions are tying library funding to the use of filtering software, while others have discussed imposing fines on anyone providing children access to pornography.

At the heart of this debate is nothing less than the definition of the role of the public library. We must never forget that public libraries belong to the public. We hold them in trust for present and future generations, and ultimately public libraries will be what the public wants them to be. If we want the community to hear and understand our position on these issues, we must hear and understand theirs. We must search together for a solution that will enable parents to continue to send their children to the public library with confidence without eroding our ability to meet the information needs of adults with vastly different opinions and orientations.

Within the profession we must treat each other with respect as well and avoid saying—as one prominent ALA representative said to a librarian in a public meeting in Ohio last year—that the librarian should "look for another career" because he dared to disagree with the Association's position on this topic. We need the best thinking of everyone, even—maybe especially—those who are not repeating conventional wisdom.

What is censorship in this environment? Censorship is what happens if we are forced to pull the plug on the Internet because legal or financial constraints make it impossible for us to do anything else. Censorship occurs if we deny citizens who are unable to afford computers access to a world of information now found on those 34 million Web sites (a number that is doubling every three months), thereby effectively redlining people because of their economic condition. Censorship is providing nothing to anyone because we are unwilling or unable to search for new solutions appropriate to an electronic age.

TOPICS FOR DISCUSSION AND WRITING

1. Discuss what Mason describes as the distinction between "selection" and "censorship." Which of these two approaches do you think is the wisest?

2. What does Mason mean when she says that we are trying to solve current problems "with old paradigms"? What new paradigms do we need?

Keeping Libraries User- and Family-Friendly: The Challenge of Internet Pornography

Robert Marshall

Robert Marshall, a representative to the Virginia House of Delegates, submitted the following essay to The Family Research Council in Washington, D.C., an organization that advocates positions promoting family values. Among such positions is the question of pornography and how to protect children, and other family members, from offensive material on the Internet. Marshall is interested in Internet access in both public and school libraries. He wrote this article after the defeat of the Communications Decency Act but before Congress adopted the Child Online Protection Act (1998)—considered by some to be a Communication Decency Act II—and before the courts ruled, once again, to overturn it (1999). But his remarks could just as well be directed at any of the ongoing efforts to overrule Congressional legislation controlling access to the Internet. Note his repeated references to the American Civil Liberties Union which challenged the Communications Decency Act. Consider also, as you read, the ways in which both the ACLU and Robert Marshall cite the First Amendment in support of their opposing viewpoints.

Last year when the Library Board of Trustees of Loudoun County, Virginia, moved to purchase computer software to screen sexually provocative Internet sites in public libraries, the action immediately provoked a lawsuit challenging the constitutionality of any community effort aimed at mediating in public settings the prodigious amount of material and resources accessible on the latest technological marvel, the information superhighway. While this particular case will not be resolved for some time, municipalities, libraries, and public schools all over the country have been placed on the defensive in the interim. Even as they seek to explore and experiment with policies that promote the common good in relation to new information technologies, small municipalities and school boards across the nation face not only legal battles but an uphill public relations war against such Goliaths as the American Civil Liberties Union and the American Library Association, two national advocacy groups demanding full access to the Internet, including obscenity harmful to women and children, in all public places.

How local governments and school boards can succeed in their desire to put a brake on Internet obscenity available to patrons and students, as well as effectively meet the legal and public relations struggle, is the subject of this issue of *Family Policy*. The American Civil Liberties Union and the American Library Association notwithstanding, case law and constitutional considerations clearly support the right of local, mediating institutions—whether library or school boards—to select, buy, catalog, and place in their stacks or computer terminals the kind of information and material they believe best serves the interests of the communities they serve. No matter how powerful, no outside professional association or legal advocacy group can lawfully coerce educational institutions of local governments to carry material they believe does not serve their mission.

While the issue may seem as simple as the right of self-government and determination of local institutions to set their own policies in their own communities, the issue is a bit more complicated. Fond as Americans are of modern technology, the computer has achieved a near-sacred status. Many have embraced the information age with unthinking reverence, believing the Internet, the latest step in a long line of tools that aid information presentation and retrieval, will magically create a better society. In the world of education, private and public schools alike have responded to the calls of President Bill Clinton and House Speaker Newt Gingrich, installing computers with Internet access into classrooms across the country in hopes of reversing the sagging academic achievement of the last two generations.

Therefore, any attempt, no matter how reasonable or prudent, to interfere with the rush into the computer age may face opposition, if not from the American Civil Liberties Union or the American Library Association, from the emotional fear that regulating traffic on the information superhighway will stand in the way of progress. But just as the *Atlantic Monthly* has warned about the "the computer delusion," claiming that no solid evidence supports the presumption that a computer in every classroom will improve teaching and learning,[1] local communities would be wise not to entertain the empty rhetoric of angry interest groups demanding (and suing for) unlimited Internet access in the name of the First Amendment.

LIBRARIES AND THE CONSTITUTION

Contrary to the claims of the American Library Association and the American Civil Liberties Union, restrictions on Internet resources in a public setting like a library do not violate the First Amendment. If they did, every single procedure and policy by which public libraries operate would be unconstitutional as well. If a library board or staff cannot be selective regarding what comes into the library via the computer, it has no right to be selective in regards to books, magazines, tapes, and cassette disks that come in through the mail and delivery truck. Librarians, for example, are under no constitutional mandate to catalog one book on the Civil War by a reputable scholar and another by an amateur for "balance" out of fear that selecting only one might violate the constitution.

Whereas in the past the very nature of book publishing was selective—publishers accepted some manuscripts and rejected others—therefore making the librarian's job less taxing, the very nature of the Internet has no built-in selection process. Anyone with a computer and software knowledge can publish anything he or she wants on the Internet. As a result, a prodigious amount of unauthenticated, uncredentialed, and unedited junk rides the information superhighway that a generation ago would never pass a junior editor in a reputable publishing house.

One key responsibility of a librarian is to use her professional judgment in evaluating competing claims for library resources; as a result, some items are chosen, others are rejected. The mere rejection of some material is not a First Amendment problem if done on the basis of content and not the author's viewpoint. In other words, libraries are free to regulate their holdings based on subject matter, but not based upon a book's position regarding subject matter. This critical distinction is often purposely disregarded by those opposed to Internet filtering when they argue that Internet filtering is "viewpoint" discrimination (and therefore unconstitutional) when in fact it is "content" discrimination, as Bruce Taylor and Robert Flores, attorneys with the National Legal Center, have demonstrated.[2]

The Supreme Court has already placed itself on record supporting the right of public libraries to screen certain material from the Internet. In *American Civil Liberties Union v. Reno,* a case that challenged the Communications Decency Act of 1996, the court left intact a provision of the federal law that specifically grants immunity from liability to Internet service providers, including state and local governments, public libraries, and schools, for screening certain material. The provision states:

> No provider or user of an interactive service shall be held liable on account of (A) any action voluntarily taken in good faith to restrict access to or availability of material that the provider or user considers to be obscene, lewd, lascivious, filthy, excessively violent, harassing, or otherwise objectionable, whether or not such material is constitutionally protected; or (B) any action taken to enable or make available to information content providers or others the technical means to restrict access to material.[3]

Restrictions can include the monitoring by library employees of public computer use, the placement of computers in a library, honor codes, time limits, the ability to print or save material as a computer file, and the installation and use of Internet filters to screen disruptive material.

Not only are libraries free to place on their shelves whatever resources they deem appropriate, they are likewise free to remove from circulation whatever they deem not appropriate. When a public school district in New York State removed certain books from a school library in the early 1980s, some parents sued. The issue eventually made it to the U.S. Supreme Court, which acknowledged in the *Pico* decision that certain classes of books could be removed from a school library even if they were already part of an established collection:

> Respondents implicitly concede that an unconstitutional motivation would not be demonstrated if it were shown that petitioners [school board] had decided to remove the books at issue because those books were pervasively vulgar. . . . And again, respondents concede that if it were demonstrated that the removal decision was based solely upon the "educational suitability" of the books in question, then their removal would be "perfectly permissible" . . . in respondents' view, such motivations, if decisive of petitioners' actions, would not carry the danger of an official suppression of ideas, and thus would not violate respondents' First Amendment rights . . . . Nothing in our decision today affects in any way the discretion of a local school board to choose books to add to the libraries of their schools.[4]

The American Civil Liberties Union and the American Library Association claim the *Pico* decision prevents a library from using an Internet screen because filtering is the same as removing a book from a collection based upon the viewpoint of the author. But even if filtering were "viewpoint" discrimination, the analogy does not fit. A computer filter does not remove an electronic or virtual book, article, magazine, or picture from a library because the item was never cataloged in the first place. A filter that screens obscenity, child pornography, or other illegal sexually explicit material is simply a tool that assists the normal selection and acquisition process; it essentially performs the work of a librarian. Consequently, most material excluded through a computer filter is material that would have never been acquired via the routine selection process.

Nor does established case law suggest that libraries are under any constitutional mandate to provide exhaustive resources to patrons who demand them.

In a case where state inmates were held to have a right to access a prison law library as a means to secure civil and due process rights, prisoners sued to have additional library resources available to them. But the Supreme Court denied the request in a 1996 case.

> Because Bounds [a previous case] did not create an abstract, free-standing right to a law library or legal assistance, an inmate cannot establish relevant actual injury simply by establishing that his prison's law library or legal assistance program is sub-par in some theoretical sense. . . . In other words, Bounds does not guarantee inmates the wherewithal to transform themselves into litigating engines capable of filing everything from shareholder derivative actions to slip-and-fall claims.[5]

If prisoners seeking to restore their liberty do not have a constitutional right to unlimited library resources, then citizens who merely want to satisfy their personal curiosity or secure information faster or more conveniently have no constitutional right to unlimited Internet access at public expense.

ARE LIBRARIES PUBLIC FORUMS?

At the heart of the Internet access controversy is the extent to which public and school libraries are considered public forums. While the American Library Association and the American Civil Liberties Union claim schools and libraries are public forums and therefore cannot place any restriction whatsoever on speech, Supreme Court precedent provides a more nuanced understanding, suggesting that schools and libraries are only public forums in a very restricted sense. In *Hazelwood School District v. Kuhlmeier,* the Supreme Court stated that public schools should not be considered public squares. They do not possess all the attributes of streets, sidewalks, parks, and other traditional public forums that have "been used for purposes of assembly, communicating thoughts between citizens, and discussing public questions."[6] Nor does a public library qualify as an open public space that has "immemorially been held in trust for the use of the public and, time out of mind, been used for purposes of assembly, communicating thoughts between citizens, and discussing public questions."[7]

Unlike true public forums where almost anything is acceptable, public schools, claims the high court, "posses significant discretion to determine the content of their school libraries."[8] The same applies to public libraries, which also have a more defined purpose than a public square. According to the Supreme Court, a public library exists to make available books, research tools, and supplemental educational opportunities to citizens. It is "a place dedicated to quiet, to knowledge, and to beauty."[9] Unlike public forums, a public library is not a place where a person is free to make noise, disseminate propaganda, or interfere with the pursuit of knowledge.

Just because citizens are permitted freely to visit a library or school does not make the institution a public forum. Nor does a school or library become a public forum simply because the buildings are sometimes used for public speeches, public gatherings, or town meetings. Schools and libraries have more defined purposes with rules and regulations, including the control of noise and voices, to create an atmosphere that is safe and conducive to their intended purpose. A public forum, on the other hand, is created "intentionally" with a decision by a government body to open "a nontraditional forum for public discourse."[10]

Even the very location of schools and libraries on property that is separate from public squares has a bearing on what constitutes a public forum. According to the court, the physical environment of a library suggests it is a special enclave and therefore subject to greater restriction than what would normally be allowed in a public forum.[11] Patrons, for example, are not free to enter every area of the library nor to engage in every activity they might permissibly engage in on the sidewalk outside the library. Loud talking, disruptive behavior, or failure to conform to library rules are all violations which may result in the immediate exclusion of the violator, though such conduct would, absent harm or threats to public safety, be permitted in the streets outside. Thus, that a library is intentionally sited so as to protect against the distractions of the outside world provides further basis that a library is different than a public forum.

The very existence of library policies and rules supports this argument. A library, for example, limits borrowing privileges to residents who have been issued a library card that signifies that a patron is a responsible member of the community and is willing to abide by library regulations. The regulations include time limits on use of materials, from a few minutes or hours of computer time to several weeks for printed materials. The bigger the library, the more complicated the borrowing and usage policies. Large libraries with multiple or rare book collections do not place all their books in general circulation; some are restricted to authorized patrons who must demonstrate additional qualifications or reasons, a particular need, or even written permission that indicates that the materials will be safe in the care of the patron.

How these principles apply to Internet filtering devices is clear. Where a library or school has purchased and installed a computer system, it has done so to make the system available as a nonpublic forum to a limited number of authorized patrons for academic, research, and learning purposes. Library patrons may use it, but only according to the rules and regulations set by the library staff or board. The computer does not "belong" to patrons; it belongs to the library that makes it available for limited public use. Patrons would not be permitted to operate a commercial enterprise on the library Internet computer, nor could they set time limits for themselves. Such library policies are reasonable and do not conflict with constitutional principles even though a patron might be permitted to use the library's computer to engage in research in support of his commercial or professional endeavors. Consequently, the prerogative held by a public library to block receipt of or restrict access to hard-core sexually provocative Internet addresses is within the boundaries it created when it established the limitations of this nonpublic forum, the computer. . . .

Therefore a local library board has every right to specify that its library computers, including Internet access, be used for academic and research purposes only. To fulfill that purpose, a library board or staff can lawfully prohibit patrons from accessing certain sites that do not suit those purposes, using screens or filters to prevent access to materials that do not meet the criteria the library uses to select books, magazines, and other literature in general circulation. Specifically, the library should formally proscribe access to Internet sites that depict: (1) the lewd or lascivious exhibition of genitals; (2) adults engaged in sexual intercourse, masturbation, or simulated masturbation; (3) sexual acts where penetration is clearly visible; (4) sexual acts between humans and animals; (5) bondage or sadomasochistic abuse; (6) ultimate sexual acts; (7) minors engaged in sexual acts; (8) coprophilia or urophilia; and (9) other prohibited sexual or excretory acts as described in the state code. However, the filter cannot prevent access to electronic material on the Internet to which the library has a corresponding hard copy on the shelves.

In contrast to the right of libraries, the patron who seeks access to pornographic Internet sites without a legitimate purpose has absolutely no right to demand that a library buy or provide his pornography for him. The pornography aficionado has to fend for himself in the marketplace, to the extent permitted by law or tolerated by law enforcement. On the other hand, a parent, researcher, news reporter, or student with a bona fide need for such access would simply be required to obtain assistance from library staff to disable filters or otherwise access the necessary materials, a service librarians are able to provide. Legitimate or even controversial sexual or disease information need not and should not be excluded or restricted. A sexual organ in an AIDS prevention pamphlet or website is not obscene or harmful to minors simply because its subject is sexuality or the genitals. But the combination of prurience and offensiveness to the average person and lack of educational value distinguishes illegal commercial pornography from sexually graphic information used for educational reasons. In either case, the general exclusion of hard-core sexually explicit materials from Internet access on a library's computer system is not viewpoint discrimination, but content selection, resource management, compliance with the law, and the exercise of reasonable policy and practice rights of the library itself.

Private citizens and interest groups have a legal right to advocate for the legalization of all forms of adult and child pornography and for the repeal of all federal and state laws on the subject. But library and school boards, as well as librarians and teachers, have the right to reject the calls of groups that electronic pornography be available, even to children. Not only do public libraries have the right to place restrictions on Internet access, they have a duty to comply with federal and state obscenity law and protect the public interest, including the young minds of the next generation. No reasonable person will advocate that making hard-core and child pornography available on library computers will benefit the common good.

The action of public institutions to limit access to illegal and unwanted pornography—except for legitimate academic or research purposes—is a reasonable, prudent, and perfectly legal response to the deluge of sexually provocative materials that drenches the Internet. Such action also complies with the high educational, aesthetic, and community-building purposes for which libraries exist.

Mediating institutions, whether public schools, libraries, or universities, are stewards of the public trust and public resources. They must fulfill their responsibilities to ensure that criminal violations do not occur with their knowledge or concurrence so that their limited resources are enjoyed by all citizens, whether young or old, male or female. Their policies of selection, purchase, cataloging, and placing on the shelf of books—whether in electronic or physical form—is not censorship, but sponsorship. The law fully protects the rights of a library and its staff to call the shots—not the rights of patrons to demand whatever they want. It may use filterware to mediate the Internet so that only material and resources that are keeping with the institution's purpose come into the library. That prudent response to Internet obscenity will not only help prevent community libraries from digressing into virtual adult bookstores, but will help ensure that libraries remain a haven dedicated, in the words of the Supreme Court, "to quiet, to knowledge, and to beauty."

ENDNOTES

1. Todd Oppenheimer, "The Computer Delusion," *Atlantic Monthly* (July 1997), pp. 45–46.

2. For a complete legal brief prepared by the National Legal Center, visit the web site, www.filteringfacts.org/.

3. Communications Decency Act of 1996, ¶509 (c), Pub. L. No. 104, February 8, 1996.

4. U.S. 853, *Board of Education, Island Trees Union Free School District No. 26, et al. v. Pico, by His Next Friend Pico, et al.,* Certiorari to the United States Court of Appeals for the Second Circuit No. 80-2043, argued March 2, 1982, decided June 25, 1982: "[W]e hold that local school boards may not remove books from school library shelves simply because they dislike the ideas contained in those books and seek by their removal to 'prescribe what shall be orthodox in politics, nationalism, religion, or other matters of opinion.'" Vigorous dissents were filed by three justices who believed the decision considerably diminished the power of school boards.

5. *Lewis, Director, Arizona Department of Corrections, et al. v. Casey et al.* Certiorari to the U.S. Court of Appeals for the Ninth Circuit. No. 94-1511. Argued November 29, 1995; decided June 24, 1996.

6. U.S. 260, 267 (1988) (quoting *Hague v. Committee for Industrial Organization,* 307 U.S. 496, 515 (1939)).

7. Id. 679 (quoting from *Hague,* 307 U.S. 496, 515, 516 [1939]).

8. *Pico,* 457 U.S. 869.

9. *Brown v. Louisiana,* U.S. 131, 142 (1966).

10. *Greer v. Spock,* 424 U.S. 828 (1976).

11. International Society, 680 (citing *United States v. Grace,* 461 U.S. 171, 179–180 [1982]). . . .

TOPICS FOR DISCUSSION AND WRITING

1. Write a summary of Marshall's arguments, clarifying his principal premises and conclusions. (See Summaries and Premises and Conclusions in Chapter 3.)

2. Marshall cites a provision of the Communications Decency Act not included in the excerpts above. What does this provision allow?

What did the *Pico* decision specify regarding selection of books in school libraries? What, according to Marshall, is the distinction between "viewpoint" and "content" in a library's evaluation of a book?

3. Much of Marshall's argument depends on what is already established policy regarding selection and use of books and restrictions on behavior in libraries. Do you agree with him that these limitations should also apply to Internet filtering devices? Explain your position.

From His Dorm Room, a Vanderbilt Junior Becomes a Force Against Internet Regulation

Jeffrey R. Young

As a Vanderbilt University junior, Bennett Haselton founded an organization called Peacefire (www.peacefire.org) to campaign against any form of Internet censorship and enlist teenagers to his cause. Like the Internet itself, Haselton is bursting with youthful energy, confident that other young people will share his strong views. As you will see, his opinion differs markedly from Robert Marshall's.

A homemade sign over Bennett Haselton's door at Vanderbilt University reads "Bennett the Unseen." Mr. Haselton, at 18 already a junior, rarely emerges from his tiny dorm room. He spends almost all of his time in front of his computer, logged on to the Internet.

Although Mr. Haselton goes nearly unseen on the campus here, he has made a name for himself in cyberspace as a vigorous defender of young people's on-line interests. His message: Stop locking kids out of portions of the Net. He says measures designed to protect minors from "cyberporn" do more harm than good, because they also block sites that could be critically important to some young people—sites offering information about women's issues, safer sex, and support groups for homosexuals, for instance.

So Mr. Haselton is using the Internet to give high-school and college students a voice in the debate over freedom of speech in cyberspace. He's organized a band of young people 500 strong into a group called Peacefire. Its members oppose the use of blocking software in schools and libraries; laws that regulate "indecent" material on the Net; and rating systems for Internet content.

Since Mr. Haselton founded Peacefire last summer, it has been involved in some high-profile protests. For instance, it is a plaintiff in the American Civil Liberties Union's legal challenge to a New York law that would restrict a wide range of on-line materials deemed harmful to minors. The group has started boycotts of blocking-software programs and is conducting letter-writing campaigns decrying the use of such programs in schools and libraries.

WORKING THE INTERNET

But the center of all this activity is a messy room. Computer books and magazines carpet the floor, along with clothes, loose papers, and cereal boxes. The clearest surface is the desk, where the computer sits. Mr. Haselton seems comfortable at the center of this universe of stuff, where almost everything he owns can be reached without leaving his chair.

When he's not in class he's most likely here, wearing jeans and a T-shirt, his curly red hair pulled back in a pony tail. Running Peacefire means working the Internet—searching the Web for the latest information about blocking software, answering e-mail from members and reporters, and making Web pages that present the group's message (http://www.peacefire.org/).

Mr. Haselton started Peacefire after becoming frustrated with on-line debates over whether Internet content should be regulated. In the debates, he sees blocking software widely praised, even by free-speech advocates. Many such advocates say the software provides a personal alternative to government-mandated restrictions. But to Mr. Haselton, even blocking software is too restrictive.

"Minors' interests in free speech on the Internet were being overlooked," he says. Parents who use blocking software effectively turn over the job of raising their children to a software company, he argues. "It's like telling their children, 'I trust a software company more than I trust my child,'" he says.

So he formed Peacefire and began checking out the software programs for himself. He installed one, called CYBERsitter, on his computer and began surfing to see what it blocked. He found that a wide range of material was excluded, including the home page for the National Organization for Women and pages describing support groups for homosexuals. He tried some other programs and found similar sites blocked, although he says he found CYBERsitter the most restrictive.

"These programs block more than any law could have removed from the Internet," he says. Peacefire has posted criticisms of the company on its Web site and is calling for a boycott, spreading the phrase "Don't Buy CYBERsitter" across the Internet.

Brian Milburn, president of the company that makes CYBERsitter, Solid Oak Software, says it's no secret that the program blocks more than pornography. "Our customers simply do not want their children to have access to homosexual resources," he says. The program also locks out violent material, sites that encourage illegal activity, information that appears to come from pedophiles, and sites that criticize blocking software—including the Peacefire Web site. "If you want your kids to have access to it, you shouldn't buy our product," he says.

Mr. Milburn says the company did make an effort to address Peacefire's concerns. It set up an electronic mailing list for customers who disagree with its blocking policies, but only a handful of people subscribed. As for Mr. Haselton's boycott, Mr. Milburn says: "Quite honestly, our sales have doubled since he started doing it."

"POLITICALLY SLANTED SOFTWARE"

The plot has thickened in recent months, as a number of communities have begun requiring blocking software on computers in public schools and libraries. "Using politically slanted software to filter access on a taxpayer-funded computer terminal steps out of the bounds of the Constitution," Mr. Haselton writes on the Peacefire Web site.

In Orlando, Fla., the Orange County Library System recently installed blocking software on all of its networked computers. Legislators in Minnesota are considering a law that would force all schools and public libraries to equip their machines with similar software. And in Boston, Mayor Thomas M. Menino has ordered that a blocking program called Cyber Patrol be used on computers in the city's schools, libraries, and community centers. Peacefire encourages its members to send letters to officials urging them to reverse such policies.

Mr. Haselton believes that the Internet offers some minors the only possibility of finding information that could help them work though serious issues they can't, or won't, talk to their parents about. And, he says, "Blocking out the word homosexual is a sure-fire way to teach intolerance." Though he agrees that children should be discouraged from viewing pornography, he says the drawbacks of blocking software outweigh any benefits. "I don't think it is an acceptable price to pay for something as silly as trying to control everything your child sees before they're 18."

UNINTENDED CONSEQUENCES

Mr. Haselton grew up in Copenhagen, Denmark, though he is an American citizen. He says that in Denmark, children can see pornography in shops and on newsstands, and attitudes toward such material are more casual. "By blocking it out you just make it more alluring." he argues. "If you don't make a big deal out of these pictures, it's just not something special." He says he didn't have access to the Internet until he came to Vanderbilt, but he believes that his parents would not have installed blocking software on their home computer.

When Mr. Haselton isn't running Peacefire, he plugs away at his computer-science and mathematics courses. He says he loves the exactness of math, and he enjoys solving problems for his courses on theoretical calculus, numerical analysis, and topology. He admits he doesn't have much of a background in politics or activism. "I've never been involved in anything this political," he says.

He does spend some time outside of his room, of course. He's a member of Alpha Phi Omega, a co-ed service organization, and he eats his meals at a language table where students are required to speak German. He says his favorite area of the Net is Internet Relay Chat, where people can have conversations on line. He says he's learned to type fast by spending hours in chat rooms for teen-agers.

He says he hopes the efforts of Peacefire will show that minors have a lot to offer the on-line community. "We're almost fighting for the credibility of minors to organize themselves and get something done on a huge scale," he says.

To that end, he's organized a fund raiser to let Peacefire members show off their Web savvy and, at the same time, help the organization's cause. Members are offering to design Web pages for $10 per hour, with all the money going to the A.C.L.U. They hope to help pay for their part in the lawsuit challenging New York's law against "indecent" content on line. So far, about a dozen individuals and organizations have hired the Peacefire members to make Web pages.

NO FORMAL STRUCTURE

Peacefire doesn't have a board of directors or any kind of formal structure. Instead, members discuss business on an electronic mailing list. Big decisions, such as accepting the A.C.L.U.'s invitation to join the New York lawsuit, are made by Mr. Haselton after he consults with other members. Occasionally, Peacefire holds a meeting over Internet Relay Chat. At the first such meeting last month, about a dozen members, most of them high-school students, gathered to talk about the goals of the group, about how to organize their fundraising work better, and even about their homework.

Some people find it hard to take an organization of young people seriously, however. "He's just a kid. How seriously are we supposed to take him?" asks Mr. Milburn of Solid Oak Software. "He's just having his fun. Maybe next year he'll get a girlfriend and he'll spend his time with that."

And sometimes you do get the idea that Mr. Haselton views cyber-activism as a kind of game. "It's all fun," he says. "All of it is enjoyable." And some of his protests could be considered, well, juvenile. For instance, he set up a rating system for Internet content called RSUCKY that lets users label their pages as excessively geeky. The name is a spoof on a rating system by a group called the Recreational Software Advisory Council, or RSAC.

But he argues that the nature of the Internet is to judge material by its merits, not by the age of the speaker. It's one advantage of the Internet that he hopes to preserve: In cyberspace, Mr. Haselton has shown that an unseen 18-year-old who is committed to his ideas can stir up plenty of controversy.

TOPICS FOR DISCUSSION AND WRITING

1. What reasons does Haselton offer in support of his position against any kind of Internet blocking software?

2. Haselton says he "is almost fighting for the credibility of minors." Do you think this is an important fight? Why? Do you know of any students engaging in First Amendment and the Internet activities on your campus? If so, seek them out and write a report on what you discover.

3. Visit Bennett Haselton's Internet Web site at www.peacefire.org to see what specific issues he or his successor is addressing at this date.

If Haselton has moved on, try to find a current site, run by a college student, which addresses the same issues. (As of summer, 2000, the site remained active.)

4. Conduct a survey of parents with young children to determine (1) whether they use filtering software to protect their children, (2) whether or not they think such filtering software is effective, and (3) what they would recommend be done about protecting their children from indecent material on the Internet. (See Generalization, as well as Conducting a Survey in Chapter 7.)

Free Speech or Hate Crime?

With the rise in deadly violence in schools, the nation, particularly parents and school authorities, has become increasingly worried about violent expressions in cyberspace and what students themselves post. Concern escalated after authorities discovered that a Web site designed by Eric Harris and Dylan Klebold before the Littleton, Colorado shootings promoted violence and hate.

Schools Challenge Students' Internet Talk

Tamar Lewin

Even when the issue starts with what was supposed to be a joke about a dog, schools can become concerned. The following story reminds us once again that school-imposed authority and First Amendment-sanctioned free speech can conflict.

Aaron Smith's troubles grew out of a drawing that he made in the school computer lab, one that his friend said looked like a chihuahua being killed. That remark, hilarious to a group of 13-year-old boys, became a kind of standing joke that led Aaron and his computer-nerd pals to go home and create a "C.H.O.W." Web page—a place for Chihuahua Haters of the World to share tidbits like the tale of the seven-foot boa constrictor that ate a chihuahua.

"The whole C.H.O.W. Web page was just for fun, but it was my creation and I loved it," said Aaron, whose site included a statement that he and his friends did not imagine how it would evolve "when we started this in the Dowell Middle School computer lab in McKinney, Tex."

But it was not hilarious to a Fort Worth chow breeder who visited the page and became so incensed that she contacted the school, threatening an animal-rights protest.

"I must have gotten 50 E-mails," said the Superintendent, Jack Cockrill. "We believed it was a product of the computer lab and we immediately began an investigation."

Hauled into the principal's office, Aaron quickly volunteered to take out the reference to the school. But that was not enough. School officials suspended him for the day; transferred him out of his favorite class, the computer lab where he was an aide, and told him to take down the Web site and post an apology.

Much like the underground newspapers of past generations, student-created Web pages are increasingly creating conflicts between students and schools, with students asserting their right to free speech on their personal sites while schools seek to control content that concerns them.

"As more and more people get on line and more out-of-school on-line conduct gets tracked back to the school, we're seeing more of these cases," said Ann Beeson, a lawyer with the American Civil Liberties Union. "Schools are trying to control what kids with on line or punish them for it, when they have no right to."

Ms. Beeson said the first such case that came to her attention occurred several years ago in Bellevue, Wash., where a bright high school senior, Paul Kim, created a Web site, on his own time, that was a parody of the high school newspaper.

School officials told him they did not like the parody, Ms. Beeson said, but they did not tell him that because of it they were withdrawing his recommendation for a National Merit Scholarship. With legal help from the A.C.L.U., the boy won a "very favorable settlement," Ms. Beeson said.

In Aaron's case, too, the civil liberties organization has reached a settlement, under which he was allowed to return to the computer class, with no mention of the Web page incident to appear on his record.

"This was a bizarre intrusion on his free speech rights," Ms. Beeson said. "It was a Web site created off campus, completely unrelated to school, and he has every right to announce to the world that he goes to that school. It doesn't give the school any right to exert any power over his Web page."

Ms. Beeson is still negotiating with Geocities, the Web server that had carried the chihuahua site but took it down after Aaron posted his apology, apparently because the way the apology was posted created a technical violation of Geocities guidelines.

And Aaron is still hoping to get the C.H.O.W. site going again, with missives like this boa story from Aug 11:

"Today in the California region a 7-ft boa constrictor was caught devouring a chihuahua. I have repeatedly called the snake's home to tell him what a great job our operatives are doing out there, but he won't answer the phone. If anyone can relay this information to him C.H.O.W. would be grateful."

If schools worry about that kind of silliness, they become absolutely enraged about sites created specifically as forums to criticize school policies or personnel.

One of the knottiest cases arose in December in Statesboro, Ga., where a 15-year-old student was arrested and charged with making terroristic threats against the principal of Statesboro High School, Darryl Dean, and his family, on a Web site that caused concern from the start.

It was not a pleasant site, laced with obscenity and invitations to click on links to other sites, where browsers could find out about "cool bands, how to make bombs and even how to kill yourself."

And it promised trouble to Mr. Dean, 36, in his first year as principal, with suggestions for shooting him, kidnapping his 7-year-old daughter, scratching his car with keys and putting Superglue in the locks at school. Other students posted their critiques of the principal and the school, often in the most crude language that they could muster.

The school came down hard: the district not only suspended the creator of the site but also turned over the case to the police for criminal investigation. The boy's name was not released because the charges, still pending, are in juvenile court.

The school also suspended several students who had posted negative comments. Although the suspensions have all been completed, some of the students are seeking to have their disciplinary records expunged.

Civil libertarians contend that the school wrongly punished the students. "Our position is that the school system cannot discipline students for off campus free-speech activity," said Gerald Weber, legal director of the Georgia Civil Liberties Union. "You can't stop students or anyone else from saying what they want unless there's a credible threat of imminent harm. It was a complete overreaction to suggest that this was a real threat. It was all hyperbole, not a realistic threat."

Louisa Abbot, a lawyer for one of the suspended students, said the school should not have treated the Web site as a real threat.

"These are not students who have been a problem in school, and they were just expressing the kind of dislike of authority that every generation feels," Ms. Abbot said. "It's interesting to speculate whether, if there'd been a more temperate use of language, this would have provoked such an extreme reaction."

Both Mr. Dean and the lawyer for the school board, Vanderver Pool, declined to discuss the case, citing student confidentiality.

The boy charged with the threats, who is generally described as well behaved, also declined to discuss the case, saying he hoped that the charges would "blow over." So did his lawyer, Gates Peed.

People familiar with the case said the charges might have been as much a matter of timing as of any real perception of a threat. The Statesboro boy's arrest followed closely on the heels of national publicity about a 14-year-old in West Paducah, Ky., who fired on classmates at a prayer circle, killing three girls and injuring five others.

In that climate, the people in Statesboro said, school authorities may have felt that they could not afford to ignore anything that might be a harbinger of violence.

TOPICS FOR DISCUSSION AND WRITING

1. The conflict in this article is compared to clashes between unautho-rized school newspapers and school officials in the past. Do you think this is a fair comparison? Why or why not? (See False Analogy in Chapter 6.)

2. School officials suspended Aaron Smith, took him out of the com-puter lab, which was his favorite class, and made him remove his site from the Web and post an apology. But as attorney Ann Beeson said, "Schools are trying to control what kids write online or punish them for it, when they have no right to." In Aaron's particular case, do you support Aaron or his school? Write a paper explaining your position, being sure to take into consideration the rights of the Chi-huahua breeder.

Is Hate Young and New on the Web?

Jean Winegardner

Far beyond the case of a childish prank turned harmful, each year we read of unimaginable hate crimes against individuals because of their race or sexual orienta-tion. A black man was dragged to his painful death behind a truck; a gay college stu-dent was savagely murdered by a group of young men. Such behavior is deemed criminal and the perpetrators were brought to trial. But when hate speech is directed against individuals or groups on the Web, the authors claim First Amendment pro-tection and a serious conflict of interest develops.

In the following article, Jean Winegardner, a staff writer with the *Online Journalism Review* (www.ojr.org), a publication of the Annenberg School of Communication at the University of Southern California, addresses the issue of hate speech on the Internet. As you read, think critically about whose rights come first when the issues are so sensitive.

Is hate young and new on the Web? Has a fresh generation of hate-mongers found a home on the Net?

A cursory review of the Internet reveals a plethora of resources for hate-mongers. Typing any number of hate-related key words into a search engine will bring up thousands of hits. Type "hate niggers" into the Yahoo! search engine and you will come up with 65,659 hits. Type "white power" or "holocaust lie,"and you will come up with many more. It can be terrifying and disturbing to browse through these sites.

"This site is best viewed with Microsoft Internet Explorer. Download Inter-net Explorer! And Heil Hitler!"

These are the first words that appear when the Teen White Supremacist Movie Critic Web site appears on a computer screen.

The 17-year-old responsible for this page reviews one film a day, writing a short review of each and rating it with his system—four swastikas is a must-see, one swastika means it is terrible. Recently reviewed films include "Triumph of the Will"—four swastikas: "The film is a stunning piece of work by director Leni Reifenstahl, who is good even though she is a woman. The Fuhrer is no less than brilliant. All you need to do is watch to see the grandeur and majesty of the Third Reich"— and "Malcolm X"—one swastika: "This movie is about a Black Negro who forgets his place and starts trying to make other Black Negroes angry like he is."

On the page, the teen includes a biography. "This year, besides my pages on the net, I have learned bomb-making and I have become interested in starting my own militia. My studies are mostly White history, which I learn about by reading pamphlets and watching television." He also offers a tongue-in-cheek tip on how to write to him: "Get some friends and some guns and storm your local post office. You'll be surprised at how much inside help you'll get."

This is one example of hate speech on the Internet. There is much, much more out there. And it's easy to find.

There is another issue at play, however. Just as the Anti-Defamation League has the First Amendment right to publish a Web site, so does the Ku Klux Klan. In this new medium that has the power to reach so much of the world so quickly, groups that never had access to the masses now do. But where does censorship begin? Does it start with a law forbidding this speech on the Internet or with a home-installed software filter that keeps hate sites off your personal computer?

Or does it start with Internet service providers pulling hate sites off their servers? Some ISPs integrate an anti-hate speech clause into their contracts and pull sites that fall into that category. America Online is one such ISP. The Anti-Defamation League does not feel that this is censorship. Sue Stengel, western states counsel for that organization, says simply that if an ISP has an anti-hate speech section in their contract, then they should abide by it. Stengel says that although the ADL does not think these sites are good things, her organization also does not believe in censorship. "We believe in fighting bad speech with good speech," said Stengel. The ADL monitors hate speech on the Internet, then tries to inform the public about sites featuring hate speech through their own site and by publishing documents and conducting seminars. They are also working with the Learning Co. to publish a Net filter that would direct users to ADL's site if they try to access a hate site.

Don Black, 44, a white nationalist since the age of 15, runs a site many would put in the hate speech category. He is the founder of Stormfront, a white nationalist Web site. Stormfront has been on the Internet for nearly three years and gets more than 1,500 hits each weekday. Don Black reports that on some days they have gotten as many as 2,500.

He says he started the Web site to provide an alternative news media and to serve as a means for those attracted to the white nationalist movement to stay in touch and form a virtual community.

Part of the danger of sites such as Stormfront, according to Stengel, is that they can recruit through the Internet. Black seems to agree. "Most of those visiting our site have never been in touch with any white nationalist organizations or publications."

Black called groups like the ADL and the Simon Wiesenthal Center the "Internet Thought Police" and went on to say that they want the news media to remain "a controlled monopoly, where ideas they find "offensive" are suppressed." He says he understands their agenda, but says it is not in the best interest of the American people.

Kim Alleyn Badynski, Grand Dragon in the Ku Klux Klan and regional organizer for five states in the Pacific Northwest, is a researcher for a Ku Klux Klan Web site, a site he says is intended to encourage Klan members and other "white Christian patriots" to migrate to the Pacific Northwest to establish a regional power base.

The Klan has been online since late 1996. KKK.com is new, having only been on the Net since December, 1997. He calls the anti-hate sites dangerous to the Constitution and the American tradition of freedom.

Recent history has shown us that attempts to control Internet content angers users. The medium is perhaps the most democratic to appear in the 20th century and users seem to resent any effort by lawmakers—or service providers—to control it.

There is the concern that the censoring of hate speech on the Internet is the proverbial foot in the door that could lead to more censorship, based on political or moral reasoning.

Don Black says that there are lots of sites on the Internet that he would consider dangerous. "But I don't think prior restraint of otherwise legal sites promoting moral degencracy or national suicide is practical."

Badynski agrees when he says: "In the United States we have a Constitution, which guarantees freedom of speech and religion. We should have the same freedom on the Internet. If someone does not like what we have to say, they do not have to look."

This conflict between hate speech and the First Amendment is likely to continue. Groups promoting white power have been struggling to affirm their rights under the Constitution for years. What seems clear is that these sites will stay on the Internet for a long time. It is up to the computer users to decide what sites to call up with their Internet connection.

"[Hate speech on the Internet] is dangerous because of the people it reaches in so short a time," said Stengel. "That is the benefit as well as the cost of the Internet."

TOPICS FOR DISCUSSION AND WRITING

1. Winegardner suggests several ways in which censorship of hate sites on the Web might begin. What are these different methods? Which do you think would be preferable, if any?

2. The author cites specific sites on the Web where you can find both hate speech and organizations that monitor and try to combat such speech. With a partner from your class, explore some of these sites, making sure you look at sites that represent both points of view. Together, write a report on your findings. Include how you felt when reading such material. Confronting inflammatory language and racist images can be extremely disturbing, but knowledge of the world as it can be represented in cyberspace may prepare you to find ways to combat hate speech.

Racism, Racial Discrimination, Xenophobia and Related Intolerance

The United Nations Commission on Human Rights

In late 1997, the United Nations Commission on Human Rights met in Geneva, Switzerland, to address racism on the Internet. They released a lengthy report examining their discussion of the problem. Excerpts from this report, which was circulated on the Internet, follow. As we can see, questions of free speech, especially as they relate to the First Amendment of the U.S. Constitution, grow ever more complex when the international community enters the picture. The global reach of the World Wide Web has the potential to put one nation's laws in conflict with those of other governments.

. . . 5. The seminar was opened on behalf of the Secretary-General by the Acting Deputy High Commissioner for Human Rights, Mr. Ralph Zacklin. In his opening statement, Mr. Zacklin said that the Internet, as a means of communication, bore great potential, notably for improving education techniques, circulating health-related information, facilitating the debate between distant cultures, encouraging dialogue and nurturing comprehension among peoples in our divided world. However, while conceived as a means of celebrating a variety of freedoms, the Internet was also being used as a means of vilifying groups and/or individuals in society. In North America, in particular, "high-tech hate," or "cyber-racism," was growing at an alarming rate. The major challenge for the international community today was how to avoid restrictions on the freedom of expression while continuing to provide proper legal protection to the rights of groups and individuals. . . .

10. After a brief historical overview of how individuals and organizations had used the technology of the Internet to promulgate what was deemed to be "offensive" or "hate" speech, Ms. Guzman [Executive Director of the Human Rights Information Network] provided information and examples of how the human rights activist community had been using this communication tool. Some of the thinking by industry leaders about the notion of regulating the Internet in order to prevent abuses on it was also briefly outlined. The general consensus of the

computer communications leaders canvassed was that it should not—not that it cannot—be regulated. Opinions by online activists worldwide as to regulation were offered and again, the consensus was that there should be no regulation. . . .

13. The starting point for any discussion of the rights of United States citizens, and of the powers (and restrictions) that attached to the United States Government, was the United States Constitution. The First Amendment to the Constitution provided that "Congress shall make no law . . . abridging the freedom of speech, or of the press. . . ." Through its explicit guarantee of freedom of expression, the First Amendment established a general rule that neither the federal Government nor the governments of the states could criminalize speech (or burden it, as by imposing civil penalties) on the basis of content. Like the Universal Declaration of Human Rights, which also recognized a right to free expression, the First Amendment proceeded from the understanding that Governments must permit vigorous (and often competing) speech in the "marketplace of ideas." The First Amendment commanded that Government refrain from penalizing one viewpoint at the expense of another. This was the case even where the "exposition of ideas" included expression that the average citizen might find irrational or even repugnant.

14. The animating principle of First Amendment jurisprudence was that such expression would meet with opposing expression—often described succinctly as "more speech"—and that citizens could discern for themselves the truth or falsity of the contending viewpoints. That tolerant attitude to expression found its roots deep in the traditions of humanism itself, which proceeded from the fundamental belief that each person was (and must be) a moral actor. Under that philosophical approach, it was not the role of the State to dictate the views a citizen must hold; rather, each person must exercise his innate capacity for independent reason. As a corollary, however, Government must accept that not every person will arrive at the same judgement.

15. This is precisely the relation in which the First Amendment stood vis-à-vis racist speech, whether it occurred on the Internet or in the physical world. Even where the United States Government found the views expressed to be misguided and repugnant, the Constitution commanded that we neither prohibit nor regulate speech merely "because of disapproval of the ideas expressed." The broad speech guarantee of the First Amendment had been interpreted to extend well beyond the expression of personally held beliefs. In addition, it extended in many cases to speech advocating conduct even when the conduct itself would be illegal.

16. Thus, in the landmark decision in *Brandenburg v. Ohio*, 395 U.S.444 (1969), the Supreme Court held unanimously that "the constitutional guarantees of free speech and free press do not permit a State to forbid or proscribe advocacy of the use of force or of law violation except where such advocacy is directed to inciting or producing imminent lawless actions and is likely to incite or produce that action." For similar reasons, racist speech on the Internet—even when it was directed towards a specific victim—was protected by the First Amendment.

17. It was well settled that threats of harm (physical or otherwise) received no First Amendment protection, and this was no less true for threats involving racial epithets or those motivated by racial animus. Thus, a threatening electronic mail message sent to a victim, or even a public announcement (via the World Wide

Web) of an intention to commit acts of racially motivated violence could, in many cases, be punished. Even here, however, the Constitution had been construed as requiring that any such punishment be applied only to "true threats." Thus, in *Watts v. United States,* 394 U.S. 705 (1969), the Supreme Court upheld the constitutionality of a federal law against threatening the President, but in the same case vacated the defendant's conviction as inconsistent with the First Amendment. . . .

19. In the United States legal tradition, the proper response to racist books was not to ban or burn them; rather, it was to leave open avenues of expression for a diverse array of views, with the knowledge that racist dogma will be soundly rebutted. In that tradition, it is through a clash of views in vigorous debate, and not through government censorship, that equality was well served. . . .

47. In the United States, anti-Semitic and racist speech on the Internet was protected by the First Amendment guarantee of freedom of expression. Consequently, material that was treated as illegal in most other democracies, including racist and defamatory statements, could be posted on the Internet in the United States and, as a result, become accessible to virtually everyone around the globe, regardless of existing local laws and morals. As the Supreme Court had noted, while the "chat rooms" and Web sites existed at fixed geographical locations on the Internet, users could transmit and receive messages without revealing anything about their identities, or indeed disguising them.

48. To what extent could democratic Governments regulate the material that passed through the Net? The Internet providers could, if they wished, refuse service. They could also screen content with the aid of technologies that were evolving rapidly. *The Economist,* in its issue of 19 October 1996, stated: "Governments need to force Internet service providers, many of which will in the future be big telephone companies, to take responsibility for what they knowingly carry on their sites."

49. The aim was to penalize racist propaganda on the Internet, not pre-censorship. That in no way implied that racist propaganda should not also be dealt with by monitoring and refutation. Multiple strategies were called for to counter racism and racial discrimination on the Internet. . . .

67. It was noted that consideration of the right to freedom of expression was beyond the mandate of the seminar. Instead, the seminar was meant to find ways and means to use the Internet responsibly in light of States' obligations under the Convention. As racism was clearly illegal under article 4, the seminar should focus on ways of achieving a prohibition of racist propaganda and racial discrimination on the Internet. It was quite clear that the Internet could and was being used irresponsibly. The seminar should therefore turn its attention to ways of locating and prosecuting the perpetrators of racist propaganda.

68. However, freedom of expression could not be discounted at such a seminar, despite its terms of reference. All human rights had to be viewed and balanced in the context of other human rights and these were sometimes in competition. At the same time, undue consideration should not be given to United States law. The seminar was concerned with international law and the international rules of law were not those set down by the United States

Supreme Court. International laws were generally to be considered as complementary to national laws although there were, at times, disputes. Many years ago, the International Law Commission stated that constitutional law was not superior to the principles of international law. If there was a discrepancy, a State could always hold a reservation to certain provisions of an international convention. However, the fact that States held reservations to provisions of international conventions could make the world's commitment to human rights merely a formal one.

69. Many countries, certainly most Western European countries, had criminalized racist hate speech and propaganda. The question for those States was not how to balance freedom of expression with other obligations but how to enforce the laws in existence. However, censorship by the State could lead to repressive government. The freedom of expression was paramount and must be respected for democracy to function effectively. . . .

TOPICS FOR DISCUSSION AND WRITING

1. When issues of First Amendment rights arise, conflicts of personal and legal dimensions often baffle the experts. Explain the conflict of laws in the 1969 case of *Watts v. The United States* in light of remarks in this report (see item number 17).

2. What are the international concerns at issue in the Commission on Human Rights' efforts to limit racist hate speech and propaganda on the Internet?

3. Jean Winegardner concludes her article, "Is Hate Young and New on the Web?" with the statement that hate speech on the Internet "is dangerous because of the people it reaches in so short a time. That is the benefit as well as the cost of the Internet." Review Winegardner's article as well as the United Nations report on hate speech on the Internet and explain what Winegardner means.

4. If you were appointed to be a member of the UN Commission, what position would you advocate for controlling hate speech on the Net? You may want to incorporate your response to this question into a paper addressing topic number 3.

The First Amendment—Concluding Topics

1. Write an essay in which you address one of the following questions at issue:

   Do you think freedom of speech should be abridged in order to protect children from pornography on the Internet?

   Do you think freedom of speech should be abridged in order to protect people from hate speech on the Internet?

   You may wish to confine your paper to the issue of public and/or school libraries. Should libraries have the power to filter material available to children—or to anyone—on library computers?

   After narrowing your topic, summarize the problem, then present both sides of the issue, and conclude with a discussion of your position. (See Focusing Your Topic as well as Shaping a Written Argument in Chapter 4.)

2. Since the Supreme Court ruling in 1997 and subsequent court decisions overturning Internet legislation and the proliferation of PICS labeling programs, new approaches to the issue of controlling material on the Internet have arisen. Research the directions that government and society have taken and write a report updating the topic. In particular, what new software has appeared to provide broader options for filtering and tagging specific material on the Internet? And has any server or software manufacturer been able to solve the problem of unrated sites being automatically blocked? What new issues have emerged in the public media?

3. At the conclusion of its report to the United Nations, The Commission for Human Rights posed the following "questions on the effectiveness of a code of conduct for the Internet." Write a report in which you try to answer these questions. You may concentrate on both hate speech and material offensive for children, or you may choose one area only.

   Should there be control and regulation of the Internet?

   How would restrictions impact the right to freedom of opinion and expression?

   Is control technically feasible? At what cost?

   How would regulation be enforced and by whom?

   How effective would regulation be, given the nature of the Internet?

   Would there be any conflict with the right to privacy and freedom of association?

   What would be the geographical range or ranges of this regulation?

4. Research the growth in "hate" sites on the Internet, particularly ones targeting specific racial groups. In 1999, the Simon Wiesenthal Center, a research and educational organization based in Los Angeles, released an interactive CD-ROM that tracks such sites and might be a useful place to start. You might also check for a Web site. Write a report on the current status of "hate" sites, whether or not efforts to limit them have been successful, and how such efforts have been met by advocates of First Amendment Rights.

5. A challenging assignment: Milos Forman in his address to the National Press Club, see above, quotes from *Areopagitika*, a celebrated political essay by seventeenth-century English poet John Milton (available in your library). Read this essay, summarize Milton's main points, and write your own response to his argument. What would today's Supreme Court members have to say about Milton's position?

6. An ambitious synthesis: Throughout this section on freedom of speech, writers repeatedly invoke the First Amendment. In particular, arguments surrounding the film, *The People vs. Larry Flynt;* the Supreme Court decision on the Communications Decency Act, and reactions to it; the reactions to Internet filters; reports on student Aaron Smith's Web page and more serious questions of hate speech—all are concerned with freedom of expression. Review all these sets of essays, list major points writers have made on both sides of the First Amendment guarantees, and write a report in which you summarize and comment on the variety of issues that evoke the crucial rights guaranteed under this Amendment. You may wish to conclude with a discussion of your own view of what the First Amendment guarantees. (For guidance on this topic you will want to review material on writing Summaries in Chapter 3 and Written Argument in Chapter 4.)

CHAPTER 11

Bioethics in a Changing World

Business Week says we are moving into the "biotech century." According to Nobel Prize-winner Robert F. Curl of Rice University, the twentieth century was "the century of physics and chemistry [atomic physics in particular]. But it is clear that the twenty-first century will be the century of biology," its premier technology, genetic engineering. Jeremy Rifkin, a leading voice of skeptical concern and caution in this world of biotechnical advances, claims in his book called *The Biotech Century:*

> Never before in history has humanity been so unprepared for the new technological and economic opportunities, challenges, and risks that lie on the horizon. Our way of life is to be more fundamentally transformed in the next several decades than in the previous one thousand years. By the year 2025, we and our children may be living in a world utterly different from anything human beings have ever experienced in the past. . . . These changes represent a turning point for civilization. We are in the throes of one of the great transformations in world history.

Time was when we knew, or thought we knew, what human life was, and learned as children how babies were conceived and born and where their genes came from. We understood that much of who we are and what we look like came directly from our parents and grandparents, even if, in the case of adoption, we didn't know our biological parents. We also believed strongly that the environment in which we grew up had an important influence on who we became. But in the background of our lives scientists were working on the frontiers of biology, exploring the nature of our genetic codes. In 1968 the world thrilled to the book, *The Double Helix,* James Watson and Francis Crick's vividly readable explanation of the structure of DNA (the main component of chromosomes, the material that transfers genetic characteristics). In 1962, Watson and Crick had won the Nobel Prize for the research described in their book. What the world didn't yet know was that natural human curiosity and intellectual drive were leading scientists on an inevitable quest to map the genetic make-up of each individual and to gain control over the molecular construction of our genes. To these ends, in 1988 two government agencies, the National Institutes of Health and the Department of Energy, joined forces on the Human Genome Project. In the 1990s, at least two private companies entered the race to map the genome, with lucrative rewards for the winner and for drug companies looming on the horizon. In June, 2000, the public consortium, headed by the National Institutes of Health with Francis Collins at the helm, and the private company Celera, headed by J. Craig Venter, announced to much fanfare that they had completed a "working draft" of the human genome.

It is no wonder then that each year brings new breakthroughs in reproductive biology and the study of genetics. Chromosomes, present in every cell and the bearers of the genes, can be isolated, removed, replaced, and finally combined by means of recombinant DNA. It is now possible to move the bird call of a quail to the brain of a chicken while it's still an embryo in the egg, and take the light from a firefly and, by inserting it into a tobacco plant, make its leaf glow. We are used to the once-astonishing feat of human eggs selectively fertilized outside the womb. The eggs of one woman can be implanted in the womb of another. "Undesirable" genes can be exchanged for "preferable" ones or combined across species. Scientists can manipulate the building blocks of life, which, until recently, were assumed to be forever predetermined.

As a result of this biological revolution, once unthought-of steps are taken every day. Women unable to conceive can bear children not of the mother's genetic heritage and at ages thought, until now, well beyond the possible. New genetically engineered treatments for serious medical conditions are emerging at a rapid rate. In highly controversial research which could lead to enormous financial profit for the companies financing the research, scientists have isolated and cultured human stem or "master" cells, cells with the potential to grow new human parts on demand and thus provide cures for many diseases. In 1997, scientists cloned a sheep and surprisingly soon after, a calf, then mice, and then six calves. Early in the spring of 2000, scientists reported the production of six cloned calves destined to outwit the perils of aging. In December 1998, biologists in South Korea had already claimed to have made the ultimate breakthrough: cloning a cell from a thirty-year-old woman, creating an embryo that is her exact genetic copy. They did not allow this embryo to develop, but the technology appears to be in place. We can be sure that each year, if not each month, will bring new headlines about cloning. On a lighter note, unidentified pet owners donated $2.3 million to the College of Veterinary

"Genetic engineering got us into this mess,
and genetic engineering will get us out of it."

Medicine at Texas A&M University in hopes that their beloved dog Missy can be cloned. This donation led to Genetic Savings and Clone, a company that can store your aging pet's DNA so that one day you might have a clone, for about $200,000. From the frightening to the ridiculous, the cloning pendulum keeps swinging and the ethical questions multiply.

But the issue of cloning—and all the radical changes in our concept of "life" and cellular reproduction that the biotech revolution has spawned—has led to serious, complex, ethical questions. As Jeremy Rifkin continues in *The Biotech Century:*

> The biotech revolution will affect every aspect of our lives. The way we eat; the way we date and marry; the way we have our babies; the way our children are raised and educated; the way we work; the way we engage in politics; the way we express our faith; the way we perceive the world around us and our place in it—all of our individual and shared realities will be deeply touched by the new technologies of the biotech century. Surely, these very personal technologies deserve to be widely discussed and debated by the public at large before they become a part of our daily lives.

To determine the moral boundaries and legislative necessities of such a totally new biological landscape, all of us must become aware of and knowledgeable about the issues that this new landscape creates. In the articles that follow, you will have an opportunity to *read and think critically, discuss,* and ultimately *write about* this unprecedented frontier as you weigh the risks and the blessings.

The Ethical Dilemmas of Cloning

A Prophecy

Moving Toward Clonal Man: Is This What We Want?

James D. Watson

In 1971, molecular biologist, James Watson (author of *The Double Helix,* mentioned earlier) wrote a prophetic article for the *Atlantic Monthly,* an article referred to by William Safire in his definition of the term *clone* cited below. Working on the cutting edge of genetic research, Watson, who won the Nobel Prize in 1962, was for several decades a professor of molecular biology at Harvard University and is currently direc-tor of the Cold Spring Harbor Laboratory. He discusses in this essay many of the in-novative procedures that we consider common place today and helps shed light on the genesis of current breakthroughs in genetic engineering. For those of you who are not biology students, you may need to look up a few terms (*blastocyst, diploid nu-clei, enucleated,* for example), but otherwise you will find that Watson writes clearly for lay people about complex scientific issues.

The notion that man might sometime soon be reproduced asexually upsets many people. The main public effect of the remarkable clonal frog produced some ten years ago in Oxford by the zoologist John Gurdon has not been awe of the elegant scientific implication of this frog's existence, but fear that a similar experiment might someday be done with human cells. Until recently, however, this foreboding has seemed more like a science-fiction scenario than a real prob-lem which the human race has to live with.

For the embryological development of man does not occur free in the placid environment of a freshwater pond, in which a frog's eggs normally turn into tadpoles and then into mature frogs. Instead, the crucial steps in human embryology always occur in the highly inaccessible womb of a human female. There the growing fetus enlarges unseen, and effectively out of range of almost any manipulation except that which is deliberately designed to abort its exis-tence. As long as all humans develop in this manner, there is no way to take the various steps necessary to insert an adult diploid nucleus from a pre-existing hu-man into a human egg whose maternal genetic material has previously been re-moved. Given the continuation of the normal processes of conception and de-velopment, the idea that we might have a world populated by people whose genetic material was identical to that of previously existing people can belong only to the domain of the novelist or moviemaker, not to that of pragmatic sci-entists who must think only about things which can happen.

Today, however, we must face up to the fact that the unexpectedly rapid progress of R. G. Edwards and P. S. Steptoe in working out the conditions for routine test-tube conception of human eggs means that human embryological development need no longer be a process shrouded in secrecy. It can become instead an event wide-open to a variety of experimental manipulations. Already the two scientists have developed many embryos to the eight-cell stage, and a few more into blastocysts, the stage where successful implantation into a human uterus should not be too difficult to achieve. In fact, Edwards and Steptoe hope to accomplish implantation and subsequent growth into a normal baby within the coming year.

The question naturally arises, why should any woman willingly submit to the laparoscopy operation which yields the eggs to be used in test-tube conceptions? There is clearly some danger involved every time Steptoe operates. Nonetheless, he and Edwards believe that the risks are more than counterbalanced by the fact that their research may develop methods which could make their patients able to bear children. All their patients, though having normal menstrual cycles, are infertile, many because they have blocked oviducts which prevent passage of eggs into the uterus. If so, *in vitro* growth of their eggs up to the blastocyst stage may circumvent infertility, thereby allowing normal childbirth. Moreover, since the sex of a blastocyst is easily determined by chromosomal analysis, such women would have the possibility of deciding whether to give birth to a boy or a girl.

Clearly, if Edwards and Steptoe succeed, their success will be followed up in many other places. The number of such infertile women, while small on a relative percentage basis, is likely to be large on an absolute basis. Within the United States there could be 100,000 or so women who would like a similar chance to have their own babies. At the same time, we must anticipate strong, if not hysterical, reactions from many quarters. The certainty that the ready availability of this medical technique will open up the possibility of hiring out unrelated women to carry a given baby to term is bound to outrage many people. For there is absolutely no reason why the blastocyst need be implanted in the same woman from whom the pre-ovulatory eggs were obtained. Many women with anatomical complications which prohibit successful childbearing might be strongly tempted to find a suitable surrogate. And it is easy to imagine that other women who just don't want the discomforts of pregnancy would also seek this very different form of motherhood. Of even greater concern would be the potentialities for misuse by an inhumane totalitarian government.

Some very hard decisions may soon be upon us. It is not obvious, for example, that the vague potential of abhorrent misuse should weigh more strongly than the unhappiness which thousands of married couples feel when they are unable to have their own children. Different societies are likely to view the matter differently, and it would be surprising if all should come to the same conclusion. We must, therefore, assume that techniques for the *in vitro* manipulation of human eggs, are likely to become general medical practice, capable of routine performance in many major countries, within some ten to twenty years.

The situation would then be ripe for extensive efforts, either legal or illegal, at human cloning. But for such experiments to be successful, techniques would have to be developed which allow the insertion of adult diploid nuclei into human eggs which previously have had their maternal haploid nucleus removed.

At first sight, this task is a very tall order since human eggs are much smaller than those of frogs, the only vertebrates which have so far been cloned. Insertion by micropipettes, the device used in the case of the frog, is always likely to damage human eggs irreversibly. Recently however, the development of simple techniques for fusing animal cells has raised the strong possibility that further refinements of the cell-fusion method will allow the routine introduction of human diploid nuclei into enucleated human eggs. Activation of such eggs to divide to become blastocysts, followed by implantation into suitable uteri should lead to the development of healthy fetuses, and subsequent normal-appearing babies.

The growing up to adulthood of these first clonal humans could be a very startling event, a fact already appreciated by many magazine editors, one of whom commissioned a cover with multiple copies of Ringo Starr, another of whom gave us overblown multiple likenesses of the current sex goddess, Raquel Welch. It takes little imagination to perceive that different people will have highly different fantasies, some perhaps imagining the existence of countless people with the features of Picasso or Frank Sinatra or Walt Frazier or Doris Day. And would monarchs like the Shah of Iran, knowing they might never be able to have a normal male heir, consider the possibility of having a son whose genetic constitution would be identical to their own?

Clearly, even more bizarre possibilities can be thought of, and so we might have expected that many biologists, particularly those whose work impinges upon this possibility, would seriously ponder its implication, and begin a dialogue which would educate the world's citizens and offer suggestions which our legislative bodies might consider in framing national science policies. On the whole, however, this has not happened. Though a number of scientific papers devoted to the problem of genetic engineering have casually mentioned that clonal reproduction may someday be with us, the discussion to which I am party has been so vague and devoid of meaningful time estimates as to be virtually soporific.

Does this effective silence imply a conspiracy to keep the general public unaware of a potential threat to their basic ways of life? Could it be motivated by fear that the general reaction will be a further damning of all science, thereby decreasing even more the limited money available for pure research? Or does it merely tell us that most scientists do live such an ivory-tower existence that they are capable of thinking rationally only about pure science, dismissing more practical matters as subjects for the lawyers, students, clergy, and politicians to face up to?

One or both of these possibilities may explain why more scientists have not taken cloning before the public. The main reason, I suspect, is that the prospect to most biologists still looks too remote and chancy—not worthy of immediate attention when other matters, like nuclear-weapon overproliferation and pesticide and auto-exhaust pollution, present society with immediate threats to its orderly continuation. Though scientists as a group form the most future-oriented of all professions, there are few of us who concentrate on events unlikely to become reality within the next decade or two.

To almost all the intellectually most adventurous, geneticists, the seemingly distant time when cloning might first occur is more to the point than its far-reaching implication, were it to be practiced seriously. For example, Stanford's celebrated geneticist, Joshua Lederberg, among the first to talk about cloning as a practical matter, now seems bored with further talk, implying that we should channel our limited influence as public citizens to the prevention of the wide-scale, irreversible damage to our genetic material that is now occurring through increasing exposure to man-created mutagenic compounds. To him, serious talk about cloning is essentially crying wolf when a tiger is already inside the walls.

This position, however, fails to allow for what I believe will be a frenetic rush to do experimental manipulation with human eggs once they have become a readily available commodity. And that is what they will be within several years after Edwards-Steptoe methods lead to the birth of the first healthy baby by a previously infertile woman. Isolated human eggs will be found in hundreds of hospitals, and given the fact that Steptoe's laparoscopy technique frequently yields several eggs from a single woman donor, not all of the eggs so obtained, even if they could be cultured to the blastocyst stage, would ever be reim-planted into female bodies. Most of these excess eggs would likely be used for a variety of valid experimental purposes, many, for example, to perfect the Edwards-Steptoe techniques. Others could be devoted to finding methods for curing certain genetic diseases, conceivably through use of cell-fusion methods which now seem to be the correct route to cloning. The temptation to try cloning itself thus will always be close at hand.

No reason, of course, dictates that such cloning experiments need occur. Most of the medical people capable of such experimentation would probably steer clear of any step which looked as though its real purpose were to clone. But it would be shortsighted to assume that everyone would instinctively recoil from such purposes. Some people may sincerely believe the world desperately needs many copies of really exceptional people if we are to fight our way out of the ever-increasing computer-mediated complexity that makes our individual brains so frequently inadequate.

Moreover, given the widespread development of the safe clinical proce-dures for handling human eggs, cloning experiments would not be prohibitively expensive. They need not be restricted to the superpowers. All smaller countries now possess the resources required for eventual success. Furthermore, there need not exist the coercion of a totalitarian state to provide the surrogate moth-ers. There already are such widespread divergences regarding the sacredness of the act of human reproduction that the boring meaninglessness of the lives of many women would be sufficient cause for their willingness to participate in such experimentation, be it legal or illegal. Thus, if the matter proceeds in its current nondirected fashion, a human being born of clonal reproduction most likely will appear on the earth within the next twenty to fifty years, and even sooner, if some nation should actively promote the venture.

The first reaction of most people to the arrival of these asexually produced children, I suspect, would be one of despair. The nature of the bond between parents and their children, not to mention everyone's values about the individ-ual's uniqueness, could be changed beyond recognition, and by a science which they never understood but which until recently appeared to provide more good than harm. Certainly to many people, particularly those with strong religious backgrounds, our most sensible course of action would be to de-emphasize all those forms of research which would circumvent the normal sexual reproductive process. If this step were taken, experiments on cell fusion might no longer be supported by federal funds or tax-exempt organizations. Prohibition of such research would most certainly put off the day when diploid nuclei could satisfactorily be inserted into enucleated human eggs. Even more effective would be to take steps quickly to make illegal, or to reaffirm the illegality of, any experimental work with human embryos.

Neither of the prohibitions, however, is likely to take place. In the first place, the cell-fusion technique now offers one of the best avenues for understanding the genetic basis of cancer. Today, all over the world, cancer cells are being fused with normal cells to pinpoint those specific chromosomes responsible for given forms of cancer. In addition, fusion techniques are the basis of many genetic efforts to unravel the biochemistry of diseases like cystic fibrosis or multiple sclerosis. Any attempts now to stop such work using the argument that cloning represents a greater threat than a disease like cancer is likely to be considered irresponsible by virtually anyone able to understand the matter.

Though more people would initially go along with a prohibition of work on human embryos, many may have a change of heart when they ponder the mess which the population explosion poses. The current projections are so horrendous that responsible people are likely to consider the need for more basic embryological facts much more relevant to our self interest than the not-very-immediate threat of a few clonal men existing some decades ahead. And the potentially militant lobby of infertile couples who see test-tube conception as their only route to the joys of raising children of their own making would carry even more weight. So, scientists like Edwards are likely to get a go-ahead signal even if, almost perversely, the immediate consequences of their "population-money"-supported research will be the production of still more babies.

Complicating any effort at effective legislative guidance is the multiplicity of places where work like Edwards' could occur, thereby making unlikely the possibility that such manipulations would have the same legal (or illegal) status throughout the world. We must assume that if Edwards and Steptoe produce a really workable method for restoring fertility, large numbers of women will search out those places where it is legal (or possible), just as now they search out places where abortions can be easily obtained.

Thus, all nations formulating policies to handle the implications of *in vitro* human embryo experimentation must realize that the problem is essentially an international one. Even if one or more countries should stop such research, their action could effectively be neutralized by the response of a neighboring country. This most disconcerting impotence also holds for the United States. If our congressional representatives, upon learning where the matter now stands, should decide that they want none of it and pass very strict laws against human embryo experimentation, their action would not seriously set back the current scientific and medical momentum which brings us close to the possibility of surrogate mothers, if not human clonal reproduction. This is because the relevant experiments are being done not in the United States, but largely in England. That is partly a matter of chance, but also a consequence of the advanced state of English cell biology, which in certain areas is far more adventurous and imaginative than its American counterpart. There is no American university which has the strength in experimental embryology that Oxford possesses.

We must not assume, however, that today the important decisions lie only before the British government. Very soon we must anticipate that a number of biologists and clinicians of other countries, sensing the potential excitement, will move into this area of science. So even if the current English effort were stifled, similar experimentation could soon begin elsewhere. Thus it appears to me most desirable that as many people as possible be informed about the new ways of human reproduction and their potential consequences, both good and bad.

This is a matter far too important to be left solely in the hands of the scientific and medical communities. The belief that surrogate mothers and clonal babies are inevitable because science always moves forward, an attitude expressed to me recently by a scientific colleague, represents a form of laissez-faire nonsense dismally reminiscent of the creed that American business, if left to itself, will solve everybody's problems. Just as the success of a corporate body in making money need not set the human condition ahead, neither does every scientific advance automatically make our lives more "meaningful." No doubt the person whose experimental skill will eventually bring forth a clonal baby will be given wide notoriety. But the child who grows up knowing that the world wants another Picasso may view his creator in a different light.

I would thus hope that over the next decade wide-reaching discussion would occur, at the informal as well as formal legislative level, about the manifold problems which are bound to arise if test-tube conception becomes a common occurrence. A blanket declaration of the worldwide illegality of human cloning might be one result of a serious effort to ask the world in which direction it wished to move. Admittedly the vast effort, required for even the most limited international arrangement, will turn off some people—those who believe the matter is of marginal importance now, and that it is a red herring designed to take our minds off our callous attitudes toward war, poverty, and racial prejudice. But if we do not think about it now, the possibility of our having a free choice will one day suddenly be gone.

TOPICS FOR DISCUSSION AND WRITING

1. What achievements that we take for granted today did Watson accurately predict in 1971?

2. What reasons does Watson offer for predicting that no legal steps will be taken to slow genetic research leading to cloning? (See Premises and Conclusions in Chapter 3.)

3. Now try your hand at playing prophet. Write a shorter version of Watson's article, predicting a few genetic breakthroughs down the

road and providing current evidence to support your guesses about the future. You may want to look ahead through other articles in this chapter for additional ideas.

The Story of Dolly the Sheep and Her Aftermath

In the February, 1997 issue of the prestigious scientific journal *Nature,* Scottish embryologist Ian Wilmut and his colleagues at the Roslin Institute, near Edinburgh, astonished not only the biomedical community but the whole world with their announcement that they had cloned a six-year-old sheep. Using a single cell taken from the udder of a pregnant six-year-old ewe, they produced an exact replica and whimsically named her Dolly in honor of the famously endowed celebrity, Dolly Parton. In Wilmut's words, "The lamb born after nuclear transfer from a mammary gland cell is, to our knowledge, the first mammal to develop from a cell derived from an adult tissue." This made her the only mammal ever born that was identical to her biological mother. While several attempts to clone cells from animal embryos had been successful, never before had a cell from an adult mammal reproduced itself without fertilization. The key biological issue revolved around the nature of how genes develop as cells grow and differentiate. Until Dolly, most biologists thought that only at the embryonic stage could a cell reproduce itself. It is difficult to assess the potential of an embryo; cloning the unknown would presumably have limited advantages.

"Ewe again?"

But selecting choice adult specimens could lead to interesting advances or, on the other hand, to dangerous meddling in evolution, God's will, nature's way—or however you view the orchestration of the universe. One of the many puzzling questions about Dolly is whether she will assume the life expectancy of a newborn or of a six-year-old. Regardless, she arrived in the world as a newborn lamb, with no biological father and two mothers, one the celebrated donor ewe, the other a Scottish Blackface surrogate.

After Decades and Many Missteps, Cloning Success

Michael Specter with Gina Kolata

When the news of Dr. Wilmut and Dolly broke, the *New York Times* put it on page one and gave the story in-depth coverage for a wide audience. Journalist Michael Specter and Gina Kolata the author of the book *Clone: The Road to Dolly and the Path Ahead* and an expert on cloning and other bioethical issues, provided all the details in language their lay readers could readily understand. (See Audience and Purpose in Chapter 1.)

Midlothian, Scotland, March 2—Charles Darwin was so terrified when he discovered that mankind had not been specially separated from all other animals by God that it took him two decades to find the courage to publish the work that forever altered the way humans look at life on Earth. Albert Einstein, so out-

Dolly the lamb with her surrogate mother.

Photo reprinted with permission from *Nature* Vol. 385, pp. 810–813. Copyright © 1997 Macmillan Magazines Limited/Photo by Ian Wilmut.

wardly serene, once said that after the theory of relativity stormed into his mind as a young man, it never again left him, not even for a minute.

But Dr. Ian Wilmut, the 52-year old embryologist who astonished the world on Feb. 2 by announcing that he had created the first animal cloned from an adult—a lamb named Dolly—seems almost oblivious to the profound and disquieting implications of his work. Perhaps no achievement in modern biology promises to solve more problems than the possibility of regular, successful genetic manipulation. But certainly none carries a more ominous burden of fear and misunderstanding.

"I am not a fool," Dr. Wilmut said last week in his cluttered lab, during a long conversation in which he reviewed the fitful 25-year odyssey that led to his electrifying accomplishment and unwanted fame. "I know what is bothering people about all this. I understand why the world is suddenly at my door. But this is my work. It has always been my work, and it doesn't have anything to do with creating copies of human beings. I am not haunted by what I do, if that is what you want to know. I sleep very well at night."

Yet by scraping a few cells from the udder of a 6-year-old ewe, then fusing them into a specially altered egg cell from another sheep, Dr. Wilmut and his colleagues at the Roslin Institute here, seven miles from Edinburgh, have suddenly pried open one of the most forbidden—and tantalizing—doors of modern life.

People have been obsessed with the possibilities of building humans for centuries, even before Mary Shelley wrote "Frankenstein" in 1818. Still, so few legitimate researchers actually thought it was possible to create an identical genetic copy of an adult animal that Dr. Wilmut may well have been the only man trying to do it, a contrast with the fiery competition that has become the hallmark of modern molecular biology.

Dr. Wilmut, a meek and affable researcher who lives in a village where sheep outnumber people, grew more disheveled and harried as the pressure-filled week wore on. A $60,000-a-year government employee at the institute, Scotland's leading animal research laboratory, Dr. Wilmut does not stand to earn more than $25,000 in royalties if his breakthrough is commercially successful.

"I give everything away," he said. "I want to understand things."

Dr. Wilmut has made no conscious effort to improve on science fiction in his work; he said, in fact, that he rarely read it. A quiet man whose wife is an elder in the Church of Scotland but who says he "does not have a belief in God," Dr. Wilmut is the least sensational of scientists. Asked the inevitable questions about cloning human beings, he patiently conceded that it might now become possible but added that he would "find it repugnant."

Dr. Wilmut's objectives have always been prosaic and direct: he has spent his life trying to make livestock healthy, more efficient and better able to serve humanity. In creating Dolly, his goal—like that of many other researchers around the world—was to turn animals into factories churning out proteins that can be used as drugs. Even though the work is early and tentative, and it needs many improvements before it can be used, no scientists have stepped forward to say that they doubt its authenticity.

Many scientists say they are certain that the day will eventually come when humans can also be cloned. Already, scientists in Oregon say they have cloned rhesus monkeys from very early embryo cells. That is not the same as cloning the more sophisticated cells of an adult animal, or even a developing fetus. But any kind of cloning in primates brings the work closer to human beings. That is why what has happened here has rapidly begun to resonate far beyond the tufted glens and heather hills of Scotland. In much the way that the Wright Brothers at Kitty Hawk freed humanity of a restriction once considered eternal, human existence suddenly seems to have taken on a dramatic new dimension.

The eventual impact of this particular experiment on business and science may not be known for years. But it will almost certainly cast important new light on basic biological science.

Already, even the simplest questions about the creation of Dolly provoke answers that demonstrate how profound and novel the research here has been. Asked if the lamb should be considered 7 months old, which is how long she has been alive, or 6 years old, since it is a genetic replica of a 6-year-old sheep, Dr. Wilmut's clear blue eyes clouded for a moment. "I can't answer that," he said. "We just don't know. There are many things here we will have to find out."

THE GOAL

Aim Is Barnyard, Not Nursery

The Scots have an old tongue twister of an adage that says "many a mickle make a muckle," or, little things add up to big things. It is certainly true of the cloning of Dolly, who had her conceptual birth in a conversation in an Irish bar more than a decade ago and who was born after a series of painstaking experiments, years of doubt and several final all-night vigils—one bleating little lamb among nearly 300 abject failures.

While the world has become transfixed by the idea of creating identical copies from frozen cells, that was not the result that Dr. Wilmut, or any other scientists interviewed for this article, considers the most significant part of the research.

The true object of those years of labor was to find better ways to alter the genetic make-up of farm animals to create herds capable of providing better food or any chemical a consumer might want. In theory, genes could be altered so animals would produce better meat, eggs, wool or milk. Animals could be made more resistant to disease. Researchers here even talk about breeding cows that could deliver low-fat milk straight from the udder.

"The overall aim is actually not, primarily, to make copies," Dr. Wilmut said, interrupted constantly by the institute's feed mill as it noisily blew off steam. "It's to make precise genetic changes in cells."

Obscure as he may seem to those outside his field, Ian Wilmut has been quietly pushing the borders of reproductive science for decades. In 1973, having just completed his doctorate at Cambridge, he produced the first calf born from a frozen embryo. Cows give birth to no more than 5 or 10 calves in a lifetime. By taking frozen embryos produced by cows that provide the best meat and milk, thawing them and transferring them to surrogate mothers, Dr. Wilmut enabled cattle breeders to increase the quality of their herds immensely.

Since then, while always harboring at least some doubt that cloning was really possible, he has struggled to isolate and transfer genetic traits that would improve the utility of farm animals.

In 1986, while in Ireland for a scientific meeting, Dr. Wilmut heard something during a casual conversation in a bar that caught his attention and convinced him that cloning large farm animals was indeed possible "It was just a bar-time story," he recalled this week, in the slight brogue he has acquired after living here for 25 years. "Not even straight from the horse's mouth."

What he heard was the rumor—true, it turned out—that another scientist had created a lamb clone from an already developing embryo. It was enough to push him in a direction that had already been abandoned by most of his colleagues.

By the early 1980's, many researchers had grown discouraged about the practicalities of cloning because of a hurdle that had come to seem insurmountable. Every cell in the body originates from a single fertilized egg, which contains in its DNA all the information needed to construct a whole organism. That fertilized egg cell grows and divides. The new cells slowly take on special properties, developing into skin, or blood or bones, for example. But each cell, however specialized, still carries in its nucleus a full complement of DNA, a complete blueprint for an organism.

The problem for scientists was stark and unavoidable: It was assumed that the nucleus of a mature cell, which has developed, or differentiated, so it could carry out a specific function in the body, simply could not be made to function like the nucleus of an embryo that had yet to begin the process of learning to play its special role. Even though the DNA, with all the necessary genes, was in the differentiated cell, the issue was how to turn it on so it would direct the process of growth that begins with the egg. The essential question for cloning researchers was whether the genes in an adult cell could still be used to create a new animal with the same genes.

The pivotal rumor Dr. Wilmut heard at the meeting in Ireland was that a Danish embryologist, Dr. Steen M. Willadsen, then working at Grenada Genetics in Texas, had managed to clone a sheep using a cell from an embryo that was already developing.

The story, which came from a veterinarian named Geoff Mahon, who worked at the same company, went beyond the research that Dr. Willadsen would publish later that year on cloning sheep from early embryos, Dr. Willadsen said in a telephone interview from his home in Florida that he had indeed done the more advanced work but had never published it.

What he did publish was the result of successfully cloning sheep from very early embryo cells: the first cloning of a mammal. Dr. Willadsen tried that experiment with three sheep eggs. In each case, he removed the egg's nucleus, with all its genetic information, and fused that egg, now bereft of instructions on how to grow, with a cell from a growing embryo. If the egg could use the other cell's genetic information to grow itself into a lamb, the experiment would be a success. It worked.

"The reality is that the very first experiment I did, which involved only three eggs, was successful," Dr. Willadsen said. "It gave me two lambs." They were dead on arrival, but the next one we got was alive." The paper was eventually published in *Nature,* the influential British science journal that last week published Dr. Wilmut's news of Dolly, and it created a sensation.

But it was the rumor of the unpublished work that captivated Dr. Wilmut. If it was possible to clone using an already differentiated embryonic cell, it was time to take another look at cloning an adult, Dr. Wilmut decided. "I thought if that story was true—and remember, it was just a bar-time story—if it was true, we could get those cells from farm animals," he said. And, he thought, he might even be able to make copies of animals from more mature embryos or eventually from an adult.

When Dr. Wilmut flew back to Scotland, he was already dreaming of Dolly. When he was flying back over the Irish Sea with a colleague, he said. "We were already making plans to try to get funds to start this work."

THE QUEST

From Daydreams to Successes

Dr. Wilmut's dominance of the field grew from that day, almost by default. He was nearly alone, out on a limb. His tumultuous field seemed to have run out of steam. Many of its leaders and its students had departed, going to medical school and becoming doctors or accepting lucrative positions at in vitro fertilization centers, helping infertile couples have babies. Two of its stars published a famous paper concluding that cloning an adult animal was impossible, dashing cold water on their eager colleagues. Companies, formed in a flush of enthusiasm a decade earlier, folded by the early 1990's.

Most of the few cloning researchers left were focused on a much easier task. They were cloning cells from early embryos that had not yet specialized. And even though some had achieved stunning successes, none were about to try cloning an adult or even cells from mature embryos. It just did not seem possible.

The idea of cloning had tantalized scientists since 1938. When no one even knew what genetic material consisted of, the first modern embryologist, Dr. Hans Spemann of Germany, proposed what he called a "fantastical experiment": taking the nucleus out of an egg cell and replacing it with a nucleus from another cell. In short, he suggested that scientists try to clone.

But no one could do it, said Dr. Randall S. Prather, a cloning researcher at the University of Missouri in Columbia, because the technology was not advanced enough. It would be another 14 years before anyone could try to clone, and then they did it with frogs, whose eggs are enormous compared with those of mammals, making them far easier to manipulate. Dr. Spemann, who died in 1941, never saw his idea carried to fruition.

In fact, frogs were not successfully cloned until the 1970's. The work was done by Dr. John Gurdon, who now teaches at Cambridge University. Even though the frogs never reached adulthood, the technique used was a milestone.

He replaced the nucleus of a frog egg, one large cell, with that of another cell from another frog.

It was the beginning of nuclear transfer experiments, which had the goal of getting the newly transplanted genes to direct the development of the embryo. But the frog studies seemed to indicate that cloning could go only so far. Although scientists could transfer nuclei from adult cells to egg cells, the frogs only developed to tadpoles, and they always died.

Most researcher at the time though even that sort of limited cloning success depended on something special about frogs. "For years, it was thought that you could never do that in mammals," said Dr. Neal First of the University of Wisconsin, who has been Dr. Wilmut's most devoted competitor.

In 1981, after some rapid advances in technology, two investigators published a paper that galvanized the world. It seemed to say that mammals could be cloned—at least from embryo cells. But, in a crushing blow to those in the field, the research turned out to be a fraud.

The investigators, Dr. Karl Illmensee of the Univeristy of Geneva and Dr. Peter Hoppe of the Jackson Laboratory in Bar Harbor, Me., claimed that they had transplanted the nuclei of mouse embryo cells into mouse eggs and produced three live mice that were clones of the embryos. Their mice were on the cover of the prestigious journal *Science,* and their work created a sensation.

"Everyone thought that article was right," said Dr. Brigid Hogan, a mouse embryologist at Vanderbilt University in Nashville. Dr. Illmensee, the senior author, "was getting enormous publicity and exposure, and accolades," Dr. Hogan said.

Two years later, however, two other scientists, Dr. James McGrath and Dr. Davor Solter, working at the Wistar Institute in Philadelphia, reported in *Science* that they could not repeat the mouse experiment. They concluded their paper with the disheartening statement that the "cloning of mammals by simple nuclear transfer is impossible." After a lengthy inquiry, it was discovered that Dr. Illmensee had faked his results.

Leaders in the field were shattered. Dr. McGrath gave up cloning, got an M.D. degree and is now a genetics professor at Yale University. Dr. Solter gave up cloning and is now the director of the Max Planck Institute in Freiburg, Germany. Most research centers abandoned the work completely.

"Man, it was depressing," said Dr. James M. Robl, a cloning researcher at the University of Massachusetts in Amherst. After the paper by Dr. Illmensee, "we all thought we would be cloning animals like crazy," Dr. Robl said. He had pursued research to try to clone cows and pigs. Suddenly, it seemed as though he was wasting his time.

"We had a famous scientist come through the lab," Dr. Robl said. "I showed him with all enthusiasm all the work I was doing. He looked at me with a very serious look on his face and said, 'Why are you doing this?'"

But not everyone was despondent. A few investigators forged on. One of them was Dr. Keith Campbell, a charismatic 42-year-old biologist at the institute here who specializes in studying the life cycle of the cell. Dr. Campbell, who joined the institute in 1991, said in an interview last week, "I always believed that if you could do this in a frog, you could do it in mammals." Dr. Campbell, who said he had enjoyed the cloning fantasy "The Boys From Brazil," responded to questions about his earlier work on cloning in an interview last summer, saying "We're only accelerating what breeders have been doing for years."

Soon he had convinced his colleagues at the institute to try the experiments that eventually led to their success with Dolly. "But at that point, we still had much to learn," he said.

The most important step would be to find a way to grow clones from cells that had already developed beyond the very earliest embryonic stage. Whenever cloning had been tried with more specialized cells in the past, it had ended in failure. Until Dolly was born, nobody could be sure whether those failures were because older cells have switched off some of their genes for good or because nobody knew how to make them work properly in an egg.

Because no one knew whether cloning was even possible, it was hard to speculate about what the hurdles might be. But Dr. Campbell had what turned out to be the crucial insight. It could be, he realized, that an egg will not take up and use the genetic material from an adult cell because the cell cycles of the egg and the adult cell might be out of synchrony. All cells go through cycles in which they grow and divide, making a whole new set of chromosomes each time. In cloning, Dr. Campbell speculated, the problem might be that the egg was in one stage of its cycle while the adult cell was in another.

Dr. Campbell decided that rather than try to catch a cell at just the right moment, perhaps he could just slow down cellular activity, nearly stopping it. Then the cell might rest in just the state he wanted so it could join with an egg.

"It dawned on me that this could be a beneficial way of utilizing the cell cycle," he said, in what may turn out to be one of scientific history's great understatements.

What he decided to do was to force the donor cells into a sort of hibernating state, by starving them of some nutrients.

In Wisconsin, Dr. First had actually beaten the Scottish group to cloning a mammal from cells from an early embryo; that occurred when a staff member in the laboratory forgot to provide the nourishing serum, inadvertently starving the cells. The result, in 1994, was four calves. But even Dr. First and his colleagues did not realize the significance of how the animals had been created.

Two years later, Drs. Wilmut and Campbell tried the starvation technique on embryo cells to produce Megan and Morag, the world's first cloned sheep and, until now, the most famous sheep in history. Their creation really laid the foundation for what happened with Dolly, for Dr. Campbell succeeded in doing an end run around the problem of coordinating the cycles of the donor cell with the recipient egg.

Today, Megan and Morag munch contentedly in the same straw-covered pen with the new star of the Roslin Institute, angelic little Dolly. Megan and Morag seem completely normal, if slightly spoiled.

Megan is now expecting, and she got pregnant the old-fashioned way. "It will always be the preferred way of having children," Dr. Campbell said jokingly.

"Why would anyone want to clone, anyway? It's far too expensive and a lot less fun than the original method."

When the scientists moved on to cloning a fully grown sheep, they decided to use udder, or mammary, cells, and that is how Dolly got her name. She was named after the country singer Dolly Patron, whose mammary cells, Dr. Wilmut said, are equally famous.

In the experiment that produced Dolly, Dr. Wilmut's team removed cells from the udder of a 6-year-old sheep. The cells were then preserved in test tubes so the investigators would have genetic material to use in DNA fingerprinting—required to prove that Dolly was indeed a clone. In fact, by the time Dolly was born, her progenitor had died.

The trick, Dr. Wilmut said, was the starvation of the adult cells. "You greatly reduce serum concentration for five days," Dr. Wilmut said. "That's the novel approach. That's what we submitted a patent for." And that is why the team was silent about the lamb's birth for months. Until the patent was applied for, nobody wanted the news to spread.

But success is a relative concept. Even Dr. Campbell's technique has failed far more often than it has succeeded. Dolly was the only lamb to survive from 277 eggs that had been fused with adult cells. Nobody knows, or can know, until the work is repeated, whether the researchers were lucky to get one lamb—whether in fact that one lamb was one in a million and not just one in 277 or whether the scientists will become more proficient with more refinement.

The cell fusion that produced Dolly was done in the last week of January 1996. When the resulting embryo reached the six-day stage, it was implanted in a ewe. Dolly's existence as a growing fetus was first discovered on March 20, the 48th day of her surrogate mother's pregnancy. After that, the ewe was scanned with ultrasound, first each month and then, as interest grew, every two weeks.

"Every time you scanned, you were always hoping you were going to get a heartbeat and a live fetus," said John Bracken, the researcher who monitored the pregnancy.

"You could see the head structure, the movement of the legs, the ribs," he said. "And when you actually identified a heart that was beating, there was a great sense of relief and satisfaction. It was as normal a pregnancy as you could have."

On July 5 at 4 P.M., Dolly was born in a shed down the road from the institute. Mr. Bracken, a few members of the farm staff and the local veterinarian attended. It was a normal birth, head and forelegs first. She weighed 6.6 kilograms, about 14-1/2 pounds, and she was healthy.

Because it was summer, the few staff members present were very busy. There was no celebration.

"We phoned up the road to inform Ian Wilmut and Dr. Campbell," Mr. Bracken said.

But Dr. Wilmut does not remember the call. He does not even remember when he heard about Dolly's birth.

"I even asked my wife if she could recall me coming home doing cartwheels down the corridor, and she could not," he said. . . .

THE PUBLICITY

The tiny center has been contending with the overwhelming and often hostile descent of the news media.

On Friday, as Dr. Wilmut looked deeply uncomfortable in a suit and tie, television crews from around the globe flung themselves at him as if he were an indicted government official. "Do you have any idea of the implications of this research?" a woman from German television shouted at him, becoming the thousandth person to do so. Dr. Wilmut squirmed, shrugged and simply said, "Yes."

One reporter from Greek television demanded permission to jump into the pen with Dolly, Megan and Morag so she could prove to the viewers at home that she was truly on the scene. She did not get it. Other reporters, ignoring completely the fact that this research is new and has been conducted only in sheep, pounded Dr. Wilmut relentlessly about the prospects for cloning human beings.

After all that, Dr. Wilmut now seems to understand that he is struggling with something beyond his control.

"People have sensationalized this in every way," he said, too tired of hearing the worries of everyone from the Vatican to President Clinton to muster any further outrage. He admitted dismay at learning that the leaders of the Euorpean Union had called for an investigation and that the British Government was considering cutting the highly respected institute's financing as a result of the work.

"People say that cloning means that if a child dies, you can get that child back," he said, tugging nervously at his neatly trimmed beard. "It's heartwrenching. You could never get that child back. It would be something different. You need to understand the biology. People are not genes. They are so much more than that.". . .

THE ROAD AHEAD

Hopes and Fears for the Future

Six years ago, animal rights activists burned down two of Roslin's laboratories. It was the first time the public became aware that Dr. Wilmut and his colleagues were trying to do something momentous.

Even before that, cloning had already become a shorthand way to talk about all that many fear in science. It hardly matters that many of the tomatoes and apples sold in grocery stores are the products of genetic engineering or that advances in reproductive technology have brought new hope to millions of potential parents. To most people, the idea of cloning is frightening; it is evidence of technology speeding out of control, an Orwellian universe where the essence of humanity has been lost and the fact of it has been cheapened.

And the race to follow Dr. Wilmut's lead has now begun in earnest. In Wisconsin on Saturday, Dr. First—one of the United States' leading experts in the field—decided to try cloning a cow by the method Dr. Wilmut used.

When he called his technician to ask her to start starving some skin cells from a fetal calf to prepare them for cloning, the technician had already begun. She, too, had heard the news.

Dr. First said he doubted that his lab was alone. He suspects that all over the world, he said, people who know how to clone will "do like we did—grab whatever cells they have" growing in the laboratory and try to repeat Dr. Wilmut's work.

TOPICS FOR DISCUSSION AND WRITING

1. On the basis of the Specter and Kolata article above, write a report in which you summarize the cloning of a sheep to produce Dolly, explaining what made this event so ground-breaking and why it is different from previous cloning experiments. In addition, briefly describe the earlier research that led to Dr. Wilmut's breakthrough and consider what Dr. Wilmut describes as the true object of his early work and the distinction between cloning from embryonic versus adult differentiated cells. You will be summarizing and synthesizing a quantity of information. Use your own words as much as possible. When you find it necessary to quote short passages, be sure to use quotation marks and cite the source. (See Summaries in Chapter 3.)

2. After the birth of Dolly became public, Dr. Wilmut was besieged by reporters from around the world, some quite hostile to what he had done. Why were these critics so upset?

3. One Critic asked Dr. James Robl, an American cloning researcher, "Why are you doing this?" What seems to be the answer for Dr. Wilmut and his colleagues in Scotland and around the world?

4. Explain what Dr. Wilmut meant when he said: "You need to understand the biology. People are not genes. They are so much more than that." Do you see a connection between that remark and his claim earlier in the article, "I am not haunted by what I do. . . . I sleep very well at night"?

5. Kolata has quoted Russian novelist Dostoevsky in connection with cloning: "Man gets used to everything—the beast." Are you astonished by scientific creations such as Dolly the sheep and the cloned animals that have followed her? Or are you growing used to the startling new developments in the natural sciences? Think critically about your own reactions. After class discussion, write a paper exploring your attitude toward cloning and state your position on cloning. You may want to suspend the written part of this assignment until after you have read the selections on the subject which follow in the next section, The Debate, starting on page 356.

Cloned Cows Have Younger-Than-Normal Cells

....

The April 28, 2000 issue *Science,* America's leading journal of scientific research, carried news of the latest breakthrough in the ongoing cloning saga. Reported widely in the press, the story is summarized here in a report from the Web site News from Health-central.com. Particularly exciting are the implications for treating a number of diseases and controlling the aging process, something the cloning of Dolly left unanswered.

New York (Reuters, Health)—One of the problems with the cloned sheep Dolly was that she was born with cells that appeared to be prematurely aged. Now researchers report that a set of six cloned calves seem to have discovered the fountain of youth. Compared with calves the same age, these cloned cattle have cells that appear younger—in some cases, even younger than newborn calves.

"Cloning cells can take cells back in time," the study's lead author, Dr. Robert P. Lanza, of Advanced Cell Technologies in Worcester, Massachusetts, told Reuters Health in an interview. The findings "pave the way" for using cloned cells to form replacements for diseased tissue, he said.

Lanza and colleagues report in the April 28th issue of *Science* that, unlike Dolly, the cloned cows had telomeres—structures at the tip of chromosomes that shorten with each cell division—that were longer than in normal calves the same age and in some cases, longer than those seen in newborn calves. Individual cells divide only a finite number of times (usually 75 to 80 divisions), and each time the telomeres lose a bit of their length. When the telomere reaches a certain length, the cell dies—a natural process that rids the body of old and worn out tissue. It's not clear what impact telomere length has on the lifespan of the entire organism.

One reason that the calves' cells seem younger than Dolly's could be that the animals were produced in different ways, according to Lanza. The researchers who produced Dolly cloned the sheep using adult mammary cells that had been starved to make them enter a resting state. Lanza and his colleagues used connective tissue cells that were at the end of their lifespan. The cells had about four divisions left before their number was up. In contrast, the telomere length of the cloned calves suggested that cells had up to 90 divisions before they were scheduled to self-destruct.

"We've proven that it's possible to create young healthy cells from old cells," Lanza said in the interview.

According to Lanza, the cloned cells may be ideal for treating a number of diseases including Parkinson's disease, diabetes and heart disease. For example, cells taken from a person with diabetes could be cloned to form cells that produce insulin and then re-injected into the person, he said. Or cells could be cloned to form heart cells that could be used to form a "patch" to repair damaged heart tissue, according to Lanza.

Treating disease with cells cloned from a person's own cells would have a special advantage over using cells taken from another person, Lanza said, since they would not be rejected by the immune system. He also noted that one of the obstacles currently preventing the development of replacement tissues is the difficulty in growing enough cells. With the youthful, cloned cells, which divide rapidly, however, growing enough cells would be much easier, according to Lanza.

Since the cells appear to have the properties of much younger cells, Lanza said, "Any structure you create from these cells would outlive the normal life-span of the patient."

In his comments to Reuters Health, Lanza said that the next step is to see what effects these younger-appearing cells have on the calves as they grow.

"We're wondering what that means for the lifespan of the whole animal," he said. A longer lifespan would have implications for not only medicine but also agriculture, he said.

TOPICS FOR DISCUSSION AND WRITING

1. What, according to scientist Robert Lanza, is particularly gratifying about the latest cloning experiments?

2. How could cloning make treating diseases like Parkinson's and diabetes more effective than current methods?

3. Developments in cloning are so fast-breaking that it's difficult to stay current on the latest information. Use the Internet and other media to research new developments in animal cloning and discuss what seem to be the advantages of each cloning breakthrough. Write a report in which you bring the articles included in "The Story of Dolly and Her Aftermath" up to date. (See Chapter 9 for help in research strategies.)

Another View of Cloning

Russell Baker

Humorist Russell Baker, in one of his columns on contemporary life, inserted a welcome note of laughter after learning about the successful cloning of mice in the summer of 1998. Perhaps he has a point.

We truly live in wonderful times, but now and then when Old Devil Skeptic jumps on my back, he starts me asking myself questions. . . . Scientists who work with genes have just cloned some mice. It was big news, but can somebody tell me: Why does the world need more mice? Aren't there already enough mice for everybody? Are so many people complaining of mice shortages that we have to clone them? Can't we curb the childish exuberance of the world's cloners? Don't misread me. Cloning is a wonderful, wonderful thing, but where will we end up when the cloners clone what they're absolutely dying to clone just to show they can do it; to wit, people? Why make rush-hour traffic worse just because you've got the knowhow? That's just, showing off, isn't it? Instead of glutting the landscape with more mice and people, why don't biologists clone creatures facing extinction? Frogs and toads, for instance, are much in the news just

© 1999 Mike Twohy. Dist. by Washington Post Writers Group.

7-24   m. Twohy

"Come look, honey. They've successfully introduced the newscaster gene into a sheep."

now. They are dying en masse of a mysterious worldwide affliction. You cloners ought to be making frogs and toads, not mice. Shouldn't you?

The Debate

> *"Did you know that a woman can now have children without a man?"*
> *"But what on earth for?"*
> *"You can apply ice to a woman's ovaries, for instance. She can have a child. Men are no longer necessary to humanity."*
> *At once Ella laughs, and with confidence, "But what woman in her senses would want ice applied to her ovaries instead of a man?"*
>
> DORIS LESSING, *THE GOLDEN NOTEBOOK*

Lessing makes much the same observation as Dr. Wilmut did in his interview included above. But, in the words of a recent advertising campaign, "If it can be imagined, it can be done." And so, inevitably, research in genetics will continue to go forward, right or wrong, whether we want it or not, just as it has in the past.

Following the announcement of Dolly's birth, U.S. government officials and medical ethicists were quick to take up the thorny issue of limiting or banning research that could lead to advancements in cloning, and journalists framed and reframed the questions for the general public. A Time/CNN poll indicated that 93 percent of Americans disapproved of attempts to clone humans, 66 percent disapproved of cloning animals. In March, 1997, the President imposed a ban on the use of federal money for cloning and appointed an ethics panel to study the issue. In June, the panel recommended making human cloning a criminal offense, extending the restrictions to private as well as publicly funded research. Clinton then proposed legislation to ban cloning and directed the National Bioethics Advisory Commission to report back in 2002.

Gregory E. Pence, a professor of bioethics at the University of Alabama's medical school, took a strong minority position in his book, *Who's Afraid of Cloning?*, claiming freedom of reproduction was at issue. And Chicago scientist, G. Richard Seed, startled the nation in an interview on National Public Radio, where he announced that "It is our objective to set up a human clone clinic in Greater Chicago here, make it a profitable fertility clinic." He said he would be using the techniques pioneered by the Scottish scientists who created Dolly. His argument centered on the following deduction:

> God made man in his own image.
> God intended for man to become one with God.
> Cloning and the reprogramming of DNA is the first serious step in
>   becoming one with God.

(For a discussion of deductive argument, see Chapter 7.)

In quick response to Dr. Seed, both Republicans and Democrats came up with anti-cloning bills. But in spite of strong support from the right-to-life movement, concerns about inhibiting research on cancer and other diseases stalled the legislation, at least temporarily.

A number of more serious voices on both sides have joined the argument. A selection of their articles follows. As you read, you will want to notice which side of the issue each author takes, what their principal premises are, and how strong you find their arguments.

Clonalities

William Safire

Safire is known both as a prominent political columnist leaning toward the conservative point of view and as a leading interpreter of the English language and how it is used today. Not to be left behind in the flurry of excitement surrounding the proliferation of biotechnical wonders, he saw it necessary to pin down the meaning of the term *clone* in one of his "On Language" newspaper columns.

> The noun means "replica, duplicate"; in biology, "an organism produced asexually from a single ancestor"—which, up to now, most often meant "grafting," a nonpolitical term used by botanists. A duplicated cell can be good or bad: when the body produces cells to fight infection, they are *clones;* but so, on the other

hand, are cancer cells. The essence of the word is "same genetic makeup"—more "replication" than "reproduction," and not involving sex.

The noun produced a verb, *to clone,* meaning "to propagate so as to form a genetic duplicate," which first appeared in the magazine *Nature* in 1959. The adjective *clonal* was coined in 1968. . . . Another sense is "robot, automation, android" (and I'll be beamed up by Mr. Spock's fans for that). In cyberlingo, a *clone* is a competitor's computer.

In his essay, "Clonalities," Safire muses on cloning, this time referring us to William Blake, an English poet of the eighteenth century. Before reading the essay, you may want to read Blake's poem, "Tyger," to see what Safire is referring to in his discussion of fearsome Tyger and gentle Lamb and the issue of who makes what many refer to as "God's creatures." Note that Safire concludes with the question, "Little clone, who will make thee?"

Two centuries ago, when William Blake posed the question "Little lamb, who made thee?" the answer the mystic poet gave seemed obvious: the same gentle God who fathered Jesus made, and blessed, the lamb.

But in counterpoint to his "Songs of Innocence," Blake, in his "Songs of Experience," followed up that question—with a more troubling one about a terrifying creature: "Tyger, tyger, burning bright/ In the forests of the night/ . . . Did he who made the Lamb make thee?"

Some of us who study the Old Testament Book of Job, as Blake did, think the poet was dealing with the duality of the God of mercy and the God of wrath—searching for answers to why a just God permitted evil to afflict innocent people.

I ran this thought past Harold Bloom, a classmate 50 years ago at the Bronx High School of Science; he's now the great professor of humanities at Yale. (Neither of us made it in science.) He sees the Lamb and Tyger as satiric images of each other, and that Blake's Man makes both Tyger and Lamb: In "the forests of the night," or mental darkness, we mortals create our fearsome Tyger, but in the open vision of day we make our gentle Lamb.

These head-breaking thoughts about good and evil, God and humanity, are stimulated, of course, by the creation of Dolly, the lamb formed by cellular biologists in Scotland and fused into life by electric shock, as was the Monster in Mary Shelley's "Frankenstein."

The first reaction to this epochal news ranged from the defensively comic (Jay Leno's "Can clones make campaign donations without violating election laws?") to the offensively bureaucratic (the President bucks the issue to a bioethical committee).

Pollsters immediately reported a split decision about cloning animals for medical use, but a huge majority of people, reacted like sheep—that is, without thinking—against the cloning of human beings.

Moralists are torn: Who is to deny infertile or bereaved parents another chance at a child, or a life-saving animal organ to a dying human, versus Who has the right to play God by creating life, and what are the moral obligations of the creator?

Of this we're sure: *Knowledge unstoppably begets more knowledge.* In the May 1971 *Atlantic Monthly,* Dr. James Watson, a Nobel winner a decade before for co-discovering the structure of DNA, titled a seminal article "Moving Toward the Clonal Man." He explained how it could be done, and tried to awaken people to "a matter far too important to be left solely in the hands of the scientific and medical communities."

I'm a fan of Watson's at the Dana Alliance for Brain Initiatives, so I called him: "This could have been in 1938," he says of the stunning Scottish sheep trick; "it's moving cells, not DNA." He thinks it may take biologists a while to clone primates, but won't take a huge investment.

I take that to mean human cloning could happen in the coming decade. And if it can be done, it will be done—right or wrong, openly or secretly, dangerous or not.

In the necessary debate about how we direct the transmission of the life we now possess, we must remember:

First, that a human clone is only a blueprinted person; his or her upbringing, perhaps more than genetic code, develops personality and helps fulfill the potential of the copied genes.

Next, that a clone must be respected as a human being with the freedom and rights of every other. No slave; no organ factory; no discrimination.

Third, although a clone is an exact genetic reproduction, even a perfect copy of a person does not help perfect the human species; on the contrary, cloning's identicality would restrict evolution.

Homo sapiens sapiens is only about 1,000 generations old; our subspecies has a long way to go. We don't want to stop with copies of geniuses like the Blooms and the Watsons; the continued interplay of genes, propelled by love and protected by family, is central to human kind's progress.

Little clone, who will make thee? The same mysterious amalgam of beauty and terror that made the Lamb and the Tyger.

TOPICS FOR DISCUSSION AND WRITING

1. Safire suggests three important points to remember as we approach the moral issue of cloning humans. State what these points are and explain in your own words what he means. By the end of his essay, what is his principal argument?

2. Following the structure of a complex metaphor can be challenging, but try your hand at explaining what Safire is saying about the meaning of the tiger and the lamb in Blake's poem. How does he relate this poem to the issue of human cloning? (See Metaphor, Simile, and Personification in Chapter 14.)

Will We Follow the Sheep?

....

Jeffrey Kluger

Shortly after the announcement of Dolly's birth, journalist Jeffrey Kluger of *Time* magazine began to weigh the inevitability of scientific progress against the moral risks involved in cloning. Note how he interweaves his analysis with brief fictional episodes to illustrate his points. .

It's a busy morning in the cloning laboratory of the big-city hospital. As always, the list of people seeking the lab's services is a long one—and, as always, it's a varied one. Over here are the Midwestern parents who have flown in specially to see if the lab can make them an exact copy of their six-year-old daughter, recently found to be suffering from leukemia so aggressive that only a bone-marrow transplant can save her. The problem is finding a compatible donor. If, by reproductive happenstance, the girl had been born an identical twin, her matching sister could have produced all the marrow she needed. But nature didn't provide her with a twin, and now the cloning lab will try. In nine months, the parents, who face the very likely prospect of losing the one daughter they have, could find themselves raising two of her—the second created expressly to help keep the first alive.

Just a week after Scottish embryologists announced that they had succeeded in cloning a sheep from a single adult cell, both the genetics community and the world at large are coming to an unsettling realization: the science is the easy part. It's not that the breakthrough wasn't decades in the making. It's just that once it was complete—once you figured out how to transfer the genetic schematics from an adult cell into a living ovum and keep the fragile embryo alive throughout gestation—most of your basic biological work was finished. The social and philosophical temblors it triggers, however, have merely begun.

Only now, as the news of Dolly, the sublimely oblivious sheep, becomes part of the cultural debate, are we beginning to come to terms with those soulquakes. How will the new technology be regulated?

What does the sudden ability to make genetic stencils of ourselves say about the concept of individuality? Do the ants and bees and Maoist Chinese have it right? Is a species simply an überorganism, a collection of multicellular parts to be die-cast as needed? Or is there something about the individual that is lost when the mystical act of conceiving a person becomes standardized into a mere act of photocopying one?

Last week President Clinton took the first tentative step toward answering these questions, charging a federal commission with the task of investigating the legal and ethical implications of the new technology and reporting back to him with their findings within 90 days. Later this week the House subcommittee on basic research will hold a hearing to address the same issues. The probable tone of those sessions was established last week when Harold Varmus, director of the National Institute of Health (NIH), told another subcommittee that cloning a person is "repugnant to the American public."

Though the official responses were predictable—and even laudable—they may have missed the larger point. The public may welcome ways a government can regulate cloning, but what's needed even more is ways a thinking species can ethically *fathom* it. "This is not going to end in 90 days," says Princeton University president Harold Shapiro, chairman of President Clinton's committee. "Now that we have this technology, we have some hard thinking ahead of us."

> Also waiting in the cloning lab this morning is the local industrialist. Unlike the Midwestern parents, he does not have a sick child to worry about; indeed, he has never especially cared for children. Lately, however, he has begun to feel different. With a little help from the cloning lab, he now has the opportunity to have a son who would bear not just his name and his nose and the color of his hair but every scrap of genetic coding that makes him what he is. Now that appeals to the local industrialist. In fact, if this first boy works out, he might even make a few more.

Of all the reasons for using the new technology, pure ego raises the most hackles. It's one thing to want to be remembered after you are gone; it's quite another to manufacture a living monument to ensure that you are. Some observers claim to be shocked that anyone would contemplate such a thing. But that's naïve—and even disingenuous. It's obvious that a lot of people would be eager to clone themselves.

"It's a horrendous crime to make a Xerox of someone," argues author and science critic Jeremy Rifkin. "You're putting a human into a genetic straitjacket. For the first time, we've taken the principles of industrial design—quality control, predictability—and applied them to a human being."

But is it really the first time? Is cloning all that different from genetically engineering an embryo to eliminate a genetic disease like cystic fibrosis? Is it so far removed from in vitro fertilization? In both those cases, after all, an undeniable reductiveness is going on, a shriveling of the complexity of the human body to the certainty of a single cell in a Petri dish. If we accept this kind of tinkering, can't we accept cloning? Havard neurobiologist Lisa Geller admits that intellectually, she doesn't see a difference between in vitro technology and cloning. "But," she adds, "I admit it makes my stomach feel nervous."

More palatable than the ego clone to some bioethicists is the medical clone, a baby created to provide transplant material for the original. Nobody advocates harvesting a one-of-a-kind organ like a heart from the new child—an act that would amount to creating the clone just to kill it. But it's hard to argue against the idea of a family's loving a child so much that it will happily raise another, identical child so that one of its kidneys or a bit of its marrow might allow the first to live. "The reasons for opposing this are not easy to argue," says John Fletcher, former ethicist for the NIH.

The problem is that once you start shading the cloning question—giving an ethical O.K. to one hypothetical and a thumbs-down to another—you begin making the sort of ad hoc hash of things the Supreme Court does when it tries to define pornography. Suppose you could show that the baby who was created to provide marrow for her sister would forever be treated like a second-class sibling—well cared for perhaps, but not well loved. Do you prohibit the family from cloning the first daughter, accepting the fact that you may be condemning her to die? Richard McCormick, a Jesuit priest and professor of Christian ethics at the University of Notre Dame, answers such questions simply and honestly when he says, "I can't think of a morally acceptable reason to clone a being."

In a culture in which not everyone sees things so straightforwardly, however, some ethical accommodation is going to have to be reached. How it will be done is anything but clear. "Science is close to crossing some horrendous boundaries," says Leon Kass, professor of social thought at the University of Chicago. "Here is an opportunity for human beings to decide if we're simply going to stand in the path of the technological steamroller or take control and help guide its direction."

> Following the local industrialist on the appointments list is the physics laureate. He is terminally ill. When he dies, one of the most remarkable minds in science will die with him. Reproductive chance might one day produce another scientist just as gifted, but there is no telling when. The physics laureate does not like that kind of uncertainty. He has come to the cloning lab today to see if he can't do something about it.

If the human gene pool can be seen as a sort of species-wide natural resource, it's only sensible for the rarest of those genes to be husbanded most carefully, preserved so that every generation may enjoy their benefits. Even the most ardent egalitarians would find it hard to object to an Einstein appearing every 50 years or a Chopin every century. It would be better still if we could be guaranteed not just *an* Einstein but *the* Einstein. If a scientific method were developed so that the man who explained general relativity in the first half of the [20th] century could be brought back to crack the secrets of naked singularities in the second, could we resist using it? And suppose the person being replicated were researching not just abstruse questions of physics but pressing questions of medicine. Given the chance to bring back Jonas Salk, would it be moral not to try?

Surprisingly, scientific ethicists seem to say yes, "Choosing personal characteristics as if they were options on a car is an invitation to misadventure," says John Paris, professor of bioethics at Boston College. "It is in the diversity of our population that we find interest and enthusiasm."

Complicating things further, the traits a culture values most are not fixed. If cloning had existed a few centuries ago, men with strong backs and women with broad pelvises would have been the first ones society would have wanted to reproduce. During the industrial age, however, brainpower began to count for more than muscle power. Presumably the custodians of cloning technology at that historical juncture would have faced the prospect of letting previous generations of strapping men and fecund women die out and replacing them with a new population of intellectual giants. "What is a better human being?" asks Boston University ethicist George Annas. "A lot of it is just fad."

Even if we could agree on which individuals would serve as humanity's templates of perfection, there's no guarantee that successive copies would be everything the originals were. Innate genius isn't always so innate, after all, coming to nothing if the person born with the potential for excellence doesn't find the right environment and blossom in it. A scientific genius who's beaten as a child might become a mad genius. An artist who's introduced to alcohol when he's young might merely become a drunk. A thousand track switches have to click in sequence for the child who starts out toward greatness to wind up there. If a single one clicks wrong, the high-speed rush toward a Nobel Prize can dead-end in makeshift shack in the Montana woods. Says Rabbi Moshe Tendler, professor of both biology and biblical law at Yeshiva University in New York City: "I can make myself an Albert Einstein, and he may turn out to be a drug addict."

> The despot will not be coming to the cloning lab today. Before long, he knows, the lab's science will come to him—and not a moment too soon. The despot has ruled his little country for 30 years, but now he's getting old and will have to pass his power on. That makes him nervous; he's seen what can happen to a cult of personality if too weak a personality takes over. Happily, in his country that's not a danger. As soon as the technology of the cloning lab goes global— as it inevitably must—his people can be assured of his leadership long after he's gone.

This is the ultimate nightmare scenario. The Pharaohs built their pyramids, the Emperors built Rome, and Napoleon built his Arc de Triomphe—all, at least in part, to make the permanence of stone compensate for the impermanence of the flesh. But big buildings and big tombs would be a poor second choice if the flesh could be made to go on forever. Now, it appears, it can.

The idea of a dictator's being genetically duplicated is not new—not in pop culture, anyhow. In Ira Levin's 1976 book *The Boys from Brazil* a zealous ex-Nazi bred a generation of literal Hitler Youth—boys cloned from cells left behind by the Führer. Woody Allen dealt with a similar premise a lot more playfully in his 1973 film *Sleeper,* in which a futuristic tyrant is killed by a bomb blast, leaving nothing behind but his nose—a nose that his followers hope to clone into a new leader. Even as the fiction of one decade becomes the technology of another, it's inevitable that this technology will be used—often by the wrong people.

"I don't see how you can stop these things," says bioethicist Daniel Callahan of the Hastings Center in Briarcliff Manor, New York. "We are at the mercy of these technological developments. Once they're here, it's hard to turn back."

Hard, perhaps, but not impossible. If anything will prevent human cloning —whether of dictator, industrialist or baby daughter—from becoming a reality, it's that science may not be able to clear the ethical high bar that would allow basic research to get under way in the first place. Cutting, coring and electrically jolting a sheep embryo is a huge moral distance from doing the same to a human embryo. It took 277 trials and errors to produce Dolly the sheep, creating a cellular body count that would look like sheer carnage if the cells were human. "Human beings ought never to be used as experimental subjects," Shapiro says simply.

Whether they will or not is impossible to say. Even if governments ban human cloning outright, it will not be so easy to police what goes on in private laboratories that don't receive public money—or in private ones offshore. Years ago, Scottish scientists studying in vitro fertilization were subjected to such intense criticism that they took their work underground, continuing it in seclusion until they had the technology perfected. Presumably, human-cloning researchers could also do their work on the sly, emerging only when they succeed.

Scientists don't pretend to know when that will happen, but some science observers fear it will be soon. The first infant clone could come squalling into the world within seven years according to Arthur Caplan, director of the Center for Bioethics at the University of Pennsylvania. If he's right, science had better get its ethical house in order quickly. In calendar terms, seven years from now is a good way off; in scientific terms, it's tomorrow afternoon.

TOPICS FOR DISCUSSION AND WRITING

1. Kluger raises several questions surrounding the ethics of cloning. Briefly summarize each of these issues. (See Summaries in Chapter 3.)

2. Explain how the narrative episodes illustrate the major points he is making. Do you find this technique effective for argument?

Ethical Fears Aside, Science Plunges On

George Johnson

George Johnson has written widely on contemporary scientific topics for lay readers, including books on science and faith, on artificial intelligence, and on how we construct memory, as well as working as a science correspondent for the *New York Times*. As you read this piece, think about how Johnson's ideas fit in with those of Kluger and how they differ.

With the prospect of human cloning becoming less unthinkable by the day, it seems almost quaint that a mere decade ago people were up in arms over the perils of spraying strawberries with bacteria genetically altered to prevent frost.

At about the same time, a Montana scientist, hounded by cries that he was tampering with nature, tearfully chopped down a grove of trees he had carefully injected with bacteria whose genes had been rejiggered to fight Dutch elm disease. For all the outrage and apprehensions, one would have thought he was playing with something as dangerous as the Andromeda Strain.

Gene-splicing, artificial insemination, in vitro fertilization, bovine growth hormone, genetically engineered tomatoes—all jolted people to dig out their yellowed copies of Aldous Huxley and Michael Crichton and tremble before the certainty that the worst was yet to come. Genies were being let out of bottles. Brave new worlds were approaching.

And in the end, all the bioethical agonizing was largely beside the point. The scientists kept quietly, deliberately working away, incrementally improving the technology. What seemed scary to people slowly started to seem interesting, and maybe useful. Looking back over the years, it's hard to find a case in which the unthinkable remained unthinkable for very long.

Earlier this year, with the sudden appearance of Dolly, the genetically duplicated lamb, it seemed that science had finally come up against an unbreachable moral barrier. Against many of their own expectations, scientists had shown that it was possible to take a cell from an adult mammal and use it as the seed for a new creature. But one scientist after another vowed that cloning would never be done with people. Finally, it seemed, science would not try to do something just because it could.

In the midst of the panic, President Clinton called an obscure group known as the National Bioethics Advisory Commission into action. Moralizing under the pressure of a Presidentially imposed 90-day deadline, the panel gravely concluded that human cloning was wrong and called for a moratorium. Mr. Clinton, armed with the latest in family-value issues, declared that the practice would violate "the sacred family bonds at the very core of our ideals and our society" and "make our children objects rather than cherished individuals."

MONKEY SEE, HUMAN DO

Bills were debated in Congress, professional ethicists convened conferences and wrote books and articles. California banned human cloning. Meanwhile, the real action was quietly going on in the laboratories, outside the periphery of the public eye. Federally supported experiments in cloning monkeys for use in AIDS vaccine and other research was continuing outside the limelight. What can be done with monkeys can probably be done with people. "We are laying the groundwork," one of the scientists said.

Dr. Steen Willadsen, who developed techniques used to make Dolly, said it was "just a matter of time" before the first human is cloned. Anticipating that cloning will inevitably become an accepted medical procedure, he is now working in a fertility clinic, perfecting techniques that could eventually be used for the ultimate in reproductive freedom—making a younger copy of yourself.

It's the same old story. The terror of Jurassic Park dinosaurs on the loose in San Diego or the eerie absurdity of cloning multiple Hitlers in "The Boys From Brazil" gives way to practical questions. Infertile couples wonder whether cloning one of their cells to make a baby is really any more unnatural than taking fertility drugs and ending up with septuplets.

Could it be that cloning a cancer victim to harvest a bone marrow donor is less an abomination than an act of human charity? If the evolutionary psychologists can be believed, such a clone, sharing an identical set of genes, would feel closer than brother to sister or parent to child. One might very well want to help the other with an organ donation. The notion of genetically engineered slaves kept in a closet for spare parts starts to seem like bad science fiction.

ETHICAL CONCERNS

No one should be Pollyannish about this. Before human cloning becomes as acceptable as implanting frozen embryos, all kinds of moral and legal dilemmas would have to be dealt with. Should we worry about the undue pressures a clone might feel to give up a body part? Would knowing that you were conceived for utilitarian purposes be psychologically upsetting? Or would it be no worse than learning you were an accident, or adopted, or conceived in a petri dish? If history is a guide, the answers to these questions will come only after cloning is a fait accompli.

Over time, all the dire warnings and predictions seem to have the opposite of the intended effect. People become inured to the predictable hand-wringing and begin to feel that every new development is accompanied by an obligatory round of chilling scenarios, which often turn out to be wrong. Each new pill for better or worse, is just a little bit easier to swallow. One wonders whether in 10 years, or in 5 or 3, the outrage over cloning will seem as misguided as medieval bans on dissecting cadavers in medical schools. What was the big deal, anyway?

With each new development the labyrinth of possibilities expands. New channels of thought open up. Trying to recreate an old moral mindset becomes as difficult as imagining why Beethoven at first sounded shocking, or remembering why mood rings and pet rocks once seemed cool.

It's almost as though society wants its scientists to spring these surprises on them. And people know deep down that, like it or not, what can be done probably will. From the time the first caveman, obsessed with the image of a circle, picked up a chisel and turned a block of stone into a wheel, ideas—good ones and bad—have had a way of breaking loose from the mind. Thought inevitably crystallizes into action, ideas into things, and even notions that seem frighteningly dangerous have to be tried at least once before they are accepted, regulated or, occasionally, banned.

Some of the scientists of the Manhattan Project, working on the first hydrogen bomb, worried that it might set off a global chain reaction and turn the earth into a burning star. After a round of marathon calculations convinced them that this probably wouldn't happen, they crossed their fingers and exploded the bomb anyway. Then the world was left to deal with the mess.

"When you see something that is technically sweet you go ahead and do it," the physicist Robert Oppenheimer said later. "And you argue about what to do about it only after you have had your technical success."

TOPICS FOR DISCUSSION AND WRITING

1. Johnson quotes Robert Oppenheimer, considered the "father" of the atomic bomb, as saying, "When you see something that is technically sweet, you go ahead and do it, and you argue about what to do about it only after you have had your technical success." Johnson

is making a connection to the ethical debate surrounding the possibility of human cloning. Explain the analogy and discuss whether or not it helps to clarify issues in the debate over cloning. (See False Analogy in Chapter 6 and Analogy in Chapter 14).

2. Johnson asks, "would knowing that you were conceived for utilitarian purposes [such as to help a sibling survive with a kidney or bone marrow transplant] be psychologically upsetting?" How would you answer this question? If you were a parent who created a clone "for utilitarian purposes," how would you respond to such a child's questions concerning her birth? Can you think of other situations in which people are conceived for utilitarian purposes, and if so, how do these examples change your view of cloning?

Overcoming Yuk

Oliver Morton

Adopting an entirely different tone, *Wired* magazine contributing editor Oliver Morton, in a breezy style appropriate to the emergent computer world, introduces a fresh new term to examine our distaste for scientific meddling. Through his choice of language alone you will pick up his attitude toward the issue. As you read, think about how his style affects your reactions.

We might as well start with Dolly. The past five years have seen plenty of other breakthroughs, from bacterial genome sequences to headless frogs, but none has had quite the same impact as the little woolly clone. Maybe that's because, in an odd way, we were prepared for her. Unlike homeotic genes, or DNA hybridization arrays, or secondary cellular messengers, or most of the rest of the stuff of the new biology, cloning is something we think we understand. And there's something deeply emblematic about it, too. Inasmuch as she's just another sheep, Dolly's completely natural; inasmuch as she's a clone of one particular other sheep, she's utterly unnatural. So there she stands, nature and artifice wrapped up into one bundle. Welcome to the future. Ecce ovo. (Behold the egg.) Baaa.

The fact that she was a clone was actually not the most interesting thing about Dolly. Being able to Xerox single creatures is not a particularly interesting skill in most circumstances. The important thing about Dolly is that a nucleus was taken from a cell in a laboratory test tube and put into an egg. Manipulating the genes of cells in laboratories is something molecular biologists are getting better and better at. The Dolly technique means that these manipulated genes can now be slotted into eggs much more precisely. From the laboratory and the clinic, the new biology is now poised to move into the field, or the barnyard, or the home. The first practical applications will be sheep with valuable proteins in their milk. Then there may be pigs that make organs for transplanting into humans. Then pets with engaging predetermined characters and advertising logos growing in their fur.

The first of those two applications is pretty widely acceptable. The second is still disgusting to many. It falls prey to what Tom Wilkie, who runs the biomedical ethics section of the Wellcome Trust in London, calls "the Yuk factor." The Yuk factor governs the initial public response to almost every biomedical advance that can easily be understood as being unnatural. Women giving birth after 60? Yuk! Pigs as organ donors? Yuk!

The Yuk factor feels instinctual, primal, a law of nature. Yet it can pass quite quickly. Take the cornea. In the 1950s it was against the law in Britain to save a patient's sight by grafting a dead person's corneas onto the patient's eyes. This was not just a legal oversight; people found the idea quite deeply Yuk, and it took a prolonged journalistic campaign to get the law changed. (Every contact lens wearer goes through the same process on a personal level. At first there is a definite Yuk to touching the eye; soon it becomes utterly commonplace.)

The Yuk factor boils down to a disgust at what seems unnatural. As we live with the unnatural, though, we begin first to accommodate it, then to accept it, then to appreciate it. That's just as well, because our success as a species rests on ever greater unnaturalness. Sheep were a product of our willingness to disregard nature long before we started cloning them, bred as they were for wool, for mutton, for a willingness to be herded. And what we do to sheep is nothing compared to what we're willing to do to ourselves with the help of qualified doctors and pharmaceutical prowess. The Yuks that surround the new biology reflect its ability to take our unnaturalness to hitherto impossible heights; but our enthusiasm for medicine will overcome them.

Biology, after all, is about life, not nature. It's just an accident of history that, until recently, everything alive was more or less natural. Nature is a record of 4 billion years of life's successes, written in the language of the genes. Biology's new strength comes from being able to read that record; cracking the genetic code has ushered in one of those wonderful eras of scientific progress when new discoveries keep leading to new techniques with which yet more discoveries can be made. From the ability to splice genes comes the monoclonal antibodies that recognize proteins, the DNA amplifiers that pick up genetic signals previously inaudible, the probes that tell one gene from another, the techniques for making mutations ever more subtle and specific. What used to be a Nobel Prize-worth of research is now a couple of months of PhD drudgery; what PhDs used to do with pride is now done by robots with efficiency. The past five years have seen the knowledge machines blur into ever faster productivity.

That knowledge is beginning to be put to use in unnatural wonders all around the world. There's Dolly. There are millions of other genetically engineered animals, and countless billions of cells in culture, some of them pumping out life-giving medicines under the auspices of biotechnology companies. There's a young woman named Louise Brown, and thousands of children created through in vitro fertilization after her. There's a girl called Ashanti DeSilva who was the first child to be deliberately infected with a virus that was supposed to knit a new gene into her cells. And this is all just the beginning.

It's unnatural; it's Yuk; but it is not bad. The natural has no special moral status; it merely has a practical pedigree. That which is natural has the advantage of having been shown to work, and we should bear that in mind. But no gene ever knew what would work in advance, or applied itself to a greater purpose than its own replication; the choices recorded in the genome are not moral choices. Morality has only now come to the genome, because only now is the genome open to deliberate action by people with foresight and responsibility. We can choose life in ways nature could not. But we should not be bound by it.

Humanity is used to power over nature. Physics has given us abilities that most of our ancestors would have reserved for the gods; the power to visit new worlds, to end this one, to see everything, and to be heard everywhere. All this in barely a hundred years. Biological power will bring changes as profound—and choices with consequences as grave. Unfortunately, most people do not understand that these choices are becoming increasingly possible; they see nature as a set of bonds they cannot break.

The material basis of human nature is more widely accepted today than ever before, largely due to the new biology. The mind has been dissected; thoughts have been imaged; moods are altered. At an intellectual level, human nature, long exiled by social theorists, has made a comeback. To think of the mind as an evolved organ, its patterns of thought as biological as the metabolic pathways of the liver, is now to be at the vanguard of what is called evolutionary psychology, a field that over the past five years has grown from the obsession of a few to the intellectual fashion of many. While its findings may sometimes be fallacious, its foundations are clearly true: If the mind was not shaped by God, then it was shaped by evolution and culture.

Add to this a misleading way of talking about genetics that involves tagging genes with the problem that accompanies their dysfunction—genes "for" obesity, aggression, dyslexia, and addiction, and their more obviously medical cousins, the genes "for" cancer, Alzheimer's, and high cholesterol—and you get a world where people begin to think that their genes hold road plans for their lives. That their nature controls them.

But the organism is not specified by its genes as a car is specified by its blueprints; it is always already a work in progress. A living being is an information processor that continuously remakes itself, an interaction between matter and information in which neither can take priority. It is a dance of form and substance, of nature and nurture, of matter and information.

At the moment we know a lot about data in our genes, because we recently learned how to read it. We know far less about the processes that use that data to make cells, organs, behaviors, people. That means that, at the moment, people can be faced with the dilemma of knowledge that brings with it little power; they can know they face an increased risk of breast cancer thanks to a faulty gene, thanks to a recently developed test, but not know what to do with that knowledge.

This is a temporary problem. There is every reason to think that we can develop ever subtler ways to change the environment—the social environment, the global environment, the environment in our guts or our blood or our brainstem. And so we can change the way the genetic information is processed.

In some cases we already know how to do this. There is a genetic defect called phenylketonuria (PKU) that disrupts the ability to metabolize the amino acid phenylalanine. Left to itself, it leads to severe mental retardation; in that much, it is a gene "for" imbecility. These days, though, it is not left to itself. In America and much of the rest of the world, every newborn child is tested for PKU, and those who have it are then put on a special diet, one low in phenylalanine. The diet is not pleasant, and sticking with it is hard (it may become easier when cows are engineered to produce phenylalanine-free milk, a development project already under way). But stick with the diet and the child can develop pretty normally. Knowing about nature lets you change nurture to match. The two can be made to mesh.

PKU is a somewhat simple example. But the principle it embodies is one that should guide us through all the new knowledge and pseudo-knowledge about human nature and the workings of the mind that biology is producing at ever greater rates. Knowing the score is the first step toward putting the process back on the rails. Knowledge about genes is the beginning, not the end—the point from which you can start making choices about how to shape your world.

Addressing a conference at Caltech a few years ago, physicist and science fiction author Gregory Benford imagined the perplexity of historians 50 years hence. "They'll look back at our abortion debates and they'll laugh; they won't see how we could get so worked up about such a simple choice when their biological choices are far, far more complex."

Perhaps the biggest choices will be about children. Better environments tailored for their genes are one thing; but what about better genes, too? Wholesale engineering of human children seems unlikely, for a range of practical, social, and ethical reasons to do with creating human life as an experiment. Much more likely is widespread "genotype choice"—a sort of decentralized, do-it-yourself eugenics.

A couple goes to a clinic and provides some sperm and some eggs. The clinic turns them into embryos and analyzes the different mixtures of the parents' genes each embryo carries. The parents are given the embryos' genetic profiles and advice on how the genes relate to various traits, both physical and mental, in various different conditions. At present, such a profile would be expensive and crude, capable of spotting genes for serious genetic disabilities but not much more. But with better DNA-analysis tools and much more knowledge about which genes do what—both fields that are growing exponentially—the pictures will get sharper and sharper. The parents choose the profile they like, on whatever criteria appeal to them; the chosen embryo is grown a bit further in the test tube, a few cells are snipped out to provide tissue for repairs in later life, and then the pregnancy gets under way. No engineering; just choice.

Many people, including some of the scientists who have made it possible, see this as unethical, the creation of a life as a commodity. Yet people create lives for self-centered purposes—such as support in old age—all the time. Genotype choice would undoubtedly be deeply unnatural. But so is birth in a hospital, not to mention contraception. It would give parents a real power over the sort of people their children will turn out to be. But parents have that power already, to a large degree—through attitudes, affection, and school choice.

Eugenics—the favoring of the reproduction of some genes over others—has a vile history. If genotype choice were to be in the hands of the state, it would likely be a continuation of that history, and a thing to fear and reject. But there is no need for it to be in the hands of the state, and every reason to fight against any strict control the state might try to exercise. Genotype choice should be a matter for individuals, a personal choice about what sort of life they want their children to have.

There would be effects beyond the level of the individual in such a world, as various traits became more common. Symmetrical features would seem a good bet, along with strong immune systems and some types of intelligence. Judging by personal ads, a gene for a good sense of humor would spread like wildfire. Severe genetic disorders would disappear. None of these is clearly a bad thing. Perhaps the most worrying potential by-product of genotype choice would be a skewed sex ratio—and that is already upon us. In India, China, and other countries, ultrasound imaging has led to the preferential abortion of female fetuses on quite a large scale. What can be done about this, though, is not clear. Sex tests are easy enough for a black market to spring up easily; so is abortion. It may be that the only thing to do is to proselytize for women's rights, to convince people that a girl is as valuable as a boy. And to remember that over time, if sex selection swings a long way in one direction, it is bound to swing back.

The other major social impact of genotype choice is far further off: longer lives. Aging research has already become a hot topic; the boomer generation that grew up with routine vaccination and with drugs that actually worked has started to face mortality. This is a huge constituency for advanced medical technology. A few years ago, a biotech lobbyist told me that every conversation he has with a legislator sooner or later turns to a specific affliction that has struck the lawmaker's family or friends. One look at the U.S. Senate tells you that the National Institutes of Health can more or less write its own ticket when it comes to prostate cancer. Even a not very good Alzheimer's treatment is a sure bet for an enterprising drug company.

There's no doubt that medicine and smart environments can and will prolong life. Tools that are now imaginable—things like tailored viruses, cellular grafting, artificial glands, and artificial organs—could have a major effect; so could genotype choice. Medicine may not stretch out the baby boomers' lives much further than they can already expect (which is still longer than any other generation has been granted), but their children, or their children's children, could live a fair stretch longer, not least because it's probably going to be easier to preserve youth than to reverse decline. I'd be surprised if some of the younger readers of this article are not still in pretty good shape when it's time to see in the 22nd century, though I don't anticipate joining in the festivities myself. It's conceivable that if your children choose your grandchildren's genes well, some of them may see the 24th.

It's a happy coincidence of iconography that the double helix was a medical icon long before the discovery of DNA. The two twisted snakes of the caduceus have been with doctors since Hippocrates, as has the sacred symbol of Mercury, god of messages, of choices, of crossroads.

Now medicine can offer us more than ever before; more benefits and more choices. Better biology will not solve everything. Warding off many forms of cancer will not make the world perfect; nor will delaying the onset of Alzheimer's by a few decades, or even a century. Better understanding of the relief of emotional suffering will not make us all happy, and new techniques for maximizing the power of the intellect will not make everyone an Einstein. But the past five years suggest that all these things are conceivable over the next century—I'd say quite likely. We need to face them, decide how much we want them, look at ways we can spread their benefits widely, look at what they might cost us.

Nature has been making choices for 4 billion years; every base in the human genome is a result of those natural selections, just as every byte of a computer program is a choice between yes and no. This record has given us our knowledge, but it is no guide to how to use it. Those choices must be made not on the basis of what has worked before—which is all nature can ever offer us—but on the basis of what we want, individually and collectively. From now on the caduceus is ours.

So are the crossroads.

TOPICS FOR DISCUSSION AND WRITING

1. Explain what Morton means by "the Yuk factor" and discuss where you draw the line between acceptable biology and procedures that qualify as "Yuk."

2. Morton is very optimistic about the new breakthroughs in biotechnology. Why? Do you share his enthusiasm?

Human Cloning and the Challenge of Regulation

John A. Robertson

The New England Journal of Medicine, preeminent among medical journals, weighed in on the cloning debate with lawyer Robertson addressing issues of regulation. To fully understand the medical arguments in this essay, you will want to look up the meaning of *gamete, mitochondria,* and *somatic-cell nuclear transfer.* The term *genome* has appeared in more than one of the readings earlier in this chapter. Otherwise, this essay avoids the kind of medical terminology we would expect in a medical journal. (Note how his argument structure reflects the principles laid out in A Dialectical Approach to Argument in Chapter 4.)

The birth of Dolly, the sheep cloned from a mammary cell of an adult ewe, has initiated a public debate about human cloning. Although cloning of humans may never be clinically feasible, discussion of the ethical, legal, and social issues raised is important. Cloning is just one of several techniques potentially available to select, control, or alter the genome of offspring.[1-3] The development of such technology poses an important social challenge: how to ensure that the technology is used to enhance, rather than limit, individual freedom and welfare.

A key ethical question is whether a responsible couple, interested in rearing healthy offspring biologically related to them, might ethically choose to use cloning (or other genetic-selection techniques) for that purpose. The answer should take into account the benefits sought through the use of the techniques and any potential harm to offspring or to other interests.

The most likely uses of cloning would be far removed from the bizarre or horrific scenarios that initially dominated media coverage.[4] Theoretically, cloning would enable rich or powerful persons to clone themselves several times over, and commercial entrepreneurs might hire women to bear clones of sports or entertainment celebrities to be sold to others to rear. But current reproductive techniques can also be abused, and existing laws against selling children would apply to those created by cloning.

There is no reason to think that the ability to clone humans will cause many people to turn to cloning when other methods of reproduction would enable them to have healthy children. Cloning a human being by somatic-cell nuclear transfer, for example, would require a consenting person as a source of DNA, eggs to be enucleated and then fused with the DNA, a woman who would carry and deliver the child, and a person or couple to raise the child. Given this reality, cloning is most likely to be sought by couples who, because of infertility, a high risk of severe genetic disease, or other factors, cannot or do not wish to conceive a child.

Several plausible scenarios can be imagined. Rather than use sperm, egg, or embryo from anonymous donors, couples who are infertile as a result of gametic insufficiency might choose to clone one of the partners. If the husband were the source of the DNA and the wife provided the egg that received the nuclear transfer and then gestated the fetus, they would have a child biologically related to each of them and would not need to rely on anonymous gamete or embryo donation. Of course, many infertile couples might still prefer gamete or embryo donation or adoption. But there is nothing inherently wrong in wishing to be biologically related to one's children, even when this goal cannot be achieved through sexual reproduction.

A second plausible application would be for a couple at high risk of having offspring with a genetic disease.[5] Couples in this situation must now choose whether to risk the birth of an affected child, to undergo prenatal or preimplantation diagnosis and abortion or the discarding of embryos, to accept gamete donation, to seek adoption, or to remain childless. If cloning were available, however, some couples, in line with prevailing concepts of kinship, family, and parenting, might strongly prefer to clone one of themselves or another family member. Alternatively, if they already had a healthy child, they might choose to use cloning to create a later-born twin of that child. In the more distant future, it is even possible that the child whose DNA was replicated would not have been born healthy but would have been made healthy by gene therapy after birth.

A third application relates to obtaining tissue or organs for transplantation. A child who needed an organ or tissue transplant might lack a medically suitable donor. Couples in this situation have sometimes conceived a child coitally in the hope that he or she would have the correct tissue type to serve, for example, as a bone marrow donor for an older sibling.[6,7] If the child's disease was not genetic, a couple might prefer to clone the affected child to be sure that the tissue would match.

It might eventually be possible to procure suitable tissue or organs by cloning the source DNA only to the point at which stem cells or other material might be obtained for transplantation, thus avoiding the need to bring a child into the world for the sake of obtaining tissue.[8] Cloning a person's cells up to the embryo stage might provide a source of stem cells or tissue for the person cloned. Cloning might also be used to enable a couple to clone a dead or dying child so as to have that child live on in some closely related form, to obtain sufficient numbers of embryos for transfer and pregnancy, or to eliminate mitochondrial disease.[5]

Most, if not all, of the potential uses of cloning are controversial, usually because of the explicit copying of the genome. As the National Bioethics Advisory Commission noted, in addition to concern about physical safety and eugenics, somatic-cell cloning raises issues of the individuality, autonomy, objectification, and kinship of the resulting children.[5] In other instances, such as the production of embryos to serve as tissue banks, the ethical issue is the sacrifice of embryos created solely for that purpose.

Given the wide leeway now granted couples to use assisted reproduction and prenatal genetic selection in forming families, cloning should not be rejected in all circumstances as unethical or illegitimate. The manipulation of embryos and the use of gamete donors and surrogates are increasingly common. Most fetuses conceived in the United States and Western Europe are now screened for genetic or chromosomal anomalies. Before conception, screening to identify carriers of genetic diseases is widespread.[9] Such practices also deviate from conventional notions of reproduction, kinship, and medical treatment of infertility, yet they are widely accepted.

Despite the similarity of cloning to current practices, however, the dissimilarities should not be overlooked. The aim of most other forms of assisted reproduction is the birth of a child who is a descendant of at least one member of the couple, not an identical twin. Most genetic selection acts negatively to identify and screen out unwanted traits such as genetic disease, not positively to choose or replicate the genome as in somatic-cell cloning.[3] It is not clear, however, why a child's relation to his or her rearing parents must always be that of sexually reproduced descendant when such a relationship is not possible because of infertility or other factors. Indeed, in gamete donation and adoption, although sexual reproduction is involved, a full descendant relation between the child and both rearing parents is lacking. Nor should the difference between negative and positive means of selecting children determine the ethical or social acceptability of cloning or other techniques. In both situations, a deliberate choice is made so that a child is born with one genome rather than another or is not born at all.

Is cloning sufficiently similar to current assisted-reproduction and genetic-selection practices to be treated similarly as a presumptively protected exercise of family or reproductive liberty.[10] Couples who request cloning in the situations I have described are seeking to rear healthy children with whom they will have a genetic or biologic tie, just as couples who conceive their children sexually do. Whether described as "replication" or as "reproduction," the resort to cloning is similar enough in purpose and effects to other reproduction and genetic-selection practices that it should be treated similarly. Therefore, a couple should be free to choose cloning unless there are compelling reasons for thinking that this would create harm that the other procedures would not cause.[10]

The concern of the National Bioethics Advisory Commission about the welfare of the clone reflects two types of fear. The first is that a child with the same nuclear DNA as another person, who is thus that person's later-born identical twin, will be so severely harmed by the identity of nuclear DNA between them that it is morally preferable, if not obligatory, that the child not be born at all.[5] In this case the fear is that the later-born twin will lack individuality or the freedom to create his or her own identity because of confusion or expectations caused by having the same DNA as another person.[5,11]

This claim does not withstand the close scrutiny that should precede interference with a couple's freedom to bear and rear biologically related children.[10] Having the same genome as another person is not in itself harmful, as widespread experience with monozygotic twins shows. Being a twin does not deny either twin his or her individuality or freedom, and twins often have a special intimacy or closeness that few non-twin siblings can experience.[12] There is no reason to think that being a later-born identical twin resulting from cloning would change the overall assessment of being a twin.

Differences in mitochondria and the uterine and childhood environment will undercut problems of similarity and minimize the risk of overidentification with the first twin. A clone of Smith may look like Smith, but he or she will not be Smith and will lack many of Smith's phenotypic characteristics. The effects of having similar DNA will also depend on the length of time before the second twin is born, on whether the twins are raised together, on whether they are informed that they are genetic twins, on whether other people are so informed, on the beliefs that the rearing parents have about genetic influence on behavior, and on other factors. Having a previously born twin might in some circumstances also prove to be a source of support or intimacy for the later-born child.

The risk that parents or the child will overly identify the child with the DNA source also seems surmountable. Would the child invariably be expected to match the phenotypic characteristics of the DNA source, thus denying the second twin an "open future" and the freedom to develop his or her own identity?[5,11,13] In response to this question, one must ask whether couples who choose to clone offspring are more likely to want a child who is a mere replica of the DNA source or a child who is unique and valued for more than his or her genes. Couples may use cloning in order to ensure that the biologic child they rear is healthy, to maintain a family connection in the face of gametic infertility, or to obtain matched tissue for transplantation and yet still be responsibly committed to the welfare of their child, including his or her separate identity and interests and right to develop as he or she chooses.

The second type of fear is that parents who choose their child's genome through somatic-cell cloning will view the child as a commodity or an object to serve their own ends.[5] We do not view children born through coital or assisted reproduction as "mere means" just because people reproduce in order to have company in old age, to fulfill what they see as God's will, to prove their virility, to have heirs, to save a relationship, or to serve other selfish purposes.[14] What counts is how a child is treated after birth. Self-interested motives for having children do not prevent parents from loving children for themselves once they are born.

The use of cloning to form families in the situations I have described, though closely related to current assisted-reproduction and genetic-selection practices, does offer unique variations. The novelty of the relation—cloning in lieu of sperm donation, for example, produces a later-born identical twin raised by the older twin and his spouse—will create special psychological and social challenges. Can these challenges be successfully met, so that cloning produces net good for families and society? Given the largely positive experience with assisted-reproduction techniques that initially appeared frightening, cautious optimism is justified. We should be able to develop procedures and guidelines for cloning that will allow us to obtain its benefits while minimizing its problems and dangers.

In the light of these considerations, I would argue that a ban on privately funded cloning research is unjustified and likely to hamper important types of research.[3] A permanent ban on the cloning of human beings, as advocated by the Council of Europe and proposed in Congress, is also unjustified.[15,16] A more limited ban—whether for 5 years, as proposed by the National Bioethics Advisory Commission and enacted in California, or for 10 years, as in the bill of Senator Dianne Feinstein (D-Calif.) and Senator Edward M. Kennedy (D-Mass.) that is now before Congress—is also open to question.[5,17,18] Given the early state of cloning science and the widely shared view that the transfer of cloned embryos to the uterus before the safety and efficacy of the procedure has been established is unethical, few responsible physicians are likely to offer human cloning in the near future.[5] Nor are profit-motivated entrepreneurs, such as Richard Seed, likely to have many customers for their cloning services until the safety of the procedure is demonstrated.[19] A ban on human cloning for a limited period would thus serve largely symbolic purposes. Symbolic legislation, however, often has substantial costs.[20,21] A government–imposed prohibition on privately funded cloning, even for a limited period, should not be enacted unless there is a compelling need. Such a need has not been demonstrated.

Rather than seek to prohibit all uses of human cloning, we should focus our attention on ensuring that cloning is done well. No physician or couple should embark on cloning without careful thought about the novel relational issues and child-rearing responsibilities that will ensue. We need regulations or guidelines to ensure safety and efficacy, fully informed consent and counseling for the couple, the consent of any person who may provide DNA, guarantees of parental rights and duties, and a limit on the number of clones from any single source.[10] It may also be important to restrict cloning to situations where there is a strong likelihood that the couple or individual initiating the procedure will also rear the resulting child. This principle will encourage a stable parenting situation and minimize the chance that cloning entrepreneurs will create clones to be sold to others.[22] As our experience grows, some restrictions on who may serve as a source of DNA for cloning (for example, a ban on cloning one's parents) may also be defensible.[10]

Cloning is important because it is the first of several positive means of genetic selection that may be sought by families seeking to have and rear healthy, biologically related offspring. In the future, mitochondrial transplantation, germ-line gene therapy, genetic enhancement, and other forms of prenatal genetic alteration may be possible.[3,23,24] With each new technique, as with cloning, the key question will be whether it serves important health, reproductive, or family needs and whether its benefits outweigh any likely harm. Cloning illustrates the principle that when legitimate uses of a technique are likely, regulatory policy should avoid prohibition and focus on ensuring that the technique is used responsibly for the good of those directly involved. As genetic knowledge continues to grow, the challenge of regulation will occupy us for some time to come.

REFERENCES

1. Silver LM. Remaking Eden: cloning and beyond in a brave new world. New York: Avon Books, 1997.

2. Walters L. Palmer JG. The ethics of human gene therapy. New York: Oxford University Press, 1997.

3. Robertson JA. Genetic selection of offspring characteristics. Boston Univ Law Rev 1996;76:421–82.

4. Begley S. Can we clone humans? Newsweek, March 10, 1997:53–60.

5. Cloning human beings: report and recommendations of the National Bioethics Advisory Commission. Rockville, Md.: National Bioethics Advisory Commission, June 1997.

6. Robertson JA. Children of choice: freedom and the new reproductive technologies. Princeton, N.J.: Princeton University Press, 1994.

7. Kearney W, Caplan AL. Parity for the donation of bone marrow: ethical and policy considerations. In: Blank RH, Bonnicksen AL, eds. Emerging issues in biomedical policy: an annual review, Vol. 1. New York: Columbia University Press, 1992:262–85.

8. Kassirer JP. Rosenthal NA. Should human cloning research be off limits? N Engl J Med 1998:338:905–6.

9. Holtzman NA. Proceed with caution: predicting genetic risks in the recombinant DNA era. Baltimore: Johns Hopkins University Press, 1989.

10. Robertson JA. Liberty, identity, and human cloning. Texas Law Rev 1998;77: 1371–456.

11. Davis DS. What's wrong with cloning? Jurimetrics 1997;38:83–9.

12. Segal NL Behavioral aspects of intergenerational human cloning: what twins tell us. Jurimetrics 1997;38:57–68.

13. Jonas H. Philosophical essays: from ancient creed to technological man. Englewood Cliffs, N.J.: Prentice-Hall, 1974:161.

14. Heyd D. Genethics: moral issues in the creation of people. Berkeley: University of California Press, 1992.

15. Council of Europe. Draft additional protocol to the Convention on Human Rights and Biomedicine on the prohibition of cloning human beings with explanatory report and Parliamentary Assembly opinion (adopted September 22, 1997). XXXVI International Legal Materials 1415 (1997).

16. Human Cloning Prohibition Act, H.R. 923, S.1601 (March 5, 1997).

17. Act of Oct. 4, 1997, ch. 688, 1997 Cal. Legis. Serv. 3790 (West, WESTLAW through 1997 Sess.).

18. Prohibition on Cloning of Human Beings Act, S. 1602, 105th Cong. (1998).

19. Stolberg SG. A small spark ignites debate on laws on cloning humans. New York Times. January 19, 1998:A1.

20. Gusfield J. Symbolic crusade: status politics and the American temperance movement. Urbana: University of Illinois Press, 1963.

21. Wolf SM. Ban cloning? Why NBAC is wrong. Hastings Cent Rep 1997; 27(5):12.

22. Wilson JQ. The paradox of cloning. The Weekly Standard. May 26, 1997:23–7.

23. Zhang J, Grifo J, Blaszczyk A, et al. In vitro maturation of human preovulatory oocytes reconstructed by germinal vesicle transfer. Fertil Steril 1997:68:Suppl:S1. abstract.

24. Bonnicksen AL. Transplanting nuclei between human eggs: implications for germline genetics. Politics and the Life Sciences. March 1998:3–10.

TOPICS FOR DISCUSSION AND WRITING

1. Robertson mentions "two types of fear" held by the National Bioethics Advisory Commission. What are these two fears and how does Robertson refute them?

2. What does Robertson suggest as the best direction for the Commission?

3. What importance do you place on the fact that this article appeared in *The New England Journal of Medicine*? Research the Journal's recent history to learn what other articles on ethical or social (in other words, non-medical) issues the *Journal* has published. Can you discern themes or patterns that unite these kinds of articles?

The Biotech Century

....

Jeremy Rifkin

In his book on biotechnology, *Harnessing the Gene and Remaking the World: The Biotech Century,* Jeremy Rifkin, president of the Foundation on Economic Trends in Washington, sounds a strong note of skepticism and caution in the field. He maintains that "for now, the most important issue at hand is to make the new science and technology an issue of considerable public attention." In the excerpts that follow, Rifkin discusses some of his misgivings about cloning and other issues of genetic engineering discussed later in *Bioethics,* emphasizing the potential for discrimination and the threat of eugenics. For a more complete discussion of his point of view, you might want to turn to his book in its entirety. You would be interested to see how his interest in biotechnology intersects with the exponential growth in computers and so connects with some of the issues discussed in Chapter 10.

A 1996 survey of genetic discrimination in the United States, conducted by Dr. Lisa N. Geller, et al., of the Department of Neurobiology and Division of Medical Ethics at Harvard Medical School, suggests that the practice is already far more widespread than previously thought. Genetic discrimination is being practiced by a range of institutions including insurance companies, health care providers, government agencies, adoption agencies, and schools. Researchers surveyed individuals at risk—or related to people at risk—for Huntington's disease, mucopolysaccharidosis (MPS), phenylketonuria (PKU), and hemochromatosis. Huntington's disease is a fatal disorder whose symptoms appear in middle age. MPS is associated with mental retardation and organomegaly. PKU also results in mental retardation but can be treated with special diets after birth. Hemochromatosis is an iron storage disorder.[38]

Of the 917 individuals surveyed in the study, 455 reported that they had experienced some form of discrimination based on their genetic makeup and genetic predispositions. Insurance companies and health providers were the most likely to practice genetic discrimination.[39] In one instance, a health maintenance organization refused to pay for occupational therapy after an individual was diagnosed with MPS-I, arguing that it was a preexisting condition. In another case, a twenty-four-year-old woman was refused life insurance because her family had a history of Huntington's disease, despite the fact that she had never been tested for the disease.[40] A *Newsweek* study of discrimination in the insurance industry found similar instances of abuse. One family had its entire coverage canceled when the insurance company discovered that one of its four children was afflicted with fragile X disease. The rest of the children were free of the disease but lost their coverage anyway.[41] . . .

Couples desiring to adopt children have also been discriminated against because of their genotypes. In one reported instance, a couple was denied adoption because the wife was "at risk" of coming down with Huntington's disease. In another case a birth mother with Huntington's disease was not allowed to put up her child for adoption through a state adoption agency. Still another couple, one of whom was at risk of developing Huntington's, was denied adoption of a normal baby but was allowed to adopt a baby at risk of coming down with Huntington's disease.[46] The very idea that genetically "at risk" couples should only be paired with genetically "at risk" babies, and vice versa, is still another early warning sign of what might potentially develop into a kind of informal genetic caste system in the coming century.

Equally troubling is the prospect of discriminatory genotyping of racial and ethnic groups in the Biotech Century. As scientists gain more information on the workings of the human genome, they will succeed in identifying an increasing number of genetic traits and predispositions that are unique to specific ethnic and racial groups, opening the door to the possibility of genetic discrimination of entire peoples. Already, for example, we know that Armenians are more prone to Familial Mediterranean Fever disease. Jews are carriers of Tay-Sachs and Gaucher's disease, and Africans carry the sickle-cell gene.[47] Might not this kind of ethnic- and race-specific genetic information be used as well by institutions as a tool of discrimination, segregation, and abuse?

Employers are also becoming more interested in using genetic screening tests to screen prospective employees. Their reasons run the gamut. Some chemical companies are interested in screening workers to assess their genetic sensitivity to highly toxic work environments. Worried over the high cost of health insurance coverage, disability compensation claims, and absenteeism, companies are interested in weeding out workers who may be more susceptible to illness. Matching workers' genotypes to the workplace would be a less costly alternative to cleaning up the sites and making them safe for all the workers, regardless of their susceptibilities. . . .

For its most ardent supporters, engineering life to improve humanity's own prospects is, no doubt, seen as the highest expression of ethical behavior. Any resistance to the new technology is likely to be castigated by the growing legion of true believers as inhuman, irresponsible, morally reprehensible, and perhaps even criminal.

On the other hand, the new genetic engineering technologies raise one of the most troubling political questions in all of human history. To whom, in this new era, would we entrust the authority to decide what is a good gene that should be added to the gene pool and what is a bad gene that should be eliminated? Should we entrust the government with that authority? Corporations? University scientists? From this perspective, few of us would be able to point to any institution or group of individuals we would entrust with decisions of such import. If, however, we were asked whether we would sanction new biotech advances that could enhance the physical, emotional, and mental well-being of our progeny, many of us would not hesitate for a moment to add our support. . . .

. . . Human gene screening and therapy raise the very real possibility that, for the first time in history, we might be able to reengineer the genetic blueprints of our own species and begin to redirect the future course of our biological evolution on Earth. The prospect of creating a new eugenic man and woman is no longer just the dream of wild-eyed political demagogues but rather a soon-to-be-available consumer option and a potentially lucrative commercial market.

Genetic engineering technologies are, by their very nature, eugenics tools. Because the technology is inseparably linked to eugenics ideas, no thoughtful discussion of the new technology revolution can occur without raising eugenics issues. The term "eugenics" was conceived by Sir Francis Galton, Charles Darwin's cousin, in the nineteenth century and is generally divided along two lines. Negative eugenics involves the systematic elimination of so-called undesirable biological traits. Positive eugenics is concerned with the use of selective breeding to "improve" the characteristics of an organism or species. . . .

The history of the American eugenics movement needs to be publicly aired, especially in light of the many new scientific discoveries and inventions that now make possible the kind of eugenics society that earlier eugenics reformers only could have dreamed of achieving. At a time when so many mainstream politicians, scientists, academicians and editorial writers discount the likelihood of a eugenics movement emerging in the twenty-first century, America's eugenics past is a sobering reminder that "it can happen here."

AMERICA'S EUGENIC PAST

Some day we will realize that the prime duty, the inescapable duty of the good citizen of the right type is to leave his or her blood behind him in the world; and that we have no business to permit the perpetuation of citizens of the wrong type. The great problem of civilization is to secure a relative increase of the valuable as compared with the less valuable or noxious elements in the population. . . . The problem cannot be met unless we give full consideration to the immense influence of heredity. . . . I wish very much that the wrong people could be prevented entirely from breeding; and when the evil nature of these people is sufficiently flagrant, this should be done. Criminals should be sterilized and feeble minded persons forbidden to leave offspring behind them. . . . the emphasis should be laid on getting desirable people to breed.[1]

This quote could have come from the lips of countless political functionaries at party rallies and meetings throughout Nazi Germany in the 1930s. But it didn't. It was uttered by the twenty-sixth President of the United States. Theodore Roosevelt, and it represented the "enlightened" 'view of millions of Americans caught up in an ideological movement that has been virtually written out of American history books. . . .

By the early 1990s, a torrent of breathtaking new discoveries and applications were being announced in the biotech field. Most people found themselves unprepared to assess the full social implications of the many new genetic breakthroughs that seemed to be challenging so many well-established customs and conventions. Today, scientists are developing the most powerful set of tools for manipulating the biological world ever conceived. The newfound power over the life force of the planet is, once again, raising the specter of a new eugenics movement. This is the troubling reality that so few policy makers, and even fewer biologists, are willing to acknowledge.

The new genetic engineering tools are, by definition, eugenics instruments. Whenever recombinant DNA, cell fusion, and other related techniques are used to "improve" the genetic blueprints of a microbe, plant, animal, or human being, a eugenics consideration is built into the process itself. In laboratories across the globe, molecular biologists are making daily choices about what genes to alter, insert, and delete from the hereditary code of various species. These are eugenics decisions. Every time a genetic change of this kind is made, the scientist, corporation, or state is implicitly, if not explicitly, making decisions about which are the good genes that should be inserted and preserved and which are the bad genes that should be altered or deleted. This is exactly what eugenics is all about. Genetic engineering is a technology designed to enhance the genetic inheritance of living things by manipulating their genetic code. . . .

. . . The biotech revolution will affect every aspect of our lives. The way we eat; the way we date and marry; the way we have our babies; the way our children are raised and educated; the way we work; the way we engage in politics; the way we express our faith; the way we perceive the world around us and our place in it—all of our individual and shared realities will be deeply touched by the new technologies of the Biotech Century. Surely, these very personal technologies deserve to be widely discussed and debated by the public at large before they become part of our daily lives. . . .

NOTES

38. Geller, Lisa N., Joseph S. Alper, Paul R. Billings, Carol I. Barash, Jonathan Beckwich, and Marvin R. Natowicz, "Individual, Family, and Societal Dimensions of Genetic Discrimination: A Case Study Analysis," *Science and Engineering Ethics,* vol. 2, no. 1, 1996, pp. 71–74.

39. Ibid., pp. 75–76.

40. Ibid.

41. Cowley, Geoffrey, "Flunk the Gene Test and Lose Your Insurance," *Newsweek,* December 23, 1996. p. 49.

. . .

46. Geller et al., "Individual, Family, and Societal Dimensions of Genetic Discrimination." p. 77.

47. Gostin, Larry, "Genetic Discrimination: The Use of Genetically Based Diagnostic and Prognostic Tests by Employers and Insurers," *American Journal of Law and Medicine,* vol. 17, nos. 1 and 2, 1991, P. 137; Goldstein, Joseph F., and Michael S. Brown, "Genetic Aspects of Disease," in K. Isselbacher, R. Adams, E. Braunwald, R. Peterdorf, and J. Wilson, eds., *Harrison's Principles of Internal Medicine,* 9th ed., vol.1 (New York: McGraw-Hill, 1980). p. 293.

. . .

1. Roosevelt, Theodore, to Charles B. Davenport, January 3, 1913, "Charles B. Davenport Papers," Department of Genetics, Cold Spring Harbor, NY; Roosevelt, Theodore, "Birth Reform, from the Positive, Not the Negative Side," in *The Works of Theodore Roosevelt,* vol. 21 (New York: Charles Scribner's Sons, 1923–26), p. 163; Roosevelt, Theodore, "Twisted Eugenics," *The Works of Theodore Roosevelt,* vol. 12, p. 201.

TOPICS FOR DISCUSSION AND WRITING

1. Rifkin raises concerns about how cloning could lead to discrimination. Discuss each of these different areas of discrimination, and, if writing a paper, add your own opinion on these issues. You may draw on personal experience if you or those you know have experienced similar forms of discrimination or if you see the threats Rifkin fears as potentially real threats to you.

2. In his discussion of eugenics, Rifkin claims that "the history of the American eugenics movement needs to be publicly aired" First, write a detailed definition of the term "eugenics." (See Writing Assignment 13 on page 133.) Then discuss what is particularly surprising in the history of eugenics in America. Why has the potential for eventually cloning humans made our awareness of eugenics so important today?

3. Compare Rifkin's outlook with that of Robertson in "Human Cloning and the Challenge of Regulation" above. Do you find differences between the style of lawyer Robertson and social critic Rifkin?

To Clone or Not to Clone

Jean Bethke Elshtain

Jean Bethke Elshtain is a Professor of Social and Political Ethics at the University of Chicago. Her essay is included in a collection titled *Clones and Clones: Facts and Fantasies about Human Cloning,* edited by Martha C. Nussbaum and Cass R. Sunstein. In a slightly different form, it appeared first in the *New Republic,* a magazine that features articles on politics and social issues. Note how she shares some of Jeremy Rifkin's concerns about cloning, detailing more specific concerns than appear in our excerpt from Rifkin's book.

Cloning is upon us. The techno-enthusiasts in our midst celebrate the collapse of yet another barrier to human mastery and control. But for most of us, this is an extraordinarily unsettling development. Talk to the man and woman in the street and you hear murmurs and rumblings and much dark musing about portents of the end-times and "now we've gone too far." The airwaves and the street win this one hands down, a welcome contrast to the celebratory glitz of *USA Today* trumpeting "Hello Dolly!"—Dolly being the name of the fetching ewe that faced the reader straight-on in a front page color photo announcing her cloned arrival. The subhead read, "Sheep cloning prompts ethical debate," The sheep looked perfectly normal, of course, and not terribly exercised about her historic significance. That she was really the child of no one—no one's little lamb—will probably not haunt her nights and bedevil her days. But we—we humans—should be haunted, by Dolly and all the Dollies to come and by the prospect that others are to appear on this earth as the progeny of our omnipotent striving, our yearning to create without pausing to reflect on what we are destroying.

When I pondered cloning initially, a Chicago Bulls game was on television. The Bulls were clobbering the Spurs. Michael Jordan had just performed a typically superhuman feat, an assist that suggested he has eyes in the back of his head and two sets of arms. To one buoyant citizen—a rare optimist among the worriers—who called a local program to register his two cents worth on cloning, the prospect of "more Michael Jordans" made the whole "cloning thing" worthwhile. "Can you imagine a whole basketball team of Michael Jordans?" he queried giddily. Unfortunately, I could. It seemed to me then and seems to me now a nightmare. If there were basketball teams fielding Jordans against Jordans, we wouldn't be able to recognize the one, the only, Michael Jordan. It's rather like suggesting that forty Mozarts are better than one. But there would be no Mozart were there forty Mozarts. We know the singularity of the one; the extraordinary genius—a Jordan, a Mozart—because they stand apart from and above the rest. Absent that irreducible singularity, their gifts and glorious, soaring accomplishments would come to mean nothing as they would have become the norm, just commonplace. Another dunk; another concerto. In fact, lots of callers made this point, or one similar to it, reacting to the Michael Jordan Clontopia scenario.

A research librarian at a small college in Indiana, who had driven me to her campus for the purpose of delivering a lecture, offered a spontaneous, sustained, and troubled critique of cloning that rivals the best dystopian fictions. Her cloning nightmare was a veritable army of Hitlers, ruthless and remorseless bigots and killers who kept reproducing themselves and were one day able to finish what the historic Hitler failed to accomplish. It occurred to me that an equal number of Mother Theresas would probably not be a viable deterrent, not if the Hitler clones were behaving like, well, Hitlers.

But I had my own nightmare scenario to offer. Imagine, I suggested to my librarian driver, a society that clones human beings to serve as spare parts. Because the cloned entities are not fully human, our moral queasiness could be disarmed and we could "harvest" organs to our heart's content—and organs from human beings of every age, race, phenotype at that. Harvesting organs from anencephalic newborns would, in that new world, be the equivalent of the Model T—an early and, it turns out, very rudimentary prototype of glorious, gleaming things to come.

Far-fetched? No longer. Besides, often the far-fetched gets us nearer the truth of the matter than all the cautious, persnickety pieces that fail to come anywhere close to the pity and terror this topic evokes. Consider Stanislaw Lem's *The Star Diaries,* in which his protagonist; Ijon Tichy, described as a "hapless Candide of the Cosmos," ventures into space encountering one weird situation after another. Lem's "Thirteenth Voyage" takes him to a planet, Panta, where he runs afoul of local custom and is accused of the worst of crimes, "the crime of personal differentiation." The evidence against him is incriminating. Nonetheless, Tichy is given an opportunity to conform. A planet spokesman offers a peroration to Tichy concerning the benefits of his planet, on which there are no separate entities—"only the collective."

For the denizens of Panta have come to understand that the source of all "the cares, sufferings and misfortunes to which beings, gathered together in societies, are prone" lies in the individual, "in his private identity." The individual, by contrast to the collective, is "characterized by uncertainty, indecision, inconsistency of action, and above all—by impermanence." Having "completely eliminated individuality," on planet Panta they have achieved "the highest degree of social interchangeability." It works rather the way the Marxist utopia was to function. Everyone at any moment can be anything else. Functions or roles are interchangeable. On Panta you occupy a role for twenty-four hours only: one day a gardener, the next an engineer, then a mason, now a judge.

The same principle holds with families. "Each is composed of relatives— there's a father, mother, children. Only the functions remain constant; the ones who perform them are changed every day." All feelings and emotions are entirely abstract. One never needs to grieve or to mourn as everyone is infinitely replaceable. "Affection, respect, love where at one time gnawed by constant anxiety, by the fear of losing the person held dear. This dread we have conquered. For in point of fact whatever upheavals, diseases or calamities may be visited upon us, we shall always have a father, a mother, a spouse, and children." As well, there is no "I." And there can be no death "where there are no individuals. We do not die." Tichy can't quite get with the program. Brought before a court, he is "found guilty and condemned to life identification." He blasts off and sets his course for Earth.

Were Lem writing an addendum for his brilliant tale, he might show Tichy landing, believing he is at last on terra firma in both the literal and metaphorical sense, only to discover that the greeting party at the rocket-port is a bit strange: There are forty very tall basketball players all in identical uniforms wearing No. 23 jerseys, on one side and, on the other, forty men in powdered wigs, suited up in breeches and satin frock coats and playing identical pieces on identical harpsichords. Wrong planet? No more.

Sure, it's amusing, up to a point. But it was anything but amusing to overhear the speculation that cloning might be made available to parents about to lose a child to leukemia or, having lost a child to an accident, in order that they might reproduce and replace that lost child. This image borders on an obscenity. Perhaps we need a new word to describe what it represents, to capture fully what order of things the cloning of children in order to forestall human loss and grief violates. We say to little Tommy, in effect: "Sorry to lose you. But Tommy 2 is waiting in the wings." And what of Tommy 2? What happens when he learns he is the pinch hitter? "There was an earlier Tommy, much loved, so Mommy and Daddy had a copy made." But it isn't really Mommy and Daddy—it's the two people who placed the order for him and paid a huge sum. He's their little product; little fabricated Tommy 2, a techno-orphan. And Tommy 1 lies in the grave unmourned; undifferentiated in death; un-remembered because he had been copied and his individuality wrenchingly obliterated.

The usual nostrums are of no use here. I have in mind the standard cliché that, once again, our "ethical thinking" hasn't caught up with technological "advance." This is a flawed way to reflect on cloning and so much else. The problem is not that we must somehow catch our ethics up to our technology. The problem is that technology is rapidly gutting our ethics. And it is *our* ethics. Ethical reflection belongs to all of us—all those agitated radio callers—and it is the fears and apprehension of ordinary citizens that should be paid close and re-spectful attention. The ethicists are cut from the same cloth as everybody else. They breathe the same cultural air. They, too, are children of the West, of Ju-daism, Catholicism, the Renaissance, the Reformation, the Enlightenment. In the matter of cloning, we cannot wait for the experts. The queasiness the vast ma-jority of Americans feel at this "remarkable achievement" is appropriate and should be aired and explored fully.

Perhaps something remarkable will finally happen. We will put the genie back into the bottle for a change. We will say, "No, stop, we will not go down this road." This doesn't make us antiscience or antiprogress or stodgy sticks-in-the-mud. It makes us skeptical, alert, and, yes, frightened citizens asking the question: Whatever will become of the ancient prayer, "That I may see my chil-dren's children and peace upon Israel," in a world of cloned entities, peopled by the children of No Body, copies of our selves? These poor children of our fan-tasies and our drive to perfect and our arrogant search for dominion: What are we to say to them? Forgive us, for we knew not what we were doing? That tastes bitter on the tongue. We knew what we were doing and we did it anyway. Of whom will we ask forgiveness? Who will be there to listen? Who to absolve?

Are these the musings of an alarmist, a technophobe, a Luddite? Consider that there are now cloned calves in Wisconsin and cloned rodents in various lab-oratories worldwide. Cloned company is bursting out all over: thus far none of it human. The clone enthusiasts will surely find a way, however. Dolly's creator or producer or manufacturer—hard to know what to call him—thinks human cloning is a bad idea. But others are not nearly so reticent. Consider, then, some further developments on the cloning and related fronts that promise, or threaten, to alter our relation to our bodies, our selves.

A big story of the moment—and a huge step toward human cloning—lies in the fertile field of infertility science: the world of human reproductive technol-ogy. Many procedures once considered radical are by now routine. These in-clude in vitro fertilization, embryo flushing, surrogate embryo transfer, and sex preselection, among others. Now comes Dr. Mark Sauer, described by the *New York Times* as "an infertility expert at Columbia Presbyterian Medical Center in New York" who "dreams of offering his patients a type of cloning some day." It would work like this. You take a two- or three-day-old human embryo and use its cells—there are only about eight at this stage—to grow identical embryos where once there was only one. The next step is to implant "some" of these embryos in a woman's uterus immediately and freeze the extras. And what are the plans for the clonettes in cold storage? Well, initial attempts at impregnation may fail. So you have some spare embryos for a second, third, or fourth try. Suppose the woman successfully carries the initial implants to term. She may want more babies—identical babies—and the embryos are there for future use. The upshot, of course, is that a woman could wind up with "identical twins, triplets, or even quadruplets, possibly born years apart."

And why would anyone want this, considering the potentially shattering questions it presents to the identity and integrity of the children involved? Dr. Sauer has an answer. Otherwise there "might be no babies at all." To be sure, the premise of this procedure isn't as obviously morally repugnant as the scenario noted above, the speculation that cloning might be made available to parents about to lose a child to leukemia or, having lost a child to an accident, in order that they might reproduce and replace that child, as I noted already.

Rather, the debate about this latest embryo cloning scenario, by contrast, rages around whether or not this is, in fact, cloning at all or whether it is a version of cloning that is more or less questionable than the standard or classic form: the Dolly scenario. Dr. Sauer and other enthusiasts say that because cloning is a "politically dirty word"—there is, apparently, no real ethical issue here—they hope that their proposed method of crypto-cloning may slip under the radar screen. Besides, he avers, it's much better for the women involved: You don't have to give them lots of drugs to "force their ovaries to pump out multiple eggs so that they could fertilize them and create as many embryos as possible."

Again, why are so many women putting themselves through this? And why has this been surrounded by the halo of "rights"? You can be sure, once word gets around, that the more "attractive" idea (in the words of another infertility specialist) of replicating embryos will generate political demands. A group will spring up proclaiming "embryo duplication rights" just as an outfit emerged instantly after Dolly was announced arguing that to clone oneself was a fundamental right. Several of the infertility specialists cited in the *Times* piece, all male doctors, interestingly enough, spoke of the pleading of women, of "the misery my patients are living through." But surely a good bit of that misery comes from having expectations lifted out of all proportion in relation to chances of success (with procedures like in vitro), only to find, time and time again, that the miracle of modern medicine has turned into an invasive, expensive, mind-bending, heart-rending dud. A doleful denouement to high-tech generated expectations and the playing out of "reproductive freedom."

Whatever happened to accepting embodied limits with better grace? There are many ways to enact what the late Erik Erikson called "generative" projects and lives. Biological parenthood is one but not the only one. Many of the women we call great from our own history—I think here of one of my own heroes—Jane Addams of Hull-House—were not mothers although they did an extraordinary amount of mothering. Either through necessity or choice, she and many others offered their lives in service to civic or religious projects that located them in a world of relationships over the years with children not their own that involved loving concern, care, friendship, nurture, protection, discipline, pride, disappointment: all the complex virtues, habits, and emotions called forth by biological parenting.

And there is adoption, notwithstanding the frustrations many encounter and the fear instilled by such outrageous violations of decency as the holding in the "Baby Richard" and other recent cases in which children were wrenched from the only family they had ever known in order to be returned to a bio-parent claimant who had discovered belatedly the overwhelming need to be a father or mother. How odd that biology now trumps nearly all other claims and desires. In several texts I've encountered recently, adoption is surrounded with a faintly sinister odor and treated as an activity not all that different from baby selling. Somehow all these developments—the insistent urge to reproduce through any means necessary and the emergence of a multimillion-dollars-a-year specialty devoted to precisely that task; the diminution of the integrity of adoption in favor of often dubious claims from bio-parents; the possibility, now, of cloning embryos in order to guarantee more or less identical offspring to a desperate couple—are linked.

What common threads tie these disparate activities together? How does one account for the fact that the resurgence of feminism over the past thirty years and enhanced pressures on women, many of them placed on women by themselves, to reproduce biologically have emerged in tandem? Why are these developments surrounded by such a desperate aura and a sense of misery and failure—including the failure of many marriages that cannot survive the tumult of infertility high-tech medicine's intrusion into a couple's intimate lives? Let's try out one possible explanation. Here at the end of the twentieth century we all care mightily about identity: who we are. Sometimes this takes the form of identity politics in which one's own identity gets submerged into that of a group, likely a group defined in biological or quasi-biological terms on grounds of sex, race, or ethnicity. That's problematic enough as a basis for politics, to say the least. But we've further compounded the biological urgencies, upping the ante to bear one's "own" child as a measure of the success or failure of the self.

Mind you, I do not want to downplay how heartbreaking it is for many couples who want to have a baby and cannot. But, again, there are many ways to parent and many babies desperate for loving families. Rather than to expand our sense of gracious acceptance of those who may not be our direct biological offspring, which means accepting our own limits but coming to see that these open up other possibilities, we rail against cruel fate and reckon ourselves nigh-worthless persons if we fail biologically. Perhaps with so much up for grabs, in light of the incessant drumbeat to be all we can be, to achieve, to produce, to succeed, to define our own projects, to be the sole creators of our own destinies, we have fallen back on the bedrock of biology. When all that is solid is melting into air, maybe biology seems the last redoubt of solidity, of identity. But, of course, this is chimerical. In demanding of our bodies what they sometimes cannot give, our world grows smaller, our focus more singular if not obsessive, and identity itself is called into question: our own and that of our future, identical offspring.

TOPICS FOR DISCUSSION AND WRITING

1. Explain the relevance of Michael Jordan and Mozart to Elshtain's argument about the ethical dangers of cloning.

2. Explain what Elshtain means when she says, "And it is *our* ethics."

3. Elshtain takes a strong position on the moral issues surrounding cloning. She does, however, make concessions as she argues her point. Identify where she concedes and discuss the effect of this strategy on the strength of her argument. (See A Dialectical Approach to Argument in Chapter 4 and also the essays "Second Thoughts on Cloning" by Laurence Tribe in Chapter 3 and "Human Cloning" by John Robertson for more examples of concession.)

4. After reading Jeremy Rifkin and Jean Elshtain's arguments against human cloning, reread Oliver Morton and John Robertson's endorsements in "Overcoming Yuk" and the article from *The New England Journal of Medicine.* Use Rifkin's and Elshtain's arguments to write a refutation of Morton's and Robertson's defenses of human cloning. (See Refutation in Chapter 4.)

Can Souls Be Xeroxed?

Robert Wright

Shortly after the announcement of Dolly's birth, journalist Robert Wright questioned a fundamental assumption about what makes a person an individual. Note how this discussion relates to the debate surrounding cloning.

The world has had a week to conjure up nightmare scenarios, yet no one has articulated the most frightening peril posed by human cloning: rampant self-satisfaction. Just consider, If cloning becomes an option, what kind of people will use it? Exactly—people who think the world could use more of them; people so chipper that they have no qualms about bestowing their inner life on a dozen members of the next generation; people, in short, with high self-esteem. The rest of us will sit there racked with doubt, worried about inflicting our tortured psyches on the innocent unborn, while all around us shiny, happy people proliferate like rabbits. Or sheep, or whatever.

Of course, this assumes that psyches get copied along with genes. That seems to be the prevailing assumption. People nod politely to the obligatory reminder about the power of environment in shaping character. But many then proceed to talk excitedly about cloning as if it amounts to Xeroxing your soul.

What makes the belief in genetic identity so stubborn? In part a natural confusion over headlines. There are zillions of them about how genes shape behavior, but the underlying stories spring from two different sciences. The first, behavioral genetics, studies genetic differences among people. (Do you have the thrill-seeking gene? You do? Mind if I drive?) Behavioral genetics has demonstrated that genes matter. But does that mean that genes are destiny, that your clone is you?

Enter the second science, evolutionary psychology. It dwells less on genetic difference than on commonality. In this view, the world is already chock-full of virtual clones. My next-door neighbor—or the average male anywhere on the globe—is a 99.9%-accurate genetic copy of me. And paradoxically, many of the genes we share empower the environment to shape behavior and thus make us different from one another. Natural selection has preserved these "malleability genes" because they adroitly tailor character to circumstance.

Thus, though some men are more genetically prone to seek thrills than others, men in general take fewer risks if married with children than if unattached. Though some people may be genetically prone to high self-esteem, everyone's self-esteem depends heavily on social feedback. Genes even mold personality to our place in the family environment, according to Frank Sulloway, author of *Born to Rebel,* the much discussed book on birth order. Parents who clone their obedient oldest child may be dismayed to find that the resulting twin, now lower in the family hierarchy, grows up to be Che Guevara.

This malleability could, in a round-about way, produce clones who are indeed soul mates. Your clone would, after all, look like you. And certain kinds of faces and physiques lead to certain kinds of experiences that exert certain effects on the mind. Early in this century, a fledgling effort at behavioral genetics divided people into such classes as mesomorphs—physically robust, psychologically assertive—and ectomorphs —skinny, nervous, shy. But even if these generalizations hold some water, it needn't mean that ectomorphs have genes for shyness. It may just mean that skinny people get pushed around on the junior-high playground and their personality adapts. (This is one problem with those identical twins-reared-apart studies by behavioral geneticists: Do the twins' characters correlate because of "character genes" or sometimes just because appearance shapes experience which shapes character?)

People who assume that genes are us seem to think that if you reared your clone, you would experience a kind of mind meld—not quite a fusion of souls, maybe, but an uncanny empathy with your budding carbon copy. And certainly empathy would at times be intense. You might know exactly how nervous your frail, gawky clone felt before the high school prom or exactly how eager your attractive, athletic clone felt.

On the other hand, if you really tried, you could similarly empathize with people who weren't your clone. We've all felt an adolescent's nervousness, and we've all felt youthfully eager, because these feelings are part of the generic human mind, grounded in the genes that define our species. It's just that we don't effortlessly transmute this common experience into empathy except in special cases—with offspring or siblings or close friends. And presumably with clones.

But the cause of this clonal empathy wouldn't be that your inner life was exactly like your clone's (it wouldn't be.) The catalyst, rather, would be seeing that familiar face—the one in your high school yearbook, except with a better haircut. It would remind you that you and your clone were *essentially* the same, driven by the same hopes and fears. You might even feel you shared the same soul. And in a sense, this would be true. Then again, in a sense, you share the same soul with everyone.

TOPICS FOR DISCUSSION AND WRITING

1. According to Robert Wright, what peril of human cloning has thus far gone unrecognized? On what assumption does this particular peril lie? What flaw does Wright find in this assumption? What does Wright mean by the terms *commonality* and *malleability*? Do you agree with his analysis of the soul as it relates to the cloning issue?

2. Do Wright's observations simplify the debate over cloning or complicate it?

3. Look ahead to Nature Versus Nurture and note how "Can Souls Be Xeroxed?" ties into that debate.

4. Review each article under "The Debate" starting on page 356 and briefly summarize each writer's position on cloning. (See Summaries in Chapter 3.)

5. Updating information on the Internet: Since these articles were assembled, further developments in the field will have expanded and broadened the possibilities and the controversies. To add current findings to the material offered here, go to the Internet or your library and find two articles on cloning and on the bioethical questions this issue raises. Summarize the facts and moral issues addressed in these articles, discuss in what ways they continue the debate occasioned by the birth of Dolly, and then address any new questions raised. By the year 2001, the National Bioethics Advisory. Committee should be preparing to issue the results of its investigations on cloning. (See The Debate, starting on page 356.

Many readings in this book came from research done on computer databases or the Internet. (See Chapter 9 for help in research strategies.)

Nature Versus Nurture

With the rise of genetic research and increasing public as well as scientific interest in DNA, the age-old debate over nature versus nurture has taken on new life—do our genes determine who we are and how we behave or does the environment in which we develop exert a greater influence? This question leads on to the next: What are the social, economic, and political consequences of such a debate? The selections that follow explore some of these issues.

Nature vs. Nurture

Art Spiegelman

Cartoonist and social satirist Art Spiegelman has fun with the nature versus nurture debate.

TOPICS FOR DISCUSSION AND WRITING

1. What is Spiegelman's conclusion on the nature versus nurture debate? What popular theory of child rearing is he satirizing?

2. The controversy surrounding the nature versus nurture debate lies at the center of many feminist issues. Spiegelman is playing off this question in his cartoon above. From your own observations, where do you stand on the roles of nature and nurture in determining gender-based behaviors? Before discussing this issue, you may want to read ahead in Nature Versus Nurture.

3. For the artists among you: Can you create your own cartoon on a subject related to nature versus nurture or on some other issue connected to cloning? This exercise could wait until you have read all the material in this chapter.

Aristotle to Zoos: A Philosophical Dictionary of Biology

P. B. and J. S. Medawar

The Medawars, two British biologists, a husband and wife team, discuss nature and nurture and offer definitions in their instructive and entertaining dictionary, a selection from which follows. P. B. Medawar won the Nobel Prize for medicine and physiology in 1960.

The antithetical use of the terms "nature" and "nurture" probably derives from Sir Francis Galton's *English Men of Science: Their Nature and Nurture* (London, 1874), but in *The Tempest,* act 4, scene 1, Shakespeare puts into Prospero's mouth the description of Caliban as "a devil on whose nature nurture can never stick." Robert Nisbet in his essay on "Anomie" in *Prejudices: A Philosophical Dictionary* (Cambridge, Massachusetts, 1982), feels that the antithesis is foreshadowed by an antagonism dating from the fifth century B.C. between *physis* (having much the connotation of "nature") and *nomos* (meaning a pasture for cattle, a nurturing environment we assume). The usage is, in any event, long established and well understood.

In the modern application of these terms, an organism's nature is that which it is by reason of its genetic makeup. Its nurture is the sum total of the factors that have entered into its environment and its upbringing. Laymen are apt to think of the distinction in competitive terms and have been wont to ask themselves what fractions nature and nurture respectively contribute to a certain character difference—say, a difference of intelligence. We can only proffer a general rule about attempts to attach exact percentages to the two contributions: the more confident and dogmatic the attempt, the more likely it is to be wrong—or, more often, wrongheaded. Indeed, the estimated contribution made by nature may vary from 0 to 100 percent according to environment, that is according to the contribution of nurture—and vice versa. . . .

[The Medawars go on to suggest a theorem] which declares that the contribution of nature to any character difference is a function of nurture and [the contribution] of nurture is a function of nature, a theorem of which there are an infinitude of illustrations. For example, in many crustaceans the degree of pigmentation of the eye depends both upon the genetic makeup and upon the temperature at which development proceeds: it is possible to fix upon a temperature at which the differences between having white, black, red, or dusky eyes present themselves as wholly genetic in origin, and it is possible to choose genotypes in which the color of the eyes is determined almost wholly by environmental influences. Exactly the same argument in principle applies to the number of facets in the compound eye of insects: this too is under genetic control but also influenced by temperature.

If in these simple and straightforward cases it is seen to be quite impossible to attach exact figures to the contribution of nature and nurture to character differences, must this not apply a fortiori to those weary attempts by IQ psychologists to demonstrate that intelligence is 75 to 80 percent genetically controlled and only influenced to the tune of 20 to 25 percent by education and nurture? Such pronouncements have had a profound influence upon politicians and through them upon legislation. . . .

The argument that has been outlined above, that the contribution of nature is a function of nurture and of nurture a function of nature, is not in principle a very difficult argument. Nevertheless, to understand it requires a certain strength of comprehension which seems in the past to have been beyond the capacity of many psychologists, high though their IQ scores may have been.

There is a strong political coloration to the inclination to attribute inequalities of intellectual performance to nature rather than to nurture. For if the poor and needy have become so by reason of their genes, there is nothing very much we can do about it: their poverty and inadequacy are not of our doing, and we have no moral compulsion to take social steps to remedy their condition. If, on the other hand, like dedicated modern Marxists we categorically deny that there are inborn differences among human capabilities so that a human being is only what his environment and upbringing can make of him, then in a just society it is an obligation upon the state to provide for the education and upbringing of its citizens. . . .

TOPICS FOR DISCUSSION AND WRITING

1. The Medawars quote the Duke Prospero talking about the strange character Caliban in Shakespeare's *The Tempest.* Examine the quotation and explain what Prospero means. You may find it helpful to read the play, or at least the scene quoted from, if you want to elaborate on the remark.

2. How do the Medawars describe the relationship between nature and nurture? What significance do they suggest arises from the debate? What position do you think the Medawars take on nature versus nurture?

3. In your own words, describe the point the Medawars make about the eyes of crustaceans and insects.

Born That Way

William Wright

While acknowledging that nurture plays a role in human development, William Wright, in his comprehensive study of research on the influence of genes on human behavior, comes down firmly on the side of nature. Wright is first a writer rather than a scientist, but his interest in the issue of nature versus nurture dates back four decades to his undergraduate days at Yale University, when he considered psychology as a major. Put off by the purely behaviorist approach (nurture as the only important part of the equation), Wright abandoned the field, not to return to the issue until research brought new emphasis to the genetic view of behavior. These brief selections from his book (published in 1998 when biotechnology had begun to capture public attention more than ever) introduce some of his arguments.

The interaction between genes and environment is, we now know, essential to the developing child—and for psychologists the term "environment" means every influence on an organism that is not genetic. Not only in children, but in adults too, the environment can have powerful effects. But to a greater degree than ever before realized, the genetic influences on behavior, barring an extraordinary childhood (malnutrition, social deprivation, prolonged abuse), express themselves pretty much as configured before birth.

Scholars have traditionally divvied up the human into an array of discrete vantage points—anatomy, psychology, anthropology, sociology, economics, political science, history. We now see these disciplines converging on a component of our physical selves that mounting evidence indicates is the underlying basis of it all: the twenty-three pairs of chromosomes, containing approximately 100,000 genes, that exist in every human cell. Whatever the term—chromosomes, genes, DNA, the double helix, nucleic acids, ribosomes, alleles—all refer to our biochemical blueprints.

Genetic discoveries have been receiving so much press that non-scientists can be forgiven for seeing the DNA furor as a fad, a New Thing steamroller, this year's channeling or biorhythms. The world appears so in the grip of a double-helix dither that less excitable types shrug it off as a hyped-up media ploy to make the news of the day appear different from the news of last week. Unfortunately for people already bored with gene palaver, the ramifications of this scientific earthquake will continue unfolding, and making news, well into the next century. And the possibilities this knowledge opens up are vast.

Many of the most riveting findings have been of a high-priority medical nature, the genetic roots of birth defects and diseases that, throughout time, have plagued humanity. Because of the widespread suffering caused by these genetic mishaps—British geneticist Steve Jones states that one child in thirty is born with a genetic irregularity of one sort or other—the excitement over genetic therapies is understandable. More recently, the sensational news about cloning a sheep from a mature cell has seized the spotlight from even the landmark medical breakthroughs.

Important as these advances are, they have overshadowed a concurrent, and in some ways more momentous, revolution—the burgeoning understanding of genetic links to personality and behavior. A mass of research that has been building over the past two decades has forced most psychologists and other social scientists to acknowledge what they had long denied: Genes influence not just physical characteristics such as hair color and susceptibility to cancer but our personalities, temperaments, behavioral patterns—even personal idiosyncrasies, the quirks and foibles that make each person unique.

Since behavior is the subject of this book, and the term is broad enough to glaze the eyes of nonprofessionals, it might be a good idea to consider what the word means to scientists. For them, behavior is everything the organism does and thinks—from crying for its mother to delivering a Nobel acceptance speech. Ambition is behavior; so are laziness, rebellion, and compassion. Patriotism, sexism, hating your boss, and loving the Lakers—all are forms of behavior. Virtually anything the individual does, any product of the brain, any action, any mood, emotion, mannerism, or tie, is lumped under the umbrella word "behavior."

From the beginning of the brief hundred years that the mechanics of inheritance have been unfolding, science understood that genes were the building plans for our bodies and brains, the human machine that seemed to be able to think and behave in unlimited numbers of ways. Patterns and constraints were imposed on behavior from the external world, especially from the culture and its primary agents, parents. Now we see that this picture is not accurate. Many patterns and constraints are imposed by culture, but many others, the new evidence shows—along with batteries of impulses, leanings, attitudes, susceptibilities, aptitudes—are born with us.

It is hard enough for nonscientists to conceive of a few microscopic specks of nucleic acid containing the instructions for growing an arm, an ear, or a kidney. Now research says we must grasp as well that similar specks can also go far toward determining if we are to be happy or morose, passive or aggressive, bright or dim, liberal or conservative, religious or atheistic. "Phenotype" is the word scientists use for each genetic manifestation. (Genotype refers to an organism's entire complement of genes, the overall blueprint for each species.) A leg is a phenotype; so are arms, ears, and kidneys. Geneticists have come to consider behavior (or behavioral propensities) just another phenotype.

Among those pursuing this research, some focus on specieswide traits, seeking out the evolved behavioral template shared by everyone. These are the evolutionary psychologists and sociobiologists who try to identify the broad traits that have evolved to make up human nature—aggression, competitiveness, sociality, and altruism would be a few. Behavioral geneticists, on the other hand, are more interested in individual differences. They are ferreting out the genetic influences, if any, that make one person fearful, another bold, one optimistic, one pessimistic, one placid, one fretful. They are also seeking the specific genetic configurations that abundant evidence indicates interact with the environment to produce such common behavioral problems as depression, addiction, obesity, and autism.

An unexpected product of this research is the ever-narrower behavioral nooks and crannies that reveal a genetic component. For most of us it is not difficult to accept at least partial genetic orchestration of broad categories of temperament such as shyness, pessimism, and boldness, among others. Narrower traits, however, such as compassion, extravagance, rule-flouting, and risk-taking, can, without too great an effort of the imagination, also be nominated for biochemical underpinnings. But our minds rebel at the news that genes can induce such behavioral minutiae as hand gestures, pet-naming, and nervous giggles. According to recent research, this appears to be the case. Whether aimed at individual differences or specieswide traits, both behavioral genetics and evolutionary biology are in the business of seeking genetic paths to behavior, and both are bringing about a new perspective on the human complex.

Therapeutic promise is not the only reason the news about gene therapy and cloning has overshadowed the news concerning behavior. The genetic insights about physical defects and dysfunctions are filling a void of knowledge or deepening existing understanding. This sort of information is welcomed by everyone. Findings about the gene-behavior dynamic, on the other hand, are overturning existing truths and demolishing assumptions upon which fifty years of psychological theory has been based. Totally different answers are emerging to questions many experts were confident had long been answered. It is this apostate cast to the behavioral findings that has caused turmoil in the academic community and provoked angry debate. It has also contributed to the early media caution in announcing the discoveries.

The largest body of hard data to establish the genetic roots of behavior has come from comparisons of fraternal with identical twins and comparisons of adopted with biological siblings. For thirty years these investigations have been progressing quietly in scores of kinship studies in the United States and abroad and building a mountain of evidence of the gene-behavior relationship. Of all this research, the most persuasive as well as the most dramatic has been an eighteen-year examination at the University of Minnesota of identical twins who were separated shortly after birth and raised in different homes. The study has examined over seventy sets of separated identical twins and more than fifty sets of fraternals. The telling results startled not only the scientific world but the Minnesota researchers themselves. This was not so much for the degree of genetic influence on traits, which has already been established by other studies, but by the highly specific nature of some genetic expressions. Some of these stories are astounding and dramatically extend the possibilities of genetic string-pulling.

Conclusive as these overall twin findings were for many of the extensive gene-personality links, even harder scientific evidence corroborating this data is just now beginning to emerge from molecular biologists who are tracking the DNA itself to locate explicit chromosomal segments that lead to particular behaviors. While twin and adoption studies measure and compare individuals to establish genetic influence, molecular biologists can be seen as approaching human behavior "from the other end," seeking out the individual genes that might contribute to a particular trait. Such gene pinpointing brings us much closer to interventions–enhancing, fixing, blocking. The possibilities are endless. . . .

On the face of it, all of this may not seem too revolutionary. Everyday chitchat abounds in behavioral geneticist thinking. "She got her extravagance from her mother." Or, "the musical talent comes from his father's side." Or, "he's a crook just like his granddaddy." Whether consciously or not, such remarks suggest DNA strings that lead to spending sprees, piano-playing, and crookedness. While we may have gut feelings of genetic transmission of personality traits—animal breeders have known about it for centuries—such thinking has been abhorrent to prevailing scientific thought for much of this century. Back-porch philosophers and animal breeders could believe whatever they wished; science *knew* we humans were creatures of our rearing environments. Experience and learning determined who we are, nothing else.

This is no minor artifact of intellectual history to be tossed quickly into the bin marked "Earlier Mistakes." The behaviorist belief in an all-powerful environment has for many decades dominated enlightened thinking and been the basis of our society's approaches to childrearing, education, social dysfunctions—and, of course, psychological problems. All the leading psychotherapists, from Freud to

Joyce Brothers, might have disagreed about *which* environmental influences made you wet your bed, bite your nails, expose yourself—but none had any doubts that it was *something* in the environment. Always the environment. And this view is still very much with us, if more as a habit of thought than a conscious idea. . . .

The new information about genes is not just a matter of fresh dogma replacing old. The discoveries of behavioral genetics have shown the earlier environment-is-everything model to be half true, but a view of human functioning so myopic, so lopsided as to invalidate most of the findings based on it. It also caused considerable harm. A prime example would be the psychodynamic "cures" imposed on sufferers of conditions we now know can have genetic roots—calamities like schizophrenia, autism, obesity, and an array of neurotic symptoms. Harm was also inflicted when parents were blamed for childhood problems that stemmed from genetic irregularities. In addition to the injustice involved, placing blame in the wrong place moved practitioners further from remedies. For nailing down the cause of psychological problems, genetic knowledge now provides an additional suspect: pesky bits of nucleic acid contained in the genes that the parents may have provided but over which they have little or no control. . . .

CONCLUSIONS

Whether or not the young science of behavioral genetics finds the root cause of behaviors we deplore, like war and racism, this field of inquiry, along with its sister science of evolutionary psychology, is arriving at a broad new understanding of our species. In addition to seeing ourselves as products of culture, education, and upbringings, we can also see ourselves as blinking switchboards of gene-

"Not guilty by reason of genetics, Your Honor. I come from a long line of scumbags."

CARTOON COPYRIGHT © 1999, THE WASHINGTON POST WRITERS GROUP. REPRINTED WITH PERMISSION.

fired impulses, some older than the species itself, some weak, others powerful, some ever-present, others sporadic—but all waiting their moment to take charge of the entire vessel, to move us to an action that evolution at one period in our four-million-year history decided increased chances of survival.

After only two decades of concerted research into this aspect of our makeup, we can now address human dysfunctions, contradictions, and self-destructiveness armed with a grasp of an important new component, perhaps the most important of all: the powerful effect on behavior of the human genome, the twenty-three pairs of chromosomes that produced our eyes, feet, and kidneys, and play a role in every aspect of our behavior.

NOTES

1. "One child in thirty": *The Language of Genes* by Steve Jones, Anchor Books, 1994. . . .

TOPICS FOR DISCUSSION AND WRITING

1. William Wright cites a particular "momentous revolution" in genetic discoveries. To what is he referring?

2. How does Wright define behavior? What distinctions does he make between evolutionary biology and behavioral genetics? What significance does Wright see in the recent findings in behavioral genetics?

3. What does Wright cite as the "harm" resulting from years of the "environment-is-everything" model which has dominated behavioral psychology? If you are taking or have taken a psychology class, can you make any comparisons between what Wright believes and the theories expressed in the texts used in such a class?

4. In your library or on the Internet, look up the University of Minnesota twin study that Wright refers to and discuss some of the findings that support his claims.

Do Parents Matter?

Malcolm Gladwell

In her book, *The Nurture Assumption,* published in the fall of 1998, Judith Harris acknowledges the powerful role that genes play in determining human behavior, but her study turns on a particular theory of nurture. New in the field of developmental psychology is her emphasis on the environment outside the home, particularly a child's peer group, rather than on parents, traditionally seen as central in determining what kind of person their child becomes. She begins, "This book has two purposes: first, to dissuade you of the notion that a child's personality—what used to be called 'character'—is shaped or modified by the child's parents; and second, to give you an alternative view of how the child's personality is shaped." She admits her position is still a theory awaiting further corroboration, but Malcolm Gladwell, writing in *The New Yorker* magazine, is enthusiastic about her ideas in his report, "Do Parents Matter?" Brief excerpts from his article follow.

Judith Harris's big idea—that peers matter much more than parents—runs counter to nearly everything that a century of psychology and psychotherapy has told us about human development. Freud put parents at the center of the child's universe, and there they have remained ever since. "They fuck you up, your mum and dad./ They may not mean to, but they do," the poet Philip Larkin memorably wrote, and that perspective is fundamental to the way we have been taught to understand ourselves. When we go to a therapist, we talk about our parents, in the hope that coming to grips with the events of childhood can help us decipher the mysteries of adulthood. When we say things like "That's the way I was raised," we mean that children instinctively and preferentially learn from their parents, that parents can be good or bad role models for children, that character and personality are passed down from one generation to the next. Child development has been, in many ways, concerned with understanding children *through* their parents.

In recent years, however, this idea has run into a problem. In a series of careful and comprehensive studies (among them the famous Minnesota studies of twins separated at birth) behavioral geneticists have concluded that about fifty percent of the personality differences among people—traits such as friendliness, extroversion, nervousness, openness, and so on—are attributable to our genes which means that the other half must be attributable to the environment. Yet when researchers have set out to look for this environmental influence they haven't been able to find it. If the example of parents were important in a child's development, you'd expect to see a consistent difference between the children of anxious and inexperienced parents and the children of authoritative and competent parents, even after taking into account the influence of heredity. Children who spend two hours a day with their parents should be different from children who spend eight hours a day with their parents. A home with lots of books should result in a different kind of child from a home with very few books. In other words, researchers should have been able to find some causal link between the specific social environment parents create for their children and the way those children turn out. They haven't.

One of the largest and most rigorous studies of this kind is known as the Colorado Adoption Project. Between 1975 and 1982, a group of researchers at the University of Colorado, headed by Robert Plomin, one of the world's leading behavioral geneticists, recruited two hundred and forty-five pregnant women from the Denver area who planned to give up their children for adoption. The researchers then followed the children into their new homes, giving them a battery of personality and intelligence tests at regular intervals throughout their childhood and giving similar tests to their adoptive parents. For the sake of comparison, the group also ran the same set of tests on a control group of two hundred and forty-five parents and their biological children. For the latter group, the results were pretty much as one might expect: in intellectual ability and certain aspects of personality, the kids proved to be fairly similar to their parents. The scores of the adopted kids, however, had nothing whatsoever in common with the scores of their adoptive parents: these children were no more similar in personality or intellectual skills to the people who reared them, fed them, clothed them, read to them, taught them, and loved them all their lives than they were to any two adults taken at random off the street.

Here is the puzzle. We think that children resemble their parents because of both genes and the home environment, both nature and nurture. But, if nurture matters even a little, why don't the adopted kids have at least some greater-than-chance similarities to their adoptive parents? The Colorado study says that the only reason we are like our parents is that we share their genes, and that—by any measures of cognition and personality—when there is no genetic inheritance there is no resemblance.

This is the question that so preoccupied Harris on that winter morning four and a half years ago. She knew that most people in psychology had responded to findings like those of the Colorado project by turning an ever more powerful microscope on the family, assuming that if we couldn't see the influence of parents through standard psychological measures it was because we weren't looking hard enough. Not looking hard enough wasn't the problem. The problem was that psychologists weren't looking in the right place. They were looking inside the home when they should have been looking outside the home. The answer wasn't parents; it was peers. . . .

Not long ago, Anne-Marie Ambert, a sociologist at York University, in Ontario, asked her students to write short autobiographies describing, among other things, the events in their lives which made them most unhappy. Nine percent identified something that their parents had done, while more than a third pointed to the way they had been treated by peers. Ambert concluded:

> There is far more negative treatment by peers than by parents. . . . In these autobiographies, one reads accounts of students who had been happy and well adjusted, but quite rapidly began deteriorating psychologically, sometimes to the point of becoming physically ill and incompetent in school, after experiences such as being rejected by peers, excluded, talked about, racially discriminated against, laughed at, bullied, sexually harassed, taunted, chased or beaten.

This is Harris's argument in a nutshell: that whatever our parents do to us is overshadowed, in the long run, by what our peers do to us. In "The Nurture Assumption," Harris pulls together an extraordinary range of studies and observations to support this idea. Here, for example, is Harris on delinquency. First, she cites a study of juvenile delinquency—vandalism, theft, assault, weapons possession, and so on—among five hundred elementary-school and middle-school boys in Pittsburgh. The study found that African-American boys, many of them from poor, single-parent, "high-risk" families, committed far more delinquent acts than the white kids. That much isn't surprising. But when the researchers divided up the black boys by neighborhood the effect of coming from a putatively high-risk family disappeared. Black kids who didn't live in the poorest, underclass neighborhoods—even if they were from poor, single-parent families—were no more delinquent than their white, mostly middle-class peers. At the same time, Harris cites another large study—one that compared the behavior of poor inner-city kids from intact families to the behavior of those living only with their mothers. You'd assume that a child is always better off in a two-parent home, but the research doesn't bear that out. "Adolescent males in this sample who lived in single-mother households did not differ from youth living in other family constellations in their alcohol and substance use, delinquency, school dropout, or psychological distress," the study concluded. A child is better off, in other words, living in a troubled family in a good neighborhood than living in a good family in a troubled neighborhood. Peers trump parents. . . .

All these findings become less perplexing when you accept one of Harris's central observations; namely, that kids aren't interested in becoming copies of their parents. Children want to be good at being children. How, for example, do you persuade a preschooler to eat something new? Not by eating it yourself and hoping, that your child follows suit. A preschooler doesn't care what you think. But give the food to a roomful of preschoolers who like it, and it's quite probable that your child will happily follow suit. From the very moment that children first meet other children, they take their cues from them. . . .

Already, Harris has helped wrench psychology away from its single-minded obsession with chronicling and interpreting the tiniest perturbations of family life. The nurture assumption, she says, has turned childhood into parenthood: it has turned the development of children into a story almost entirely about their parents. "Have you ever thought of yourself as a mirror?" Dorothy Corkille Briggs asks in her pop-psychology handbook "Your Child's Self-Esteem." You are one—a psychological mirror your child uses to build his identity. And his whole life is affected by the conclusions he draws," And here are Barbara Chernofsky and Diane Gage, in "Change Your Child's Behavior by Changing Yours," on how children relate to their parents: "Like living video cameras, children record what they observe." This is the modern-day cult of parenting. It takes as self-evident the idea that the child is oriented, overwhelmingly, toward the parents. But why should that be true? Don't parents, in fact, spend much of their time interacting with their children not to act like adults—that they cannot be independent, that they cannot make decisions entirely by themselves, that different rules apply to them because they are children?

"If developmental psychology were an enterprise conducted by children there is no question that peer relationships would be at the top of the list," Peter Gray, a psychologist at Boston College, told me. "But because it is conducted by adults we tend, egocentrically, to believe that it is the relationship between us and our children that is important. But just look at them. Whom do they want to please? Are they wearing the kind of clothing that other kids are wearing or the kind that their parents are wearing? If the other kids are speaking another way, whose language are they going to learn? And, from an evolutionary perspective, whom should they be paying attention to? Their parents—the members of the previous generation—or their peers, who will be their future mates and future collaborators? It would be more adaptive for them to be better attuned to the nuances of their peers' behavior. That just makes a lot of sense. . . ."

TOPICS FOR DISCUSSION AND WRITING

1. In what ways does Harris depart from the traditional view of "nurture"? In the brief excerpts quoted by Gladwell in his article, what evidence does she give in support of her theory?
2. Using yourself or someone in your family, apply Harris's theory of child development. Do your findings support her ideas? Discuss to what degree, if any, you would agree with Harris.

Politics of Biology

Wray Herbert

Addressing the scientific, political and personal implications of the nature versus nurture debate, journalist Wray Herbert of *U.S. News and World Report* provides an overview of some of the complexities inherent in determining what is hereditary and what is environmentally induced in human behavior.

Laurie Flynn uses the technology of neuroscience to light up the brains of Washington lawmakers. As executive director of the National Alliance for the Mentally Ill, she marshals everything from cost analysis to moral pleading to make the case for laws banning discrimination against people with mental illness. But her most powerful advocacy tool by far is the PET scan. She takes a collection of these colorful brain images up to Capitol Hill to put on a show, giving lawmakers a window on a "broken" brain in action. "When they see that it's not some imaginary, fuzzy problem, but a real physical condition, then they get it: 'Oh, it's in the brain.'"

The view of mental illness as a brain disease has been crucial to the effort to destigmatize illnesses such as schizophrenia and depression. But it's just one example of a much broader biologizing of American culture that's been going on for more than a decade. For both political and scientific reasons—and it's often impossible to disentangle the two—everything from criminality to addictive disorders to sexual orientation is seen today less as a matter of choice than of genetic destiny. Even basic personality is looking more and more like a genetic legacy. Nearly every week there is a report of a new gene for one trait or another. Novelty seeking, religiosity, shyness, the tendency to divorce, and even happiness (or the lack of it) are among the traits that may result in part from a gene, according to new research.

This cultural shift has political and personal implications. On the personal level, a belief in the power of genes necessarily diminishes the potency of such personal qualities as will, capacity to choose, and sense of responsibility for those choices—if it's in your genes, you're not accountable. It allows the alcoholic, for example, to treat himself as a helpless victim of his biology rather than as a willful agent with control of his own behavior. Genetic determinism can free victims and their families of guilt—or lock them in their suffering.

On the political level, biological determinism now colors all sorts of public-policy debates on issues such as gay rights, health care, juvenile justice, and welfare reform. The effort to dismantle social programs is fueled by the belief that government interventions (the nurturing side in the nature-nurture debate) don't work very well—and the corollary idea that society can't make up for every unfortunate citizen's bad luck. It's probably no coincidence that the biologizing of culture has accompanied the country's shift to the political right, since conservatives traditionally are more dubious about human perfectability than are liberals. As Northeastern University psychologist Leon Kamin notes, the simplest way to discover someone's political leanings is to ask his or her view on genetics.

Even so, genetic determinism can have paradoxical consequences at times, leading to disdain rather than sympathy for the disadvantaged, and marginalization rather than inclusion. Cultural critics are beginning to sort out the unpredictable politics of biology, focusing on four traits: violence, mental illness, alcoholism and sexual orientation.

THE NATURE OF VIOLENCE

To get a sense of just how thorough—and how politicized—the biologizing of culture has been, just look at the issue of urban gang violence as it is framed today. A few years ago, Frederick Goodwin, then director of the government's top mental health agency, was orchestrating the so-called Federal Violence Initiative to identify inner-city kids at biological risk for criminal violence, with the goal of intervening with drug treatments for what are presumed to be nervous-system aberrations. Goodwin got himself fired for comparing aggressive young males with primates in the jungle, and the violence initiative died in the resulting furor. But even to be proposing such a biomedical approach to criminal justice shows how far the intellectual pendulum has swung toward biology.

The eugenics movement of the 1930s was fueled at least in part by a desire to get rid of habitual criminals, and many attempts have been made over the years to identify genetic roots for aggression, violence, and criminality. A 1965 study, for instance, found that imprisoned criminals were more likely than other people to have an extra Y chromosome (and therefore more male genes). The evidence linking this chromosomal aberration to crime was skimpy and tenuous, but politics often runs ahead of the evidence: Soon after, a Boston hospital actually started screening babies for the defect, the idea being to intervene early with counseling should personality problems become apparent. The screening was halted when further study showed that XYY men, while slightly less intelligent, were not unusually aggressive.

An with many psychopathologies, criminal aggression is difficult to define precisely for research. Indeed, crime and alcohol abuse are so entangled that it's often difficult to know whether genetic markers are associated with drinking, criminality—or something else entirely, like a personality trait. A 1993 National Research Council study, for example, reported strong evidence of genetic influence on antisocial personality disorder, but it also noted that many genes are probably involved. Getting from those unknown genes to an actual act of vandalism or assault—or a life of barbaric violence—requires at this point a monstrous leap of faith.

Yet it's a leap that many are willing to make. When geneticist Xandra Breakefield reported a possible genetic link to violent crime a few years ago, she immediately started receiving phone inquiries from attorneys representing clients in prison; they were hoping that such genetic findings might absolve their clients of culpability for their acts.

MUTATIONS AND EMOTIONS

Just two decades ago, the National Institute of Mental Health was funding studies of economic recession, unemployment, and urban ills as possible contributors to serious emotional disturbance. A whole branch of psychiatry known as "social psychiatry" was dedicated to helping the mentally ill by rooting out such pathogens as poverty and racism. There is no longer much evidence of these sensibilities at work today. NIMH now focuses its studies almost exclusively on brain research and on the genetic underpinnings of emotional illnesses.

The decision to reorder the federal research portfolio was both scientific and political. Major advances in neuroscience methods opened up research that wasn't possible a generation ago; and that research has paid off in drugs that very effectively treat some disorders. But there was also a concerted political campaign to reinterpret mental illness. A generation ago, the leading theory about schizophrenia was that this devastating emotional and mental disorder was caused by cold and distant mothering, itself the result of the mother's unconscious wish that her child had never been born. A nationwide lobbying effort was launched to combat such unfounded mother blaming, and 20 years later that artifact of the Freudian era is entirely discredited. It's widely accepted today that psychotic disorders are brain disorders, probably with genetic roots.

But this neurogenetic victory may be double edged. For example, family and consumer groups have argued convincingly that schizophrenia is a brain disease like epilepsy, one piece of evidence being that it is treatable with powerful antipsychotic drugs. Managed-care companies however, have seized upon the disease model, and now will rarely authorize anything but drug treatment: it's efficient, and justified by the arguments of biological psychiatry. The American Psychiatric Association just this month issued elaborate guidelines for treating schizophrenia including not only drugs but an array of psychosocial services—services the insurance industry is highly unlikely to pay for.

The search for genes for severe mental disorders has been inconclusive. Years of studies of families, adoptees, and twins separated at birth suggest that both schizophrenia and manic-depressive illness run in families. But if that family pattern is the result of genes, it's clearly very complicated, because most of the siblings of schizophrenies (including half of identical twins, who have the same genes) don't develop the disorder. Behavioral geneticists suspect that several genes may underlie the illness, and that some environmental stress—perhaps a virus or birth complications—also might be required to trigger the disorder.

On several occasions in the past, researchers have reported "linkages" between serious mental illness and a particular stretch of DNA. A well-known study of the Amish for example, claimed a link between manic-depression and an aberration on chromosome 11. But none of these findings has held up when other researchers attempted to replicate them.

Even if one accepts that there are genetic roots for serious delusional illnesses, critics are concerned about the biologizing of the rest of psychiatric illness. Therapists report that patients come in asking for drugs claiming to be victims of unfortunate biology. In one case, a patient claimed he could "feel his neurons misfiring"; it's an impossibility, but the anecdote speaks to the thorough saturation of the culture with biology.

Some psychiatrists are pulling back from the strict biological model of mental illness. Psychiatrist Keith Russell Ablow has reintroduced the idea of "character" into his practice, telling depressed patients that they have the responsibility and capacity to pull themselves out of their illness. Weakness of character, as Ablow sees it, allows mental illness to grow. Such sentiment is highly controversial within psychiatry, where to suggest that patients might be responsible for some of their own suffering is taboo.

BESOTTED GENES

The best that can be said about research on the genetics of alcoholism is that it's inconclusive, but that hasn't stopped people from using genetic arguments for political purposes. The disease model for alcoholism is practically a secular religion in this country, embraced by psychiatry, most treatment clinics, and (perhaps most important) by Alcoholics Anonymous. What this means is that those seeking help for excessive drinking are told they have a disease (though the exact nature of the disease is unknown), that it's probably a genetic condition, and that the only treatment is abstinence.

But the evidence is not strong enough to support these claims. There are several theories of how genes might lead to excessive drinking. A genetic insensitivity to alcohol, for example, might cause certain people to drink more; or alcoholics might metabolize alcohol differently; or they may have inherited a certain personality type that's prone to risk-taking or stimulus-seeking. While studies of family pedigrees and adoptees have on occasion indicated a familial pattern for a particular form of alcoholism (early-onset disorder in men, for example), just as often they reveal no pattern. This shouldn't be all that surprising, given the difficulty of defining alcoholism. Some researchers identify alcoholics by their drunk-driving record, while others focus on withdrawal symptoms or daily consumption. This is what geneticists call a "dirty phenotype"; people drink too much in so many different ways that the trait itself is hard to define, so family patterns are all over the place, and often contradictory.

Given these methodological problems, researchers have been trying to locate an actual gene (or genes) that might be involved in alcoholism. A 1990 study reported that a severe form of the disorder (most of the subjects in the study had cirrhosis of the liver) was linked to a gene that codes for a chemical receptor for the neurotransmitter dopamine. The researchers even developed and patented a test for the genetic mutation, but subsequent attempts to confirm the dopamine connection have failed.

The issues of choice and responsibility come up again and again in discussions of alcoholism and other addictive disorders. Even if scientists were to identify a gene (or genes) that create a susceptibility to alcoholism, it's hard to know what this genetic "loading" would mean. It certainly wouldn't lead to alcoholism in a culture that didn't condone drinking—among the Amish, for example—so it's not deterministic in a strict sense. Even in a culture where drinking is common, there are clearly a lot of complicated choices involved in living an alcoholic life; it's difficult to make the leap from DNA to those choices. While few would want to return to the time when heavy drinking was condemned as strictly a moral failing or character flaw, many are concerned that the widely accepted disease model of alcoholism actually provides people with an excuse for their destructive behavior. As psychologist Stanton Peele argues: "Indoctrinating young people with the view that they are likely to become alcoholics may take them there more quickly than any inherited reaction to alcohol would have."

SYNAPSES OF DESIRE

It would be a mistake to focus only on biological explanations of psychopathology; the cultural shift is much broader than that. A generation ago, the gay community was at war with organized psychiatry, arguing (successfully) that sexual orientation was a lifestyle choice and ought to be deleted from the manual of disorders. Recently the same community was celebrating new evidence that homosexuality is a biological (and perhaps genetic) trait, not a choice at all.

Three lines of evidence support the idea of a genetic basis for homosexuality, none of them conclusive. A study of twins and adopted siblings found that about half of identical twins of homosexual men were themselves gay, compared with 22 percent of fraternal twins and a 11 percent of adoptees; a similar pattern was found among women. While such a pattern is consistent with some kind of genetic loading for sexual orientation, critics contend it also could be explained by the very similar experiences many twins share. And, of course, half the identical twins did not become gay which by definition means something other than genes must be involved.

A well-publicized 1991 study reported a distinctive anatomical feature in gay men. Simon LeVay autopsied the brain of homosexual men and heterosexual men and women and found that a certain nucleus in the hypothalamus was more than twice as large in heterosexual men as in gay men or heterosexual women. Although LeVay couldn't explain how this neurological difference might translate into homosexuality, he speculates that the nucleus is somehow related to sexual orientation. The hypothalamus is known to be involved in sexual response.

The only study so far to report an actual genetic connection to homosexuality is a 1993 study by Dean Hamer, a National Institutes of Health biologist who identified a genetic marker on the X chromosome in 75 percent of gay brothers. The functional significance of this piece of DNA is unknown, and subsequent research has not succeeded in duplicating Hamer's results.

Homosexuality represents a bit of a paradox when it comes to the intertwined issues of choice and determinism. When Hamer reported his genetic findings, many in the gay community celebrated, believing that society would be more tolerant of behavior rooted in biology and DNA rather than choice. LeVay, himself openly gay, says he undertook his research with the explicit agenda of furthering the gay cause. And Hamer testified as an expert witness in an important gay-rights case in Colorado where, in a strange twist, liberals found themselves arguing the deterministic position, while conservatives insisted that homosexuality is a choice. The argument of gay-rights advocates was that biological status conveyed legal status—and protection under the law.

HISTORY'S WARNING

But history suggests otherwise, according to biologist and historian Garland Allen. During the eugenics movement of the 1920s and 1930s, both in the United States and Europe, society became less, not more, tolerant of human variation and misfortune. Based on racial theories that held Eastern Europeans to be genetically inferior to Anglo-Saxon stock, Congress passed (and Calvin Coolidge signed) a 1924 law to restrict immigration, and by 1940 more than 30 states had laws permitting forced sterilization of people suffering from such conditions as "feeblemindedness," pauperism, and mental illness. The ultimate outcome of the eugenics craze in Europe is well known; homosexuals were not given extra sympathy or protection in the Third Reich's passion to purify genetic stock.

Allen is concerned about the possibility of a "new eugenics" movement, though he notes that it wouldn't be called that or take the same form. It would more likely take the form of rationing health care for the unfortunate. The economic and social conditions today resemble conditions that provided fertile ground for eugenics between the wars, he argues; moreover, in Allen's view, California's Proposition 187 recalls the keen competition for limited resources (and the resulting animosity toward immigrants) of the '20s. Further, Allen is quick to remind us that eugenics was not a marginal, bigoted movement in either Europe or the United States; it was a Progressive program, designed to harness science in the service of reducing suffering and misfortune and to help make society more efficient.

These concerns are probably justified, but there are also some signs that we may be on the crest of another important cultural shift. More and more experts, including dedicated biologists, sense that the power of genetics has been oversold and that a correction is needed. What's more, there's a glimmer of evidence that the typical American may not be buying it entirely. According to a recent *U.S. News*/Bozell poll, less than 1 American in 5 believes that genes play a major role in controlling behavior; three quarters cite environment and society as the more powerful shapers of our lives. Whether the behavior under question is a disorder like addiction, mental illness, or violence, or a trait like homosexuality, most believe that heredity plays some role, but not a primary one. Indeed, 40 percent think genes play no role whatsover in homosexuality, and a similar percentage think heredity is irrelevant to drug addition and criminality. Across the board, most believe that people's lives are shaped by the choices they make.

These numbers can be interpreted in different ways. It may be that neurogenetic determinism has become the "religion of the intellectual class," as one critic argues, but that it never really caught the imagination of the typical American. Or we may be witnessing a kind of cultural self-correction, in which after a period of infatuation with neuroscience and genetics the public is becoming disenchanted, or perhaps even anxious about the kinds of social control that critics describe.

Whatever's going on, it's clear that this new mistrust of genetic power is consonant with what science is now beginning to show. Indeed, the very expression "gene for" is misleading, according to philosopher Philip Kitcher, author of *The Lives to Come.* Kitcher critiques what he calls "gene talk," a simplistic shorthand for talking about genetic advances that has led to the widespread misunderstanding of DNA's real powers. He suggests that public discourse may need to include more scientific jargon—not a lot, but some—so as not to oversimplify the complexity of the gene-environment interaction. For example, when geneticists say they've found a gene for a particular trait, what they mean is that people carrying a certain "allele"—a variation in a stretch of DNA that normally codes for a certain protein— will develop the given trait in a standard environment. The last few words—"in a standard environment"—are very important, because what scientists are *not saying* is that a given allele will necessarily lead to that trait in every environment. Indeed, there is mounting evidence that a particular allele will not produce the same result if the environment changes significantly; that is to say, the environment has a strong influence on whether and how a gene gets "expressed."

It's hard to emphasize too much what a radical rethinking of the nature-nurture debate this represents. When most people think about heredity, they still think in terms of classical Mendelian genetics: one gene, one trait. But for most complex human behaviors, this is far from the reality that recent research is revealing. A more accurate view very likely involves many different genes, some of which control other genes, and many of which are controlled by signals from the environment. To complicate matters further, the environment is very complicated in itself, ranging from the things we typically lump under nurture (parenting, family dynamics, schooling, safe housing) to biological encounters like viruses and birth complications, even biochemical events within cells.

The relative contributions of genes and the environment are not additive, as in such-and-such a percentage of nature, such-and-such a percentage of experience; that's the old view, no longer credited. Nor is it true that full genetic expression happens once, around birth, after which we take our genetic legacy into the world to see how far it gets us. Genes produce proteins throughout the lifespan, in many different environments, or they don't produce those proteins, depending on how rich or harsh or impoverished those environments are. The interaction is so thoroughly dynamic and enduring that, as psychologist William Greenough says. "To ask what's more important, nature or nurture, is like asking what's more important to a rectangle, its length or its width."

The emerging view of nature–nurture is that many complicated behaviors probably have some measure of genetic loading that gives some people a suscepti-bility—for schizophrenia, for instance, or for aggression. But the development of the behavior or pathology requires more, what National Institute of Mental Health Director Stephen Hyman calls an environmental "second hit." This second hit op-erates, counterintuitively, through the genes themselves to "sculpt" the brain. So with depression, for example, it appears as though a bad experience in the world— for example, a devastating loss—can actually create chemical changes in the body that affect certain genes, which in turn affect certain brain proteins that make a person more susceptible to depression in the future. Nature or nurture? Similarly, Hyman's own work has shown that exposure to addictive substances can lead to biochemical changes at the genetic and molecular levels that commandeer brain circuits involving volition—and thus undermine the very motivation needed to take charge of one's destructive behavior. So the choice to experiment with drugs or alcohol may, in certain people, create the biological substrate of the addictive disorder. The distinction between biology and experience begins to lose its edge.

NURTURING POTENTIALS

Just as bad experiences can turn on certain vulnerability genes, rich and chal-lenging experiences have the power to enhance life, again acting through the genes. Greenough has shown in rat studies that by providing cages full of toys and complex structures that are continually rearranged—"the animal equivalent of Head Start"—he can increase the number of synapses in the rats brains by 25 percent and blood flow by 85 percent. Talent and intelligence appear extraordi-narily malleable.

Child-development experts refer to the life circumstances that enhance (or undermine) gene expression as "proximal processes," a term coined by psychol-ogist Urie Bronfenbrenner. Everything from lively conversation to games to the reading of stories can potentially get a gene to turn on and create a protein that may become a neuronal receptor or messenger chemical involved in thinking or mood. "No genetic potential can become reality," says Bronfenbrenner, "unless the relationship between the organism and its environment is such that it is *per-mitted* to be expressed." Unfortunately, as he details in his new book, *The State of Americans,* the circumstances in which many American children are living are becoming more impoverished year by year.

If there's a refrain among geneticists working today, it's this: The harder we work to demonstrate the power of heredity, the harder it is to escape the po-tency of experience. It's a bit paradoxical, because in a sense we end up once again with the old pre–1950s paradigm, but arrived at with infinitely more-sophisticated tools: Yes, the way to intervene in human lives and improve them, to ameliorate mental illness, addictions, and criminal behavior, is to enrich impoverished environments, to improve conditions in the family and society. What's changed is that the argument is coming not from left-leaning sociologists, but from those most intimate with the workings of the human genome. The goal of psychosocial interventions is optimal gene expression.

So assume for a minute that there is a cluster of genes somehow associated with youthful violence. The kid who carries those genes might inhabit a world of loving parents, regular nutritious meals, lots of books, safe schools. Or his world might be a world of peeling paint and gunshots around the corner. In which environment would those genes be likely to manufacture the biochemical underpinnings of criminality? Or for that matter, the proteins and synapses of happiness?

TOPICS FOR DISCUSSION AND WRITING

1. What is meant by "genetic" or "biological determinism"?
2. Quoting Northeastern University psychologist Leon Kamin, the author says, "The simplest way to discover someone's political leaning is to ask his or her view of genetics." What do Kamin and thus Herbert mean by this?
3. What does Herbert imply by the phrase "the unpredictable politics of biology"?
4. Where does Herbert stand on the nature versus nurture debate?
5. How, according to Herbert, does the nature versus nurture discussion relate to the eugenics movement of the 1920s and '30s? (See also Jeremy Rifkin, *The Biotech Century*, quoted above.)
6. Choose one of the four traits Herbert discusses: violence, mental illness, alcoholism, or homosexuality. Write a paper in which you first summarize Herbert's analysis and then do further research in current literature and on the Internet to expand on what she says about the roles of nature and nurture. If, after your research, you have formulated your own point of view on the issue, conclude your essay with this opinion. To support your position, you may want to include your own observations and experience.

Learning Right from Wrong

Sharon Begley with Claudia Kalb

Begley and Kalb, writing for *Newsweek* magazine, prepared this analysis of the moral issues surrounding the shooting of a first grade girl by her six-year-old classmate. The schoolyard shooting took place near Flint, Michigan, in March, 2000, and raised once again the question of why children turn to violence. When the child is as young as six, we are tempted to ask whether he was born a "bad seed" or whether the difficult circumstances of his home-life led to the tragedy. Begley and Kalb attempt to fit these questions into the current debate of nature versus nurture and draw on experts in the field to bring some clarification. Sharon Begley, a senior editor and science writer at *Newsweek,* is widely known among journalists for her ability to break down complex scientific theories and write about them clearly for a lay readership.

To the legal system, the answer is clear: children have the requisite moral sense—the ability to tell right from wrong—by age 7 to 15, depending on which state they live in, and so can be held responsible for their actions. The Roman Catholic Church pegs it at the early end of that range: children reach the "age of reason" by the tender age of 7, a milestone marked by their first confession of sin and holy communion. Developmental psychologists and other researchers who study the question are not so sure. How old a child must be to both know in his mind and feel in his heart that lying, stealing, cheating, hurting—let alone murdering—are morally wrong is a matter of scientific debate.

But the question of when is not nearly so fraught as the question of how. Although they pretty much agree that living in a crack house—with people who respond to challenges with violence, and bereft of parental love, supervision and models of moral behavior—can leave a child's conscience stillborn, scientists are struggling toward a definitive answer to the question of how children develop a sense of right and wrong. "If there is any consensus, it is that conscience is a combination of head, heart and hand," says Marvin Berkowitz, professor of character development at the University of Missouri, St. Louis. "It is knowing the good, loving the good and doing the good. And that requires both congnitive and emotional components."

The emotional piece falls into place first. "All children are born with a running start on the path to moral development," says psychologist William Damon of Stanford University. The reason is that empathy, the key emotion supporting a sense of right and wrong, emerges early and, it seems, naturally. Babies cry in response to the wails of other babies, "and not just because it's a sound that upsets them," notes Carolyn Zahn-Waxler of the National Institute of Mental Health. "They cry more in response to human cries than to other aversive sounds. Somehow, there's a built-in capacity to respond to the needs of others." Babies as young as 1 try to console others in distress. Toddlers offer their security blanket to a teary-eyed parent or a favorite toy to a distraught sibling, as if understanding that the very object that brings them comfort will do the same to another.

Although there seems to be some heritable component to empathy—identical twins, who have identical genes, show more similarity in their response to others distress than fraternal twins do—it can be twisted, warped or crushed like a fragile sprout. Empathy means, at heart, the ability to respond to another's distress in a way more appropriate to her situation than to your own. "The development of empathy has a lot to do with how children experience emotions and how people respond to their emotional states," argues Berkowitz. "It's not automatic." If a child's sadness is met with stony silence rather than a hug, if her loneliness is met with continued abandonment, then she is in danger of losing her natural empathy. Kids who, as 14-month-olds, exhibit high levels of empathy typically become less empathetic after only six months if they live in homes filled with conflict, and if they seldom feel a mother's love, finds Zahn-Waxler.

The other emotional ingredients of conscience are that quaint pair, guilt and shame. Although some child advocates insist that no child should ever be shamed, scientists who study moral development disagree. "Guilt and shame are part of conscience," says Berkowitz. In young children the sense of right and wrong is born of the feeling that you have disappointed someone you love, usually your parents. If there is no one whose love you need, whose disapproval breaks your heart, you are missing a crucial source of the emotions that add up to knowing right from wrong and acting on it.

Important as emotions are in the development of conscience, the heart can falter without the head. The very thought of shooting a little girl inspires in most people a profound feeling of horror. But feelings can fail us when we face more ambiguous moral choices, such as whether it is right to help a struggling friend cheat on a test. Much as children pass through stages of cognitive reasoning, so they pass through six stages of moral reasoning. In the model developed by the late Lawrence Kohlberg and still accepted today, children's first glimmer of conscience comes in the form of thinking, "I won't do this; Mommy will punish me if I do." That gives way to a positive spin: "I won't do this bad thing, because I want a reward for being good." Both forms of reasoning at this early stage, which roughly coincides with toddlerhood, turn on self-interest. But most preschoolers also grasp and believe in abstract ideas like fairness and reciprocity. When asked, as part of an experiment, how to distribute a pile of toys or a box of cookies to a group of children, many respond with explanations such as "We should all get the same," reports Stanford's Damon.

Also in the early years, roughly until 6 to 7, "most children make moral judgments on the basis of the damage done," says David Elkind, professor of child development at Tufts University. They condemn the child who broke three glasses while helping Mom load the dishwasher more than the child who broke one glass while playing with the good crystal. But after the age of 7 or 8, children begin to make judgments based on intent: they know that smashing the Waterford while using it as a Barbie pool will land them in more trouble than shattering an entire place setting while clearing the table.

By middle childhood, if all goes well, children begin to seek social approval. This shows up as "I won't do this because I want people to like me," and then "I won't do this because it is against the law." By 8, children generally understand that retaliation is wrong, and their brain's so-called judgment circuit, centered in the prefrontal cortex, approaches maturity. In the final stage, one that even many adults fall short of, abstract ideals guide moral reasoning. Ideally, the adolescent recognizes a social contract ("I won't do it because I am obliged not to") and something like universal rights ("I won't do this because it is simply wrong").

The age at which a child reaches these milestones of moral reasoning varies with how he is raised and how those around him act. Unlike empathy, full-fledged conscience does not seem innate. Children acquire the cognitive understanding of right and wrong by observing the behavior of the people most important to them, usually (and hopefully) their parents. If Dad reacts to injured pride—"He dissed me!"—with violence, that becomes the model for his son. And that is only the beginning of a parent's influence.

Different styles of parenting seem to nourish, or beat down, a child's nascent conscience. Both autocratic and permissive parenting, although they seem like opposites, tend to shape the same behavior and attitudes in children. Children of permissive parents often struggle to learn the limits of acceptable behavior. They typically develop poor self-control, perhaps because anything-goes parenting conveys the message that none is needed. Autocratic parenting says that the course of control is outside the child—namely, parents—so there is no need to develop an inner moral compass.

Sitting in the sensible middle is "authoritative" parenting that, say numerous studies, nurtures a child's respect for rules. Authoritative means setting firm limits, letting your child know your views of right and wrong, but "explaining instead of forcing," says Berkowitz. Authoritative falls short of the "do it because I say so!" autocratic school of parenting. For that reason, many cultural conservatives blame authoritative parenting for everything from kids who kill to gangsta rap, but authoritative does not mean permissive. It does not mean negotiating over whether a 12-year-old can leave the house at 9 p.m. clutching a six-pack. And it does not mean trying to lay out the fine points of retributive justice to a 2-year-old who just shoved the playmate who "pushed me first!" But parents who explain their moral reasoning provide a model their child can emulate. "If you want a kid who respects and cares about others," says Berkowitz, "You have to first give him respect and show that you care about him."

The community, too, shapes a child's conscience. It will come as no surprise to parents that children have built-in hypocrisy detectors. ("But Mommy, if it's wrong to lie, why did you tell her she looked beautiful?") If the football coach preaches winning above all, and if Mom lies to get her child excused from class in order to take another day of vacation, and if Dad reams out a teacher who reprimanded his daughter for cheating, "children learn not to take moral messages seriously," says Damon.

Heart and head will take a child only so far, however. "I suspect that if you sat down [the first-grade shooter] when he was quiet and calm, before this happened, and asked, 'Is it bad to shoot someone?' he would have said yes," says psychologist Laurence Steinberg of Temple Universty and director of a MacArthur Foundation program on juvenile justice. How much he understood about the consequences of shooting and the finality of death is unknown. But choosing not to undertake a horrific act requires the third ingredient of conscience: a gut-wrenching aversion to wrong. "Gut-wrenching" is not merely a figure of speech: it means the racing heart, sweaty palms and churning stomach that moral individuals would feel if forced to, say, burglarize a house.

Some people simply lack this stress response, but probably not because of a genetic defect. When Adrian Raine of the University of Southern California recorded now 15-year-olds' heart rates, EEGs (a measure of brain activity) and other factors changed in response to stress, he found some cool customers who were not fazed by anything. Compared with kids with a normal stress response, they had a greater chance of being criminals at the age of 24. Perhaps low arousability makes kids seek out excitement and danger, Raine suggests. Or maybe it makes them fearless. "Kids who come from a bad home environment, who are battered from pillar to post, may become inoculated to stress," says Raine. "Their nervous system may simply not be wired to ring a warning bell" when they are about to do something dangerous—or wrong. This brain wiring may be what's missing in kids who "know" right from wrong but fail to act on it.

When do the heart, the head and the gut come together to produce, if not a moral philosopher, at least a moral child? "My hunch is that it's probably not complete until a child is close to 12," says Steinberg. "But a lot of these things are still developing at 15." And sometimes, as any glance at the headlines will tell you, they fail to develop at all.

TOPICS FOR DISCUSSION AND WRITING

1. Stanford psychologist William Damon and Carolyn Zahn-Waxter of the National Institute of Mental Health claim there is one essential moral sense that is inherited by all. What is this trait? Marvin Berkowitz of the University of Missouri, on the other hand, says this trait is "not automatic." Explain both positions, including where the two sides might find common ground.

2. The authors say that "Some people simply lack this stress response ['a gut-wrenching aversion to wrong'], but probably not because of a genetic defect." Explain what they think is the cause of such behaviors. Do you agree with Begley and Kalb's position on the genetic influence in this situation?

3. Each school-yard shooting further inflames the on-going debate over gun-control. How does the gun-control controversy connect to the nature versus nurture issue?

4. Look back at all the selections that address the issue of nature versus nurture and then, in light of these observations, write a personal essay in which you discuss your own profile. Which of your characteristics do you think come from your genes, which from your environment? Is it difficult to separate the influences of the two? What features of your environment do you consider the most important in shaping you?

If you wish, you may substitute another family member, perhaps your own child if you are a parent, or a close friend or relative if you do not know your own biological parents or you prefer not to examine your own life.

In your conclusion, you may want to consider whether you (or your chosen subject) have been fairly judged by others in terms of nature and nurture.

Further Frontiers in Biotechnology

As advancements in cloning and the controversy surrounding such research continues, and as the nature versus nurture debate goes on, frontiers of human biology keep expanding at a rapid rate. Fertility remains a central issue for scientist and ethicist alike; the race to map the complete human genome has ramifications that will echo throughout the century; ethical questions surrounding therapies available with new gene technology keep growing. What follows is just a tiny sampling of the ever-increasing range of issues facing biologists and bioethicists today.

Marketing Fertility

A married woman of 63 gives birth to a daughter fathered by her husband with another woman's egg. A single woman of 51 delivers her first child, a son created from a donor egg and a donor sperm nurtured in her uterus. A small industry has grown up around women who serve as surrogate mothers. Using frozen sperm, doctors help men give life after they have died. In Boston, a man citing "wrongful birth" sued his ex-wife for conceiving a child by implanting a frozen embryo fertilized before their divorce and then demanding child support. Beyond in vitro fertilization, considered almost routine today, a mother can order a custom-tailored embryo, even select a child's sex. Fertilized eggs, frozen and waiting, are now available for "adoption." And in two emerging technologies, an artificial uterus offers safe haven for an at-risk fetus or for a woman who does not want to experience pregnancy, while genetic enhancement may offer opportunities for selecting or improving an embryo's traits. By the time you read this, who can predict what new technologies will be available? The biotech revolution keeps pushing the frontiers of reproductive engineering toward limits scarcely imagined a generation ago. But all of these choices come at a price.

Clinics Selling Embryos Made for Adoption

Gina Kolata

Gina Kolata, *New York Times* writer now celebrated for her book *Clone: The Road to Dolly and the Path Ahead,* reports on desperate would-be-parents turning in increasing numbers to fertility clinics that offer frozen, "premade human embryos." Her story sets the stage for the two pieces that follow it.

Kathy Butler, a 47-year-old New Jersey woman, is pregnant with triplets. But the babies bear no relationship to her or to her husband, Gary. Instead, they are growing from ready-made embryos that the Butlers selected and paid for at Columbia-Presbyterian Medical Center in Manhattan.

Doctors there had mixed human eggs and sperm to make a variety of embryos with different pedigrees, then froze them. The idea was to allow prospective parents to select embryos whose parents resemble them physically or have the same ethnic background and are well educated—the best possible sperm and egg donors for those who cannot have babies of their own.

The Butlers are part of a quiet but fast-emerging new world of assisted reproduction in the United States. Doctors have become skilled at creating human embryos, and anguished infertile couples are more than willing to pay for whatever infertility clinics can offer. The new technique has resulted in an unknown number of births over the last several years.

Ms. Butler said she and her husband had few options. They had spent all their money on other infertility treatments, and so when they discovered that they could select a group of premade frozen embryos for $2,750, they were overjoyed.

For many who venture into the doors of leading infertility clinics, what the Butlers have done will be understandable, even enviable. After all, those few centers with embryos that are up for what the doctors euphemistically call "adoption" have waiting lists for them.

Premade human embryos are rare and largely confined to a handful of burgeoning centers like the one at Columbia-Presbyterian, where doctors quietly tell patients about the embryos but do not advertise them. "If you talk to smaller centers, they'll say they never heard of such a thing," said Dr. Mark Sauer of Columbia-Presbyterian.

Some embryos are custom made by doctors; others have been made by doctors for infertile couples and then not used by couples who ended up with more than they needed. The clinics offer these embryos to people who cannot afford the more than $16,000 it would cost for an attempt at pregnancy with sperm and egg donors they select themselves.

Is there something chilling about the idea of making embryos on speculation and selecting egg and sperm donors according to their looks, education and ethnicity?

"It does seem like a supermarket approach to embryos," said Lori B. Andrews, a professor of law at Chicago-Kent College of Law.

Doctors who treat infertility say such questions are beside the point.

"It's normal human nature" to want to choose donors of eggs and sperm, Dr. Sauer said. "Behind closed doors, the most liberal-minded people are about as discriminating as you can get. So don't accuse us of playing God."

The premade embryos appear to inhabit ambiguous legal territory, Ms. Andrews said. Laws governing sperm and egg donors vary from state to state, and many states have no laws. And the law has not addressed such questions as the status of embryos formed in the laboratory, or who the guardians of the frozen embryos may be, she added.

So, too, the technique seems to raise a tangle of ethical issues, like the potential, in theory, for siblings to be raised by separate parents without any knowledge that they have brothers or sisters.

Freezing eggs is still not a completely reliable art. But once eggs are fertilized, the embryos can be readily frozen, stored indefinitely and survive the thawing process for placement in a woman's womb.

It is the distress of frustrated would-be parents that drives the recruitment of sperm and eggs donors. Infertility clinics and even some individuals advertise in newspapers at elite colleges and universities, knowing that a woman who is a student at Princeton or Stanford or the University of Pennsylvania will seem especially desirable to recipients.

Dr. Lee Silver, a molecular biologist at Princeton University, spotted an advertisement in the school's student newspaper that read: "Loving infertile couple (Yale '80 grad and husband) wanting to start family needs a healthy, light-haired, Caucasian woman (ages 21–32) willing to be an egg donor. Reimbursed

$2,000 plus expenses for time and effort. Comprehensive physical at leading NYC hospital included."

Dr. Silver mentioned the advertisement to a class he was teaching. "Sex, Babies, Genes and Choices." A few women in the class said they had considered responding to it, explaining that the money was nice but that they also liked the idea of helping other people and "the idea that they could seed the world in some way."

Eggs donors agree to inject themselves with drugs to stimulate their ovaries, making the ovaries swell with ripening eggs. It is not a totally benign experience, said Dr. Mitchell Tucker, who is scientific director at Reproductive Biology Associates in Atlanta. On rare occasions, he said, the woman's ovaries become over-stimulated.

"Her estrogen levels go through the roof, and she goes into a nonphysiological crisis where you get fluid retention," he added. "In the severest cases, the kidneys shut down," and, very rarely, women have died.

Dr. Sauer of Columbia-Presbyterian said he creates embryos for adoption when an infertile woman who has selected and contracted for an egg donor suddenly changes her mind. In a large program like his, with about 150 to 200 egg donations a year, it is not uncommon for the recipient to back out at the last minute, Dr. Sauer said.

When the recipient backs out, the egg donor is left with ovaries that are bursting with eggs, waiting for a final hormone shot that will allow the eggs to be released. One option is for the donor to forgo that shot. Her ovaries would then shrink from the size of grapefruits to their normal walnut size over the next few weeks.

But, Dr. Sauer said, "it would be a waste of eggs not to retrieve them." So he tells the egg donor that he plans to create embryos anyway, using several donors. Then he gives the woman the final hormone injection, removes the eggs and fertilizes what may be 20 to 30 ripe eggs with a variety of sperm from a commercial sperm bank, looking for a donor with blue eyes and one with brown, one with dark hair and one who is fair.

Doctors at other leading infertility centers said that it was rare to have unused donor eggs. But when they do, they too make embryos.

Dr. Tucker of Reproductive Biology Associates said that one woman at his clinic who paid for an egg donor recently backed out when one of her parents died. "It seemed totally inappropriate to give the eggs up," he said, so he created embryos for adoption.

Dr. Joseph Schulman, director of the Genetics and IVF Institute in Fairfax, Va., never has unused eggs, he said, because he makes the women who want donor eggs pay in full for egg retrieval and in vitro fertilization before the egg donor begins the series of injections. "No one backs out," Dr. Schulman said.

But, he said, some who carefully select egg and sperm donors end up with more embryos than they need and allow Dr. Schulman to offer their embryos to other couples.

Ms. Butler, the patient of Dr. Sauer's has a 21-year-old son from her first marriage, but when she married Gary Butler, they wanted a baby of their own. She ran into fertility problems, though.

They were too old for adoption agencies in the United States, and they were wary of private and international adoptions, Ms. Butler said. They tried an egg donor, paying $16,500 to have embryos made with the donor eggs and Mr. Butler's sperm. But the embryos did not survive. "It wiped us out financially," Ms. Butler said.

Then Dr. Sauer mentioned that there was a small pool of embryos available. The Butlers, who both have Irish ancestors, wanted the sperm and egg donors to have Irish backgrounds, "or at least light hair and light eyes," Ms. Butler said. But all the available embryos had a mother who was Italian, with brown hair and brown eyes. Five of her eggs were fertilized with sperm from a man of Russian, Romanian and Hungarian heritage, and two others with sperm from a man of Welsh background.

Ms. Butler, who is half Welsh, and her husband decided it was more important to have more embryos to give themselves a greater chance that one would survive. (Most embryos produced in the laboratory, or the womb, do not survive; that is why doctors implant several.) So they chose the Russian-Romanian-Hungarian father.

Three of the five embryos survived after thawing, and two survived when they were put in Ms. Butler's uterus. One of those split into identical twins, leaving Ms. Butler pregnant with triplets. Her due date is June 6.

"It's an adoption, but we have control," Ms. Butler said. "We don't have to worry about the birth mother changing her mind. We don't have to worry that she'll take drugs while she's pregnant."

TOPICS FOR DISCUSSION AND WRITING

1. In what ways are the embryos similar to a traditional adoption and in what ways are they different?

2. Kolata poses the question, "Is there something chilling about the idea of making embryos on speculation and selecting egg and sperm donors according to their looks, education and ethnicity?" Write an essay in which you answer Kolata's question. You may want to reread Jeffrey Kluger's essay, "Will We Follow the Sheep?" for further insights on these questions, or wait until you have read the two selections which follow.

Fertility for Sale

As donor eggs become a valuable commodity, the controversy over the price tag and also the health risks is heating up. Here, experts discuss whether or not women should be able to sell their eggs.

As reproductive technology has advanced, the law of supply and demand has inevitably clicked in. Some clinics have had trouble finding women to donate their eggs for implantation in infertile women. That has led to a medical and ethical debate over whether donors should charge for their eggs and, if so, how much. The St. Barnabas Medical Center in Livingston, N.J., recently accelerated that debate by offering $5,000 for donors, double the rate of many clinics. A variety of experts were asked whether women should be permitted to sell their eggs on the open market:

Robert Wright is the author of "The Moral Animal: Evolutionary Psychology and Everyday Life."

Is a woman who gets several thousand dollars for a few eggs being exploited? The claim is not on its face ridiculous; a donor undergoes an unpleasant and risky procedure that is invasive both physically and in a less tangible sense. What *is* ridiculous is the idea that the woman is more exploited if she gets $5,000 than if she gets $2,000. Yet that is the implicit logic of some who argue for limiting fees lest we degrade women by turning their eggs into commodities.

Critics of high fees say it's all right to compensate donors, just not to entice them. But that distinction faded years ago, when infertile women began paying more than a few hundred dollars for eggs. They found that if they didn't pay real money, they'd get no eggs. This is the market at work: a willing buyer, a willing seller. Is there any reason to get between them?

Sometimes society plausibly says yes, as with drug sales and prostitution. Personally, I don't see a comparably strong argument in this case. If there is one, maybe we should take eggs off the market. But what's the point of pretending they aren't already there?

Cynthis Gorney is the author of "Articles of Faith: A Frontline History of the Abortion Wars."

A precedent for limiting compensation for egg donation was set 15 years ago, when the most heated argument in infertility circles was about surrogate mothers—woman who volunteered to undergo artificial insemination and carry a baby to term for infertile couples. The ethical consensus then was that if a woman offers to lend out her own reproductive system because she wants to help someone else, we suppose we can't stop her, but she shouldn't be tempted to do it because she wants or needs money: a surrogate should be paid for medical expenses and lost time at work, and perhaps offered some modest extra cash to offset the physical discomfort of pregnancy. But the money should not be generous enough to make surrogacy an attractive line of work.

And as a rule, surrogate mothers still don't collect much money, nor should they. To be sure, this is partly because they deliver up fully developed human beings, which by law and venerable tradition may not be bought and sold. But it is also because surrogate mothers deliver up their own bodily organs—their eggs and the use of their wombs—and we have equally venerable tradition forbidding people to sell their body parts for profit.

Galloping technology and the escalating hopes of infertile couples are working together to push us much too far, too fast. There has got to be a point at which society declares to the infertile couple: We are sorry for your situation, but you cannot buy everything you want. We will not let you offer that young woman $10,000 for some of her eggs, just as we will not let you offer her brother $10,000 for one of his kidneys. The potential cost to both of them—and to all the rest of us—is too high.

Lee M. Silver, *a biology professor at Princeton, is the author of "Remaking Eden: Cloning and Beyond in a Brave New World."*

Why are physicians and bioethicists—who are mostly male—trying to limit monetary compensation to women who donate their eggs? In no other part of the economy do we limit the amount of money that can be paid to people who participate in risky or demeaning activities. Indeed, college students have long been enticed by high fees into participating in risky medical experiments.

But society expects women to be altruistic, not venal. And it insists that women be protected from themselves, on the assumption that they are unable to make rational decisions about their own bodies. And perhaps men feel threatened by the idea that women now also have a way to spread their seed upon the earth.

Robert Coles, *a physician, is a professor of social ethics at Harvard and the author, most recently, of "The Youngest Parents: Teen-Age Pregnancy as It Shapes Lives."*

We really don't know the long-term medical consequences for women who donate their eggs. There have been a few reports of serious side effects, like renal failure. But have researchers studied carefully enough what exposure to these fertility drugs does to women? If poor women become repeat donors because the process keeps getting more lucrative, will they increase their risk down the line for ovarian cancer? These are unanswered questions.

Most important, the widening divide between the rich and the poor poses an ethical dilemma: can we condone the "harvesting" of eggs from poor women, who may be putting their health at risk, for the benefit of the affluent?

Elizabeth Bartholet, *a professor at Harvard Law School, is the author of "Family Bonds: Adoption and the Politics of Parenting."*

The selling of human eggs puts at risk the donors' health and sacrifices their human dignity. It also encourages women to bear children who are not genetically related to them, so that their mates can have genetic offspring. This practice produces children who have lost one genetic parent—in a world that already has an abundance of orphans who need homes.

We need to call a halt to further commercialization of reproduction to give policy makers a chance to consider the ethical issues involved in reproductive technology like egg selling, cloning and sex selection. We should follow the lead of other countries and establish a national commission to resolve these issues rather than leave them to the market.

Lori Arnold *is a doctor at the Fertility and I.V.F. Center of Miami.*

Most women who donate their eggs at our clinic do so because they want to help provide the gift of life. Many have children of their own: they want to help others experience the joys of motherhood.

The motive is altruistic, but that should not blind anyone to the practical difficulties. Donors are required to undergo treatment with fertility drugs, counseling, screening, ultrasound monitoring, blood work and numerous office visits. It takes weeks. And retrieving the eggs from their ovaries is a surgical procedure.

Also worth factoring in is that the donors are giving a couple the chance to have a family, with a child who has the father's genetic makeup. The donor also gives the recipient a chance to experience pregnancy, delivery and breast-feeding, thereby facilitating mother-baby bonding.

Thus compensation given to an egg donor is well deserved. Of course, there comes a point when a fee becomes self-defeating, since the cost is paid by the recipient—few couples can afford to pay an unlimited amount. But donors deserve something more than a token. Ours receive $1,500 to $2,000: no one should begrudge them that.

TOPICS FOR DISCUSSION AND WRITING

1. Examine each argument in "Fertility for Sale" and in a sentence state each author's position.

2. Where you see a connection, discuss the relationship of each author's professional qualifications with the position he or she takes in the debate.

3. Add your own capsule opinion on the issue to the views expressed here.

Eggs for Sale

Rebecca Mead

As scientists refine their techniques for the donation of eggs to infertile women, the economic element is escalating. Rebecca Mead lays out the issues in the story of one young woman who has decided to fund her education through the sale of her eggs. By giving a name and face to this new technology, Mead reveals some of the reasons women are willing to undergo what is at best an uncomfortable procedure and what could have far-reaching medical and personal repercussions.

The first time I met Cindy Schiller, at the Hungarian Pastry Shop on Amsterdam Avenue and 111th Street one morning this winter, she told me that she wasn't feeling quite herself, on account of what she called "the whole menopause thing." Her short-term memory was out of whack, she was lethargic, and she'd been finding herself suddenly drenched in sweat. "Hot flashes sound like they're no big deal, but hot flashes kick your ass," she said.

Schiller is a student at Columbia University Law School, and at twenty-six she should be only halfway to menopause. But she had been undergoing an artificially induced change of life over the previous weeks, which was precipitated by an array of drugs and an unusually relaxed attitude about sticking needles into herself. For three weeks, she had injected her stomach with a drug called Lupron, which shut down her ovaries, so that none of her eggs ripened and none of her egg follicles developed that month. Then menopause was suddenly over, she switched medications, and started injecting a combination of Pergonal and Metrodin—follicle-stimulating hormones—into her hip every morning. This kicked her quiescent ovaries into overdrive, swelling them to the size of oranges, and brought a cluster of her eggs to the brink of ripeness. After eight days, Schiller took a final shot of a hormone called human chorionic gonadotropin, or H.C.G., and exactly thirty-six hours later she went to the office of a fertility doctor on Central Park West. There she was put under general sedation, and an ultrasound probe was introduced into her vagina and threaded up through her uterus, so that a needle could be inserted into each of her ovaries and the eggs sucked out, one by one. Twelve eggs were whisked away, to be fertilized in a petri dish with the sperm of a man Schiller wasn't especially fond of, in preparation for transfer to the uterus of a woman she didn't really know, in the hope that at least one would grow into a child whom Schiller would probably never see.

Schiller, whose name has been changed in this article at her request, is a lively young woman with blue eyes, long light-brown hair, and very pale skin, unmarked except for five tattoos—tattoos that her mother, back home in the southwest, has been begging her to remove with laser surgery. She also has sixteen piercings, including several of the kind that only real intimates or fertility doctors get to see.

If she were your daughter, you, too, would probably want her to have the tattoos removed, because in other respects Schiller is such a nice girl: she doesn't drink, she doesn't smoke, she doesn't take drugs, she's pretty and quick to laugh, and she has a lovely singing voice. I went to a basement college dining hall one evening to listen to a performance by a musical group she belongs to, and I found her there in jeans and a low-cut T-shirt, singing harmony with a look of blithe pleasure in her eyes and with a stud through her tongue flashing in the fluorescent lighting. Schiller wants to be a civil-rights lawyer when she graduates, but this year she has been much too busy with a panoply of left-wing and feminist causes to spend much time in the library. The first time I phoned her apartment, her answering machine advised me to leave a message for "Cindy Schiller, the National Day of Appreciation Task Force, or Stop Police Brutality." Within a couple of months, the list had morphed into "Cindy Schiller, the Courageous Resister Committee, Students for Reproductive Freedom, the Housing Law Workshop, or Task Force against Police Brutality."

Not long after she arrived at Columbia last fall, Schiller read a notice pinned to a bulletin board in the law school by an infertile couple who were seeking an egg donor. For a woman who is trying to get pregnant and has no viable eggs of her own, donor eggs are a last resort. Schiller had signed up with an egg-donor agency while she was an undergraduate in her home state and had twice donated eggs there. She was now eager to do it again, even though the last time she had "hyper-stimulated," which means that she had produced too many eggs (more than thirty, in her case) and had suffered so much abdominal pain and nausea that she could hardly get out of bed for two days. On both occasions, she had been selected as a donor immediately, no doubt because she is fair and blue-eyed and has a good academic record.

Schiller donates her eggs because she thinks that it's a worthy thing to do, and because it's a worthy thing to do for which she can be paid in sums that seem handsome to a heavily indebted student. Schiller's parents, who are divorced, know that she donates eggs, and they are not opposed to her doing it, though they are concerned about its effect on her health. They aren't especially wealthy, and Schiller says she would rather support herself with eggs than ask them to help her out.

She does, however, have the political objections to the trade which you might expect from someone with an answering-machine message like hers. She thinks it would be "really cool" to donate to a gay couple, say, rather than to the upper-middle-class wives and husbands who are the typical recipients of donor eggs. She also disapproves of the preference for egg donation over adoption. "It's the fact that I'm helping a white-supremacist system work," she told me earnestly. "People are getting these fair, blue-eyed children, and that does bother me philosophically." Still, she had earned twenty-five hundred dollars for each of her earlier donations, and by last fall the going rate in New York was five thousand dollars, so when she saw the ad she called the couple and arranged to meet them at a café on Broadway.

They turned out to be a professional Manhattan couple old enough to be Schiller's parents, and they bought her lunch and quizzed her about her interests and skills. She told them about her expertise in martial arts and music, and about the fact that she was really good at math and science and was also a decent writer. It was a bit like a job interview, she told me, though she hadn't done some of the things that a career counsellor might have advised, like removing her nose ring or the stud in her tongue. The hardest part of the interview came when it was time to negotiate the fee, and the couple asked her to name her price. "The husband wouldn't, like, name a figure, so I had to," she said, "Five thousand was the amount that I needed to make in this period of time, and he jumped at it. I probably could have asked for more and got it."

This past February, in the middle of Schiller's fertility-drug regimen, she heard about an advertisement that had been placed in several Ivy League school newspapers offering fifty thousand dollars to a donor who was athletic, had S.A.T. scores of 1400 or more, and was at least five feet ten inches tall. She was a few inches too short to apply, but it made her think that there might be someone who was willing to pay such a premium for her eggs, thereby making her next year at Columbia a whole lot easier. "I'm only now beginning to realize that I could tap into some cash here," she said.

In 1984, a woman gave birth to a child who was genetically unrelated to her for the first time, after a donor's egg had been fertilized in a petri dish in the laboratory of Dr. Alan Trounson, an embryologist at Monash University, in Melbourne, Australia, and transferred to another woman's womb. This year, there will probably be around five thousand egg donations in the United States.

In the early days of egg donation, very few patients could take advantage of the procedure. These recipients were given whatever eggs clinics could lay their hands on: some were leftover eggs donated by women who had undergone in-vitro fertilization, which involves the same kind of ovary-stimulating hormonal regimen as egg donation; a few came from women who were having their tubes tied and agreed to give away the eggs they would no longer be using. Some infertile women were helped by their younger sisters, or by friends. There was little concern about matching donor's and recipients beyond the broadest categories of race, One recipient I spoke with, who is dark-haired, olive-skinned, and Jewish, received donor eggs ten years ago from a woman who was tall, blond, and Nordic.

These days, such a match would be unlikely, although if a dark, Jewish recipient wanted to introduce a little Nordic blood into her family stock, she would certainly be able to find an egg-donor agency happy to oblige. Nowadays, donors and recipients are matched with remarkable precision, right down to tanning ability and hair texture. There are around two hundred private egg-donations agencies and clinics in the United States, and they are intensely competitive, offering patients donor data bases that may include as many as three hundred women. Different agencies specialize in different kinds of donors; one bicoastal agency is known for signing up donors who are in their late twenties and early thirties, are married, and have children of their own; a former actress in Los Angeles runs an agency that specializes in donors who are models and actresses; at another Los Angeles agency, the two proprietresses accompany donors to their medical appointments and have had dinner and flowers delivered to them on the night after the surgery.

Marketing strategies are ingenious. A New York egg-donation program advertises in movie theatres, inviting would-be donors to dial 1–877-BABY-MAKERS. A new company in Los Angeles called the Center for Egg Options hired a hip advertising agency to write catchy ad copy. Instead of variations on the usual "give the gift of life" theme, one ad reads simply, "Pay your tuition with eggs." Another, which appeared in the magazine *Backstage*, says, "Get paid $4,000 for a small part." The same company is known for sending fertility doctors promotional giveaways that consist of shrink-wrapped egg cartons filled with chocolate eggs.

Many agencies direct would-be recipients to log on to Internet sites and browse through pictures of willing donors which are accompanied by detailed profiles that include the donors' health history, educational background, ambitions, and interests. One popular Web site that is unaffiliated with an agency invites donors and recipients to post classified advertisements, which are by turns poignant and outlandish. There are pleas for help from women who cannot afford to use donor agencies which typically charge around twenty-five hundred dollars for their matching services, and examples of unabashed hawking: one recent posting read, "I donated to a famous couple, WHY NOT YOU!"

The United States is the only country in the world in which the rules of the marketplace govern the trade in gametes and genes. In parts of Europe, and in most of South America, egg donation is illegal, often because of the influence of

the Catholic Church, which holds that only intercourse should lead to conception. (Muslim law also forbids egg donation; Judaism generally has a more flexible view toward methods of assisted reproduction.) In other countries, egg donation is legal only under certain circumstances. A recent British law allows
patients of in-vitro fertilization to sell their leftover eggs, thereby offsetting the
cost of the original I.V.F. procedure, but it is against the law to pay women to
undergo voluntary egg retrieval. Many foreigners seeking fertility treatments
travel to the United States, which is seen by overseas patients as the place where
their prayers may be answered and by their overseas doctors as something of a
rogue nation. Robert Jansen, a prominent Australian fertility doctor, character-
izes the American egg trade as "a thoroughly commercial activity," and regrets
that "people are not even pretending anymore that it is an altruistic act to donate eggs." He adds, "Personally, I am frightened by it."

In the United States, though, the controversy has centered less on whether
donors should be paid than on how much they should earn. When Thomas
Pinkerton, a San Diego lawyer, placed the fifty-thousand-dollar-egg-donor advertisement earlier this year on behalf of an anonymous client, he was accused
of exercising unreasonable influence over students who may be hard-up. Television news magazines grilled him about his ethics, and the Academy of Assisted
Reproductive Technology, an organization on whose legal advisory board he
sits, was troubled by the controversy. But Pinkerton's clients aren't alone in looking for high-end eggs: last year, a donor in Los Angeles received thirty-five thousand dollars for her eggs.

Escalating fees are causing doctors in this county, somewhat belatedly, to
express reservations about the commercial traffic in eggs. At a recent conference
on infertility that I attended in Sydney, Australia, Dr. Mark V. Sauer, who is the
director of reproductive endocrinology at Columbia Presbyterian Medical Center
in New York, addressed the issue. "First of all, we have to recognize that we have
a problem," he said. "It is like saying at A.A. meetings, 'I am an alcoholic.' Well,
I am an egg-donor man, and I do pay my donors, and I pay them too much,
and I recognize that, so what are we going to do about it?"

Doctors are concerned that high prices are attracting women who aren't mature enough to be able to make the kind of philosophical decision implicit in donating eggs; but they are also worried about the interests of their infertility patients, many of whom are being priced out of the market. Egg donation is generally
not covered by insurance, and the price for one retrieval (known as a cycle) in New
York City, including donor fees and medications for both participants, is currently
twenty thousand dollars, with the chances of success being around fifty percent.
Some patients undergo as many as three cycles in their efforts to become parents.

The ethical quandary that doctors now find themselves in, however, is one
of their own making. It has long been accepted that gametes have a monetary
value, ever since commercial sperm donation took off in the nineteen-sixties.
(Although there are laws against the commodification of body parts, a curious
legislative loophole has enabled a market in eggs and sperm to emerge. There
is no doubt that if such a loophole existed for the market in, say, kidneys, you
would be able to order them on the Internet from donors who would provide

detailed accounts of their families' excellent urological history.) The average sperm-donor fee is fifty dollars per deposit, which works out to about 0.00001 cent per spermatozoon. Part of the reason that egg-donor fees are higher than sperm-donor fees is that the effort required is so much greater. Being an egg donor can be inconvenient, because, unlike sperm, eggs cannot easily be frozen, so there are no "egg banks"; instead the donor takes drugs to synchronize her reproductive system with the recipient's. What's more, as Cindy Schiller found out, the process can be painful, and it can be dangerous as well: hyperstimulation can, in very rare instances, lead to stroke. Donating eggs does not deplete a donor's own reserves, since the eggs that are taken would otherwise have been wasted that month; but it is too early in the history of egg donation to know what the long-term side effects might be. Ovarian scarring may compromise a donor's own fertility, and one medical study, which has since been disputed, has suggested that there might be an association between fertility drugs and ovarian cancer.

All of these factors have led some doctors to argue that egg donors are actually underpaid. Dr. Jamie Grifo, who heads New York University's infertility clinic, says, "If you consider the hourly wage for a sperm donor and the hourly wage for an egg donor—my God, five thousand dollars is about ten times too little."

In its egg-donor guidelines, the American Society for Reproductive Medicine stipulates that donors be paid not for the actual eggs but for the "inconvenience, time, discomfort, and for the risk undertaken." Agencies reject potential donors who say they are doing it just for the money, in part because most recipients wouldn't want a donor who appears to be mercenary; they would prefer a donor who has chosen to perform this service out of the goodness of her heart. (In the euphemistic parlance of the industry, eggs are "donated," never "sold.") The ideal egg donor embodies all sorts of paradoxes: she is compassionate toward an infertile stranger but feels no necessary attachment to her own genetic kin; she is fecund but can easily divorce the reproductive from the maternal.

Before Cindy Schiller was allowed to become an egg donor, she underwent psychological counselling and testing. Egg-donor programs generally reject any young women who view their eggs as protochildren. "They always ask what you are going to do when in eighteen years' time someone comes knocking at your door," Schiller told me, her tone implying that she thought the question was a silly one to ask of someone her age. "How would I know what I'm going to do?"

Donors who advertise their services directly on the Internet are not prescreened. I spoke to one would-be donor, a student near Chicago, who had just turned twenty and was planning to work with two couples who had responded to her ad, "Beauty Queen looking to help infertile couple." If she had applied to one of the big egg-donation programs, she might well have been weeded out by a psychologist. She was interested in donating only to a religious couple, she said, "because I want to someday see these kids up in Heaven with me." She went on to say, "That would be awesome. I probably won't have any contact with them until then, so that will be my first time meeting him or her." It also turned out that this young woman's religious convictions included a prohibition on premarital sex, so if she went ahead with the donation she would have genetic offspring before she had lost her virginity. "Yep," she said brightly and a bit shyly. "It's kind of cool, huh?"

Cindy Schiller was nonchalant when discussing the children who might result from her donations. "I'm really getting a good bargain, because I don't have to raise them," she said, half seriously. Schiller had nonetheless become deeply invested in the pregnancies of the women she was helping. (The agency back in her home state didn't tell Schiller whether her donations were successful, but she did receive a thank-you card from one couple, telling her that they now had a son.) "Of course, you are doing it for the money," she said, "but I always hope it works. I really hope it works."

In the weeks after we first met, Schiller had sent away for an application form from a large West Coast agency called Options. Most agencies do not allow women to donate eggs more than four or five times, because of the health risks, and Schiller was approaching her limit; she hoped that Options would help her market herself for what might be the last time. She was asked to provide head shots, and was taken aback by a number of other details that Options expected. "They even ask whether your grandparents had acne," she marvelled. "I can see why you would want to know about diseases and stuff, but acne? *Please*, I know they're paying top dollar here for the genes, but if acne is your biggest problem you're good to go."

Options is one of the largest egg-brokering agencies in the country: it can offer around two hundred and fifty donors to recipients worldwide at any given moment, and it conducts almost all of its business on the Internet. I went to visit the Options offices, which are located in a nondescript building on an anonymous street in the Los Angeles area; before I was provided with the address, I was required to sign a nondisclosure agreement stating that I would not reveal it. Teri Royal, who runs the company, said that she kept her address secret in order to preserve the security of her records, some of which deal with high-profile clients in Hollywood and in Washington.

The place had the feeling of a cottage industry that needs to move into a mansion: partitions had been set up to divide small spaces into even smaller ones, and there was hardly room to turn around without bumping into another woman with a phone clamped to her ear and a computer screen glowing in front of her. Royal is a stout thirty-nine-year-old woman with strawberry-blond hair. She explained that Options donors are carefully selected for their marketability as well as for their general health; Options does not accept donors older than thirty, for instance, because recipients shy away from them. But when it comes to accepting recipients into the program, Royal practices reproductive free trade.

"We would never turn somebody down," she said, "It is none of my business how someone wants to make her baby, so long as all parties are informed and give their consent. So I'm not going to turn away homosexuals, bisexuals, transracials, single parents, older couples." She showed me a photograph of twins born to a couple who had been rejected by another agency before coming to Options because they were both Asian but wanted a Caucasian donor. "They thought the mix was beautiful," Royal said. The agency's oldest would-be mother had been sixty-eight years old; she and her husband, both of whom already had grown children, recruited an egg donor and also a gestational surrogate to carry the new baby. "Everyone realized that the mother wasn't going to be around for the whole of the child's life," Royal said, "but the rest of the family planned to step in and be there for the parenting of this child, and it was a wonderful thing." Royal sees herself as a service provider, and she cites a higher authority for her policy of nonintervention: "In the Bible, Sarah didn't conceive until she was ninety. So I figure that until I get someone over ninety I am not going to say no to them, because if God thinks it's O.K., then who am I to say it's not?"

Using Options is expensive. The agency charges eighteen hundred and sixty-five dollars for bringing donors and recipients together. Administrative and legal costs are close to another thousand dollars. Then there is the compensation for the donor. Options donors are among the best paid in the country: those who appear on the Internet data base receive between thirty-five hundred and five thousand dollars, and others who are recruited through private advertisements placed for specific couples earn still more. Last year, Options placed a cap of sixty-five hundred dollars on payments, because would-be recipients were trying to outbid one another in the pages of the same college newspapers. "We had recipients saying they wanted to offer ten thousand, fifteen thousand, twenty thousand," Royal said. It turns out that the cap is not screwed on very tightly, however: Options still allows recipients to reward donors with additional "gifts." The *Columbia Daily Spectator* recently featured an Options ad seeking a donor who was "5'5" or taller, Caucasian, slim with dark hair, intelligent and kind"; the ad also stated that "although our gratitude cannot be measured in dollars, if we were in your shoes, the least we would expect is: $6,500 plus expenses (and a gift)."

"We have had some fabulous gifts," Royal told me. "We have had donors sent on cruises, we have had a year of tuition paid. The donor doesn't know what the gift is going to be. She just knows that there will be a gift, so that way she's still giving her eggs without undue compensation or any form of bribery." She can also, perhaps, experience the same anticipatory thrill and anxiety that a lottery player feels as he waits to see if his numbers have come up.

As egg donation has changed from being an experimental procedure to being just one of a range of infertility treatments, consumers have begun to demand more from agencies like Options. They expect to be offered donors who are not just healthy but bright and accomplished and attractive. One recent morning, I attended a matching session at Saint Barnabas Medical Center, in New Jersey, where the members of the egg-donation team were going over the wish lists of various recipients. (Like all the New York-area egg-donation programs, Saint Barnabas practices anonymous donation, in which recipients and donors are matched by nurses and psychologists; the recipients never see a picture of the woman who is chosen for them.) It felt like a good-humored, girls-only swap meet, although the scarcity of the right kinds of donors was obvious. "She wants Jewish," the program's psychologist said of one would be recipient, and one of the nurses snorted, "She can wait; she'll be waiting a long time."

Someone else asked, "Do we have someone small and dark? And Irish?" Another participant read a wish list of characteristics: "She wants no cat allergies. 'Tall, dark-haired, healthy, athletic, animal-loving.' And a partridge in a pear tree."

Most of the egg-donation professionals I talked to had similar stories of highly specific requests from prospective parents. Dr. Sauer, at Columbia Presbyterian, told me that when he was in charge of an egg-donation program at the University of Southern California, he was approached by a couple from Nebraska, and the husband introduced himself as a former college football player—a Cornhusker. "He had the red pants on and everything," Sauer said. "Because we were the U.S.C. program, he figured that we had very athletic donors, or could get them. He didn't want just a good athlete; he wanted someone who was on one of the actual teams. I said, 'I am not going to go down to the track and find you a donor,' and he got quite indignant." Sauer went on to tell me that he had couples who tried to make special deals, as if there were under-the-counter eggs to be had: "They come in and say, 'I know this is what you usually pay, but if we pay more, will you give us something better?' It's as if they were buying a puppy, or something."

Egg-donor recipients bridle at the suggestion that they are shopping for genes, but the agencies and the programs provide so much personal information about donors that recipients are invited to view eggs as merchandise. After all, most modern parents do everything they can to give a child its best start in life—from taking folic acid while trying to conceive to not drinking during pregnancy to drilling a toddler with flash cards and sending a ten-year-old to tennis camp. So it is not surprising that egg recipients are particularly choosy before conception even takes place. Lyne Macklin, the administrator of an agency in Beverly Hills, the Center for Surrogate Parenting and Egg Donation, told me that there's a great temptation among recipients to engage in a kind of genetic upgrading. "It's like shopping," she said, "If you have the option between a Volkswagen and a Mercedes, you'll select the Mercedes."

It is impossible to determine just how likely a child is to inherit such characteristics as academic ability or athleticism or musicality. Still, would-be parents can play the odds. Robert Plomin, a behavioral geneticist at the University of London, says that a recipient probably ought to pay attention to such characteristics as cognitive ability, which is about fifty percent heritable. "I generally try to be a scientist and say, 'These are populations and averages, and we can't make very good predictions for an individual,'" he told me. "But I do let friends know that some of these things are heritable."

Egg-donation specialists tend to tell their patients that they should not worry too much about behavioral genetics. Nonetheless, there is some speculation that paying donors high rates might have an effect on the character of the children produced. Robert Jansen, the Australian fertility doctor, told me, "As the price rises and becomes more and more of a motivating factor, and we also appreciate the genetics of personality and character, you start to ask, 'Do you really want to bring up a little girl whose biological mother was someone who decided to charge ten thousand dollars for eggs?'"

Jansen's question suggests a profound anxiety about the new reproductive territory that egg donation has opened up. Egg donation makes it possible, for the first time, for a woman's procreative capacity to be detached from any maternal investment on her part. Though men have always been able to father children they may never meet, the fact that an egg donor might, by semantic equivalence, mother a child she will never know confounds both the dictionary and an ingrained assumption about the maternal instinct.

One day, I asked Schiller whether she had any idea how she would be raising the money for law school if she weren't selling her eggs. "Some idea," she said. "I might be working at Hooters." In an earlier era, Schiller's youth and her fertility would have served her well in the matrimonial marketplace. Because she can now choose an education and a career, deferring marriage and children, her reproductive capital has been made otherwise available—to women who have themselves preferred an education and a career over early childbearing. Schiller told me that she couldn't imagine being ready to have children for at least a decade, if then, and it had occurred to her that she might need reproductive assistance herself one day. "What a sweet irony that would be," she said.

In the years before the birth-control pill and *Roe v. Wade,* a woman like Schiller might have provided an infertile couple not with eggs but with an actual baby—the product of an unwanted pregnancy, given up for adoption. Indeed, the rising demand for donor eggs—most of which come from white, middle-class women—coincides with a decline in the number of adoptable American infants born to white, middle-class women. Some donors have undergone abortions, and they may see egg donation as a way of making amends. The Options data base features several such women, including Jennifer, a twenty-four-year-old medical assistant. "I had to terminate two pregnancies at ages nineteen and twenty," Jennifer explained, "I felt really bad about it. I want to help someone who cannot have children. I would feel a lot better about my own decisions if I could do that."

The babies who might have resulted from Jennifer's pregnancies would have been highly adoptable (her forebears are European), but her eggs are even more desirable, because they allow a recipient couple to have a baby who is genetically related to one parent. And with egg donation, as opposed to adoption, there is no extraneous birth mother to deal with—as long as Jennifer continues to have no interest in her genetic offspring, that is, and as long as no law is introduced to give donor children the right to track down their genetic mothers.

As the egg-donation industry grows, however, legal changes are expected. "There is currently no controlling federal legislation," Sean Tipton, a spokesman for the American Society for Reproductive Medicine, explains. Donors sign a consent form saying that they are relinquishing any claim to their retrieved eggs. Five states—Florida, North Dakota, Oklahoma, Texas, and Virginia—have passed legislation that releases donors from responsibility for the children born from their eggs. "In most cases, people should be confident that they are giving up those rights," Tipton says, "But it is not clear whether it would survive a court challenge."

Legal scholars expect that, in years to come, lawsuits will be brought by donors who develop regrets about having sold their eggs back in their student days. Karen Synesiou, the co-owner of the Center for Surrogate Parenting and Egg Donation, told me, "If you get an eighteen- or nineteen-year-old who has been stimulated four or five times and her ovaries stop functioning because of all the scarring, she is going to want to sue someone for being infertile." At least one donor has threatened to sue a fertility clinic after being hyperstimulated, but the suit was dropped when the clinic agreed to pay her medical expenses.

Schiller, who as a law student might be expected to be aware of her rights and responsibilities concerning her eggs, seemed vague when I asked her whether she had made any legal arrangement with the couple who had just bought her eggs. She had signed the consent form waiving her rights, she said, but she had not come to any agreement about whether she would have future contact with the family. She seemed to have very little idea of what the couple expected from her; she had never discussed with them whether they planned to tell the child of its origins, and she did not know whether they expected her to be available to the child if it later wanted to know its genetic mother. She wasn't even sure whether they would notify her of a pregnancy, or of a baby's birth, and said that she had never felt that she could ask about these issues. "Ultimately, until it's over and you get paid you feel, 'I had better not say anything,'" she told me.

So far, there has been very little case law in which egg donation plays a role. One notorious case that does involve an egg donor is known as *Buzzanca v. Buzzanca.* John and Luanne Buzzanca were both infertile, so they obtained an embryo that was left over from an I.V.F. cycle performed on an infertile woman, using a donor egg and her husband's sperm. The embryo was transferred to the womb of a gestational surrogate whom the Buzzancas had hired. During the pregnancy, the Buzzancas separated; shortly after the baby's birth, John claimed that he was exempt from paying child support, because the child was not genetically related to him and had not been born to his wife. A lower court agreed with John Buzzanca that he was not the little girl's parent, but it declined to say who, precisely, was; however, a higher court ruled that John and Luanne were indeed the child's father and mother. The child now lives with Luanne Buzzanca, and she receives child support from John Buzzanca. Some legal scholars have suggested that the original egg donor, who seemed to be unaware that her eggs had been passed on to yet another infertile couple, might have had a claim if she had decided to sue her clinic.

The Buzzanca case has implications not just for the field of assisted reproduction but also for the contemporary cultural definition of parenthood. According to the Buzzanca ruling, parenthood is not a biological category but a conceptual one: its defining characteristic is that of intent. John and Luanne Buzzanca were the child's parents because at one point they had meant to be her parents. This reasoning—the idea that intent trumps biology—makes for some remarkably slippery values. A woman who bears an egg-donor child is encouraged to believe that carrying the fetus is the crucial component of motherhood. But a woman who hires a surrogate to carry her fertilized egg to term for her is encouraged to believe the opposite: that the important thing is the genetic link to the baby, and not the womb out of which the baby came. Biologically, an egg donor's situation is identical to that of a woman who uses a surrogate. But egg donors are encouraged to believed that what makes a woman into a mother is the wish to be a mother—to be what is known in the infertility business as "the social parent."

The American fertility industry is based upon the conviction that a person is the agent of his or her own destiny—that fate and fortune are fashioned, not inflicted. Effective contraception has made it possible for people to believe that all pregnancies can be planned, and that children are chosen. The corollary of that belief is the conviction that choosing to have a child is a right, and that the desire to have one, even when pregnancy is against the odds, should command the utmost attention and effort and resources. The jargon of the reproductive-services industry, which talks about "nontraditional family-building" and "creating families," illustrates this very American idea: that sleeves-rolled-up diligence is what makes people into parents—rather than anything as unreliable as chance, or fate, or luck, or God.

In late June, Schiller finally heard from the couple who had received her eggs four months earlier: the woman had failed to conceive. So far, they hadn't asked her to donate eggs a second time, but they seemed to want to stay in touch, and she wondered whether they might call upon her to repeat the process.

Meanwhile, in the final week of the spring semester, a new advertisement had appeared in the *Columbia Daily Spectator* for a donor who was five feet seven inches tall and had S.A.T. scores of 1300 or more; the ad offered fifty thousand dollars. When we first met, Schiller had told me that she was five feet six; now, she thought, she might be five feet seven, barely. She had contacted the office of the attorney who placed the ad, had sent off a batch of photographs of herself as a baby, as a child, and as an adult, and was waiting to hear whether she would fill the bill.

The attorney was Thomas Pinkerton, the lawyer who had placed the first fifty-thousand-dollar ad, several months earlier. I called Pinkerton at his office in San Diego. He told me that he had started out as a real-estate attorney but that his personal life had redirected his professional life: he and his wife, Darlene, had contracted with his sister for her to carry a surrogate pregnancy for them using Darlene's egg and Pinkerton's sperm. The health department wanted the birth certificate to carry the names of Pinkerton and his sister as the child's parents, but Pinkerton obtained a court order, the first of its kind in San Diego, allowing Darlene to be named as the child's mother.

Pinkerton defended the high fee that his clients were offering by noting that they had been unable to find a donor who met their specifications through the usual agencies and programs. He said that he saw nothing wrong with a client's paying premium rates for hard-to-come-by goods. "People have asked, 'How can a donor make an informed choice about undertaking the risk of going through a medical procedure when there is so much money at stake?'—as if she weren't going to be able to use her mind any more," Pinkerton said. "But put it in the context of what we are offering other youngsters, such as football players —is that unethical? It is almost an assault on womanhood to say that this woman can't make a decision because there's fifty thousand dollars at stake."

More than two hundred women had responded to Pinkerton's first ad; another hundred had called after the second ad. And, although Pinkerton says that this wasn't his original intention, he is now doing what some in the fertility business had told me they suspected was behind the advertisements all along. He's creating his own Internet data base—a kind of blue-chip directory of donors, which, for a fee, recipients will be able to inspect. Pinkerton has kept the operation small: by mid-July, he said, he was working with ten couples. But he expects it to grow, and he is planning to approach a California business school to assign as a class project the drafting of a business plan for his new agency.

Pinkerton explained that his data base, unlike the on-line agencies, does not list prices for any of the donors. A donor can put herself on the egg market, find out what she's worth, and privately negotiate the fee for her genes—eggBay, so to speak. So far, donors have been settling for considerably less than the fifty-thousand-dollar fee they hoped for when they sent in their original applications; but in theory a donor will be able to command a price even higher than fifty thousand dollars. "We can give a couple access to the data base with the profiles and pictures, and then they can make an offer," Pinkerton said. "They can settle on a figure with her that is totally undirected by us."

As of July, only a month before fall registration, Schiller had not been chosen by one of Pinkerton's recipients, and she had begun to investigate the possibility of putting up her own classified advertisement on one of the Internet's egg-donor sites. She browsed the advertisements that had been placed by couples who were looking for donors. "Gosh, these ads are really sad," she told me. "Most people have to be really desperate before they will even try something like this." There was one couple who had lost many family members in the Holocaust and wanted a Jewish donor to continue the bloodline; another woman had suffered serious damage to her reproductive organs after being in a car accident.

Schiller had recently heard from Columbia's Financial Aid office that she'd be receiving more funds than she expected this academic year, so she hadn't yet decided whether to go through with a fourth donation. But just in case, she had looked into taking a Mensa test in order to have proof of her intelligence, and she had decided one thing: "If someone offers me something really high, and they are an asshole, I won't do it." In any case, Schiller has no regrets about her adventures in the egg marketplace. "It's almost like a hobby now," she said. "This is weird, isn't it? But it is a very interesting experience. I don't think I would trade it for anything."

TOPICS FOR DISCUSSION AND WRITING

1. Cindy Schiller is conflicted over her role as egg donor. What are the sources of her conflict and how does she justify her choice?

2. Why do you think reproductive agencies use the term "donated" rather than "sold" when discussing the exchange of a woman's eggs?

3. In legal terms, what is the difference for the hopeful parents between a baby given up for adoption, a baby born to a surrogate mother, and a baby born of a donated egg?

4. Do you find any features of the current market in egg donors that reflect larger trends in our society today? If so, explain.

5. Only in the United States do "rules of the marketplace govern the trade in gametes and genes." Discuss the issue of egg donation as a commercial enterprise and explain your position on the subject. (For direction in setting up an argument on this subject, see Writing Assignments 9, 10, and 11 in Chapter 4.)

6. Harvard professor of government Michael Sandel has been struck "by the readiness of a large majority of students to allow the buying and selling of sperm and eggs and of surrogacy." Are you surprised by his students' reaction? You and your classmates might want to conduct a survey of your class, or even of a larger group on your campus, to determine their attitude on this issue. (See Conducting a Survey: A Collaborative Project in Chapter 7.)

Decoding the Human Genome

On June 26, 2000, President Clinton called a press conference at the White House to celebrate the completion of the human genome map. Flanked by Dr. Francis Collins of the Human Genome Project and Dr. J. Craig Venter of Celera Genomics and linked by satellite to Britain's Prime Minister Tony Blair, the President praised the public and private efforts that led to sequencing almost all of the three billion letters that make up the genetic code. It was a landmark moment in human biology with competing public and private scientists sharing the spotlight. The article that follows, written shortly before the final breakthrough, describes the nature of the human genome project and outlines a little of its history. The article provides some background and introduces a few of the questions this research raises. One interesting feature of the project rests on the intense competition between (1) Craig Venter, the founder and CEO of Celera Genomics, the private company that aspired to be first with the complete map, and (2) the consortium of mostly American and British scientists working at the different academic sites of the Human Genome Project funded by the National Institutes of Health in the United States and the Wellcome Trust of London. In particular, Francis Collins, the director of the National Human Genome Research Institute in Bethesda, Maryland, found himself going head-to-head with Venter in this competition. One ardent critic of Venter is James Watson (see his article "Moving Toward Clonal Man"), who is concerned about public access to the scientific and medical breakthroughs flowing from the new understanding of our genes. Some raise the question, if one private company controls the data, will profit dictate who uses the data? Providing a little color to the contest, Venter is described as an ex-surfer who came to science late and brought new urgency to the venture. Perhaps it's no accident that his company is named Celera, derived from the Latin for "quick." Both economics and ethical concerns were at stake in this race and remain at the forefront of ongoing genomic research.

Two Groups on Verge of Reading the Entire Human Gene Code

Tom Abate

As the race to complete the map of the human genome drew to a close, news of its completion spilled over from scientific journals into the media, which gave full coverage to the unfolding events. The *San Francisco Chronicle* put the story on its front page. Much is at stake, as news writer Abate explains in the following excerpts from his story.

At the center of almost every human cell sit the long strands of DNA that contain the complete instructions for making a person. Known as the human genome, these DNA strands might be thought of as a software program evolved over 4 billion years. Now, after more than a decade of effort by thousands of scientists the world over, humanity is on the verge of decoding this genetic instruction book.

Within weeks, either the publicly funded Human Genome Project or a rival, private effort by Celera Genomics will complete a first draft of the human genetic code—identifying the estimated 100,000 genes that influence every aspect of human disease, development and behavior. Whoever finishes first, the effort promises to revolutionize medicine in the 21st century. Such knowledge will help scientists understand more about the causes of human ailments and fashion powerful new treatments. But some fear that the knowledge will be misused. The Human Genome Project could give scientists potent tools to manipulate human traits and behavior before society has sorted out the implications.

"For the first time we've rolled back the big stone and peered into the sepulcher with our tiny flashlights, reading the sacred script off the tablet," said Elbert Branscomb, director of the Joint Genome Institute in Walnut Creek [California], one of five main centers of the public project. Branscomb's lab recently completed "reading" the chemical letters of three of the 23 human chromosomes, a big step toward completion of the public project. Like other public genome centers, Branscomb's lab posted the text on the Internet.

Across the country in Maryland, Celera appears poised to beat the public project to the finish line. Craig Venter, the company's maverick founder, says researchers at his company will complete their rough draft before the public project is scheduled to complete its in June [2000].

Deciphering the human genome has been an epic task. Human DNA is made up of a chain 3 billion chemical letters in length. Scientists have used the most powerful computers and developed a new generation of automated machines to read the letters.

Deciphering the human genome has been likened to putting a man on the moon. But if today's world seems preoccupied with genes and unraveling the secrets of DNA, it seems worth recalling that it wasn't always that way.

Fifteen years ago, finding a single gene was an interminable process. Genes are small sections of DNA that tell cells how to function. Each gene contains instructions on producing or controlling a specific protein. The proteins, in turn, carry out the cell's work in the body. As the 1980s drew to a close, biologists in several quarters began to campaign for a systematic gene discovery program. But the proposal proved elusive because of divergent agendas and ideas. . . .

A 1988 National Research Council report largely settled the scientific debate. A committee headed by former University of California at San Francisco professor Bruce Alberts recommended a 15-year, $3 billion program to decipher the entire genome. Congress followed the NRC strategy when it funded the Human Genome Project in 1990, and appointed James Watson—the co-discoverer of DNA—its first leader. [See James Watson's predictive article earlier in this section] . . .

Now, a decade after its inception, the Human Genome Project is closing in on its most important milestone: a rough draft of the entire genome; full of holes, to be sure, but ahead of schedule. But reading the chemical letters in the human genome is only the beginning. Researchers have yet to determine what many of the genes do and how they work in the body.

"A hundred years from now scientists will still be making discoveries in the genome," said Craig Venter, founder of Celera Genomics, which appears poised to beat the public project in finishing the first draft. "It will take most of this century to analyze this information."

The first drafts will show genetic sequences that are considered normal. The next step, already under way in public and private labs, is to look for the many slight differences in the genetic codes of any two humans. Scientists call these differences single nucleotide polymorphisms, or SNPs. SNPs (pronounced "snips") may help explain why some people, and not others, are susceptible to complex diseases like schizophrenia, which are likely to be caused by an interplay between genes and environmental factors. [For more on genetics versus environment influences, see Nature Versus Nurture starting on page 392.]

"The ultimate goal is creating a genetic profile of every individual," Venter said. "If we gave you your genetic code on a DVD, and you saw the differences between your genome and the reference genome, it would aid in diagnosing and treating disease."

Doctors hope to learn how to repair the faulty genes responsible for illnesses like cystic fibrosis and hemophilia. New drugs that enhance the activity of some genes and block others may be used to treat cancer and heart disease. Drug companies already talk about using SNPs to tailor remedies to individuals and thereby lessen the side effects that come from one-size-fits-all medicine.

Scientists say the genome project marks a new era in which they are beginning to see the body much the way engineers see the working of a complex machine. . . .

But just as genetic knowledge will lead to better medicine, the advent of the genomic era raises fears that this knowledge will be misused. Since 1990, the public genome project has funded research into the "ethical, legal and social implications" of its work. Topping the list of concerns is the question of genetic privacy. What's to stop employers, insurers or anyone else from using your genetic information as the basis for decisions that could lead to discrimination?

[Eric] Lander [of the Whitehead Institute, Massachusetts Institute of Technology] offers a scenario about privacy invasion that is apropos of a Presidential election year: How long, he asks, before someone filches a saliva sample from the cocktail napkin of each presidential candidate, and reveals which candidate has the gene for Alzheimer's?

Genetic testing could also raise the societal anxiety level. Tests for genes that cause cancer and other human ailments will become available relatively soon. But it will take much longer to develop treatments for these diseases.

"Welcome to the problem," said Trevor Hawkins, deputy director of the Joint Genome Institute in Walnut Creek. "There's going to be this tidal wave of diagnostic tests which can be produced very, very easily," he said. "Then there will be a huge gap between the tests and being able to do anything about it."

UC Berkeley sociologist Troy Duster, who spent seven years consulting with the genome program, said his greatest fear is the emergence of genetic determinism, the belief that any success or failure, any health or illness, can be explained by our genes. Duster believes many will feel an irresistible tug to use genetics to "improve" the human species. Already, during in-vitro fertilization, doctors create several embryos and pick the one devoid of known defects. It's just a short leap from there to inserting genes that might give a child an edge. Duster recalled Doogie, the "smart mouse" that a Princeton researcher created last year by giving embryos an extra copy of a gene that stimulated brain cells.

"If that insertion technology could make children smarter for the SAT or LSAT, I have no doubt that some part of the population would move toward it," Duster said.

Lander, the Whitehead Institute geneticist, said scientists today aren't capable of making such precise genetic fixes on human embryos, and most would abhor the notion of tinkering with human inheritance. . . .

But just because decoding the "Book of Life" is fraught with potential perils does not mean we should—or can—shy away from doing so, said Francis Collins, who oversees the public effort as director of the National Human Genome Research Institute in Bethesda, Maryland.

"As someone whose faith is important to him,"Collins said, "I am somewhat repelled by the notion that we will reduce human beings to a parts list and a set of chemical reactions, that we will reduce ourselves to predetermined, DNA-driven robots, that love will become a series of chemical reactions and that God will become irrelevant.

"I'm interested in this project for the reason that healers have always been interested in learning more," he said. "So that they will be able to make sick people better. To argue that you shouldn't do this seems to be most unethical. That would be the greatest disappointment of all."

TOPICS FOR DISCUSSION AND WRITING

1. Briefly summarize the Human Genome Project and explain what is so groundbreaking in this endeavor.

2. What, according to this article, are the major concerns surrounding the work of the genome project and the knowledge that will emerge?

3. Investigate current progress in gene research, both public and private, and write an updated report. Explore the ethical issues currently facing scientists as genes for specific human illnesses and personality traits are identified. Does the competition between government funded and private projects continue? If so, what impact does such competition have?

Gene Therapy

The powerful new tools available to scientists today continue to pose difficult questions for all of us. We might assume that curing disease and helping the disabled would be universally applauded. But once again, conflicting imperatives cloud the picture. News from France of successful gene therapy for babies suffering from a potentially lethal immune system disease was hailed as a marvel. However, a few gene therapy procedures in the United States have gone wrong, leading to the death of more than one young person. An article summarizing the good news from Paris and a report of a debate in Congress over possible perils present the dilemmas posed by emerging gene therapies.

Long-awaited Gene Therapy Success Restores Two Babies to Health

In April, 2000, the prestigious journal *Science* (see "Cloned Cows Have Younger than Normal Cells" on page 354), reported the story of the two babies in France who appear to have been saved by gene therapy. The on-line site HealthCentral.com picked up the "translation" for non-scientists from the Associated Press.

In an exciting and long-awaited success, gene therapy has restored apparently normal immune systems to two French babies born with a rare, lethal immune disease sometimes called the "bubble boy disease." It's too soon to know if the babies are cured, experts cautioned. But the experiment, reported in Friday's edition of the journal *Science*, finally provides evidence that gene therapy can succeed—at a time when skeptics are harshly criticizing the field.

"The clinical benefits we observed had never been achieved before," Dr. Alain Fischer, the Paris physician who performed the gene therapy, said at a news conference Thursday, describing his sickly patients' rebound into healthy toddlers.

"It looks like this really worked," agreed Dr. Jennifer Puck, a geneticist at the U.S. National Institutes of Health who plans to start a similar gene therapy study this fall with doctors at North Carolina's Duke University. "This is a very important milestone." The babies have SCID, or "severe combined immunodeficiency disease," a devastating, rare disease. Their bodies cannot make lymphocytes, the immune cells crucial for warding off infection—meaning they can die from the most minor of germs.

The best-known victim of SCID was David, Houston's famous "bubble boy," who lived in a germ-proof plastic enclosure until his death at age 12. Today, bone marrow transplants keep many SCID babies from having to live in sterile bubbles. Transplants provide them with healthy stem cells, special cells that reside in the bone marrow and produce lymphocytes. Transplants have cured some babies and extended the lives of others. But they're not always successful, so scientists hope gene therapy could offer an alternative.

The French babies never tried a transplant, and lived the first months of their lives inside sterile bubbles. They have the most common form of SCID, caused by a defective gene that blocks a cell receptor needed to trigger lymphocyte formation. Lift that roadblock, and the body should generate normal, working immune cells. Fischer, of the Hospital Necker-Enfants Malades in Paris, took bone marrow from the babies when they were ages 8 months and 11 months, respectively. He culled some of their stem cells, and bathed them in fibronectin, a protein believed to make them more receptive to gene therapy. Then he took a normal version of the immune system gene the babies were missing, and added it to a harmless virus. In a lab dish, he infected the babies' stem cells with the gene-carrying virus for three days. Then he transplanted the stem cells back into their bodies. Soon, the babies started making germ-killing immune cells. Three months later, they went home from the hospital without antibiotics or any additional treatment—and 11 months later, both have levels of immune system cells comparable to healthy children their age, Fischer said.

Neither suffered any side effects from the gene therapy. Their immune systems reacted properly when they were vaccinated against polio and other diseases. A third patient who had the treatment four months ago is also doing well, he said.

It is "the first significant success" in gene therapy in 10 years of experiments with over 4,000 people, said Dr. W. French Anderson of the University of Southern California, who performed the world's first gene therapy attempt.

What's especially important here: Scientists have long wanted to correct gene detects at the stem cell level because healthy stem cells should continue producing a working immune system for years. Plus, unlike the challenge with genetic diseases that affect other types of cells, every stem cell doesn't have to take up the new gene—only a few healthy stem cells are required to work.

"You can't call it a cure" until the children are older and the disease doesn't return, Anderson cautioned, but it is a possibility. "It does look like gene therapy might finally be turning the corner."

If so, it comes at a crucial time. Gene therapy has come under harsh criticism since September, when a different gene therapy experiment killed an Arizona teenager. Skeptics questioned if the field was too risky and would ever cure anyone, and the public outcry slowed new experiments as regulators and doctors alike started double-checking safety procedures.

"I had my heart in my throat watching this trial go on," Puck said of the French study, worried that any side effects could threaten her own pending study. Instead, she said, "They did great."

TOPICS FOR DISCUSSION AND WRITING

1. Why do doctors think that gene therapy in the treatment of children with severe combined immunodeficiency disease, or SCID, is so important?

2. Look up the case of the Arizona teenager and other failed gene therapy cases. Write a report in which you discuss the controversies

that erupted after each death. One case in Pennsylvania led to a serious reevaluation of such treatments. Bring this debate up to date with current data.

Stem Cell Research Debated at Senate Hearing

Since human embryonic stem cells, the primordial human cells from which all life grows, were isolated in 1998, a clash of competing values has set off a new round of debate between political conservatives in government and the larger community on one side and scientists involved in human embryo research and their supporters on the other. The hope of these researchers is that through manipulating embryonic stem cells they will gradually build up a kind of repair kit for treating genetic flaws and thus a whole array of illnesses and disabilities. The controversy centers on two potential sources of stem cells—from surplus or "spare" embryos created in fertility clinics and, more distasteful to critics, actually creating embryos artificially just for the purpose of harvesting stem cells. Some critics oppose any procedure that requires destroying an embryo. In the spring of 2000, Congress began to consider funding for stem cell research. Increasingly, technical issues of this nature are being debated by lawmakers and discussed for the general public in the media. Keeping up with science is becoming a required part of our civic life.

Proponents and opponents of federal funding of research on stem cells derived from human embryos, including paralyzed actor Christopher Reeve, faced off at a Senate subcommittee hearing Wednesday, setting the stage for a likely Senate floor debate later this spring.

Congress has for the past 5 years banned research on human embryos. In 1999, however, lawyers for the Department of Health and Human Services said that research using human pluripotent stem cells derived from embryos could be funded, as long as the cells were not removed from the embryos using federal funds. But the National Institutes of Health (NIH) has still not issued the guidelines that would allow such funding to proceed.

In the meantime, Sens. Arlen Specter (R-PA) and Tom Harkin (D-IA) have introduced the "Stem Cell Research Act of 2000," which would allow federal funding of research using stem cells derived from embryos obtained from in vitro fertilization clinics. Specter and Harkin are the chairman and ranking Democrat, respectively, on the Senate appropriations subcommittee that funds the NIH.

Reeve, paralyzed in a horse riding accident, said that it is imperative that the government fund stem cell research and not merely leave it to the private sector. "That will avoid abuses by for-profit corporations, avoid secrecy and destructive competition between laboratories, and ensure the widest possible dissemination of scientific breakthroughs," he told the subcommittee. Among others testifying in favor of the bill at Tuesday's hearing, the subcommittee's fifth on the subject, were the heads of two NIH institutes. "Virtually every institute at the NIN has an intense interest in stem cell research," Dr. Gerald

Fischbach, head of the National Institute of Neurological Disorders and Stroke, told the subcommittee. "The potential in this regard is exciting and unlimited."

Opponents of the research suggested that recent advances in deriving stem cells from adults and other nonembryonic sources might eliminate the need to use embryos. But Dr. Allen Spiegel, head of the National Institute of Diabetes and Digestive and Kidney Diseases, disagreed. Both avenues need to be explored further, he said, and to pursue only nonembryonic stem cell research "would be tying one hand behind our back." But foes of the research insisted that destroying embryos is tantamount to murder. "It is never acceptable to deliberately kill an innocent human being in order to help another," said Sen. Sam Brownback (R-KS). When asked by Specter why it is unethical to use embryos that are going to be discarded in any case, Brownback likened it to the atrocities perpetrated on Jews in the Second World War. "You had the Nazis in World War II say, "'These people are going to be killed anyway. Why not experiment on them,'" he said.

The full Senate is expected to debate the bill to allow stem cell research sometime before Memorial Day [2000].

TOPICS FOR DISCUSSION AND WRITING

1. Present in standard form the premises proposed by both sides in the congressional debate over funding for research on human embryo stem cells. In your opinion, which side has the strongest argument? Why? (See Standard Form in Chapter 3.)

2. To more fully understand the debate, research a fuller meaning of "stem cell" than the brief description offered in this article. (See Definition in Chapter 5.)

3. Senator Sam Brownback of Kansas compares the destruction of embryos for science to Nazi atrocities against Jews during World War II. Look up scientific experiments conducted in concentration camps in World War II and evaluate Browback's analogy. (See False Analogy in Chapter 6 and Analogy in Chapter 14.)

Science into Fiction

Long before science suggested that animal cloning or gene replacement was possible, the human imagination had foreshadowed recent events. In his short story "The Birthmark," Nathaniel Hawthorne deals provocatively with the human desire to control human life and death. Aldous Huxley bred moronic Epsilons to serve as worker-drones for upper caste Alphas and Betas in *Brave New World.* In *The Boys from Brazil,* the infamous Dr.

Josef Mengele cloned a gang of Hitlers from the dead dictator's blood. In her novel *The Cloning of Joanna May,* novelist Fay Weldon created a demonic nuclear engineer who makes multiple clones of the beautiful Joanna May, his unfaithful wife. Woody Allen, in *Sleeper,* foiled attempts to clone a mad dictator from the dead man's nose. An episode of TV's *X-Files* included a woman trying to reproduce herself. In the movie *Multiplicity,* one man found he couldn't cope with all the roles he had to play in contemporary life and so kept cloning himself until he was four men. The film, *Gattaca,* offers a future world populated by a ruling class of superior people genetically engineered. Envisioning a biotech twenty-first century, novelist Philip Dick created synthetically produced slaves, who were translated to the screen in the epoch-making science fiction film *Blade Runner.* Both novel and movie deal head-on with bioengineering. And most notable of all, Mary Shelley, in 1816, created the scientist Frankenstein who in turn fashioned his celebrated monster, the idea of such a creation coming to her in a dream. In an introduction to her novel, she wrote, "The event on which this fiction is founded has been supposed, by Dr. Darwin [evolutionist Charles Darwin's father], and some of the physiological writers of Germany, as not of impossible occurrence." Her remarkable story was composed as part of a competition inspired by the poets Lord Byron and her husband, Percy Bysshe Shelley. She seems to have won.

Clone Your Wife

Arthur Hoppe

In a short column, humorist Arthur Hoppe creates an up-to-the minute science fiction tale with an amusing cautionary conclusion.

It was a beautiful wedding. Hobart and Melody, both 21, plighted their troth with true love glowing in their eyes. He was handsome, she was gorgeous. The match seemed made in Heaven.

Melody was particularly touched when, on their honeymoon, Hobart asked for a lock of her hair. "I want to carry it in my wallet so that part of you will always be with me," he whispered.

"Oh, Hobart, you're so romantic!" Melody cried joyously.

Hobart did put the lock in his wallet as promised—all but one hair. That hair he took to a noted scientist, Dr. Fred N. Stein, who extracted Melody's DNA and injected it into a surrogate mother.

When the child was born, Hobart named her Melody II and found a kindhearted old couple, Mr. and Mrs. Kindheart, who agreed to adopt her and raise her as their very own.

The years passed. No marriage was more ideal than Hobart's and Melody's. He was the perfect husband, rarely watching football on television, always remembering the anniversary of the day they met and never chipping a dish. Melody, in turn, was the perfect wife, rubbing his neck without being asked, never criticizing his growing bald spot and always laughing at his little witticisms.

Meanwhile, Melody II was growing up as beautiful as Melody I. The Kindhearts would send snapshorts of her to Hobart, and he would compare them with old photos in his wife's album.

"A perfect match!" he would gloat.

More years passed. Melody I was in the kitchen baking a cake for her 42d birthday when Hobart entered, smiling broadly. "There's something I want to give you on this happy occasion," he said taking her in his arms.

"Not another diamond tiara?" teased Melody.

"No," said Hobart, "a divorce."

Melody was stunned. Hobart tried to explain. "It's only because I loved you so much the day we were wed. But you now have three gray hairs on your left temple, a crow's foot by each eye and a touch of arthritis in your second finger. You are no longer the girl that I married."

"You didn't expect me to grow older?" demanded Melody angrily.

"But I did," said Hobart. "And that's why I had you cloned. I love you so much that I plan to marry you again just as you were 21 years ago. I can think of no higher compliment than wanting to re-live our wonderful marriage."

Unfortunately, Melody didn't take it that way. What she took was an abalone whacker from a kitchen drawer which she applied liberally to Hobart's head. When the lumps subsided, he bought a bouquet, sucked in his paunch and called at the Kindhearts' to claim his trophy wife.

He sat with Melody II on a garden bench. Taking her hand, he explained how she owed her very existence to his brilliant concept and careful planning. "So you see," he said. "I have spent the past 21 years waiting for this precious moment."

"To do what?" asked Melody II suspiciously.

"Why, to ask you to plight our troth in a beautiful wedding ceremony," said Hobart confidently.

"What?" cried Melody, aghast. "Marry a balding, pot-bellied old geezer like you?"

And the very next day, she ran off with a handsome, 21-year-old skateboarder instructor.

TOPICS FOR DISCUSSION AND WRITING

1. How far is Hoppe stretching credibility by having a human clone grow from a single hair? Look back at the article "After Decades and Many Missteps, Cloning Success" for scientific information. You may also want to search for more current news about developments on cloning.

2. The 1997 science fiction film, *Gattaca*, focuses on the consequences of genetically engineered children. The film actually presents an argument. After viewing the film (this might be fun to do as a class), summarize what that argument is—its conclusions and

premises—and then write a review of the film for an audience who has not seen it, including the argument in your review. To prepare your readers, you will need to write a short summary of the plot without giving away the resolution. For a sense of the conventions of film reviews (if you are not already familiar with them), turn to your local newspaper or to national magazines such as *Newsweek*, *Time*, *The New Yorker*, *Vanity Fair*. As an alternate choice you might select *Blade Runner*. Not for the fainthearted, this film projects a twentieth century view of our new twenty-first. (Did novelist Philip Dick and the director, Ridley Scott, get it right?)

3. Consider reading Mary Shelley's *Frankenstein* (available in paperback) and discuss her novel of terror in light of current scientific findings. As part of your paper, include a brief biographical sketch of Mary Shelley.

4. Aldous Huxley in *Brave New World* (also available in paperback) suggests that new technologies are enslaving us. Read *Brave New World* and discuss Huxley's view of a technologically controlled future in light of what scientists have achieved in biotechnology today. How close to the scientifically possible do you think he came? In April 1998, a cable TV channel found *Brave New World* sufficiently up-to-date to air the first-ever film of the novel—more than sixty years after it was written in 1932. And a few months later, the novel was selected by a panel at Random House Publishing as number 5 on a list of the 100 best English-language novels of the twentieth century.

5. Now it is your turn to try your hand at a science fiction tale tied to the current issues of genetic research and discoveries presented in the selections above. Write a short story in which such an issue plays a role, perhaps following Arthur Hoppe's "Clone Your Wife" in suggesting unforseen consequences of bioengineering.

Bioethics—Concluding Topics

1. Look back at the essay "Moving Toward the Clonal Man" by James Watson above. What, in 1971, did Watson think scientists and politicians should do about the new developments in genetic engineering? After reading the articles that follow his essay and thinking about the astonishing breakthroughs that scientists have made and continue to

make, discuss the significance of his predictions and whether or not we have followed his advice. Were his recommendations wise? What would you recommend for our scientists and politicians today?

2. A Concluding Written Argument

STEP 1: After reading the selections on the ethical, social, political, and practical concerns surrounding cloning and other related issues of genetic engineering in this chapter, write out in *standard form* the premises for and against further cloning research. You will be synthesizing information and ideas from a number of different articles. (See Standard Form in Chapter 3.)

STEP 2: What at one time would have been topics for specialized biologists alone have now become issues for us all. Such a shift means that we, as ordinary citizens, will be asked to express opinions and will possibly even have to vote on cloning and related genetic research. Drawing on the readings and your list of premises for and against cloning and on further research to bring the issues up to date, write a position paper stating whether or not, and under what circumstances, you would support research that could lead to the cloning of humans. (See Chapter 4. If you are not ready to take a simple pro or con position on such a question, look at Writing Assignment 11 on page 118.)

3. You may want to construct a poll on specific facets of cloning, reproductive engineering, or replacement therapy. To focus your survey, you will want to narrow the topic to a single question at issue. Such a poll could be taken among a select population on your campus, on a random sample of your campus as a whole, or on an area in your community. You may find the results of this poll useful if you are writing a paper under Step 2 above. (See Conducting a Survey: A Collaborative Project in Chapter 7 and The Question at Issue in Chapter 4.)

4. As our genes are identified and mapped, the number of new therapies keeps growing. One biotech company, Geron, set its sights on a gene which could provide immortality for our cells and thus for ourselves. Such a gene, if found and cloned, could greatly extend human life expectancy. Research current progress on producing such a key to aging and discuss your own opinion on these developments. Note advancements in control of aging in "Cloned Cows Have Younger-Than-Normal Cells."

5. Throughout the world and especially in Europe and the United States, the controversy is growing over genetically engineered food. With world populations exploding, new sources of food are imperative for human survival. But the growing development of genetically

engineered foods designed to increase and improve yields has set off a fierce debate over their safety. In this chapter, we have not explored the agricultural aspect of bioethics, but if you find this topic interesting, look up current data, discuss both sides of the issue and come to as much of a conclusion as the information and your own understanding allow.

CHAPTER 12

Sexual Harassment

In October of 1991, Clarence Thomas appeared before the United States Senate to have his appointment to the Supreme Court confirmed. When the FBI conducted a routine but thorough background check of Thomas, they came across Anita Hill, a young lawyer who worked for Thomas at the Department of Education and the Equal Employment Opportunity Commission. As a witness at these confirmation hearings, she revealed that Thomas, her superior, often used sexually explicit language in her presence, making her extremely uncomfortable. She never protested, however, because she feared that doing so would threaten her career.

Despite these allegations, Clarence Thomas's appointment was confirmed—he is now a Supreme Court Justice—but the issues raised by Anita Hill's charges against him continue to have a profound impact on American culture. These televised hearings captured the nation's attention and "sexual harassment" became a national obsession. This national obsession was then fueled by another incident, the Tailhook Scandal, which occurred in 1991 in Las Vegas where, at the annual convention of naval aviators, dozens of the women present were forced to run the gauntlet—a hotel hallway lined with men—who tore at the women's clothes, grabbed their breasts and buttocks and yelled obscenities at them. Of the dozens of women attacked, only one came forward to file a complaint against the officers involved. At the end of three years of hearings and reports, none of the 43 men who faced administrative action were charged with assaulting or molesting women, and whistle blower Navy Lieutenant Paula Couglin resigned from the Navy.

Since the confirmation of Thomas and the Tailhook Scandal, a U.S. Senator has resigned, high ranking military officers have been forced into early retirement, professors have lost their tenured positions, and in one case, a seven million dollar judgment was levied against a law firm, all as a consequence of sexual harassment charges. Indeed, a President of the United States, Bill Clinton, has had to face sexual harassment charges.

In the workplace, on college campuses, on military bases, charges of sexual harassment continue to proliferate, prompting us to ask, has the behavior between men and women changed so drastically or have the relationships between the sexes been redefined?

Hearing Hill's charges against Thomas, Senator Metzenbaum of Ohio exclaimed, "If that's sexual harassment, half the Senators on Capital Hill could be accused." This response, shared by many, indicates that behavior once considered acceptable is acceptable no longer. But what constitutes sexual harassment? What behavior or behaviors can be classified as sexual harassment? How does one distinguish between flirtation and sexual harassment? Some feel that sexual harassment is to the nineties what communism was to the fifties—a witch hunt. In fact, there have been cases of women filing false charges against employers in an effort to win large sums of money from sympathetic jurors. Some men take exception with the assumption that it is only men who sexually harass women. Don't women harass men? And what about same-sex harassment? Can a man harass a man, a woman harass a woman? These questions are explored in the following collection of readings.

Before Sexual Harassment

The term "sexual harassment" became part of our national dialogue after the Clarence Thomas confirmation hearings, but one of the first places it appeared was in a book called *The Harassed Worker* written by medical anthropologist Carroll Brodsky in 1976. She based her analysis on a thousand cases in which employees sought unemployment benefits because they were unable to work due to harassment. She saw the sexual nature of this harassment not only in the form of sexual advances but in any instance in which sexuality was used to torment those who felt "discomfort about discussing sex or relating sexually."

Legal scholars and social critics cite women's increased presence in the workplace after the women's movement of the 1960s for the recognition of this problem. Because of the ingrained nature of this behavior, it has taken since 1976 to legally address it.

We offer two selections to give our readers a sense of the way things were before the Clarence Thomas hearings and political correctness, first a short personal essay and then three cartoons from the archives of *The New Yorker* magazine.

A Long Road to Women's Freedom

Merrill Joan Gerber

This short essay by writer and teacher Gerber illustrates the secondary status often assigned to women prior to the feminist movement of the late 1960s. At that time, the term "sexual harassment" did not exist though you will discover that Gerber, in one of the incidents she describes, was a victim of sexual harassment.

When I went away to graduate school in 1959, I was required, as were all the students, to have a physical exam.

The women in my group lined up in the hall of the infirmary, wearing only their slips, and one by one we entered a room where a young male doctor examined us.

The doctor had us sit on a table and stood between our legs. While he ostensibly looked into our ears and felt for swollen glands, he rubbed his body against ours. He moved his stethoscope over our breasts for what seemed an exceedingly long time. Each girl, as she came out to the hall in a state of shock, recounted this nightmare to the others. We had no avenue of escape. Our clothes were in a different room.

We had no one to whom to report this—and anyway, what could we say? The exam was required, the man was a doctor, he had license to examine our bodies and he "didn't really do anything." The exam took only 10 or 15 minutes. We had to take it. It wouldn't kill us.

In 1960, after I finished the course work for my Masters degree, I applied for a grant to go on for my Ph.D. The head of my department at that time (a famous man, you would know his name) called me into his office and said, "Your grades are as good as any man's, you're just as smart. But you're only a girl (and only a writer) and the men students have more need of these grants than you do." I was shocked, but I nodded my head. I had to take it. It wouldn't kill me.

In 1962, when I was awarded a Stegner creative writing fellowship to Stanford University, my husband and I and our new baby arrived at the married student housing office. I went inside and requested an apartment that was available at low prices to married students.

I was told by the secretary, "We only offer housing to married male students and their families."

I went out to the car where my husband was waiting for me with the baby, and I took her in my arms to nurse her. As I sat there, thinking of what had transpired, I began to cry (female that I was), but at the same time I thought, "I don't have to take this! It is killing me!"

I marched back into the office with my baby in my arms, and said to the secretary, "I want to write a letter to the president. We have nowhere to live. I demand to have a student apartment."

She got me some stationery led me to a typewriter, and held my daughter while I wrote an impassioned letter to the president. Two days later we got a call that an arrangement had been made. We could have an apartment in Stanford Village (rent $52 a month.)

Thus I was able to stay on and study with Wallace Stegner, and that year (though I was "only a girl") sell my first story to *The New Yorker*.

It has taken too many years for us to figure out we don't have to tolerate, as a people, segregation, or discrimination, or, at another level, smoke being blown into our faces, or having to leave our young children alone for surgery in hospitals.

Let us hope that in the future it won't take as long as it has taken between the time we understand we deserve equal access to the entitlements of human life and the time it takes these freedoms to be afforded to all of us. Just remember that we don't have to take it. It could kill us.

TOPICS FOR DISCUSSION AND WRITING

1. Young women are often accused of taking for granted rights gained for them by the struggles and political protests of earlier generations of feminists. Do you think this is true? To aid you in your response to this question, list any changes that you are aware of in women's status since the sixties.

2. Interview a woman—a relative, friend, or coworker—who is at least 15 years older than you are on the subject of equal rights for women. Can she remember incidents of sexual discrimination in school, sports, or the workplace? Was she ever sexually harassed? Ask her to describe the changes in women's status that she has observed in the course of her lifetime. Write a short essay based on this interview and include your own reaction to it.

Three Cartoons from the Archives of The New Yorker *Magazine*

1. RICHARD TAYLOR, 1958

"Three more months and he reaches mandatory retirement age, thank God."

2. PETER ARNO, 1944

*"Young woman, do you realize my
time is worth thirty dollars a minute."*

3. WHITNEY DARROW, JR., 1954

*"Notice, class, how Angela circles, always
keeping the desk between them. . ."*

TOPICS FOR DISCUSSION AND WRITING

1. What do these cartoons suggest about relationships between men and women in the workplace of the 1940s and 50s? (See What Is an Inference? in Chapter 2.)

2. Collect from a current issue of the *The New Yorker* magazine cartoons that address relationships between men and women. What assumptions are they based on? How do these assumptions compare to those of the earlier cartoons? (See Hidden Assumptions in Argument in Chapter 3.)

A Legal History of Sexual Harassment

Catharine MacKinnon, a legal scholar and currently a professor of law at the University of Michigan Law School, wrote *Sexual Harassment of Working Women* in 1979. Jeffrey Toobin in "The Trouble with Sex," an essay included in this section, calls this book "one of the most influential law books of the late twentieth century." We include MacKinnon's introduction to that book in which she makes clear the connection between Title VII of The Civil Rights Act of 1964 and sexual harassment law, a fundamental connection to which several articles in this section refer. Toobin's aforementioned "The Trouble with Sex" brings us up-to-date on sexual harassment law. Law professor Vicki Shultz finds fault with sexual harassment law for its emphasis on sex rather than gender in her "Reconceptualizing Sexual Harassment." We also include a significant Supreme Court decision involving "hostile environment," *Harris v. Forklift* by Justice Sandra Day O'Connor, and then return to Vicki Shultz as she takes the court to task for its decision in her critique, "The Supreme Court's Decision in *Harris v. Forklift*." We conclude this brief legal history with an essay by Harvard professor Henry Louis Gates, Jr. in which he focuses on the semantics of sexual harassment.

Sexual Harassment of Working Women

Catharine MacKinnon

In this introduction to her seminal work on sexual harassment law, MacKinnon points out that sexual harassment follows from a "social context," from women's position in the work force and "the relationship between the sexes in American society as a whole." Keep in mind as you read this selection that is was written over twenty years ago and ask yourself if the conditions MacKinnon refers to have changed.

Intimate violation of women by men is sufficiently pervasive in American society[1] as to be nearly invisible. Contained by internalized and structural forms of power, it has been nearly inaudible. Conjoined with men's control over women's material survival, as in the home or on the job, or over women's learning and educational advancement in school, it has become institutionalized. Women employed in the paid labor force,[2] typically hired "as women," dependent upon their income and lacking job alternatives, are particularly vulnerable to intimate violation in the form of sexual abuse at work. In addition to being victims of the practice, working women have been subject to the social failure to recognize sexual harassment as an abuse at all. Tacitly, it has been both acceptable and taboo; acceptable for men to do, taboo for women to confront, even to themselves. But the systematic silence enforced by employment sanctions is beginning to be broken. The daily impact upon women's economic status and work opportunities, not to mention psychic health and self-esteem, is beginning to be explored, documented, and, increasingly, resisted.

Sexual harassment, most broadly defined, refers to the unwanted imposition of sexual requirements in the context of a relationship of unequal power. Central to the concept is the use of power derived from one social sphere to lever benefits or impose deprivations in another. The major dynamic is best expressed as the reciprocal enforcement of two inequalities. When one is sexual, the other material, the cumulative sanction is particularly potent. American society legitimizes male sexual dominance of women and employer's control of workers, although both forms of dominance have limits and exceptions. Sexual harassment of women in employment is particularly clear when male superiors on the job coercively initiate unwanted sexual advances to women employees; sexual pressures by male coworkers and customers, when condoned or encouraged by employers, might also be included. Lack of reciprocal feeling on the woman's part may be expressed by rejection or show of disinclination. After this, the advances may be repeated or intensified; often employment retaliation ensues. The material coercion behind the advances may remain implicit in the employer's position to apply it. Or it may be explicitly communicated through, for example, firing for sexual noncompliance or retention conditioned upon continued sexual compliance.

Sexual harassment may occur as a single encounter or as a series of incidents at work. It may place a sexual condition upon employment opportunities at a clearly defined threshold, such as hiring, retention, or advancement; or it may occur as a pervasive or continuing condition of the work environment. Extending along a continuum of severity and unwantedness, and depending upon the employment circumstances, examples include

> verbal sexual suggestions or jokes, constant leering or ogling, brushing against your body "accidentally," a friendly pat, squeeze or pinch or arm against you, catching you alone for a quick kiss, the indecent proposition backed by the threat of losing your job, and forced sexual relations.[3]

Complex forms include the persistent innuendo and the continuing threat which is never consummated either sexually or economically. The most straight-forward example is "put out or get out."

Typically, employers, husbands, judges, and the victims themselves have understood and dismissed such incidents as trivial, isolated, and "personal," or as universal "natural" or "biological" behaviors. This book interprets sexual ha-rassment in the context of women's work and sex roles, in which women as a group are seen to occupy a structurally inferior as well as distinct place. Sexual harassment is argued to derive its meaning and detrimental impact upon women not from personality or biology, but from this *social* context. The defin-ing dimensions of this social context are employer-employee relations (given women's position in the labor force) and the relationship between the sexes in American society as a whole, of which sexual relations are one expression.

If sexual harassment is a product of social factors, it might be expected to be a common occurrence. Preliminary indications, although tentative, suggest that it is pervasive, affecting in some form perhaps as many as seven out of ten women at some time in their work lives.[4] Yet sexual harassment of women in employment has provided explicit grounds for legal action in only a handful of cases.[5] Why has so apparently massive a social problem surfaced so seldom within the legal system? The reasons are probably not limited to the lack of le-gitimized or sympathetic channels for complaint short of the courts, or to women's learned reticence, enforced through fear of reprisals, although these would seem deterrent enough. It is probably not because the problem has been adequately handled socially. That there has not been *even one* reported case un-til very recently implicates the receptivity of the legal system.

Applicable legal concepts, with the social relations they reify, have tended to turn women's differences from men at once into special virtues and special re-straints. In effect, if not intent, the law has conceptualized women workers ei-ther in terms of their "humanity," which has meant characteristics women share with men, or in terms of their womanhood, which has meant their uniqueness. These two standards have been mutually exclusive. When women have been de-fined "as women" their human needs have often been ignored. An example is "protective" laws that, in shielding women's femininity from work stress, often excluded women from desperately needed jobs or job benefits.[6] Alternatively, when women have been analyzed as "human," their particular needs as women have often been ignored. An example is employment insurance plans that cover virtually every work disability (including many unique to men) except preg-nancy.[7] In a long-ignored analysis that can be applied to the legal conceptual-izations of women both "as human" and "as woman," the sociologist Georg Simmel observed:

> Man's position of power does not only assure his relative superiority over the woman, but it assures that his standards become generalized as generically hu-man standards that are to govern the behavior of men and women alike. . . . Almost all discussions of women deal only with what they are in relation to men in terms of real, ideal, or value criteria. Nobody asks what they are for themselves.[8]

On the whole, the legal doctrine of "sex discrimination" as interpreted by the courts has implicitly used such standards and criteria. In the analysis to follow, legal interpretations that give concrete meaning to the sex discrimination prohibition are reconsidered in their theoretical underpinnings, both for their potential in prohibiting sexual harassment and for their limitations, as the issue of sexual harassment reveals them.

The legal argument advanced by this book is that sexual harassment of women at work is sex discrimination in employment. The argument proceeds first by locating sexual harassment empirically in the context of women's work, showing that the structure of the work world women occupy makes them systematically vulnerable to this form of abuse. Sexual harassment is seen to be one dynamic which reinforces and expresses women's traditional and inferior role in the labor force. Next, reports of sexual harassment are analyzed with a focus upon the dimensions of the experience as women undergo it. This is followed by an account of those few legal cases that have raised the problem of sexual harassment at work. Once the problem has been defined within its material context and as experienced, and the legal attempts to address it have been initially explored, the central legal question can be confronted: is sexual harassment sex discrimination?

Two distinct concepts of discrimination, which I term the "differences" approach and the "inequality" approach, emerge as approaches to answering this question.[9] These conceptions are not strictly legal doctrines in the sense that judges recognize them as alternative views on the meaning of discrimination. Rather, they are the result of an attempt to think systematically about the broader concepts that underlie the logic and results of the discrimination cases as a whole, with particular attention to discrimination law's most highly developed application: the cases on race. Applied to sex, the two approaches flow from two underlying visions of the reality of sex in American society. The first approach envisions the sexes as socially as well as biologically *different* from one another, but calls impermissible or "arbitrary" those distinctions or classifications that are found preconceived and/or inaccurate. The second approach understands the sexes to be not simply socially differentiated but socially *unequal.* In this broader view, all practices which subordinate women to men are prohibited. The differences approach, in its sensitivity to disparity and similarity, can be a useful corrective to sexism; both women and men can be damaged by sexism, although usually it is women who are. The inequality approach, by contrast, sees women's situation as a structural problem of enforced inferiority that needs to be radically altered.

The view that discrimination consists in arbitrary differentiation dominates legal doctrine and scholarly thinking on the subject, reaching an epiphany in the Supreme Court's majority opinion in *Gilbert v. General Electric* (1977).[10] General Electric excluded only pregnancy and pregnancy-related disabilities from risks covered under an employee disability insurance plan. Had the case been approached with an awareness of the consequences of pregnancy and motherhood in the social inequality of the sexes, the Court would have found such a rule discriminatory. More narrowly, only women are excluded from insurance coverage against a detriment in employment due to temporary disability, creating unequal employment security on the basis of sex. Taking the differences approach, however, the Court thought that, although all pregnant persons are women, because pregnancy is unique (but not universal) to women, excluding it from coverage was not a distinction "based on sex," hence not discriminatory. Because women actually had *different* disabilities from men, it was not discriminatory to fail to insure them. By contrast, the result (although not every feature of the reasoning) in a 1978 case, *City of Los Angeles v. Manhart*,[11] illustrates the inequality approach. There, the Supreme Court found that requiring women to make larger contributions to their retirement plan was discriminatory, in spite of the proved sex difference that women on the average outlive men. A real difference between the sexes was not allowed to obscure or excuse socially unequal consequences.

Implicit in the distinction in approach are different conceptions of reasonable comparability: must women and men be able to be compared on the variable in question? Further, exactly what the variable in question is defined to be is decided by the approach which is taken. Under the differences approach, if the context is defined so that the sexes cannot be reasonably compared, discrimination cannot be seen to be sex-based. By contrast, the inequality approach comprehends that women and men may, due to sex or sexism, present noncomparabilities. In this view, lack of comparability is not a permissible basis for socially perpetuating women's disadvantages.

In terms of the social context discussed, and under the legal doctrines that context has produced, sexual harassment is argued in this book to be not simply abusive, humiliating, oppressive, and exploitative, but also to be sex discrimination in employment. Specifically, this is argued under Title VII of the Civil Rights Act of 1964, as amended, and the Equal Protection Clause of the Fourteenth Amendment. In relevant part, Title VII states:

> a. It shall be an unlawful employment practice for an employer—
>   1. to fail or refuse to hire or to discharge any individual, or otherwise to discriminate against any individual with respect to his compensation, terms, conditions, or privileges of employment because of such individual's. . . sex. . . ; or
>   2. to limit, segregate, or classify his employees or applicants for employment in any way which would deprive or tend to deprive any individual of employment opportunities or otherwise adversely affect his status as an employee, because of such individual's. . . sex.[12]

The Equal Protection Clause of the Fourteenth Amendment to the Constitution guarantees that no state shall "deny to any person within its jurisdiction the equal protection of the laws."[13] Sexual harassment is argued to be sex discrimination under these sections according to both the inequality approach, which is favored, and the differences approach, which is criticized.

Both arguments can be briefly stated. Under the inequality approach, sexual harassment is seen to disadvantage women as a gender, within the social context in which women's sexuality and material survival have been constructed and joined, to women's detriment. Under the differences approach, sexual harassment is sex discrimination *per se* because the practice differentially injures one gender-defined group in a sphere—sexuality in employment—in which the treatment of women and men can be compared. Sexuality is universal to women, but not unique to them. All women possess female sexuality, so the attribute in question is a gender characteristic. But men also possess sexuality and could be sexually harassed. When they are not, and women are, unequal treatment by gender is shown. If only men are sexually harassed, that is also arbitrary treatment based on sex, hence sex discrimination. If both sexes are, under this argument the treatment would probably not be considered gender-based, hence not sex discriminatory. Thus, sexual harassment of working women is treatment impermissibly based on sex under both approaches.

Sexual harassment is also discrimination in employment. Current cases are analyzed in which courts have found sexual harassment "personal," "biological," "not a policy," and thus (implicitly) not employment discrimination as well as not based on sex. These objections are found uncompelling, mutually inconsistent, without weight in analogous areas of law, and ideologically sexist. Although some of the cases which rely on these formulations have been reversed on appeal, most of these assertions, which represent deep and broadly held social views on women's sexuality, have not been squarely controverted by the courts and continue to arise in litigation. The Supreme Court has yet to hear its first sexual harassment case.

Opposing sexual harassment of women at work through the legal system deserves evaluation from a social standpoint. Sexual harassment is addressed in this book in terms of employment, and women's employment status in terms of sexual harassment, not because work is the only place women are sexually harassed nor because sexual harassment is women's only problem on the job. Legally, women are not arguably entitled, for example, to a marriage free of sexual harassment any more than to one free of rape, nor are women legally guaranteed the freedom to walk down the street or into a court of law without sexual innuendo. In employment, the government promises more.

Work is critical to women's survival and independence. Sexual harassment exemplifies and promotes employment practices which disadvantage women in work (especially occupational segregation) and sexual practices which intimately degrade and objectify women. In this broader perspective, sexual harassment at work undercuts woman's potential for social equality in two interpenetrated ways: by using her employment position to coerce her sexually, while using her sexual position to coerce her economically. Legal recognition that sexual harassment is sex discrimination in employment would help women break the bond between material survival and sexual exploitation. It would support and legitimize women's economic equality and sexual self-determination at a point at which the two are linked.

NOTES

1. Sexism is by no means unique to American culture. This discussion, for purposes of application to American law, focuses upon its forms in this culture.

2. Houseworkers (paid and unpaid) are excluded from this discussion of working women not because I think they do not work, nor because they do not suffer from sexual harassment. Most are not covered by Title VII's limitation to workplaces with fifteen or more employees. For one review of quantitative studies which discuss the contribution of unpaid housework to the Gross National Product, see Juanita Kreps, *Sex in the Marketplace: American Women at Work* (Baltimore: Johns Hopkins University Press, 1971), chap. 2.

3. "Sexual Harassment on the Job: Questions and Answers" (Ithaca, N.Y.: Working Women United Institute, 1975 [mimeograph]).

4. Lin Farley, testimony given before the Commission on Human Rights of the City of New York, Hearings on Women in Blue-Collar, Service and Clerical Occupations, "Special Disadvantages of Women in Male-Dominated Work Settings," April 21, 1975 (mimeograph). The data are based upon the study reported at chap. 3. *infra*, note 5.

5. *Barnes v. Costle*, 13 F.E.P. Cases 123 (D.D.C. 1974), *rev'd*, 561 F.2d 983 (D.C. Cir. 1977); *Williams v. Saxbe*, 413 F. Supp. 654 (D.D.C. 1976) *sub nom. Williams v. Bell*, Nos. 76–1833, 76–1994 (D.C. Cir. September 19, 1978) (slip opinion); *Corne v. Bausch & Lomb*, 390 F. Supp. 161 (D. Ariz 1975), *vacated and remanded*, 562 F. 2d 55 (9th Cir. 1977); *Miller v. Bank of America*, 418 F. Supp. 233 (N.D. Cal. 1976), *appeal docketed*, No. 76–3344 (9th Cir. 1976); *Tomkins v. Public Service Electric & Gas Co.*, 422 F. Supp. 553 (D.N.J. 1976), *rev'd*, 568 F.2d 1044 (3rd Cir. 1977); *Garber v. Saxon Business Products, Inc.*, 552 F. 2d 1032 (4th Cir. 1977); *Munford v. James T. Barnes & Co.*, 441 F. Supp. 459 (E.D. Mich. 1977); *Elliott v. Emery Air Freight*, No. C-C–75–76 (W.D.N.C. June 21, 1977): *Heelan v. Johns-Manville Corp.*, 451 F. Supp. 1382 (D. Colo. 1978). A case of sexual harassment brought as a contract action is *Monge v. Beebe Rubber*, 316 A. 2d 549 (N.H. 1974). Three unreported actions for unemployment compensation are based upon allegations of sexual harassment. *In re Nancy J. Fillhouer*, App. No. 75–5225, California Unemployment Insurance Appeals Board (July 25, 1975); *In re Carmita Wood*, App. No. 207, 958, New York State Department of Labor, Unemployment Insurance Appeals Board (October 6, 1975); *Cathy Hamilton v. Appleton Electric Co.*, E.R.D. Case 7301025, State of Wisconsin Department of Industry, Labor and Human Relations (October 1, 1976). In education, see *Alexander v. Yale*, 459 F. Supp.1 (D. Conn. 1977), *supplemented*, June 30, 1978.

6. Ann Hill, "Protective Labor Legislation for Women: Its Origin and Effect" (unpublished paper, Yale Law School, 1970); Ann Hill, "Protection of Women Workers and the Courts: A Legal Case History" (unpublished paper prepared for the Conference on Protective Legislation and Women's Employment, Smith College, Northampton, Massachusetts, November 3–5, 1977); Ronnie Steinberg Ratner, "The Paradox of Protection: Changes in Hours Legislation in the United States" (unpublished paper, prepared for the same conference.)

7. The Supreme Court has held that disability insurance plans that do not cover pregnancy or pregnancy-related disabilities in employment are not illegal sex discrimination. *Geduldig v. Aiello*, 417 U.S. 484 (1974) (state plans, under the Fourteenth Amendment); *Gilbert v. General Electric*, 429 U.S. 125 (1976) (private plans, under Title VII). In October 1978, the House of Representatives agreed to the conference report on S. 995, a bill to amend Title VII to prohibit discrimination on the basis of pregnancy as sex discrimination. *Congressional Record Daily Digest*, vol. 124, no. 168, part V, October 14, 1978, D 1574 (*Congressional Record* at H13494–H13496). Congress (with the approval of the President) can thus modify the result of *Gilbert*, but it cannot so directly alter the reasoning on the meaning of sex discrimination which produced it. (The Congressional action also leaves the *Geduldig* result standing.)

8. Georg Simmel, *Philosophische Kultur* (Leipzig: Werner Klinkhardt, 1911), quoted in Lewis A. Coser, "Georg Simmel's Neglected Contributions to the Sociology of Women," *Signs: Journal of Women in Culture and Society*, vol. 2, no. 4 (Summer 1977), at 872, 873.

9. Professor Fiss, in a recent article, develops a similar distinction in his examination of equal protection cases on race. Owen Fiss, "Groups and the Equal Protection Clause,"5 *Philosophy and Public Affairs* 108 (1976). His article provided labels for the two theories and advanced and clarified them. The two theories, as I develop them, differ from his in several respects. Most obvious is that he does not directly consider whether women could be a "disadvantaged" group. The essential purpose of his theory is to justify affirmative action for blacks in higher education. The outside requirements for a group to be "disadvantaged" are not clear, especially where the criteria of biology and mutability are involved. At one point, apparently stating reasons that qualify the case for some groups to be considered disadvantaged groups, he states that "some . . . socially disadvantaged groups can be defined in terms of characteristics that do not have biological roots and that are not immutable; the Clause might protect certain language groups and aliens." This clouds whether it is biology and immutability that qualify blacks as disadvantaged (and would also qualify women), or whether, as he more generally seems to think, blacks are disadvantaged because of their social characteristics. He continues, " the court may even develop variable standards of protection. . . . it may tolerate disadvantaging practices that would not be tolerated if the group was a 'pure' specially disadvantaged group. Jews or women may be entitled to less protection than American Indians, though nonetheless entitled to some protection" (155) (citations omitted). Treatment of the poor, a group that is, after all, totally socially created, is grudging to the point of exclusion. However strategic this may have been—in order to promote affirmative action for blacks, it is necessary to convince courts that they are not opening the door to redress of all inequalities—it does not bode well for women. His interpretation of equal protection disadvantagement would allow a legislative judgment that "the plight of the poor may be bad but, so the legislator or administrator should be allowed to say, not as bad as that of the blacks" (162). Given that the majority of blacks are poor, this recognizes as disadvantagement only that poverty which is attributable to racial, as distinct from economic, causes, a difficult distinction to make. Since poverty is not seen to be completely all-pervasive, cultural, disabling, maintained by false consciousness, and as difficult to change as the meaning of being black, it seems unlikely that women would fare well under this interpretation.

10. 429 U.S. 125 (1976).

11. *City of Los Angeles, Department of Water and Power, et al. v. Manhart, et al.,* 98 S. Ct. 1370 (1978).

12. Title VII of the Civil Rights Act of 1964, as amended by the Equal Employment Opportunity Act of 1972, Section 703 (a) (1) and (2), codified at 42 U.S.C. Section 2000 e (2) (a) (1) and (2). (Hereinafter, "Title VII" refers to this quoted section, unless specifically noted otherwise.) Section (b) applies the quoted section to employment agencies, (c) to labor organizations, and (d) to training programs. Section (e) provides for an exception under which sex may be shown a bona fide occupational qualification; Section (h) excepts bona fide seniority and merit systems; Section (j) prohibits "preferential treatment" based upon existing numerical or percentage imbalance.

13. *United States Constitution,* Amendment XIV.

TOPICS FOR DISCUSSION AND WRITING

1. MacKinnon claims that "working women have been subject to the social failure to recognize sexual harassment as an abuse at all."

How do the previous two selections, Merrill Joan Gerber's "A Long Road to Women's Freedom," and the cartoons from *The New Yorker* magazine support MacKinnon's claim?

2. How does MacKinnon define sexual harassment? What is your evaluation of this definition? (See Logical Definition in Chapter 5.)

3. What connection is MacKinnon trying to establish between sexual harassment and Title VII of the Civil Rights Act of 1964 and the Equal Protection Clause of the Fourteenth Amendment?

The Trouble with Sex

Jeffrey Toobin

Jeffrey Toobin is a lawyer, a legal analyst for ABC News, and the author of two books —*A Young Lawyer's First Case; The United States v. Oliver North* and *The Run of His Life: The People v. O.J. Simpson*. In this essay he provides us with both a history and a critique of sexual harassment law, referring extensively to the work of legal scholars Catherine McKinnon and Vicki Shultz, whose writings are included in this section.

Only a month ago, it would have been difficult to imagine a more luridly embarrassing accusation against a President of the United States than the one at the center of the case of *Paula Corbin Jones v. William Jefferson Clinton*. But that stew, however unsavory, was still simmering on what is known in Washington as the back burner. Then, on January 20th, the news broke of Monica Lewinsky's tape-recorded descriptions of her purported affair with the President. In a flash, the sexual pot boiled over, blew its lid, and left every one in the kitchen scalded and dripping.

Jones claims that Clinton grossly propositioned her; Lewinsky has apparently said that Clinton asked her to lie under oath about their relationship. But two sets of accusations have a good deal in common, beyond the fact that both allege spectacular sexual impropriety. They both emerge out of the law of sexual harassment—a legal area that has come to be invoked almost automatically whenever a case involves a sexual intrigue (real or imagined, consummated or thwarted) between two people at different levels of a chain of workplace command. In legal if not Biblical terms, Paula begat Monica.

As is demonstrated by the history of scandal from Helen of Troy to Monica of Beverly Hills, sex has a way of befogging the higher intellectual faculties; and, as is demonstrated by the prosperity of the legal profession, the law in general is not always a model of unambiguous clarity. Little wonder, then, that the legal doctrine of sexual harassment is mired in murk. And now that the murk is threatening to engulf the White House itself, the moment seems right to pause and examine just what the law is and how it got that way.

Sexual harassment is a form of discrimination. Perpetrators discriminate against their victims—by punishing or threatening to punish them, directly or indirectly, if they don't submit sexually, or simply by making life so difficult that victims can't do their work. This may sound simple, but the doctrine of sexual harassment, in its relatively brief life, has become one of the most politicized areas in American law. As always, the law reflects the times. Sexual-harassment law came into being at a time of great change and uncertainty in relations between the sexes. But, like most laws, sexual harassment law works best as a crude tool to deal with the most extreme and obvious cases. At other times, the result can be chaos.

No law, of course, can sort out the explosive relationships between men and women—not even in the relatively structured environment of an office. But in the nineteen-seventies the creators of the doctrine of sexual harassment, who had a clear political agenda as well as a legal one, thought otherwise. Their work blurred the difference between consensual sex and harassment, suggesting that sex between a woman and a man in the workplace almost inevitably entailed a form of coercion, generally from a man in a position of authority. For the first time, women could use the courts to fight an ancient form of oppression. But there was an unintended consequence of the emphasis on sexual advances as a form of discrimination. While feminists were arguing that there is no sex without harassment, the conservative judges who interpreted the law tended to respond that there is no harassment without sex. As a result, many judges have ruled against women who have suffered terrible mistreatment in the workplace—just not of an overtly sexual kind. As it stands now, sexual harassment law can punish innocent parties and it can deny relief to women who have been discriminated against.

The Paula Jones case is a good example of the confusion engendered by sexual harassment litigation. Is the law intended to protect women from sexual impropriety or from job discrimination? Jones's lawsuit rests almost entirely on the former proposition. Her case seems noticeably slim on evidence that she suffered any kind of professional setback as a result of her encounter with Clinton. The President's lawyers will shortly have their final chance to ask Judge Susan Webber Wright to dismiss Jones's case before it goes to trial. (That motion was originally due on March 13th, but last week the Clinton team asked Judge Wright to move up both this date and the start of the trial, which had been set for May 27th.) In essence, the President's motion for summary judgment will argue that even if Jones is telling the truth about what went on in Little Rock's Excelsior Hotel on May 8, 1991, those facts do not amount to sexual harassment because she wasn't fired or demoted or deprived of any benefits or promotions that were due her.

The Supreme Court has already decided to hear four sexual-harassment cases this term. On January 23rd, three days into the current scandal, the Court agreed to address perhaps the most important of them. A woman named Kimberly Ellerth says that she quit her job at Burlington Industries after a vice-president at the company made sexual advances toward her and threatened to hurt her chances at the company, although his threats were never carried out and she didn't complain to the company at the time. Can an employee sue for sexual harassment if she rebuffed her supervisor's advances but suffered no adverse consequences on the job as a result? The decision in this case may clarify—or further muddle—a critical area of the law.

It would be comforting to think that the focus of all the energy spinning out of the Jones case could create the pressure to channel the law in a more productive direction. To judge from how the story has unfolded so far, however, a bad situation seems about to get worse.

Modern sexual-harassment law was invented by accident. During the debate over the Civil Rights Act of 1964, one of the leading reactionaries of the twentieth-century House of Representatives, Howard W. Smith, a Dixiecrat from Virginia, filed a last-minute amendment to try to kill the bill. Title VII of that act sought to ban racial discrimination in employment, and on February 8th of that year Smith rose in the House to propose that the act ban discrimination on the basis of sex as well as race. In his remarks in the well of the House, Smith suggested snidely that his amendment would protect the "right of every female to have a husband of her own" and "protect our spinster friends in their right to a nice husband and family."

"The Southerners thought if they could put sex in there, it would drag down the whole bill," Norbert Schlei, a senior official in the Justice Department at the time, told me recently. Schlei, who was in the House gallery on the day that Smith proposed his amendment, recalled, "They thought it was a joke. They didn't think there was any discrimination against women that mattered. They were laughing down on the floor as they were talking about it."

But Smith's proposal drew an unexpected reaction from the few women who had seats in Congress at the time. Martha Griffiths, a Michigan Democrat, backed the amendment by the Virginia segregationist, and so did several other liberals. Following a brief but passionate debate, the Smith amendment came up for a vote, and it passed, 168 to 133. "Most of the people who voted for the amendment actually wound up voting against the whole bill, which Smith was trying to kill," Schlei said. "The part about sex never really got debated after that one day, and it wound up becoming part of the law. But the last thing Smith wanted to do was give women any rights."

Title VII came into being when the nation nearly went to war over race. Sex fit into the picture awkwardly, if at all. There were no clear and undeniable biological differences between the races, but there were plenty of differences between the sexes—the ability to get pregnant, for one—that the courts had to struggle to address under Title VII. Furthermore, the law changed at a time when relations between men and women were undergoing a volcanic upheaval. Women were not only pouring into the workforce in dramatically larger numbers; they were changing the social dynamics there, too. As more women arrived, there was still sexual harassment. But there was also sex, which was welcomed by some women as well as by some men. Above all, the coming of age of the baby boomers created a social and political transformation, and the legal system tried gamely to keep pace. Sorting all this out was a task of some subtlety —a task that Catharine MacKinnon decided to take on.

MacKinnon holds joint appointments at the law schools of the Universities of Michigan and Chicago. Tall, slim, regal in bearing, and possessed of a Sontag-style stripe of gray in a mane of reddish-blond hair, she has always been a provocateur, and has had a far more public and controversial career than most law professors. (In the early nineteen-nineties, when she was widely known as one of the country's most articulate and militant feminists, she was engaged to the Freud scholar Jeffrey Masson.) MacKinnon has no affection for reporters, since, she says, they have consistently misrepresented her work—especially her crusade against pornography, through much of which her comrade-in-arms has been the essayist and critic Andrea Dworkin. "It became extremely important to publish only defamatory statements about me," MacKinnon told me recently with some bitterness. "Some people have even said I didn't create the law of sexual harassment."

MacKinnon's ideas came very clearly from a specific time and place—New Haven in the mid-nineteen-seventies. Like Berkeley and Cambridge, the city had an unending supply of smart and motivated young people arriving every year. In 1970, one of those new arrivals was MacKinnon, who enrolled as both a graduate student in political science and as a student at Yale Law School. The politics of the time had a brittle edge in New Haven. In 1971, a rancorous trial of the Black Panther leader Bobby Seale on murder and kidnapping charges ended in a hung jury, and the aftermath of the case left a residue of suspicion between students and law-enforcement officials that lingered for years. In addition, the first women graduated from Yale College that year, and co-education was met on campus with less than universal support. The passionately committed and endlessly energetic MacKinnon thrived in this volatile mix. Thanks to her, Yale would become a kind of laboratory for the invention and application of the doctrine of sexual harassment. (Coincidentally, three other pivotal figures in the history of sexual harassment—Bill Clinton, Clarence Thomas, and Anita Hill—were also law students at Yale during the nineteen-seventies.)

MacKinnon spent some seven years at Yale. She worked toward both a Ph.D. and a law degree, taught a series of undergraduate courses, created the first women's-studies course at the college, worked with unions, and co-founded a progressive collective in which she practiced law with a handful of like-minded young attorneys. In addition, she travelled around the country as a guitar-playing folksinger. According to MacKinnon, she learned at least as much from being on the road as she did in the classroom. "We were performing at all the women's centers, and they'd put us on their lists to get their newsletters," MacKinnon told me recently. "The only real thinking I was coming across in those days was in the newsletters. We did a music night at Cornell, and sometime in 1975 we got a newsletter from the women's center there, and it had a story about a woman named Carmita Wood. She had been a secretary in a laboratory at Cornell, and her employer had been all over her sexually, and she quit. She applied for workers' comp, but they told her that since her reasons for leaving the job were 'personal' she wasn't eligible. The newsletter asked, 'Does anyone have any ideas for Carmita?' When I read that, my mind just went. This is it. It was an epiphany experience. Everything I had heard about what sex inequality is, is not it. This is it."

Of course, MacKinnon was not the first woman to recognize the phenomenon that came to be called sexual harassment. (The first use of that precise term seems to have been at a 1975 conference at Cornell when a group of feminists based in Ithaca held a "Speak-Out on Sexual Harassment.") A pioneering survey of working women which was published by *Redbook* magazine in 1976 raised the issue before a mass audience, and two years later an activist from Ithaca named Lin Farley wrote a book on the subject, entitled "Sexual Shakedown." But, in the mid-seventies, very few women successfully sued their employers under Title VII for sexual harassment they had suffered on the job. As in Carmita Wood's case, the courts said that sexual overtures from superiors were "personal," and did not constitute sex discrimination.

"The courts had said the ability to get pregnant was just a difference between men and women, and where there's a difference you can't have sex discrimination," MacKinnon explained. "I realized sexual harassment was really the same thing. It was a difference between men and women in their working lives. But these differences did not mean that sex discrimination could not exist. It was just the opposite. In these differences were the very essence of sex discrimination."

When MacKinnon had nearly completed a paper on sexual harassment which she was preparing for an independent-study course at Yale, she heard about a lawsuit at the federal appeals court in Washington that raised precisely the issues she was addressing. In *Barnes v Costle*, Paulette Barnes, a clerk at the Environmental Protection Agency, had sued her employer under Title VII because, she said, her supervisor had retaliated against her for her refusal to sleep with him. The district court had dismissed her case on the familiar ground that the harassment was personal. MacKinnon gave a copy of her paper to a law clerk on the case in the federal appeals court, and, she claims, "it became the basis of the decision." In 1977, the three-judge panel on the case reversed the district court and produced, as MacKinnon later wrote, "the most explicit treatment of the issues to date and a holding that sexual harassment is sex discrimination in employment." (The late George MacKinnon, Catharine's father—and a conservative Republican—was one of the judges on the panel.)

MacKinnon turned the paper into a book, "Sexual Harassment of Working Women," which was published in 1979. Now in its twelfth paperback printing, it surely ranks as one of the most influential law books of the late twentieth century. (On February 27th, Yale will host a conference of sexual-harassment scholars marking the upcoming twentieth anniversary of its publication.) Dense, closely argued, and relentlessly polemical, MacKinnon's book is dedicated to the proposition that "sexual harassment, the experience, is becoming 'sexual harassment,' the legal claim." The book even includes a primer for lawyers to use in writing briefs to bring sexual harassment cases under Title VII. MacKinnon defines two categories of sexual harassment. The first is "quid pro quo" harassment, which is, she writes, "the more or less explicit exchange: the woman must comply sexually or forfeit an employment benefit. . . 'put out or get out.'" The second category covers "hostile environment" cases, of which she writes, "Less clear, and undoubtedly more pervasive, is the situation in which sexual harassment simply makes the work environment unbearable."

During the late seventies and early eighties, MacKinnon's bottom line—that sexual harassment is a form of discrimination—was evolving into conventional wisdom. In 1977, Anne Simon, a member of MacKinnon's law collective, filed a lawsuit that forced Yale to establish guidelines for sexual harassment on campus—and nearly every university in the country eventually followed suit. Several other appellate courts adopted the reasoning of the Barnes v. Costle appellate decision, and in 1980 the Equal Employment Opportunity Commission issued the first comprehensive guidelines on gender-based harassment. Those guidelines defined such harassment in part as unwelcome "sexual advances, requests for sexual favors, and other verbal or physical conduct of a sexual nature. "The women who were groped and humiliated in the "boom boom room" of Smith Barney's Garden City, New York, office—or the employees of Mitsubishi's Normal, Illinois, plant who say that their male superiors taped some women to factory carts and threatened to kill others during oral sex—have been, in effect, working from a template drawn by MacKinnon.

As the years passed, however, more judges and scholars came to regard the underlying basis of MacKinnon's position as idiosyncratic. In her book and in her subsequent work, including her writings on pornography, MacKinnon portrays men and women in a constant state of war—a war that the men are winning. MacKinnon has long argued that in a patriarchal society, the notion of consent has no real meaning for women. The real question, as she put it in her book, is "whether women have a chance, structurally speaking and as a normal matter, even to consider whether they want to have sex or not." In the light of the argument of her book, MacKinnon's question is clearly rhetorical. But her implication is clear: consent is a myth; all sex is harassment.

The courts would never go this far. Although they never adopted the extreme definition of all sex as harassment, they did deem sexual overtures to be the sine qua non of sexual-harassment claims. In case after case, judges rejected women's claims of sex-based discrimination unless they could prove that their male bosses made sexual advances or sexual remarks toward them. In one notorious 1982 case in Rhode Island, a judge dismissed a sexual-harassment claim even though male workers sabotaged a women's projects, interfered with her efforts to do her job, and disparaged the efforts of women generally in the workplace. The court concluded that such conduct did not constitute "sexual harassment as that term has come to be defined." There had to be a sexual come-on if conduct was to be a violation of the law.

The early debates over sexual-harassment law went on in the relative privacy of little-publicized court decisions and little-read law-review articles, but then came the epic Clarence Thomas-Anita Hill hearings before the Senate Judiciary Committee, in 1991, and the subject was introduced to the general public. The introduction, however, came in a very peculiar way. At the hearings, both Thomas's supporters and his opponents agreed that if Hill was telling the truth about what had occurred during her tenure as Thomas's assistant, the nominee was unquestionably guilty of sexual harassment. The Republicans who sponsored Thomas's nomination to the Supreme Court chose not to quibble about the definition of sexual harassment but, rather, just to attack Hill's version of the facts.

As a result, Hill's accusations became known as the paradigmatic case of sexual harassment, But, as many feminist scholars acknowledge today, the case against Thomas would have been a close one. His alleged requests for dates and his occasional bizarre sex talk may have amounted only to distasteful but legal office banter. In theory, Hill could have claimed that Thomas created a hostile work environment. But to do so she would have had to prove, as the Supreme Court put it in 1986, that Thomas went so far as to "alter the conditions of [the victim's] employment and create an abusive working environment"—a difficult task. Yet the distinction was never aired before the public during the hearings. The message that emerged was that risqué banter and suggestive overtures were what made harassment sexual. What mattered, it seemed, was the grossness of Thomas's conduct, and not his impact on Hill's ability to do her job.

In this way, then, the Thomas hearings may have made a case like Paula Jones's inevitable. Jones accused Governor Clinton of bad behavior. But would Clinton's alleged behavior have made Jones a victim of employment discrimination? In Jones's initial complaint, filed in May of 1994, she asserted that Clinton's solicitation served "to impose a hostile work environment" on her. Jones mentioned quid-pro-quo harassment in that complaint, but she made a clearer claim of retribution in an amended complaint, which was filed in October of 1997. The amended complaint says that Jones was denied "appointments, benefits, advancements, raises [and] promotions. . . because she would not accede to Defendant Clinton's repeated solicitations of sex from her." (Clinton's lawyers will surely argue that, since Jones added the claim only last fall, it apparently took her more than six years to realize that she had been retaliated against.)

At first, Clinton's defenders took much the same tack as Thomas's supporters. In public, Robert S. Bennett, Clinton's lead lawyer, stressed that Jones's claims were simply false. There is a sign, however, that the magnitude of the Lewinsky disclosures has prompted Bennett to recast his approach. In view of Lewinsky's allegations, a jury may be more inclined to believe that Clinton did proposition Jones. So Bennett may be backtracking to a position that asserts that, even if Clinton did behave inappropriately, Jones suffered no legal harm. In the motion, filed last Monday, asking for an earlier trial date in the Jones case, Bennett wrote, "Paula Jones did not suffer any detriment at the hands of President Clinton; she cannot prove either *quid pro quo* or hostile environment sexual harassment; she cannot prove there was a conspiracy between Mr. Clinton and Trooper Danny Ferguson to deprive her of her civil rights; and she did not experience severe emotional distress as a result of anything President Clinton is alleged to have done to her." In this litany, Bennett conspicuously omits the defense's primary claim that Clinton did not proposition Jones. The irony is that such an approach may have been the right one all along. A proposition alone isn't—and shouldn't be—sex discrimination.

In *Burlington Industries v. Ellerth*, the case that the Supreme Court recently agreed to decide, the question presented is whether a woman is entitled to damages if she quits a company after a supervisor made sexual advances toward her but before she either submitted to them or suffered untoward consequences for refusing them. The case raises a fundamental question in sexual-harassment law: Should the law presume that a sexual advance causes harm or should it require some proof that a woman has suffered injury?

Yale for its part, has just taken another look at questions of this sort. It has done so in the most difficult of contexts—regarding sex between teachers and students. Of course, the rules governing such relationships do not precisely duplicate those concerning employers and subordinates. Yale, in view of its quasi-parental role, took what seems to be, on the surface of it, a commonsensical step. Last November, the university officially banned all sexual relations between teachers and their students. But in a painful and public controversy over its sexual-harassment policy, Yale also discovered the difficulties of regulating consensual sex.

In January of 1996, a Yale freshman whom I will call Nancy Smith was unhappy at the school and was thinking of dropping out. She sought the advice of a resident dean in her dormitory, and in the course of her conversation with him she said that during her first semester at Yale, when she was seventeen, she had an affair with her mathematics professor, Jay Jorgenson, which began after he started giving her special assistance in his class "Introduction to Differential Equations." Smith acknowledged from the start that she was a willing participant in any relationship she had with Jorgenson, but Yale launched a sexual harassment investigation nonetheless. It was conducted by the Grievance Board for Student Complaints of Sexual Harassment, the same administrative body that the university had established in response to the feminist law collective's court victory of two decades earlier. The inquiry was especially tricky because Jorgenson denied that he had any sexual relationship with Smith. So the members of the board recovered E-mail between Smith and Jorgenson from Yale's central computer and pondered the significance of a message by the professor which concluded "xoxoxo"; they interviewed Smith's roommates and discussed whether Jorgenson was the mysterious "Alan" who sometimes left phone messages; they asked, as the board put it in its final report, "if there were any physical characteristics that [Smith] could describe which would indicate that they had had an intimate relationship."

Ultimately, the board concluded that Smith and Jorgenson had indeed had sexual intercourse. But Richard H. Brodhead, the dean of Yale College and the ultimate arbiter in the case, didn't quite concur. In a letter to Jorgenson dated September 16, 1996, he wrote that the professor and student had had a "sexually-charged relationship," but he withheld final judgement on whether they had actually had sex with one another. Still, Brodhead concluded that "your conduct constituted sexual harassment, and it would have done so whether or not you and [Smith] engaged in sexual intercourse." The dean issued a "stern reprimand" for the professor's "deeply inappropriate" behavior.

In the fall of 1996, Smith returned for her sophomore year and discovered that the board had vindicated her and reprimanded Jorgenson, but that he was still teaching a class of undergraduates. "It wasn't my intention to ruin Jay's plans and his whole life and publicity humiliate him," she told me, "but I didn't think he should be teaching." So Smith talked to the Yale *Daily News,* and it broke her story on October 25th. The article, written by a student named Erin White, identified Jorgenson and withheld Smith's name (as I have done, following journalistic convention), but it quoted "the student" as saying, "I felt so betrayed, so used. . . . He's going to Ohio next year, and he's just going to cut his swath across campus there too." On the day the story appeared, Jorgenson checked into the psychiatric ward of St. Raphael's Hospital, in New Haven, where he remained for four days.

At the time Smith filed her complaint, Jay Jorgenson was thirty-two years old, held a Ph.D. from Stanford, and was a highly promising mathematician. He had written or collaborated on more than twenty scholarly papers, and he had accepted a tenure-track position at Ohio State University, which was to begin in the 1997 spring semester. Beyond his scholarly work, during his seven years as an assistant professor at Yale Jorgenson had earned a reputation as an extraordinary teacher. When news of the accusations broke, scores of faculty colleagues and students rushed to defend him publicly. Still, shortly after Ohio State learned of the reprimand by Brodhead, the university withdrew its offer to Jorgenson. He has sent applications to more than thirty universities but has received no other offers. When I met with Jorgenson, in New York, he was looking for a job in the financial sector. "As far as I am concerned, my academic career is over, " he told me.

In response to the publicity stirred by the Jorgenson case, the provost of the university appointed a committee to revise and clarify the campus rules on sexual harassment. At the time, the rules had been somewhat ambiguous, prohibiting only such relationships between faculty and students as "unreasonably interfer[e] with an individual's work or academic performance or creat[e] as intimidating or hostile academic or work environment." In the new guidelines, which were issued last November, teachers are officially forbidden to have sexual relationships with students over whom they have or are likely to have a supervisory relationship—"regardless of whether the relationship is consensual." According to William Sledge, the professor of psychiatry who chaired the committee that drafted the new policy, "the trend in universities around the country is toward prohibiting all student-faculty sex." The reasoning behind Yale's new policy was nearly a word-for-word parsing of MacKinnon's almost two-decade-old work: "The unequal institutional power inherent in this relationship heightens the vulnerability of the student and the potential for coercion." Between students and their teachers at Yale, there is now, officially, no sex without harassment.

For better or worse, teachers have been sleeping with their students since the days of Plato; presumably, notwithstanding the new rules, they still occasionally will. Given the current punitive climate surrounding the subject of sexual harassment, professors who are found to be in these relationships can expect, like Jay Jorgenson, to have their careers destroyed. This will be even more true now that Yale and other universities are embracing categorical prohibitions on student-faculty sex. But it is worth pausing to consider the costs of policing consensual sex. They include expanding the university's responsibility for private, intimate conduct; they institutionalize the university's role as bedroom snoop; and, perhaps most important, they apply the rules of sexual harassment—a law that is supposed to concern discrimination—to what are often victimless crimes.

The frenzy of public interest in the details of Clinton's alleged encounter with Paula Jones (and his possible relationship with Monica Lewinsky) may still drown out any serious discussion of the real meaning of sexual harassment. But that would be too bad, because some of the most thoughtful and original work in the field of sexual harassment is going on right now. This work, too, is being done at Yale, in one of the turreted Gothic towers of the law-school building, but its focus and its emphasis differ considerably from those of the administrators who have just banned all faculty-student sex. In April of this year, a law professor named Vicki Schultz will publish a groundbreaking article in the Yale Law Journal entitled "Reconceptualizing Sexual Harassment," which is part of a large-scale reassessment of the law in light of the Thomas-Hill case. At the heart of her work is a deceptively simple idea. It is discrimination—not sex—that the law ought to be preventing.

Schultz, the forty-year-old daughter of a hairdresser and an Air Force enlisted man, has the manner of a pleasantly strict elementary-school teacher— friendly, almost bubbly, but with a noticeable aversion to cant and imprecision. Instead of clerking on an appellate court, she spent two years as a clerk on a federal district court, watching jury trials. Instead of writing appellate briefs, she spent three years trying civil-rights cases in the Department of Justice during the Reagan Administration. Schultz told me that her experiences "gave me a fundamental interest in and respect for facts. If you want to understand how a law works, you can't just look at what the Supreme Court or any court is doing but how it actually works in the real world."

Schultz researched sexual-harassment law for four years, and she learned that it was not functioning successfully in the real world. Her critique doesn't fit into any clear ideological pigeon-hole. She devotes a substantial part of her article to debunking the notion that there is no sex without harassment. "By focusing on sexual advances as the quintessential harassment, the paradigm encourages courts to extend protection to women for the wrong reasons," she writes. "Rather than emphasizing the use of harassment law to promote women's empowerment and equality as workers, it subtly appeals to judges to protect women's sexual virtue or sensibilities." Schultz argues that sex is a right—and a responsibility—that women themselves must decide how to exercise.

Yet Schultz also demolishes the claim that there is no harassment without sex. Such a view, she writes, seriously understates the amount of real sexual discrimination in the work place: "Much of what is harmful to women is difficult to construe as 'sexual' in design." She told me, "The focus of harassment law shouldn't be on sexuality as such. We should worry more about making sure women have opportunities in the workplace and less about regulating who sleeps with whom. We can't pretend that all sexual interaction is non-consensual, and we shouldn't try to stop sexual interaction that really is consensual."

Unlike most law-review articles, Schultz's is full of actual stories having to do with working women. She quotes a welder from Mary Walshok's 1981 book, "Blue-Collar Women," who said, "It's a form of harassment every time I pick up a sledgehammer and that prick laughs at me, you know. It's a form of harassment when a journeyman is supposed to be training me and it's real clear to me that he does not want to give me any information whatsoever." Schultz describes the case of Margaret Reynolds, an electrician who was appointed subforeman of a crew at the Atlantic City Convention Center. Her male subordinates would not work with her and laughed while she unloaded heavy boxes. She endured verbal abuse and obscene gestures. A union official refused to arrange for locks to be put on the shower that she and another woman on her work crew used. When the Miss America Pageant came to town, an exhibitor asked that Reynolds be removed from the floor—"Apparently the incongruity between the images of the pageant contestants and the tradeswomen was too much for the exhibitor," Schultz observes—and Reynolds was replaced by a male co-worker. She lost her hostile-work-environment claim, because, the court said, in essence, "Not enough sex."

What Schultz is doing is returning sexual harassment to its roots as an anti-discrimination law. She points out that whether or not Margaret Reynolds' superiors sexually harassed her, they discriminated against her because of her gender—and that's what should really matter. Women have always been able to sue under Title VII, claiming discrimination in hiring, firing, and promotions; that's called "disparate treatment." But courts have been slow to find hostile work environments except when women were subject to explicitly sexual treatment. "What I'm trying to do is go back to the fundamental recognition of why there was a law of hostile work environment in the first place—the notion that one can be discriminated against in the atmosphere in which one works," Schultz says. "The hostile environment may include sexual advances, but they're not necessary. Sexuality isn't the only tool of discrimination," she says.

But as unions and businesses have begun to devise ways to address the problem of sexual harassment, Schultz fears that some of the remedies show just how badly people misconstrue it. "I recently heard that there is a training program for masons near New Haven where they are teaching the men what they call the 'five-second rule,'" she told me. That means that men are not allowed to look at a fellow-worker who is a woman for more than five seconds because to do so might be sexual harassment. But that's a form of discrimination itself—trying to set women off in a category so that you can't even look at them. That's not what women care about."

Schultz's reassessment of the law is no panacea. No set of legal standards will obviate the need to make difficult judgments about individual behavior. But that may ultimately be the most important point of all. Human sexuality combines, among other things, passion, nuance, irrationality, and lust. Any attempt to purge sexuality from any part of human life—including the classroom, the courtroom, and the factory floor—is doomed to failure. The legal system, it seems, would do better simply to try to measure real and identifiable harms. It is hubris to think that this most baffling realm of life can be regulated with much precision or fairness. Sexual-harassment law will never end the battle of the sexes. Perhaps it will help make sure that women can do their jobs in peace. That's hard enough.

TOPICS FOR DISCUSSION AND WRITING

1. What has been the public understanding of sexual harassment as a result of the Clarence Thomas confirmation hearings? According to Toobin, what problems has this understanding led to?

2. What are the two categories of sexual harassment identified by lawyer Catharine MacKinnon? What problems do you see either or both categories presenting?

3. MacKinnon asks "whether women have a chance, structurally speaking and as a normal matter, even to consider whether they want to have sex or not." The implication of MacKinnon's work on sexual harassment is that there is no such thing as consensual sex between a man with power and a woman without power. What unstated assumptions underlie this belief about men, women, power, and sex? List as many as you can. (See Hidden Assumptions in Argument in Chapter 3.)

4. Write an essay on your reaction to MacKinnon's views. Do you agree with her or not? Explain your reasoning.

5. Toobin asks the following rhetorical question: "Can an employee sue for sexual harassment if she rebuffed her supervisor's advances but suffered no adverse consequences on the job as a result?" Write a considered response to this question perhaps as the conclusion to an in-class discussion. Then find the U.S. Supreme Court's answer to this question in its response to *Burlington Industries v. Ellerth*, a case it heard in the spring of 1998 and compare it to your own response. Finally, write a paper for an audience unfamiliar with the case, summarizing the Court's decision and including your reaction to it.

6. In November 1997, Yale University revised its guidelines concerning sexual harassment, forbidding teachers to have sexual relationships with students they supervise or are likely to supervise, "regardless of whether the relationship is consensual." How does this prohibition reflect Catherine MacKinnon's view of sexual relationships between men and women? What problems might result from such a rule?

7. Write a paper in which you urge your campus administration to adopt or reject a rule similar to Yale's forbidding sexual relationships between professors and students.

Reconceptualizing Sexual Harassment

Vicki Shultz

In the previous selection, "The Trouble with Sex," Toobin refers to this piece by Shultz as "a groundbreaking article. . . which is part of a large-scale reassessment of the law in light of the Thomas-Hill case." Shultz, a law professor, studied sexual harassment law for four years before publishing this in-depth critical analysis of it in the *Yale Law Journal*. We include here the introduction to this lengthy journal article.

It's a form of harassment every time I pick up a sledgehammer and that prick laughs at me, you know. It's a form of harassment when a journeyman is supposed to be training me and it's real clear to me that he does not want to give me any information whatsoever. He does not want me to be there at all. . . . They put me with this one who is a lunatic . . . he's the one who drilled the hole in my arm. . . . It's a form of harassment to me when the working foreman puts me in a dangerous situation and tells me to do something in an improper way and then tells me, Oh, you can't do that! It's a form of harassment to me when someone takes a tool out of my hand and says, I'll show you how to do this, and he grabs the sledgehammer from my hand and he proceeded to try to show me how to do this thing . . . you know, straighten up a post . . . it's nothing to it, you just bang it and it gets straight . . . It's a form of harassment to me when they call me honey and I have to tell them every day, don't call me that, you know, I have a name printed right on my thing. . . . Ah, you know, it's all a form of harassment to me. It's not right. They don't treat each other that way. They shouldn't treat me that way. It's a form of harassment to me when this one asks me to go out with him all the time. You know, all this kind of stuff. It's terrible.[1]

How should we understand sex-based harassment on the job? Its existence is now part of the national consciousness. Over the past twenty years, feminists have succeeded in naming "sexual harassment" and defining it as a social problem.[2] Popular accounts abound: Newspapers, movies, and television programs depict women workers who are forced to endure sexual advances and decry the fact that these women must contend with such abuse.[3] The legal system, too, has recognized the problem. The Supreme Court, on two separate occasions,[4] has affirmed that workplace sexual harassment violates Title VII of the Civil Rights Act.[5] and the lower federal courts have created a massive body of doctrine detailing the law's protection. All the while, public awareness of legal rights has continued to develop, and workers have filed sexual harassment complaints in increasing numbers.[6]

That feminists (and sympathetic lawyers) have inspired a body of popular and legal opinion condemning harassment in such a brief period of time is a remarkable achievement. Yet the achievement has been limited because we have not conceptualized the problem in sufficiently broad terms. The prevailing paradigm for understanding sex-based harassment places sexuality—more specifically, male-female sexual advances—at the center of the problem. Within that paradigm, a male supervisor's sexual advances on a less powerful, female subordinate represent the quintessential form of harassment.

Although this sexual desire-dominance paradigm represented progress when it was first articulated as the foundation for quid pro quo sexual harassment, using the paradigm to conceptualize hostile work environment harassment has served to exclude from legal understanding many of the most common and debilitating forms of harassment faced by women (and many men) at work each day.[7] The prevailing paradigm privileges conduct thought to be motivated by sexual designs—such as sexual advances—as the core sex- or gender-based harassment.[8] Yet much of the gender-based hostility and abuse that women (and some men) endure at work is neither driven by the desire for sexual relations nor even sexual in content.

Indeed, many of the most prevalent forms of harassment are actions that are designed to maintain work—particularly the more highly rewarded lines of work—as bastions of masculine competence and authority. Every day, in workplaces all over the country, men uphold the image that their jobs demand masculine mastery by acting to undermine their female colleagues' perceived (or sometimes even actual) competence to do the work. The forms of such harassment are wide-ranging. They include characterizing the work as appropriate for men only; denigrating women's performance or ability to master the job; providing patronizing forms of help in performing the job; withholding the training, information, or opportunity to learn to do the job well; engaging in deliberate work sabotage; providing sexist evaluations of women's performance or denying them deserved promotions; isolating women from the social networks that confer a sense of belonging; denying women the perks or privileges that are required for success; assigning women sex-stereotyped service tasks that lie outside their job descriptions (such as cleaning or serving coffee); engaging in taunting, pranks, and other forms of hazing designed to remind women that they are different and out of place; and physically assaulting or threatening to assault the women who dare to fight back. Of course, making a woman the object of sexual attention can also work to undermine her image and self-confidence as a capable worker. Yet, much of the time, harassment assumes a form that has little or nothing to do with sexuality but everything to do with gender. As the female welder quoted above put it, "Ah, you know, it's all a form of harassment to me. . . . They don't treat each other that way. They shouldn't treat me that way."[9]

In spite of the female welder's intuitive understanding that all these actions are gender-based forms of harassment, there has been little or no recognition of such a perspective in the law. Most feminists and other scholars sympathetic to working women have either explicitly advocated or implicitly accepted the prevailing sexual desire-dominance paradigm. This is not surprising, for feminists played a prominent role in creating it. The focus on sexual conduct emerged from an early radical feminist critique of heterosexual relations as a primary producer of women's oppression. These early feminists saw rape as a central metaphor for men's treatment of women, and they compared sexual harassment to rape.[10] More recently, feminist legal scholars have analogized the law governing workplace harassment to rape law, criticizing harassment law for its disregard of women's perspectives on sexuality and for its failure to appreciate the unique harm inherent in the fact that harassment is a sexual violation.[11] Just as feminist analyses have conceived of harassment as sexual abuse, most scholars who have addressed same-sex harassment have characterized it in sexualized terms, analogizing same-sex harassment to heterosexual sexual advances as an argument for legal regulation.[12] Thus, even the most critical accounts of harassment law, like other accounts of workplace harassment,[13] have assumed a sexuality-centered perspective that portrays sexual advances and other sexually oriented conduct as the core of the problem.[14] They are rooted in the prevailing paradigm.[15]

This Article challenges the sexual desire-dominance paradigm. A comprehensive examination of Title VII hostile work environment harassment cases demonstrates the paradigm's inadequacy. Despite the best intentions of its creators, the paradigm has compromised the law's protection. Principal among its drawbacks, the paradigm is underinclusive: It omits—and even obscures—many of the most prevalent forms of harassment that make workplaces hostile and alienating to workers based on their gender. Much of what is harmful to women in the workplace is difficult to construe as sexual in design. Similarly, many men are harmed at work by gender-based harassment that fits only uneasily within the parameters of a sexualized paradigm. The prevailing paradigm, however, may also be overinclusive. By emphasizing the protection of women's sexual selves and sensibilities over and above their empowerment as workers, the paradigm permits—or even encourages—companies to construe the law to prohibit some forms of sexual expression that do not promote gender hierarchy at work. The focus of harassment law should not be on sexuality as such. The focus should be on conduct that consigns people to gendered work roles that do not further their own aspirations or advantage.

NOTES

1. Mary Lindenstein Walshok, Blue Collar Women: Pioneers on the Male Frontier 221–22 (1981) (quoting a female welder).

2. Working Women United (WWU) is the first group known to have used the term "sexual harassment." In May of 1975, WWU held a "Speak-Out on Sexual Harassment," for purposes of which it defined sexual harassment as "the treatment of women workers as sexual objects." Dierdre Silverman, *Sexual Harassment: Working Women's Dilemma,* Quest: Feminist Q., Winter 1976–1977, at 15, 15.

3. For examples of recent newspaper articles depicting sexual harassment in negative terms, see Jane Daugherty, Sexual Harassment Takes a Devastating Toll, Detroit News, Jan. 28, 1997, at D1; Lisa Hoffman, Sex Harassment Last Straw for Career Soldier: Woman Finally Left Army out of Frustration, Anger, *Rocky Mountain News,* Feb.16, 1997, at 3A; and A Mission for the Military, Boston Globe, Feb. 7, 1997, at A18. The Lifetime television network produced a movie told from the perspective of Kerry Ellison, the plaintiff in *Ellison v. Brady,* 924 F. 2d 872 (9th Cir. 1991). See *Hostile Advances: The Kerry Ellison Story* (Lifetime television broadcast, May 27,1996). But see David Mamet, Oleanna (1992) (depicting sympathetically a male professor accused of sexual harassment by a female college student).

4. See *Harris v. Forklift Sys., Inc.,* 510 U.S. 17 (1993); *Meritor Sav. Bank v. Vinson,* 477 U.S. 57 (1986).

5. 42 U.S.C. §2000e (1994). Title VII reads in relevant part: "It shall be an unlawful employment practice for an employer . . . to fail or refuse to hire or to discharge any individual, or otherwise to discriminate against any individual with respect to his com-

pensation, terms conditions, or privileges of employment, because of such individual's race, color, religion, sex, or national origin; or . . . to limit, segregate, or classify his employees or applicants for employment in any way which would deprive or tend to deprive any individual employee of employment opportunities or otherwise adversely affect his status as an employee, because of such individual's race, color, religion, sex, or national origin."
Id.§ 2000e–3.

6. See Kirstin Downey Grimsley, Worker Bias Cases Are Rising Steadily; New Laws Boost Hopes for Monetary Awards, *Wash. Post*, May 12, 1997, at A1 (noting that the fastest growing area of employment discrimination complaints is sexual harassment, up from 6127 complaints in 1990 to 15,342 complaints in 1996); Allen R. Myerson, As Federal Bias Cases Drop, Workers Take Up the Fight, *N.Y. Times*, Jan. 12, 1997, § 1, at 1 (noting that the new bias cases often are more about pay, promotion and harassment than about hiring, and increasingly concern sex rather than race).

7. Title VII jurisprudence recognizes two different types of sex-based harassment: (1) quid pro quo harassment, in which a supervisor seeks to condition employment benefits on a subordinate's grant of sexual favors: and (2) hostile work environment harassment, in which supervisors or coworkers engage in conduct that is "sufficiently severe or pervasive to alter the conditions of [the victim's] employment and create an abusive working environment." Vinson, 477 U.S. at 67 (quoting *Henson v. City of Dundee*. 682 F. 2d 897, 904 (11th Cir. 1982)).

8. Throughout this Article, I use the terms "gender" and "sex" interchangeably. I use the terms to refer to the complex process of socializing human beings into the identities of men and women, to the element of social relationships based on differences that society attributes to people with those two identities, and to the process of signifying power through those identities. See Joan Wallach Scott, *Gender and the Politics of History* 28–50 (1988), for the views that come perhaps closest to capturing my own.

For many years, feminists distinguished between "sex"—the biological sex of a human being—and "gender"—the different social and cultural expectations and roles assigned to the sexes. Recently, this distinction has come under challenge, as some feminists have questioned whether it makes sense to refer to "sex" as an ontologically given category that we can comprehend free of perceptions that have already been gendered. See e.g., Judith Butler, *Gender Trouble: Feminism and the Subversion of Identity* (1990). For purposes of this Article, I need not take a position in this debate. Regardless of whether something endowed by nature called "sex" can be known with any certainty, it is clear that the legal system cannot ascertain it with any certainty. Thus, Title VII's protection against discrimination based on "sex" has ultimately, and necessarily, been construed to protect people from discrimination based on "gender," even though some courts may cling to the notion that they can discover natural sex differences that justify differential treatment. See Katherine M. Franke, The Central Mistake of Sex Discrimination Law: The Disaggregation of Sex from Gender, 144 *U. Pa. L. Rev.* 1 (1995) (arguing that antidiscrimination law incorrectly proceeds from the assumption of biological sex difference).

9. Walshok, supra note 1, at 222; see supra text accompanying note 1.

10. See infra notes 58–69 and accompanying text.

11. One of the clearest statements of this position appears in Susan Estrich's powerful article. Susan Estrich, Sex at Work, 43 *Stan. L. Rev.* 813 (1991). As Estrich writes:
What makes sexual harassment more offensive, more debilitating, and more dehumanizing to its victims than other forms of discrimination is precisely the fact that it is sexual. Not only are men exercising power over woman, but they are operating in

a realm which is still judged according to a gender double standard, itself a reflection of the extent to which sexuality is used to penalize women. In my view, [harassment] cases are such a disaster in doctrinal terms precisely because, as with rape, they involve sex and sexuality.

Id. at 820. For additional examples of this perspective, see Caroline Forell, Essentialism, Empathy, and the Reasonable Woman, 1994 *U. Ill. L. Rev.* 769; Ann C. Juliano, Note, Did She Ask for It?: The "Unwelcome" Requirement in Sexual Harassment Cases, 77 *Cornell L. Rev.*1558 (1992); and Miranda Oshige, Note, What's Sex Got To Do with It?, 47 *Stan. L. Rev.* 565 (1995). Cf. Richard A. Posner, An Economic Analysis of Sex Discrimination Laws, 56 *U. Chi. L. Rev.* 1311, 1318 (1989) (arguing that sexual harassment is "more clearly akin to . . . rape than to misogynistic refusal to accept women workers").

12. See, e.g., Charles R. Calleros,The Meaning of "Sex": Homosexual and Bisexual Harassment Under Title VII, 20 *Vt. L. Rev.* 55 (1995); Samuel A. Marcosson, Harassment on the Basis of Sexual Orientation: A Claim of Sex Discrimination Under Title VII, 81 *Geo. L.J.* 1 (1992); Lisa Wehren, Note, Same-Gender Sexual Harassment Under Title VII: Garcia v. Elf Atochem Marks a Step in the Wrong Direction, 32 *Cal. W. L.* Rev. 87 (1995).

13. Most of the large-scale empirical studies of sex-based harassment have also used a sexualized definition of harassment limited to sexual advances and other conduct of a sexual nature. See, e.g., Barbara Gutek, Sex and the Workplace: The Impact of Sexual Behavior and Harassment on Women, Men, and Organizations (1985); U.S. Merit Sys. Protection Bd., Sexual Harassment in the Federal Government: An Update (1988) [hereinafter Sexual Harassment in the Federal Government]; U.S. Merit Sys. Protection Bd., Sexual Harassment in the Federal Workplace: Is It a Problem? (1981) [hereinafter Sexual Harassment in the Federal Workplace]; Walshok, supra note 1; see also Patricia A. Frazier et al., Social Science Research on Lay Definitions of Sexual Harassment, 51 *J. Soc. Issues* 21 (1995) (citing numerous studies of harassment that utilize a sexualized definition).

14. A few writers have urged courts to construe Title VII broadly to prohibit all forms of gender-based harassment, rather than focusing narrowly on sexual advances and other sexual conduct. See, e.g., L. Camille Hebert, Sexual Harassment is Gender Harassment, 43 *U. Kan. L. Rev.* 565 (1995); Frank S. Ravitch, Contextualizing Gender Harassment: Providing an Analytical Framework for an Emerging Concept in Discrimination Law, 1995 *Det. C.L.* Rev. 853. Even such writers, however, have found it difficult to escape the prevailing sexual paradigm. Some, for example, continue to make an artificial analytical distinction between gender-based harassment and sexual harassment. See, e.g., Ravitch, supra, at 856–57. Others subtly continue to highlight the sexual nature of harassment as a reason for condemning it, even though they purport to understand harassment as a form of sexism rather than sexuality. See, e.g., Hebert. supra. at 587. None of these writers advances an account of harassment that highlights its role in preserving job segregation by constructing gender- based differences in work competence, as I do here.

15. A notable exception is Carlin Meyer, Feminism, Work and Sex: Returning to the Gates (1995) (unpublished manuscript, on file with author). Meyer insightfully discusses how feminist legal theorists' emphasis on sexual harassment has neglected other fundamental work-related problems of concern to women, such as sweatshops, occupational health and safety, pension issues, and the rise of home work and contingent labor. See id. at 8–10. This Article, by contrast, shows how the courts' utilization of a feminist-inspired paradigm to regulate sexual forms of harassment has neglected equally pernicious, nonsexual forms of gender-based misconduct in the workplace—particularly conduct that denigrates women's competence and thereby preserves work along gendered lines.

TOPICS FOR DISCUSSION AND WRITING

1. What does Shultz mean by "the sexual desire-dominance paradigm" of sexual-harassment law?

2. Why does she see this paradigm as limiting our understanding of sexual harassment and compromising the law's ability to protect us from it?

Harris v. Forklift Systems, Inc.
Opinion of the Supreme Court

Justice Sandra Day O'Connor

Teresa Harris v. Forklift Systems, Inc. is one of the more significant cases in the legal battle over sexual harassment. On July 7, 1989, Teresa Harris filed suit against her employer, Forklift Systems, for sexual harassment, claiming that the president of the company, Charles Hardy, created a sexually hostile work environment because of her gender, a violation of Title VII of the Civil Rights Act of 1964.

The first court to hear this case, the District Court, concluded that Hardy's comments did not create an abusive environment because they were not "so severe as to . . . seriously affect [Harris'] psychological well-being" or lead her to "suffer injury." When this decision was appealed by Harris, the Court of Appeals affirmed the lower court's decision. But the Supreme Court disagreed and on November 9,1993, over-turned the Court of Appeals, finding that abusive work environment harassment need not "seriously affect [an employee's] psychological well-being" or lead the plaintiff to "suffer injury."

When the Supreme Court reaches a decision on a case, one or more justices write the opinion or opinions of the Court, often and certainly in this case, setting precedents for future legal cases. Justice O'Connor delivered the opinion for a unanimous Court.

In this case we consider the definition of a discriminatorily "abusive work environment" (also known as a "hostile work environment") under Title VII of the Civil Rights Act of 1964, 78 Stat. 253, as amended, *42 U.S.C. § 2000e* et seq. (1988 ed., Supp. III).

I

Teresa Harris worked as a manager at Forklift Systems, Inc., an equipment rental company, from April 1985 until October 1987. Charles Hardy was Fork-lift's president.

The Magistrate found that, throughout Harris' time at Forklift, Hardy often insulted her because of her gender and often made her the target of unwanted sexual innuendos. Hardy told Harris on several occasions, in the presence of other employees, "You're a woman, what do you know" and "We need a man as the rental manager"; at least once, he told her she was "a dumb ass woman." App. to Pet. for Cert. A-13. Again in front of others, he suggested that the two of them "go to the Holiday Inn to negotiate [Harris'] raise." Id., at A-14. Hardy occasionally asked Harris and other female employees to get coins from his front pants pocket. Ibid. He threw objects on the ground in front of Harris and other women, and asked them to pick the objects up. Id., at A-14 to A-15. He made sexual innuendos about Harris' and other women's clothing. Id., at A-15.

In mid-August 1987, Harris complained to Hardy about his conduct. Hardy said he was surprised that Harris was offended, claimed he was only joking, and apologized. Id., at A-16. He also promised he would stop, and based on this assurance Harris stayed on the job. Ibid. But in early September, Hardy began anew: While Harris was arranging a deal with one of Forklift's customers, he asked her, again in front of other employees, "What did you do, promise the guy. . . some [sex] Saturday night?" Id., at A-17. On October 1, Harris collected her paycheck and quit.

Harris then sued Forklift, claiming that Hardy's conduct had created an abusive work environment for her because of her gender. The United States District Court for the Middle District of Tennessee, adopting the report and recommendation of the Magistrate, found this to be "a close case," id. at A-31, but held that Hardy's conduct did not create an abusive environment. The court found that some of Hardy's comments "offended [Harris], and would offend the reasonable woman," id., at A-33, but that they were not

> so severe as to be expected to seriously affect [Harris'] psychological well-being. A reasonable woman manager under like circumstances would have been offended by Hardy, but his conduct would not have risen to the level of interfering with that person's work performance.
>
> Neither do I believe that [Harris] was subjectively so offended that she suffered injury. . . . Although Hardy may at times have genuinely offended [Harris], I do not believe that he created a working environment so poisoned as to be intimidating or abusive to [Harris]. Id., at A-34 to A-35.

In focusing on the employee's psychological well-being, the District Court was following Circuit precedent. See *Rabidue v. Osceola Refining Co., 805 F.2d 611, 620 (CA6 1986)*, cert. denied, *481 U.S. 1041 (1987)*. The United States Court of Appeals for the Sixth Circuit affirmed in a brief unpublished decision.

We granted certiorari, 507 U.S. (1993), to resolve a conflict among the Circuits on whether conduct, to be actionable as "abusive work environment" harassment (no quid pro quo harassment issue is present here), must "seriously affect [an employee's] psychological well-being" or lead the plaintiff to "suffer injury." Compare Rabidue (requiring serious effect on psychological well-being); *Vance v. Southern Bell Telephone & Telegraph Co., 863 F.2d 1503, 1510 (CA11 1989)* (same); and *Downes v. FAA, 775 F.2d 288, 292 (CA Fed. 1985)* (same), with *Ellison v. Brady, 924 F.2d 872, 877–878 (CA9 1991)* (rejecting such a requirement).

II

Title VII of the Civil Rights Act of 1964 makes it "an unlawful employment practice for an employer . . . to discriminate against any individual with respect to his compensation, terms, conditions, or privileges of employment, because of such individual's race, color, religion, sex, or national origin." *42 U.S.C. §2000e-2*(a)(1). As we made clear in *Meritor Savings Bank v. Vinson, 477 U.S. 57 (1986)*, this language "is not limited to 'economic' or 'tangible' discrimination. The phrase 'terms, conditions, or privileges of employment' evinces a congressional intent 'to strike at the entire spectrum of disparate treatment of men and women' in employment," which includes requiring people to work in a discriminatorily hostile or abusive environment. *Id., at 64,* quoting *Los Angeles Dept. of Water and Power v. Manhart, 435 U.S. 702, 707, n. 13 (1978)* (some internal quotation marks omitted). When the workplace is permeated with "discriminatory intimidation, ridicule, and insult," *477 U.S., at 65,* that is "sufficiently severe or pervasive to alter the conditions of the victim's employment and create an abusive working environment," *Id., at 67* (internal brackets and quotation marks omitted), Title VII is violated.

This standard, which we reaffirm today, takes a middle path between making actionable any conduct that is merely offensive and requiring the conduct to cause a tangible psychological injury. As we pointed out in Meritor, "mere utterance of an . . . epithet which engenders offensive feelings in a employee," ibid. (internal quotation marks omitted) does not sufficiently affect the conditions of employment to implicate Title VII. Conduct that is not severe or pervasive enough to create an objectively hostile or abusive work environment—an environment that a reasonable person would find hostile or abusive—is beyond Title VII's purview. Likewise, if the victim does not subjectively perceive the environment to be abusive, the conduct has not actually altered the conditions of the victim's employment, and there is no Title VII violation.

But Title VII comes into play before the harassing conduct leads to a nervous breakdown. A discriminatorily abusive work environment, even one that does not seriously affect employees' psychological well-being, can and often will detract from employees' job performance, discourage employees from remaining on the job, or keep them from advancing in their careers. Moreover, even without regard to these tangible effects, the very fact that the discriminatory conduct was so severe or pervasive that it created a work environment abusive to employees because of their race, gender, religion, or national origin offends Title VII's broad rule of workplace equality. The appalling conduct alleged in Meritor, and the reference in that case to environments "'so heavily polluted with discrimination as to destroy completely the emotional and psychological stability of minority group workers,'" supra, at 66, quoting *Rogers v. EEOC, 454 F.2d 234, 238 (CAS 1971)*, cert. denied, *406 U.S. 957 (1972)*, merely present some especially egregious examples of harassment. They do not mark the boundary of what is actionable.

We therefore believe the District Court erred in relying on whether the conduct "seriously affected plaintiff's psychological well-being" or led her to "suffer injury." Such an inquiry may needlessly focus the factfinder's attention on concrete psychological harm, an element Title VII does not require. Certainly Title VII bars conduct that would seriously affect a reasonable person's psychological well-being, but the statute is not limited to such conduct. So long as the environment would reasonably be perceived, and is perceived, as hostile or abusive, Meritor, supra, at 67, there is no need for it also to be psychologically injurious.

This is not, and by its nature cannot be, a mathematically precise test. We need not answer today all the potential questions it raises, nor specifically address the EEOC's new regulations on this subject, see *58 Fed. Reg. 51266 (1993)* (proposed 29 CFR § § 1609.1, 1609.2); see also 29 CFR § 1604.11 (1993). But we can say that whether an environment is "hostile" or "abusive" can be determined only by looking at all the circumstances. These may include the frequency of the discriminatory conduct; its severity; whether it is physically threatening or humiliating, or a mere offensive utterance; and whether it unreasonably interferes with an employee's work performance. The effect on the employee's psychological well-being is, of course, relevant to determining whether the plaintiff actually found the environment abusive. But while psychological harm, like any other relevant factor, may be taken into account, no single factor is required.

III

Forklift, while conceding that a requirement that the conduct seriously affect psychological well-being is unfounded, argues that the District Court nonetheless correctly applied the Meritor standard. We disagree. Though the District Court did conclude that the work environment was not "intimidating or abusive to [Harris]," App. To Pet. For Cert. A-35, it did so only after finding that the conduct was not "so severe as to be expected to seriously affect plaintiff's psychological well-being," id., at A-34, and that Harris was not "subjectively so offended that she suffered injury," ibid. The District Court's application of these incorrect standards may well have influenced its ultimate conclusion, especially given that the court found this to be a "close case," id., at A-31.

We therefore reverse the judgment of the Court of Appeals, and remand the case for further proceedings consistent with this opinion.

So ordered.

TOPICS FOR DISCUSSION AND WRITING

1. Write a short summary of Justice O'Connor's reasoning in overturning the lower courts' decisions. (See Summaries in Chapter 3.)

2. How does O'Connor define a hostile work environment?

3. Do you agree with the Supreme Court's decision? Why or why not?

The Supreme Court's Decision in Harris v. Forklift Systems, Inc.

Vicki Shultz

In another excerpt from "Reconceptualizing Sexual Harassment"—the introduction to this *Yale Law Journal* article is included earlier in this section—Shultz expresses her disappointment in a Supreme Court opinion which missed the opportunity "to expand the legal understanding of hostile work environment harassment."

In *Harris v. Forklift Systems, Inc.,*[128] the Supreme Court had an opportunity to expand the legal understanding of hostile work environment harassment. Theresa Harris was the rental manager in a company that sold, leased, and repaired forklift equipment. She was one of only two female managers; the other was the daughter of the company president, Charles Hardy. During Harris's tenure, Hardy subjected her to various treatment undermining her authority as a manager, such as denying her an individual office, a company car, and a car allowance; paying her on a different basis from the other managers; refusing to give her more than a cursory annual review; and forcing her to bring coffee into meetings, which he never asked male managers to do. Hardy made it plain that he considered women inadequate as managers. He frequently denigrated the plaintiff in front of other employees with such remarks as, "You're a woman, what do you know"; "You're a dumb ass woman"; and "We need a man as the rental manager."[129] Hardy made other comments that demeaned Harris as a professional, suggesting that the two of them go to the Holiday Inn to negotiate her raise and intimating that she must have promised sex to a client in order to obtain an account. In addition, Hardy denigrated Harris's managerial role by subjecting her to the same sort of sophomoric, sexually oriented conduct that he directed at lower-level women employees (but not male employees), such as asking her to retrieve coins from his front pocket and making suggestive comments about her clothing.[130]

Despite Hardy's conduct, the district court adopted the magistrate's conclusion that the harassment did not rise to the level of a hostile work environment.[131] The Sixth Circuit affirmed. Harris's appeal to the Supreme Court emphasized only one aspect of the case: Harris urged that the lower court had erred in requiring her to prove that the harassment had seriously affected her psychological well-being or otherwise caused her psychological injury. The Supreme Court found for Harris, rejecting the lower court's narrow subjective psychological harm requirement and holding that a plaintiff need show only that a reasonable person would have perceived, as Harris did, that the harassment was sufficiently severe or pervasive to create a hostile or abusive work environment.[132]

In focusing on the abstract standards, however, both the Supreme Court and the lawyers failed to address the real problem in the case: the lower court's application of those standards from an overly narrow, sexualized perspective. The magistrate made the classic analytical move made by courts that have adopted the sexual desire-dominance paradigm: disaggregation. He began by parceling out the sexual and nonsexual conduct into separate claims. The nonsexual conduct, such as denying Harris a car, car allowance, office, and annual review, was not considered part of the harassment claim, but was examined under a separate claim of disparate treatment.[133] For purposes of the hostile work environment claim, the magistrate concluded that only Hardy's "sexually crude comments" met the EEOC guidelines' definition of actionable harassment.[134] After limiting his focus to these comments, the magistrate then trivialized them by emphasizing that they do not sufficiently resemble the sexual advances at the core of the sexual desire-dominance paradigm. The Holiday Inn comment, for instance, was a bad joke, "but it was not a sexual proposition."[135] According to the magistrate, Harris's harassment was similar to that of another Sixth Circuit plaintiff who had also been subjected to harassment that was "vulgar and crude," but who lost because "the sexual conduct was not in the form of sexual propositions or physical touching."[136] Winning cases "involved sexual harassment . . . in the form of requests for sexual relations or actual offensive touching."[137] Thus, it was the comparison of Harris's mistreatment to an imagined case of sexual advances that led the magistrate and the lower courts to conclude that the mistreatment was not sufficiently injurious to be actionable.

Harris provided a clear opportunity to transcend this unduly restrictive focus. The case presented a chance to expand the concept of hostile work environment harassment to include all conduct that is rooted in gender-based expectations about work roles and to recognize that harassment functions as a way of undermining women's perceived competence as workers. From such a perspective, Charles Hardy's conduct looks like the central sex discimination that Title VII was intended to dismantle. Taken together, Hardy's conduct—from the "sexual" conduct that reduced Harris to a sexual object as she struggled to fulfill her work role, to the nonsexual but gender-biased conduct that denigrated her capacity to serve as a manager, to the facially gender-neutral conduct that denied her the perks, privileges, and respect she needed to do her job well—had the purpose and effect of undermining Harris's status and authority as a manager on the basis of her sex. These actions fit a classic pattern of harassment often directed at women who try to claim male-dominated work as their own.[138] Yet, neither the Supreme Court, the Sixth Circuit, the district court. Harris's counsel,[139] nor most amici curiae[140] saw the case in these terms or even perceived the magistrate's narrow obsession with the lack of direct sexual advances on Harris as problematic.

Notes

128. 510 U.S. 17 (1993).

129. *Harris v. Forklift Sys., Inc.,* 60 Empl. Prac. Dec. (CCH) P 42,070, at 74,247 (M.D. Tenn. 1991), aff'd, 976 F.2d 733 (6th Cir. 1992) (per curiam), rev'd, 510 U.S. 17 (1993).

130. See id. This form of behavior—treating women alike even though some have jobs or roles of much different or higher status—is referred to as "status-leveling" in the relevant literature. See Rosabeth Moss Kanter, Men and Women of the Corporation 231-32 (rev. ed. 1993); cf. *Dothard v. Rawlinson,* 433 U.S. 321, 343-44 & n.3 (1977) (Marshall, J., concurring in part and dissenting in part) (objecting to the majority's use of attacks by prison inmates on an untrained female clerical worker and a female

student touring a facility to support its proposition that trained female correctional officers would be vulnerable to sexual assault by inmates).

131. See Harris, 60 Empl. Prac. Dec. (CCH) at 74,249.

132. See Harris, 510 U.S. at 22.

133. See Harris, 60 Empl. Prac. Dec. (CCH) at 74,251. This, of course, is the same move made by the Seventh Circuit in *King v. Board of Regents of the University of Wisconsin System,* 898 F.2d 533 (7th Cir. 1990). See supra Chapter I.C.

134. Harris, 60 Empl. Prac. Dec. (CCH) at 74,249.

135. Id. at 74,250.

136. Id. (citing *Rabidue v. Osceola Ref. Co.,* 805 F.2d 611 (6th Cir. 1986)).

137. Id. (emphasis added.)

138. See infra Sections IV. A-B.

139. Indeed, Harris's counsel argued from within the sexual desire-dominance paradigm, emphasizing the sexually explicit nature of some of Hardy's conduct. See Petitioner's Brief at 33, *Harris v. Forklift Sys., Inc.,* 510 U.S. 17 (1993) (No. 92–1168). This strategy, of course, invited counsel for Forklift Systems to stress that much of the conduct was not sexual in nature and that such nonsexual conduct rarely rises to the level of affecting the terms and conditions of employment. See Respondent's Brief at 28. Only in the reply brief, presumably after seeing the point raised by a couple of amici, see infra note 140, did Harris's counsel argue that Hardy's denigration of Harris's competence was "especially demeaning to a person in a managerial position." Petitioner's Reply Brief at 9.

140. See, e.g., Brief Amici Curiae of the Employment Law Center et al. in Support of Petitioner; Brief Amici Curiae in Support of Petitioner on Behalf or National Conference of Women's Bar Associations and Women's Bar Association of the District of Columbia: Brief Amici Curiae of the NAACP Legal Defense and Educational Fund, Inc. and the National Council of Jewish Women in Support of Petitioner; Brief Amicus Curiae of the National Employment Lawyers Association in Support of Petitioner: Brief of Amici Curiae NOW Legal Defense and Education Fund et al.; Brief of the Southern States Police Benevolent Association and the North Carolina Police Benevolent Association, as Amici Curiae; Brief of the Women's Legal Defense Fund et al.

　　Two exceptions stand out. The brief filed by Feminists for Free Expression urged the Court to clarify that the definition of hostile work environment harassment includes all gender-based conduct, not only conduct of a "sexual" nature as suggested in the EEOC guidelines. See Brief of Amicus Curiae Feminists for Free Expression in Support of Petitioner at *7, available in LEXIS, Genfed Library, Briefs File. The group argued that the courts' current focus on sexuality perpetuates a harmful stereotype that women need to be protected from sexual speech and risks prohibiting speech that is protected by the First Amendment. See id. The brief filed by the United States and the EEOC urged the Court to reject a psychological injury requirement in favor of a requirement of proof that the harassment was sufficiently severe or pervasive to interfere with a reasonable person's job performance. See Brief for the United States and the Equal Employment Opportunity Commission as Amici Curiae at *8, available in LEXIS, Genfed Library, Briefs File. The brief pointed out that harassment could include nonsexual conduct and that even explicitly sexual conduct can be understood to inhibit job performance by "hamper[ing] [a woman's] opportunity to succeed vis-a-vis her male peers or den[ying] her credit for her achievements." Id. at *12.

TOPICS FOR DISCUSSION AND WRITING

1. What is Shultz's criticism of the Supreme Court's decision?

2. According to Shultz, how should the courts define "hostile work environment"?

3. Based on the Supreme Court decision by Sandra Day O'Connor and Vicki Shultz's critique of that decision, write an essay about the *Harris v. Forklift* case for an audience unfamiliar with the case. (See Hidden Assumptions—Audience Awareness in Chapter 3.)

Men Behaving Badly

Henry Louis Gates, Jr.

Writer and professor Henry Louis Gates, Jr. is the director of the W. E. B. Du Bois Institute of Afro-American Research at Harvard. In his essay, "Men Behaving Badly," he argues that the meaning of "sex" in sexual harassment has undergone "a process of semantic drift," leading to undesirable legal consequences.

History is, in no small part, a chronicle of formerly acceptable outrages. Once upon a time, perfectly decent folk took it for granted that watching two gladiators hack each other to death was just the thing to do on a summer afternoon, that co-religionists with whom you had teensy doctrinal differences were best roasted on an open fire, that making slaves of Africans was a good deal for all concerned, and that participation in politics should be restricted to male landowners. What were they thinking? You could say that posterity is a hanging judge, except that sooner or later capital punishment, too, will turn up on that chronicle of outrages.

These days, members of a cultural derrière-garde—perplexed by new rules applying to sexual harassment, acquaintance rape, and the like—often complain that sexual intimacy has been "politicized." In truth, it always had been. What has changed is the balance of power. Women no longer feel obliged to tolerate the kind of sexual condescension that was once prevalent in the workplace. And if you think the date-rape issue has been overplayed, consider the legal environment that prevailed before modern feminism. Many states required corroborating evidence before there could be a conviction in a rape case (there usually isn't any), and essentially denied the possibility that a person could be raped by an acquaintance. What were they thinking?

We've come a long way. Today, even that most conservative of institutions, the United States Army, has come to terms with feminist arguments about sexual harassment and the abuse of power. Consider the ongoing hearings against

Sergeant Major of the Army Gene C. McKinney, America's top enlisted soldier. Brenda L. Hoster, the retired Sergeant Major whose accusations prompted McKinney's fall from grace, has testified that he once tried to pressure her into having sex, and several other women have turned up to bolster her account. One, a Navy Chief Petty Officer, testified that he'd offered to "show me passion like I'd never known." Another, a female sergeant, recalled his saying, "Men, women, we have needs." Yet another woman, an Army recruiter based in Florida, says he asked her whether she wanted to kiss him. ("Hell, no that's the last thing I want to do" was her response.) It is clearly a shameful abuse of authority for an army officer to solicit sex from subordinates, and the Army has rightly taken a dim view of it. Indeed, if it has its way, Sergeant Major Gene C. McKinney could be sentenced to prison for fifty-six years. All told, the McKinney case might seem to mark a victory for ideas of sexual equity that had once existed only on the fringes of American culture.

So why don't we feel more victorious? The trouble goes back to a tension between an animating concern with sexual abuse and the use of antidiscrimination law to address it. The "sexual" in the phrase "sexual harassment"—as opposed to, say, the "sexual" in "sexual misconduct"—was supposed to refer to the category of citizen harassed: Title VII of the Civil Rights Act of 1964 prohibited harassment that was gender-specific, as opposed to amorous in content. Through a process of semantic drift, though, the one sense of "sexual" shaded into the other. The goalposts had moved: sexual etiquette, as distinct from discriminatory treatment, has become the subject of legal scrutiny.

That was a lesson learned from *Mackenzie v. Miller Brewing Co.,* the now famous case of the beer executive and the "Seinfeld" episode. One day in 1993, the executive, Jerold Mackenzie, told a female co-worker the plot of the "Seinfeld" show he'd seen the night before. (In the episode, Seinfeld has a new woman friend, but he can't remember her name—just that it vaguely rhymes with a female body part. Only after she realizes that he's forgotten her name and storms off does he remember it and shout "Dolores!"). When the co-worker complained of sexual harassment, Mackenzie, who had served nineteen years with the company, was fired.

And why not? This is a country in which harassment complaints were lodged against a library employee who had posted a *New Yorker* cartoon in his cubicle. (The cartoon, published shortly after the Lorena Bobbitt incident, showed one besuited man saying to another, "What's the big deal? I lopped off my own damn penis years ago.") The Mackenzie case was noteworthy because the original overreaction was repaid by another: last month, a mostly female jury awarded the "Seinfeld"-watching executive 26.6 million dollars for wrongful dismissal. But what Mackenzie's original firing offense has in common with the librarian's banished cartoon and a host of similar instances—and what the jury may have been reacting to—is that it had precious little to do with discrimination on the basis of gender.

What has happened is that a whole range of offensive conduct—some of it plainly opprobrious, some merely in poor taste—has been squeezed into the purview of antidiscrimination law. Brenda L. Hoster's testimony last week was actually a wrenching account of what it was like to work for a Boss from Hell. She recounted an incident that occurred long before any sexual advances were made, when McKinney banged his fist on the table and yelled at her for failing to prepare him adequately for a press conference—even though he'd previously told her that he didn't need any preparation. Little wonder that she sounded nearly as outraged about the blatant injustice of that episode ("No matter what I did," she testified, "I wasn't going to be able to do it right") as about the time in an Oahu hotel when he made a fumbling play for her and told her—look, see!— that she aroused him. Both forms of conduct seem abusive, but, because there is no obvious legal remedy for generic abuse, a sort of amalgam grievance is the result. Another Boss from Hell, this time a casino manager in Nevada, routinely referred to the men in his employ as "assholes" and worse, but only in referring to women as "cunts" did he run afoul of federal law. In a range of cases, using antidiscrimination law against abusive bosses has become a judicial expedient akin to siccing the I.R.S. on Al Capone.

What's most troubling about the way we've sexualized sexual harassment, though, is that it puts victims of gender discrimination at a disadvantage when the abusive conduct *isn't* sexual in nature. Required by Title VII to protect women from a "hostile environment" in the workplace, the courts have failed to recognize the existence of hostile environments that don't involve sexual content—and this can mean giving the plain old unsexy kind of sex discrimination a free pass. As it happens, the category of "sex" was added to Title VII, just hours before its adoption, by Southern senators intent on sabotage. To those benighted souls—the original Guys Who Don't Get It—the notion of protecting citizens against gender discrimination was a ludicrous prospect. But when civil liberties are pitted against civil rights, when the heavy weight of antidiscrimination law falls on Bobbit cartoons, when sexual content, and not disparate treatment, becomes the measure of the offense, you start to wonder about posterity's perspective. What are *we* thinking?

TOPICS FOR DISCUSSION AND WRITING

1. Gates lists gladiators, religious persecution, slavery and the restriction of the vote to male landowners as some of the "acceptable outrages" that history chronicles. Can you add to this list of "acceptable outrages"?

2. What, according to Gates, is the problem with the term "sexual harassment" as it has been used in recent court cases? What problems result from the use of this ambiguous term?

3. What do you think Gates means by "plain old unsexy kind of sex discrimination"? Can you think of any examples?

Higher Barriers Between Men and Women

Sexual Separatism

Diana Trilling

Diana Trilling was the wife of literary scholar Lionel Trilling. She and her husband were members of a group of writers who dominated the intellectual scene of New York in the fifties. She died not long after this piece appeared in *Newsweek* where she expressed her fear that sexual harassment would contribute to a "spiraling discord" between men and women.

I find it difficult to think about the issue of sexual harassment without recalling my mother's account of her first job in America. At 18 she had come to this country alone, from Poland. With no knowledge of English, but a good figure, she had become a model in the New York City garment district. But she soon wearied of having to fend off the advances of the male buyers. She gave up modeling to become a milliner's apprentice.

There was no note of insult or injury in my mother's report of this experience. She even seemed to have been mildly flattered by the overtures that had been made to her. But she had found them a nuisance to handle.

The distinction between sexual nuisance and harassment is a crucial one, but it has all but disappeared in a feminist culture which appears to be bent upon raising always-new and higher barriers between men and women. While there are many forms of male behavior which legitimately call for censure and even for the intervention of law—they include not only any imposition of physical force but the kind of indignity which our female naval officers at Tailhook were made to suffer—the legitimate effort to guard women against gender-initiated mistreatment now reaches the point where the most casual expression of male interest in women, whistling at a woman on the street or remarking on her dress, is taken to be an infringement of her "personhood." She has been made into a mere "object."

Yet one wonders what enterprise there is in our society to which women are more universally and urgently dedicated than to being the objects of male notice and desire. A first imperative of our society is that women make themselves attractive to men. Our cosmetic and clothing industries are driven by it; our newly thriving fitness industry depends upon it. Indeed, sex has come to displace sport as our national obsession. Slyly or overtly, it riddles our fiction, our television and movies, our advertising.

In the past, because of our country's background in Puritanism, Americans were often accused of sexual hypocrisy. Today, we are less guilty of sexual hypocrisy than of sexual paradox and disingenuousness. Even while our college campuses ring with the cry of date rape, our female students cheerily invite male students to all-night study sessions in their rooms. In a culture which demands that women have equal access with men to positions of authority and power in business and the professions, we encourage women to feel that they need the protection of society against a man who tells them a dirty joke.

We recall, for instance, Anita Hill's remarkable appearance before the Senate Judiciary Committee at the hearings for Clarence Thomas and her account of Judge Thomas's pursuit of her with dirty stories. Charming in speech and manner, backed by parents of incontestable respectability, Miss Hill was the very image of maidenly modesty. Yet the forthrightness with which she repeated to the Committee and to an audience of untold millions of television listeners Judge Thomas's dirty jokes in all their tasteless detail would have done credit to a truck driver.

A half century ago, the gifted humorist James Thurber created a cartoon series "The War Between Men and Women" in which he satirized the often-bizarre marital struggle between the sexes. We have only to compare Thurber's bloodless war with the death-dealing spirit which animates the sexual manual which was recently drafted by the students of Antioch Collage to recognize the dangerous distance we have traveled in the relation of men and women. According to the Antioch rules, verbal permission must be requested and received before one's sexual partner may proceed from one "level" (their word) to the next in sexual intimacy. Although the manual is at pains to address itself to men as well as women, it does a poor job of disguising its basic assumption that men are natural predators and that women are at one and the same time sacred vessels, shatterable at a touch, and the traffic managers of love.

This is scarcely a useful axiom to disseminate in our society, but for several years now it has been establishing itself in our sexual culture, and it accounts, of course, for the increase in charges now being brought by women against men, the most recent and unpleasant of them the charge of sexual harassment brought by Paula Jones against President Clinton. A woman who doesn't flinch at alleging that the president of the United States attempted to seduce her by letting down his pants demands legal and financial recompense for the damage which this is supposed to have done to her delicate sensibility!

We live in a world which runs with the blood of hostility between racial and religious groups, between ethnic and national groups. To these lamentable separations among people, we now add another division, a separatism of the sexes. Where it used to be that the act of love (as it was then called) was regarded as an aspect, and even a celebration, of our shared humanity, it now becomes a dehumanized exercise and a new arena for conflict.

Black separatism came into existence in this country in the late '60s as an effort of prideful self-assertion. In claiming its separate identity, the black minority undertook to assert its equality with the white majority. At the time, the program may perhaps have had its symbolic use, but with the passage of the years we see its sorry consequences. Far from contributing to racial harmony, it has produced only a spiraling racial antagonism. Is this what we are aiming for in the relation of men and women: a spiraling discord?

It is still possible for this trend to be reversed in our society if feminism will take warning from all the other separatisms which now divide our world. Surely nothing is gained for society, nothing is gained for either men or women, by fostering the idea that men are ruthless aggressors against women and that women need to keep themselves in cautionary command of any relation which they have with men. Ours is not a moment in history in which to widen the divisions among people.

TOPICS FOR DISCUSSION AND WRITING

1. Diana Trilling claims that "the distinction between sexual nuisance and harassment is a crucial one. . . ." How does she define that distinction? How would you define it?

2. Trilling states that "feminist culture . . . appears to be bent upon raising always-new higher barriers between men and women." Do you agree with this statement? What impact do you observe the feminist movement having—directly or indirectly—on relationships between men and women?

3. She criticizes female college students who are upset about date rape yet "invite male students to all-night study sessions in their rooms." First, identify the hidden assumptions in her statement, and then answer her criticism. Is it justified or not? (See Hidden Assumptions in Argument in Chapter 3.)

A Call for Lustiness

Camille Paglia

Professor of Humanities at the University of the Arts in Philadelphia, social critic Camille Paglia, the author of three books on art and feminism, is known for outrageous opinions dramatically expressed. In this essay published in *Time* magazine, she expresses her concern about the impact of sexual harassment law on civil liberties and shares with Diana Trilling a concern that such laws relieve women of individual responsibility.

Liberal Democrats, who supported Anita Hill against Clarence Thomas in 1991, are waking up to the police state that their rigid rules have created. Now, as allegations fly about presidential sex, we can finally distinguish between genuine sexual coercion and free expression of sexual thought.

As a college teacher, I've long held that no person in power should demand sexual favors in return for a high grade or promotion. Nor should subordinates sexually involved with teachers or managers enjoy an unfair advantage over their peers. Those principles are a genuine contribution to feminist history.

But the secondary "hostile environment" policy, which allows employees to file lawsuits on nebulous grounds of psychological distress, is grotesquely totalitarian. It offends free-speech rights and is predicated on a reactionary female archetype: the prudish Victorian lady who faints at a sexual innuendo. This isn't feminism: it's Puritanism.

The Anita Hill case, far from expanding women's rights, was a disaster for civil liberties. That Hill, an articulate graduate of the Yale Law School, could find no job-preserving way to communicate to her employer her discomfort with mild off-color banter strained credulity. That Thomas could be publicly grilled about trivial lunchtime conversations that occurred 10 years earlier was an outrage worthy of Stalinist Russia.

An antiseptically sex-free workplace is impossible and unnatural. We want a sophisticated art of seduction. Feminist excesses have paralyzed and neutered white, upper-middle-class young men, as should be obvious to any visitor to the campuses of the élite schools. I want a society of lusty men and lusty women whose physical and mental energies are in exuberant free flow. While men must behave honorably (Governors and Presidents should not be dropping their pants in front of female employees or secretly preying on buxom young interns), women must also watch how they dress and behave. For every gross male harasser, there are 10 female sycophants who shamelessly use their sexual attractions to get ahead. We don't want a society of surveillance by old maids and snitches. The proper mission of feminism is to encourage women to take personal responsibility without running to parental authority figures for help.

The fanatic overprotection of women is fast making us an infantile nation. We need to treat sex with greater realism and imagination. Women should be taught not that they are passive wards of the state but that sex is a great human comedy where the joke is always on us.

TOPICS FOR DISCUSSION AND WRITING

1. How would Camille Paglia define sexual harassment?
2. What are her objections to sexual harassment cases which are based on a "hostile environment"?
3. Why does she see the Anita Hill case as "a disaster for civil liberties"?
4. What negative consequences for both men and women does she see resulting from current sexual harassment law?
5. In her essay "On Date Rape" (see page 163), Paglia also writes about relationships between men and women. What parallels do you find between the opinions expressed there and those in this essay?
6. Write a letter to Professor Paglia in response to her essay. You may agree or disagree with her conclusions (or some combination of both), but you need to be specific and to show awareness of your audience. (See Audience and Purpose in Chapter 1, and Hidden Assumptions in Chapter 3.)

Are Women the Only Victims of Sexual Harassment?

Man Handling

Harsh Luthar and Anthony Townsend

Writing in the *National Review,* a journal known for its conservative point of view, two business school professors, Luthar and Townsend, take exception to the assumption that in instances of sexual harassment it is always the woman who is the victim.

Although a popular success, *Disclosure** was derided by feminists who considered its premise—sexual harassment of a man by a woman—silly at best, dangerous at worst. After all, everyone knows sexual harassment is something a man does to a woman. That assumption is reflected in the Equal Employment Opportunity Commission's guidelines on sexual harassment, where the harasser is always a "he" and the victim a "she." You have to refer to a footnote to verify that the law, in theory, protects men as well as women.

Most of the published research on sexual harassment agrees: women are victims; men are harassers. In surveys, some 40 percent of women report being harassed at work, compared to a negligible proportion of men. When men do report harassment, their harassers are often other men.

But these indicators may not give us an accurate picture of what is going on. To begin with, the leading sexual-harassment researchers are feminist ideologists who are mainly concerned with finding evidence of patriarchal oppression. They design their studies accordingly: most of the research does not even include male subjects.

More to the point, most men would not recognize sexual harassment if it hit them in the face. Ask a number of men if they have been harassed, and nine out of ten, will say, "No, but I'd like to be." Men generally do not consider teasing, sexual jokes, and lewd innuendoes from female-co-workers harassment; they are not upset by the kinds of comments and incidents that have brought female plaintiffs millions of dollars in awards for "hostile environment" claims. In a recent lawsuit against the Jenny Craig diet organization by several male employees, one of the plaintiffs said he initially liked it when the women he worked with told him he had a nice body. He and the others did not file suit until they were denied promotions, were assigned to poor sales territories, or were terminated from the organization. After examining their complaint, the Massachusetts Commission Against Discrimination found probable cause of gender bias in the organization's action against the men.

Since men are not sensitive to harassing behavior that women (or at least feminists) construe as harassment, it's not surprising that they are not filing

---

*Disclosure is a film based on a novel by Michael Crichton in which a female executive (Demi Moore) sexually harasses a male subordinate (Michael Douglas).

many harassment complaints. Consider a scenario. A young man gets a job as an assistant manager in a bank. His boss, a member of the National Association of Bank Women, often talks about the importance of mentoring young women and complains that men have created a glass ceiling that oppresses female managers. Her coffee mug is emblazoned with an anti-male statement. To top it off, she and the other women who work in the branch often tell dirty jokes in which men are portrayed derogatorily. There's little question that this man is the victim of a "hostile environment," one that may well interfere with his ability to perform his duties. But if you ask him whether he has been sexually harassed, he will probably say no.

To get beyond this barrier, male subjects in harassment surveys should be asked not whether they have been sexually harassed but whether certain kinds of behavior have occurred. When we ask male undergraduates if they have ever been sexually harassed by a female instructor, almost all of them say no. But when we ask if they have experienced specific types of treatment in a female instructor's classroom, such as derogatory or off-color comments about men, some 60 percent of them report such incidents.

As for "sleep with me or else" harassment—the kind dramatized in *Disclosure*—we are starting to see court cases indicating that some men (and women) have been pressured into sex by a predatory female boss. There is every reason to believe that more such cases will appear as more women assume positions of power.

Yet most people still snicker about female harassment of males. Several men who claimed to have been sexually harassed appeared recently on *Donahue*. Between the host's eye rolling and the audience's derision, you would have thought these men were reporting encounters with UFOs. Sometimes even juries do not take the subject seriously. In a 1991 case in Michigan, the jury agreed that a man had endured repeated fondling by his female co-workers but awarded him only $100 in damages. Compare that to the hundreds of thousands or dollars regularly awarded to female plaintiffs.

Men are doubly penalized by the current alarm about sexual harassment. On the one hand, they are weakened in any office encounter with a woman because she always holds the harassment trump card. On the other hand, the current interpretation of harassment law gives woman license to say and do things in the workplace to which men cannot respond in kind. There is an open hostility toward men in many workplaces, and no one is rushing to document or change it.

Business, which should have an interest in finding out the truth, has instead swallowed whole the received wisdom on sexual harassment and acted on it swiftly and thoroughly. Companies spend millions of dollars on "harassment training," hoping that putting employees through these programs will stave off potential problems or at least inoculate them against major liability. Although some of the harassment training is of passable quality (given the flawed evidence on which it is based), too much of the training results in resentment by male employees and "over-empowerment" of female employees. In a recent case, a group of male air-traffic controllers filed charges against the Federal Aviation Administration, claiming they were forced to observe photos of male sex organs and let female participants fondle them during harassment training.

Sexually harassed men face skepticism from both sides of the political spectrum. On the Left, no one is seriously challenging the anti-male feminist paradigm. On the Right, commentators have cautioned that men should not succumb to the harassment hysteria. Yet conservatives in particular should take a more active interest in setting the record straight, given the costs and public-policy ramifications of current erroneous theories.

WORKPLACE TENSIONS

The current approach to sexual harassment has clearly hurt working relationships between men and women. Men are retreating to the safety of their offices, avoiding private contact with female co-workers, and carefully censoring their speech. Although the evidence has not yet been collected, it seems likely that male harassment victims, like their female counterparts, are more likely to be absent from work, to be less productive, and to leave the organization. In addition, men confronted by a sexually hostile environment may lash out against female co-workers, thereby prompting sexual-harassment complaints.

Trying to document a large, invisible mass of harassed men in the work force, however, does not mean advocating a new set of entitlements. On the contrary, recognizing that women are also harassers will help control the hysteria. Public policy, judicial interpretation, and popular sentiment have been swayed by statistics fraught with paradigmatic prejudice and methodological error. It is time for responsible researchers to begin an objective reexamination of the way that men and women treat each other at work. If the research shows that both men and women are experiencing harassment, then judicial remedy and public policy can be adjusted, and the idea of a harassing class and a victim class can be discarded.

It may also be time to reconsider the extent to which government can or should try to assure a comfortable working environment. People often receive treatment at work they do not like. The problem may lie in how the individual interprets the treatment.

Differing male and female interpretations of harassing behavior led the federal courts to establish the "reasonable woman" standard in 1991. This codified what we have known all along: men and women see things differently.

According to the ruling, behavior that a man considers acceptable can constitute harassment if it is offensive to a "reasonable woman." In other words, decades of evolving feminist theory have led us back to a Victorian vision of woman; she cannot endure what man can and must be protected.

Most of the outcry over sexual harassment is not about bosses demanding sex but about men doing and saying things that some women find offensive. Perhaps women are behaving just as offensively, but men have learned to live with it. The real answer to the "hostile environment" problem may be that women should learn to live with it too.

TOPIC FOR DISCUSSION AND WRITING

> Harsh Luthar and Anthony Townsend concede that studies on sexual harassment reveal that a significant number of women but only a negligible number of men have been sexually harassed. Discuss their explanation for this imbalance, and then devise and administer—possibly with a group of other students—a short survey designed to test the authors' belief that different questions would yield different results. Write the results of your survey and your analysis of them in a short report. (See Writing Assignment 17 on page 201.)

One Man's Tale of Harassment

Robert Ward

Ward's experience as one of three men working in an office with thirty women supports Luthar and Townsend's conclusion in "Man Handling" that a double standard exists in the workplace when it comes to sexual harassment.

There has been a lot of discussion in the press lately about sexualized interactions in the workplace, some of which is welcomed, and some of which resides in what is considered sexual harassment. That workplace can be the corner warehouse or the White House.

A few months ago, the focal point of the dialogue was centered around surgeon Frances K. Conley's scalding-hot memoir of sexism at Stanford University School of Medicine. In Conley's book, "Walking Out On the Boys," she supplies her readers with a cascade of abuses she witnessed, experienced, or heard about.

Throughout all the contemporary hubba-bubba over sexual harassment, how many people actually stop to think about all the men who are targets of abuse? Everyone assumes that sexual harassment happens only to women.

When men, such as myself, are victims, lots of people—including women—have no trouble looking the other way. There is definitely a double standard.

Why is it so different for men? Why is it that our society frowns upon and punishes men for certain behaviors toward women, while it is no big deal when women exhibit those same behaviors toward men?

The activities that befell me in the office would have sent most women cart-wheeling to the nearest salivating attorney. Co-workers of mine didn't even seem to notice that I was preyed upon. I was sexually harassed and subjected to a hostile environment every workday. It was simply another day at the office for my female co-workers.

The office I worked at was predominately female, with approximately 30 women and three men. Several of the women visited my cubicle every day. One was always telling me the latest sexual joke. One once showed me the black panties she planned on wearing that night to her boyfriend's house (she was wearing the panties).

Another woman, who worked out strenuously at a local gym, often gave me updates on her physical conditioning by lifting up her blouse to show off her abs.

My rear end was slapped more than a couple times, and I often felt like I was walking a gantlet of oversexed women fueled by raging hormones.

Men I personally know, especially those who work in mixed-sex offices, claim they would never say anything degrading, demeaning, or even remotely sexual to a woman in the workplace. Not because they are the valiant sort who would spread their coats over a puddle. No. The sexual harassment lawsuits against individuals and businesses have truly done an impressive job of curtailing sexual harassment.

But these same strictures and guidelines are often ignored by a great num-ber of women. Part of the blame for the double standard may rest with several stereotypes that we, as a society, hold toward men. Males are frequently viewed as able to "take care of themselves." Men are sometimes viewed as brusque sim-pletons with base desires.

In the real world, there are perfect matchups for these stereotypical men. But it is important to remember that there is also a great number of men who don't whistle at women, men who never tell a sexual joke to anyone, men who have numerous supportive and satisfying platonic relationships with women, and men who regard women as their equal, not as an object of sex-ual conquest.

There is a marked difference in what is acceptable and not acceptable in the work environment with regards to men and women. It's acceptable in our society for women to sexually joke around with men, yet if men do the same to women, they'll be in front of a judge faster than a lightning bolt. What gives?

TOPIC FOR DISCUSSION AND WRITING

In reference to sexual harassment in the workplace, Ward poses the following question: "Why is it that our society frowns upon and punishes men for certain behaviors toward women, while it is no big deal when women exhibit those same behaviors toward men?"

What is your response to this question? In your answer, you may refer to "Man Handling," "One Man's Tale of Harassment," and your own experience and ideas.

High Court Ruling Says Harassment Includes Same Sex

....

Linda Greenhouse

Business school professors Harsh Luthar and Anthony Townsend and office worker Robert Ward all object to the assumption that only women are sexually harassed and always by men. We can imagine their positive reaction to a 1998 U.S. Supreme Court decision which ruled out gender, sexual orientation and sexual desire as relevant elements in determining sexual harassment cases.

In an important sex discrimination case, the Supreme Court ruled today that Federal law protects employees from being sexually harassed in the workplace by people of the same sex.

The unanimous decision carried the law of sexual harassment—itself largely a creation of Supreme Court rulings over the last 12 years—beyond the classic male-female context to a type of case that has only recently been making its way into largely hostile lower courts. Many lower Federal courts either have flatly rejected same-sex harassment claims as a matter or law, or have limited them to cases in which a heterosexual employee complains of harassment by a homosexual co-worker.

In his opinion for the Court today, Justice Antonin Scalia said it was the conduct itself, and not the sex or motivation of the people involved, that determined whether sexual harassment amounted to "discrimination because of sex" within the meaning of Title VII of the Civil Rights Act of 1964. Sexual desire, whether heterosexual or homosexual, is not a necessary element of such a case, he said.

Justice Scalia's unusually brief opinion, barely seven pages, offered relatively little guidance about what must be proved to win a sexual harassment case against someone of the same sex. As with the Court's initial male-female sexual harassment cases, the Justices have evidently decided to allow the finer points of the law to develop as lower courts gain experience in handling actual cases.

The decision reinstated a harassment suit by Joseph Oncale, an oil rig worker, against his employer and three members of his all-male crew, including two supervisors. He said they had singled him out for crude sex play, unwanted touching and threats of rape.

The worker resigned after company officials refused to help him. The Federal District Court and the United States Court of Appeals for the Fifth Circuit, both in New Orleans, ruled that Mr. Oncale had no case because the Civil Rights Act did not apply to same-sex harassment.

In his opinion today overturning those rulings, Justice Scalia said, "We see no justification in the statutory language or our precedents for a categorical rule excluding same-sex harassment claims from the coverage of Title VII."

Civil rights lawyers praised the decision. Martha Davis, legal director of the NOW Legal Defense Fund, said the decision's unanimity and straightforward approach sent a clear message to lower courts to take sexual harassment claims seriously without making distinctions based on the sex of the people involved.

There are no statistics on the number of same-sex sexual harassment cases; any statistics would in any event be meaningless, because lawyers in jurisdictions where such cases have been ruled out would face sanctions for frivolous litigation if they filed a same-sex harassment lawsuit.

It is clear from today's opinion that the central element Mr. Oncale will have to prove to win his case is that he was discriminated against because of his sex. "Whatever evidentiary route the plaintiff chooses to follow, he or she must always prove that the conduct at issue was not merely tinged with offensive sexual connotations, but actually constituted 'discrimination because of sex,' " Justice Scalia said.

The phrase is contained in Title VII of the Civil Rights Act of 1964, which does not mention sexual harassment but outlaws discrimination in the workplace on the basis of race, sex and religion. In a unanimous ruling in 1986, *Meritor Savings Bank v. Vinson,* and in a subsequent decision in 1993, the Supreme Court held that sexual harassment so severe and pervasive as to alter the conditions of a victim's employment was a type of sex discrimination and was covered by the law.

In his opinion today, Justice Scalia offered very general examples of how a same-sex harassment claim might be shown to be discrimination—for instance, evidence of "general hostility" to the presence of people of the victim's sex in the workplace, or "direct comparative evidence" of how the accused harasser treated members of both sexes.

Neither of those tests appear applicable to Mr. Oncale's all-male workplace, but the opinion did not indicate that these examples were the only methods of proof. Because Mr. Oncale has never had a trial, few facts of his case have yet been established. But he might be able to show, for example, that he was singled out because he did not fit the image of the typical male oil-rig roustabout.

One Federal appeals court, in a case that has been appealed to the Supreme Court, recently allowed a same-sex harassment suit to proceed to trial on the evidence that the plaintiff, a teen-age boy who wore an earring, was harassed by co-workers on a municipal work crew in Belleville, Ill., for not being sufficiently masculine. The United States Court of Appeals for the Seventh Circuit, in Chicago, said that if proved, the co-workers' behavior amounted to discrimination on account of the boy's sex.

The Justices deferred action on the city's appeal, *City of Belleville v. Doe,* No. 97-669, until after the Oncale decision. How they deal with it now—whether by permitting the suit to go to trial or by ordering the appeals court to revisit the issue— may indicate the likelihood of Mr. Oncale's success on a similar theory.

Allen Fagin, a New York lawyer who represents management in employment discrimination suits, said today that while the Justices had clearly endorsed the "self-evident proposition" that the law covered sexual harassment between people of the same sex, "how that will play out is a different question."

Mr. Fagin, co-chairman of the labor and employment department at the law firm of Proskauer Rose, said that while "the opinion is short and simple, it is most important to understand what it doesn't say." He said the Court was not opening the door to suits for anti-homosexual discrimination as such. "People have to show they were discriminated against because they are male, not because they are gay," he said, adding that "at some point in some of these cases, the line between the two is likely to be cloudy."

For their part, lawyers representing gay rights groups greeted the ruling with relief, principally because the Court adhered to a single standard for same-sex and opposite-sex harassment cases. "We're really pleased that the Court made it as clear as it did that neither sexual orientation nor sexual attraction is a necessary part of a sexual harassment claim," said Beatrice Dohrn, legal director of the Lambda Legal Defense and Education Fund.

Matt Coles, director of the American Civil Liberties Union's gay rights project, said the Court's message was that "male or female, gay or straight, nobody should have to face sexual harassment when they go to work in the morning."

In the opinion, *Oncale v. Sundower Offshore Services*, No. 96–568, Justice Scalia was in some ways more explicit about what a valid sexual harassment claim is not than about what one is. There is no danger, despite the defendant's warnings in this case, that the Court is creating a "general civility code for the American workplace," Justice Scalia said.

"We have never held that workplace harassment, even harassment between men and women, is automatically discrimination because of sex merely because the words used have sexual content or connotations," he said. "The prohibition of harassment on the basis of sex requires neither asexuality nor androgyny in the workplace; it forbids only behavior so objectively offensive as to alter the conditions of the victim's employment," he added.

Justice Scalia said that "common sense and an appropriate sensitivity to social context" were important in judges' and juries' evaluation of each case. For example, he said, a professional football player would not be harassed if his coach "smacks him on the buttocks as he heads onto the field," but the same behavior "would reasonably be experienced as abusive by the coach's secretary (male or female) back at the office."

Martha Davis, the NOW Legal Defense Fund lawyer, said she had no problem with the Court's "common sense" standard. "I don't think there's any workplace where one would expect to be raped," she said.

TOPICS FOR DISCUSSION AND WRITING

1. What must an individual prove in order to win a sexual harassment suit?

2. In his seven-page written decision, Justice Scalia advises that "common sense and an appropriate sensitivity to social context" should

guide the courts' understanding of sexual harassment cases. To support his point, he offers the example of the football player being slapped on his buttocks by his coach before a game, appropriate behavior in that context, but inappropriate in an office setting. Can you think of any other such examples? From your own experiences as a student or employee, have you ever witnessed behavior that violated "common sense and an appropriate sensitivity to social context"? Write a short paper describing these instances, and the impact, if any, they had on the individuals involved, yourself or others.

A Double Standard

In Chapter 6 we include the fallacy of "special pleading." While philosophers may prefer this term, we might call it the fallacy of the double standard since special pleading means to apply a different standard to essentially the same act. The three essays which follow all accuse others of this fallacy. As you read, ask yourself if this charge is justified.

Feminism's Double Standard

Cynthia Tucker

Cynthia Tucker, the editorial editor of the Atlanta Constitution where this essay first appeared, expresses her anger at feminists for judging Bill Clinton's behavior less harshly than they have judged others whose behavior she sees as similar.

As things stand, Bill Clinton must atone for considerable collateral damage— humiliating his family, betraying close associates, sullying the Oval Office.

But the president cannot fairly be blamed for all the wreckage that lies in the wake of his tawdry affair. He bears little responsibility, for example, for the devastation suffered by a formerly high-minded movement called "feminism." The injuries to the women's movement have been self-inflicted—the result of contorted defenses of Clinton's behavior.

On Monday, before the president even testified or issued his kinda mea culpa, National Organization for Women President Patricia Ireland issued a statement defending him. After a perfunctory denunciation of his behavior, she said, in part, ". . . consensual sex is not illegal harassment and it is not an impeachable offense. Nor is it in the best interest of our country for the president to resign."

Ireland's sentiments were similar to the Clintonesque, legalistic defense that Gloria Steinem used in March to support the president in the wake of Kathleen Willey's charges that he groped her during a meeting in which she asked for a paying job. According to Steinem, "President Clinton took 'no' for an answer," so Willey's charges, even if true, did not constitute sexual harassment.

Anita Hill, the woman who stamped the term sexual harassment on the nation's consciousness, agreed, saying her case against Clarence Thomas was "different." (She's right. She accused Thomas only of using offensive language, not groping her.)

Not even the fiercest enemies of equal rights for women could have done more to eviscerate feminism than Ireland, Steinem and Hill did with those declarations. If feminism were left to them, it would be nothing more than a sham—not a principled movement at all, but just another partisan claque.

After all, feminism has long held as one of its core values the notion that women should not be sexually exploited. In the 1970s, it was well-known feminist writers such as Steinem who introduced to the country the concept that "all politics is personal," meaning, among other things, that a man's behavior at home should be counted in the political context.

Of course, a good feminist may assume that politicians are due privacy, and their relationships with their spouses are their own business. Still, that privacy does not extend to the politician's tax-supported workplace.

Until now, it has also been a core value of feminism that a powerful executive who engages in casual sex with a subordinate has crossed the line into sexual exploitation, if not legal sexual harassment. Monica Lewinsky's age is not the major consideration here; it is, rather, her how-level status. Given Clinton's position as the most powerful CEO in the country, her "consent" is not equal to his. In many corporations, an executive engaging in that same behavior would be fired. And feminists would applaud.

That does not even begin to address Clinton's apparent attempt to rewrite the definition of "sexual relations" so that oral sex is not included. In other words, he does not even give his "consensual" acts with Lewinsky the dignity of intimacy; she just serviced him, as a prostitute might. What kind of attitude toward women does that imply?

Still, it is not the president's fault that so-called feminists so easily sold out their principles. They should have judged Clinton, a political ally, by the same standards to which they held Thomas and former Oregon Senator Bob Packwood, no matter how painful that might have been. They have not. And because of that duplicity, some of the most worthy crusades of the women's movement—such as an end to sexual harassment— have been diminished.

TOPICS FOR DISCUSSION AND WRITING

1. Would you classify Bill Clinton's treatment of Kathleen Willey and Monica Lewinsky as examples of sexual harassment? Why or why not? Support your answer with specific references to the readings in this chapter.

2. Use the Internet in order to research both the Clarence Thomas Supreme Court confirmation hearings and the U.S. Senate's case

against former Oregon Senator Bob Packwood. (See Research and Documentation in Chapter 9.) In what ways was their behavior like or unlike Clinton's?

3. Do you agree with Tucker's accusation that feminists are guilty of applying a double standard when judging Bill Clinton's behavior? Why or why not? (See Special Pleading in Chapter 6.)

High Court's Mixed Decisions

Ellen Goodman

Boston Globe columnist Ellen Goodman accuses the U.S. Supreme Court of applying a double standard in two recent sexual harassment decisions, in one case protecting workers from abusive supervisors but in another case, failing to adequately protect students from teachers who behave inappropriately.

By now it's become a summer ritual. The justices finish the term cramming as if they were still law students. They drop their final papers on the public desk and head off for vacation.

This year the Supremes majored in sexual harassment and got some pretty good marks. But at the risk of sounding like a hard grader, they also deserve some incompletes. In a series of decisions, the court made it easier for workers to sue their companies for sexual harassment than for students to sue their school districts.

In the workplace cases, a majority of the justices struck a balance that both sides—women's rights advocates and corporations alike—called a "win-win." Ruling in favor of a lifeguard in Boca Raton and a manager at Burlington Industries, they gave women a powerful tool to sue for sexual harassment. In essence, they said a company could be liable for the behavior of a supervisor even if it didn't know what he was doing.

At the same time, they gave that company a powerful defense. They said that if you have a good sexual harassment policy and the worker doesn't use it, you're off the hook.

But in the case of a high-school student harassed by a teacher, a 5-to-4 majority just about reversed the rules. They made it harder for a student to sue and easier for a school to stick its head in the sand.

The court ruled if a teacher harasses a student, the school isn't liable for damages unless those in charge both knew and acted with "deliberate indifference." The school didn't need to have any policy at all to defend itself. But the student had to complain to a person with the power to change things.

So this is where we stand at the end of this term paper. Companies are scrambling to beef up sexual harassment policies. But schools?

Indeed, if you put those two rulings together, a teacher is now better protected from harassment by a principal in her workplace, than a student is from her teacher in her studyplace.

Those of us who did not major in sexual harassment, but rather in common sense, can see a double standard. And a bizarre one at that.

After all, a worker is generally older than a student. She can get up and leave her desk, her office, her job without raising her hand. A student is younger, more vulnerable, and less likely to bring her complaint to the top. If anything, the schools, acting *in loco parentis,* funded by taxpayers, should have the higher standard.

How did the Supreme Court end up with these contradictions? The official rationale is that the sexual harassment cases at work and at school were brought under separate laws. Title IX bars sex discrimination in education and Title VII bars it in employment.

The trio of justices who switched sides looked over Title IX and decided that since there was no specific language allowing individual suits against a school system, Congress wanted it this way.

I don't believe that Congress ever intended to make the classroom easier than the office for sexual harassers. But this is where we are at the end of Sexual Harassment Spring Semester.

The good news is that Congress will soon be back in session. It's up to the folks on Capitol Hill now to eliminate the double standard.

Sex Harassment and Double Standards

....

Marcia D. Greenberger and Verna L. Williams

Marcia Greenberger, co-president, and Verna Williams, senior counsel, at the National Women's Law Center, both agree with Ellen Goodman, sharing her concern that two decisions made by the Supreme Court apply a double standard, one in the workplace, another in the classroom, leaving students vulnerable to abusive behavior.

When is a victim of sexual harassment not a victim of sexual harassment? When the victim is a student, according to several decisions by the Supreme Court this term. Indeed, the Court's rulings inadvertently created two classes of citizens: employees, who are protected from sexual harassment, and students, who are not.

In a victory for employees, the Court, in a pair of 7-to–2 decisions, ruled that employers could be held financially responsible when supervisors sexually harassed workers, whether or not the employer actually knew about the harassment.

Indeed, the Court ruled that under Title VII, the Federal law prohibiting workplace discrimination, an employee who resisted a supervisor's advances need not have suffered any kind of tangible loss, like dismissal or loss of a promotion, to be able to file a lawsuit against her company. Instead, when the harassment does not result in any loss, but causes emotional distress or other injury, then the employer must show that it had strong policies and procedures in place, that employees were informed about these policies and that the employee had unreasonably failed to use it.

Under this sound decision, if a teacher harasses an assistant and the school system fails to respond, then it can be held liable.

But what happens to a student harassed by a teacher? In *Gebser v. Lago Vista Independent School District,* the Court ruled 5 to 4 that schools or colleges do not have to pay damages for harassment of a student by a teacher unless officials specifically knew about the misconduct and responded with "deliberate indifference." It does not matter whether the school system had any policies or procedures in place or whether it did anything at all to combat harassment.

This decision creates an incentive for school officials to turn their backs on the most egregious instances of harassment like sexual assault. Officials need only insulate themselves from being informed and claim ignorance.

Why would the Court make this distinction between students and employees? Students fall under Title IX, the Federal law that prohibits sex discrimination in education. Title IX, unlike Title VII, has no specific language allowing students to sue and win damages from lawsuits—even though the Court had previously ruled that Congress intended such remedies.

The majority instead said that students were covered by another remedy under Title IX: schools can be sanctioned by the Education Department, which is authorized to investigate sexual harassment complaints and, if justified, to halt Federal financing if a school persist in allowing such harassment.

Thanks to the Education Department's efforts, many schools have complied with Title IX. But this cannot be the only remedy. The Government has limited resources and many civil rights obligations extending far beyond harassment. It cannot possibly pursue every harassment complaint. And even if the Government investigates a complaint—and a school adopts procedures to insure that complaints are addressed promptly—that does little to compensate a student for the injury he or she suffered.

Now the Government's job might be even harder, since the Court's decision has created a financial incentive for schools to hide harassment. Many schools will wait to be caught before coming into compliance with the law.

The Supreme Court has ruled, and now Congress must step in. Working with the Clinton Administration, it should define Title IX as explicitly allowing students who have been harassed to sue their schools, and to win damages. Justice requires no less.

TOPICS FOR DISCUSSION AND WRITING

1. On the basis of both the Goodman and the Greenberger and Williams editorials, write a summary, not of the articles, but of the two Supreme Court decisions which the articles focus on. (See Summaries in Chapter 3.)

2. Do you agree with the authors that the Supreme Court is guilty of creating a double standard? Why or why not? (See Special Pleading in Chapter 6.)

Sexual Harassment on Campus

Bad Behavior

Francine Prose

Novelist and teacher Francine Prose defends her friend, a college professor, accused of sexual harassment, comparing his ordeal to the Salem witch trials and the anti-communist McCarthy hearing of the 1950s. Her latest novel, *Blue Angel,* also addresses the issue of sexual harassment on campus.

Five men and women from the university community were convened in a campus conference room to decide if my friend Stephen Dobyns—a distinguished poet and novelist and a tenured creative-writing professor—was guilty of sexual harassment and should be dismissed from his job. The tone was one of such civility and high moral seriousness that I could only assume I was the only person in the room tuned in to the disturbing static beneath all this calm inquiry: the only one hearing echoes of Victorian melodrama, of badly overacted student productions of Arthur Miller's play "The Crucible."

Perhaps my alienation came from my peculiar role—as a character witness for the alleged sexual harasser. I think of myself as a feminist. I write about "women's issues." I teach in writing programs and am painfully aware of the pressures facing young (and older) female writers. I find myself more often than not taking the woman's side. I believed Anita Hill.

Two months before the hearing, at a graduate-student party, an argument erupted—and my friend splashed a drink in the face of a student who had heard him make a remark about her breasts. (Witnesses say he told another writer to "stop looking at her breasts.") The student filed a formal complaint, and two others have come forward to say that his harassment has destroyed their ability to function in the classroom and at the writing desk.

Clearly, my friend is guilty—but only of bad behavior. You don't go throwing drinks in a student's face and talking about her breasts. Since the drink-throwing incident, my friend has been sober and regularly attends A.A. meetings, but a drinking problem used to exaggerate his confrontational personality. He has spoken without considering the feelings of his audience; he sometimes connects with other men with fairly crude talk about sex. But that's not sexual harassment as I understand it.

No one suggests that he offered to trade good grades for sex. He is not accused of sleeping with or propositioning students—one says he tried to kiss her at a drunken party—or of the focused protracted hectoring we might call "harassment." The allegations all concern language: specifically, what the commit-tee calls "salty language" used outside the classroom at graduate-student par-ties. They involve attempts to be funny, and to provoke. There was one cruel sexual remark about a professor who wasn't present, and the suggestion that another might benefit from a "salty" term for a satisfactory sexual encounter.

Is this sexual harassment? Not in any clear sense, but those clear borders have been smudged by university policies that refer to "a hostile workplace," to "patterns of intimidation." "Hostile" and "intimidation" are subjectively defined, as they were by the student who testified (hilariously, I thought, though, again, no one seemed to notice) that he felt intimidated by my friend's use of a "salty" phrase. He felt he was being asked to condone a locker-room atmosphere that might offend the women present.

There was much talk of protecting women from blunt mentions of sex. And the young women who testified were in obvious need of protection. They gulped, trem-bled and wept, describing how my friend yelled at them in class or failed to encour-age their work. Victorian damsels in distress, they used 19th-century language: they had been "shattered" by his rude, "brutish" behavior. After testifying, they seemed radiant, exalted, a state of being that, like so much else, recalled "The Crucible," which used the Salem witch trials as a metaphor for the Army-McCarthy hearings.

Are these the modern women feminists had in mind? Victorian girls, Puritan girls, crusading against dirty thoughts and loose speech? I thought of all the salty words I have used in class—words that could apparently cost me my job—and of my own experience with sexual harassment: the colleague who told me that his department only hired me because I was a woman; if they could have found a black woman, they would have hired her. Such words were more damaging than anything he could have said about my breasts. But no one could have ac-cused him of harassment: he didn't make a pass at me or refer to a sexual act.

Finally, I thought of students, men and women whose lives were changed by studying with Dobyns, an excellent teacher who cares about writing, who takes women seriously and is interested in their work and not (like many male teachers who are not, strictly speaking, guilty of sexual harassment) annoyed by female intelligence and bored by the subject of female experience. But these facts were irrelevant to the discussion of whether or not my friend got drunk and said this or that dirty word.

Soon after the hearing, he was informed that he had been found guilty of making five sexually harassing remarks. The committee recommended that he be suspended from his job without pay for two years, banned from campus ex-cept to use the library, required to perform 200 hours of community service and to pay one of his accusers $600 to compensate for the wages she lost because of the mental suffering he caused her.

It's as if a nasty bubble of Puritanism has risen to the surface and burst. There's been a narrowing of parameters—not of what can be done, but of what can be said by writers whose subject (one might think) is language. In an effort to protect the delicate ears of the gentle sex, a career has been damaged with casual glee. Feminists, academics, intellectuals—those who stand to lose the most from restrictions on free expression—are ignoring the possible consequences of the precedent they are setting. They must be choosing not to imagine the terrible swift ease with which our right to free speech can simply crumble away, gathering momentum as the erosion process begins—until human rights and women's rights are subjects too salty to mention.

TOPICS FOR DISCUSSION AND WRITING

1. Why does Francine Prose think her friend, Stephen Dobyns, is being treated unfairly? Do you agree or disagree? Support your answer with specific details from the essay.

2. What does the writer see as the ultimate consequence of behavior such as Dobyn's being categorized as sexual harassment? Could she be accused of slippery slope reasoning or are her fears justified? (See Slippery Slope in Chapter 6.)

This Is Teaching?

Linda Hirshman

In the following two essays paired in the same issue of the *American Bar Association Journal,* Michael S. Greve, director of the Center for Individual Rights in Washington, D.C., and Linda Hirshman, a law professor at the Illinois Institute of Technology, debate the case of Donald Silva, a writing instructor at the University of New Hampshire, who lost his position at the University as a result of his female students complaining about the sexual metaphors he used to teach writing. As you read about Silva's behavior, imagine yourself in his class, and ask yourself what impact, if any, his behavior would have on you.

I belong to the Ruth Bader Ginsburg generation of liberal feminists. I read "The Feminine Mystique" when it was published, was one of eight women in law school, and thought I could be as good a lawyer as any man. So, for a long time, I thought the focus of Catherine MacKinnon on sexual subordination and harassment was eccentric. Equal pay, reproductive rights—those were my issues.

But, in the last few years, the teachers who talk dirty to their female students have made a believer out of me. I began to ask what conceivable justification there could be for Professor J. Donald Silva to have to teach his students that writing "is like sex. You seek a target. You zero in on your target. You move from side to side. You close in on the subject. . . . You and the center become one."

In this post-*Harris v. Forklift** era, can you imagine your law partner describing legal writing to your associates this way? College tuition these days is a pretty

---

*A reference to a sexual harrassment case in which the Supreme Court ruled that a work environment can be considered abusive even if it does not "seriously affect [an employee's] psychological well-being" or lead her to "suffer injury."

high price to pay for something you can get from a 900 number for a lot less money. Worse still, if Greve has his way, and the colleges can't offer students alternatives to Silva's sex talk, the students will continue to be his captive audience.

Professors like Silva and their defenders say that the students should lighten up. Such sex talk is important, they say. Yet the more I know about the offending teachers, the more I realize that what really matters to them is the privilege of sexual abuse. The academics' attachment to acting out has made me realize the importance of this issue.

Another tactic is to compare people who oppose the harassment to Hitler. Legal commentators argue that law suddenly loses all capacity for sensible distinctions when sex is involved. Don't believe it. First calling someone Hitler (the "reductio ad Hitlerium") is a desperate move, which people make only because their other arguments aren't very good. Historical exceptions to the First Amendment—for instance, limiting lawyers soliciting captive clients at bedside—exist to this day. Free countries like Canada and Britain regulate pornography and defamation without turning into the Third Reich.

EDUCATION NEEDN'T BE X-RATED

Constitutional law aside, the professors' defenders invoke the serious and worthy value of "academic freedom," implying that nothing less than the future of Western civilization rests on the freedom to engage in such exhibitions. This suggestion defames the very concept of "teachers."

Since women entered higher education in numbers, a whole generation of American women have been lucky enough to know teachers who managed to achieve excellence without insulting female students.

Consider these examples from my past: During the 1960s, philosophy students at Harvard would copy drafts of John Rawls' work in progress and send them to other departments around the country so students elsewhere could study them as soon as possible. When it came out, Rawls' "A Theory of Justice" almost single-handedly revived the subject of political philosophy.

No one has ever suggested that John Rawls felt compelled to compare any aspect of his magisterial and revolutionary theory of political philosophy to sexual intercourse.

My own First Amendement teacher and one of its greatest advocates, Harry A. Kalven Jr., of the University of Chicago, derived his love of free speech from its role in the 1960s enabling black Americans to march for full citizenship after centuries of subordination.

None of us who were privileged to sit in Harry's classroom could remotely imagine him offering to relieve an 18-year-old student of her virginity, as did 54-year-old William Kerrigan of the University of Massachusetts in a recent issue of *Harper's*.

In Europe, liberal equality put an end to droit du seigneur, the feudal lord's privilege of sexual access to the females on his lands. University campuses are one of the last refuges of the practice, and it's beyond time for the Middle Ages to come to an end there, too.

Call It What It Is—Censorship

Michael S. Greve

J. Donald Silva is a pastor at the New Castle Congregational Church in New Castle, N.H. Until April 1993, he was also a creative writing teacher at the University of New Hampshire. His 30-year tenure was terminated for having created a "hostile environment." The evidence consisted of two offbeat remarks Silva had made in class—one comparing "focus" in the writing process to sexual activity, the other elucidating the meaning of simile with a famed belly dancer's description of her craft.

Silva v. University of New Hampshire may be unique in its particulars. But it shows that the current untempered enthusiasm for stamping out "hostile environment" harassment may produce huge social costs, including the suppression of free speech.

To date, First Amendment concerns have played only a marginal role in sexual harassment litigation, and the Supreme Court ignored them in its recent decision in *Harris v. Forklift Systems.* But this is changing rapidly. Complaints over a hostile work or learning environment are proliferating on college campuses, which are disproportionately populated by individuals with exquisite sensibilities or, less charitably but perhaps more to the point, with a politically and sexually correct agenda.

Conflicts between harassment claims and free speech will be much sharper on campus than in the ordinary employment context, and effort to produce a harmonious environment by means of civil rights litigation will entail far higher social costs in the form of "lost" speech.

Widget Inc. and its employees will function with or without pin-up posters and other forms of employee "speech" that have occasionally attracted harassment complaints. In higher education, in contrast, free speech is central both to the purpose of the institution and to the employee's profession and performance.

Academia cannot function under a legal regime that punishes speech in the name of combating a "hostile environment." This, alas, is the legal regime we have. One may argue that Professor Silva is a rare exception. But the question is not what Professor Silva said; it is what professors and students on campuses across the country will refrain from saying.

VAGUE RULES STIFLE SPEECH

The current legal rules, which define a "hostile environment" on the basis of a case-by-case, multifactor analysis and with reference to the perception of a "reasonable person," are exceedingly vague. By that very virtue, they deter not only genuine harassment but also harmless and desirable speech; faced with legal uncertainty, individuals will avoid any speech that might be interpreted as creating a hostile environment.

Nor is it enough that the innocent victims of the anti-harassment campaign eventually can obtain judicial relief; mere complaints of misconduct, and their adjudication at university committees that operate with less than mathematical precision and are fearful of EEOC sanctions and investigations by the Office of Civil Rights, are in and of themselves a powerful deterrent.

A more reasonable set of rules would afford comprehensive First Amendment protection for all academic speech: Subject to liability only speech that is targeted at particular individuals and amounts to an intentional infliction of severe emotional distress; and authorize disciplinary measures and compensatory damages against individuals who knowingly bring false and frivolous charges of harassment (much like some "hate crime" statues impose liability for such charges).

This arrangement would have the great advantage of curbing genuine harassment without intrusion into free speech and academic freedom. Naturally, it would fail to satisfy the apostles of sexual correctness, who view the First Amendment as merely one more policy consideration and the delicate sensibilities of freshwomen as an absolute limit to academic discourse.

But, as any student with strong religious convictions can testify, we have never considered subjective perceptions of a "hostile environment" as a limit to robust dialogue. Professor Silva's case illustrates why we should not do so now.

TOPICS FOR DISCUSSION AND WRITING

1. Summarize the positions of Hirshman and Greve. (See Summaries in Chapter 3.)

2. Write a paper stating your own position on this particular case. Do you believe that the University of New Hampshire was right to let Silva go, or that he should be allowed to continue to teach? In defending your position, draw from the arguments of Hirshman and Greve as well as from your own personal experience and reading.

3. Compare the case of Professor Silva with other cases of harassment detailed in this chapter. Which cases do you consider to have the greatest consequences?

Oleanna

David Mamet

David Mamet is one of America's most acclaimed playwrights. Among his plays are *Speed-the-Plow, American Buffalo, Sexual Perversity in Chicago* and *Glengarry Glen Ross,* which won the Pulitzer Prize. He is also a screenwriter (his screenplay for *The Verdict* was nominated for an Oscar), an essayist and a poet. His play *Oleanna* has only two characters: John, a male college professor and Carol, a female student. Their interaction created a great deal of controversy when the play was first performed, leaving members of the audience arguing with one another about political correctness and sexual harassment after the final curtain came down. In reaction to this phenomenon, some theater companies invited audiences to stay after the performance to discuss the play and debate the issues with the actors.

The question most hotly debated at these after-the performance discussions was this: Is Carol a legitimate victim of sexual harassment or a manipulative woman with a political agenda? Keep this question in mind as you read the play.

Characters

Carol   A woman of twenty

John   A man in his forties

The play takes place in John's office.

ONE

John is talking on the phone. Carol is seated across the desk from him.

JOHN   (*on phone*): And what about the land. (*Pause*) The land. And what about the land? (*Pause*) What about it? (*Pause*) No. I don't understand. Well, yes, I'm I'm . . . No, I'm *sure* it's signif . . . I'm sure it's significant. (*Pause*) Because it's significant to mmmmmm . . . did you call Jerry? (*Pause*) Because . . . no, no, no, no, no. What did they say . . . ? Did you speak to the *real* estate . . . where is she . . . ? Well, well, all right. Where are her notes? Where are the notes we took with her. (*Pause*) I thought you were? No. No, I'm sorry, I didn't mean that, I just thought that I saw you, when we were there . . . What . . . ? I thought I saw you with a *pencil*. WHY NOW? is what I'm say . . . well, that's why I say "call Jerry." Well, I can't right now, be . . . no, I *didn't* schedule any . . . Grace: I *didn't* . . . I'm well aware . . . Look: Did you call Jerry? Will you call Jerry . . . ? Because I can't now. I'll be there, I'm sure I'll be there in fifteen, in twenty. I intend to. No, we aren't *going* to lose the, we aren't *going* to lose the house. Look: Look I'm not minimizing it. The "easement." Did she say "easement"? (*Pause*) What did she *say; is* it a "term of art," are we *bound* by it . . . I'm sorry . . . (*Pause*) are: we: yes. *Bound* by . . . Look: (*He checks his watch.*) before the other side *goes home,* all right? "a term of art." Because: that's right (*Pause*) The yard for the boy. Well, that's the whole . . . Look: I'm going to meet you there . . . (*He checks his watch.*) Is the realtor there? All right, tell her to show you the basement again. Look at the *this* because . . . Bec . . . I'm leaving in, I'm leaving in ten or fifteen . . . Yes. No, no, I'll meet you at the new . . . That's a good. If he thinks it's necc . . . you tell Jerry to meet . . . All right? We *aren't* going to lose the deposit. All right? I'm sure it's going to be . . . (*Pause*) I hope so. (*Pause*) I love you, too. (*Pause*) I love you, too. As soon as . . . I will.

(*He hangs up.*) (*He bends over the desk and makes a note.*) (*He looks up.*) (*To Carol:*) I'm sorry . . .

CAROL: (*Pause*) What is a "term of art"?

JOHN: (*Pause*) I'm sorry . . . ?

CAROL: (*Pause*) What is a "term of art"?

JOHN: Is that what you want to talk about?

CAROL: . . . to talk about . . . ?

JOHN: Let's take the mysticism out of it, shall we? Carol? (*Pause*) Don't you think? I'll tell you: when you have some "thing." Which must be broached. (*Pause*) Don't you think . . . ? (*Pause*)

CAROL: . . . don't I think . . . ?

JOHN: Mmm?

CAROL: . . . did I . . . ?

JOHN: . . . what?

CAROL: Did . . . did I . . . did I say something wr . . .

JOHN: (*Pause*) No. I'm sorry. No. You're right. I'm very sorry. I'm somewhat rushed. As you see. I'm sorry. You're right. (*Pause*) What is a "term of art"? It seems to mean a *term,* which has come, through its use, to mean something *more specific* than the words would, to someone *not acquainted* with them . . . indicate. That, I believe, is what a "term of art," would mean. (*Pause*)

CAROL: You don't know what it means . . . ?

JOHN: I'm not sure that I know what it means. It's one of those things, perhaps you've had them, that, you look them up, or have someone explain them to you, and you say "aha," and, you immediately *forget* what . . .

CAROL: You don't do that.

JOHN: . . . I . . . ?

CAROL: You don't do . . .

JOHN: . . . I don't what . . . ?

CAROL: . . . for . . .

JOHN: . . . I don't for . . .

CAROL: . . . no . . .

JOHN: . . . forget things? Everybody does that.

CAROL: No, they don't.

JOHN: They don't . . .

CAROL: No.

JOHN: (*Pause*) No. Everybody does that.

CAROL: Why would they do that . . . ?

JOHN: Because. I don't know. Because it doesn't interest them.

CAROL: No.

JOHN: I think so, though. (*Pause*) I'm sorry that I was distracted.

CAROL: You don't have to say that to me.

JOHN: You paid me the compliment, or the "obeisance"—all right—of coming in here . . . All right. *Carol.* I find that I am at a *standstill.* I find that I . . .

CAROL: . . . what . . .

JOHN: . . . one moment. In regard to your . . . to your . . .

CAROL: Oh, oh. You're buying a new house!

JOHN: No, let's get on with it.

CAROL: "get on"? (*Pause*)

JOHN: I know how . . . *believe* me. I know how . . . potentially *humiliating* these . . . I have no desire to . . . I have no desire other than to help you. But: (*He picks up some papers on his desk.*) I won't even say " but." I'll say that as I go back over the . . .

CAROL: I'm just, I'm just trying to . . .

JOHN: .. . . no, it will not do.

CAROL: . . . what? What will. . . . ?

JOHN: No. I see, I see what you, it . . . (*He gestures to the papers.*) but your work . . .

CAROL: I'm just: I sit in class I . . . (*She holds up her notebook.*) I take notes . . .

JOHN: (*simultaneously with* "notes"): Yes. I understand. What I am trying to tell *you* is that some, some basic . . .

CAROL: . . . I . . .

JOHN: . . . one moment: some basic missed communi . . .

CAROL: I'm doing what I'm told. I bought your book, I read your. . .

JOHN: No, I'm sure you . . .

CAROL: No, no, no. I'm doing what I'm told. It's *difficult* for me. It's *difficult* . . .

JOHN: . . . but . . .

CAROL: I don't . . . lots of the *language.* . .

JOHN: . . . please . . .

CAROL: The *language,* the "things" that you say . . .

JOHN: I'm sorry. No. I don't think that that's true.

CAROL: It *is* true. I . . .

JOHN: I think . . .

CAROL: It *is* true.

JOHN: . . . I . . .

CAROL: Why would I . . . ?

JOHN: I'll tell you why: you're an incredibly bright girl.

CAROL: . . . I . . .

JOHN: You're an incredibly . . . you have no problem with the . . . Who's kidding who?

CAROL: . . . I . . .

JOHN: No. No. I'll tell you why. I'll tell . . . I think you're *angry*, I . . .

CAROL: . . . why would I . . .

JOHN: . . . wait one moment. I . . .

CAROL: It *is* true. I have *problems* . . .

JOHN: . . . every . . .

CAROL: . . . I come from a different *social* . . .

JOHN: . . . ev . . .

CAROL: a different economic . . .

JOHN: . . . Look:

CAROL: No. I: when I *came* to this school:

JOHN: Yes. Quite . . . (*Pause*)

CAROL: . . . does that mean nothing . . . ?

JOHN: . . . but look: look . . .

CAROL: . . . I . . .

JOHN: (*Picks up paper.*) Here: Please: Sit down. (*Pause*) Sit down. (*Reads from her paper.*) "I think that the ideas contained in this work express the author's feelings in a way that he intended, based on his results." What can that mean? Do you see? What . . .

CAROL: I, the best that I . . .

JOHN: I'm saying, that perhaps this course . . .

CAROL: No, no, no, you can't, you can't . . . I have to . . .

JOHN: . . . how . . .

CAROL: . . . I have to pass it . . .

JOHN: Carol, I:

CAROL: I *have* to pass this course, I . . .

JOHN: Well.

CAROL: . . . don't you. . .

JOHN: Either the . . .

CAROL: . . . I . . .

JOHN: . . . either the, I . . . either the *criteria* for judging progress in the class are . . .

CAROL: No, no, no, no, I have to pass it.

JOHN: Now, look: I'm a human being, I . . .

CAROL: I did what you told me. I did, I did everything that, I read your *book*, you told me to buy your book and read it. Everything you *say* I . . . (*She gestures to her notebook.*) (*The phone rings.*) I do . . . . Ev . . .

JOHN: . . . look:

CAROL: . . . everything I'm told . . .

JOHN: Look. Look. I'm not your *father*. (*Pause*)

CAROL: What?

JOHN: I'm.

CAROL: Did I say you were my father?

JOHN: . . . no . . .

CAROL: Why did you say that . . . ?

JOHN: I . . .

CAROL: . . . why . . . ?

JOHN: . . . in class I . . . (*He picks up the phone.*) (*Into phone:*) Hello. I can't talk now. Jerry? Yes? I underst . . . I can't talk now. I know . . . I know . . . Jerry. I can't *talk* now. Yes, I. Call me back in . . . Thank you. (*He hangs up.*) (*To Carol:*) What do you want me to do? We are two people, all right? Both of whom have subscribed to . . .

CAROL: No, no . . .

JOHN: . . . certain arbitrary . . .

CAROL: No. You have to help me.

JOHN: Certain institutional . . . you tell me what you want to do . . . You tell me what you want me to . . .

CAROL: How can I go back and tell them the *grades* that I . . .

JOHN: . . . what can I do . . . ?

CAROL: *Teach* me. *Teach* me.

JOHN: . . . I'm trying to teach you.

CAROL: I read your book. I read it. I don't under . . .

JOHN: . . . you don't understand it.

CAROL: No.

JOHN: Well, perhaps it's not well *written* . . .

CAROL (*simultaneously with* "written"): No. No. No. I want to *understand* it.

JOHN: What don't you understand? (*Pause*)

CAROL: *Any* of it. What you're trying to say. When you talk about . . .

JOHN: . . . yes . . . ? (*She consults her notes.*)

CAROL: "Virtual warehousing of the young" . . .

JOHN: "Virtual warehousing of the young." If we artificially prolong adolescence . . .

CAROL: . . . and about "The Curse of Modern Education."

JOHN: . . . well . . .

CAROL: I don't . . .

JOHN: Look. It's just a *course*, it's just a *book*, it's just a . . .

CAROL: No. No. There are *people* out there. People who came *here*. To know something they didn't *know*. Who *came* here. To be *helped*. To be *helped*. So someone would *help* them. To *do* something. To *know* something. To get, what do they say? "To get on in the world." How can I do that if I don't, if I fail? But I don't *understand*. I don't *understand*. I don't understand what anything means . . . and I walk around. From morning 'til night: with this one thought in my head. I'm *stupid*.

JOHN: No one thinks you're stupid.

CAROL: No? What am I . . . ?

JOHN: I . . .

CAROL: . . . what am I, then?

JOHN: I think you're angry. Many people are. I have a *telephone* call that I have to make. And an *appointment*, which is rather *pressing*; though I sympathize with your concerns, and though I wish I had the time, this was not a previously scheduled meeting and I . . .

CAROL: . . . you think I'm nothing . . .

JOHN: . . . have an appointment with a *realtor*, and with my wife and . . .

CAROL: You think that I'm stupid.

JOHN: No. I certainly don't.

CAROL: You said it.

JOHN: No. I did not.

CAROL: You did.

JOHN: When?

CAROL: . . . you . . .

JOHN: No. I never did, or never would say that to a student, and . . .

CAROL: You said, "What can that mean?" (*Pause*) "What can that mean?" . . . (*Pause*)

JOHN: . . . and what did that mean to you . . . ?

CAROL: That meant I'm stupid. And I'll never learn. That's what that meant. And you're right.

JOHN: . . . I . . .

CAROL: But then. But then, what am I doing here . . . ?

JOHN: . . . if you thought that I . . .

CAROL: . . . when nobody wants me, and . . .

JOHN: . . . if you interpreted . . .

CAROL: Nobody *tells* me anything. And I *sit* there . . . in the *corner*. In the *back*. And everybody's talking about "this" all the time. And "concepts," and "precepts" and, and, and, and, and, WHAT IN THE WORLD ARE YOU *TALKING* ABOUT? And I read your book. And they said, "Fine, go in that class." Because you talked about responsibility to the young. I DON'T KNOW WHAT IT MEANS AND I'M *FAILING* . . .

JOHN: May . . .

CAROL: No, you're right. "Oh hell." I failed. Flunk me out of it. It's garbage. Everything I do. "The ideas contained in this work express the author's feelings." That's right. That's right. I know I'm stupid. I know what I am. (*Pause*) I know what I am, Professor. You don't have to tell me. (*Pause*) It's pathetic. Isn't it?

JOHN: . . . Aha . . . (*Pause*) Sit down. Sit down. Please. (*Pause*) Please sit down.

CAROL: Why?

JOHN: I want to talk to you.

CAROL: Why?

JOHN: Just sit down. (*Pause*) Please. Sit down. Will you, please . . . ? (*Pause. She does so.*) Thank you.

CAROL: What ?

JOHN: I want to tell you something.

CAROL: (*Pause*) What?

JOHN: Well, I know what you're talking about.

CAROL: No. You don't.

JOHN: I think I do. (*Pause*)

CAROL: How can you?

JOHN: I'll tell you a story about myself. (*Pause*) Do you mind? (*Pause*) I was raised to think myself stupid. That's what I want to tell you. (*Pause*)

CAROL: What do you mean?

JOHN: Just what I said. I was brought up, and my earliest, and most persistent memories are of being told that I was stupid. "You have such *intelligence*. Why must you behave so *stupidly*?" Or, "Can't you *understand*? Can't you *understand*?" And I could *not* understand. I could *not* understand.

CAROL: What?

JOHN: The simplest problem. Was beyond me. It was a mystery.

CAROL: What was a mystery?

JOHN: How people learn. How *I* could learn. Which is what I've been speaking of in class. And of *course* you can't hear it. Carol. Of *course* you can't. (*Pause*) I used to speak of "real people," and wonder what the *real* people did. The *real* people. Who were they? *They* were the people other than myself. The *good* people. The *capable* people. The people who could do the things, I could not do: learn, study, retain . . . all that *garbage*—which is what I have been talking of in class, and that's *exactly* what I have been talking of—If you are told . . . Listen to this. If the young child is told he cannot understand. Then he takes it as a *description* of himself. What am I? I am *that which can not understand*. And I saw you out there, when we were speaking of the concepts of . . .

CAROL: I can't understand any of them.

JOHN: Well, then, that's *my* fault. That's not your fault. And that is not verbiage. That's what I firmly hold to be the truth. And I am sorry, and I owe you an apology.

CAROL: Why?

JOHN: And I suppose that I have had some *things* on my mind . . . We're buying a *house*, and . . .

CAROL: People said that you were stupid . . . ?

JOHN: Yes.

CAROL: When?

JOHN: I'll tell you when. Through my life. In my childhood; and, perhaps, they stopped. But I heard them continue.

CAROL: And what did they say?

JOHN: They said I was incompetent. Do you see? And when I'm tested the, the, the *feelings* of my youth about the *very subject of learning* come up. And I . . . I become, I feel "unworthy," and "unprepared." . . .

CAROL: . . . yes.

JOHN: . . . eh?

CAROL: . . . yes.

JOHN: And I feel that I must fail. (*Pause*)

CAROL: . . . but then you *do* fail. (*Pause*) You have to. (*Pause*) Don't you?

JOHN: A *pilot*. Flying a plane. The pilot is flying the plane. He thinks: Oh, my *God,* my mind's been drifting! Oh, my God! What king of a cursed imbecile am I, that I, with this so precious cargo of *Life* in my charge, would allow my attention to wander. Why was I born? How deluded are those who put their trust in me, . . . et cetera, so on, and he crashes the plane.

CAROL: (*Pause*) He could just . . .

JOHN: That's right.

CAROL: He could say:

JOHN: My attention *wandered* for a moment . . .

CAROL: . . . uh huh . . .

JOHN: I had a *thought* I did not like . . . but now:

CAROL: . . . but now it's . . .

JOHN: That's what I'm telling you. It's time to put my attention . . . see: it is not: this is what I learned. It is Not Magic. Yes. Yes. *You.* You are going to be frightened. When faced with what may or may not be but which you are going to perceive as a test. You will become frightened. And you will say: "I am incapable of . . ." and everything *in* you will think these two things. "I must. But I can't." And you will think: Why was I born to be the laughingstock of a world in which everyone is better than I? In which I am entitled to nothing. Where I can not learn.

(*Pause*)

CAROL: Is that . . . (*Pause*) Is that what I have . . . ?

JOHN: Well, I don't know if I'd put it that way. Listen: I'm talking to you as I'd talk to my son. Because that's what I'd like him to have that I never had. I'm talking to you the way I wish that someone had talked to me. I don't know how to do it, other than to be *personal,* . . . but . . .

CAROL: Why would you want to be personal with me?

JOHN: Well, you see? That's what I'm saying. We can only interpret the behavior of others through the screen we . . . (*The phone rings.*) Through . . . (*To phone:*) Hello . . . ? (*To Carol:*) Through the screen we create. (*To phone:*) Hello. (*To Carol:*) Excuse me a moment. (*To phone:*) Hello? No, I can't talk nnn . . . I know I did. In a few . . . I'm . . . is he coming to the . . . yes. I talked to him. We'll meet you at the No, because I'm with a *student.* It's going to fff . . . This is important, too. I'm with a *student,* Jerry's going to . . . Listen: the sooner I get off, the sooner I'll be down, all right. I love you. Listen, listen, I said "I love you," it's going to work *out* with the, because I feel that it is, I'll be right down. All right? Well, then it's going to take as long as it takes. (*He hangs up.*) (*To Carol:*) I'm sorry.

CAROL: What was that?

JOHN: There are some problems, as there usually are, about the final agreements for the new house.

CAROL: You're buying a new house.

JOHN: That's right.

CAROL: Because of your promotion.

JOHN: Well, I suppose that that's right.

CAROL: Why did you stay here with me?

JOHN: Stay here.

CAROL: Yes. When you should have gone.

JOHN: Because I like you.

CAROL: You like me.

JOHN: Yes.

CAROL: Why?

JOHN: Why? Well? Perhaps we're similar. (*Pause*) Yes. (*Pause*)

CAROL: You said "everyone has problems."

JOHN: Everyone has problems.

CAROL: Do they?

JOHN: Certainly.

CAROL: You do?

JOHN: Yes.

CAROL: What are they?

JOHN: Well. (*Pause*) Well, you're perfectly right. (*Pause*) If we're going to take off the Artificial *Stricture*, of "Teacher," and "Student," why should *my* problems be any more a mystery than your own? Of *course* I have problems. As you saw.

CAROL: . . . with what?

JOHN: With my *wife* . . . with *work*. . . .

CAROL: With work?

JOHN: Yes. And, and, perhaps my problems are, do you *see*? *Similar* to yours.

CAROL: Would you tell me?

JOHN: All right. (*Pause*) I came *late* to teaching. And I found it Artificial. The notion of "I know and you do not"; and I saw an *exploitation* in the education process. I told you. I hated school, I hated teachers. I hated everyone who was in the position of a "boss" because I *knew*—I didn't *think*, mind you, I *knew* I was going to fail. Because I was a fuckup. I was just no goddamned good. When I . . . late in life . . . (*Pause*) When

I *got out from under* . . . when I worked my way out of the need to fail. When I . . .

CAROL: How do you do that? (*Pause*)

JOHN: You have to look at what you are, and what you feel, and how you act. And, finally, you have to look at how you act. And say: If that's what I *did*, that must be how I think of myself.

CAROL: I don't understand.

JOHN: If I fail all the time, it must be that I think of myself as a failure. If I do not want to think of myself as a failure, perhaps I should begin by *succeeding* now and again. Look. The tests, you see, which you encounter, in school, in college, in life, were designed, in the most part, for idiots. *By* idiots. There is no need to fail at them. They are not a test of your worth. They are a test of your ability to retain and spout back misinformation. Of *course* you fail them. They're *nonsense*. And I . . .

CAROL: . . . no . . .

JOHN: Yes. They're *garbage*. They're a *joke*. Look at me. Look at me. The Tenure Committee. The Tenure Committee. Come to judge me. The Bad Tenure Committee.

The "Test." Do you see? They put me to the test. Why, they had people voting on me I wouldn't employ to wax my car. And yet, I go before the Great Tenure Committee, and I have an urge, to *vomit*, to, to, to puke my *badness* on the table, to show them: "I'm no good. Why would you pick *me*?"

CAROL: They granted you tenure.

JOHN: Oh no, they announced it, but they haven't *signed*. Do you see? "At any moment . . ."

CAROL: . . . mmm . . .

JOHN: "They might not *sign*." . . . I might not . . . the *house* might not go through . . . Eh? Eh? They'll find out my "dark secret." (*Pause*)

CAROL: . . . what is it . . . ?

JOHN: There *isn't* one. But *they* will find an index of my badness . . .

CAROL: Index?

JOHN: A ". . . pointer." A "Pointer." You see? Do you see? I *understand* you. I. Know. That. Feeling. Am I entitled to my job, and my nice *home*, and my *wife*, and my *family*, and so on. This is what I'm saying: That theory of education which, that *theory*:

CAROL: I . . . I . . . (*Pause*)

JOHN: What?

CAROL: I . . .

JOHN: What?

CAROL: I want to know about my grade. (*Long pause*)

JOHN: Of course you do.

CAROL: Is that bad?

JOHN: No.

CAROL: Is it bad that I asked you that?

JOHN: No.

CAROL: Did I upset you?

JOHN: No. And I apologize. Of *course* you want to know about your grade. And, of course, you can't concentrate on anyth . . . (*The telephone starts to ring.*) Wait a moment.

CAROL: I should go.

JOHN: I'll make you a deal.

CAROL: No, you have to . . .

JOHN: Let it ring. I'll make you a deal. You stay here. We'll start the whole course over. I'm going to say it was not you, it was I who was not paying attention. We'll start the whole course over. Your grade is an "A." Your final grade is an "A." (*The phone stops ringing.*)

CAROL: But the class is only half over . . .

JOHN: (*simultaneously with* "over"): Your grade for the whole term is an "A." If you will come back and meet with me. A few more times. Your grade's an "A." Forget about the paper. You didn't like it, you didn't like writing it. It's not important.

What's important is that I awake your interest, if I can, and that I answer your questions. Let's start over. (*Pause*)

CAROL: Over. With what?

JOHN: Say this is the beginning.

CAROL: The beginning.

JOHN: Yes.

CAROL: Of what?

JOHN: Of the class.

CAROL: But we can't start over.

JOHN: I say we can. (*Pause*) I say we can.

CAROL: But I don't believe it.

JOHN: Yes, I know that. But it's true. What is The Class but you and me? (*Pause*)

CAROL: There are rules.

JOHN: Well. We'll break them.

CAROL: How can we?

JOHN: We won't tell anybody.

CAROL: Is that all right?

JOHN: I say that it's fine.

CAROL: Why would you do this for me?

JOHN: I like you. Is that so difficult for you to . . .

CAROL: Um . . .

JOHN: There's no one here but you and me. (*Pause*)

CAROL: All right. I did not understand. When you referred . . .

JOHN: All right, yes?

CAROL: When you referred to hazing.

JOHN: Hazing.

CAROL: You wrote, in your book. About the comparative . . . the comparative . . . (*She checks her notes.*)

JOHN: Are you checking your notes . . . ?

CAROL: Yes.

JOHN: Tell me in your own . . .

CAROL: I want to make sure that I have it right.

JOHN: No. Of course. You want to be exact.

CAROL: I want to know everything that went on.

JOHN: . . . that's good.

CAROL: . . . so I . . .

JOHN: That's very good. But I was suggesting, many times, that that which we wish to retain is retained oftentimes, I think, *better* with less expenditure of effort.

CAROL: (*Of notes*) Here it is: you wrote of *hazing*.

JOHN: . . . that's correct. Now: I said "hazing." It means ritualized annoyance. We shove this book at you, we say read it. Now, you say you've read it? I think that you're *lying*. I'll *grill* you, and when I find you've lied you'll be disgraced, and your life will be ruined. It's a sick game. Why do we do it? Does it educate? In no sense. Well, then, what is higher education? It is something other-than-useful.

CAROL: What is "something-other-than-useful?"

JOHN: It has become at ritual, it has become an article of faith. That all must be subjected to, or to put it differently, that all are entitled to Higher Education. And my point . . .

CAROL: You disagree with that?

JOHN: Well, let's address that. What do you think?

CAROL: I don't know.

JOHN: What do you think, though? (*Pause*)

CAROL: I don't know.

JOHN: I spoke of it in class. Do you remember my example?

CAROL: Justice.

JOHN: Yes. Can you repeat it to me? (*She looks down at her notebook.*) Without your notes? I ask you as a favor to me, so that I can see if my idea was interesting.

CAROL: You said "justice" . . .

JOHN: Yes?

CAROL: . . . that all are entitled . . . (*Pause*) I . . . I . . . I . . .

JOHN: Yes. To a speedy trial. To a fair trial. But they needn't be given a trial *at all* unless they stand accused. Eh? Justice is their right, should they choose to avail themselves of it, they should have a fair trial. It does not follow, of necessity, a person's life is incomplete without a trial in it. Do you see?

My point is a confusion between equity and *utility* arose. So we confound the *usefulness* of higher education with our, granted, right to equal access to the same. We, in effect, create a *prejudice* toward it, completely independent of . . .

CAROL: . . . that it is prejudice that we should go to school?

JOHN: Exactly. (*Pause*)

CAROL: How can you say that? How . . .

JOHN: Good. Good. *Good.* That's right! Speak up! What is a prejudice? An unreasoned belief. We are all subject to it. None of us is not. When it is threatened, or opposed, we feel anger, and feel, do we not? As you do now. Do you not? Good.

CAROL: . . . but how can you . . .

JOHN: . . . let us examine. Good.

CAROL: How . . .

JOHN: Good. Good. When . . .

CAROL: I'M SPEAKING . . . (*Pause*)

JOHN: I'm sorry.

CAROL: How can you . . .

JOHN: . . . I beg your pardon.

CAROL: That's all right.

JOHN: I beg your pardon.

CAROL: That's all right.

JOHN: I'm sorry I interrupted you.

CAROL: That's all right.

JOHN: You were saying?

CAROL: I was saying . . . I was saying . . . (*She checks her notes.*) How can you say in a class. Say in a college class, that college education is prejudice?

JOHN: I said that our predilection for it . . .

CAROL: Predilection . . .

JOHN: . . . you know what that means.

CAROL: Does it mean "liking"?

JOHN: Yes.

CAROL: But how can you say that? That College . . .

JOHN: . . . that's my *job,* don't you know.

CAROL: What is?

JOHN: To provoke you.

CAROL: No.

JOHN: Oh. Yes, though.

CAROL: To provoke me?

JOHN: That's right.

CAROL: To make me mad?

JOHN: That's right. To force you . . .

CAROL: . . . to make me mad is your job?

JOHN: To force you to . . . listen: (*Pause*) Ah. (*Pause*) When I was young somebody told me, are you ready, the rich copulate less often than the poor. But when they do, they take more of their clothes off. Years. Years, mind you, I would compare experiences of my own to this dictum, saying, aha, this fits the norm, or ah, this is a variation from it. What did it mean? Nothing. It was some jerk thing, some school kid told me that took up room inside my head. (*Pause*)

Somebody told *you,* and you hold it as an article of faith, that higher education is an unassailable good. This notion is so dear to you that when I question it you become angry. Good. Good, I say. Are not those the very things which we should question? I say college education, since the war, has become so a matter of course, and such a fashionable necessity, for those either of or aspiring *to* to the new vast middle class, that we *espouse* it, as a matter of right, and have ceased to ask, "What is it good for?" (*Pause*)

What might be some reasons for pursuit of higher education?

One: A love of learning.
Two: The wish for mastery of a skill.
Three: For economic betterment.
(Stops. Makes a note.)

CAROL: I'm keeping you.

JOHN: One moment. I have to make a note . . .

CAROL: It's something that I said?

JOHN: No, we're buying a house.

CAROL: You're buying the new house.

JOHN: To go with the tenure. That's right. Nice *house*, close to the *private school* . . . *(He continues making his note.)* . . . We were talking of economic *betterment* *(Carol writes in her notebook.)* . . . I was thinking of the School Tax. *(He continues writing.)* *(To himself:)* . . . *where is it written* that I have to send my child to public school . . . Is it a law that I have to improve the City Schools at the expense of my own interest? And, is this not simply *The White Man's Burden*? Good. And *(Looks up to Carol)* . . . does this interest you?

CAROL: No. I'm taking notes . . .

JOHN: You don't have to take notes, you know, you can just listen.

CAROL: I want to make sure I remember it. *(Pause)*

JOHN: I'm not lecturing you, I'm just trying to tell you some things I think.

CAROL: What do you think?

JOHN: Should all kids go to college? *Why* . . .

CAROL: *(Pause)* To learn.

JOHN: But if he does not learn.

CAROL: If the child does not learn?

JOHN: Then why is he in college? Because he was told it was his "right"?

CAROL: Some might find college instructive.

JOHN: I would hope so.

CAROL: But how do they feel? Being told they are wasting their time?

JOHN: I don't think I'm telling them that.

CAROL: You said that education was "prolonged and systematic hazing."

JOHN: Yes. It can be so.

CAROL: . . . if education is so *bad*, why do you do it?

JOHN: I do it because I love it. *(Pause)* Let's . . . I suggest you look at the demographics, wage-earning capacity, college– and non-college-educated men and women, 1855 to 1980, and let's see if we can wring some worth from the statistics. Eh? And . . .

CAROL: No.

JOHN: What?

CAROL: I can't understand them.

JOHN: . . . you . . . ?

CAROL: . . . the "charts." The *Concepts,* the . . .

JOHN: "Charts" are simply . . .

CAROL: When I leave here . . .

JOHN: Charts, do you see . . .

CAROL: No, I can't . . .

JOHN: You can, though.

CAROL: NO. NO—I DON'T UNDERSTAND. DO YOU SEE??? I DON'T *UNDER-STAND* . . .

JOHN: What?

CAROL: *Any* of it. *Any* of it. I'm *smiling* in class, I'm *smiling,* the whole time. *What* are you *talking* about? What is everyone *talking* about? I don't *understand.* I don't know what it *means.* I don't know what it means to *be* here. . . you tell me I'm intelligent, and then you tell me I should not be *here,* what do you *want* with me? What does it *mean?* Who should I *listen* to. . . I . . .
   (*He goes over to her and puts his arm around her shoulder.*)
   NO! (*She walks away from him.*)

JOHN: Sshhhh.

CAROL: No, I don't under . . .

JOHN: Sshhhhh.

CAROL: I don't know what you're *saying* . . .

JOHN: Sshhhhh. It's all right.

CAROL: . . . I have no . . .

JOHN: Sshhhhh. Sshhhhh. Let it go a moment. (*Pause*) Sshhhhh . . . let it go. (*Pause*) Just let it go. (*Pause*) Just let it go. It's all right. (*Pause*) Sshhhhh. (*Pause*) I understand . . . (*Pause*) What do you feel?

CAROL: I feel bad.

JOHN: I know. It's all right.

CAROL: I . . . (*Pause*)

JOHN: What?

CAROL: I . . .

JOHN: What? Tell me.

CAROL: I don't understand you.

JOHN: I know. It's all right.

CAROL: I . . .

JOHN: What? (*Pause*) What? *Tell* me.

CAROL: I can't tell you.

JOHN: No, you must.

CAROL: I can't.

JOHN: No. Tell me. (*Pause*)

CAROL: I'm bad. (*Pause*) Oh, God. (*Pause*)

JOHN: It's all right.

CAROL: I'm . . .

JOHN: It's all right.

CAROL: I can't talk about this.

JOHN: It's all right. Tell me.

CAROL: Why do you want to know this?

JOHN: I don't want to know. I want to know whatever you . . .

CAROL: I always . . .

JOHN: . . . good . . .

CAROL: I always . . . all my life . . . I have never told anyone this . . .

JOHN: Yes. Go on. (*Pause*) Go on.

CAROL: All of my life . . . (*The phone rings.*) (*Pause. John goes to the phone and picks it up.*)

JOHN: (*into phone*): I can't talk now. (*Pause*) What? (*Pause*) Hmm. (*Pause*) All right, I . . . I. Can't. Talk. Now. No, no, no, I *Know* I did, but . . . What? Hello. What? She *what*? She *can't,* she said the agreement is void? How, how is the agreement *void*? That's *Our House.*

I have the *paper,* when we come down, next week, with the payment, and the paper, that house is . . . wait, wait, wait, wait, wait, wait, wait: Did Jerry . . . is Jerry there? (*Pause*) Is *she* there . . . ? Does she have a *lawyer* . . . ? How the *hell,* how the *Hell.* That is . . . it's a question, you said, of the *easement.* I don't underst . . . it's not the *whole agreement.* It's just the *easement,* why would she? Put, put, put, Jerry on. (*Pause*) Jer, *Jerry:* What the *Hell* . . . that's my *house.* That's . . . Well, I'm, no, no, no, I'm *not* coming ddd . . . List, *Listen, screw* her. You *tell* her. You, listen: I want you to take *Grace,* you take Grace, and get out of that house. You *leave* her there. Her and her lawyer, and you *tell* them, we'll see them in court next . . . no. No. Leave her there, leave her to *stew* in it: You tell her, we're *getting* that house, and we are going to . . . No. I'm *not* coming down. I'll be damned if I'll sit in the same rrr . . . the next, you tell her the next time I *see* her is in court . . . I . . . (*Pause*) What? (*Pause*) What? I don't understand. (*Pause*) Well, what about the house? (*Pause*) There isn't any problem with the hhh . . . (*Pause*) No, no, no, that's all right. All ri . . . All right . . . (*Pause*) Of course. Tha. . . Thank you. No, I will. Right away. (*He hangs up.*) (*Pause*)

CAROL: What is it? (*Pause*)

JOHN: It's a surprise party.

CAROL: It is.

JOHN: Yes.

CAROL: A party for you.

JOHN: Yes.

CAROL: Is it your birthday?

JOHN: No.

CAROL: What is it?

JOHN: The tenure announcement.

CAROL: The tenure announcement.

JOHN: They're throwing a party for us in our new house.

CAROL: Your new house.

JOHN: The house that we're buying.

CAROL: You have to go.

JOHN: It seems that I do.

CAROL: (*Pause*) They're proud of you.

JOHN: Well, there are those who would say it's a form of aggression.

CAROL: What is?

JOHN: A surprise.

TWO

John and Carol seated across the desk from each other.

JOHN: You see, (*pause*) I love to teach. And flatter myself I am *skilled* at it. And I love the, the aspect of *performance*. I think I must confess that.

   When I found I loved to teach I swore that I would not become that cold, rigid automaton of an instructor which I had encountered as a child.

   Now, I was not unconscious that it was given me to err upon the other side. And, so, I asked and *ask* myself if I engaged in heterodoxy, I will not say "gratuitously" for I do not care to posit orthodoxy as a given good—but, "to the detriment of, of my students." (*Pause*)

As I said. When the possibility of tenure opened, and, of course, I'd long pursued it, I was, of course *happy,* and *covetous* of it.

I asked myself if I was wrong to covet it. And thought about it long, and, I hope, truthfully, and saw in myself several things in, I think, no particular order. (*Pause*)

That I *would* pursue it. That I *desired* it, that I was not pure of longing for security, and that that, perhaps, was not reprehensible in me. That I had duties *beyond* the school, and that my duty to my home, for instance, was, or should be, if it were not, of an equal weight. That tenure, and security, and yes, and *comfort,* were not, of themselves, to be scorned; and were even worthy of honorable pursuit. And that it was given me. Here, in this place, which I enjoy, and in which I find comfort, to assure myself of—as far as it rests in The Material—a continuation of that joy and comfort. In exchange for what? Teaching. Which I love.

What was the price of this security? To obtain *tenure.* Which tenure the committee is in the process of granting me. And on the basis of which I contracted to purchase a house. Now, as you don't have your own family, at this point, you may not know what that means. But to me it is important. A home. A Good Home. To raise my family. Now: The Tenure Committee will meet. This is the process, and a *good* process. Under which the school has functioned for quite a long time. They will meet, and hear your complaint—which you have the right to make; and they will dismiss it. They will *dismiss* your complaint; and, in the intervening period, I will lose my house. I will not be able to close on my house. I will lose my *deposit,* and the home I'd picked out for my wife and son will go by the boards. Now: I see I have angered you, I understand your anger at teachers. I was angry with mine. I felt hurt and humiliated by them. Which is one of the reasons that I went into education.

CAROL: What do you want of me?

JOHN: (*Pause*) I was hurt. When I received the report. Of the tenure committee. I was shocked. And I was hurt. No, I don't mean to subject you to my weak sensibilities. All right. Finally, I didn't understand. Then I thought: is it not always at those points at which we reckon ourselves unassailable that we are most vulnerable and . . . (*Pause*) Yes. All right. You find me pedantic. Yes. I am. By nature, by *birth,* by profession, I don't know . . . I'm always looking for a *paradigm* for . . .

CAROL: I don't know what a paradigm is.

JOHN: It's a model.

CAROL: Then why can't you use that word? (*Pause*)

JOHN: If it is important to you. Yes, all right. I was looking for a model. To continue: I feel that one point . . .

CAROL: I . . .

JOHN: One second . . . upon which I am unassailable is my unflinching concern for my students' dignity. I asked you here to . . . in the spirit of *investigation,* to ask you . . . to ask . . . (*Pause*) What have I done to you? (*Pause*) And, and, I suppose, how I can make amends. Can we not settle this now? It's pointless, really, and I want to know.

CAROL: What you can do to force me to retract?

JOHN: That is not what I meant at all.

CAROL: To bribe me, to convince me . . .

JOHN: . . . No.

CAROL: To retract . . .

JOHN: That is not what I meant at all. I think that you know it is not.

CAROL: That is not what I know. I *wish* I . . .

JOHN: I do not want to . . . you wish what?

CAROL: No, you said what amends can you make. To force me to retract.

JOHN: That is not what I said.

CAROL: I have my notes.

JOHN: Look. Look. The Stoics say . . .

CAROL: The Stoics?

JOHN: The Stoical Philosophers say if you remove the phrase "I have been injured," you have removed the injury. Now: Think: I know that you're upset. Just tell me. Literally. Literally: what wrong have I done you?

CAROL: Whatever you have done to me—to the extent that you've done it to *me,* do you know, rather than to me as a *student,* and, so, to the student body, is contained in my report. To the tenure committee.

JOHN: Well, all right. (*Pause*) Let's see. (*He reads.*) I find that I am sexist. That I am *elitist.* I'm not sure I know what that means, other than it's a derogatory word, meaning "bad." That I . . . That I insist on wasting time, in nonprescribed, in self-aggrandizing and theatrical *diversions* from the prescribed *text* . . . that these have taken both sexist and pornographic forms . . . here we find listed . . . (*Pause*) Here we find listed . . . instances " . . . closeted with a student" . . . "Told a rambling, sexually explicit story, in which the frequency and attitudes of fornication of the poor and rich are, it would seem, the central point . . . moved to *embrace* said student and . . . all part of a pattern . . . " (Pause)

(*He reads.*) That I used the phrase "The White Man's Burden" . . . that I told you how I'd asked you to my room because I quote like you. (*Pause*)

(*He reads.*) "He said he 'liked' me. That he 'liked being with me.' He'd let me write my examination paper over, if I could come back oftener to see him in his office." (*Pause*) (*To Carol:*) It's *ludicrous*. Don't you know that? It's not *necessary*. It's going to *humiliate* you, and it's going to cost me my *house,* and . . .

CAROL: It's "*ludicrous*. . ."?

(*John picks up the report and reads again.*)

JOHN: "He told me he had problems with his wife; and that he wanted to take off the artificial stricture of Teacher and Student. He put his arm around me . . . "

CAROL: Do you deny it? Can you deny it . . . ? Do you see? (*Pause*) Don't you see? You don't see, do you?

JOHN: I don't see . . .

CAROL: You think, you think you can deny that these things happened; or, if they *did*, if they *did,* that they meant what you *said* they meant. Don't you see? You drag me in here, you drag us, to listen to you "go on"; and "go on" about this, or that, or we don't "express" ourselves very well. We don't say what we mean. Don't we? Don't we? We *do* say what we mean. And you say that "I don't understand you . . . ": Then *you* . . . (*Points.*)

JOHN: "Consult the Report"?

CAROL: . . . that's right.

JOHN: You see. You see. Can't you. . . . You see what I'm saying? Can't you tell me in your own words?

CAROL: Those are my own words. (*Pause*)

JOHN: (*He reads.*) "He told me that if I would stay alone with him in his office, he would change my grade to an A." (*To Carol:*) What have I done to you? Oh, My God, are you so hurt?

CAROL: What I "feel" is irrelevant. (*Pause*)

JOHN: Do you know that I tried to help you?

CAROL: What I know I have reported.

JOHN: I would like to help you now. I would. Before this escalates.

CAROL: (*simultaneously with* "escalates"): You see. I don't think that I need your help. I don't think I need anything you have.

JOHN: I feel . . .

CAROL: I don't *care* what you feel. Do you see? DO YOU SEE? You can't *do* that anymore. You. Do. Not. Have. The. Power. Did you misuse it? *Someone* did. Are you part of that group? *Yes. Yes.* You Are. You've *done* these things. And to say, and to say, "Oh. Let me help you with your problem . . . "

JOHN: Yes. I understand. I understand. You're *hurt.* You're *angry.* Yes. I think your *anger* is *betraying* you. Down a path which helps no one.

CAROL: I don't *care* what you think.

JOHN: You don't? (*Pause*) But you talk of *rights.* Don't you see? *I* have rights too. Do you see? I have a *house* . . . part of the *real* world; and The Tenure Committee, Good Men and True. . .

CAROL: . . . Professor . . .

JOHN: . . . Please: *Also* part of that world: you understand? This is my *life.* I'm not a *bogeyman.* I don't "stand" for something, I . . .

CAROL: . . . Professor . . .

JOHN: . . . I . . .

CAROL: Professor. I came here as a *favor.* At your personal request. Perhaps I should not have done so. But I did. On my behalf, and on behalf of my group. And you speak of the tenure committee, one of whose members is a woman, as you know. And though you might call it Good Fun, or An Historical Phrase, or An Oversight, or, All of the Above, to refer to the committee as Good Men and True, it is a demeaning remark. It is a sexist remark, and to overlook it is to countenance continuation of that method of thought. It's a remark . . .

JOHN: OH COME ON. Come on. . . . Sufficient to deprive a family of . . .

CAROL: Sufficient? Sufficient? Sufficient? Yes. It is a *fact* . . . and that story, which I quote, is *vile* and *classist,* and *manipulative* and *pornographic.* It . . .

JOHN: . . . it's pornographic . . . ?

CAROL: What gives you the *right.* Yes. To speak to a *woman* in your private. . . Yes. Yes. I'm sorry. I'm sorry. You feel yourself empowered . . . you say so yourself. To *strut.* To *posture.* To "perform." To "Call me in here . . ." Eh? You say that higher education is a joke. And treat it as such, you *treat* it as such. And *confess* to a taste to play the *Patriarch* in your class. To grant *this.* To deny *that.* To embrance your students.

JOHN: How can you assert. How can you stand there and . . .

CAROL: How can you *deny* it. You did it to me. *Here.* You *did.* . . . You *confess.* You love the Power. To *deviate.* To *invent,* to transgress . . . to *transgress* whatever norms have been established for us. And you think it's charming to "question" in yourself this taste to mock and destroy. But you should question it. Professor. And you pick those things which you feel *advance* you: publication, *tenure,* and the steps to get them you call "harmless rituals." And you perform those steps. Although you say it is hypocrisy. But to the aspirations of your students. Of *hardworking students,* who come here, who *slave* to come here—you have no idea what it cost me to come to this school—you *mock* us. You call education "hazing," and from your so-protected, so-elitist seat you hold our confusion as a *joke,* and our hopes and efforts with it. Then you sit there and say "what have I done?" And ask me to understand that *you* have aspirations too. But I tell you. I tell you. That you are vile. And that you are exploitative. And if you possess one ounce of that inner honesty you describe in your book, you can look in yourself and see those things that I see. And you can find revulsion equal to my own. Good day. (*She prepares to leave the room.*)

JOHN: Wait a second, will you, just one moment. (*Pause*) Nice day today.

CAROL: What?

JOHN: You said "Good day." I think that it is a nice day today.

CAROL: *Is* it?

JOHN: Yes, I think it is.

CAROL: And why is that important?

JOHN: Because it is the essence of all human communication. I say something conventional, you respond, and the information we exchange is not about the "weather," but that we both agree to converse. In effect, we agree that we are both human. (*Pause*)

I'm not a . . . "exploiter," and you're not a . . . "deranged, what? *Revolutionary*". . . that we may, that we may have . . . positions, and that we may have . . . desires, which are in *conflict*, but that we're just human. (*Pause*) That means that sometimes we're *imperfect*. (*Pause*) Often we're in conflict . . . (*Pause*) *Much* of what we do, you're right, in the name of "principles" is *self-serving* . . . much of what we do is *conventional*. (*Pause*) You're right. (*Pause*) You said you came in the class because you wanted to learn about *education*. I don't know that I can teach you about *education*. But I know that I can tell you what I *think* about education, and then *you* decide. And you don't have to fight with me. *I'm* not the subject. (*Pause*) And where I'm *wrong* . . . perhaps it's not your job to "fix" me. I don't want to fix *you*. I would like to tell you what I *think,* because that *is* my job, conventional as it is, and flawed as I may be. And then, if you can show me some better *form,* then we can proceed from there. But, just like "nice day, isn't it . . . ?" I don't think we can proceed until we accept that each of us is human. (*Pause*) And we still can have difficulties. We *will* have them . . . that's all right too. (*Pause*) Now:

CAROL: . . . wait . . .

JOHN: Yes, I want to hear it.

CAROL: . . . the . . .

JOHN: Yes. Tell me frankly.

CAROL: . . . my position . . .

JOHN: I want to hear it. In your own words. What you want. And what you feel.

CAROL: . . . I . . .

JOHN: . . . yes . . .

CAROL: My Group.

JOHN: Your "Group" . . . ? (*Pause*)

CAROL: The people I've been talking to . . .

JOHN: There's no shame in that. Everybody needs advisers. Everyone needs to expose themselves. To various points of view. It's not wrong. It's essential. Good. Good. Now: You and I . . . (*The phone rings.*)
    You and I . . .
    (*He hesitates for a moment, and then picks it up.*) (*Into phone*) Hello. (*Pause*) Um . . . no, I know they do. (*Pause*) I know she does. Tell her that I . . . can I call you back? . . . Then tell her that I think it's going to be fine. (*Pause*) Tell her just, just hold on, I'll . . . can I get back to you? . . . Well . . . no, no, no, we're *taking* the house . . . we're . . . no, no, nn . . . no, she will nnn, it's not a *question* of refunding the dep . . . no . . . it's not a *question* of the deposit . . . will you call Jerry? Babe, baby, will you just call Jerry? Tell him, nnn . . . tell him they, well, they're to keep the deposit, because the deal, be . . . because the deal is going to go *through* . . . because I know . . . be . . . will you please? Just *trust* me. Be. . . well, I'm dealing with the complaint. Yes. Right *Now*. Which is why I . . . yes, no, no, it's really, I can't *talk* about it now. Call Jerry, and I can't talk now. Ff . . . fine. Gg . . . good-bye. (*Hangs up.*) (*Pause*) I'm sorry we were interrupted.

CAROL: No . . .

JOHN: I . . . I was saying:

CAROL: You said that we should agree to talk about my complaint.

JOHN: That's correct.

CAROL: But we *are* talking about it.

JOHN: Well, that's correct too. You see? This is the *gist* of education.

CAROL: No, no. I mean, we're talking about it at the Tenure Committee Hearing. (*Pause*)

JOHN: Yes, but I'm saying: we can talk about it *now*, as easily as . . .

CAROL: No. I think that we should stick to the process . . .

JOHN: . . . wait a . . .

CAROL: . . . the "conventional" process. As you said. (*She gets up.*) And you're right, I'm sorry if I was, um, if I was "discourteous" to you. You're right.

JOHN: Wait, wait a . . .

CAROL: I really should go.

JOHN: Now, look, granted. I have an interest. In the status quo. All right? Everyone does. But what I'm saying is that the *committee* . . .

CAROL: Professor, you're right. Just don't impinge on me. We'll take our differences, and . . .

JOHN: You're going to make a. . . look, look, look, you're going to . . .

CAROL: I shouldn't have come here. They told me . . .

JOHN: One moment. No. No. There are *norms*, here, and there's no reason. Look: I'm trying to *save* you . . .

CAROL: No one *asked* you to . . . you're trying to save *me*? Do me the courtesy to . . .

JOHN: I *am* doing you the courtesy. I'm talking *straight* to you. We can settle this *now*. And I want you to sit *down* and . . .

CAROL: You must excuse me . . . *(She starts to leave the room.)*

JOHN: Sit down, it seems we each have a . . . . Wait one moment. Wait one moment. . . just do me the courtesy to . . .

(He restrains her from leaving.)

CAROL: LET ME GO.

JOHN: I have no desire to *hold* you, I just want to *talk* to you . . .

CAROL: LET ME GO. LET ME GO. WOULD SOMEBODY *HELP* ME? WOULD SOMEBODY HELP ME PLEASE . . . ?

THREE

(At rise, Carol and John are seated.)

JOHN: I have asked you here. *(Pause)* I have asked you here against, against my . . .

CAROL: I was most surprised you asked me.

JOHN: . . . against my better *judgment*, against . . .

CAROL: I was most surprised . . .

JOHN: . . . against the . . . yes. I'm sure.

CAROL: . . . If you would like me to leave, I'll leave. I'll go right now . . . *(She rises.)*

JOHN: Let us begin *correctly*, may we? I feel . . .

CAROL: That is what I wished to do. That's why I came here, but now . . .

JOHN: . . . I feel . . .

CAROL: But now perhaps you'd like me to leave . . .

JOHN: I don't want you to leave. I asked you to come . . .

CAROL: I didn't have to come here.

JOHN: No. (*Pause*) Thank You.

CAROL: All right. (*Pause*) (*She sits down.*)

JOHN: Although I feel that it *profits*, it would *profit* you something, to . . .

CAROL: . . . what I . . .

JOHN: If you would hear me out, if you would hear me out.

CAROL: I came here to, the court officers told me not to come.

JOHN: . . . the "court" officers . . . ?

CAROL: I was shocked that you asked.

JOHN: . . . wait . . .

CAROL: Yes. But I did *not* come here to hear what it "profits" me.

JOHN: The "court" officers . . .

CAROL: . . . no, no, perhaps I should leave . . . (*She gets up.*)

JOHN: Wait.

CAROL: No. I shouldn't have . . .

JOHN: . . . wait. Wait. Wait a moment.

CAROL: Yes? What is it you want? (*Pause*) What is it you want?

JOHN: I'd like you to stay.

CAROL: You want me to stay.

JOHN: Yes.

CAROL: You do.

JOHN: Yes. (*Pause*) Yes. I would like to have you hear me out. If you would. (*Pause*) Would you please? If you would do that I would be in your debt. (*Puuse*) (*She sits.*) Thank You. (*Pause*)

CAROL: What is it you wish to tell me?

JOHN: All right. I cannot . . . (*Pause*) I cannot help but feel you are owed an apology. (*Pause*) (*Of papers in his hands*) I have read. (*Pause*) And reread these accusations.

CAROL: What "accusations"?

JOHN: The, the tenure comm . . . what other accusations . . . ?

CAROL: The tenure committee . . . ?

JOHN: Yes.

CAROL: Excuse me, but those are not accusations. They have been *proved*. They are facts.

JOHN: . . . I . . .

CAROL: No. Those are not "accusations."

JOHN: . . . those?

CAROL: . . . the committee (*The phone starts to ring.*) the committee has . . .

JOHN: . . . All right . . .

CAROL: . . . those are not accusations. The Tenure Committee.

JOHN: ALL RIGHT. ALL RIGHT. ALL RIGHT. (*He picks up the phone.*) Hello. Yes. No. I'm here. Tell Mister . . . No, I can't talk to him now . . . I'm sure he has, but I'm ff . . . I know . . . No, I have no time t . . . tell Mister . . . tell Mist . . . tell Jerry that I'm *fine* and that I'll call him right aw . . . (*Pause*) My wife . . . Yes. I'm sure she has. Yes, thank you. Yes, I'll call her too. I cannot talk to you now. (*He hangs up.*) (*Pause*) All right. It was good of you to come. Thank you. I have studied. I have spent some time studying the indictment.

CAROL: You will have to explain that word to me.

JOHN: An "indictment" . . .

CAROL: Yes.

JOHN: Is a "bill of particulars." A . . .

CAROL: All right. Yes.

JOHN: In which is alleged . . .

CAROL: No. I cannot allow that. I cannot allow that. Nothing is alleged. Every-thing is proved . . .

JOHN: Please, wait a sec . . .

CAROL: I cannot *come* to allow . . .

JOHN: If I may . . . If I may, from whatever you feel is "established," by . . .

CAROL: The issue here is not what I "feel." It is not my "feelings," but the feel-ings of women. And men. Your superiors, who've been "polled," do you see? To whom *evidence* has been presented, who have *ruled,* do you see? Who have weighed the testimony and the evidence, and have *ruled,* do you see? That you are *negligent.* That you are *guilty,* that you are found *wanting,* and in *error;* and are *not,* for the reasons so-told, to be given tenure. That you to be disciplined. For facts. For *facts.* Not "alleged," what is the word? But *proved.* Do you see? *By your own actions.*

That is what the tenure committee has said. That is what my lawyer said. That is what you did in class. For what you did *in this office.*

JOHN: They're going to discharge me.

CAROL: As full well they should. You don't understand? You're angry? What has *led* you to this place? Not your sex. Not your race. Not your class. YOUR OWN ACTIONS. And you're *angry.* You *ask* me here. What *do* you want? You want to "charm" me. You want to "convince" me. You want me to recant. I will *not* recant. Why should I . . . ? What I say is right. You tell me, you are going to tell me that you have a wife and child. You are going to say that you have a career and that you've worked for twenty years for this. Do you know what you've *worked* for? *Power*. For *power*. Do you understand? And you sit there, and you tell me *stories*. About your *house*, about all the private *schools*, and about *privilege*, and how you are entitled. To *buy*, to *spend*, to *mock*, to *summon*. All your stories. All your silly weak *guilt*, it's all about *privilege*; and you won't know it. Don't you see? You worked twenty years for the right to *insult* me. And you feel entitled to be *paid* for it. Your Home, Your Wife . . . Your sweet "deposit" on your house . . .

JOHN: Don't you have feelings?

CAROL: That's my point. You see? Don't you have feelings? Your final argument. What is it that has no feelings. *Animals*. I don't take your side, you question if I'm Human.

JOHN: Don't you have feelings?

CAROL: I have a responsibility. I . . .

JOHN: . . . to . . . ?

CAROL: To? This institution. To the *students*. To my *group*.

JOHN: . . . your "group." . . .

CAROL: Because I speak, yes, not for myself. But for the group; for those who suffer what I suffer. On behalf of whom, even if I, were, inclined, to what, forgive? Forget? What? Overlook your . . .

JOHN: . . . my behavior?

CAROL: . . . it would be wrong.

JOHN: Even if you were inclined to "forgive" me.

CAROL: It would be wrong.

JOHN: And what would transpire.

CAROL: Transpire?

JOHN: Yes.

CAROL: "Happen?"

JOHN: Yes.

CAROL: Then *say* it. For Christ's sake. Who the *hell* do you think that you are? You want a post. You want unlimited power. To do and to say what you want. As it pleases you—Testing, Questioning, Flirting . . .

JOHN: I never . . .

CAROL: Excuse me, One moment, will you?
            (*She reads from her notes.*)
            The twelfth: "Have a good day, dear."
            The fifteenth: "Now, don't *you* look fetching . . ."
            April seventeenth: "If you girls would come over here . . ." I saw you.

I saw you, Professor. For two semesters sit there, stand there and exploit our, as you thought, "paternal prerogative," and what is that but rape; I swear to God. You asked me in here to explain something to me, as a child, that I did not understand. But I came to explain something to you. You Are Not God. You ask me why I came? I came here to instruct you.

(*She produces his book.*)

And your book? You think you're going to show me some "light"? You "*maverick.*" Outside of tradition. No, no, (*She reads from the book's liner notes.*) "*of* that fine tradition of *inquiry.* Of Polite *skepticism*". . . and you say you believe in free intellectual discourse. YOU BELIEVE IN NOTHING. YOU BELIEVE IN NOTHING AT ALL.

JOHN: I believe in freedom of thought.

CAROL: Isn't that fine. *Do* you?

JOHN: Yes. I do.

CAROL: Then why do you question, for one moment, the committee's decision refusing your tenure? Why do you question your suspension? You believe in what *you call* freedom of thought. Then, fine. You believe in freedom-of-thought *and* a home, and, *and* prerogatives for your kid, *and* tenure. And I'm going to tell you. You believe *not* in "freedom of thought," but in an elitist, in, in a protected hierarchy which rewards you. And for whom you are the clown. And you mock and exploit the system which pays your rent. You're wrong. I'm not wrong. You're wrong. You think that I'm full of hatred. I know what you I think I am.

JOHN: Do you?

CAROL: You think I'm a, of course I do. You think I am a frightened, repressed, confused, I don't know, abandoned young thing of some doubtful sexuality, who wants, power and revenge. (*Pause*) *Don't* you? (*Pause*)

JOHN: Yes. I do. (*Pause*)

CAROL: Isn't that better? And I feel that that is the first moment which you've treated me with respect. For you told me the truth. (*Pause*). I did not come here, as you are assured, to gloat. Why would I want to gloat? I've profited nothing from your, your, as you say, your "misfortune." I came here, as you did me the honor to *ask* me here, I came here to *tell* you something.

(*Pause*) That I think . . . that I think you've been wrong. That I think you've been terribly wrong. Do you hate me now? (*Pause*)

JOHN: Yes.

CAROL: Why do you hate me? Because you think me wrong? No. Because I have, you think, *power* over you. Listen to me. Listen to me, Professor. (*Pause*) It is the power that you hate. So deeply that, that any atmosphere of free discussion is impossible. It's not "unlikely." It's *impossible.* Isn't it?

JOHN: Yes.

CAROL: *Isn't* it . . . ?

JOHN: Yes. I Suppose.

CAROL: Now. The thing which you find so cruel is the selfsame process of selection I, and my group, go through *every day of our lives.* In admittance to school. In our tests, in our class rankings . . . Is it unfair? I can't tell you. But, if it is fair. Or even if it is "unfortunate but necessary" for us, then, by God, so must it be for you. (*Pause*) You write of your "responsibility to the young." Treat us with respect, and that will *show* you your responsibility. You write that education is just hazing. (*Pause*). But we worked to get to this school. (*Pause*) And some of us. (*Pause*) Overcame prejudices. Economic, sexual, you cannot begin to imagine. And endured humiliations I *pray* that you and those you love never will encounter. (*Pause*) To gain admittance here. To pursue that same dream of security *you* pursue. We, who, who are, at any moment, in danger of being deprived of it. By . . .

JOHN: . . . by. . . ?

CAROL: By the administration. By the teachers. By *you.* By, say, one low grade, that keeps us out of graduate school; by one, say, one capricious or inventive answer on our parts, which, perhaps, you don't find amusing. Now you *know,* do you see? What it is to be subject to that power. (*Pause*)

JOHN: I don't understand. (*Pause*)

CAROL: My charges are not trivial. You see that in the haste, I think, with which they were accepted. A *joke* you have told, with a sexist tinge. The language you use, a verbal or physical caress, yes, yes, I know, you say that it is meaningless. I understand. I differ from you. To lay a hand on someone's shoulder.

JOHN: It was devoid of sexual content.

CAROL: I say it was not. I SAY IT WAS NOT. Don't you begin to *see* . . . ? Don't you begin to understand? IT'S NOT FOR YOU TO SAY.

JOHN: I take your point, and I see there is much good in what you refer to.

CAROL: . . . do you think so . . . ?

JOHN: . . . but, and this is not to say that I cannot change, in those things in which I am deficient. . . But, the . . .

CAROL: Do you hold yourself harmless from the charge of sexual exploitativeness. . . ? (*Pause*)

JOHN: Well , I . . . I . . . I . . . You know I, as I said. I . . . think I am not too old to *learn,* and I *can* learn, I. . .

CAROL: Do you hold yourself innocent of the charge of . . .

JOHN: . . . wait, wait, wait . . . All right. let's go back to . . .

CAROL: YOU FOOL. Who do you think I am? To come here and be taken in by a *smile.* You little yapping fool. You think I want "revenge." I don't want revenge. I WANT UNDERSTANDING.

JOHN: . . . *do* you?

CAROL: I do. (*Pause*)

JOHN: What's the use. It's over.

CAROL: Is it? What is?

JOHN: My job.

CAROL: Oh. Your job. That's what you want to talk about. (*Pause*) (*She starts to leave the room. She steps and turns back to him.*) All right. (*Pause*) What if it were possible that my Group withdraws its complaint. (*Pause*)

JOHN: What?

CAROL: That's right. (*Pause*)

JOHN: Why.

CAROL: Well, let's say as an act of friendship.

JOHN: An act of friendship.

CAROL: Yes. (*Pause*)

JOHN: In exchange for whal.

CAROL: Yes. But I don't think, "exchange." Not "in exchange." For what do we derive from it? (*Pause*)

JOHN: "Derive"

CAROL: Yes.

JOHN: (*Pause*) Nothing. (*Pause*)

CAROL: That's right. We derive nothing. (*Pause*) Do you see that?

JOHN: Yes.

CAROL: That is a little word, Professor. "Yes." "I see that." But you will.

JOHN: And you might speak to the committee . . . ?

CAROL: To the committee?

JOHN: Yes.

CAROL: Well. Of course. That's on your mind. We might.

JOHN: "If" what?

CAROL: "Given" what. Perhaps. I think that that is more friendly.

JOHN: GIVEN WHAT?

CAROL: And, believe me, I understand your rage. It is not that I don't feel it. But I do not see that it is deserved, so I do not resent it. . . . All right. I have a list.

JOHN: . . . a list.

CAROL: Here is a list of books, which we . . .

JOHN: . . . a list of books . . . ?

CAROL: That's right. Which we find questionable.

JOHN: What?

CAROL: Is this so bizarre . . . ?

JOHN: I can't believe . . .

CAROL: It's not necessary you believe it.

JOHN: Academic freedom . . .

CAROL: Someone chooses the books. If you can choose them, others can. What are you, "God"?

JOHN: . . . no, no, the "dangerous." . . .

CAROL: You have an agenda, we have an agenda. I am not interested in your feelings or your motivation, but your actions. If you would like me to speak to the Tenure Committee, here is my list. You are a Free Person, you decide. (*Pause*)

JOHN: Give me the list. (*She does so. He reads.*)

CAROL: I think you'll find . . .

JOHN: I'm capable or reading it. Thank you.

CAROL: We have a number of *texts* we need re . . .

JOHN: I see that.

CAROL: We're amenable to . . .

JOHN: Aha. Well, let me took over the . . . (*He reads.*)

CAROL: I think that . . .

JOHN: LOOK. I'm reading your demands. All right?! (*He reads.*) (*Pause*) You want to ban my book?

CAROL: We do not . . .

JOHN: (*Of list*): It says here . . .

CAROL: . . . We want it removed from inclusion as a representative example of the university.

JOHN: Get out of here.

CAROL: If you put aside the issues of personalities.

JOHN: Get the fuck out of my office.

CAROL: No, I think I would reconsider.

JOHN: . . . you think you can.

CAROL: We can and we *will.* Do you want our support? That is the only quest . . .

JOHN: to ban my *book.* . . ?

CAROL: that is correct . . .

JOHN: . . . this . . . this is a *university* . . . we . . .

CAROL: . . . and we have a statement . . . which we need you to . . . (*She hands him a sheet of paper.*)

JOHN: No, no. It's out of the question. I'm sorry. I don't know what I was thinking of. I want to tell you something. I'm a teacher. I am a teacher. Eh? It's my *name* on the door, and *I* teach the class, and that's what I do. I've got a book with my name on it. And my son will *see* that *book* someday. And I have a respon . . . No, I'm sorry I have a *responsibility.* . . to *myself,* to my *son,* to my *profession.* . . I haven't been *home* for two days, do you know that? Thinking this out.

CAROL: . . . you haven't?

JOHN: I've been, no. If it's of interest to you. I've been in a *hotel.* . . *Thinking.* (*The phone starts ringing.*) Thinking. . .

CAROL: . . . you haven't been home?

JOHN: . . . *thinking,* do you see.

CAROL: Oh.

JOHN: And, and, I owe you a debt. I see that now. (*Pause*) You're *dangerous,* you're *wrong* and it's my job . . . to say no to you. That's my job. You are absolutely right. You want to ban my book? Go to *hell,* and they can do whatever they want to me. . .

CAROL: . . . you haven't been home in two days . . .

JOHN: I think I told you that.

CAROL: . . . you'd better get that phone. (*Pause*) I think that you should pick up the phone. (*Pause*)

(*John picks up the phone.*)

JOHN: (*on phone*): Yes. (*Pause*) Yes. Wh . . . I. I. I had to be away. All ri . . . did they wor . . . did they worry ab . . . No. I'm all right, now, Jerry. I'm f . . . I got a little turned *around,* but I'm *sitting* here and . . . I've got it figured out. I'm fine. I'm fine don't worry about me. I got a little bit mixed up. But I am not sure that it's not a blessing. It cost me my job? Fine. Then the job was not worth having. Tell Grace that I'm coming home and everything is fff . . . (*Pause*) What? (*Pause*) *What?* (*Pause*) What do you *mean?* WHAT? Jerry . . . Jerry. They . . . Who, who, what can they do . . . ? (*Pause*) NO. (*pause*) NO. They can't do th . . . What do you mean? (*Pause*) But how . . . (*Pause*) She's, she's, she's *here* with me. To . . . Jerry. I don't underst . . . (*Pause*) (*He hangs up.*) (*To Carol*) What does this mean?

CAROL: I thought you knew.

JOHN: What. (*Pause*) What does it mean. (*Pause*)

CAROL: You tried to rape me. (*Pause*) According to the law. (*Pause*)

JOHN: . . . what . . . ?

CAROL: You tried to rape me. I was leaving this office, you "pressed" yourself into me. You "pressed" your body into me.

JOHN: . . . I . . .

CAROL: My Group has told your lawyer that we may pursue criminal charges.

JOHN: . . . no . . .

CAROL: . . . under the statute. I am told. It was battery.

JOHN: . . . no . . .

CAROL: Yes. And attempted rape. That's right. (*Pause*)

JOHN: I think that you should go.

CAROL: Of course. I thought you knew.

JOHN: I have to talk to my lawyer.

CAROL: Yes. Perhaps you should. (*The phone rings again.*) (*Pause*)

JOHN: (*Picks up the phone. Into phone.*) Hello? I . . . Hello . . . ? I . . . Yes, he just called. No . . . I. I can't talk to you now, Baby. (*To Carol:*) Get out.

CAROL: . . . your wife . . . ?

JOHN: . . . who it is is no concern of yours. Get out. (*To phone.*) No, no, it's going to be all right. I. I can't talk now, Baby. (*To Carol:*) Get out of here.

CAROL: I'm going.

JOHN: Good.

CAROL (*exiting*): . . . and don't call your wife "baby."

JOHN: What?

CAROL: Don't call your wife baby. You heard what I said.

(*Carol starts to leave the room. John grabs her and begins to beat her.*)

JOHN: You vicious little bitch. You think you can come in here with your political correctness and destroy my life?

(*He knocks her to the floor.*)
After how I treated you . . . ? You should be. . . *Rape you . . .* ? Are you kidding me . . . ?

(He picks up a chair, raises it above his head, and advances on her.)
   I wouldn't touch you with a ten-foot pole. You little *cunt. . .*

(She cowers on the floor below him. Pause. He looks down at her. He lowers the chair. He moves to his desk, and arranges the papers on it. Pause. He looks over at her.)
   . . . well . . .

(Pause. She looks at him.)

CAROL: Yes. That's right.

(She looks away from him, and lowers her head. To herself:) . . . yes. That's right.

END

TOPICS FOR DISCUSSION AND WRITING

1. David Mamet has told interviewers that his father, a labor lawyer and a difficult man, was obsessed with language, with word usage and clarity. Not surprisingly, language, its misuse and abuse, is a significiant theme in all of Mamet's plays. First, characterize the way in which Carol and John talk to each other and the phone conversations between John and his wife. Then write a paper about the language in *Oleanna*. What is Mamet saying about language, about "human communication," in this play?

2. Although John is a college professor, he presents an argument against higher education. Write an essay in which you state his complete argument and, as someone pursuing a degree in higher education, give your reaction to it. (See Standard Form in Chapter 3.)

3. In the charges Carol files against John, she accuses him of being "elitist," "sexist," and of "wasting time, in non-prescribed, in self-aggrandizing and theatrical *diversions* from the prescribed *text*." What is your evaluation of John as a teacher? In your response, consider John's reasons for becoming a teacher.

4. Several critics have seen Carol's transformation from a timid mouse in Act I to a roaring lion in Act III as a flaw in the play. What do think? Is Carol's transformation plausible?

5. Is Carol a legitimate victim of sexual harassment or a manipulative woman with a political agenda? Write an essay in which you answer this question using all the available and relevant evidence the play provides.

6. Compare the relationship between the fictional professor, John, and his student Carol, to the relationship Jeffery Toobin describes between Yale mathematics professor Jay Jorgenson and one of his female students in "The Trouble with Sex." How are they similar? How are they different?

Defining Sexual Harassment on Campus

The first and often the biggest problem facing colleges as they attempt to deal with charges of sexual harassment is determining exactly what behavior qualifies. The first step in making this determination is a clear definition of what sexual harassment is. Read the following two examples.

From the Policy on Sexual Harassment and Complaint Resolution Procedures of the University of California

Unwelcome sexual advances, requests for sexual favors, and other verbal or physical conduct of a sexual nature constitute sexual harassment when:

1. submission to such conduct is made either explicitly or implicitly a term or consideration of instruction, employment, or participation in other University activity;

2. submission to or rejection of such conduct by an individual is used as a basis for evaluation in making academic or personnel decisions affecting an individual; or

3. such conduct has the purpose or effect of unreasonably interfering with an individual's performance or creating an intimidating, hostile, or offensive University environment.

From the Antioch College Sexual Offense Policy

Insistent and/or persistent sexual harassment: Any insistent and/or persistent emotional, verbal, or mental intimidation or abuse found to be sexually threatening or offensive. This includes, but is not limited to, unwelcome and irrelevant comments, references, gestures, or other forms of personal attention which are inappropriate and which may be perceived as persistent sexual overtones or denigration.

TOPICS FOR DISCUSSION AND WRITING

1. Discuss these definitions with other members of your class. Is Mamet's fictional professor, John, guilty according to these definitions? What about Professor Jay Jorgenson ("The Trouble with Sex"), Professor Stephen Dobyns ("Bad Behavior") and Professor Donald Silva ("Do 'Hostile Environment' Charges Chill Academic Freedom?") discussed earlier in this chapter? Do you find these definitions too broad or too narrow? If so, how would you revise them?

2. Find a copy of your college's official policy on sexual harassment and cull from this statement the precise definition of sexual harassment on which it is based. How adequate is this definition?

3. As a final exercise on this issue, write a definition of sexual harassment you would like your campus to adopt. (See Writing Assignment 13 on page 133.)

Student-on-Student Sexual Harassment

In May of 1999, the United States Supreme Court made yet another landmark decision in the area of sexual harassment law, ruling in a 5 to 4 decision that public schools may be sued for failing to deal with students who sexually harass other students. The decision is based on a broad interpretation of the federal law known as Title IX, which bars discrimination on the basis of sex in any educational institution receiving federal funds and until now, has been used primarily to equalize school athletic programs. The ruling was condemned by Justices who dissented from the majority opinion. Justice Anthony Kennedy argued that the decision will usurp the state's role in education by placing the federal courts "center stage in America's classrooms" and create "an avalanche of liability" for schools, further eroding their limited resources. Martha Davis, a representative of the National Organization of Women, disagrees: "There's a difference between teasing and the sort of behavior that really contributes to gender discrimination."

The selections that follow, excerpts from Justice Sandra Day O'Connor's majority opinion and Justice Kennedy's dissenting opinion, and "Teaching Johnny the Appropriate Way to Flirt," by Cynthia Gorney on the incidents that have led to this critical ruling, will enable you to decide for yourself if the Court's decision was a good one or not.

From the Supreme Court's Decision on Student-on-Student Sexual Harassment

Justices Sandra Day O'Connor and Anthony M. Kennedy

JUSTICE SANDRA DAY O'CONNOR'S MAJORITY OPINION

We consider here whether a private damages action may lie against the school board in cases of student-on-student harassment. We conclude that it may, but only where the funding recipient acts with deliberate indifference to known acts of harassment in its programs or activities. Moreover, we conclude that such an action will lie only for harassment that is so severe, pervasive and objectively offensive that it effectively bars the victim's access to an educational opportunity or benefit. . . .

In [a 1998 ruling] we concluded that a recipient of federal education funds may be liable in damages under Title IX where it is deliberately indifferent to known acts of sexual harassment by a teacher.

JUSTICE ANTHONY M. KENNEDY'S DISSENT

The only certainty flowing to the majority's decision is that scarce resources will be diverted from educating of our children and that many school districts, desperate to avoid Title IX peer harassment suits, will adopt whatever federal code of student conduct and discipline the Department of Education sees fit to impose upon them.

The nation's schoolchildren will learn their first lessons about federalism in classrooms where the federal government is the ever-present regulator. The federal government will have insinuated itself not only into one of the most traditional areas of state concern but also into one of the most sensitive areas of human affairs.

Perhaps even more startling than its broad assumptions about school control over primary and secondary school students is the majority failure to grapple in any meaningful way with the distinction between elementary and secondary schools, on the one hand, and universities on the other. . . .

We can be assured that like suits will follow—suits, which in cost and number, will impose serious financial burdens on local school districts, the taxpayers who support them and the children they serve.

Teaching Johnny the Appropriate Way to Flirt

Cynthia Gorney

In this article from *The New York Times Magazine,* Gorney describes the incident which led to the Supreme Court decision as well as other incidents of student harassment and the schools' reaction to them.

What follows is a very small story, lightly censored but entirely true, that comes with a lot of very big stories attached. The setting for the very small story, which we will refer to as the Milk-Bag Incident for purposes of the arguments it is likely to set off, is a public middle-school cafeteria in Duluth, Minn. The time of year is mid-February. Because it is lunchtime, numerous schoolchildren are crowded together at the tables with their food and their milk, which in Duluth is doled out not in cartons but in single-serving plastic bags with straws.

At one cafeteria table, set together in close quarters amid the commotion: several boys, two girls, a milk bag. One of the boys picks up the milk bag. No violence is about to erupt; this is a story about schoolchildren that contains no guns or homicidal rages. All the boy does next is shape the milk bag into a recognizable replica of manly genitalia, including scrotum. The boy announces his achievement to everyone within earshot, which includes the girls at his table, and points out that the genitalia he has sculptured is fully tumescent. (The boy's exact choice of words will not be printed here, but fits into what would probably qualify as "age appropriate" disgusting language for a modern American sixth grader, which is to say: *really* disgusting language.) The boy and his friends, brandishing the tumescent milk bag, fall about in general hilarity. The bell rings. Lunch period comes to a close.

Sometime in the course of the next few days, the girls—like the boys, these are sixth graders, 12 years old—appear at the office of the school vice principal to report that they wish to make a complaint. Do the girls use the term "sexual harassment"? Possibly, for they have encountered these words in a middle-school assembly and one or two contemporary novels assigned at their grade level, but probably not. Maybe they use the word "harassment." Maybe they use the word "gross." In any case they understand that there is a Procedure, and the vice principal, having paid close attention to the training that instructed her to do so, now sets the Procedure into motion: she pulls out a harassment complaint form. (*Sexual harassment, sexual advances or other forms of religious, racial or sexual harassment by any pupil, teacher, administrator or other school personnel, which create an intimidating, hostile or offensive environment, will not be tolerated under any circumstances.*) She asks the girls whether they want to fill out the form and sign it. They do. She calls up the Duluth school system harassment specialist.

The school system harassment specialist, who has a job title that a decade ago did not exist in the Duluth public schools—or, for that matter, in any other school system in the United States—is a small, cheerful, sturdy-looking 58-year-old former special-education teacher named Judy Gillen. Gillen has short-cropped reddish hair and half-rimmed trifocals and a wild, merry guffaw that is audible some distance away. She works out of the Duluth school administration headquarters, a turreted brick building on the downtown streets that overlook Lake Superior. Gillen's office is a 6-by-10-foot enclosure wedged into half a small room and decorated with teddy bears, puppets, framed photographs of her grandchildren, a Women's History Month poster and a big bright sign, affixed to the front of a file cabinet, that reads: SEXUAL HARASSMENT—IT'S ILLEGAL.

There's a great deal of printed material in Gillen's office, too—books, pamphlets, videotape guides, visual aids for overhead projection. "Sexual Harassment in Our School: What Parents and Teachers Need to Know to Spot It and Stop It." "Girls and Boys Getting Along: Teaching Sexual Harassment Prevention in the Elementary Classroom." "The Hostile School Bus." "Sexual Harassment: Pay Attention!" There are copies of a districtwide newsletter Gillen composes, which used to be called Harassment News Notes until she changed the title, in a flush of optimism, to Prevention News Notes. And there's an active complaints folder, inside one of the file drawers; that's where the Milk-Bag incident harassment form will be parked while the middle-school vice principal, with Judy Gillen monitoring the situation from the downtown office, considers what to do.

Until late last month, when the words "student-on-student sexual harassment" suddenly appeared on newspaper front pages accompanied by the sober countenance of Supreme Court Justice Sandra Day O'Connor, there was probably not much question about the sort of response the Milk-Bag Incident would have provoked in most outsiders coming across it for the first time. It would have made them say: Come *on.* It would have made them say: 12–year-old girls running straight for the office because somebody *offended* them, vice principal nodding soberly and handing over *forms* to fill out, have these people completely lost their bearings? It would have made them say: These are children. They're *supposed* to conduct themselves from time to time like hormonally over-stimulated jerks.

Then, on May 24, in a case called *Aurelia Davis v. Monroe Country Board of Education,* the Supreme Court ruled 5 to 4 that any school receiving Federal money can face a sex-discrimination suit for failing to intervene energetically enough when a student complains of sexual harassment by another student. The Davis case started as a lawsuit brought by the mother of a Georgia schoolgirl who was in fifth grade when she began experiencing what her family describes as prolonged sexual harassment—that was the label from the outset, sexual harassment, even though the two children involved were 10 and 11 years old—by the boy who sat beside her in class.

The Supreme Court options in Davis were lengthy and complicated, as Supreme Court opinions often are, but at the center was a rather remarkable and contentious back-and-forth between Justice O'Connor, writing for the majority, and Justice Anthony Kennedy, writing for the minority. O'Connor said "student-on-student sex harassment" could be a deeply serious matter, affecting a child's ability to learn; Kennedy said "student-on student sex harassment" was in essence a phrase that made no sense. O'Connor said school officials who ignored protracted and serious harassment could be sued under Title IX, the Federal law prohibiting sex discrimination in educational institutions; Kennedy said the U.S. Supreme Court had no business poking around in matters of local school discipline. "After today," Kennedy wrote, "Johnny will find that the routine problems of adolescence are to be resolved by invoking a Federal right to demand assignment to a desk two rows away."

Kennedy had more to say. He said "sex harassment" is a term that properly applies to the behaviour of adults, not to children "who are just learning to interact with their peers." He said one published harassment manual advises that one student's saying "You look nice" to another could be construed as sex harassment, depending on the tone of voice and another variables. He did not say, but suggested by the indignation in some of his memorable prose, that he believes the banner of "student-on-student sex harassment" is being carried at the present time in our legal and social history by meddling, litigation-happy, over-reaching hysterics placing impossible demands upon schools that have their hands full teaching children how to read and write.

Judy Gillen is familiar with the harassment manual Kennedy quoted so disapprovingly; it's called "Flirting or Hurting?", it has sold about 20,000 copies to schools all over the United States since it was first published in 1994 and Gillen uses elements of it when she conducts sex-harrassment workshops for middle- and high-school students. The line Kennedy lifted is part of a chart used to inspire student argument about possible differences between flirting and harassment. Flirting, suggests the chart: "You look nice." "Like your hair." "Wink." "Wave." Harassment, suggests the chart: "Ho." "Grab own crotch." "Pinch." "Lip licking." And may be, depending on the tone of voice, the facial expression and who else is around: "You look nice."

Justice Kennedy may have a real problem with this. A great many thoughtful people, already working hard to understand the boundary lines defining sexual harassment among adults, may have a real problem with this. But Gillen has no problem with it at all. "I mean, get real," says Gillen, who read every word of *Davis v. Monroe Country,* including the long dissent, the afternoon the decision was handed down. "We *need* to teach responsibility, we who work directly with kids, and shaping kids' behavior and kids' lives. Because behavior is learned. We *can't* accept that kind of behavior."

HOW THE HARASSMENT SPECIALIST SPENDS HER SCHOOL DAY

Judy Gillen is one of the banner carriers—that's why she's a harassment specialist. Quite a few public schools consult harassment specialists these days; they're supposed to, or somebody will have a problem and nobody will know what to do about it and there'll be a complaint and state or Federal investigators and a lawsuit against the school district and maybe an expensive settlement. There were at least a dozen reported lower court lawsuits even before the Davis ruling, with its announcement that student-to-student Title IX suits may proceed if it can be shown that school officials exhibited "deliberate indifference" to sex harassment that took place on their watch. Now there will be many more, as school officials scramble to figure out what "deliberate indifference" means.

But for some time now one of the numerous anti-lawsuit maneuvers recommended by experts in these matters has been: Get a specialist. Often the specialist is an outside professional who comes in with manuals and case studies in student harassment. It's unusual for a school district to invent a wordy systemwide job title that includes "Harassment Curriculum," but Minnesota is particularly aggressive in what is referred to by its adherents as "gender equity," and besides, as far as is publicly known, Duluth Public Schools was the first district in the country to pay out a monetary settlement in a student-to-student sex harassment case.

"My first title was just Harassment Specialist," Gillen says. "The standing joke was, 'Judy knows how to do *that* well.'" But she takes her work extremely seriously. She follows legal cases; she studies updates in the education press; she travels out of state to harassment conferences: she gets up in front of classrooms and spends 45 minutes at a shot saying things like: "*Unwelcome.* And *unwanted.* Somebody doesn't *like* it. That's what makes it harassment." She's a hybrid, a product of bewildering and litigious times: part teacher, part mediator, part agitator, part cop. Here's a Judy Gillen work list, the week the Milk-Bag Incident report comes in:

She runs three harassment workshops, one for an eighth-grade health class, one for a high-school health class and one for bus drivers, who as employed agents of the school district are legally liable for reporting anything that looks like harassment on their buses, even if it takes place behind their backs.

She summons a principals' meeting to introduce a new campaign called Safe Harbor, to beef up the idea that harassment protections apply to gay kids too—that schoolchildren are not supposed to be able to get away with yelling "faggot" at somebody just because everybody else is doing it and previous generations thought it was O.K. She invites as a surprise guest speaker a young Wisconsin man who was recently awarded a $962,000 settlement from school officials found by a jury to have violated the young man's constitutional rights by failing to stop what happened to him in junior high and high school after he acknowledged being gay: the boy was taunted, shoved, sworn at, laughed at, beaten up, subjected to mock rape and cornered in the bathroom while other boys urinated on him.

She holds an early-morning counseling session with a 10th-grader reported for lurking in the hallways, hissing sexual epithets at girls and trying to grab them in inappropriate ways. She rides herd on a gang of high-school boys using obscene anti-gay epithets to pick on a special-education boy who is in fact heterosexual, but feels taunted nonetheless. She keeps close watch on a high-school girl whose ex-boyfriend has been shoving and cursing her in the hallway. (The harassment report filed by the girl reads: "name-calling: 'bitch,' 'slut,' 'whore,' 'ugly bitch,' pushed me, threatened to punch me.") Gillen has the local police on alert for that one.

She follows up on a new complaint report, a boy and girl in the ninth grade going at each other in a mode somewhat unclear to observers and also probably to themselves; the girl told the boy she was going to file a harassment report on him if he didn't leave her alone, whereupon the boy turned around and filed a harassment report on her. "I talked to the principal today and said, 'Get some mediation for these two clowns,'" Gillen says. "You gotta keep a good healthy outlook on life. Because otherwise you'd get torqued out every day, thinking about what kids do."

She's chuckling. She's accelerating her red Subaru up the long hill that leads back from the school-bus office to central headquarters. The expression on her face and the set of her shoulders is just: Ahh, schoolkids, you adore them and you agonize over them and they make you completely crazy, which is something most of us already know. But we don't know it in quite the way somebody like Judy Gillen knows it.

Gillen knows what's in the transcribed proceedings of that Wisconsin lawsuit brought by the young gay man, including the part where school administrators are described as having advised the boy's parents that trouble of this nature is to be "expected" when a student is openly gay. She knows the pertinent narratives that float up from the central pages of other harassment lawsuits as well: the large-breasted California girl who was regularly greeted at the school doorway and followed through the hall by boys making mooing noises at her; the eighth-grade Texas girl who was repeatedly groped on the school bus by a boy who kept demanding to know what size bra and underpants she was wearing; the seventh-grade California girl who became the subject of a rollicking school-wide rumor, spread by both boys and girls, about sexual acts performed with her dogs; the school bus in Minneapolis—in a district down near Minneapolis—in which 8-year-old girls were being called "bitches" and urged to go home and perform fellatio on their fathers.

That famous North Carolina story about the 6-year-old who was suspended from school three years ago for kissing a classmate on the cheek? Sure. She knows that one too. Gillen rolls her eyes. "For a while I got asked that question just about every place I went," she says, "'And what do you think about that? How stupid can they be?' And frankly, I agreed with them. It was stupid." For the record: the school subsequently recanted the suspension, and the Lexington, N.C. school district revised its sex-harassment policy to take into account the age and maturity of the accused harasser. But that's not what lingers in the memory about the North Carolina story, is it? There's a reason people latched on with such enthusiasm to the image of school officials banishing a 6-year-old for kissing his classmate on the cheek: it was simple. Norman Rockwell felled by the overreaching hysterics. *Much* simpler to think about than packs of junior-high-school boys mooing at a schoolgirl's breasts.

HOW AWFUL BEHAVIOR GOT WORSE AND BECAME HARASSMENT

When Judy Gillen is called upon to explain herself before gatherings of parents—not hostile gatherings as a rule, they don't exactly mind that there's a specialist, but the very phrase "student-to-student sexual harassment," which nobody had ever heard of 15 years ago, perplexes people and makes them start invoking their own sensible, litigation-free childhoods, when lawyers didn't hover in the wings waiting for children to complain that their feelings had been hurt—she has three things to say.

First: It's worse now, being a kid, what goes on in schools. It's worse not just because students have access to assault weapons, but also because the culture heaves raw, explicit sexual imagery at children from sources as diverse as prime-time television, pop music, video games, movies, billboard advertising, the Internet and talk radio. When people old enough to have children now were in school, kids were offensive to one another, kids wounded one another emotionally, kids were raucous and lewd and spread rumors and talked about sex when they thought they could get away with it—but not like this. In the Davis case, what the boy accused of harassment did—what the Georgia school officials are accused of ignoring, despite repeated pleas for help from the girl and her family—was to spend five months directly and explicitly pressuring his classmate to have sex with him. From the Davis plaintiff's brief to the Court: ". . . repeatedly attempted to touch LaShonda's breasts and vaginal area, . . . told her in vulgar terms that he want[ed], . . . to get in bed with her, . . . placed a doorstop in his pants and behaved in a sexually harassing manner."

All of these allegations have yet to be proved in a court of law; the two sides in Davis were fighting about whether harassment charges could be brought under Title IX. But the suggestion that an 11-year-old boy might make advances as crude and aggressive as a grown man's comes as no surprise to Judy Gillen, nor to anybody else who has read the details of those lawsuits; something truly has changed, she tells those gatherings of the perplexed, and it starts far younger than you think, and it's not confined to rough inner-city schools. "The kids today are not the same kids we dealt with 15 years ago," Gillen says. "One of our assignments has been just to send kids home to watch television for an evening, and put down hatch marks for every swear word, every put-down, every direct sexual reference, everything that is derogatory against another person. And the fallout the next day is: 'Can you believe it?'"

Second: At the same time that students' behavior was growing more aggressive and lewd, a new vocabulary was being imported into the schools to describe certain forms of sexually charged hostile interaction between students, and this vocabulary—this way of thinking about the rights and obligations of individual students and the adults who are supposed to supervise them—comes directly from sex-harassment litigation in the workplace. For a lot of reasons, this makes for a troubling and imperfect fit. But here it is, and parents need to get used to it, the way we're getting used to the idea that a business executive can't go on thinking it's cute to pat his female colleagues on the buttocks as they walk by. Under the schoolhouse code of conduct implicit in the new vocabulary, the boys don't get to move their seats away from the lone girl in the auto mechanics class and let themselves be overheard muttering, "The bitch might break a nail and start crying" (that's from a sexual-harassment curriculum manual); girls don't get to humiliate a boy on the school bus by speculating loudly as to the modest size of his penis (that's from a drivers' instructional video), and boys don't get to pass around annotated lists of the school's 25 Most [expletive] Females (that's from an actual case brought before the Minnesota Department of Human Rights—the financial settlement, paid by the school district to the senior class girl who brought the complaint, was $40,000).

The expression "boys will be boys" frequently comes up at this point in the discussion, even though in Gillen's experience the perps, especially in the vicious-mouth department, are as likely as not to be girls. And Gillen's job is to answer: Not that way. Not anymore. "It's a whole new set of game rules," Gillen says. "The fun between all of us has sort of taken on a new dimension. You have to be so careful. You feel like you're walking on eggs: 'If I wanted to flirt with you, how would I go about it without offending you?' 'My God, maybe I just better not do anything anymore.' "That's been a lot of the typical responses I've had."

Third: As an employee of the Duluth Public Schools, Gillen has a closer for the unconvinced, more in the nature of a blunt instrument. If this still doesn't make sense to you, if you're still not seeing the wisdom of requiring young people to learn at school some version of the behavior protocols the workplace will demand of them, too bad. There *are* lawyers hovering out there. Parents retain them. The lawsuits show up in a variety of forms: negligence, violation of state discrimination laws, deprivation of constitutional rights and sex discrimination under Title IX. "When I cite court cases, and the outcomes, and the emotional damage the harassment has done to victims," Gillen says, "I don't get much argument."

Which bring us to the student-to-student sex-harassment settlement that helped inspire Judy Gillen's Job. The harassment involved bathroom graffiti; Gillen is discreet about discussing it in any detail, since a number of the suit's central characters remain her colleagues to this day. This bathroom graffiti story was broadcast years ago as an ABC movie for television; it was slightly fictionalized, given the title "Boys Will Be Boys" and run as an afternoon special, deliberately timed to reach a national audience of children. Sample exchange from the script:

> ALI: (*nervously*) . . . which is why I was hoping maybe you could do something about it.
>
> MR. PRITCHARD: You know, Ali, boys do that kind of thing. No one believes any of it.
>
> ALI: (*respectfully*) But they do. People look at me . . . they talk about me and tease me all day long. They treat me like it's true.
>
> MR. PRITCHARD: I'm sorry to hear that. But we can't stop boys from writing in the bathroom. It's . . . impossible.

HOW THE GRAFFITI ABOUT KATY LYLE CHANGED EVERYTHING

There's a legal principle hiding in those lines of "Boys Will Be Boys" dialogue, although it isn't fully unveiled until later in the plot. The legal principle, which has informed every one of the scores of lawsuits, administrative complaints and Office for Civil Rights rulings that have accumulated under the general label "student-to-student sex harassment," can be impertinently condensed as:

Mr. Pritchard, You Have to Stop It—or at Least You Have to Try. A lot of people are still arguing about this principle, Justices Kennedy and O'Connor most recently and famously among them, and to understand its controversial primary tenet—that the law ought to force the Mr. Pritchards of the world to sit up and pay attention when one student complaints of harassment by another—it may be helpful to go back a decade and recap what happened to the real Ali, whose name is Katy Lyle.

Lyle is 27 now, an attractive and articulate young woman who continues to live in the Duluth area. She teaches music to elementary-school children. She was 15, a sophomore at Duluth Central High School, when friends advised her in the spring of 1988 that someone had written obscene graffiti about her on the wall of a stall in the second floor boys' bathroom.

The way Katy Lyle tells the story, it was not long afterward that she saw how certain boys were staring at her, or shying away from her in the hallways, or snickering when she walked past. "And that's when I stared thinking: 'What's wrong with me?' Lyle says. "You know, the way girls do. 'Am I fat? Is it my hair?' "But then when the *girls* stared shying away, that's when I started making the connection."

In the short history of sex-harassment law, 1988 was a long time ago, and it bears remembering how novel many people still found the terminology then, even when it was being used to describe the behavior of adults. The phrase "sexual harassment" was invented during the mid–1970's by a group of Cornell University women looking for a way to characterize the treatment of a campus employee who had been refused repeated requests to be transferred away from a colleague who was hounding her. In 1986, two years before Lyle discovered the graffiti about her, the Supreme Court handed down its very first ruling on sexual harassment in the workplace, in *Meritor Savings Bank v. Vinson,* a case brought by a bank employee who testified that for four years she had been aggressively pursued, fondled and forced into sex by a male supervisor at the bank. The court's unanimous ruling in Meritor contained two crucial findings. One: Workplace sex harassment is illegal because it's a form of sex discrimination in employment, prohibited under Federal law by Title VII of the 1964 Civil Rights Act. Two: Illegal workplace sex harassment comes in two forms, either "quid pro quo"—this for that, more commonly understood as "sleep with me if you want the promotion"— or "hostile environment," a term that was to be argued over in many subsequent cases. The broader meaning was alarmingly clear to many employers: if the sexual atmosphere in your workplace makes even one person feel bad enough, it's going to cost you a lot of money.

Lyle v. Independent School District 709, the complaint filed by Katy Lyle's parents with the Minnesota Department of Human Rights in October 1989, was one of the first efforts in the United States to try out the proposal that students in school might be legally held to the same sex-harassment standards as employees in a workplace—that a high school full of teenagers, some of them brutish or foulmouthed or willing to write personalized obscenities on a bathroom wall, might be legally regarded as a form of "hostile environment." This is an idea that might fill some adults with careering, comically horrible memories of their own school years (well, of *course* it's a hostile environment, anybody who ever went to school knows that, adolescence *itself* is a hostile environment, but so what?), and even Katy Lyle says she was startled when a local rape crisis counselor, whom Katy had called for advice even though no physical assault had taken place, first used the new legal vocabulary to describe what was happening to Katy at school. "I always thought 'sexual harassment' happened in the workplace," Lyle says. "Those are the pictures they show you: a guy with a suit and tie, a secretary with a short skirt, and he tells her she has to do certain things or she'll get fired. I remember thinking about that, when I first found out what this was."

Exactly what did happen to Lyle at Central High remains under dispute, as Duluth public-school officials have never publicly agreed with the Lyles' account, and the school principal, the real-life official fictionalized as Mr. Pritchard, who has since moved on to a districtwide supervisory job, politely but emphatically denies interview requests. Everybody does agree that someone wrote obscene graffiti about Katy Lyle in the boys' bathroom; the Lyles say they never learned who wrote it or why, but at one point, long after Katy's mother placed her first distressed call to the principal, she entered the bathroom on a day when school was out so that she could see for herself the writing that covered a substantial portion of one stall's inside wall. "Slut" was the mildest, most old-fashioned of the slurs; there were pornographic references to dogs, to farm animals, to Katy engaging in sexual relations with her brother. "It took my breath away." Carol Lyle says. "I just burst into tears." The graffiti stayed up—not all of it, but enough for some portion of the obscenities to remain legible—for 16 months, encompassing two full summers and Katy's entire junior year.

So here's where the Mr. Pritchard principle comes in. It was not actually the writing of the graffiti that most infuriated Katy Lyle's parents; it was not the obscene drawings that began landing on Katy's desk during class, nor the folded notes demanding sex, nor the kids doubling up in laughter at the sight of Katy eating a banana in the cafeteria, nor the boy who yelled across the school's crowded entrance hall. "Hey, Katy, I took a [expletive] in your stall this morning!" What most infuriated Katy's parents was the school official who, in a district that actually had a written public-school sex-harassment policy in place, could not seem to *do* anything—who for nearly a year and half could not manage what seemed to the Lyles the simple act of cleaning graffiti off a bathroom wall. The Lyles began keeping an increasingly agitated record of their pleas to have the graffiti removed (July 14, 1989: "To our total disbelief, the graffiti was still there!").

Eventually the Duluth schools' lawyer was obliged to assemble a written chronicle, too, and between the two records there are hints as to the nature of the long delay: the principal's assurances that something would be done; the custodial crew not getting around to it; a janitor finally washing off the graffiti that was inked on the wall (as opposed to being scratched into the paint; more graffiti reappearing after the washing: Katy's older brother, who was in college, storming into the high-school bathroom with some cleaning chemicals to scrub at the graffiti himself; the wall not undergoing a paint job to cover the scratched-in graffiti because by contract custodians didn't paint.

Veterans of sexual-harassment theory, the academics and lawyers who developed the earliest lawsuits and training manuals, like to talk about the power of naming, of changing the nature and dimension of an act by calling it something new. ("That seemed very important," says Eleanor Linn, a University of Michigan gender equity specialist who participated during the mid–1980's in some of the first student-on-student studies. "We talked a lot about it: the thing that is not named is not recognized.") And a decade ago, even in the earnestly well-intentioned city of Duluth, the Katy Lyle graffiti problem was "viewed as a physical plant issue," as the schools' attorney, Elizabeth Storaasli, puts it. There is no evidence that anyone actually said, "Boys will be boys," but Carol Lyle remembers a custodian trying gruffly to comfort her as she was standing in the boys' bathroom staring at the scrawled-up wall. "After all, this is a high school," Carol Lyle says the custodian told her. "This kind of thing ought to be expected."

Properly contracted painters did eventually come to Central, the graffiti disappeared and Katy finished her senior year without further incident and moved on to the University of Minesota campus in Duluth. But her parents, who say they spent too many evenings watching Katy shut herself into her room to cry, decided to do what now comes naturally to American citizens who want to kick an institution they believe has done them wrong: they got a lawyer.

Their claim to the Minnesota Department of Human Rights, which the Lyles filed in anticipation of a lawsuit in state court, asserted that leaving offensive graffiti visible for so long constituted a form of illegal sex discrimination—in essence that the principal at Central bore the same ethical and legal responsibility as an employer who lets men leave obscene notes and pictures on a female co-worker's desk. And when state investigators released a finding siding with the Lyles, the Duluth school board elected to make history by settling rather than making history by carrying the battle into court. "It was clear that the state was going to see this as a test case," Storaasli says. "And at that point the board had determined that they did not want to become the test case."

Under the Lyle settlement, the Duluth school board agreed to a payment of $15,000 as a compensation for what the paperwork carefully referred to as Katy's "alleged pain and suffering." Jim Lyle recalls feeling uncertain about how much to ask for; some workplace sex harassment cases were commanding spectacular jury verdicts and settlements, sums of six and seven figures, but the Lyles decided that if they were going to set national precedent by making a public-school district pay for its own attitude problem—for its failure to see a certain kind of injury as urgent and serious and worthy of immediate intervention—the dollar amount ought to be both big enough to attract attention and modest enough to keep from outraging taxpayers. Jim Lyle thought $20,000 sounded about right. When the district suggested $5,000, the Lyles dismissed the offer as insulting. "It didn't dig deep enough," Carol Lyle says. "It had to be more than that to *say* something."

HOW STUDENT HARASSMENT GOT TO THE SUPREME COURT

When the Supreme Court took up the issue during the Davis oral argument last January, the justices, most of whom have reared children themselves, all of whom have *been* children themselves, at times sounded flummoxed. Here was Justice O'Connor, asking the first question of the argument, grilling the National Women's Law Center attorney, Verna L. Williams: "I'm sure that schoolchildren nationwide tease each other, and little boys tease little girls, and so forth throughout their years in school. And is every one of those incidents going to lead to some kind of a lawsuit?"

No, replied Williams, who was representing the family of the Georgia schoolgirl, LaShonda Davis; there are workplace code words now to help us draw the line: "severe," "pervasive," "objectively offensive to a reasonable person." But Justice Antonin Scalia persisted: "Gee, but little girls always tease little boys and little boys always tease little girls. That's pervasive." Williams: "It's pervasive, but it is not severe." Scalia: "In my experience it's severe."

And Williams began to answer, but Scalia interrupted: "Are you going to apply a reasonable—a 'reasonable teen-ager' standard? Is *that* the criteria?" There was chuckling in the courtroom, but Scalia had gone straight to the imperfect fit problem—the challenge of trying to lift rules and principles devised for adult workplaces and somehow force them onto the messy emotional lives of schoolchildren. A good many laws and legal terms are being tossed around in these cases, but nearly every one of them was first articulated before it had occurred to anybody to think of the behavior of teen-agers, or fifth graders, or children even younger, as the kind of "harassment" that might be addressed in court. Title IX, for example, was adopted as part of the 1972 Federal education amendments; it prohibits sex discrimination in any educational institution receiving Federal funds. The word " harassment" does not appear anywhere in Title IX, which was drafted by people worrying about more conventionally measured forms of discrimination in education—things like unequal allocation of scholarship money or athletic opportunities.

Twice in the years before Davis, when asked whether a school's failure to stop the sexual harassment of a student could be regarded as discrimination for purposes of a Title IX lawsuit, the Supreme Court ruled that it could—and that a person bringing such a lawsuit could collect monetary damages as compensation. But the harassers in those cases, one decided in 1992 and the second in 1998, were adults. Nasty allegations, too: young female students (one in 10th grade, one in 8th), older male teachers, "coercive intercourse" in private offices at school, student and teacher caught *in flagrante* by the police.

The justices argued among themselves about how high to set the bar for such cases, about how difficult it should be to bring a harassment-based Title IX suit against a school district, but there was no argument at all about the working label for these girls' experiences—about whether a 14-year-old schoolchild could legitimately be said to have been sexually harassed. Adult teacher, in a position of power, repeated intercourse: no issue.

Then Davis threw the Mr. Pritchard question at them—one kid going after another, school officials unwilling or professing helplessness to intervene—and the consensus fell apart. On the basis of the allegations in the complaint, *Davis v. Monroe County Board of Education* looks like one more case with details to wince over: LaShonda Davis complaining repeatedly that a boy identified as "G.F." has been propositioning her in class; the children's teacher refusing for three months LaShonda's requests to be moved from her assigned seat beside G.F.; LaShonda's grades dropping and her father learning that she has written a suicide note; G.F. subjected to no school discipline at all until Mrs. Davis finally has him charged with sexual battery, to which he pleads guilty.

Nonetheless, they're *both children.* Is the law capable of fashioning a rule for hanging the "sexual-harrassment" label on the things an 11-year-old boy says and does to the girl in the next seat?

Justice O'Connor's majority opinion used the "severe, pervasive, objectively offensive" language—it has to be disruptive enough to keep a kid from the equal educational opportunities Title IX guarantees—but Kennedy wouldn't buy it. "Schools are not workplaces, and children are not adults," Justice Kennedy protested in his adamant Davis dissent, which Scalia joined, along with William Rehnquist and Clarence Thomas. "A teacher's sexual overtures toward a student are always inappropriate; a teen-ager's romantic overtures to a classmate (even when persistent and unwelcome) are an inescapable part of adolescence."

Well, that's the crux of it, isn't it? "An inescapable part of adolescence." When Judy Gillen printed *Davis v. Monroe County Board of Education* from her computer the afternoon the ruling was announced, she marked up that passage in bright orange highlighter, it made her so mad. "I almost came out of my chair when I read that," she says. Here she is with all her materials, bulleting the principles she's trying to get across—

Harassment may include:

- Unwanted touching
- Verbal comments, name-calling
- Spreading sexual rumors
- Gestures, jokes or cartoons
- Too personal a conversation or note

—and here are four justices of the United States Supreme Court insisting on the "inescapable part of adolescence" argument, as though surviving into adulthood carried with it some implicit, immutable risk of being mooed at or urinated on or leered at by a boy with a door stop in his pants. "It's like: It's been O.K in the past, it was O.K. for me, it's been O.K for my kids, so what's so bad about it?" Gillen says. "They haven't got a clue how degrading these remarks can be."

It's an enormously difficult thing that people like Judy Gillen are trying to do in modern schools—to teach children and adults alike a vocabulary that somehow separates benign vulgarity and flirting from behavior that escalates into humiliation or fear. But at its core the message she has to deliver—the message rephrased over and over in the harassment manuals, including the comic-book-style kids' pamphlets with cover exhortations like "Nobody has to live with sexual harassment at school"—is simpler and less elusive than many of its critics give it credit for. The message is: There is a certain kind of lousy feeling that ought not be inescapable, at least not in school, not when adults are supposed to be watching out for you. "Talk to a trusted adult," reads one manual. "Get help from an adult if you need it," reads another. "Tell someone and keep telling," reads "Flirting or Hurting?" the manual mentioned in the Davis minority opinion, adding a checklist of other suggestions for the student who might in an earlier era have been advised to lighten up and take it like a kid: telling the harasser directly to stop, keeping a written record of the incidents as they accumulate; writing a letter to the harasser and having it delivered by an adult.

A final suggestion from this checklist: Get a lawyer. The language in the manual is actually much less pugnacious than that ("You have the right to file a complaint with the U.S Department of Education's Office for Civil Rights . . . or to bring a lawsuit under federal law Title IX"), but in the end it is the threat of a lawsuit that has pushed this enterprise the hardest and fastest.

And it's a real nuisance, that threat, no question about it. Invisible hovering lawyers make oppressive officemates for anybody who works in a public school, especially since legislation and legal definitions generally organize human behavior into categories far neater than the ragged multipart dramas that traipse in and out of a typical school counselor's office. Is there a complaint form for "Made me feel like quitting school by repeatedly inviting everybody except me to parties?" No. Is there a complaint form for "Spent every football practice for the last two years sidling up to me and hissing that I was a stupid geek who had no business being on the team?" No. The complaint forms, and the new post-Davis big Federal stick of deal-with-this-or-risk-a-lawsuit, kick in only for the verbal and emotional wounds that can be fit somehow into one of the legally recognized categories of discrimination—gender, race, religion, ethnicity, sexual orientation. There's no working warranty that everybody makes it to age 18 with spirits intact; maybe there should be, but that seems to be beyond the conceptual reach of the law, which has so far laid out what even the National School Boards Association agrees is a fairly reasonable base line for school administrators trying to avoid getting sued: Don't ignore a complaint.

That's the essence of the Davis instruction: Don't ignore it. You don't have to fix everything successfully; you don't have to create a school in which nobody ever looks down blouse fronts or draws crotch pictures on binder covers; you don't have to turn all schoolchildren into sensitive, caring, gender-enlightened New Persons. But you must take it seriously, when they come to you with the thing that's troubling them, and if it is bad, then you must intervene at least actively enough to avoid being accused of "deliberate indifference." You must, at risk of a Federal lawsuit charging your school with sex harassment under Title IX, "respond to peer harassment in a manner that is not clearly unreasonable."

It will take a great many lawyers a very long time to work out precisely what all that language means; that's what usually happens when new legal standards are set, and in the meantime some of those lawyers will end up costing school boards good defense money that might have been put to better use elsewhere. Children and teen-agers are going to go right on being crude to one another; school counselors and principals are going to go right on being asked to undo attitudes and incivilities that are hammered into their students the other 18 hours of the day, and teachers like Judy Gillen will right on knowing that their careful harassment presentations are being delivered at least some of the time to bored schoolchildren who roll their eyes and chortle about it afterward—or who file away select parts of the message as potential weaponry against classmates who happen to tick them off.

HOW THE MILK-BAG CASE WAS SETTLED

There's one way of looking at those 12-year-old girls signing complaint papers on the milk-bag boy from the Duluth school cafeteria: as tattletales, classroom scolds, the inevitable byproducts of a generation being taught to take umbrage at just about anything. But here's what happened after the girls filed their complaint. The boys at the center of the action were summoned to the principal's office for a mild chewing-out, told that behavior of this nature was offensive and unacceptable in school and sentenced to an in-school suspension, which required taking one day's classes and lunch in a detention room. The girls were told that their complaint had been attended to, were reminded in passing to keep their language out of the gutter, too, and were given to understand what in an ideal world all schoolchildren ought to know—that some grown-up at school is ready to listen, seriously, without shooing them away amid dismissive reassurances about the inescapable parts of adolescence.

Repercussions? None, so far. Event over. "I think we've done an excellent job of educating kids, that they're willing to report that," Judy Gillen says, "I don't think we'll see those boys involved in anything again." If she's right, then maybe this is how the system, clumsy and heavy-footed as it is, is supposed to work.

TOPICS FOR DISCUSSION AND WRITING

1. What single concern of Justice Kennedy's is voiced in his dissenting opinion which is not addressed in Justice O'Connor's majority opinion or in Gorney's article?

2. This Supreme Court decision was made in May of 1999. Conduct research on student-on-student harassment to discover if Justice Kennedy's prediction that "like suits will follow—suits, which in cost and number, will impose serious financial burdens on local school districts" has been proven true.

3. How does sexual harassment specialist Judy Gillen justify her role in the schools to parent groups? List these justifications and your reactions to them.

4. Gorney refers to "the power of naming." What is that power? Can you think of other examples of it?

5. Write an essay in which you side with the majority or the dissenting opinion in the Supreme Court decision, citing specifics from both opinions and from Gorney's article.

Sexual Harassment—Concluding Topic

How a court will rule in any particular case of sexual harassment will depend on its definition of the term, a definition which is based in law but not in stone. The definition is modified as courts rule on individual cases. As a culminating assignment for this chapter, review all of the selections which include definitions of sexual harassment—your answers to the "Topics for Discussion and Writing" should prove helpful here—and list all definitions of sexual harassment and any criticisms of these definitions you find. Then construct a paper based on this list in which you analyze the various definitions and what others have said about them, and conclude with what seems to you to be the best definition of sexual harassment on which to try sexual harassment cases. (See Logical Definition in Chapter 5.)

CHAPTER 13

Romance and Marriage

Romance and marriage may strike some readers as unusual topics for a critical thinking textbook, but we see no reason for exempting one's personal life from the benefits of critical thinking. Indeed, with sexual harassment and political correctness sometimes straining relationships between men and women, we may all benefit from a greater critical awareness of the assumptions that surround romance and marriage.

Our first selection in The Dating Game, *The Rules* by Ellen Fein and Sherrie Schneider, a strategy for women to catch a husband, is seen by some as emblematic of the antipathy that exists between men and women. Nevertheless, commentator Shann Nix in "Girl Talk" expresses her approval of "the rules," claiming her father taught them to her when she was eight years old. *The Rules* and other similar self-help books stress the differences between men and women and imply that game-playing and manipulation are required as men and women negotiate their way in and out of relationships. In fact, *The Rules* prompted a reply in the form of *The Code,* a book by two young men who counsel other men on strategies to avoid marriage. Determined to marry, a woman featured in a Wall Street Journal article approaches dating as a business proposition, employing in her search for a husband the strategies that made her successful in business. In "Dating In Cyberspace," we look at technology's impact on dating as couples meet and court on the Internet only to find real space quite different from cyberspace.

The readings in Marriage offer a variety of viewpoints as well as a variety of genres—two expository essays, a personal essay, two poems and one short story—from which to examine the institution. The selections in What's In a Name? include four essays which look carefully and critically at the tradition of women taking their husbands' name when they marry. We conclude with several selections on the controversial subject of same-sex marriage. The courts are addressing this question as homosexuals gain power as a political group and fight for what they believe is a right guaranteed them by the Constitution.

The Dating Game

The Rules

Ellen Fein and Sherrie Schneider

The book *The Rules* by Ellen Fein and Sherrie Schneider tells women how to get a husband by playing hard to get. Thirty-five axioms make up *The Rules,* and their authors urge women to follow them religiously if they want to "catch" a man. Many women reject these "Rules," believing they imply that a woman must be manipulative and dishonest in order to find a partner. Others swear by them, giving them credit for changing their lives.

The controversy and debate engendered by these rules is evident on the Amazon Books Web site (Amazon.com), where customers are encouraged to submit on-line book reviews. The number of reviews attests to the interest readers have in the book with their reactions varying greatly—some praise the book, others condemn it. You may want to read some of these reviews as you think through your own reaction to *The Rules.* We also encourage you to join the public debate by submitting your own on-line review.

How many times have you heard someone say, "She's nice, she's pretty, she's smart . . . why isn't she married?" Were they talking about you, perhaps? Ever wonder why women who are not so pretty or smart attract men almost effortlessly?

"*Katherine left me. She decided to make 'The Rules' retroactive.*"

Frankly, many women we know find it easier to relocate to another state, switch careers, or run a marathon than get the right man to marry them! If this sounds like you, then you need *The Rules!*

What are *The Rules?* They are a simple way of acting around men that can help any woman win the heart of the man of her dreams. Sound too good to be true? We were skeptical at first, too. Read on!

The purpose of *The Rules* is to make Mr. Right obsessed with having you as his by making yourself seem unattainable. In plain language, we're talking about playing hard to get! Follow *The Rules,* and he will not just marry you, but feel crazy about you, forever! What we're promising you is "happily ever after." A marriage truly made in heaven.

If you follow *The Rules,* you can rest assured that your husband will treat you like a queen—even when he's angry with you. Why? Because he spent so much time trying to get you. You have become so precious to him that he doesn't take you for granted. On the contrary, he thinks of you constantly. He's your best friend, your Rock of Gibraltar during bad times. He's hurt if you *don't* share your problems with him. He is always there for you—when you start your new job, if you need surgery. He even likes to get involved in mundane things, such as picking out a new bedspread. He always wants to do things *together.*

When you do *The Rules,* you don't have to worry about him chasing other women, even your very attractive neighbor or his bosomy secretary. That's because when you do *The Rules,* he somehow thinks you're the sexiest woman alive! When you do *The Rules,* you don't have to worry about being abandoned, neglected, or ignored!

A woman we know who followed *The Rules* is now married to a wonderful man who doesn't try to get rid of her to go out with the guys. Instead, he becomes slightly jealous when she does her own thing. They are very good friends, too.

Men are different from women. Women who call men, ask them out, conveniently have two tickets to a show, or offer sex on the first date destroy male ambition and animal drive. Men are born to respond to challenge. Take away challenge and their interest wanes. That, in a nutshell, is the premise of *The Rules.* Sure, a man might marry you if you don't do *The Rules,* but we can't guarantee that yours will be a good marriage.

This is how it works: if men love challenge, we become challenging! But don't ask a man if he loves challenge. He may think or even say he doesn't. He may not even realize how he reacts. *Pay attention to what he does, not what he says.*

As you read this book, you may think that *The Rules* are too calculating and wonder, "How hard to get do I have to be? Am I never to cook him dinner or take him to a Broadway show? What if I just feel like talking to him? Can't I call? When may I reveal personal things about myself?"

The answer is: Read *The Rules.* Follow them completely (not à la carte) and you will be happy you did. How many of us know women who never quite trust their husbands and always feel slightly insecure? They may even see therapists to talk about why their husbands don't pay attention to them. *The Rules* will save you about $125 an hour in therapy bills.

Of course, it's easy to do *The Rules* with men you're not that interested in. Naturally, you don't call them, instantly return their calls, or send them love letters. Sometimes your indifference makes them so crazy about you that you end up marrying one of them. That's because you did *The Rules* (without even thinking about it) and he proposed!

But settling for less is not what this book is about. The idea is to do *The Rules* with the man you're *really* crazy about. This will require effort, patience, and self-restraint. But isn't it worth it? Why should you compromise and marry someone who loves you but whom you're not crazy about? We know many women who face this dilemma. But don't worry—this book will help you marry only Mr. Right!

Your job now is to treat the man you are really, really crazy about like the man you're not that interested in—don't call, be busy sometimes! Do all of this from the beginning—from day one! Do it from the second you meet him—or should we say, the second he meets you! The better you do *The Rules* from the beginning, the harder he will fall for you.

Keep thinking, "How would I behave if I weren't that interested in him?" And then behave that way. Would you offer endless encouragement to someone you didn't really like? Would you stay on the phone with him for hours? Of course not!

Don't worry that busyness and lack of interest will drive him away. The men you don't like keep calling after you've turned them down, don't they?

Remember, *The Rules* are not about getting just any man to adore you and propose; they're about getting the man of your dreams to marry you! It's an old-fashioned formula, but it really works!

We understand why modern, career-oriented women have sometimes scoffed at our suggestions. They've been MBA-trained to "make things happen" and to take charge of their careers. However, a relationship with a man is different from a job. In a relationship, the man must take charge. He must propose. We are not making this up—biologically, he's the aggressor.

Some women complain that *The Rules* prevent them from being themselves or having fun. "Why should dating be work?" some ask. But when they end up alone on Saturday night because they did not follow The Rules, they always come back to us saying, "Okay, okay, tell me what to do."

Doing what you want to do is not always in your best interest. On a job interview, you don't act "like yourself." You don't eat cake if you're serious about losing weight. Similarly, it is not wise to let it all hang out and break *The Rules* as soon as you begin dating a man.

In the long run, it's not fun to break *The Rules!* You could easily end up alone. Think long term. Imagine a husband you love, beautiful sex, children, companionship, and growing old with someone who thinks you're a great catch.

Think about never having to be alone on Saturday nights or having to ask your married friends to fix you up. Think about being a couple! Unfortunately, however, you must experience some delayed gratification in the first few months of the relationship to achieve this marital bliss. But has wearing your heart on your sleeve ever gotten you anywhere?

There are many books and theories on this subject. All make wonderful promises, but *The Rules* actually produce results. It's easy to know what's going on when you do *The Rules.* It's very simple. If he calls you, pursues you, asks you out, it's *The Rules.* If you have to make excuses for his behavior—for example, he didn't call after the first date because he's still hung up on his ex-girl-friend—and you have to think about very word he said until your head hurts and you call him, it's not *The Rules.* Forget what he's going through—for example, "fear of commitment" or "not ready for a relationship." Remember, we don't play therapist when we do *The Rules.* If he calls and asks you out, it's *The Rules.* Anything else is conversation.

THE RULES-AT-A-GLANCE

Rule 1   Be a "Creature Unlike Any Other"

Rule 2   Don't Talk to a Man First (and Don't Ask Him to Dance)

Rule 3   Don't Stare at Men or Talk Too Much

Rule 4   Don't Meet Him Halfway or Go Dutch on a Date

Rule 5   Don't Call Him and Rarely Return His Calls

Rule 6   Always End Phone Calls First

Rule 7   Don't Accept a Saturday Night Date after Wednesday

Rule 8   Fill up Your Time before the Date

Rule 9   How to Act on Dates 1, 2, and 3

Rule 10   How to Act on Dates 4 through Commitment Time

Rule 11   Always End the Date First

Rule 12   Stop Dating Him if He Doesn't Buy You a Romantic Gift for Your Birthday or Valentines' Day

Rule 13   Don't See Him More than Once or Twice a Week

Rule 14   Not More than Casual Kissing on the First Date

Rule 15   Don't Rush into Sex and Other *Rules* for Intimacy

Rule 16   Don't Tell Him What to Do

Rule 17   Let Him Take the Lead

Rule 18   Don't Expect a Man to Change or Try to Change Him

Rule 19   Don't Open Up Too Fast

Rule 20   Be Honest but Mysterious

Rule 21   Accentuate the Positive and Other *Rules* for Personal Ads

Rule 22   Don't Live with a Man (or Leave Your Things in His Apartment)

Rule 23   Don't Date a Married Man

Rule 24   Slowly Involve Him in Your Family and Other *Rules* for Women with Children

TOPICS FOR DISCUSSION AND WRITING

1. Write a short paper in support of, or in opposition to, *one* of "The Rules." Choose one that strongly engages you, either because you wholeheartedly agree or vehemently disagree.

2. Write a response to *one* of these two questions: Women, would you follow *"The Rules"*? Why or why not? Men, what is your reaction to *"The Rules"*?

Girl Talk

Shann Nix

Writer and radio talk show host Nix is a firm believer in *"The Rules"*; she has followed them herself and urges her female readers to do the same.

It was bound to happen.

After all the unisex flower children with their long hair, bell bottoms and drug-induced, come-'n'-get-it nookie, after the wedgie-wearing bra-burners who pretended to hate men even if they *didn't,* really, after the hordes of angry women who boarded the bus to work in their Peter Pan collars and sneakers, carrying their high heels in leather bags, girding their (hidden and androgynously caparisoned) loins and locking their jaws for a monstrous fight in an unevenly male world:

It was bound to happen.

And it has.

The girls are back.

Not the Lipstick Lesbians, the Guerrilla Grrrls, or any other trendy recasting of some now long-defunct, kitsch-ily resuscitated, politically-incorrect-on-purpose kind of girls.

These are the real thing. Nicely dressed to take out the garbage, sweet, light and breezy, pleasant but distant, never-ever-call-him-first, hard to get, Rules Girls.

And if you've got a man who hasn't yet proposed, they'll take him and kick your butt.

The Rules Girls, spawned by the highly controversial best-seller, "The Rules," know something that mamma should have told you, but didn't. While you were busy climbing trees, getting pine cones tangled in your curls and plotting your first corporate takeover at the age of 25, authors Ellie Fein and Sherrie Schneider had sussed out the following points.

Number One: Modern women have to "face it: as much as we loved being powerful in business, that just wasn't enough. Like our mothers and grandmothers before us, we also wanted husbands who would be our best friends."

Number Two: "Nineties women simply have not been schooled in the basics—The Rules of finding a husband or at least being very popular with men."

Number Three: "Men are different from women. Men are born to respond to challenge. Take away challenge and their interest wanes."

So if the latest stock market update isn't warming your professional but still biologically female heart, then heed The Rules and . . . Don't talk to a man first. Don't stare at him or ask him to dance. Don't go Dutch on a date. Don't call him and rarely return his calls. Always end phone calls first. Don't accept a Saturday night date after Wednesday. Don't see him more than once or twice a week. Don't open up too fast. Be honest but mysterious.

No f------duh.

Anyone who has a driblet of Southern blood in their veins already knows this stuff. My father taught these "rules" to me when I was seven, and I snagged my first boyfriend when I was eight. It's how I got my first husband. Any woman who has the sense God gave an ashtray knows in her feminine bones that this is true, and further, *THAT IT WORKS.*

Boil it down.

Play hard to get.

Men love the chase.

You doubt it?

Try it . . . .

Get this—men are so panicked about women getting hip to their little drag-her-by-the-hair inner desires, that they've written a rebuttal: "The Code." The Code informs a man that there is a "a growing army of sex-withholders, a radical band of women that want to play by the old rules. This book is a not-so-subtle assurance that we can answer (or not!) in kind." The Code stages a counter-offensive against the devastatingly effective dictates of The Rules by offering men antimarriage advice like "Be a Beast," "The Only Rules Are Your Rules," and "Women Are Natural-Born Spies."

It is to laugh. As if their puny, pathetic efforts at resistance could ever stem the rising tide of Rules Girls who've got their number.

The military terminology used by the poor two-headed darlings may sound extreme, but in truth, the Rules *do* advise women to "Remember, early on in a relationship, the man is the adversary (if he's someone you really like)."

This is war, girlfriend. Arm thyself.

Oh, I know.

You're a modern, self-actualized, professional, therapeutically experienced, honest-with-your-feelings, unwilling to play games, woman of the '90s. You've done your 12-step programs, soaked in your spa. You've wrestled with the child within, and blown its nose. You've journaled and Jungian-dreamed and even, briefly, flirted with crystals and the Tarot. You have far too much respect for yourself and your fellow, male or otherwise, human beings to engage in humiliating pre-Sexual Revolution games. After all, we're all adults now, right? Equal and free, marching arm in androgynous arm into the sanitized future of shared responsibility and joint checking accounts.

The Rules has one brief and blindingly revealing question to ask you.

Are you married?

Do you want to be?

The Census Bureau reports that a record number of adults today are single. More than ever before. Edging up towards 40 percent.

We have ignored our biological truths for far too long. You can see the consequences in the recent Aberdeen military scandals. The Army proceeded on the dangerous assumption that since we're all equal, it was OK to put male trainers in charge of women trainees, then stood back and were shocked when the inevitable biological sparks flew, and the equally inevitable sexual abuses of power occurred.

MEN AND WOMEN ARE DIFFERENT.

Reality is the anathema of a politically correct society. We love to posture and insist that as long as we assert that we have evolved beyond biology, then we will—*POOF!*—phase into androgynous robots who think the same, act the same, fantasize the same things, have the same DNA-driven desires.

Get a clue.

Men love power, control and the chase. Men love sex. Women love romance.

Men want to get laid. Women want to get married. Biologically, the male imperative is to spread the seed. This reproduces the genome effectively.

Women have a greater stake in this biological roulette. For each pregnancy, they risk their life. They cannot fish, hunt, gather or word-process while in labor. They need someone to take care of them when they are nursing, with an infant in their arms. They need a husband, who has pledged his faith in sexually happier times. Being married is a step towards a guarantee that you won't be abandoned when you're helpless.

The psychological validity behind The Rules is this: A confident, self-contained woman who is ever-so-slightly evasive because she is involved in her own interesting and fulfilling life, is far more attractive than a pustulant, sucking sinkhole of need. Hunger is the great man-repellant.

But go ahead.

Go on that first date, and invite him up to your apartment. Rail at him for being half an hour late, and explain to him that this activates all the abandonment issues from your last relationship, by those guys who constantly undervalued your time. Be up front about your needs. Demand to be valued. Go out for dinner and a movie, and then suggest dancing when his interest starts to flag. During dinner, tell him all about your horrible past and plan for the space he could occupy in your closet. Tell him that he's the one for you. Insist on picking up the tab.

At the end of the evening, suggest a trip to your place. Sleep with him. In the morning, bring him coffee and orange juice and be honest about your feelings and expectations for the future. Tell him that your mother is waiting to meet him, and explain that you have a lot of issues with that. Walk him to the door. Insist on a good-bye kiss.

Wait for him to call.

Keep waiting.

In the meantime, I'll be sitting in front of the fire with my husband and our two dogs. You see, I'm a Rules Girl.

TOPIC FOR DISCUSSION AND WRITING

Shann Nix states unequivocally that "MEN AND WOMEN ARE DIFFERENT." Write a summary of the argument she offers in support of this conclusion and a response to her argument. Do you agree with Nix? Why or why not? (See Summaries in Chapter 3.)

Breaking the Rules

Nate Penn and Lawrence LaRose

Two men, Nate Penn and Lawrence LaRose, objected so strongly to *The Rules* that they wrote *The Code* in response, a book which tells men how to "Just say no to marriage." In the following excerpt Penn and LaRose urge men to avoid commitment at all costs.

Simply, The Code is a time-honored set of behaviors and misbehaviors that guarantees fulfillment in your relations with women—without your having to sign binding legal agreements, miss a single Yankees game or buy a Lexus' worth of precious gems. The Code shows you how to keep all your options open all the time, how to have a life of possibility with a capital P. Are we from Mars? We were skeptical at first, too. Read on!

How many times have you heard someone say, "He's sociable, he's handsome, he's smart . . . why is he married?" Could he have some as-yet-undetected character flaw, is he overcompensating, or is he the victim of a hoodwinking that would wow the Symbionese Liberation Army? Simply, how did a man of such promise fall to this?

Frankly, many men find it easier to cross continents, subdue natives, erect empires or diversify mutual funds than to Just Say No to marriage. If you find yourself slipping, thinking nice thoughts of nuptials, then you need The Code.

Traditionally, the Code has been a tacit letter of intent among men, the unspoken agreement, the secret society, the world wide *Weltanschauung* of noncommitment. It demands a written explanation because of the cultural confusion which we find ourselves in. That is, at the same time that feminism has made sex more readily available and less confined to the padded cell of matrimony, there is also a growing army of sex-withholders, a radical band of women that want to play by the old rules. This book is a not-so-subtle assurance that we can answer (or not!) in kind. Many women believe anew that if they keep you hungry they are more likely to ensnare you—forever.

Pressure for wedlock marks a return to the Victorian schoolmarm's pinched morality. Commitment squanders the critical hunter-gatherer skills we are justly famous for. Without conquest, the open road meets a dead end, the journeyman becomes a Fix Flats nine-to-fiver. We're not talking hard to get, but impossible to pin down!

In a word, men and women are different, and it is important to pay attention to those differences so you don't get caught with your pants up. One major difference is that we don't communicate in the same way women do; hell, we don't communicate at all if we can get away with it. We don't recount last night's sexual play-by-play, simply the touchdown; we don't talk about feelings, simply the touchdown. The Code will remind you when to talk, what to talk about, and the fatal dangers of plain speaking.

The Code is worldly advice, a realistic road map, not some shadowy prescription for wish fulfillment and self-delusion. Plenty of people will continue to sigh and speak of unions ordained on high, but ask yourself a question: If this marriage was made in heaven, why is everyone getting so worked up about Tiffany's?

Many women would rather "ring" you into dependence, but a man stands or falls on his own merits and meretriciousness, seeking his own path. But even though each is on his own road, there still have to be some traffic regulations. Well, there's only one, if you really think about it: it is verboten to pitch woo to another man's girlfriend—all else goes. And even here, there is a disclaimer: should she voice her dissatisfaction, it is understood that she has declared herself "in play."

Some will be wary that The Code is heartless and insulting to women, and, well, if you're that far gone we can't help you. But if you want to enjoy the charms of the female sex without having to sign your life away, The Code is your Fodor's to fornication.

A good friend of ours (since deceased) obeyed the Code and his life never lacked for adventure. Once a leader of a major Western power, he did as he pleased (despite being married), flirted indiscriminately, threw his weight around fuzzy gnomic leaders of small islands, tweaked the noses of mob bosses by bedding their wives, and even threw a star-studded party for himself where a Madonna lookalike (also since deceased) sang him Happy Birthday. Code guy deluxe, he was the envy of the neighborhood. Still is.

Like our friend, adherents to The Code know full well that the half-life for any ecstatic relationship is roughly three months—the rest is just emotional fallout. Duck and cover! To put it another way, The Code means, on all levels, get in, get out, get in, get out.

Should you find your resolve crumbling, if you dream domestically of Crate & Barrel, if you muse unbidden about the charms of raking leaves and cleaning the gutters, thinking that yes, you could be happy with one woman for the rest of your life, read The Code. Read The Code more religiously than the Pentateuch. Immerse yourself entirely, remove yourself from the company of matrimonial namby-pambies, page through fashion magazines and stare at ads on the sides of phone booths, force yourself into tony bars packed with buxom Bambis, and, if you feel ready, buy our new videocassette: "Code Calisthenics For Emotional Hardening" ($49.95).

Just remember not to overdo it—you still occasionally have to affect a lust for kitchen appliances or you'll find yourself on a cold bus stop with no hope for any attention whatsoever for Mr. Winky. Men do have emotions; it is simply the smart men who know how to get rid of them, how not to fall to Cupid's curare.

So this is how it works: you've spent some time—maybe ten minutes, maybe two weeks—with a lissome beauty, and it doesn't look like she's heading for the door. What do you do? You beware, that's what you do! Don't get dealt the commitment card from the bottom of the deck! The Code states that if women seek commitment, we let them know that we are wildly, deeply, sincerely confused. Read The Code and you'll know why you should never be so thickheaded as to feign commitment, or testify too ardently.

You will learn how to seem supremely, manifestly focused on her, to treat her like she's the only woman in the world. And perhaps most critically, The Code will teach you: Don't pay attention to what she says she wants, pay attention to what you know she wants. (See Article II: She's Only after One Thing, and It Ain't between Your Legs.)

Hey! Don't overthink this! You may wonder: Should I tell her I love her? Should I make plans more than five hours in advance? Should I stop saying "I need my privacy"? Would she like to borrow my cellular phone for the weekend? Can I leave my golf clubs and fish tackle at her place? Can I ever admit to cooking for myself?

The answer, stupid, is know The Code. Read The Code, be The Code. You can waste your time and try to think things through for yourself, but that's gonna cut into ESPN time, and then where will you be? It is easier to read The Code: it has always worked and, despite great cosmetic changes in sexual relations, always will. Try to navigate the shoals of modern romance and you'll only Titanic yourself with too much thinking; do what comes naturally: be a Beast.

Every relationship can turn into a hostage crisis; don't be Jimmy Carter!

TOPICS FOR DISCUSSION AND WRITING

1. Though the authors of *The Rules* and *The Code* are advocating opposing goals—to marry in one case, not to marry in the other—they agree on several points about men and women. What are these points of agreement? What is your view of these beliefs?

"What's the rush to settle down? You're only fifty-four."

2. Both of these books are based on the same two assumptions, one, that women want to marry, two, that men are less enthusiastic about marriage. Do you accept these two assumptions? Why or why not? If you agree that women are more interested in getting married than men are, speculate on why this might be so.

Dating as a Business Venture

If You Can't Get a Man with a Gun, Big Bucks Might Work

Robert McGough

In this piece published in *The Wall Street Journal*, staff reporter Robert McGough tells us of a woman looking for a husband who does not follow *"The Rules"* but the rules of business which made her extremely successful in her career. As you read, consider your reaction to this unusual approach to dating.

Lesley Friedman made a tidy $21 million when she sold a temporary-lawyer business she had built in New York over the course of eight stressful years.

Opting to retire early, she settled down at her Palm Beach, Fla., home. Her investment portfolio swelled in the bull market. Life was good.

But entrepreneurs yearn for new challenges. And Ms. Friedman, attractive, energetic, and unmarried, is no exception.

What has she chosen for a second career? "I'm dating," she says.

This is a new vocation for Ms. Friedman, who has never really dated much. Dating certainly wasn't a big part of her high-school years in a Los Angeles suburb where good grades were of utmost importance. And later, at Mount Holyoke College and New York University law school, she was a classic over-achiever. Too busy for fun and games. Then she became an obsessive business owner. Through it all, Ms. Friedman, who admits to 39 years but occasionally lets slip that she's in her early-to-mid 40s, never seriously got around to dating. There was never any time.

But she has plunged into her new full-time endeavor "of trying to find a husband" with a vengeance: In the past 12 months, she has had 73 blind dates—"More than one a week!" she exclaims—not to mention a fair number of repeat dates.

She attributes her high date-count to a novel approach: She is treating dating like a business venture. She even has a five-year plan. Find the right dating markets—high-brow charities and Democratic Party fund-raisers, for example. Network. Get married by 2002. "In business, it's very important to have a vision—what could be, what will be," she says. "That translates to dating: I never say that something's impossible. And I'm trying to learn from each situation."

A DIFFERENT BALLGAME

Ms. Friedman is used to playing rough—in the business world. When she was still running her firm, Special Counsel International, she battled competitors and even took on the local bar, which had concerns about the use of temporary lawyers and once tried to put her out of business. But her new career is far more bruising. "I had a much tougher skin about business ups and downs than I have about relationship ups and downs," Ms. Friedman says, "I take everything personally."

It is, after all, an unknown, often scary, world. "I've never understood men," she confesses. This time around, it's no different. She's appalled at what she sees as their lack of manners, their narcissism, their fixation on extreme youth and thinness. She worries about gold diggers.

Most of all, she struggles with a very contemporary dilemma: molding her appearance and personality to fit traditional notions of femininity, or exhibiting her forceful, businesslike nature.

She admits that relationships with men are "this whole area of my life I haven't succeeded at." But she is aiming high—very high: "Because I am a high-net-worth individual and very educated and all of that, I am looking for very intelligent, high-powered and successful men." She thinks she'll get along best with a self-made wealthy man—rather than someone who inherited wealth—because they will have the same bootstrap sensibility.

This summer and fall, after dabbling with dating in niche markets like London, Florida and the south of France, Ms. Friedman took her marketing campaign to the biggest, toughest turf of all: New York. She booked digs at the upscale University Club in midtown Manhattan and rented a house in the Hamptons, the Long Island summer playground of Manhattan's elite.

One advantage to New York is that some of her key consultants are located here. "When I was in business, I had a bunch of lawyers, accountants and consultants who I used to run things by," she says. Now her consultants are "people who give me advice on my social life, fix me up, help me with this process." Some of her consultants are friends; others are specialists whom she pays.

CONSULTANTS IN LOVE

In July, not long after she arrives in New York, she drops in on her key paid consultant, Sheila Grant.

"Lesley, you can look very casual-chic. You dress up something by throwing a sweater over it," says Ms. Grant, her "re-imaging" consultant.

Ms. Friedman is standing in Ms. Grant's airy Sutton Place living room, with its scenic vistas of Manhattan's East River. A tall woman in her 50s, Ms. Grant sits with erect posture on the edge of a sofa, offering a running commentary on a one-woman fashion show starring Ms. Friedman and her new wardrobe. Ms. Grant thinks the wide belt Ms. Friedman is wearing around a sleeveless shift draws attention to her hips. Remove the belt, she says, and the eye is drawn to Ms. Friedman's bustline and face—her best features.

Ms. Grant ladles out encouragement with her pointers: "You are the beautiful woman who is dying to come out," she says. Ms. Friedman, who once ran her business with an iron grip, permits herself a nervous but grateful smile.

"Do men realty notice this stuff?" Ms. Friedman asks.

"Absolutely," Ms. Grant insists.

"Men will say, 'She's so put together, she dresses so beautifully.'"

Ms. Friedman first hired Ms. Grant, who charges $250 for an initial consultation, $100 an hour after that, last year when she was preparing for her assault on the global dating scene. She now consults her frequently, even calling for fashion advice before dates. It's a business relationship, but the two women seem honestly fond of each other. After their initial meeting, Ms. Friedman shipped her entire wardrobe, by UPS, from Palm Beach to New York for Ms. Grant to inspect. The consultant tossed almost everything out. Most of the outfits were too large—Ms. Friedman had lost 25 pounds thanks to a diet-and-exercise regimen. But they also were too frumpy.

To drape Ms. Friedman's newly svelte physique, Ms. Grant took her on a three-day, 16-hour shopping spree—they hit Bergdorf Goodman, Escada and Pilar Rossi—that yielded a 77-piece fall and winter wardrobe, including shoes and accessories. Out went the baggy pants and floppy, matronly tops. In came tight pants, stiletto heels (that took some getting used to) and strapless cocktail dresses. "She was scared," Ms. Grant recalls. "She would say, 'No, I could never wear that.'" But Ms. Grant prevailed, and the scariest outfits were ordered—sometimes in several different colors.

"I thought professional, intelligent women should be very modest." Ms. Friedman says, "I didn't have one sexy outfit." She still harbors misgivings about her sartorial makeover: "I can't believe I spend my time at the tailor. But I've gotten some great dates." It's a function of giving the customer what he wants, she says.

In her living room, Ms. Grant suggests cosmetic dentistry as a possibility. (Ms. Friedman agrees and has some work done.) And she's not satisfied with Ms. Friedman's hair style, which she deems unflattering: "She was getting her haircuts in Palm Beach without me," Ms. Grant murmurs.

SOMETHING OF A SETBACK

Not all business plans work, and Ms. Friedman's summer in the Hamptons proves unsuccessful.

Her strategy is to take a share in a house in East Hampton (monthly cost for the whole house: $10,000) and wangle invitations to charity and sports events she figures are frequented by wealthy New York men. At the Mercedes-Benz Polo Challenge, a polo tournament, she gets into the VIP tent area with the *creme de la creme.* She's invited to the "Huggy Bears" celebrity-tennis charity fund-raiser, sponsored by Wall Street's Forstmann brothers.

But she complains that the men have their eyes on the waiflike 20-something models who tend to populate these types of events. Ms. Friedman is attractive—"one of the most beautiful women I've ever seen," one New York man gushed to a mutual acquaintance recently—but she feels she just can't compete with the youngsters.

Moreover, it disturbs her that the only time she attracted attention from men at a Hamptons event was when she wore an outfit displaying some cleavage.

She frets that her search is turning her mind to mush. "I've got to read" again, she says. She considers options—perhaps volunteering at a charity. Anything to reactivate her intellect. "All I do is focus on my physical appearance and look for men," she laments. "I've become a bimbo."

Frankly, she has the most luck meeting men when friends fix her up. Going to parties in the Hamptons and waiting to get picked up just doesn't work, she concludes.

She has some success with the strategy one late-summer night at a Manhattan restaurant called San Pietro—she chose it because it's a favorite of deal-making businessmen. Indeed, a 52-year-old law-firm partner wanders over to the table where she and a married girlfriend are dining.

But Ms. Friedman immediately focuses on his shortcomings. He has a beard—probably too scratchy to kiss. Besides, "he probably has a fifth, a sixth the money I have," which leads her to worry that he might be a gold digger. Worst of all, he initially tries to pick up her friend.

Still, when he calls Ms. Friedman a few days later, she agrees to go out with him because she feels they have "a lot in common. He is well-educated, having gone to Columbia Law School," and he's "very intellectual and smart."

INITIAL PRIVATE OFFERING

The first date goes "fabulously." Their dinner is filled with "intellectual, stimulating conversation." It turns a bit awkward later when he suggests going out for a drink—and they end up outside his apartment building. "Let's go up," he tells her.

"I hardly know you," she replies.

He urgently wants to show Ms. Friedman his rare-book collection.

She demurs, and he gallantly sees her home in a cab, which she judges is "a very gentlemanly thing to do."

A few days later, they meet again. "If you really liked me, you would sleep with me" tonight, he tells her over drinks.

Ms. Friedman is insulted and disappointed: She's wearing $3,000 worth of clothes, and has schlepped into Manhattan from the Hamptons to meet him. When she says no, his response is, "Why does this have to be all on your terms? What about my needs and feelings?"

Aha! Ms. Friedman realizes: the language of negotiation! Familiar terrain.

"Maybe we could meet both of our needs," Ms. Friedman tells him. "I'm willing to sleep with you tonight, but I want to know you're not going to just drop me." In return, she asks for "12 weeks of monogamy." She has a fallback position: She's actually willing to settle for six weeks of monogamy.

But negotiating makes her date nervous: "I wouldn't have wanted to come up against you at the negotiating table," he says. After a less-than-sparkling dinner at a nearby restaurant, the bearded lawyer accompanies her home, gives her a peck on the cheek, says, "I've heard your terms"—and disappears into the night.

They go out a few more times, but the pizzazz is gone; their final date ends in a quarrel. "I was just so disappointed," Ms. Friedman says later. "Here was someone I thought I would love to get to know better."

Getting pressured for sex is a recurring problem, she says. Men, particularly New York men, expect to jump into bed with her right away. Besides being turned off by their pushiness, Ms. Freidman, who is accustomed to the clear-cut edges of the business world believes there's no economic basis for their position.

Just run the numbers, she says. The cost of buying a woman dinner at one of the fancy New York restaurants she prefers is about $150. "A high-class prostitute probably costs $500 per, ah, an encounter, whatever you call it," she says. The economic conclusion: "These guys are getting off cheap" if they expect sex after just one or two dates. "It's not fair.

"Any man who tries to get a woman to sleep with him on the first or second date, when he has no long-term interest in her, deserves having women go after him just for his money," she declares. "It's a two-way street." But she worries that the social economics of New York are different from what her calculations allow.

"I expect to be courted, I expect to be taken out nicely. I expect someone to wait for 10 dates before they have sex with me," she says. "And a lot of people are telling me, especially in New York, this is just not realistic. That people are very immediate here, they're very goal-oriented. Either it works or it doesn't work."

POLITICAL PARTYING

On a crisp October evening, Ms. Friedman is back at Sheila Grant's apartment surrounded by a group of devoted Democrats. Ms. Grant's husband, a real-estate developer, is hosting a fund-raiser for U.S. Sen. Patty Murray, the incumbent Democrat from Washington state.

Ms. Friedman, who's fairly apolitical, is here to find her own big spender. But "it's kind of a bust," she complains in a low voice made scratchy from a cold. "There are only two good-looking men here." One of them, a natty, white-bearded man in a double-breasted suit, is wearing a wedding ring. But she does chit-chat with the other man. He's tall, strong-featured, with curly hair. He smiles. He's a lawyer—good!

But, once again, she goes into fault-finding mode. She's disappointed to discover that he's an in-house lawyer for a not-for-profit organization. Surely he doesn't have much money, she quickly reasons, and he probably failed to make partner at a law firm. When he tries to exchange numbers with her, she discovers an urgent task elsewhere, and slips away into the crowd.

In sales, she recalls, it takes a lot of networking to come up with a good prospect. "The more you're out there, and the more you're networking, ultimately the more clients you get," she says. It's a tiring process: In her business, "For every 10 prospects, I got one client."

The same seems to apply to her new career. Some politicians here are in their 30s—too young. A money manager and his girlfriend promise to introduce her to a friend who has gotten divorced.

Ms. Friedman writes a check for Sen. Murray's campaign. On the way out, she stops to chat with a Democratic fundraiser. If he introduces her to a man she marries, she says, she will give the Democratic party $100,000.

A few heads turn as the fund-raiser exclaims loudly, "It's a deal!" and grips her hand in both of his.

Just like business, Ms. Friedman later explains: "I had to incentivize my sales force."

There's no question Ms. Friedman has made an enormous start-up investment in her new vocation. There's the new wardrobe, complete with $1,200 Escada jackets and $3,000 Christian Dior suits. In the past 12 months, she easily spent "in the six figures" on clothes. "I have such a tremendous investment in my wardrobe, I have to wear it."

Then there are the continuing expenses. "Do you know how much it costs to get a manicure every week? I think a manicure is $25. A pedicure, $25 to $60. Women are paying $50 to $60 a week."

That's not all: There's a bikini wax; a haircut every four to five weeks; and hair coloring. "The beauty salon is very expensive," she says. "My accountant, he's been telling me to cut back on the beauty parlor. He tells me. 'Can't you blow dry your own hair?'"

All this is why she thinks women deserve perquisites—such as free meals and a modicum of chivalry—in return for "the upkeep a woman needs to do for a man."

LACKLUSTER RESULTS

Another disappointing date: Perfect resume, lousy personality. "I like him on paper," Ms. Friedman says.

This prospect—the result of a fix-up by an acquaintance—was divorced in the past 14 months, is in his mid–50s and works for a top New York law firm. That means he's probably making between $1 million and $2 million a year—a statistic she garners from American Lawyer.

On their first date, at San Pietro, Ms. Friedman frets that her dress is to low-cut, that it gives "the wrong impression." A slip of the tongue doesn't help matters: They run into someone her date knows who tells Ms. Friedman what a terrific guy he is. "I seduced that—I meant deduced!" she stumbles.

The men roar with laughter. "I turned so red," she says.

But as the date goes on, she likes him even more. He's smart and has a degree from an Ivy League law school. He doesn't brag about himself and seems "folksy," saying he "hates to dress up." She concludes that "this is a normal man who happens to be bright and successful." He says he never cheated on either of his previous wives. He likes to travel—another plus.

On the downside, he has a young child. "I don't know how I feel about that," says Ms. Friedman. The date lasts three-and-a-half hours. Later, he tries to get her to invite him up to her room for the night. This bothers her a bit, and she says no. But all in all, it was a fun evening.

Things are iffy in the following days. She learns that he speaks critically of her to the person who fixed them up, saying she seems to be "floundering" with her life. In her view, he takes too long—10 days—before calling her for another date. Then, when he finally calls, he wants her to go out that same day—which to her seems rude. Still, they go, yet he seems aloof.

After a few more weeks, when she hasn't heard from him, she invites him to lunch and asks for feedback. He chastises her, saying she shops all day and goes to parties every night—a comment she would shrug off more easily if he had anything positive to say about her.

Later on, this lawyer, who asks not to be identified, says Ms. Friedman's being "totally focused on finding a mate" was a turnoff for him. He doesn't like that they were introduced by a matchmaking staffer of a charity to whom Ms. Friedman has promised a big donation if the match ends in marriage; this isn't the right reason to get involved in a charity, he argues.

He also repeats his criticism that her search is centered on all the wrong things. "She goes to parties in the Hamptons and parties in Palm Beach, and she's worrying about the niceties of fancy lunches and who sits where," he says.

Ms. Friedman finds this disappointing, saying her interest in the charity she works with is genuine and predates her husband search. She doesn't think she's frivolous. "I'm very loyal, I work very hard on things, I've always been at the top of my class," she protests. She decides to take his criticisms as a sign that he's still depressed about his divorce and not ready for another relationship.

Ms. Friedman, though, gets better feedback from Jonathan Farkas, a New York investor and socialite, whom she met after he spotted her out of the corner of his eye at the bar of Mar-a-Lago, Donald Trump's club in Palm Beach. They had three or four dates before deciding they would simply remain friends—Mr. Farkas was also getting over a bad breakup. And though he didn't know of her five-year plan back then, he doesn't hold it against her and, in fact, hopes she'll succeed. "I thought she was really attractive," he says. But he does worry that Ms. Friedman, a novice at dating, may be underestimating the risks: While you can put business setbacks behind you, he says, "there's no exact science for emotional pain."

RETHINKING STRATEGY

As November grows colder, Ms. Friedman is having self-doubts.

"Maybe I'm barking up the wrong tree with this whole crazy thing," she says. "I think maybe I have to face the fact that I kind of missed the boat when I was in my 20s." Perhaps, she worries, "I made a choice to be a career woman, and that means I'm precluded from certain types of relationships with men."

She adds: "I'm also getting a little bored. It's just not very intellectually stimulating—this whole process. It's taking so much time just to get ready for the dates."

Some of her friends and "consultants" perceive that Ms. Friedman is going through the types of dating pains they experienced when they were younger. Freddie Corley, a friend in Palm Beach, sees Ms. Friedman as a "wonderful woman whose life has been abbreviated."

"Many women have done this for years, and they start very early," Ms. Corley says, "the whole dating thing, the question of being alluring and really, the mating game, so to speak. She delayed all that. And of course, being smarter, and having more means than most women, she can do this very expeditiously now." But Ms. Friedman's expectations are high, she says, and "she needs to be patient."

Ms. Friedman is preparing to leave New York for a couple of weeks. In the past few days, she has been feeling a bit more upbeat. "I had a breakthrough—that's what I call it when in business something moves to the next level," she reports.

It's not an earth-shattering breakthrough. Just a couple of fun dates with nice guys who respected her boundaries. Then again, to a single woman in Manhattan, that qualifies as earth-shattering.

Her epiphany? First, fewer dates but higher-quality ones. No more run-of-the-mill law-firm partners for her, she says: "I have to date guys who are really extremely successful, which is what I've been wanting to do, because they treat me better." She's going to start "prequalifying" her dates, much as she became more selective about clients as her business grew.

Second, "I just think I have to start being much more confident about who I am and really trying to be myself, and not try to be what I think the guy wants me to be." She then excuses herself, flashing her new smile. It's time to get ready for another date.

TOPICS FOR DISCUSSION AND WRITING

1. List all the parallels Lesley Friedman draws between dating and running a business.

2. In a short essay, write your opinion of the analogy Friedman draws between dating and business. Are these activities similar? Do you think this approach to dating is a good one? (See False Analogy in Chapter 6.)

Dating in Cyberspace

Virtual Love

Meghan Daum

While dating according to "the rules" strikes many as a return to the past, dating on the Internet is a prominent feature of our high-tech present. A popular 1998 film, *You've Got Mail*, is based on this phenomenon of individuals meeting and forging relationships on the Internet. In "Virtual Love," writer Meghan Daum tells us her experience of dating in cyberspace.

It was last November; fall was drifting away into an intolerable chill. I was at the end of my twenty-sixth year, and was living in New York City, trying to support myself as a writer, and taking part in the kind of urban life that might be construed as glamorous were it to appear in a memoir in the distant future. At the time, however, my days felt more like a grind than like an adventure: hours of work strung between the motions of waking up, getting the mail, watching TV with roommates, and going to bed. One morning, I logged on to my America Online account to find a message under the heading "is this the real meghan daum?" It came from someone with the screen name PFSlider. The body of the message consisted of five sentences, written entirely in lower-case letters, of perfectly turned flattery: something about PFSlider's admiration of some newspaper and magazine articles I had published over the last year and a half, something about his resulting infatuation with me, and something about his being a sportswriter in California.

I was engaged for the thirty seconds that it took me to read the message and fashion a reply. Though it felt strange to be in the position of confirming that I was indeed "the real meghan daum," I managed to say, "Yes, it's me. Thank you for writing." I clicked the "Send Now" icon, shot my words into the void, and forgot about PFSlider until the next day, when I received another message, this one headed "eureka."

"wow, it is you," he wrote, still in lower case. He chronicled the various conditions under which he'd read my few-and-far-between articles—a boardwalk in Laguna Beach, the spring-training pressroom for a baseball team that he covered for a Los Angles newspaper. He confessed to having a crush on me. He referred to me as "princess daum." He said he wanted to have lunch with me during one of his two annual trips to New York.

The letter was outrageous and endearingly pathetic, possibly the practical joke of a friend trying to rouse me out of a temporary writer's block. But the kindness pouring forth from my computer screen was bizarrely exhilarating, and I logged off and thought about it for a few hours before writing back to express how flattered and "touched"—this was probably the first time I had ever used that word in earnest—I was by his message.

I am not what most people would call a computer person. I have no interest in chat rooms, newsgroups, or most Web sites. I derive a palpable thrill from sticking a letter in the United States mail. But I have a constant low-grade fear of the telephone, and I often call people with the intention of getting their answering machines. There is something about the live voice that I have come to find unnervingly organic, as volatile as live television. E-mail provides a useful antidote for my particular communication anxieties. Though I generally send and receive only a few messages a week, I take comfort in their silence and their boundaries.

PFSlider and I tossed a few innocuous, smart-assed notes back and forth over the week following his first message. Let's say his name was Pete. He was twenty-nine, and single. I revealed very little about myself, relying instead on the ironic commentary and forced witticisms that are the conceit of so many E-mail messages. But I quickly developed an oblique affection for PFSlider. I was excited when there was a message from him, mildly depressed when there wasn't. After a few weeks, he gave me his phone number. I did not give him mine, but he looked it up and called me one Friday night. I was home. I picked up the phone. His voice was jarring, yet not unpleasant. He held up more than his end of the conversation for an hour, and when he asked permission to call me again I granted it, as though we were of an earlier era.

Pete—I could never wrap my mind around his name, privately thinking of him as PFSlider, "E-mail guy," or even "baseball boy"—began phoning me two or three times a week. He asked if he could meet me, and I said that that would be O.K. Christmas was a few weeks away, and he told me that he would be coming back East to see his family. From there, he would take a short flight to New York and have lunch with me.

"It is my off-season mission to meet you," he said.

"There will probably be a snow storm," I said.

"I'll take a team of sled dogs," he answered.

We talked about our work and our families, about baseball and Bill Clinton and Howard Stern and sex, about his hatred for Los Angeles and how much he wanted a new job. Sometimes we'd find each other logged on simultaneously and type back and forth for hours.

I had previously considered cybercommunication an oxymoron, a fast road to the breakdown of humanity. But, curiously, the Internet—at least in the limited form in which I was using it—felt anything but dehumanizing. My interaction with PFSlider seemed more authentic than much of what I experienced in the daylight realm of living beings. I was certainly putting more energy into the relationship than I had put into many others. I also was giving Pete attention that was by definition undivided, and relishing the safety of the distance between us by opting to be truthful instead of doling out the white lies that have become the staple of real life. The outside world—the place where I walked around avoiding people I didn't want to deal with, peppering my casual conversations with half-truths, and applying my motto "Let the machine take it" to almost any scenario—was sliding into the periphery of my mind.

For me, the time on-line with Pete was far superior to the phone. There were no background noises, no interruptions from "call waiting," no long-distance charges. Through typos and misspellings, he flirted maniacally. "I have an absurd crush on you," he said. "If I like you in person, you must promise to marry me." I was coy and conceited, telling him to get a life, baiting him into complimenting me further, teasing him in a way I would never have dared to do in person, or even on the phone. I would stay up until 3 A.M. typing with him, smiling at the screen, getting so giddy that when I quit I couldn't fall asleep. I was having difficulty recalling what I used to do at night. It was as if he and I lived together in our own quiet space—a space made all the more intimate because of our conscious decision to block everyone else out. My phone was tied up for hours at a time. No one in the real world could reach me, and I didn't really care.

Since my last serious relationship, I'd had the requisite number of false starts and five-night stands, dates that I wasn't sure were dates, and emphatically casual affairs that buckled under their own inertia. With PFSlider, on the other hand, I may not have known my suitor, but, for the first time in my life, I knew the deal: I was a desired person, the object of a blind man's gaze. He called not only when he said he would call but unexpectedly, just to say hello. He was protected by the shield of the Internet; his guard was not merely down but nonexistent. He let his phone bill grow to towering proportions. He told me that he thought about me all the time, though we both knew that the "me" in his mind consisted largely of himself. He talked about me to his friends, and admitted it. He arranged his holiday schedule around our impending date. He managed to charm me with sports analogies. He didn't hesitate. He was unblinking and unapologetic, all nerviness and balls to the wall.

And so PFSlider became my everyday life. All the tangible stuff fell away. My body did not exist. I had no skin, no hair, no bones. All desire had converted itself into a cerebral current that reached nothing but my frontal lobe. There was no outdoors, no social life, no weather. There was only the computer screen and the phone, my chair, and maybe a glass of water. Most mornings, I would wake up to find a message from PFSlider, composed in Pacific time while I slept in the wee hours. "I had a date last night," he wrote. "And I am not ashamed to say it was doomed from the start because I couldn't stop thinking about you."

I fired back a message slapping his hand. "We must be careful where we tread," I said. This was true but not sincere. I wanted it, all of it. I wanted unfettered affection, soul-mating, true romance. In the weeks that had elapsed since I picked up "is this the real meghan daum?" the real me had undergone some kind of meltdown—a systemic rejection of all the savvy and independence I had worn for years, like a grownup Girl Scout badge.

Pete knew nothing of my scattered, juvenile self, and I did my best to keep it that way. Even though I was heading into my late twenties. I was still a child, ignorant of dance steps and health insurance, a prisoner of credit card debt and student loans and the nagging feeling that I didn't want anyone to find me until I had pulled myself into some semblance of an adult. The fact that Pete had literally seemed to discover me, as if by turning over a rock, lent us an aura of fate which I actually took half-seriously. Though skepticism seemed like the obvious choice in this strange situation, I discarded it precisely because it was the obvious choice, because I wanted a more interesting narrative than cynicism would ever allow. I was a true believer in the urban dream: the dream of years of struggle, of getting a break, of making it. Like most of my friends, I wanted someone to love me, but I wasn't supposed to need it. To admit to loneliness was to smack the face of progress, to betray the times in which we lived. But PFSlider derailed me. He gave me all of what I'd never even realized I wanted.

My addiction to PFSlider's messages indicated a monstrous narcissism, but it also revealed a subtler desire, which I didn't fully understand at the time. My need to experience an old-fashioned kind of courtship was stronger than I had ever imagined. And the fact that technology was providing an avenue for such archaic discourse was a paradox that both fascinated and repelled me. Our relationship had an epistolary quality that put our communication closer to the eighteenth century than to the impending millennium. Thanks to the computer, I was involved in a well-defined courtship, a neat little space in which he and I were both safe to express the panic and the fascination of our mutual affection. Our interaction was refreshingly orderly, noble in its vigor, dignified despite its shamelessness. It was far removed from the randomness of real-life relationships. We had an intimacy that seemed custom-made for our strange, lonely times. It seemed custom-made for me.

The day of our date, a week before Christmas, was frigid and sunny. Pete was sitting at the bar of the restaurant when I arrived. We shook hands. For a split second, he leaned toward me with his chin, as if to kiss me. He was shorter than I had pictured, though he was not short. He struck me as clean-cut. He had very nice hands. He wore a very nice shirt. We were seated at a very nice table. I scanned the restaurant for people I knew, saw none, and couldn't decide how I felt about that.

He talked, and I heard nothing he said. I stared at his profile and tried to figure out whether I liked him. He seemed to be saying nothing in particular, but he went on forever. Later, we went to the Museum of Natural History and watched a science film about storm chasers. We walked around looking for the dinosaurs, and he talked so much that I wanted to cry. Outside, walking along Central Park West at dusk, through the leaves, past the yellow cabs and the splendid lights of Manhattan at Christmas, he grabbed my hand to kiss me and I didn't let him. I felt as if my brain had been stuffed with cotton. Then, for some reason, I invited him back to my apartment. I gave him a few beers and finally let him kiss me on the lumpy futon in my bedroom. The radiator clanked. The phone rang and the machine picked up. A car alarm blared outside. A key turned in the door as one of my roommates came home. I had no sensation at all—only a clear conviction that I wanted Pete out of my apartment. I wanted to hand him his coat, close the door behind him, and fight the ensuing emptiness by turning on the computer and taking comfort in PFSlider.

When Pete finally did leave, I berated myself from every angle: for not kissing him on Central Park West, for letting him kiss me at all, for not liking him, for wanting to like him more than I had wanted anything in such a long time. I was horrified by the realization that I had invested so heavily in a made-up character—a character in whose creation I'd had a greater hand than even Pete himself. How could I, a person so self-congratulatingly reasonable, have been sucked into a scenario that was more akin to a television talk show than to the relatively full and sophisticated life I was so convinced I led? How could I have received a fan letter and allowed it to go this far?

The next day, a huge bouquet of FTD flowers arrived from him. No one had ever sent me flowers before. I forgave him. As human beings with actual flesh and hand gestures and Gap clothing, Pete and I were utterly incompatible, but I decided to pretend otherwise. He returned home and we fell back into the computer and the phone, and I continued to keep the real world safely away from the desk that held them. Instead of blaming him for my disappointment, I blamed the earth itself, the invasion of roommates and ringing phones into the immaculate communication that PFSlider and I had created.

When I pictured him in the weeks that followed, I saw the image of a plane lifting off over an overcast city. PFSlider was otherworldly, more a concept than a person. His romance lay in the notion of flight, the physics of gravity defiance. So when he offered to send me a plane ticket to spend the weekend with him in Los Angeles I took it as an extension of our blissful remoteness, a three-dimensional E-mail message lasting an entire weekend.

The temperature on the runway at J.F.K. was seven degrees Fahrenheit. Our DC–10 sat for three hours waiting for deicing. Finally, it took off over the frozen city, and the ground below shrank into a drawing of itself. Phone calls were made, laptop computers were plopped onto tray tables. The recirculating air dried out my contact lenses. I watched movies without the sound and told myself that they were probably better that way. Something about the plastic interior of the fuselage and the plastic forks and the din of the air and the engines was soothing and strangely sexy.

Then we descended into LAX. We hit the tarmac, and the seat-belt signs blinked off. I hadn't moved my body in eight hours, and now I was walking through the tunnel to the gate, my clothes wrinkled, my hair matted, my hands shaking. When I saw Pete in the terminal, his face seemed to me just as blank and easy to miss as it had the first time I'd met him. He kissed me chastely. On the way out to the parking lot, he told me that he was being seriously considered for a job in New York. He was flying back there next week. If he got the job, he'd be moving within the month. I looked at him in astonishment. Something silent and invisible seemed to fall on us. Outside, the wind was warm, and the Avis and Hertz buses ambled alongside the curb of Terminal 5. The palm trees shook, and the air seemed as heavy and palpable as Pete's hand, which held mine for a few seconds before dropping it to get his car keys out of his pocket. He stood before me, all flesh and preoccupation, and for this I could not forgive him.

Gone were the computer, the erotic darkness of the telephone, the clean, single dimension of Pete's voice at 1 A.M. It was nighttime, yet the combination of sight and sound was blinding. It scared me. It turned me off. We went to a restaurant and ate outside on the sidewalk. We strained for conversation, and I tried not to care that we had to. We drove to his apartment and stood under the ceiling light not really looking at each other. Something was happening that we needed to snap out of. Any moment now, I thought. Any moment and we'll be all right. These moments were crowded with elements, with carpet fibres and automobiles and the smells of everything that had a smell. It was all wrong. The physical world had invaded our space.

For three days, we crawled along the ground and tried to pull ourselves up. We talked about things that I can no longer remember. We read the Los Angeles *Times* over breakfast. We drove north past Santa Barbara to tour the wine country. I felt like an object that could not be lifted, something that secretly weighed more than the world itself. Everything and everyone around us seemed imbued with a California lightness. I stomped around the countryside, an idiot New Yorker in my clunky shoes and black leather jacket. Not until I studied myself in the bathroom mirror of a highway rest stop did I fully realize the preposterousness of my uniform. I was dressed for war. I was dressed for my regular life.

That night, in a tiny town called Solvang, we ate an expensive dinner. We checked into a Marriott and watched television. Pete talked at me and through me and past me. I tried to listen. I tried to talk. But I bored myself and irritated him. Our conversation was a needle that could not be threaded. Still, we played nice. We tried to care, and pretended to keep trying long after we had given up. In the car on the way home, he told me that I was cynical, and I didn't have the presence of mind to ask him just how many cynics he had met who would travel three thousand miles to see someone they barely knew.

Pete drove me to the airport at 7 A.M. so I could make my eight-o'clock flight home. He kissed me goodbye—another chaste peck that I recognized from countless dinner parties and dud dates. He said that he'd call me in a few days when he got to New York for his job interview, which we had discussed only in passing and with no reference to the fact that New York was where I happened to live. I returned home to frozen January. A few days later, he came to New York, and we didn't see each other. He called me from the plane taking him back to Los Angeles to tell me, through the static, that he had got the job. He was moving to my city.

PFSlider was dead. There would be no meeting him in distant hotel lobbies during the baseball season. There would be no more phone calls or E-mail messages. In a single moment, Pete had completed his journey out of our mating dance and officially stepped into the regular world—the world that gnawed at me daily, the world that fostered those five-night stands, the world where romance could not be sustained, because so many of us simply did not know how to do it. Instead, we were all chitchat and leather jackets, bold proclaimers of all that we did not need. But what struck me most about this affair was the unpredictable nature of our demise. Unlike most cyber-romances, which seem to come fully equipped with the inevitable set of misrepresentations and false expectations, PFSlider and I had played it fairly straight. Neither of us had lied. We'd done the best we could. Our affair had died from natural causes rather than virtual ones.

Within a two week period after I returned from Los Angeles, at least seven people confessed to me the vagaries of their own E-mail affairs. This topic arose, unprompted, in the course of normal conversation. I heard most of these stories in the close confines of smoky bars and crowded restaurants, and we all shook our heads in bewilderment as we told our tales, our eyes focused on some point in the distance. Four of these people had met their correspondents, by travelling from New Haven to Baltimore, from New York to Montana, from Texas to Virginia, and from New York to Johannesburg. These were normal people, writers and lawyers and scientists. They were all smart, attractive, and more than a little sheepish about admitting just how deeply they had been sucked in. Mostly, it was the courtship ritual that had seduced us. E-mail had become an electronic epistle, a yearned-for rule book. It allowed us to do what was necessary to experience love. The Internet was not responsible for our remote, fragmented lives. The problem was life itself.

The story of PFSlider still makes me sad, not so much because we no longer have anything to do with each other but because it forces me to see the limits and the perils of daily life with more clarity than I used to. After I realized that our relationship would never transcend the screen and the phone—that, in fact, our face-to-face knowledge of each other had permanently contaminated the screen and the phone—I hit the pavement again, went through the motions of everyday life, said hello and goodbye to people in the regular way. If Pete and I had met at a party, we probably wouldn't have spoken to each other for more than ten minutes, and that would have made life easier but also less interesting. At the same time, it terrifies me to admit to a firsthand understanding of the way the heart and the ego are snarled and entwined like diseased trees that have folded in on each other. Our need to worship somehow fuses with our need to be worshipped. It upsets me still further to see how inaccessibility can make this entanglement so much more intoxicating. But I'm also thankful that I was forced to unpack the raw truth of my need and stare at it for a while. It was a dare I wouldn't have taken in three dimensions.

The last time I saw Pete, he was in New York, three thousand miles away from what had been his home, and a million miles away from PFSlider. In a final gesture of decency, in what I later realized was the most ordinary kind of closure, he took me out to dinner. As the few remaining traces of affection turned into embarrassed regret, we talked about nothing. He paid the bill. He drove me home in a rental car that felt as arbitrary and impersonal as what we now were to each other.

Pete had known how to get me where I lived until he came to where I lived: then he became as unmysterious as anyone next door. The world had proved to be too cluttered and too fast for us, too polluted to allow the thing we'd attempted through technology ever to grow in the earth. PFSlider and I had joined the angry and exhausted living. Even if we met on the street, we wouldn't recognize each other, our particular version of intimacy now obscured by the branches and bodies and falling debris that make up the physical world.

TOPICS FOR DISCUSSION AND WRITING

1. Given the success of their cyberspace relationship, how do you account for the failure of Daum and PFSlider's romance?

2. Why does Daum find e-mail superior to the telephone? Can you add to her list? Which do you prefer—e-mail or the phone? Why?

3. Write an essay in which you weigh the relative merits of e-mail and the telephone as forms of communication. Feel free to draw from your personal experience in developing this essay.

Marriage

While the Internet adds a completely new way for men and women to meet each other, what isn't new is the need men and women have to find partners. Even in the face of a 50 percent divorce rate, marriage as an institution remains undiminished in its appeal for most people. Indeed, a central political issue for gays and lesbians is their struggle for the right to marry.

But before we debate same-sex marriage, we take a historical look at the role money and property played in choosing a partner in "The Marriage Market" by E. J. Graff. Then Barbara Graham in "The Marriage Trap" looks at the past and present, and concludes that our expectations of marriage have increased dramatically. Next we turn to the poets, one a Victorian, Mary Elizabeth Coleridge, the other a contemporary, Anne Stevenson, for their views of marriage.

In marriage, partners come to know each other very well, often measuring themselves against one another. Italian writer Natalia Ginzburg in "He and I" compares herself to her husband, giving her readers a picture of both husband and wife and the marriage they inhabit. On a less harmonious note, novelist Rosellen Brown's short story, "What Does the Falcon Owe?" depicts a marriage gone wrong in the form of a police report on a missing person.

One of the first decisions a couple who decides to marry must face is the choice of a name. Will the woman adopt her husband's name or will she decide to keep her own? Or will the couple create a new name by combining their surnames? Casey Miller and Kate Smith in "Beginning with Names" and Anne Bernays and Justin Kaplan in "Maiden Names" trace the history of women's surnames and urge women to keep theirs when they marry. When Liz Shankland, a public relations executive, married and kept her own name, the reaction was so negative that she bought a newspaper ad defending her decision in "Mr., Make No Mistake, This Mrs. Is Decidedly Ms." Jenny McPhee in "A Mother's Name," challenges tradition not only by keeping her own name but by passing that name, rather than her husband's, on to her son.

We begin "Same-Sex Marriage" with Carol Ostrom's "Why Get Married?" In this piece, Ostrom attempts to answer her question by listing the advantages and disadvantages of marriage for heterosexuals and homosexuals alike. In "Let Gays Marry" Andrew Sullivan argues that the political struggle for same-sex marriage is a conservative rather than a radical cause. A true conservative, William Bennet, could not disagree more. In "Leave Marriage Alone," he argues that same-sex marriage would greatly undermine the institution of marriage. Frank Browning, a gay man, surprisingly agrees with Bennet that gay marriage is a bad idea, but his reasons are quiet different from Bennet's.

The Marriage Market

E. J. Graff

In this excerpt from her book *What Is Marriage For?* journalist Graff examines the historical role played by money and property in choosing a marriage partner and warns us not to "feel *too* superior to our predecessors' financial finagling." She suggests that in contemporary life, one's "education [works] much like a traditional dowry."

Just about every human language has words for the various portions exchanged or promised in the marriage transaction: bride price, dowry, dower,
antefactum, arras, asura, biblu, bridewealth, *chidenam, coemptio, coibche,* cur-
tesy, *dahej, desponsatio,* dower, *donatio ante* or *propter nuptias, dos ex marito,
exovale, faderfio, hedna, lobola, loola, maritagium, matan, meta, metfio, mor-
gengabe, mohar, mundium, nedunia, nudunnu, pherne, proix, stridhan, sulka, ter-
cia, tinól, tinnscra, titulo dotis, vara-dakshina, yautaka.* Exactly in what directions
that alphabet of money will travel when a couple marries—and whether as
cash, cattle, cowrie shells, farm implements, furniture, houses, labor, land,
linens, orchards, pigs, plate, quilts, or some other gift—varies among cultures
and classes. Usually social systems have either dowry or bridewealth. Dowry
travels from the bride's family to the groom or his father, while bridewealth or
bride price travels from the groom's family to the bride or her father. Almost
always, there are other gifts or feasts traveling in additional directions as well,
whether they be farm service owed to the new brother-in-law, or mementos
given to every wedding guest. Some of that money is compensating one family or the other for the loss of a worker; some is celebratory potlach; some is
roped off as "dower" to guarantee the bride support when she's deserted or
widowed—when, in other words, she's a dowager. As one historian puts it,
"marriage for love has traditionally been assumed to be the dubious privilege
of those without property." Without the marriage exchange, most traditional
economies would cease to turn.

The rules in these exchanges are so varied and intricate that any informed
anthropologist or historian will wince at how this brief section simplifies them
into a few principles. But anyone within any given group knows how their own
system works—and finds that system quite "natural." Everyone knows that exactly what changes hands when two people marry must be explicitly haggled
over by the families involved and discussed all over town. If, for instance, a
young premodern French bourgeois made her debut and was not married
within the year, there'd be some nasty gossip about . . . the size of her dowry.
Of one particular seventeenth-century match, one pair of historians write, "It did
not matter that anyone of good society in Annecy was capable of providing a
fairly exact assessment of the two [orphaned and sole heirs] young people's 'expectations' (each had 70,000 livres in property) or that their marriage had been
taken for granted by everyone for ages: the actual finalization of the marriage
took many long months." "Finalization" is a softer word for *haggling*—exactly
what would go to whom, and when. During most of the history of the West, the
engagement feast was when the two families finished negotiations and finally
signed, witnessed, and notarized the marriage contract (and perhaps let the two
start living together). The marriage ceremony itself was usually when money (or
its stand-in, the ring) actually changed hands, a ceremony that was—at least in
classes where enough money changed hands for this to matter—for many years
overseen by a notary, not a priest.

All this sounds abominably mercenary and soulless now, so much so that we
may feel smugly superior to this prostitution of something so sacred and personal as one's life partner. But for thousands of years, the marriage bargain your

parents made for you was more comparable to today's college education than to today's marriages. Any responsible middle- or upper-class parent (or class aspirant) will at his child's birth start worrying about, and maybe saving for, tuition, often with some investment from the grandparents. It's all very well to say *you can be anything you want to be when you grow up,* but achieving that will be a lot harder if you go to your local community college than if you go to Yale. In fact, for the first twenty or so years that women could take a college education for granted, it was still seen as a dowry; she was there to get not a career but her "MRS" degree.

In the same way, traditionally one's offspring would have a much better chance of marrying, and therefore living, well in every sense if they brought a hefty marriage portion. Perhaps no era's parents can guarantee their children's future—charm, talent, smarts, looks, luck, and effort all matter on the career market as on the marriage market—but parents rightly worry about giving their children the best possible start.

Of course, your parents and siblings cared about your marriage not just for your sake, but also for their own. It's hard to imagine now how fully your marriage could define the future of all your relatives and allies—who they would socialize with, who they could call on in hard times, who would be able to present them at Court, which cows would be left for their own inheritance. "Many marriages have been, as everyone knows, causes of a family's ruin, because concluded with quarrelsome, litigious, proud, or malevolent individuals," wrote one fifteenth-century Tuscan. Not an individual—*individuals*. That marriage was a critical group merger was simply common wisdom. Every marriage was such an important shift in the social and economic landscape that when Florence put a cap on dowries, it was essentially an antitrust law. (Those good free-market capitalists the Medici revoked the cap, stating that "marriages must be free, and everyone should be free to endow his daughters, sisters, and other female relatives as he sees fit and as he likes, because one must be able to arrange his affairs in his way." Move over, Steve Forbes!) And so your marriage choice was not simply your own. Your family and friends were your board of directors, experienced people with a direct stake in guiding you to a successfully concluded merger. Breach of contract suits were seriously enforced because not just emotions and reputations but money and property—very serious things indeed—had been painstakingly engaged, and while negotiations had been going on the merchandise (not just the girl but property on both sides) had been taken off the market during selling season.

In other words, for most of history the phrase "a good marriage" meant something more like the phrase "a good education" or "a good job" than the shimmering rainbow of emotions that phrase implies today. Sure, marriage—like education or work—brought emotional satisfaction, but how could that satisfaction be disentangled from other, more practical rewards? Not without reason did people talk about marriage markets, marriage brokers, and marriage bargains: marriage was society's economic linchpin. For millennia, until there was a marriage contract—*cartas de arras, ketubah, pacta dotalia*—ensuring the new family's future against penury and starvation, nobody married.

If nobody could marry without money, and if large amounts of money changed hands at marriage, society cared about dowries in a way far more urgent than we might think from its quaint, white-lace associations. Not only did every marriage bargain reshuffle social and economic power, but without marriages there would be no legitimate babies and the state (or religion) would collapse for lack of citizens or parishioners. "It is a matter of state concern that women should have secure dowries," one Roman legal scholar wrote. Medieval peasant widows contributed to funds for poor girls' dowries, as philanthropists in our time might adopt an inner-city class and guarantee their college tuitions. In 1425 the city of Florence—concerned that, after several plagues, there weren't enough marriages and births—launched a savings-bond institution (the Monte delle Doti, or Dowry Fund) in which a family could invest for a daughter's future dowry with returns of up to 15.5 percent compounded annually, with both capital and interest paid to the husband after consummation (and immediately taxable). Eighteenth-century Spanish legislation tried to limit dowry to no more than twelve times the annual income of the head of household. And suits over dowry—either because the cooking pot, two carpets, and six shillings were never paid, or because the silk promised to be worth 900 florins was assessed at only 750 florins—fill every era's records. The economic world simply couldn't keep turning if the marriage bargain wasn't kept.

Not only did societies worry explicitly over the size and transfer of marriage payments, but—naturally—so did families. Dante famously noted that fathers in his time were appalled by the birth of a daughter—already anxious, in an era of extreme dowry inflation (much like tuition inflation at prestigious American colleges today), about how they would raise the fortune needed to marry a girl off. No wonder a Florentine father started sweating at each daughter's birth, aware that he might have to liquidate goods from an entire mercantile voyage in order to marry off Maria, and knowing that the higher his daughter's dowry (which everyone in town would know) the higher his credit rating and status could rise. Meanwhile, Maria's younger sisters had to be prepared to end up in convents, which required far smaller dowries, unless there came a dowry-bequest from some widowed aunt or godmother's will—known to us as the fairy godmother who magically got her goddaughter to the ball.

Sons as well as daughters might be unable to marry because of a family's limited treasury. Historian Lawrence Stone has shown that, among the families of sixteenth-century British gentry, male heirs married (and almost all of them did) by an average age of twenty-one or twenty-two, while their younger brothers, who would inherit little or nothing, didn't marry until their early thirties. That's because the younger brothers might take ten years to earn enough to attract a socially acceptable (and acceptably dowried) wife. Depending on the era, from one-fifth to one-fourth of the British gentility's younger sons never married at all; before 1650, three-quarters of the daughters of Milan's aristocracy were sent to convents; and in the eighteenth century—a time of dowry inflation—one-third of the daughters of the Scottish aristocracy stayed single.

Some of these exchanges would strike us as particularly crude. Marriages in the early Germanic clans were distinctly financial transactions: when his family handed over the money, her family handed over the girl. And if your family had money and ambition, you certainly might be married off to a toad. Maybe you'd be allowed to reject one or two suitors suggested by your family or "friends" (those people with a financial or political interest in your family's estate); you might even, if you were male, be able to say no to up to half a dozen brides—but sooner or later you had to say yes. In a famous fifteenth-century letter a British woman, Agnes Paston, writes proudly that, after her daughter obstinately refused to marry on command, the girl was confined with no visitors and "hath since Easter the most part been beaten once in the week or twice, and sometimes twice on a day, and her head broken in two or three places." If you were male, the more traditional method of persuading you to marry was to withhold your inheritance—keeping you a household subject, constantly waiting on your allowance with almost no way to make an extra dollar (or pound or lira). The authority and cohesion of the traditional family, in other words, depended in no small part on the fact that you were dependent—not just for tax purposes but in fact.

The more money involved, the younger (and more tractable) you were likely to be when married. Your Genovese mercantile family might want to go into shipping with a particular prosperous family—and so you'd be engaged by age eight or ten or at most twelve and sent to live with his family (perhaps as his sexual playmate), so that by the time you were officially married you'd have been raised in, and accustomed to, his household's habits. Or your sixteenth century Corsican clan might decide that engaging you to your father's murderer (and sending you to his house as security, even before the official marriage and payment) was the only way to stop the *vendetta*. Or your eighteenth-century British merchant father might want his grandchildren to be nobility and therefore marry you to the son of an impoverished earl who needed to pay off his mortgage or cancel his gambling debts without cutting back on his lavish parties. (To marry up the social scale, you had to fork over a sharply higher dowry: as Gatsby knew, social climbing costs extra.) Money, in other words, could be a proxy for status and power—and the more your family had, the less voice you had in your marriage.

Today, money management is the number one source of tension between spouses. Imagine how much more tension there could be when not just you and your husband but both families were involved. A Roman father-in-law could peremptorily take back his daughter—and deprive his son-in-law's estate or business of her dowry—if said son-in-law did something he disliked. Even among medieval feudal folks, your family's stake in your dowry could actually protect you from mistreatment: if your husband ran off with some young thing your family could insist he return your dowry, which might ruin his business or estate. (Of course, if *you* were the one who took a lover, you were out on your heels, no cash back.) On the other end of the social scale, a girl married off without a dowry or dower was often no better than a sexual slave, with no say in her new household, no support from her own family, and nowhere to go if the new husband died or tired of her. Billie Holliday was saying nothing new when she sang, "God bless the child that's got her own."

We shouldn't let ourselves feel *too* superior to our predecessors' financial finagling. Think of all the lawyers you know married to other lawyers, doctors to doctors, or others who've married in a comparable strata—an architect to a playwright, a truckdriver to a file clerk, Tom Cruise to Nicole Kidman, Harold Evans to Tina Brown. As free as your choice may feel, your education really has worked much like a traditional dowry. What else, after all, do dating services do but (like traditional marriage brokers) match age, class, income, and ethnic background—via such proxies as whether you listen to Nirvana or Serena or Amy Grant, eat mesclun or cream-of-mushroom-based casseroles or *kimchi?* Love *isn't* blind: it's easiest to get along with people who have similar back-grounds and interests. (Which is not to say mixed marriage—whether mixed by religion, class, race, gender, or some other variable—can't work; its just that besides bridging ordinary family and personality differences, couples also have to leap the extra cultural gap.) This might be why Samuel Johnson insisted that "marriages would in general be as happy, and often more so, if they were all made by the Lord Chancellor, upon a due consideration of the characters and circumstances, without the parties having any choice in the matter." Reverend Moon would approve. "The arranged marriage works far less badly than those educated in a romantic culture would suppose . . . partly because it is a fact that sentiment can fairly easily adapt to social command," writes historian Lawrence Stone—at least so long as everyone expects companionship instead of intimacy and passion. Since you could not marry without others' financial contributions (not to mention the haggling and string-pulling to get into the presence of, and to get a favorable contract with, a family worth marrying); since your marriage had to be concluded in a way that wouldn't deprive others of their inheritances; since the entire town was involved in enforcing the exchange—how could anyone possibly consider your marriage an entirely private romance?

TOPICS FOR DISCUSSION AND WRITING

1. What does Graff see as the modern day equivalent of the dowry? What are the parallels? Do you think this analogy is valid? Why?

2. Graff states the commonly held belief that "it's easiest to get along with people who have similar backgrounds and interests." Do you agree with this statement? Explain your answer.

3. Historian Lawrence Stone notes that "The arranged marriage works far less badly than those educated in romantic culture would suppose . . . partly because it is a fact that sentiment can fairly easily adapt to social command." Can you think of any other examples of "sentiment easily [adapting] to social command"?

The Marriage Trap

Barbara Graham

In this essay, Graham places marriage in a historical context and asks if passion and marriage are compatible.

In a snapshot taken at my first "wedding," I look deliriously happy. I'm a picture-book bride, dressed all in white—except for my tennis shoes—with one of my mother's silky half slips draped over my head like a veil. My groom is wearing short pants and has one hand on his hip; the other hand rests in mine. We are 6 years old. The setting is a pier on the bay in Miami Beach, with inky water in the background. We're looking squarely at the camera, but my beloved is angling his body away from me and, in contrast to my blissed-out grin, has a look on his face that suggests he'd rather be swallowing worms. I don't seem to notice. Neither did my mother, who wrote "the Boyfriend!" on the border of the photograph before preserving it in the family album.

We pin our hopes for happiness on romantic love so early. In elementary school, before my faux nuptials in Miami Beach, I desperately wanted to marry Danny Harris, a fellow kindergartner. Later, when I was 12 and *Exodus* had just been released, I believed with all my heart that if Paul Newman ever laid eyes on me I would be his forever. So I did what I had to do: I found out where he lived in New York City and spent the better part of my weekends camped on the sidewalk in front of his apartment building, until the temperature dropped below freezing and I was forced to tether my dreams of true love to another hero.

Freud and his psychoanalytic descendants are no doubt correct in their assessment that the search for ideal love—for that one perfect soulmate—is the futile wish of a not-fully-developed self. But it also seems true that the longing for a profound, all-consuming erotic connection (and the heightened state of awareness that goes with it) is in our very wiring. The yearning for fulfillment through love seems to be to our psychic structure what food and water are to our cells.

Just consider the stories and myths that have shaped our consciousness: Beauty and the Beast, Snow White and her handsome prince, Cinderella and Prince Charming, Fred and Ginger, Barbie and Ken. (Note that, with the exception of the last two couples, all of these lovers are said to have lived happily ever after—even though we never get details of their lives after the weddings, after children and gravity and loss have exacted their price.) Still, it's not just these lucky fairy-tale characters who have captured our collective imagination. The tragic twosomes we cut our teeth on—Romeo and Juliet, Tristan and Iseult, Launcelot and Guinevere, Heathcliff and Cathy, Rhett and Scarlett—are even more compelling role models. Their love is simply too powerful and anarchic, too shattering and exquisite, to be bound by anything so conventional as marriage or a long-term domestic arrangement.

If recent divorce and remarriage statistics are any indication, we're not as astute as the doomed lovers. Instead of drinking poison and putting an end to our love affairs while the heat is still turned up full blast, we expect our marriages and relationships to be long-running fairy tales. When they're not, instead of examining our expectations, we switch partners and reinvent the fantasy, hoping that this time we'll get it right. It's easy to see why: despite all the talk of family values we're constantly bombarded by visions of perfect romance. All you have to do is turn on the radio or TV or open any magazine and check out the perfume and lingerie ads.

"Our culture is deeply regressed," says Florence Falk, a New York City psychotherapist. "Everywhere we turn we're faced with glamorized, idealized versions of love. It's as if the culture wants us to stay trapped in the fantasy and does everything possible to encourage and expand that fantasy." Trying to forge an authentic relationship amid all the romantic hype, she adds, makes an already tough proposition even harder.

What's most unusual about our culture is our feverish devotion to the belief that romantic love and marriage should be synonymous. Starting with George and Martha, continuing through Ozzie and Harriet right up to the present day, we have tirelessly tried to formalize, rationalize, legalize, legitimize, politicize and sanitize rapture. This may have something to do with our puritanical roots, as well as our tendency toward oversimplification. In any event, this attempt to satisfy all of our contradictory desires under the marital umbrella must be put in historical context in order to be properly understood.

"Personal intimacy is actually quite a new idea in human history and was never part of the marriage ideal before the 20th century." says John Welwood, a San Francisco-based psychologist and author, most recently, of *Love and Awakening.* "Most couples throughout history managed to live together their whole lives without ever having a conversation about what was going on within or between them. As long as family and society prescribed the rules of marriage, individuals never had to develop any consciousness in this area."

In short, marriage was designed to serve the economic and social needs of families, communities and religious institutions, and had little or nothing to do with love. Nor was it expected to satisfy lust.

In *Myths to Live By* Joseph Campbell explains how the sages of ancient India viewed the relationship between marriage and passion. They concluded that there are five degrees of love. The first degree has to do with the relationship of the worshiper to the divine. The next three degrees of love, in order of importance, are friendship, the parent-child relationship, and marriage. The fifth and highest form is passionate, illicit love. "In marriage, it is declared, one is still possessed of reason." Campbell writes. "The seizure of passionate love can be, in such a context, only illicit, breaking in upon the order of one's dutiful life in virtue as a devastating storm."

No wonder we're having problems. The pressure we place on our tender unions are unprecedented. Even our biochemistry seems to militate against long-term sexual relationships. Dr. Helen Fisher, an anthropologist at Rutgers University and author of *Anatomy of Love,* believes that human pair bonds originally evolved according to "the ancient blueprint of serial monogamy and clandestine adultery" and are originally meant to last around four years—long enough to raise a single dependent child through toddlerhood. The so-called seven-year itch may be the remains of a four-year reproductive cycle, Fisher suggests.

Increasingly Fisher and other researchers are coming to view what we call love as a series of complex biochemical events governed by hormones and enzymes. "People cling to the idea that romantic love is a mystery, but it's also a chemical experience," Fisher says, explaining that there are three distinct mating emotions and each is supported in the brain by the release of different chemicals. Lust, an emotion triggered by changing levels of testosterone in men and women, is associated with our basic sexual drive. Infatuation depends on changing levels of dopamine, norepinephrine and phenylethylamine, also called the "chemicals of love." They are natural and addictive amphetamine chemicals that stimulate euphoria and make us want to stay up all night sharing our secrets. After infatuation and the dizzying highs associated with it have peaked—usually within a year or two—this brain chemistry changes and a new chemical system made up of oxytocin, vasopressin and maybe endorphins kicks in and supports a steadier, quieter, more nurturing intimacy. In the end, regardless of whether biochemistry accounts for cause or effect in love, it may help to explain why some people—those most responsive to the release of the attachment chemicals—are able to sustain a long-term partnership, while thrillseekers who feel depressed without regular hits of dopamine and phenylethylamine are likely to jump from one liaison to the next to maintain a buzz.

But even if our biochemistry suggests that there should be term limits on love, the heart is a stubborn muscle and, for better or worse, most of us continue to yearn for a relationship that will endure. As a group, Generation Xers—many of whom are children of divorce—are more determined than any other demographic group to have a different kind of marriage than their parents and to avoid divorce, says Howard Markman, author of *Fighting for Your Marriage*. What's more, lesbians and gay men who once opposed marriage and all of its heterosexual, patriarchal implications, now seek to reframe marriage as a more flexible, less repressive arrangement. And, according to the U.S. National Center for Health Statistics, in one out of an estimated seven weddings, either the bride or the groom—or both—are tying the knot for at least the third time—nearly twice as many as in 1970. There are many reasons for this, from the surge in the divorce rate that began in the '70s to our ever-increasing life span. Even so, the fact that we're still trying to get love right—knowing all we know about the ephemeral nature of passion, in a time when the stigmas once associated with being divorced or single have all but disappeared—says something about our need to connect.

And, judging by the army of psychologists, therapists, clergy and other experts who can be found dispensing guidance on the subject, the effort to save—or reinvent, depending on who's doing the talking—love and marriage has become a multimillion-dollar industry. The advice spans the spectrum. There's everything from *The Rules* by Ellen Fein and Sherrie Schneider, a popular new book that gives '90s women '50s-style tips on how to catch and keep their man, to Harville Hendrix's *Getting the Love You Want* and other guides to "conscious love." But regardless of perspective, this much is clear: never before have our most intimate thoughts and actions been so thoroughly dissected, analyzed, scrutinized and medicalized. Now, people who fall madly in love over and over are called romance addicts. Their disease, modeled on alcoholism and other chemical dependencies, is considered "progressive and fatal."

Not everyone believes the attempt to deconstruct love is a good thing. The late philosopher Christopher Lasch wrote in his final (and newly released) book, *Women and the Common Life:* "The exposure of sexual life to scientific scrutiny contributed to the rationalization, not the liberation of emotional life." His daughter, Elizabeth Lasch-Quinn, a historian at Syracuse University and the editor of the book, agrees. She contends that the progressive demystification of passionate life since Freud has promoted an asexual, dispassionate and utilitarian form of love. Moreover, like her father, she believes that the national malaise about romance can be attributed to insidious therapeutic modes of social control—a series of mechanisms that have reduced the citizen to a consumer of expertise. "We have fragmented life in such a way as to take passion out of our experience," she says.

Admittedly, it's a stretch to picture a lovesick 12th century French troubadour in a 12-step program for romance addicts. Still, we can't overlook the fact that our society's past efforts to fuse together those historically odd bed fellows—passionate love and marriage—have failed miserably. And though it's impossible to know whether all the attention currently being showered on relationships is the last gasp of a dying social order—marriage—or the first glimmer of a new paradigm for relating to one another, it's obvious that something radically different is needed.

For one thing, many of us raised in the stultifying, claustrophobic nuclear families that were glorified in '50s and '60s sitcoms but were, in fact, far less than glorious, have tried it all; Bob and Carol; Bob and Carol and Ted and Alice; Bob and Ted, Carol and Alice; and just plain Bob. Or Alice. And still we're searching.

In his latest work, *A Little Book on Love*, philosopher and San Francisco State University professor Jacob Needleman writes that "the social and sexual revolutions of the 20th century have shown us that relaxing marriage laws and customs, in the end, simply replaced one sort of suffering with another. If we love who and when we want and then break the bond whenever the impulse to do so is strong, we see that it brings no happiness to our lives. Nor, of course, did it bring happiness tensely to maintain the old rules, the old customs. So the meaning of living together in love cannot lie in either direction."

But while the experimentation of the '60s and '70s unquestionably wreaked havoc, it was a vital and creative havoc, without which we might have remained trapped in old, unsatisfying patterns of relating. "Two important developments in the '60s laid the ground for a more adult stage of couple consciousness, which we seem to be entering now," says Welwood. "The women's movement cast off old stereotypes and made relationships more egalitarian. And the dissemination of psychological ideas into the culture—mostly through pop psychology books—started to give people a new language and a new set of concepts, unavailable to previous generations, to talk about what actually goes on in a relationship." Moreover, adds Needleman, the '60s were also the beginning of an awakening, the time when people began to realize there is such a thing as transcendence.

The key to the emerging vision of love seems to be intention. Welwood, Needleman and others speak of conscious relationship, conscious marriage. Today these theorists—in their own ways—are redefining relationship as a vehicle for awakening and self-discovery. In their view genuine, enduring love is possible only when couples let go of adolescent smoke-and-mirrors fantasies of each other and the relationship and dedicate themselves to the search for truth. As Stephen Levine, author, with his wife, Ondrea, of *Embracing the Beloved,* puts it, "when your priority becomes consciousness even more than relationship, then conscious relationship is possible."

According to Harville Hendrix, founder and president of the Orlando-based Institute for Image Relationship Therapy, a primary function of marriage is for couples to help one another identify and heal unconscious childhood wounds and unmet needs. "Romantic love is a selection process based on your childhood," he explains, adding that, in spite of any conscious intent to find a partner who doesn't resemble your parents, most people are attracted to mates who have both their parents' positive and negative traits. And, typically, he says, "the negative traits carry a higher charge." Moreover, if we stay locked in unawareness, once the initial rush of romance wanes we become either mired in frustration or move on and reenact the drama with someone else. But if we stretch ourselves to help each other grow, says Hendrix, childhood vulnerabilities eventually diminish, freeing up enormous reserves of creative energy.

The new vision of love, however, is not confined to achieving psychological wholeness. Call it what you will—awakening, transcendence, connection to the divine or, in the language of the Sufis, union with the Beloved—these are also central to the vision. In this context, intimate relationship becomes a spiritual practice, a sacred, mystical union of two people connected to a larger reality. "What is sacred is the movement toward deeper truth, deeper connection, deeper understanding," says Welwood. "This involves a meeting of the human and the divine."

Though the idea of relationship as a vehicle for embodying the sacred is hardly new—especially to the tantric practices of India and Tibet, as well as in other Eastern traditions—never before has intimacy been so closely aligned with spirituality. "Now we have the opportunity to bring the sacred fully into our relationships, in a much more personal way," says Welwood—and not just for our own individual pleasure. "This is where we can start to regenerate our world. It has to begin between one person and another. How can we hope to create a better world when we can't even relate to our partner when we come home at night?"

On the one hand it sounds extraordinary—marvelous—this blending of body, mind and spirit into relationship. On the other hand it sounds like madness; we've had enough trouble bringing together body and mind, and now we want to toss in spirituality too? As Needleman points out, "the whole of human nature is an obstacle to conscious love—our unawareness and our lack of clear, deep understanding that the other person is in the same boat we're in."

Then there's the matter of the body. "My body is playing catchup with my mind and spirit," admits Mark Matousek, the author of *Sex Death Enlightenment,* who has always espoused the ideal of being sexually faithful but never believed it was possible until he entered a new relationship three years ago, with his partner, Louis. "Monogamy pushes every major button I have," Matousek says. "It brings out the best and, frequently, the worst in me. But I had to learn how to live as a sexual person on a spiritual path. Celibacy didn't work for me and neither did promiscuity. Monogamy is part of the whole search for soul."

Despite all the obstacles, maybe the sacred is the glue, the binding and holy energy that got lost—first while we tried desperately to merge marriage and passion in airtight nuclear families and, later as we turned our attention to rediscovering pleasure, as well as redefining our roles, sexual and gender identities, and traditional family structures.

But what about longing? Desire? The very human craving for delirious romance? Even when we know better, even when we've learned the hard way that no other person can possibly make us whole and we've entered into a conscious relationship, where does the longing go?

"Longing is a wonderful, very vital energy," says Florence Falk. "It's not the longing that's the problem, it's what you do with it." As we begin to reclaim our selves and find our core strength, she says, not only is it possible to develop a real, loving relationship, but the longing can be redirected to something greater than ourselves, something transcendent.

And, says Stephen Levine, "if another person is the most important thing in your life then you're in trouble and they're in trouble because they become responsible for your suffering. But if consciousness is the most important thing in our lives and relationship is a means toward that end . . . ah! Then we are approaching paradise. We are approaching the possibility of actually becoming a human being before we die." And maybe that is the future of love.

TOPICS FOR DISCUSSION AND WRITING

1. Graham refers to Freud's view of "the search for ideal love." Describe that view and discuss your reaction to it.

2. Psychotherapist Florence Falk states that "Everywhere we turn we're faced with glamorized, idealized versions of love. It's as if the culture wants us to stay trapped in the fantasy and does everything possible to encourage and expand that fantasy." Scan magazines, billboards, television and movies for examples of these "glamorized, idealized versions of love," and list as many examples as you can. Then speculate on the reasons for the numerous instances of these images in popular culture and on their impact.

3. How have expectations of marriage changed over time? What impact did the cultural revolution of the sixties have on marriage?

4. Write an essay in which you argue for or against the institution of marriage, or suggest a completely new arrangement for relationships and the raising of children. (See Shaping a Written Argument—Rhetorical Strategies in Chapter 4.)

Marriage

Mary Elizabeth Coleridge

The Marriage

Anne Stevenson

Two poets writing in different centuries, write about marriage, each poem reflective of the lives of their authors. Coleridge (1861–1907), a Victorian and the great-great-niece of the Romantic poet Samuel Taylor Coleridge, lived with her parents all of her life, never marrying. Stevenson, a contemporary, was twice married and divorced.

No more alone sleeping, no more alone waking,
  Thy dreams divided, thy prayers in twain;
Thy merry sisters to-night forsaking,
  Never shall we see thee, maiden, again.

Never shall we see thee, thine eyes glancing,
  Flashing with laughter and wild in glee,
Under the mistletoe kissing and dancing,
  Wantonly free.

There shall come a matron walking sedately,
  Low-voiced, gentle, wise in reply.
Tell me O tell me, can I love her greatly?
  All for her sake must the maiden die!

—Mary Elizabeth Coleridge

They will fit, she thinks,
but only if her backbone
cuts exactly into his rib cage,
and only if his knees
dock exactly under her knees
and all four
agree on a common angle.

All would be well
if only they could face each other.

Even as it is
there are compensations
for having to meet nose to neck

chest to scapula
groin to rump
when they sleep.

They look, at least,
as if they were going
in the same direction.

—Anne Stevenson

TOPICS FOR DISCUSSION AND WRITING

1. Mary Elizabeth Coleridge, a Victorian, never married, living with her parents all of her life. How is this experience reflected in the point of view of the poem?

2. Anne Stevenson, a contemporary poet, was twice married and divorced. How is this experience reflected in her poem?

3. Both poems express a view of marriage. Write a paragraph about each in which you summarize this view. Support your inferences with specifics from the poems. (See Writing About Fiction in Chapter 2.)

He and I

Natalia Ginzburg

Natalia Ginzburg (1916–1991) is valued as a major Italian writer, winning the Strega Prize for *Family Sayings,* an autobiographical novel. In this essay she compares herself to her husband, illustrating that two people may have different tastes, habits and abilities, and yet successfully share their lives.

He always feels hot, I always feel cold. In the summer when it really is hot he does nothing but complain about how hot he feels. He is irritated if he sees me put a jumper on in the evening.

He speaks several languages well; I do not speak any well. He manages—in his own way—to speak even the languages that he doesn't know.

He has an excellent sense of direction, I have none at all. After one day in a foreign city he can move about in it as thoughtlessly as a butterfly. I get lost in my own city; I have to ask directions so that I can get back home again. He hates asking directions; when we go by car to a town we don't know he doesn't want to ask directions and tells me to look at the map. I don't know how to read maps and I get confused by all the little red circles and he loses his temper.

He loves the theatre, painting, music, especially music. I do not understand music at all, painting doesn't mean much to me and I get bored at the theatre. I love and understand one thing in the world and that is poetry.

He loves museums, and I will go if I am forced to but with an unpleasant sense of effort and duty. He loves libraries and I hate them.

He loves travelling, unfamiliar foreign cities, restaurants. I would like to stay at home all the time and never move.

All the same I follow him on his many journeys. I follow him to museums, to churches, to the opera. I even follow him to concerts, where I fall asleep.

Because he knows the conductors and the singers, after the performance is over he likes to go and congratulate them. I follow him down long corridors lined with the singers' dressing-rooms and listen to him talking to people dressed as cardinals and kings.

He is not shy; I am shy. Occasionally however I have seen him be shy. With the police when they come over to the car armed with a notebook and pencil. Then he is shy, thinking he is in the wrong.

And even when he doesn't think he is in the wrong. I think he has a respect for established authority. I am afraid of established authority, but he isn't. He respects it. There is a difference. When I see a policeman coming to fine me I immediately think he is going to haul me off to prison. He doesn't think about prison; but, out of respect, he becomes shy and polite.

During the Montesi trial, because of his respect for established authority, we had very violent arguments.

He likes tagliatelle, lamb, cherries, red wine. I like minestrone, bread soup, omelettes, green vegetables.

He often says I don't understand anything about food, that I am like a great strong fat friar—one of those friars who devour soup made from greens in the darkness of their monasteries; but he, oh he is refined and has a sensitive palate. In restaurants he makes long inquiries about the wines; he has them bring two or three bottles then looks at them and considers the matter, and slowly strokes his beard.

There are certain restaurants in England where the waiter goes through a little ritual: he pours some wine into a glass so that the customer can test whether he likes it or not. He used to hate this ritual and always prevented the waiter from carrying it out by taking the bottle from him. I used to argue with him about this and say that you should let people carry out their prescribed tasks.

And in the same way he never lets the usherette at the cinema direct him to his seat. He immediately gives her a tip but dashes off to a completely different place from the one she shows him with her torch.

At the cinema he likes to sit very close to the screen. If we go with friends and they look for seats a long way from the screen, as most people do, he sits by himself in the front row. I can see well whether I am close to the screen or far away from it, but when we are with friends I stay with them out of politeness; all the same it upsets me because I could be next to him two inches from the screen, and when I don't sit next to him he gets annoyed with me.

We both love the cinema, and we are ready to see almost any kind of film at almost any time of day. But he knows the history of the cinema in great detail; he remembers old directors and actors who have disappeared and been forgotten long ago, and he is ready to travel miles into the most distant suburbs in search of some ancient silent film in which an actor appears—perhaps just for a few seconds—whom he affectionately associates with memories of his early childhood. I remember one Sunday afternoon in London; somewhere in the distant suburbs on the edge of the countryside they were showing a film from the 1930s, about the French Revolution, which he had seen as a child, and in which a famous actress of that time appeared for a moment or two. We set off by car in search of the street, which was a very long way off; it was raining, there was a fog, and we drove for hour after hour through identical suburbs, between rows of little grey houses, gutters and railings; I had the map on my knees and I couldn't read it and he lost his temper; at last, we found the cinema and sat in the completely deserted auditorium. But after a quarter of an hour, immediately after the brief appearance of the actress who was so important to him, he already wanted to go; I on the other hand, after seeing so many streets, wanted to see how the film finished. I don't remember whether we did what he wanted or what I wanted; probably what he wanted, so that we left after a quarter of an hour, also because it was late—though we had set off early in the afternoon it was already time for dinner. But when I begged him to tell me how the film ended I didn't get a very satisfactory answer; because, he said, the story wasn't at all important, the only thing that mattered was those few moments, that actress's curls, gestures, profile.

I never remember actors' names, and as I am not good at remembering faces it is often difficult for me to recognize even the most famous of them. This infuriates him; his scorn increases as I ask him whether it was this one or that one; "You don't mean to tell me," he says, "You don't mean to tell me that you didn't recognize William Holden!"

And in fact I didn't recognize William Holden. All the same, I love the cinema too; but although I have been seeing films for years I haven't been able to provide myself with any sort of cinematic education. But he has made an education of it for himself and he does this with whatever attracts his curiosity; I don't know how to make myself an education out of anything, even those things that I love best in life; they stay with me as scattered images, nourishing my life with memories and emotions but without filling the void, the desert of my education.

He tells me I have no curiosity, but this is not true. I am curious about a few, a very few, things. And when I have got to know them I retain scattered impressions of them, or the cadence of phrase, or a word. But my world, in which these completely unrelated (unless in some secret fashion unbeknown to me) impressions and cadences rise to the surface, is a sad, barren place. His world, on the other hand, is green and populous and richly cultivated; it is a fertile, well-watered countryside in which woods, meadows, orchards and villages flourish.

Everything I do is done laboriously, with great difficulty and uncertainty. I am very lazy, and if I want to finish anything it is absolutely essential that I spend hours stretched out on the sofa. He is never idle, and is always doing something;

when he goes to lie down in the afternoons he takes proofs to correct or a book full of notes; he wants us to go to the cinema, then to a reception, then to the theatre—all on the same day. In one day he succeeds in doing, and in making me do, a mass of different things, and in meeting extremely diverse kinds of people. If I am alone and try to act as he does I get nothing at all done, because I get stuck all afternoon somewhere I had meant to stay for half an hour, or because I get lost and cannot find the right street, or because the most boring person and the one I least wanted to meet drags me off to the place I least wanted to go to.

If I tell him how my afternoon has turned out he says it is a completely wasted afternoon and is amused and makes fun of me and loses his temper; and he says that without him I am good for nothing.

I don't know how to manage my time; he does.

He likes receptions. He dresses casually, when everyone is dressed formally; the idea of changing his clothes in order to go to a reception never enters his head. He even goes in his old raincoat and crumpled hat; a woollen hat which he bought in London and which he wears pulled down over his eyes. He only stays for half an hour; he enjoys chatting with a glass in his hand for half an hour; he eats lots of *hors d'oeuvres,* and I eat almost none because when I see him eating so many I feel that I at least must be well-mannered and show some self-control and not eat too much; after half an hour, just as I am beginning to feel at ease and to enjoy myself, he gets impatient and drags me away.

I don't know how to dance and he does.

I don't know how to type and he does.

I don't know how to drive. If I suggest that I should get a licence too he disagrees. He says I would never manage it. I think he likes me to be dependent on him for some things.

I don't know how to sing and he does. He is a baritone. Perhaps he would have been a famous singer if he had studied singing.

Perhaps he would have been a conductor if he had studied music. When he listens to records he conducts the orchestra with a pencil. And he types and answers the telephone at the same time. He is a man who is able to do many things at once.

He is a professor and I think he is a good one.

He could have been many things. But he has no regrets about those professions he did not take up. I could only ever have followed one profession—the one I chose and which I have followed almost since childhood. And I don't have any regrets either about the professions I did not take up, but then I couldn't have succeeded at any of them.

I write stories, and for many years I have worked for a publishing house.

I don't work badly, or particularly well. All the same I am well aware of the fact that I would have been unable to work anywhere else. I get on well with my colleagues and my boss. I think that if I did not have the support of their friendship I would soon have become worn out and unable to work any longer.

For a long time I thought that one day I would be able to write screenplays for the cinema. But I never had the opportunity, or I did not know how to find it. Now I have lost all hope of writing screenplays. He wrote screenplays for a while, when he was younger. And he has worked in a publishing house. He has written stories. He has done all the things that I have done and many others too.

He is a good mimic, and does an old countess especially well. Perhaps he could also have been an actor.

Once, in London, he sang in a theatre. He was Job. He had to hire evening clothes; and there he was, in his evening clothes, in front of a kind of lectern; and he sang. He sang the words of Job; the piece called for something between speaking and singing. And I, in my box, was dying of fright. I was afraid he would get flustered, or that the trousers of his evening clothes would fall down.

He was surrounded by men in evening clothes and women in long dresses, who were the angels and devils and other characters in Job.

It was a great success, and they said that he was very good.

If I loved music I would love it passionately. But I don't understand it, and when he persuades me to go to concerts with him my mind wanders off and I think of my own affairs. Or I fall sound asleep.

I like to sing. I don't know how to sing and I sing completely out of tune; but I sing all the same—occasionally, very quietly, when I am alone. I know that I sing out of tune because others have told me so; my voice must be like the yowling of a cat. But I am not—in myself—aware of this, and singing gives me real pleasure. If he hears me he mimics me; he says that my singing is something quite separate from music, something invented by me.

When I was a child I used to yowl tunes I had made up. It was a long wailing kind of melody that brought tears to my eyes.

It doesn't matter to me that I don't understand painting or the figurative arts, but it hurts me that I don't love music, and I feel that my mind suffers from the absence of this love. But there is nothing I can do about it, I will never understand or love music. If I occasionally hear a piece of music that I like I don't know how to remember it; and how can I love something that I can't remember?

It is the words of a song that I remember. I can repeat words that I love over and over again. I repeat the tune that accompanies them too, in my own yowling fashion, and I experience a kind of happiness as I yowl.

When I am writing it seems to me that I follow a musical cadence or rhythm. Perhaps music was very close to my world, and my world could not, for whatever reason, make contact with it.

In our house there is music all day long. He keeps the radio on all day. Or plays records. Every now and again I protest a little and ask for a little silence in which to work; but he says that such beautiful music is certainly conducive to any kind of work.

He has bought an incredible number of records. He says that he owns one of the finest collections in the world.

In the morning when he is still in his dressing gown and dripping water from his bath, he turns the radio on, sits down at the typewriter and begins his strenuous, noisy, stormy day. He is superabundant in everything; he fills the bath to overflowing, and the same with the teapot and his cup of tea. He has an enormous number of shirts and ties. On the other hand he rarely buys shoes.

His mother says that as a child he was a model of order and precision; apparently once, on a rainy day, he was wearing white boots and white clothes and had to cross some muddy streams in the country—at the end of his walk he was immaculate and his clothes and boots had not one spot of mud on them. There is no trace in him of that former immaculate little boy. His clothes are always covered in stains. He has become extremely untidy.

But he scrupulously keeps all the gas bills. In drawers I find old gas bills, which he refuses to throw away, from houses we left long ago.

I also find old, shrivelled Tuscan cigars, and cigarette holders made from cherry wood.

I smoke a brand of king-size, filterless cigarettes called *Stop,* and he smokes his Tuscan cigars.

I am very untidy. But as I have got older I have come to miss tidiness and I sometimes furiously tidy up all the cupboards. I think this is because I remember my mother's tidiness. I rearrange the linen and blanket cupboards and in the summer I reline every drawer with strips of white cloth. I rarely rearrange my papers because my mother didn't write and had no papers. My tidiness and untidiness are full of complicated feelings of regret and sadness. His untidiness is triumphant. He has decided that it is proper and legitimate for a studious person like himself to have an untidy desk.

He does not help me get over my indecisiveness, or the way I hesitate before doing anything, or my sense of guilt. He tends to make fun of every tiny thing I do. If I go shopping in the market he follows me and spies on me. He makes fun of the way I shop, of the way I weigh the oranges in my hand unerringly choosing, he says, the worst in the whole market; he ridicules me for spending an hour over the shopping, buying onions at one stall, celery at another and fruit at another. Sometimes he does the shopping to show me how quickly he can do it; he unhesitatingly buys everything from one stall and then manages to get the basket delivered to the house. He doesn't buy celery because he cannot abide it.

And so—more than ever—I feel I do everything inadequately or mistakenly. But if I once find out that he has made a mistake I tell him so over and over again until he is exasperated. I can be very annoying at times.

His rages are unpredictable, and bubble over like the head on beer. My rages are unpredictable too, but his quickly disappear whereas mine leave a noisy nagging trail behind them which must be very annoying—like the complaining yowl of a cat.

Sometimes in the midst of his rage I start to cry, and instead of quietening him down and making him feel sorry for me this infuriates him all the more. He says my tears are just play-acting, and perhaps be is right. Because in the middle of my tears and his rage I am completely calm.

I never cry when I am really unhappy.

There was a time when I used to hurl plates and crockery on the floor during my rages. But not any more. Perhaps because I am older and my rages are less violent, and also because I dare not lay a finger on our plates now; we bought them one day in London, in the Portobello Road, and I am very fond of them.

The price of those plates, and of many other things we have bought, immediately underwent a substantial reduction in his memory. He likes to think he did not spend very much and that he got a bargain. I know the price of that dinner service—it was £16, but he says £12. And it is the same with the picture of King Lear that is in our dining room, and which he also bought in the Portobello Road (and then cleaned with onions and potatoes); now he says he paid a certain sum for it, but I remember that it was much more than that.

Some years ago he bought twelve bedside mats in a department store. He bought them because they were cheap, and he thought he ought to buy them; and he bought them as an argument against me because he considered me to be incapable of buying things for the house. They were made of mud-coloured matting and they quickly became very unattractive; they took on a corpse-like rigidity and were hung from a wire line on the kitchen balcony, and I hated them. I used to remind him of them, as an example of bad shopping; but he would say that they had cost very little indeed, almost nothing. It was a long time before I could bring myself to throw them out—because there were so many of them, and because just as I was about to get rid of them it occurred to me that I could use them for rags. He and I both find throwing things away difficult; it must be a kind of Jewish caution in me, and the result of my extreme indecisiveness; in him it must be a defence against his impulsiveness and open-handedness.

He buys enormous quantities of bicarbonate of soda and aspirins.

Now and again he is ill with some mysterious ailment of his own; he can't explain what he feels and stays in bed for a day completely wrapped up in the sheets; nothing is visible except his beard and the tip of his red nose. Then he takes bicarbonate of soda and aspirins in doses suitable for a horse, and says that I cannot understand because I am always well, I am like those great fat strong friars who go out in the wind and in all weathers and come to no harm; he on the other hand is sensitive and delicate and suffers from mysterious ailments. Then in the evening he is better and goes into the kitchen and cooks himself tagliatelle.

When he was a young man he was slim, handsome and finely built; he did not have a beard but long, soft moustaches instead, and he looked like the actor Robert Donat. He was like that about twenty years ago when I first knew him, and I remember that he used to wear an elegant kind of Scottish flannel shirt. I remember that one evening he walked me back to the *pensione* where I was living; we walked together along the *Via Nazionale.* I already felt that I was very old and had been through a great deal and had made many mistakes, and he seemed a boy to me, light years away from me. I don't remember what we talked about on that evening walking along the *Via Nazionale;* nothing important, I suppose, and the idea that we would become husband and wife was light years away from me. Then we lost sight of each other, and when we met again he no longer looked like Robert Donat, but more like Balzac. When we met again he still wore his Scottish shirts but on him now they looked like garments for a polar expedition; now he had his beard and on his head he wore his ridiculous crumpled woollen hat; everything about him put you in mind of an imminent departure for the North Pole. Because, although he always feels hot, he has the habit of dressing as if he were surrounded by snow, ice and polar bears; or he dresses like a Brazilian coffee-planter, but he always dresses differently from everyone else.

If I remind him of that walk along the *Via Nazionale* he says he remembers it, but I know he is lying and that he remembers nothing; and I sometimes ask myself if it was us, these two people, almost twenty years ago on the *Via Nazionale,* two people who conversed so politely, so urbanely, as the sun was setting; who chatted a little about everything perhaps and about nothing; two friends talking, two young intellectuals out for a walk; so young, so educated, so uninvolved, so ready to judge one another with kind impartiality; so ready to say goodbye to one another for ever, as the sun set, at the corner of the street.

TOPIC FOR DISCUSSION AND WRITING

> Select someone you are close to—an intimate friend, a spouse, a parent, a sibling—and write your version of "He and I" or, as fits your choice, "She and I." Try using some parallel structures in the style of Ginzburg to develop your portrait and emphasize the ways in which you are similar to and different from the person you have chosen. Like Ginzburg, let your reader *see* your characters by describing them and their habits in vivid detail. (See The Importance of Specificity in Chapter 5, and Parallel Structure in Chapter 8.)

What Does the Falcon Owe?

Rosellen Brown

Rosellen Brown is a poet, a short story writer and a novelist. Her 1994 novel *Before and After* was made into a movie with Meryl Streep. Her "What Does the Falcon Owe?" is an unusual short story about an unhappy couple presented in the form of a police report on a missing person. The missing person is a wife identified by the initials MP; H refers to her husband.

F., 27, 5'5", 122 lb., hair medium brown worn long (sometimes in gold clip), eyes brown, glasses for reading (tortoise frames). Morning, 12/13 had approx. $40 (known), car keys (car left parked outside MP's apt. house). Took few clothes, overnight bag (blue plaid), portable typewriter, small b/w etching ("Clown" by Daumier), 2 small Eskimo masks, removed from bedroom wall.)

REMARKS:

MP AND H(usband) had been writing book (study of Kwamiack Indians of Saskatchewan); typed chapters were stacked neatly in basket on desk where husband says they usually were kept. On top of file was found Enclosure (C), with Enc. (A) in typewriter. Enc. (B) was taped on bathroom mirror. Enc. (D), a stapled set of yellowed newspaper clippings, was found by H on MP's pillow, which was neatly covered by bedspread. H claims apt. had been cleaned while he was out that morning. One coffee cup drying in drainer. Approx. 24 hrs. after MP disappeared, H received telegram (nightletter, sent from phone booth, this city), Enc. (E), which H identifies as Navajo prayer which he taught MP before marriage. No further communic. from MP; none of couple's friends rec'd communic. H received two bills for dept. store charge account identified as (1) Ventrillo Wonder voice-thrower (2) Furhead, a bar of soap shaped like a face, which grows a beard overnight when placed in water (3) a set of trick mirrors (4) plaster-of-paris mold outfit called "Living Death-Mask Set." Purchases totaled $14.53, which H paid.

End File. See attached Encls. A-E.

ENCL. A:

Words = Artifacts
Sentences = Ritual

First Prayer of Unbinding
†Hohman's Powwows on Arts and Remedies (Eagleton, Penna., 1837) claims
    following:

a good remedy for hysterics
a remedy to be used when anyone is falling away
a remedy for calumniation or slander
to attach a dog to a person
a sure way of catching fish
to mend broken glass
to prevent the Hessian fly from injuring the wheat
to prevent cherries from maturing before Martinmas
to prevent the worst kind of paper from blotting
to remove a wen during the crescent moon
to make a wick which is never consumed
to compel a thief to return stolen goods
against every evil influence
to charm enemies, robbers and murderers
a charm against shooting, cutting or thrusting
to prevent being cheated, charmed or bewitched
a charm to gain advantage of a man of superior strength

ENCL. B:

Dream of a hunter wearing his hooded falcon
Blind on his wrist. Then watch the bird escape.
Forgetting hunger, remembering he has wings,
He feels his way on the under edge of the sky,
Threads through the clouds,

Comes down in the safety of distance,
And wonders: The falconer is gentle,
Has fed him well, has taught him all he knows,
And keeps his sight.
Can you say what the falcon owes?

ENCL. C:

Once in a land that perhaps exists, there lived a king and his little daughter, the Princess. They lived in a regulation castle and were all the things they had to be; in fact (in spite of their perfection) they were even believed to be happy.

One day in spring the King put on the lightest cloak and crown in his closet and took the hand of his lovely little girl. "Let us go for a walk around the palace grounds," he said to her, and she threw down her golden doll and came to him with a smile of true delight. (She loved her great father perfectly and it was clear to the whole world that he reflected her love just as a still deep pool reflects a star, drinking in its light without a movement, without the hint of a ripple. He never scolded her or made her cry, he was a true king and a forgiving father.)

Hand in hand they strolled the walks in the garden, past the purple berry-bushes and the roses strung up with silver twine, past the shore of the little pond with its pearl cup of a boat tied up on the grassy beach. When they had been once around the grounds and their feet said nothing, not a word of reproach, the king suggested they walk out past the village into the country-side. The little princess had never ventured beyond the gates of the palace and she was thrilled. And she could walk longer with her splendid father, her small hand in his large one.

She was so excited that she chattered, chipped at his ear like a woodpecker. She laughed at her father's dignified silence and twitted him for talking so little. "Well," she would say, "perhaps kings are not supposed to talk as much as princesses. I'm sure that's it, and my king"—she tugged at his sleeve to reassure him—"my king always does what a king ought to." Though she was a mischievous child, often a trying one (since he never restrained her), she had no standard by which to feel herself judged. He said nothing now but walked steadily beside her. Every now and then, try as she did with her short legs beneath their heavy skirts, she could not keep in step with the king. She would run a few steps, raising the dry dust under her slippers, and match her strides to his, then she would fall behind again. Finally, feeling the pull of her hand, her father slowed his pace to match hers, and they kept on, slowly.

After some time the king stopped. He dropped his daughter's hand and said, "Dear child, I am very weary." He sat himself on a large flat stone at the roadside. "Little queen, if you want to, you can walk on a bit. Why don't you go through those trees—" He pointed to a stand of pines that loomed abruptly like an island in the flat sea of meadow—"and on the other side you will find a lovely brook full of fish with rainbows on their backs."

The princess could hardly restrain her delight. She gave her father a kiss and ran off down the road and across the spongy earth that rose and sagged beneath the trees, mountains and valleys of pine needles. She could see light pricking through the solid darkness in sudden ragged flashes like sunlight glinting off a sword, and the child ran toward it, rolling the hoop of her eagerness before her.

A low growth of bushes stood barricading her way when she approached the light, and she had to skip through it, holding her breath as each thorn scraped through her skirts and through her skin. With an anxious little sigh, she brought her leg high over the last hurdle and down with a decisive thrust, and before she could see it, she had tumbled flat on her chest into a ditch. The ground near the stream was rocky and damp and she had dirtied and torn her velvet dress in a dozen places. Winded, she shook her skirts out with a fury that was all the more painful in her throat because she was not sure where it came from or where it wanted to go.

There at least was the stream, and it would be cool on her raw ankles. It had been dusk; now the light seemed to dim and go out, and the rainbow fish had gone home, or had turned their promised lights out. If there were rainbow fish. The water darted at her bruises with cold fangs, and she waded back to the bank stung with pain in many places. Something caught at her foot, bit through with a crab's mean grip. In terror she kicked and kicked till it flew off and, wide-eyed, as she saw it arc against the black water and tumble in, she could just make out the rainbow lights winking at her. She pulled her skirts up to her knees and ran, expecting to feel a hand or a claw at her shoulder, in her hair, at her feet, as she felt her way dumbly through the fence of thorns. The forest was blacker and quieter than sleep, and cold—she felt the sudden cold as if someone had slammed a door behind her. Only the unfamiliar sounds of the night hurried her home.

When she had flown across the lawn of the castle and rattled the door open, she found her father sitting calmly with a book, wearing his heavy crown again. She could not speak.

"Child, you are home," he said to her simply, as if he were telling her something of value. "Did you see the rainbow fish?"

"Father!" The princess stood still as a thorn-tree.

"I couldn't wait for you," he said.

"Father!"

"My precious one, understand. This has always been so. You talked so much. You walked so slowly. You took so long. You could hardly expect—"

She swayed in his words. "But why did you say nothing? You said nothing at all."

"What should I have told you, little one?" He was well returned to his patience.

"I could have done something! I would have been quiet! I would have run! I would never have left you. Or I would never have come."

Her father smiled faintly, quizzically. "Ah," he said and spread his large hands wide.

ENCL. D:

VIOLINIST SCORES WITH BACH, TARTINI, BEETHOVEN, BRAHMS

Jan. 23, 1924

The splendid warmth and style of Alexei Tartakoff were again in evidence last night in a recital which brought him back from his celebrated European tour to an audience that jammed Carnegie Hall. Mr. Tartakoff chose Bach's second partita for unaccompanied violin to open his program and in the Bach and the notoriously wicked Devil's Trill sonata which followed, he showed himself again the unrivaled technical master of the era. His fingers seem to have the strength, speed and certainty of a mechanical instrument which is powered not by a motor but by a great and magnanimous heart. His tone is ripe and brilliant and he has a wealth of nuances in tone and tempo which he uses to ravishing effect. The limpidity he achieved in the slow movement of Beethoven's very familiar Spring Sonata was so lovely and cumulatively so moving that the audience applauded at the end of the movement. This crowd knew where protocol can leave off and passion begin. Mr. Tartakoff's accompanist was Frederick Hopper and his collaboration was exquisite. Mr. Tartakoff has always exercised fine judgment in picking his assistants, but there is apparently more to it: he can elicit great commitment from all who share the stage with him. His personality demands response and gets it. The audience gave it to him last night; there was a ten-minute ovation followed by four encores that left the crowd shouting for more.

August 6, 1948

The Music Shed at Tanglewood was the scene last night of a rather disheartening concert by the Boston Symphony Orchestra. The program, perhaps, was to blame. It was warhorse night, with a stable of old winners trotted out for the automatic approval of a loyal audience which, itself, is not quite as young as it used to be.

After the Leonore No. 3 and the Hayden Clock, about which there was nothing the least bit diverting or unique, Alexei Tartakoff was the soloist. Lexy, the old Russian who used to be billed as the Liszt of the violin, is still a drawing-card, whether for musical or extra-musical reasons, one cannot tell if he doesn't feel the hyponotic pull himself. (This reviewer must admit that he doesn't, but perhaps his parents did.) This reluctance to be moved by the charming smile and courtier's bow, and the still ample crown of free-floating hair, leaves one's attention, unfortunately, free to listen to the music Tartakoff produces. It is flamboyant and undisciplined and yet somehow conventional, for all the unconventionalities his sloppiness of phrasing and intonation allow. He sounds temperamental à la Russe, but it is all so familiar, could his heart really be in it? This style would be so easy for a young violinist to learn to ape, with a bit of application, from old records; and one fears that a younger, more limber man could do it better. These days, at least, we must demand more from our orchestras and our soloists than they gave us last night.

SEASON CLOSES WITH VIOLIN DUO;

TARTAKOFF FINALE SEES PUPIL BOW

April 20, 1958

Last night was a most peculiar one for all who attended the much-publicized closing concert of this season's Philharmonic at Carnegie Hall. Judging by their response, the audience was as bewildered as it had every right to be. The evening was to mark the farewell appearance of the great Alexei Tartakoff, who has appeared in New York only once in the last ten years. Mr. Tartakoff, now a worn-looking 72, has continued to concertize across the country within the last few years. Therefore, what at first announced as a return from retirement for this special concert could perhaps more honestly, if less euphemistically, be called a return from obscurity. In any event, the occurrences of the evening make one wonder what the intention really might have been, and one is at a loss even to conjecture.

A good deal of newspaper attention had been given as well to Mr. Tartakoff's plan to present at this concert his only pupil and protégé, so that the occasion was to be one of more than sentimental interest. It was to be both a farewell and a debut, and the latter, judging by Mr. Taratakoff's reluctance to sanction any other student over the years, made one quite naturally curious and hopeful that a worthy heir would be proclaimed by the abdicating king.

How to say it? To be blunt, the concert was a fiasco, and an extraordinary one. Harlan Temple, who is 23, has the manner of a master—he swept onstage and bowed from the waist, a more athletic replica of his teacher, dispensed with even the customary gesture of interest in the tuning of his instrument, strode out into the deep waters of the Dvorak A Minor, and promptly drowned. One could not attribute such fundamentally faulty playing to nervousness, especially when not a hint of discomfort was in evidence. On the contrary, Mr. Temple was more self-possessed than most proven professionals, even suspiciously so. But his technique was wretched, his intonation slapdash, his tone ugly, his general level of sensitivity and musical feeling so low it was virtually absent. This pleasant enough concerto was suddenly ghastly and endless, and when he had done with it, the soloist bowed profusely to a paralyzed audience from which a ragged little sound of applause issued briefly. But Mr. Tartakoff was onstage, clapping proudly, and the orchestra, with Rouben Der Tartesian on the podium, joined with him enthusiastically. No one but the audience looked troubled. One shook oneself to see if it might have been an acoustical fluke or an after-dinner dream. But for confirmation, the master and his pupil were paired in the Bach G Minor double concerto, and the impression persisted. And next to Tartakoff, the untalented boy was an even greater outrage. What a lovely tone and what a catsquawk juxtaposed! By comparison the aging violinist was the perfect musician again—soaring, agile, strong.

This reviewer, grieved, confused, even angry, cannot help but wonder what will happen to Harlan Temple when he is properly launched (horrible dictu!) and on his own. Considering that he already parades like a child movie-star, he has apparently been brainwashed into believing that he will have, or already has, a career ready-made for him. If so, Mr. Temple is in for a colossal disappointment.

ENCL. E:

	(H's translation):
Sike saadilil	My legs for me restore
Sitsat saadilil	My body for me restore
Sissis saaditlil	My mind for me restore
Sini saaditlil	My voice for me restore

Tadisdzin naalil sahadilil	This very day your spell for me you will take out
Naalil sahaneinla	Your spell for me is removed
Hozogo tsidisal	Happily I shall go forth
Hozogo nadedisdal	Happily I shall recover
Sana nislingo nasado	My feelings being lively may I walk
Sana nislingo nasado	

TOPICS FOR DISCUSSION AND WRITING

1. What do the Indian prayers have in common (Enclosures A, B, and E)?

2. What is the relationship between the princess and her father (Enclosure C)?

3. What is the relationship between the old and young violinists (Enclosure D)?

4. What is the relationship between the falcon and its master (Enclosure B)?

5. In what way are the items MP purchased at the department store related to the theme running through the five enclosures?

6. What can be inferred from these clues about the relationship between MP and H?

7. Why did MP leave H in this fashion—by planting subtle clues around their home—rather than by confronting him directly?

8. Now that you have studied the evidence, your task is to write an essay in which you answer this question: Why did MP leave her husband? You must play detective, drawing inferences from the police report and its various enclosures. Your response should take into account as much of the evidence as possible. (See What Is an Inference? and Making Inferences—Writing About Fiction in Chapter 2.)

What's in a Name?

The title above is taken from Shakespeare's *Romeo and Juliet,* the story of two young lovers thwarted in pursuing their love by their two families, the Capulets and the Montagues, who have long been enemies. The following exchange between the young lovers occurs as Romeo stands beneath Juliet's window (Act II, Scene ii).

Juliet: O Romeo, Romeo, wherefore art thou Romeo?
          Deny thy father and refuse thy name,

> Or, if thou wilt not, be but sworn my love
> And I'll no longer be a Capulet.

Romeo: [Aside] Shall I hear more, or shall I speak at this?

Juliet: 'Tis but thy name that is my enemy.
Thou art thyself, though not a Montague.
What's Montague? It is not hand, nor foot,
Nor arm, nor face, nor any other part
Belonging to a man. Oh, be some other name!
What's in a name? That which we call a rose
By any other name would smell as sweet.
So Romeo would, were he not Romeo called,
Retain that dear perfection which he owes
Without that title. Romeo, doff thy name,
And for thy name, which is no part of thee,
Take all myself.

Romeo and Juliet discover, tragically, that they are not able to escape their history, their families' history, all of which is symbolized by their names. One's surname is significant, linking as it does an individual to a family and to previous generations. The significance of names and the sexual politics they often demonstrate are explored in this section.

Beginning with Names

Casey Miller and Kate Swift

In this excerpt from their book, *Words and Women,* Miller and Swift provide a context, a history of the tradition of women taking their husbands' names.

In the whole name game, it is society's sanction of patronymy that most diminishes the importance of women's names—and that sanction is social only, not legal.* In the United States no state except Hawaii legally requires a woman to take her husband's name when she marries, although social pressures in the other states are almost as compelling. The very fact that until recently few women giving up their names realized they were not required to do so shows how universal the expectation is. Any married couple who agree that the wife will keep her own name are in for harassment, no matter how legal their stand; family, friends, the Internal Revenue Service, state and local agencies like motor vehicle departments and voter registrars, hotels, credit agencies, insurance companies are all apt to exert pressure on them to conform. One judge is quoted as saying to a married woman who wanted to revert to her birth name, "If you didn't want his name, why did you get married? Why didn't you live with him

*Other countries have legal requirements concerning surnames; in France, for example, it is required by law that a wife take her husband's name.

instead?" To thus equate marriage with the desire of some women to be called "Mrs." and the desire of some men to have "a Mrs." is insulting to both sexes; yet the equation is so widely accepted that few young people growing up in Western societies think in any different terms.

The judge just quoted was, in effect, defining what a family is in a patronymical society like ours where only males are assured permanent surnames they can pass on to their children. Women are said to "marry into" families, and families are said to "die out" if an all-female generation occurs. The word family, which comes from the Latin *famulus,* meaning a servant or slave, is itself a reminder that wives and children, along with servants, were historically part of a man's property. When black Americans discard the names of the slave-holders who owned their forebears, they are consciously disassociating their sense of identity from the property status in which their ancestors were held. To adopt an African name is one way of identifying with freedom and eradicating a link to bondage. The lot of married women in Western society today can hardly be called bondage, but to the degree that people's names are a part of themselves, giving them up, no matter how willingly, is tantamount to giving up some part of personal, legal, and social autonomy.

Since a surname defines a family and identifies its members, a man who marries and has children extends his family, but a woman in marrying gives up her "own" family and joins in extending another's. She may be fully aware that she brings to her new family—to her children and grandchildren—the genetic and cultural heritage of her parents and grandparents, but the lineages she can trace are ultimately paternal. Anyone who decides to look up their ancestors through marriage and birth records in town halls and genealogical societies may find paternal lines going back ten or fifteen generations or more, whereas with few exceptions maternal ones end after two or three. The exceptions are interesting for they emphasize how important the lost information from maternal lines really is. Stephen Birmingham, writing about America's blue-blooded families, notes that "'Who is she?' as a question may mean, 'What was her maiden name?' It may also mean what was her mother's maiden name, and what was her grandmother's maiden name, and so on." Blue bloods, in other words, care a lot about "maiden names," and rightly so, considering that the inputs of maternal genes and culture have as great an effect on offspring as parental inputs.

Obviously we all have as many female ancestors as male ancestors, but maternal lineages, marked with name changes in every generation, are far more difficult to trace. To most of us the identity of our mother's mother's mother's mother, and that of *her* mother, and on back, are lost forever. How is one affected by this fading out of female ancestors whose names have disappeared from memory and the genealogical records? Research on the subject is not readily availiable, if it exists at all, but it seems likely that daughters are affected somewhat differently from sons. If it is emotionally healthy, as psychologists believe, for a child to identify with the parent of the same sex, would it not also be healthy for a child to identify with ancestors of the same sex?

A boy, knowing he comes from a long line of males bearing the name Wheelwright, for example, can identify with his forefathers: Johnny Wheelwright in the 1970s, if he wants to, can imagine some medieval John in whose workshop the finest wheels in the land were fashioned, a John who had a son, who had a son, who had a son, until at last Johnny Wheelwright himself was born. No line of identifiable foremothers stretches back into the past to which his sister Mary can lay claim. Like Johhny, she is a Wheelwright, assigned by patronymy to descent from males. What neither boy nor girl will ever be able trace is their equally direct descent from, let's say, a woman known as the Healer, a woman whose daughter's daughter's daughter, through the generations passed on the skilled hands which both John and Mary may have inherited.

Imagine, in contrast to Johnny Wheelwright, a hypothetical woman of to-day whose name is Elizabeth Jones. If you were to ask, in the manner of a blue blood. "Who is she?" you might be told. "She was a Fliegendorf. Her people were Pennsylvania Dutch farmers who came over from Schleswig-Holstein in the seventeenth century." Actually, that tells a fraction of the story. This hypotheti-cal Elizabeth Jones's mother—who met her father at an Army post during the Second World War—was a Woslewski whose father emigrated from Poland as a boy, lived in Chicago, and there married a Quinn whose mother came from Canada and was a Vallière. The mother of that Vallière was the great-great-grand-daughter of a woman whose given name was the equivalent of "Deep Water" and who belonged to a group of native North Americans called the Têtes de Boule by French explorers.

Elizabeth Jones's father's mother, in Pennsylvania, had been a Bruhofer, whose mother had been a Gruber, whose mother, a Powel, was born in Georgia and was the great-great-granddaughter of a woman brought to this country from Africa in the hold of a slave ship.

Thus, although Elizabeth Jones is said to have been a Fliegendorf whose peo-ple came from Schleswig-Holstein in the sixteen hundreds, fewer than 5 per cent of her two thousand or so direct ancestors who were alive in that century had any connection with Schleswig-Holstein, and only one of those who made the pas-sage to America was born with the name Fliegendorf. The same may be said, of course, of Elizabeth Jones's brother, Ed Fliegendorf's relationship to the Fliegen-dorf family or Johnny Wheelwright's relationship to the bearers of his name. Yet so strong is our identification with the name we inherit at birth that we tend to forget both the rich ethnic mix most of us carry in our genes and the arbitrary de-finition of "family" that ultimately links us only to the male line of descent.

This concept of family is one of the reasons why most societies through most of history have placed greater value on the birth of a male child than of a female child. Ours is no exception. A recent survey reported in *Psychology Today* showed that a higher percentage of prospective parents in the United States would prefer to have a son than a daughter as a first or only child. The percent-age who feel this way, however, has dropped from what it was only twenty years ago. Responding to the report, a reader expressed his opinion that the change could be attributed to "a breakdown in the home-and-family ideal" among young parents today. "The son," he wrote in a letter to the editor, "and in particular the eldest son, is strongly tied to the archetypal family; first as its prime agent of continuation, and also as the future guardian and master of the home." Here, then, family and name are seen as synonymous, the male is the prime if not only progenitor, and even the order of birth among male children affects the model of an ideal family.

One could not ask for a better example of how patronymy reinforces the powerful myth that pervades the rest of our language—the myth that the human race is essentially male. The obvious first reaction to such a statement may be to say, "But that's absurd. No one thinks of the race as essentially male." And yet we do. As the social critic Elizabeth Janeway has pointed out, a myth does not really describe a situation; rather, it tries to bring about what it declares to exist.

A childless couple adopted a baby girl. When asked why they chose a girl rather than a boy, they explained that if she did not live up to their expectations because of her genetic heritage, "at least she won't carry on the family." Journalist Mike McGrady states the myth of racial maleness even more tellingly in an article about sperm banking: "One customer . . . gave a reason for depositing sperm that may foreshadow the future: it was to carry on the family line should his male offspring prove sterile. What we are talking about here," McGrady said, "is not fertility insurance but immortality insurance." This customer, then, believes he cannot be linked to future generations through his female offspring, should they prove fertile. His immortality, one must conclude, is not in his sperm or his genes but in his name.

"One's name and a strong devotion to it." wrote an Austrian philosopher, Otto Weininger, around the turn of the century, "are even more dependent on personality than is the sense of property. . . . Women are not bound to their names with any strong bond. When they marry they give up their own name and assume that of their husband without any sense of loss. . . . The fundamental namelessness of the woman is simply a sign of her undifferentiated personality." Weininger, whose book *Sex and Character* had a brief but powerful influence on popular psychology, is of historical interest because he articulated the myth of humanity's maleness at a time when the first wave of feminism was beginning to be taken seriously by governments, trade unions, and other institutions in England and the United States as well as in Europe. In describing the "fundamental namelessness" of woman as "a sign of her undifferentiated personality," Weininger was building support for his premise that "women have no existence and no essence . . . no share in ontological reality, no relation to the thing-in-itself, which, in the deepest interpretation, is the absolute, is God."

Otto Weininger was aware of the movement for women's rights and was deeply disturbed by it. He may well have heard of the noted American feminist Lucy Stone, whose decision to keep her birth name when she married Henry Blackwell in 1855 had created consternation on both sides of the Atlantic. An eloquent speaker with a free and fearless spirit, Stone was widely known as an antislavery crusader. After the Civil War her organizing efforts helped secure passage of the Fourteenth Amendment, which extended the vote to freed slaves who were men. She devoted the rest of her long, productive life to the cause of suffrage for women and founded and edited the *Woman's Journal,* for forty-seven years the major weekly newspaper of the women's movement.

It is especially relevant that among Lucy Stone's many important contributions to history she is best known today for her refusal to give up her name. Her explanation, "My name is the symbol of my identity and must not be lost," was a real shocker to anyone who had not considered the possibility that a married woman could have an individual identity—and in the nineteenth century that meant almost everyone. The law did not recognize such a possibility, as the famous English jurist William Blackstone made clear when he summarized the rule of "coverture," influencing both British and American law for well over a hundred years. "By marriage," he wrote, "the husband and wife are one person in the law—that is, the very being or legal existence of the woman is suspended during the marriage. . . ."

The suspended existence of the married woman came to be well symbolized in the total submersion of a wife's identity in her husband's name—preceded by "Mrs." The use of designations like "Mrs. John Jones" does not go back much before 1800. Martha Washington would have been mystified to receive a letter addressed to "Mrs. George Washington," for at that time the written abbreviation *Mrs.,* a social title applied to any adult woman, was used interchangeably with its spelled-out form *mistress* and was probably pronounced the same way. "Mistress George" would have made little sense.

Lucy Stone's example was followed in the late nineteenth and early twentieth centuries by small but increasing numbers of women, mostly professional writers, artists, and scientists. The Lucy Stone League, founded in New York in 1921, was the first organization to help women with the legal and bureaucratic difficulties involved in keeping their names after marriage. Its early leaders included Jane Grant, co-founder with her first husband, Harold Ross, of the *New Yorker* magazine, and journalist Ruth Hale who in 1926 asked rhetorically how men would respond to the suggestion that they give up *their* names. The suggestion does not often arise, but a psychologist recently described the reaction of one husband and father when someone in his family raised the possibility of changing the family name because they didn't like it:

"He suddenly realized that it was a traumatic thing for him to consider giving up his last name," according to Dr. Jack Sawyer of Northwestern University. "He said he'd never realized before that 'only men have real names in our society, women don't.' And it bothered him also that his name should be a matter of such consequence for him. He worried about his professional standing, colleagues trying to contact him—all kinds of things that women face as a matter of course when they get married. Men have accepted the permanency of their names as one of the rights of being male, and it was the first time he realized how much his name was part of his masculine self-image."

Lucy Stone, whose self-image was comfortably female but not feminine, agreed to be known as Mrs. Stone after her marriage. Through this compromise with custom she avoided the somewhat schizophrenic situation many well-known women face when they use their birth names professionally and their husbands' names socially, thus becoming both Miss Somebody and Mrs. Somebody Else. The Pulitzer-prize winning novelist Jean Stafford wants to be "saluted as *Miss* Stafford if the subject at hand has to do with me and my business or as *Mrs.* Liebling if inquiries are being made about my late husband." Miss Stafford objects to being addressed as "Ms.," a title that Lucy Stone would probably have welcomed had it existed in her time.

During the nearly two centuries in which the use of the distinguishing marital labels Miss or Mrs. for women was rigidly enforced by custom, the labels tended to become parts of women's names, in effect replacing their given names. A boarding school founded by Sarah Porter in Farmington, Connecticut, soon became known as Miss Porter's School. After the actress Minnie Maddern married Harrison Grey Fiske, she became famous as Mrs. Fiske. In the following classroom dialogue, the columnist Ellen Cohn provides a classic example of how the custom works:

> *Question:* Who is credited with discovering radium?
>
> *Answer* (all together): Madam Curie.
>
> Well, class, the woman (who was indeed married to a man named Pierre Curie) had a first name all her own. From now on let's call her Marie Curie.
>
> *Question:* Can Madam Curie ever be appropriately used?
>
> *Answer:* Of course. Whenever the inventor of the telephone is called Mr. Bell.

Through the transience and fragmentation that have traditionally character-ized women's names, some part of the human female self-image has been sacri-ficed. It is hardly surprising, therefore, that the second wave of feminist con-sciousness brought a serious challenge to patronymy and to the assignment of distinguishing marital labels to women. To be named and defined by someone else is to accept an imposed identity—to agree that the way others see us is the way we really are. Naming conventions, like the rest of language, have been shaped to meet the interests of society, and in patriarchal societies the shapers have been men. What is happening now in language seems simply to reflect the fact that, in the words of Dr. Pauli Murray. "women are seeking their own image of themselves nurtured from within rather than imposed from without."

From antiquity, people have recognized the connection between naming and power. The master-subject relationship, which corrupts the master and de-grades the subject, is foreshadowed in one of the biblical creation myths when the primal male assumes the right to name his equal, the primal female. The no-tion that the sexes were created equal and at the same time is not widely ac-cepted. As Dr. Phyllis Trible, who is a professor at Andover Newton Theological School, has demonstrated, however, when the language of the story is exam-ined outside the traditional confines of patriarchal interpretation, the evidence of full equality is inescapable.

There are two stories of creation in Genesis. In the first chapter "God cre-ated man in his own image . . . male and female created he them." In the sec-ond chapter "God formed man of the dust of the ground" and later made woman from man's rib. Scholars recognize the latter as being the earlier version, and at first glance it seems to reflect a more primitive concept of human begin-nings. But closer examination of the older story as it was recorded in the original

Hebrew reveals some significant aspects of this ancient human view of ourselves that have been lost in English translations. The "man" formed out of the dust of the ground, Professor Trible points out, is *'adham,* a generic term in ancient Hebrew for humankind. This original person is seen in the story as an androgynous being having the potentialities of both sexes. It is for the protohumam *'adham* that God plans to make a "help meet." (Even in the English of the King James Version, the adjective "meet" is not the noun "mate," as some people seem to think. "Helpmate" came into the language through what linguists call folk etymology, that is, a change in a word to make it look or sound like more familiar words, without regard to similarity in meaning. A "help meet" is a "fit helper"; a modern translation, the New English Bible, uses the word partner.)

In carrying out the plan God first creates the animals, all of which *'adham* names, thereby asserting authority over them and subjecting them to the service of humanity. The animals are helpers, but because they are not *'adham's* equals, they are not fit to be full partners. So God tries again by performing surgery on the sleeping androgynous *'adham.*

Up until this time, Trible notes, the ancient Hebrew story-teller consistently used the generic term *'adham.* Only after the rib episode are the Hebrew words specifying the human male, *'ish,* and the human female, *'ishshah,* introduced. *'Adham,* whose flesh and bones have now been sexually identified as female and male, speaks of the two sexes in the third person. "She shall be called woman (*'ishshah*), because she was *differentiated from* man (*'ish*)" provides a valid alternative for the Hebrew term usually rendered "taken out of."

In this ancient Hebrew story. "She shall be called woman" does not represent an act of naming, Trible points out. The typical formula the storyteller uses for naming is the verb *to call* coupled with the explicit object *name.* It is only later—when God has already judged the woman and man but has not yet sent them from the Garden—that the man, invoking the same formula used in naming the animals and asserting supremacy over them, "called his wife's name Eve." Trible concludes, "The naming itself faults the man for corrupting a relationship of mutuality and equality," and God then evicts the primal couple from Eden.

The recorder of that early human effort to understand the nature and meaning of existence speaks across the millenniums of patriarchy. The story is far different from the male-oriented interpretation of creation that has embedded itself in our conscious understanding and our less conscious use of language. In English the once truly generic word man has come to mean male, so that males are seen as representing the species in a way females are not. Humanity, divided against itself, becomes the norm and the deviation, the namer and the named.

TOPIC FOR DISCUSSION AND WRITING

While providing a historical context for the tradition of women taking their husband's name, authors Miller and Swift argue against the tradition.

What premises do they offer in support of their conclusion that women should keep their original names when they marry? (See Premises and Conclusions in Chapter 3.)

Maiden Names

Justin Kaplan and Anne Bernays

In this excerpt from their book *The Language of Names,* Kaplan and Bernays, who are married, explore the tradition of women taking their husband's name and, like Miller and Swift, conclude that this custom takes its toll on women's identity.

In 1881, Judge Robert A. Earl, finding for the plaintiff in *Chapman v. Phoenix National Bank,* issued a declaration that would hearten the most mean-spirited misogynist. "For several centuries," he wrote,

> by the common law among all English-speaking people, a woman, upon her marriage, takes her husband's surname. That becomes her legal name, and she ceases to be known by her maiden name. By that name she must sue and be sued, make and take grants and execute all legal documents. Her maiden name is absolutely lost, and she ceases to be known thereby.

(A century earlier, in his *Commmentaries on the Laws of England,* William Blackstone said that when a man and woman exchange marriage vows, they become one person, and "the husband is that person.") Whenever there was a legal tangle over names, Judge Earl's opinion was trotted out in support of the status quo. Although widely subscribed to and largely unchallenged until the 1940s, Judge Earl's ruling was based on nothing more than wishful thinking. In fact, the opposite is true: anyone, male or female, single or married, has a common-law right to take any name he or she wants (as long as it's considered a name).

That Judge Earl's pronouncement prevailed for so many years, in spite of its being about as reliable as a formula for turning base metals into gold, attests to both the pervasive power of resistance to change and an atavistic terror of women. But as far as they have given it any thought at all, most men believe it seemly for a woman to give up her name when she marries. Most women agree with them—yet another reason not to put all one's trust in democracy's basket.

"Light of my life, dearest girl, you have the power to make me the happiest man in the world. Oh, island of loveliness, my heart's serenity, passionate tigress, darling Jennifer, say that you will marry me."

"I thought you'd never ask, Harvey. There's just one little thing."

"And what's that, sweetest pea?"

"I think I'd like to keep my name after we're married."

"Do *what?*"

"Keep my birth name. You know: Jennifer Pickens."

"Why would you want to do a selfish thing like that, Jen? What's wrong with my name? What's wrong with Masters?"

Harvey, threatened to his very marrow, backs off. They consult a premarriage counselor. Harvey complains, "If I go along with this whacko plan, what do I do when we go out together? Do I say, 'This is my wife, Jennifer Pickens'? It sounds stupid. I can't say that. People will think, Who the hell does this dame think she is . . ."

"I'm not a dame, Harvey."

"Girl. Woman. Whatever."

The counselor gives them equal time and eventually comes down on Jennifer's side. At this, Harvey accuses his heart's serenity of being in cahoots with the therapist, and they split for good. Jennifer's well out of it, and Harvey, no doubt, will find a woman more to his taste, a girl who doesn't have an attitude problem. A freethinking woman like Jennifer doesn't belong with a man who believes that sharing a name means he shares his name while hers falls into desuetude. Poet Philip Larkin wrote:

Marrying left your maiden name disused.

Its five light sounds no longer mean your face,

Your voice, and all your vanities of grace . . .

Now it's a phrase applicable to no one.

Men like Harvey, and there are probably many more like him than not, see a she-devil rather than the love of their life as soon as they discover how reluctant she is to give up her name. These men are baffled and hurt: "If you really loved me, you'd be overjoyed to take my name." The question the woman ought to ask—but not many do—is, "Let's turn this thing around. How about giving up *your* name and taking *mine*?" Sam Howe of *The New York Times* split the difference, you might say, when he married Lisa Verhovek, the bearer of a unique surname that, since she had no male siblings, was in danger of fading out in another generation. His marriage license and all subsequent records, including his byline, transformed him into Sam Howe Verhovek. "Names mean a lot," he reflected in an "About Men" essay:

And what to do with them—keeping, changing, hyphenating them—is a problem for a lot of couples as their wedding day approaches. I feel in no way diminished by taking my wife's name, and I don't think a woman should feel diminished by taking her husband's name. Personally, I think it's a privilege to have all those names, and it's not confusing at all. Howe is my maiden name, and Verhovek is my maiden's name.

The woman who refuses to submit to the conventional practice of taking her husband's name risks having her loyalties questioned and, except in relatively sophisticated communities, being viewed as a subversive. This isn't so far off the mark, for she's tossing a custard pie in custom's face at close range. What has always been done is what's generally deemed the correct thing, whether or not it defies reason. And so, since men long ago owned their women the way they owned cows and outhouses, why not keep on doing it that way? Why change?

During the late eighties and early nineties, there was a trend, on the East and West Coasts, at any rate, identified in newspaper wedding stories by the words "The bride is keeping her name." It is probably a mistake , however, to assume this to be true of the population in general, since brides whose weddings are reported in *The New York Times,* for example, tend to be achievers and individualists who have already established their names professionally, or wish to, and see no reason to surrender them. The higher their educational level, the less likely they are to follow conventional practice. According to a 1994 survey conducted for *American Demographics,* "Fewer than 5 percent of wives who do not have a college education use something other than their husband's name, compared with 15 percent of those with bachelor's degrees and more than 20 percent of those with post-graduate degrees."

But now comes the backlash: the aggressively traditional woman who says, explaining why she took her husband's name, "I wanted to buck that feminist viewpoint that in order to be a real woman you have to have your identity, and it's defined by what you're called. I know who I am and I'm going to follow the tradition that I choose." The woman being quoted, Crystal Dozier, a black twenty-nine-year-old middle manager, went even further: "You have to look at it from the man's point of view. I think it's an ego-booster for a man to have his wife take her husband's name, especially for a professional black woman. It makes a statement to the world that even though I'm professional, I still stand by my man," the last an argument used by some black women to justify their support of O.J. Simpson regardless of his record of spousal abuse and guilt or innocence in the murders of his wife and Ronald Goldman. Dozier's statement raises the question of whether she would be so committed to standing by her man, with all that that self-effacing posture implies, if she weren't black. It also makes you wonder why Ms. Dozier thinks that it's necessary to boost her husband's ego to keep her marriage intact.

Harvey's "dame" probably has a better idea of who she is than the woman—let's call her Emily Fisher—whose embossed stationery identifies her as Mrs. Paul Johnson. Mrs. Johnson is probably not aware that Mr. Johnson has swallowed her whole, leaving no trace, not even a few bones or feathers to mark the person who was once Emily Fisher. What sort of person is Emily that she doesn't mind being invisible?

Those who embrace the traditional will haul out an argument that goes something like this: "If a woman loves a man deeply and truly, she will take his name when she marries him because a name is merely nominal. That is, it has no more significance than a label, like 'pickled beets' or 'Chanel No. 5.' What you're called matters not half as much as the quality of the relationship between this man and this woman; how they absorb life's pleasures and disappointments; how they raise their children; their respect for one another. If she's profoundly aware of both who she is and what her roles require of her, it doesn't matter what she's called, so why not stick with ways tried and true? Keeping her own name confuses rather than clarifies; the children's school doesn't know who their parents are; assuming her husband's name ensures the maintenance of a tradition that goes back centuries and unambiguously reinforces the formal structure of the nuclear family."

To continue this argument is to venture into parody. The first part of it is non-sense, ignoring as it does the profound significance a name has for the person who bears it, and the last is mischief. To blame maiden-namism for the break-down of the family is to disregard the fact that the mom-and-pop-and-the-kids type of American family is, statistically speaking, a thing of the past since almost half of today's mothers have no husbands. If a family collapses it's because one of its members is absent, not because one of them refused to change her last name.

The idea of women's independence arouses panic in otherwise reasonable men. Cultural observer Susan J. Douglas, in her 1994 book *Where the Girls Are,* found evidence of this in old television programs like *Bewitched, I Dream of Jean-nie,* and *The Flying Nun.* These long-term sitcoms featured females with super-natural powers their guys viewed as suspiciously as a pair of strange trousers hanging in the closet. "If women did use them their powers had to be confined to the private sphere," Douglas wrote. "Whenever women used these powers outside the home, in the public sphere, the male world was turned completely upside down." She blamed the news media for popularizing two feminist arche-types: the "female grotesque" and the "femme fatale."

World folklore is replete with warnings against the female, especially while she's menstruating but also, it would seem, just for the hell of it. Some African tribes believe a barren woman can blight the crops. The Bible minces no words when it comes to female toxicity:

> If a woman have conceived seed, and borne a man child, then she shall be un-clean seven days. . . . And she shall then continue in the blood of her purifying three and thirty days; she shall touch no hallowed thing, nor come into the sanctuary, until the days of her purifying be fulfilled. But if she bear a maid child, then she shall be unclean two weeks, as in her separation: and she shall continue in the blood of her purifying threescore and six days.

James Frazer theorized that the human race is slowly crawling out of the magic mode up to and through the religious and will finally emerge in the sun-light of science and rationality. Yet Frazer's demonstration of the measureless dread of women among cultures just a little less civilized than ours gives one pause; how far, in fact, have most men come from believing that "if any one drank out of the same cup [as a menstruating female] he would surely die"? To-day, an Orthodox Jewish boy still recites a morning prayer thanking God for not having made him a girl. The great white father of psychoanalysis, Sigmund Freud, alleged that woman's conscience is to a man's as a clitoris is to a penis: in other words, underdeveloped and not especially useful. What with primitive man investing his mate with magic sufficient to kill of the corn and dry up the milch herd and civilized man questioning her ability to tell right from wrong, it's not surprising so many men are more frightened of an independent woman than they are of contracting a sexually transmitted disease.

New Woman, a magazine with a surprisingly large circulation, published an article by Anne Bernays in the summer of 1993 (the editors titled it, inevitably, "What's in a Name?"). Bernays took the position that a name is too important to give up as blithely and mindlessly as most women do when they marry. "Whenever a woman marries, sheds her name, and substitutes her husband's," Bernays wrote, "she's also shedding part of herself, part of who she's been since birth. Whether she's conscious of it or not, if she changes her name her marriage will be lopsided, like a scale with five pounds of nuts on one side and two on the other." If anything, she added, a woman needs to be more herself after she marries than before, "because there's nothing that tests so often and so profoundly who you are as living with someone else in close quarters."

The piece generated a record share of reader responses, including some from an unexpectedly large number of men. Here's a sampling.

Men:

If she hadn't taken my name I would have seen it as a definite negative statement that my name wasn't good enough for her.

Women who are really adamant about not changing their name . . . don't have their children's best interest at heart.

My first wife didn't take my name. At the time I didn't mind, but in retrospect . . . well, I wonder if that didn't say something about our relationship.

A woman who is really comfortable with her identity and knows she's independent doesn't have to make a big show of it and hit everyone in the face with it.

The man's name should be used by both husband and wife to represent the idea that marriage is a melding of two into one.

It should be treated simply as a matter of preference, not a matter of power or control.

Women:

When men talk about a woman taking a man's name as a sign of "melding," they ignore the fact that the person doing the melding is the woman.

I was proud to *share* the name of a man who believes in me more than I believe in myself.

A name denotes who you are, and now that you have substituted "Mrs." for "Miss" you are a wife.

Instead of promoting a woman's right to keep her *maiden name,* why not just say she chooses to keep *her name.*

I've kept my maiden name. My husband did not seem to care one way or another, but his mother was not real happy about it.

A woman who gives up her name for her husband's has immediately created a power imbalance in the relationship.

When woman sheds her birth name, she sheds part of herself. I unthinkingly shed that part of myself when I got married but would never do it again.

A man whose feelings are hurt when a woman refuses to give up her own name is not a man at all. He's a little boy who needs to grow up.

I think that keeping your own name is just a simple, natural way to be always yourself.

My blood boils every time I hear a man imply that wives who retain their names are "uncontrollable bitches." Or, that they are simply "not committed."

As for the "melding" one of the male respondents mentioned, there's only one way to meld two into one, and that's to make a new name, an anagram composed of both their surnames, as, in our case, Barkansplaney, Plankeraybans, and Yarbankpansel would be new words—neologisms—produced by combining and mixing Bernays and Kaplan. Several couples have done this: when Skye Kerr married Deane Rynerson (hard to say which is the female and which the male), they created a new name out of old parts for both to bear: Rykerson. In the same vein, when Jennifer Lynn Wilcha married David Alan Smith, they both dropped their surnames and assumed the name Allyn, a telescoping of Lynn and Alan. In a land dedicated to egalitarianism, this practice seems to make ultimate sense, even though the newlyweds' parents may not be all that happy about the disappearance of *their* names. Other less than ideal solutions to the problem of name loss suggest themselves. One is the hyphenated name, with the woman's first. Another is the Spanish way: with *y*—and—linking his and hers. Yet a third—and, although awkward, much the fairest—is to invent an entirely new name, containing no remnants or suggestions of anything preexisting in either family, for both to take.

When he was an undergraduate at Princeton in 1939, the psychologist Robert Holt turned in an honors thesis on the bond between name and identity, focusing on what, if anything, happens to the personality after a name change. Apparently this was one of the first empirical studies to deal with the maiden name/married name problem. After interviewing thirty subjects, Holt decided that although, "severe emotional disturbances" may ensue when a man changes his name, women who don't want to take their husband's name are "usually maladjusted anyway" and are simply "projecting their difficulties." This astonishing conclusion was echoed by writer and social critic Louis Adamic in his 1942 book, *What's Your Name?* The greater part of this hymn to the United States was devoted to reassuring readers with funny foreign names that heterogeneity is the American way. Be proud of your origins, he said, and resist the temptation to become a "fake yankee." But when it comes to females, Adamic wasn't quite so reassuring. He told the story of a "real-life" professional woman who kept her own name after marriage and who, when her husband died, "suddenly realized she had no real existence apart from him. . . . Now it was pointless to retain her maiden name. To regain her identity, her existence, she took his name which had come to represent them both."

Amy and Leon Kass, both on the faculty of the University of Chicago, put the problem in a sociobiological framework, arguing that "the change of the woman's name, from family of origin to family of perpetuation, is the perfect emblem for the desired exogamy of human sexuality and generation." Their argument may sound familiar to readers of Margaret Atwood's novel *The Handmaid's Tale.* The women in Atwood's futuristic dystopia have only one function, to bear the children of the governing order; if they're not fertile, they're labeled Unwomen and shipped off to the colonies as slave labor. Ofglen (that is, Of Glen), Ofwayne, Ofwarren, and so forth are their possessive-form names, which denote the men who own them for breeding purposes. The Kasses seem to endorse a comparable order of society:

> The husband who gives his name to his bride in marriage . . . is owing up to what it means to have been given a family and a family name by his father—he is living out his destiny to be a father by saying yes to it in advance. And the wife does not so much surrender her name as she accepts the gift of his, given and received as a pledge of (among other things) loyal and responsible fatherhood

for her children. A woman who refuses this gift is, whether she knows it or not, tacitly refusing the promised devotion or, worse, expressing her suspicions about her groom's trustworthiness as a husband and prospective father.

The high nonsense content of arguments against a woman's keeping her name indicates that the antis are willing to exchange atavism for logic, something that happens whenever a social issue twangs a fragile psychic chord. In this case, it is terror of the uppity woman, the dame who thinks for herself, breathes on her own; of the woman who demands a credit card and an equal voice in how money is spent, who thinks she's capable of making administrative decisions, who insists on maintaining her own identity, keeping her own name! If we don't place this Krakatoa under wraps, we may find ourselves kissing civilization good-bye. Poor woman. Blameless, she's blamed almost as often as the Jew when society starts fracturing.

And yet, even as he resists change and choice, the reactionary is uneasily aware of the paradox in his argument that names aren't all that important. If he really means it, why doesn't he encourage his loved one to keep the name she was born with, the name her teachers knew her by, the tag on her high school diploma? Like the tryant who bans—or burns—books because he's no fool and knows the awful power of the written word, the reactionaries recognize that a name is *not* simply the label they can dismiss as peelable and that it has profound significance for its bearer. Let her wear her own name and God only knows what will happen. When a woman gives up her name at marriage, she's saying: "While I'm willing to relinquish a piece of my identity for the sake of this union, I do not ask the same of you." . . .

. . . The problem of how a woman identifies herself after marriage can be solved in any number of ways that, however irrational, nevertheless appear to satisfy the solver. Writer Susan Ferraro, née Flynn, claimed that, after she married, "changing my name meant defining myself as an adult, choosing my own label. Taking a new name was about growing up. It was about how, much as I loved him, I stopped being Daddy's little girl." That makes no sense whatsoever, for hasn't she, by analogy, transformed herself into her husband's little girl? While her "label" now read Ferraro, rather than Flynn, she didn't seem to realize that, as the saying goes, "he only married me; he didn't adopt me."

"Here I am," wrote Carol Ascher soon after her divorce from writer Philip Lopate, "thirty-six years old, a woman who has worked all her adult life, who has been in the women's movement for nearly a decade. Here I am, assertive and competent, and I can't find a name for myself." Lopate, she said, was "ugly or embarrassing. . . . I was ashamed of it, humiliated by its reminder of a discontinued legal tie." For a while she considered going back to her birth name, Bergman, when a male friend lit into her. "You just never take yourself seriously," he said. "You belittle your past, your social presence. You're a writer. If you change your name to Bergman now, it'll be like starting from scratch. Nobody will know who you are." In the end, aware that Bergman wouldn't do, she recognized an analogy Ferraro had missed: "If one can't let go of a husband, there may well be a father lurking behind." Finally, after months of chewing on the problem, she settled on her mother's family name, Ascher, although taking this name could be considered a capitulation to "Mommy." Nevertheless, Ascher felt much better, knew who she was. She also had acquired, over the drawn-out process of discovering the proper noun to call herself, a heightened awareness about names and identity. She had always assumed that name change was a problem for women only, and "now I saw that it was also a wider one: part of the suffering of so many in any disenfranchised or minority group."

Sometimes its difficult not to think: *One step forward, two steps backward.* When Hillary Rodham, Wellesley graduate, practicing lawyer, author, started campaigning for her husband Bill's 1982 reelection as governor of Arkansas, she used her married name and agreed to be identified as "Mrs. Clinton" for the first time. Did she do this because her husband's aides in the war room told her, "The gals out there—to say nothing about their husbands—aren't going to buy this maiden name crap! Bake cookies! Stand by your man!"? In spite of Rodham's capitulation (and some say she's the master politician in the family and knows by heart every intricate step of the dance), William Safire, cranky *New York Times* columnist and cultural dinosaur, took her to task in 1992 for not toeing the traditional female line and for opening her mouth on a host of other issues when he would have preferred it to stay demurely zipped. Easy as it is to understand the pragmatic motivation behind such accommodations, someone with Hillary Rodham's grit could have stuck to her precampaign guns instead and taken her chances that the voters of Arkansas, and later the entire country, wouldn't mind that Bill's wife was still Ms. and not Mrs.

Two of the three Bernays/Kaplan married daughters have kept their names, while the third, the oldest, goes back and forth. Elizabeth Taylor didn't take any of her eight husbands' names, starting with Hilton and ending with Fortensky (who, for better or worse, was not able to hang on). Radio satirist Jack Cole found the string of names acquired (but not worn) over the years by the much-married Taylor irresistible. He paid her this tribute:

> Here she comes, beat the drums, blow the trumpets,
> Dressed in white, there's delight in her stride.
> She's played queens, she's played virgins, she's played strumpets,
> Heaven knows she's equipped to play a bride.
> First came Nick, then two Mikes, then came Eddie,
> Dick came twice, then a senator named John.
> What a date, what a mate, what a Butterfield 8!
> Here comes Liz Taylor Hilton Wilding Todd Fisher
> Burton Burton Warner, with Fortensky hanging on.

The Lucy Stone League is no more. A similar organization, called Center for a Woman's Own Name, founded in 1973 and dedicated to "eliminating discrimination against women who choose to determine their own names," is now "defunct," according to the Postal Service. And even as some women, prodded by Madonna, *are* wearing their bras and panties outside, they still tend toward Mrs. when it comes to marriage.

TOPICS FOR DISCUSSION AND WRITING

1. What is the correlation between the educational level a woman reaches and her decision to take, or not take, her husband's name?

2. What are some alternatives to the wife's taking her husband's name or keeping her maiden name? What are the advantages and disadvantages of these various alternatives?

3. What do Kaplan and Bernays suggest are the reasons for people objecting to women keeping their names when they marry?

4. What paradox do the authors find in the argument of those who believe a woman should take her husband's name?

5. Design and conduct a survey of your class on this issue—possibly with a group of other students—and then write the results of your survey and your analysis of them in a short report. (See Writing Assignment 17 on page 201.)

6. *Women:* write an essay in which you address the following questions: Will you take your husband's name if you marry or keep your own? Explain your answer. If you are married, discuss the choice you made and your reasons for making it.
   Men: Write an essay in which you address the following questions: If you marry, do you expect your wife to take your name? Why or why not? Would you ever consider giving up your name and taking your wife's name? Why or why not? If you are married, how did you and your wife address this issue?

Mr., Make No Mistake, This Mrs. Is Decidedly Ms.

Sarah Lyall

The subject of this article, Liz Shankland, felt so strongly about keeping her own name that she bought a classified ad in a newspaper announcing the fact.

Cardiff, Wales—Liz Shankland, a 35-year-old public relations executive here, was thrilled to marry her longtime love, Gerald Toms, last November. But she was not thrilled when people started to call her by the name of a person she does not believe exists.

"At parties, people would say, 'This is Gerry Toms—and this is his wife, Mrs. Toms,'" she related. "They didn't even give me a Christian name. And when I said my name was Liz Shankland, they'd say: 'You can't do that. You're really Mrs. Toms.'"

The comments grew more extreme. "One woman said to me, 'Don't you think you're being rather disrespectful and rude?'" Ms. Shankland recalled—and so she decided extreme measures were called for.

The new bride, a former reporter and editor at *The Western Mail* here who knows the value of a well-timed media offensive, decided to take the unusual step of buying a classified advertisement in her old paper.

"Although she has now publicly pledged undying love for her husband, she has not changed her name to 'Mrs. Toms,'" the ad said. "Instead, she will continue to be known—personally and professionally—as Ms. Liz Shankland, and makes no apology to the misguided fuddy-duddies who believe that to be strange or unconventional."

In its small way, Ms. Shankland's situation illustrates a larger phenomenon in Britain. It is sometimes hard, women say, to convince people that you don't want to take the name of your husband (if you have one). And it is sometimes hard to get people to call you Ms., a word that while in wide use in some professions, still seems to carry connotations of the stereotypical bra-burning, man-bashing, non-leg-shaving feminists who apparently so terrorized British men in the 60's and 70's.

"They just can't cope with Ms.," said Margaret Blott, a London obstetrician in her 30's, who felt compelled to use Miss when she began practicing medicine. (Under the British system, many of the highest-qualified doctors do not call themselves Dr.) Miss Blott, the only Miss in a sea of Mr.'s on the front door of her elegant Harley Street office, said she would have much preferred Ms., but didn't want to unsettle anyone in the conservative medical establishment.

"People make all sorts of asumptions when you use Miss," she said. "They come in and expect someone who's 60 years old. On the other hand, Ms. does have connotations of aggressive feminist overtones, and a lot of people don't like it."

Why not? Kathy Lette, an expatriate Australian novelist who has made a career of poking fun at the stodgy ways of British males, said it was sexism, pure and simple. "When I say I want to be called Ms. Lette," said Ms. Lette, who is married to one of Britain's most respected human rights lawyers, Geoffrey Robertson, "they either ignore me or they just go ahead and call me Mrs. Robertson, or Mrs. Lette. When you make an issue out of it, they look at you like you've turned into Lorena Bobbitt."

Despite their trappings of enlightenment, she said, British men are unreconstructed cave dwellers.

"Women here have been lulled into a false sense of security," she said. "When I moved here, I thought I'd come to New Man planet. The men talked about gardening and opera and quoted huge whacks of poetry. They knew Shakespeare's sonnets by heart. I thought, 'Oh, they're so sensitive.' But it's a big scam—they're just as sexist as Australian men, but it's much more hidden."

Part of the problem, it seems, is that Britain has always resisted what it sees as American-style political correctness, a term derived as describing a ridiculously tortured sensitivity that has resulted in absurd changes to the language.

Britons are loath to demonstrate such sensitivity or to make such changes themselves. Thus, people who deliver the mail here are still called postmen, even if they happen to be postwomen. Michael Portillo, the former Tory Defense Minister, was routinely referred to as "the Spaniard" in newspaper reports, a reference to the fact that his father was a Spanish immigrant, and nobody seemed to object.

Feminism is a highly charged concept here, as it is to some in the United States, and many women seem almost physically afraid of the term. Margaret Jay, the leader of the House of Lords, recently declared in an interview with *The Guardian* that she was not a feminist, even though one of her jobs is to run the Government's Women's Unit, which deals with issues like education, child care and equal pay.

"In politics, feminism is seen as negative, complaining about things," said Lady Jay, who as a bona fide baroness since her elevation to the House of Lords no longer has to bother deciding whether she wants to be Mrs., Ms. or Miss.

Even Ms. Shankland, who so objected to being seen as what she calls "part and parcel of my husband," balks at the feminist label. She deliberately tried to make her ad playfully hyperbolic, she said, "so that people wouldn't think I was one of those raving feminists who doesn't agree with anything."

"I believe in equality and all the rest of it, but the word's just got such connotations," she said. "It reminds people of trade unions, of crew-cut hair and dungarees, and gives the impression that you sort of hate men."

Ms. Shankland certainly doesn't hate her husband, a superintendent in the South Wales police force, who came in for a bit of ribbing when her ad appeared, particularly because she had not told him about it in advance.

"I wasn't aware that she was going to resolve the situation in such a direct and public way," Superintendent Toms said. But he proclaimed himself unfazed by the experience, even when he found that the ad was playfully inserted into the agenda at his office's meeting the day it appeared. "I don't, as a man, need to put a tag around a woman's neck to say that I'm married to her."

Has there been any fallout? "Some people look at me like I'm somebody with two heads, but a lot of people have rung me up and said, 'Good on you,'" Ms. Shankland said. One other thing: "At Gerry's office, they're calling him Superintendent Shankland."

TOPICS FOR DISCUSSION AND WRITING

1. What is your reaction to the titles "Miss," "Mrs.," and "Ms."? Why are there no parallel forms of address for men?

2. Why are the women in the article so afraid of being identified as feminists? Is this a fear you share? Why or why not?

3. Write a definition of the word "feminist." (See Writing Assignment 13 on page 133.)

A Mother's Name

....

Jenny McPhee

In this essay, McPhee describes the reaction she receives when she breaks with tradition by giving her son her surname rather than his father's.

When I was five months pregnant with my son, I went to a dinner party in Florence, where my husband, Luca Passaleva, is from. The conversation briefly left politics when someone suggested that I name my child Silvio, after Berlusconi, the Italian Prime Minister at the time.

"No," a friend said, "Silvio Passaleva sounds terrible."

"Actually," Luca responded, "his last name will be McPhee."

Silence in a room of Italians is a rare event, but Luca's rather exotic announcement left the diners wordless for several seconds. Finally, another friend blurted out, "McPhee, McPhee, what the hell does McPhee have to do with anything?" I could think of no response to his question. All I could do was ask myself, "Yeah, what the hell does McPhee have to do with anything?"

I have been asked the same question, in milder tones, many times since that evening, and I am still not sure how to answer it. What I do know is that every time I am asked why I gave my son my name, my gut response is deep embarrassment at my own brazenness. Like Hester Prynne's A, my name becomes a symbol of shame. For a man, passing on his name is expected, traditional, unnoteworthy. For a woman to do so is a radical act, a gesture of defiance, an invitation to attack. It is also illegal for a married woman to pass on her name without a court order in some countries, like Italy. Even here, as recently as 1996, a judge in Missouri ordered a divorced woman and her son to use the father's surname. Another judge justified a similar ruling, saying, "It's a philosophical matter."

Surnames first became an issue for me during my parents' divorce, when I was 8 years old. My mother resumed using her "maiden" name, introducing me to the idea that power could be found in a name. I have since learned the origins of the male monopoly on names in our culture. In the 11th century, the Normans invaded England and established a system for recording paternal surnames. By the 14th century, it was the way property was tracked. And by the time the English colonists came to America, the custom had become entrenched as a method of determining the ownership of property—which included wives.

By the time I got to college, I was convinced that feminism had pretty much eradicated the traditional patriarchal practice of exclusively passing on the male name. But since graduation, one female friend after another has slipped on a new name. Mrs. Fred E. Green, for example, explains away her choice with, "My name was so colorless." Other friends say they are happy to get the chance to start over with a new name. (In fact, more than three-quarters of American women still take their husbands' names.) And when it comes to the children, the most frequent response is, "His name means so much more to him." Though names can mean a lot to women, girls learn very early that they will probably lose their names when they marry. If you know you will lose something, you do not get very attached to it. Thus, the connection for women between name and identity becomes insignificant and unimportant. I return to the question at the Florentine dinner party, which I am unable to answer, and I feel as if I were 5 years old again, when I would ask myself over and over, "Why am I me?"

Giving my son my name has invited all sorts of weird accusations: "He'll have trouble in school." "He's sure to be gay." "You're undetermining the integrity of the family." "You're demeaning the role of the father." "You're doing it because your father is John McPhee, a famous writer." And some people are awestruck by my powers of manipulation: "How did you finagle that one?" "Luca must be a saint." Or, most commonly, "Luca must be a pushover." And many people insist that my name is not my own to give: "It's your father's name anyway." Unlike Hester Prynne, I have always envied her A because that letter gave her a solid identity. In many ways it was horrible for her, but it was acknowledged by all to be hers, and, inasmuch as that was true, it was a source of empowerment and even pride.

On May 29, 1996, Tommaso McPhee was born. The act of naming my son after myself did something astonishing for me. By claiming my name as mine and passing it on, I have experienced something that I was not expecting, something that is at the heart of self-confidence and a strong identity—pride in myself. I know that my name is mine and that no cultural practice will take it away. I know that I can hand it on to my children and that is a wonderfully powerful sensation. Why did I give my son my name? I suppose that judge was right—it's a philosophical matter.

TOPIC FOR DISCUSSION AND WRITING

Jenny McPhee's decision to give her son her surname rather than his father's shocked many. After considering your reaction to this break with tradition, write a letter to the editor of *The New York Times Magazine* (the paper in which the essay first appeared) or to the writer, Jenny McPhee, expressing your reaction to her decision.

Before choosing your audience—the readers of *The New York Times Magazine* or the author herself—consider how these two letters would differ from one another on the basis of the audience you choose. (See Audience and Purpose in Chapter 1, and Hidden Assumptions—Audience Awareness in Chapter 3.)

Same-Sex Marriage

On June 28, 1969 at the Stonewall Inn, a gay bar in New York's Greenwich Village, the police began one of their routine raids, but this time, its patrons fought back. Thus began the gay liberation movement. Before

Stonewall, homosexuality was considered a crime by government, a mental illness by the medical establishment, and a sin by all religions. Now, thirty years after Stonewall, while the government no longer arrests homosexuals (it is still however wrestling with the issue of gays in the military as its "don't ask, don't tell" policy is debated in the courts), and the medical establishment sees homosexuality as a sexual preference, religious groups, for the most part, continue to find homosexuality objectionable.

In 1997, to express their objections, the Christian Coalition voted to boycott any films or television shows produced by Disney Studios as well as Disney's amusement parks in protest against the Disney-produced television comedy, *Ellen*, which featured an episode in which the star, Ellen DeGeneres, a lesbian, "came out" as a gay woman on the show. We can then imagine this group's reaction to one of the highest priority items on the political agenda of gay activists—same-sex marriage.

A 1996 court ruling in Hawaii suggested that same sex marriage might one day become a reality, but in 1998 Hawaii's voters passed a constitutional amendment banning same-sex unions. However, a 1999 Vermont Supreme Court decision ruled that homosexual couples deserve the same legal protections as heterosexual couples. As a result of that decision, Vermont's legislature enacted a civil union law that went into effect on July 1, 2000, granting all the rights and responsibilities of marriage to gays and lesbians. The statute also includes, however, a provision holding that marriage remains a union between a man and a woman. Gay rights activists compare their battle for same-sex marriage to the fight for interracial marriage which lasted nearly two decades—from the first state Supreme Court ruling in 1948 in California favoring interracial unions until 1967 when the U.S. Supreme Court struck down states' prohibitions of them.

Why Get Married?

Carol Ostrom

Seattle Times reporter Carol Ostrom provides an overview of the institution of marriage, its advantages and disadvantages.

Sitting in the hard pews in a church on Capitol Hill, the men and women laugh at the story the speaker is telling and exchange knowing looks. This story is funny, but it hurts, too.

She and her intended have traveled to Boston, the speaker tells the crowd, to declare their intentions to her lover's family. Facing a noisy roomful of cigarette-smoking, highball-swigging Irish Catholic extroverts, they clear their throats and begin.

"We're going to have a commitment ceremony!" one of them announces to the family.

"What?" "What did she say?" "What does that mean?" the relatives murmur, turning to each other.

"Commitment! Commitment!" the couple yell back.

"Commitment??? Aunt Lucy was committed!" comes an alarmed voice from the back, and suddenly, it's no time for semantics.

"Married!" the couple shouts, surrendering. "We're going to get married!"

"Ohhhhhhh," the crowd sighs back in relief. "Yeahhhhh!"

And, in a scene that is familiar to families from the shacks of Ecuador to the mansions of Bellevue, the relatives toast the happy couple—in this case, Seattle City Councilwoman Tina Podlodowski and her female partner, Chelle Mileur.

In this case, "married" was the magic word that provided an instant picture, a shorthand for love and commitment and sharing—a way for their families and others to understand how they felt about each other and how they wanted to live.

Addressing the primarily gay and lesbian audience attending a pro-marriage forum in the church, Podlodowski summed up her story:

"It's a word that's been used for 5,000 years—and it clicks!"

SUPPORT FOR MARRIAGE

Joining religious activists, political conservatives and social scientists, marriage's latest and loudest advocates come from a group that hasn't always promoted mainstream conventions.

Now they've added their voices to the chorus heralding marriage as an undervalued and unappreciated institution, one of society's great bargains. Straight folks, many gays and lesbians say, don't know how good they've got it.

Pundits tout marriage as a tradition worthy of a new look—a civilized custom that benefits both individuals and society, like literary salons or neighbors becoming friends.

But can marriage ratchet society into goodness two by two? Does it play a major part in our happiness?

One second-time-bride-to-be, quoting Samuel Johnson, the sharp-tongued 18th-century British social critic and wit, summed up the dilemma of marriage neatly, if wryly: "It's the triumph of hope over experience."

WHAT'S SO HOT ABOUT MARRIAGE?

Hope's part of the lure of marriage, for sure. "Happily ever after," researchers show, is a place many of us say we long to be.

But marriage has other, more tangible benefits, conferred on the institution because of "society's enormous stake in the outcome and the offspring of that marriage," says Bruce Hafen, law professor and provost of Brigham Young University.

A century ago, the U.S. Supreme Court called marriage "the foundation of the family and society, without which there would be neither civilization nor progress."

More recently, arguments have raged about the purpose of marriage. If it's for procreation, the argument goes, why should people who can't have children marry? If it's for love, why not let same-sex couples marry? If it's for the good of society, how about penalties for singleness?

But most people don't marry for societal good—they marry because there's something in it for them, individually.

And there is. Legal marriage comes with a package of goodies:

- Married couples take it for granted that they would be able to visit each other in the hospital or help make critical-care decisions for their spouse, notes Demian, a West Seattle gay man who has lived with his "life partner" for 15 years.

- Married people are protected from having to testify in court against their spouse; one can sue for loss of companionship if the other is injured or killed through negligence.

- Spouses are, in many companies, entitled to health insurance.

- If one spouse dies, the other has rights to inheritance and pension benefits as well as a presumed right to continue custody of their adopted or birth children. The surviving spouse also has the right to make burial decisions.

- Those from different countries who marry have immigration rights.

- And in case of a breakup, divorce laws may offer legal protection to the the less financially powerful spouse.

Some—but not all—of the benefits of marriage can be arranged for cohabiting partners with the help of a good lawyer, a durable power of attorney and a will. But that can take money and savvy, tools not possessed by all partners.

And many cohabiting couples have heard "horror stories," like the one about Sharon Kowalski, a Minnesota lesbian whose father stepped in after she was brain-damaged in an accident, separating her from her partner of four years. Eight years later, a court appointed her partner, Karen Thompson, to be her guardian. "Karen and Sharon are a family of affinity, which ought to be accorded respect," the judges wrote.

Married spouses likely never would have faced that battle.

MARRIAGE AND LONGEVITY

Research also shows that married people have more and better sex than singles—except for cohabiting couples. And they have better health, more money and longer life than any other group, says University of Chicago demographer Linda Waite.

How does marriage help people live longer?

First, married people tend to engage in fewer risky behaviors, including drinking and driving, substance abuse, fighting and accidents.

Second, marriage increases income and assets, which can be used to buy better medical care, diet and safer surroundings.

Third, marriage provides individuals with a network of support.

Some argue that it isn't that marriage produces these benefits. It's that women and men who have a brain bigger than a rutabaga's tend not to select drinking, drugging, fast-driving, argumentative, destitute loners as mates.

That may be, Waite says, but researchers still believe marriage itself works these wonders.

How might marriage cause a man to make more money? He becomes more productive, so the theory goes, because he has more incentive, because he's reduced negative health behavior such as drinking, or perhaps because his wife has taken over household tasks, giving him more time and energy for work.

Other benefits are harder to quantify.

Marriage traditionally has been seen as "civilizing" men. In this view, wandering, risk-taking wild men start morphing into tender homebodies when the band slips onto the finger.

The public vows, the family encouragement, the legal ties—all may help keep a couple together, learning to work out their differences, say social scientists.

For some, the most important benefit of marriage is the validation they believe society accords married couples.

It was that validation, in part, that led three couples to challenge Hawaii's law prohibiting same-sex marriages. That challenge has been upheld by the Hawaii Supreme Court, which is expected to rule again on the issue in the future.

Even if the court rules for same-sex marriage, a bill passed overwhelmingly earlier this month by the U.S. House would allow states to refuse to recognize same-sex marriages performed in other states. The bill defines marriage as a union between a man and a woman—period.

The battle for the right of same-sex couples to marry, says Lyle Rudensey, a research scientist who has been with partner Bob Allen for 15 years, "is less about rights and more about the respect that society would accord us."

Allen, a draftsman at an engineering firm, says his relationship with Rudensey has as much value as a heterosexual marriage, "and in fact, it's lasted longer than many," he adds.

"I refer to Lyle as my husband," Allen says. To him, the word simply seems the best to describe their relationship.

So marriage brings more money, longer life, better health, more satisfying sex and respect, to boot? Too good to be true, you say?

There are clues that marriage isn't a guaranteed ticket to bliss:

- There's that shelf of books in every bookstore—"Tough Marriage: How to Make a Difficult Relationship Work," say, or "Intimate Terrorism: The Deterioration of Erotic Life."

- There's that omnipresent, silently mocking statistic that four of every 10 new marriages will end in divorce.

- There's some evidence, albeit contested, suggesting that married women may be more likely to be mentally unhealthy than singles.

- While on average married women are financially better off than single women, for those who sacrifice career for family, marriage can have an economic down side, Waite notes. And if they're divorced or widowed, their income declines drastically.

- Linking your finances to another person can be risky—one spouse's credit can be ruined by a spouse's personal or business debts.

In addition, some couples have found that marriage can be a bad deal financially when one spouse has a catastrophic illness; sometimes, the only way they can keep the family home or savings is to divorce. That point is not lost on marriage advocates in the gay community, where the costs of AIDS are well known.

And, notes tax attorney Mark Bohe, for most middle-income, dual-career couples tying the knot means taking a financial hit. In the past, when the hit was even worse, Bohe says, some couples divorced on Dec. 31 and used their tax savings for a romantic vacation, where they remarried.

Others have philosophical problems with marriage.

Anne Slater of Radical Women supports the right of same-sex couples to choose marriage. But that doesn't mean she's enthusiastic about it.

Marriage, says Slater, a lesbian, "is one of the building blocks of patriarchy and the private property system. It's reactionary and sexist. It needs to be replaced by voluntary family groupings based on preference, desire and compatibility."

Then there are those like social activist Barbara Dority and environmental scientist Jim Rybock, who married in 1988 "under protest."

A few lines from their "marriage contract" (subtitled "Agreement to Have and Not to Hold"):

"We reject the concept of marriage as it presently exists in this society . . . We believe it is grossly inappropriate and intrusive for government to set the terms for the intimate relationships of its citizens."

Because Rybock's earnings were much higher than Dority's, the typical marriage penalty was reversed: tax law penalized them for not being married. And while Dority's work didn't provide health insurance, Rybock's employer offered benefits to spouses. So the two decided to make their four-year cohabitation legal—protesting every step of the way.

SEX, LIES AND PLUMBING

Historically, the roles in marriage have been rigid: plumbing, wiring, size and the fact of pregnancy had a lot to say about who did what in marriage.

In the early 1900s, cynic Ambrose Bierce defined marriage thus: "The state or condition of a community consisting of a master, a mistress and two slaves, making in all two."

In some traditional cultures, people married only if there were children, notes David Murray, a social anthropologist.

Before the Industrial Revolution, marriage was considered too important to be left to the whims of the young, according to Charles Hill, professor of psychology at Whittier College. Instead, marriages were arranged by parents based on political and economic considerations.

The Industrial Revolution changed much of that. To explain and justify marital choice, says Hill, romantic ideology was adopted.

These days, we think marriage is about individual satisfaction, says Murray, but it's still very much about politics and economics—and becoming part of a community.

We don't hope to receive tuition or a kidney from a neighbor or a colleague, but we do from relatives—and those who are married have twice as many, says Murray. Marriage, he says, links each individual to a "social security network of obligated kin."

For example: more than one fourth of new home purchases depend on gifts from parents or in-laws.

Those who focus more closely on individuals see that network slightly differently. Judith Wallerstein, author of *The Good Marriage,* says family represents acceptance, warmth and a sense of being loved and belonging.

In a time of increasing isolation, those aspects of marriage become more important to us, she theorized in *Mother Jones* magazine last year. Indeed, she says, marriage has become "the central relationship of adulthood."

Lynn Darling, writing in the May Esquire about her 10-year marriage, calls marriage a mystery.

One moment furious at marriage "for the way it buries love in the sludge of who takes out the trash," she celebrates the "poetry of dailiness" in the next.

"I see the ways my husband saved me, the ways I saved him," Darling writes. "There is still pain in the phantom limbs lost in the making of this marriage, but in that moment the loss seems a manageable part of the trade. I see only the courage and kindness that marriage elicits, not the cost, and it seems to me that it gives us our only chance to be heroes."

TOPICS FOR DISCUSSION AND WRITING

1. List the advantages and disadvantages of marriage, those enumerated by Ostrom and any others you can think of.

2. Who benefits more from marriage—men or women? Or do they benefit equally? Defend your answer with specifics. The list you created in response to the question above may come in handy here.

3. What benefits would same-sex marriage make available to gay men and women that are not available to them without that legal sanction? You may find your list helpful here as well.

4. What do you notice about the writing style of this piece? Why has the author chosen this style? What effect does the style have upon you as a reader?

Let Gays Marry

Andrew Sullivan

Using *Newsweek's* My Turn column as his forum, Sullivan, a senior editor at *The New Republic* and a gay man who is HIV positive, argues that the fight for gay marriage is a "deeply conservative cause."

"A state cannot deem a class of persons a stranger to its laws," declared the Supreme Court last week. It was a monumental statement. Gay men and lesbians, the conservative court said, are no longer strangers in America. They are citizens, entitled, like everyone else, to equal protection—no special rights, but simple equality.

For the first time in Supreme Court history, gay men and women were seen not as some powerful lobby trying to subvert America, but as the people we truly are—the sons and daughters of countless mothers and fathers, with all the weaknesses and strengths and hopes of everybody else. And what we seek is not some special place in America but merely to be a full and equal part of America, to give back to our society without being forced to lie or hide or live as second-class citizens.

That is why marriage is so central to our hopes. People ask us why we want the right to marry, but the answer is obvious. It's the same reason anyone wants the right to marry. At some point in our lives, some of us are lucky enough to meet the person we truly love. And we want to commit to that person in front of our family and country for the rest of our lives. It's the most simple, the most natural, the most human instinct in the world. How could anyone seek to oppose that?

Yes, at first blush, it seems like a radical proposal, but, when you think about it some more, it's actually the opposite. Throughout American history, to be sure, marriage has been between a man and a woman, and in many ways our society is built upon that institution. But none of that need change in the slightest. After all, no one is seeking to take away anybody's right to marry, and no one is seeking to force any church to change any doctrine in any way. Particular religious arguments against same-sex marriage are rightly debated within the churches and faiths themselves. That is not the issue here: there is a separation between church and state in this country. We are only asking that when the government gives out civil marriage licenses, those of us who are gay should be treated like anybody else.

Of course, some argue that marriage is by definition between a man and a woman. But for centuries, marriage was by definition a contract in which the wife was her husband's legal property. And we changed that. For centuries marriage was by definition between two people of the same race. And we changed that. We changed these things because we recognized that human dignity is the same whether you are a man or a woman, black or white. And no one has any more of a choice to be gay than to be black or white or male or female.

Some say that marriage is only about raising children, but we let childless heterosexual couples be married (Bob and Elizabeth Dole, Pat and Shelley

Buchanan, for instance). Why should gay couples be treated differently? Others fear that there is no logical difference between allowing same-sex marriage and sanctioning polygamy and other horrors. But the issue of whether to sanction multiple spouses (gay or straight) is completely separate from whether, in the existing institution between two unrelated adults, the government should discriminate between its citizens.

This is, in fact, if only Bill Bennett could see it, a deeply conservative cause. It seeks to change no one else's rights or marriages in any way. It seeks merely to promote monogamy, fidelity and the disciplines of family life among people who have long been cast to the margins of society. And what could be a more conservative project than that? Why indeed would any conservative seek to oppose those very family values for gay people that he or she supports for everybody else? Except of course, to make gay men and lesbians strangers in their own country, to forbid them ever to come home.

TOPICS FOR DISCUSSION WRITING

1. What concession does Sullivan grant to forces opposed to same-sex marriage? (See Refutation and Concession in Chapter 4.)

2. Sullivan bases his argument, in part, on reasoning by analogy. Identify these analogies and evaluate their effectiveness. (See False Analogy in Chapter 6.)

3. Why does Sullivan see same-sex marriage as "a deeply conservative cause"?

4. What position has your state taken on same-sex marriage? Write a paper on this position and your reaction to it. (See How to Conduct Your Research in Chapter 9.)

Leave Marriage Alone

William Bennett

Conservative William Bennett, a former Secretary of Education under George Bush and editor of *The Book of Virtues,* disagreed vehemently with Sullivan's piece published in *Newsweek* and used the same venue, *Newsweek's* My Turn column, to express his disagreement and his belief that same-sex unions will "stretch [the definition of marriage] almost beyond recognition."

There are at least two key issues that divide proponents and opponents of same-sex marriage. The first is whether legally recognizing same-sex unions would strengthen or weaken the institution. The second has to do with the basic understanding of marriage itself.

The advocates of same-sex marriage say that they seek to strengthen and celebrate marriage. That may be what some intend. But I am certain that it will not be the reality. Consider: the legal union of same-sex couples would shatter the conventional definition of marriage, change the rules which govern behavior, endorse practices which are completely antithetical to the tenets of all of the world's major religions, send conflicting signals about marriage and sexuality, particularly to the young, and obscure marriage's enormously consequential function—procreation and child rearing.

Broadening the definition of marriage to include same-sex unions would stretch it almost beyond recognition—and new attempts to expand the definition still further would surely follow. On what principled ground can Andrew Sullivan exclude others who most desperately want what he wants, legal recognition and social acceptance? Why on earth would Sullivan exclude from marriage a bisexual who wants to marry two other people? After all, exclusion would be a denial of that person's sexuality. The same holds true of a father and daughter who want to marry. Or two sisters. Or men who want (consensual) polygamous arrangements. Sullivan may think some of these arrangements are unwise. But having employed sexual relativism in his own defense, he has effectively lost the capacity to draw any lines and make moral distinctions.

Forsaking all others is an essential component of marriage. Obviously it is not always honored in practice. But it is the ideal to which we rightly aspire, and in most marriages the ideal is in fact the norm. Many advocates of same-sex marriage simply do not share this ideal; promiscuity among homosexual males is well known. Sullivan himself has written that gay male relationships are served by the "openness of the contract" and the homosexuals should resist allowing their "varied and complicated lives" to be flattened into a "single, moralistic model." But that "single, moralistic model" has served society exceedingly well. The burden of proof ought to be on those who propose untested arrangements for our most important institution.

A second key difference I have with Sullivan goes to the very heart of marriage itself. I believe that marriage is not an arbitrary construct which can be redefined simply by those who lay claim to it. It is an honorable estate, instituted of God and built on moral, religious, sexual and human realities. Marriage is based on a natural teleology, on the different, complementary nature of men and women and how they refine, support, encourage and complete one another. It is the institution through which we propagate, nurture, educate and sustain our species.

That we have to engage in this debate at all is an indication of how steep our moral slide has been. Worse, those who defend the traditional understanding of marriage are routinely referred to (though not to my knowledge by Sullivan) as "homophobes," "gay-bashers," "intolerant" and "bigoted." Can one defend an honorable, 4,000-year-old tradition and not be called these names?

This is a large, tolerant, diverse country. In America people are free to do as they wish, within broad parameters. It is also a country in sore need of shoring up some of its most crucial institutions: marriage and the family, schools, neighborhoods, communities. But marriage and family are the greatest of these. That is why they are elevated and revered. We should keep them so.

TOPIC FOR DISCUSSION AND WRITING

William Bennett believes that "broadening the definition of marriage to include same-sex unions would stretch it almost beyond recognition—and [that] new attempts to expand the definition still further would surely follow." Among these "new attempts" he suggests group marriages, polygamy and incest. Are Bennett's fears realistic or is he guilty of slippery slope reasoning? Support your answer. (See Slippery Slope in Chapter 6.) Note that the word *marriage* is one of the terms we ask you to define in Writing Assignment 13 on page 133.)

Why Marry?

Frank Browning

Browning, a gay man, is against same-sex marriage, but his reasons are quite different from William Bennet's

Thursday morning, and it's my turn to move our cars for street cleaning. Gene has already bribed the cats into silence with food.

So begins the day here in Windsor Terrace, a quiet Brooklyn neighborhood populated by many kinds of families: a lesbian couple next door—and beyond them an Italian widow who rents out rooms, an Irish-American grandmother who shares her house with her daughter's family, the multigenerational Korean family that owns the corner grocery.

We gay couples, of course, are not considered families under the law, a fact that the bishops and Buchananites insist will never change and that many gay activists have identified as America's next great civil rights struggle. Indeed, a court case in Hawaii may soon lead to that state's recognition of same-sex marriage.

I suppose it's a good thing for gay adults to be offered the basic nuptial rights afforded to others. We call that equal treatment before the law. But I'm not sure the marriage contract is such a good plan for us.

The trouble with gay marriage is not its recognition of our "unnatural unions." The problem is with the shape of marriage itself. What we might be better off seeking is civic and legal support for different kinds of families that can address the emotional, physical and financial obligations of contemporary life. By rushing to embrace the standard marriage contract, we could stifle one of the richest and most creative laboratories of family experience.

We gay folk tend to organize our lives more like extended families than nuclear ones. We may love our mates one at a time, but our "primary families" are often our ex-lovers and our ex-lovers' ex-lovers.

The writer Edmund White noticed this about gay male life 20 years ago; he called it the "banyan tree" phenomenon, after the tree whose branches send off shoots that take root to form new trunks. Nowhere has the banyan-tree family proved stronger than in AIDS care, where often a large group of people—ex-mates and their friends and lovers—tend the sick and maintain the final watch.

Modern marriage, by comparison, tends to isolate couples from their larger families and sometimes from friends—especially if they are ex-lovers. And a nuclear family with working parents has often proved less than ideal in coping with daily stresses or serious illness.

The marriage model could prove especially problematic for rearing children. In a gay family, there are often three parents—a lesbian couple, say, and the biological father. Sometimes, four or five adults are committed to nurturing the children. In such cases, a marriage between two might bring second-class status to the rest of the extended family and diminish their parental roles.

(Those who think that only a father and mother can successfully raise a child should visit Italy, Japan, Greece, Thailand or American family archives, which show that before World War II, grandparents, aunts, uncles and older siblings had vital child rearing roles.)

Precisely because homosexuals have resided outside the law, they have invented family forms that respond to late twentieth-century needs, while formulating social and moral codes that provide love, freedom and fidelity (if not always monogamy).

All I need do is look up and down Windsor Terrace to see that the family includes all sorts of relationships and obligations.

Each of us, hetero or homo, has a stake in nurturing a diverse landscape of families. Only a minority of us have marriages like Donna Reed's or Harriet Nelson's. Even Pat Buchanan knows that.

TOPICS FOR DISCUSSION AND WRITING

1. What advantages does Frank Browning see gay and lesbian relationships having over the traditional marriage? Could you add to this list? Are their disadvantages to homosexual relationships he fails to mention?

2. How might Andrew Sullivan respond to Browning's position? What would William Bennett say?

Romance and Marriage—Concluding Topics

1. As this chapter and Chapter 12—Sexual Harassment—make clear, sexual attitudes and behaviors have changed significantly in the last half of the twentieth century. Social critics see many of these changes leading to greater conflict and antagonism between men and women. As a class, update any changes in the trends or behaviors discussed in Chapters 12 and 13, and then write your own essay on the impact of these trends on relationships between men and women.

2. Review the four essays in Same-Sex Marriage and create a master list of premises in favor of same-sex marriage and a list of premises against such unions. (Feel free to paraphrase or to use quotations—whichever is easier.) Add any additional premises for either side that you would like to include. After carefully evaluating both sides of the argument, write an argument which states your position on this issue. Include in your argument the rhetorical features of counterargument, concession, refutation and Rogerian strategy. (See Premises and Conclusions in Chapter 3, and A Dialectical Approach to Argument in Chapter 4.)

CHAPTER 14

Language and Meaning

In a departure from the previous four sections which focus on argument and issues, this section asks you to think critically about language, to become more aware of how it is used and how you can use it more effectively. The readings in this section do not lend themselves to debate and argument but to analysis and consideration of the impact of language on culture and on the individual. Thus the topics, as you will see, offer more opportunities for personal and literary responses.

In Chapter 5, we discuss the slippery nature of language, noting that a word's meaning is not fixed but fluid, dependent on the speaker or writer, the listener or reader, the context, the situation, and the community and culture in which the exchange takes place. In this section we will look more closely at these factors which influence and reveal meaning. The selections ask us to look beyond the denotative level of language, to explore language in its social, cultural, and poetic complexity.

Postmodern theories of language and literature focus on the role the reader plays in determining meaning. Postmodern novelist Kurt Vonnegut comments on this phenomenon in an interview:

> One thing we used to talk about—when I was out in Iowa [teaching at the University of Iowa Writers Workshop and beginning *Slaughterhouse Five*]—was that the limiting factor is the reader. No other art requires the audience to be a performer. You have to count on the reader's being a good performer, and may write music which he absolutely can't perform—in which case it's a bust.

This view of the reader makes reading an active rather than a passive activity. The first selection, "The Voice You Hear When You Read Silently," a poem by Thomas Lux, highlights the reader's role in creating the meaning of any text he reads. Author Elizabeth Strout dramatizes this role in an excerpt from her novel, *Amy and Isabelle*. Sven Birkerts in his essay, "The Shadow Life of Reading," expands on this theme and explores the role memory plays in the act of reading.

Technology increases the reader's power, giving him the ability to enter into a writer's text. In "The End of Books," novelist Robert Coover describes hypertext in which the computer allows the reader to participate in the shaping of a text, to reorder the events in the narrative should he choose to do so. Two writers, literary critic Michiko Kakutani in "Never-Ending Saga" and on-line editor Laura Miller in "www.claptrap.com" reject this power, preferring traditional books to the hyperfiction of computers. But online publishing and the creation of e-books could one day replace traditional books.

There is no more revealing an artifact of a culture than its language. Despite political upheaval, changes in government, natural disasters, war and famine, language remains. And while language reveals culture, it also determines culture. Based on his experience as a journalist living in Beijing, Nicholas Kristof explores this connection between language and culture in "Chinese Relations." Michael Specter does much the same thing with Russian language and culture in "The Rich Idioms of Russian." Margalit Fox in "Dialects" looks at the social stigma attached to certain dialects. In "The Quare Gene," Tony Earley, who was at times socially stigmatized because of his speech, describes the Appalachian dialect of his North Carolina family, revealing not only culture but history as well. In "Today's Kids Are, Like, Killing the English Language. Yeah, Right," Kirk Johnson finds cultural significance in the slang of his two preteen sons. Linguist Geoff Nunberg highlights the role that politics plays in distinguishing a language from a dialect in "Languages Are Political Constructions."

Finally, we focus on the role poetic or figurative language plays in shaping meaning. We begin, appropriately enough, with "Simile," a poem by Rosanna Warren. We then turn our attention to metaphor, the foundation of figurative language. In fact, linguist George Lakoff and philosopher Mark Johnson in *Metaphors We Live By* believe that metaphor is not only "pervasive in everyday life" but provides the very foundation of our "conceptual system." In her book, *The Argument Culture,* sociolinguist Deborah Tannen agrees with her colleagues about the significance of metaphor, focusing on one metaphor in particular as pervasive and problematic. And Stephen Johnson in "Metaphor Monopoly" points out the role that metaphor plays in computer programs.

Analogies and symbols are related to metaphor, and we explore the use of analogy in Barbara Ehrenreich's "Getting Off Easy in Tobacco Land" and in Judith Jarvis Thomson's "In Defense of Abortion." In "Symbolism," British writer David Lodge explains symbols by looking closely at a passage from D. H. Lawrence's *Sons and Lovers*. We then turn from literature to the marketplace to study the use of symbols in several contemporary magazine ads. Finally we look at the use of figurative language in a short story, "Greasy Lake" by T. Coraghessan Boyle.

The Reader

At one time the meaning of a text was assumed to be fixed and singular—there was a particular meaning, a specific meaning residing in the text, put there by the author. Now we think of reading as an act of interpretation, one involving the author and the reader, with each reader bringing his own background and experiences to the text. Such a view of reading means that we can no longer assume that a particular interpretation is the only one possible. In fact, given the role that experience and education play in reading, we can assume that the book a person reads at eighteen as a college freshman is not the same book one reads at thirty as a newly married professional. As our experiences and knowledge expand, so do the possibilities for interpretation. Novelist and essayist Virginia Woolf comments on this phenomenon in her reading of *Hamlet:* "To write down one's impressions of *Hamlet* as one reads it year after year would be virtually to record one's own autobiography for as we know more of life, so Shakespeare comments upon what we know."

The worldview and experiences of the individual reader are not the only factors to influence interpretation; the preoccupations of a particular culture and time also play an important role. Shakespeare's *King Lear,* written in the seventeenth century, is the story of an aging king who divides his kingdom among his three daughters, a legacy which leads to alienation from his daughters and bitter rivalries between them. Rewritten in our time by Jane Smiley in her novel *A Thousand Acres,* Lear is transformed into an Iowa farmer still with three daughters among whom he divides his kingdom (a farm), but now incest lies at the heart of this troubled family. In a recent film based on Shakespeare's *Romeo and Juliet,* the lovers belong not to rival families in Padua but to rival gangs in Los Angeles. Each generation retells its culture's myths in its own terms.

Reviewing a new biography of the poet John Keats in the *New York Times Book Review,* Morris Dickstein points out that although three excellent biographies of Keats were published in the 1960s,

> biographies, like translations, are rarely provisioned to last forever, for they reflect the world of their authors as much as their subjects. Keats's Victorian admirers saw him as the ultimate esthete, a delicate pale flower nipped in the bud by harsh critics. Modern readers uncovered a more robust and manly Keats. With the return to historical criticism, scholars were drawn to Keats's neglected links to the politics and history of his times.

The concerns and preoccupations of a particular period are the lens through which an artist and his work are viewed and judged. In his book

The Kiss of Lamourette, historian Robert Darnton comments on the role time and culture play in determining how we interpret what we read.

> Reading has a history. It was not always and everywhere the same. We may think of it as a straightforward process of lifting information from a page; but if we considered it further, we would agree that information must be sifted, sorted, and interpreted. Interpretive schemes belong to cultural configurations, which have varied enormously over time. As our ancestors lived in different mental worlds, they must have read differently, and the history of reading could be as complex as the history of thinking.

In 1898, a hundred years before the role of the reader became the foundation of current literary theory, Norwegian playwright and poet Henrik Ibsen (1828–1906) commented on this phenomenon in a speech he gave to the Norwegian League for Women's Rights.

> I am not a member of the Women's Rights League. Whatever I have written has been without any conscious thought of making propaganda. I have been more the poet and less the social philosopher than people seem generally inclined to believe. . . . To me it [sexism] has seemed a problem of mankind in general. And if you read my books carefully you will understand this. Of course it is incidentally desirable to solve the problem of women; but that has not been my whole object. My task has been the description of humanity. To be sure, whenever such a description is felt to be reasonably true, *the reader will read his own feelings and sentiments into the work of the poet. These are then attributed to the poet; but incorrectly so. Every reader remolds the work beautifully and neatly, each according to his own personality. Not only those who write but also those who read are poets. They are collaborators.* [italics added]

Reading this passage in our time, we may be inclined to criticize Ibsen's phrase, "the problem of women" (were women the problem?), but on the basis of the following poem, we believe that poet Thomas Lux would agree with Ibsen that writers and readers are "collaborators," (See Language: An Abstract System of Symbols in Chapter 5.)

The Voice You Hear When You Read Silently

Thomas Lux

In this poem from Lux's book, *New and Selected Poems: 1975–1995,* we see that readers, even when reading the same text, make it uniquely their own.

is not silent, it is a speaking-
out-loud voice in your head: it is spoken,
a voice is saying it

as you read. It's the writer's words,
of course, in a literary sense
his or her "voice" but the sound
of that voice is the sound of your voice.
Not the sound your friends know
or the sound of a tape played back
but your voice
caught in the dark cathedral
of your skull, your voice heard
by an internal ear informed by internal abstracts
and what you know by feeling,
having felt. It is your voice
saying, for example, the word "barn"
that the writer wrote
but the "barn" you say
is a barn you know or knew. The voice
in your head, speaking as you read,
never says anything neutrally—some people
hated the barn they knew,
some people love the barn they know
so you hear the word loaded
and a sensory constellation
is lit: horse-gnawed stalls,
hayloft, black heat tape wrapping
a water pipe, a slippery
spilled chirrr of oats from a split sack,
the bony, filthy haunches of cows . . .
And "barn" is only a noun—no verb
or subject has entered into the sentence yet!
The voice you hear when you read to yourself
is the clearest voice: you speak it
speaking to you.

TOPICS FOR DISCUSSION AND WRITING

1. What is the difference between the voice of the writer and the voice of the reader?

2. What is the significance of the exclamation mark at the end of the following lines?

   And "barn" is only a noun—no verb
   Or subject has entered into the sentence yet!

3. Find a poem in a poetry anthology (there will be several to choose

from in your campus library) or pick one of the eleven poems in this book (six by John Cotton, two by Sylvia Plath in Chapter 2, two on marriage in Chapter 13, and one introducing figurative language in this chapter) and choose a phrase from it, describing what that phrase suggests in the poem, how it contributes to the overall meaning. Then describe what that phrase suggests to you outside of the poem. What personal associations or significance do you attach to it?

Amy and Isabelle

Elizabeth Strout

The Amy and Isabelle of the title are a single mother and her teenage daughter living in a New England mill town in the sixties. When Amy, the daughter, corrects her mother's pronunciation of a famous poet's name—"It's Yeats, mom. Not Yeets"—the humiliated mother, Isabelle, determined to educate herself, visits the "Classics" section of a local bookstore and purchases *Hamlet*. These few pages from the novel describing Isabelle's reading of the play, dramatize a reader's engagement with a text.

Tucked into bed at night, the lamp throwing a yellow pool across her quilt and the paperback *Hamlet* propped up before her, Isabelle struggled with Shakespeare. The struggle was primarily physical, for her eyelids felt glued together; really, she could barely keep them open. She tried sitting up straighter in bed, and still she couldn't make it through the second page. It was remarkable how her eyes would just flip shut. When she felt sure that Amy was asleep, she got out of bed and went downstairs to the kitchen, where she sat at the table with a cup of tea, housecoat tucked around her, her foot with its terry-cloth slipper rocking up and down as she read the lines again and again.

It was hard. Very, very difficult stuff. She hadn't expected it would be this difficult, and she had to fight a sensation of panic. "Which he stood seiz'd of, to the conqueror: Against the which, a moity competent Was gaged by our King; which had returned To the inheritance of Fortinbras, Had he been vanquisher . . ." Now what was she to make of that? The kitchen was very quiet.

She sipped her tea and glanced at the window. Where the white curtains parted slightly she could see the blackness of the windowpane, and she got up to tug the curtains together. She was not used to being down here alone at this hour. She sat at the table again, sipped her tea, and skimmed over the lines in her book. "How weary, stale, flat & unprofitable Seem to me all the uses of this world!"

Well, look at that. She could understand that. Isabelle put her finger on the page; it was Hamlet himself speaking. "How weary, stale and flat . . . seem all the uses of the world." Lord knew there were times when she felt the world to be stale and weary, and the way Hamlet said it—it was very nicely put. She felt a genuine prick of delight, as though she and Hamlet were suddenly friends.

Feeling awake now, she whispered the words that began his speech. "O, that this too, too solid flesh would melt, Thaw . . ." (Fleetingly she pictured a rump steak not taken out of the freezer in time for Sunday dinner.) She pursed her lips, sipped some tea, began again. "O, that this too, too solid flesh would melt . . ." (Hamlet was a solid, muscular man, no doubt. In a moment she'd check the drawing of him on the cover of this book.) "Thaw and resolve itself into a dew."

So far, so good; Isabelle nodded. She had certainly experienced in her own lifetime the desire to melt, to disappear. She had never longed to become *dew,* but it was a lovely idea when you thought about it, which was exactly why, after all, she was reading Shakespeare. Because he was a genius and could express things in a way the rest of us would never have thought to. She felt immensely pleased by all of this and sat up straighter in her chair. "Or that the Everlasting had not fix'd His canon 'gainst self-slaughter! O God! O God!"

She read this over a few times. Because "Everlasting" was capitalized, she assumed that Shakespeare was referring to God here, and the business of the canon of self-slaughter must be a reference to suicide: Hamlet wanted to commit suicide but he knew God had a rule against this.

Well. Isabelle looked up. Gazing at her refrigerator she wondered if Hamlet wasn't being a little melodramatic. He was certainly distraught, and of course he had reason to be. But she had been distraught herself, God knew, any number of times, and had never thought she would like to kill herself. She peered back at the book. The tea was causing a pressure on her bladder, but she would try and finish the scene. Apparently Hamlet was very sorry his father was dead. His parents had loved each other . . . but within a month his mother got over it and married Hamlet's uncle.

Isabelle touched her lips; she could see how this would be disturbing. But that line "Frailty, thy name is woman!" She didn't like that particularly; and he was talking to his mother. For heaven's sake. What did Hamlet know about being a single parent, losing the man you loved? Isabelle frowned and pushed on the cuticle of her thumb. Hamlet was pretty offensive there, frankly. Certainly those women down in Boston who had just burned their undergarments on the front steps of some court building (Isabelle had seen this on the news) wouldn't take very kindly to such a line: Frailty, thy name is woman! Isabelle tugged on her robe. Honestly, it did rile her a bit. Men had a lot to learn. There was nothing frail about women. For heaven's sake, women had been keeping things going from time in memoriam. And there was nothing frail about *her.* Nothing frail about a woman who raised her daughter alone through bleak New England winters with the roof leaking, the car needing oil.

Isabelle had to close her eyes for just a moment; she was very tired. And, in fact, she did feel frail. That was the truth, if you really wanted to know it. She sat for a moment, running her finger along the edge of the book, and then she got up and washed out her teacup in the sink, glad enough to go to bed.

TOPIC FOR DISCUSSION AND WRITING

How are your experiences as a reader like or unlike Isabelle's experience of reading *Hamlet*?

The Shadow Life of Reading

Sven Birkerts

Sven Birkerts is the author of three books of literary criticism. This selection is taken from his book *The Gutenberg Elegies,* a collection of personal essays about reading and writing and the impact of technology on both.

Reading: the term is as generous and imprecise as "love." So often it means more than just the word-by-word deciphering of the printed page. Although that definition is primary, the word's etymology (from the Anglo-Saxon *raedan*, "to make out, to interpret") points us toward open sea. We use the verb freely to denote diverse and nonspecific involvements with texts. "What are you reading now?" does not usually mean, "What book are you staring at as I address you?" More often it means, "Are you reading your way through any particular book these days?" Implicit is the understanding that most serious reading is an exertion that is interrupted and resumed and which spans an indeterminate amount of time. But there may be a still more general import to the query, allowing me to reply, "I'm reading quite a lot of modern fiction just now."

This elasticity of definition results in a certain linguistic imprecision; since "reading" signifies so many different things, why don't we have a raft of differentiated signifiers, like northern tribes are said to have for snow? But it also suggests a basic truth about the act, which is that in many vital ways it is carried on—continued—when the reader is away from the page. Thus, something more than definitional slackness allows me to tell a friend that I'm reading *The Good Solider* as we walk down the street together. In some ways I *am* reading the novel as I walk, or nap, or drive to the store for milk. When I am away from the book it lives its shadow life, its afterlife, and *that*, as the believers have always insisted, is the only life that matters.

To say that we are really reading only while our eyes are in motion, only while we are directly under the spell of the language, voicing the words to ourselves is tantamount to saying that the writer is only writing while he or she is actively putting words onto paper. What writer would not scoff at such a literal, limiting conception? We might reach a more inclusive understanding of reading (and writing) if we think in terms of a continuum. At one end, the writer—the flesh-and-blood individual; at the other, the flesh-and-blood reader. In the center, the words, the turning pages, the decoding intelligence. Writing is the monumentally complex operation whereby experience, insight, and imagination are distilled into language; reading is the equally complex operation that disperses these distilled elements into another person's life. The act only begins with the active deciphering of the symbols. It ends (if reading can be said to end at all) where we cannot easily track it, where the atmospheres of self condense into thought and action.

The ways in which reading fulfills its aims beyond the immediate verbal encounter are necessarily mysterious. In exploring them we explore, though unscientifically, some of the operations of consciousness itself, especially those having to do with perception and memory. We have to ask not only how we translate a symbolic code, but also what is the effect upon us of the translation process and the translated content? How do we make use of our own experience when we engage a novel? To what extent are we present in the content of what we read? How do we store what we've read and how do we draw upon our reading memory over time? For it is one book we close the covers on today, and quite another after some months or years have passed. The words on the page don't change, but we do, and our "reading"—the experience we had over the duration of our encounter with the book—has the plasticity of any memory.

The eyes move, the hand turns the page, but already the shadow life begins. The fact that our beam of focus is necessarily narrow and purposeful, directed at the words right in font of us, raises questions about the working of the reading memory. For we have obviously stored what we have read in the preceding pages—what we are not just now reading is what allows us to understand what we *are* reading. Without this ground, our experience would be like that of Dr. Oliver Sacks's patient for whom every moment was freshly minted because he could not remember anything that had come before.

Our reading memory must be a specialized function of our larger memory system—specialized in that it operates entirely within the sphere of language and language-produced impressions. Contextual and supple, this memory is (has to be) open to continuous modification. Indeed, the process of reading a work of fiction could be described as the creation and constant successive modification of context.

When we are reading a novel we don't, obviously, recall the preceding sentences and paragraphs—not directly. In fact, we don't generally remember the language at all, unless it is dialogue. For reading is a conversion, a turning of codes into contents. What we hold on to are the impressions and images, the overall structures of sense, that we have derived from the words. Depending on the artistic power of the work and our susceptibility to it, we fashion and then sustain a more-or-less vivid reality image.

If we are told in the early pages or a story that it is a rainy night, and if the descriptions have set us inside a drafty old house, then we naturally inhabit that context. Having brought a setting to life in our imaginations, and having invested it with the tones and shadings that are uniquely our own, we sustain it—and trust the author not to frustrate us. This is part of the implicit writer-reader contract. We do not at every moment remember the setting afresh, any more than when we sit in a restaurant we keep recalling that we are in the middle of a city. We work hard to establish the image, and then we move our attention elsewhere; the image becomes part of the context through which we filter what we read. With certain works it may figure as an ever-present backdrop, With others we forget—only when the character stands up to bid his host goodnight do we recollect that the conversation took place in a cluttered kitchen. We may put what we know out of our thoughts (and we will if we are not called upon to use it), but we do not tend to modify what we have been given until we have reason to. This is true not just for setting, but for character and narrative situation as well.

Our reading memory in many ways echoes our experiential memory, but with one crucial difference: Experiential memory is of actual people, places, and things, whereas our reading memory is of those things as we have been induced to create them in our own minds. The latter, in other words, make use of the former, creating a peculiar sort of self-referentiality about our memories of what we've read. The picture is further complicated by the feedback loop. Our real experiences, and hence our memories, are also influenced by what we carry with us from books.

The shadow life of reading begins even while we have the book in hand—begins as soon as we move from the first sentence to the second and start up a memory context. The creation and perpetuation of this context requires that we make a cognitive space, or "open a file," as it were. Here is the power, the seductiveness of the act: When we read, we create and then occupy a hitherto nonexistent interior locale. Regardless of what happens on the page, the simple fact that we have cleared room for these peculiar figments we now preside over gives us a feeling of freedom and control. No less exalting is the sensation of inner and outer worlds coinciding, going on simultaneously, or very nearly so. The awareness is enforced regularly. I am reading, caught up in my book, when the phone rings. I am shocked back into the room, forced to contend with some piece of business. Then, a moment later, I am back. I have jumped from one circuit to another. The book is there, waiting, like one of those rare dreams that I half-awaken from and then reenter. Knowing that I have the option of return, this figurative space within the literal space I occupy, changes my relation to that literal space. I am still contained in the world, but I don't feel trapped in it. Reading creates an imaginary context which then becomes a place of rescue.

TOPICS FOR DISCUSSION AND WRITING

1. What is "the shadow life of reading"?
2. What is the difference between experiential memory and reading memory?
3. What ideas do this essay, the poem "The Voice You Hear When You Read Silently," and the excerpt from the novel, *Amy and Isabelle*, have in common?

The Reader, the Computer, and Hypertext

While Ibsen and Lux see reader and author as collaborators, the computer enables the reader to take precedence over the author in determining not only meaning but plot, structure and character as well. This form of collaboration can take place only on the electronic page—not in a bound text. Does this mean that novels printed in static book form will become a thing of the past? Postmodern novelist Robert Coover suggests this possibility in "The End of Books," an essay published in *The New York Times Review of Books* in 1992. Since that time, this article has become a touchstone for literary critics to trace the progress of hyperfiction as this non-sequential, participatory, on-line form of fiction is referred to. *New York Times* literary critic Michiko Kakutani in "Never-Ending Saga" and Internet magazine editor Laura Miller in "www.claptrap.com" both refer to the Coover piece. They do not, however, share Coover's enthusiasm for this new form of literature.

The End of Books

Robert Coover

Coover is an experimental writer and a teacher at Brown University where he initiated a creative writing workshop in hypertext fiction. He found that this course produced a greater volume of creative output than any of his more traditional writing workshops. As you read this essay, see if you can explain the students' productivity and enthusiasm.

In the real world nowadays, that is to say, in the world of video transmissions, cellular phones, fax machines, computer networks, and in particular out in the humming digitalized precincts of avant-garde computer hackers, cyberpunks and hyperspace freaks, you will often hear it said that the print medium is a doomed and outdated technology, a mere curiosity of bygone days destined soon to be consigned forever to those dusty unattended museums we now call libraries. Indeed, the very proliferation of books and other print-based media, so prevalent in this forest-harvesting, paper-wasting age, is held to be a sign of its feverish moribundity, the last futile gasp of a once vital form before it finally passes away forever, dead as God.

Which would mean of course that the novel, too, as we know it, has come to its end. Not that those announcing its demise are grieving. For all its passing charm, the traditional novel, which took center stage at the same time that industrial mercantile democracies arose—and which Hegel called "the epic of the middle-class world"—is perceived by its would-be executioners as the virulent carrier of the patriarchal, colonial, canonical, proprietary, hierarchical and authoritarian values of a past that is no longer with us.

Much of the novel's alleged power is embedded in the line, that compulsory author-directed movement from the beginning of a sentence to its period, from the top of the page to the bottom, from the first page to the last. Of course, through print's long history, there have been countless strategies to counter the line's power, from marginalia and footnotes to the creative innovations of novelists like Laurence Sterne, James Joyce, Raymond Queneau, Julio Cortazar, Italo Calvino and Milorad Pavic, not to exclude the form's father, Cervantes himself. But true freedom from the tyranny of the line is perceived as only really possible now at last with the advent of hypertext, written and read on the computer, where the line in fact does not exist unless one invents and implants it in the text.

"Hypertext" is not a system but a generic term, coined a quarter of a century ago by a computer populist named Ted Nelson to describe the writing done in the nonlinear or nonsequential space made possible by the computer. Moreover, unlike print text, hypertext provides multiple paths between text segments, now often called "lexias" in a borrowing from the pre-hypertextual but prescient Roland Barthes. With its webs of linked lexias, its networks of alternate routes (as opposed to print's fixed unidirectional page-turning) hypertext presents a radically divergent technology, interactive and polyvocal, favoring a plurality of discourses over definitive utterance and freeing the reader from domination by the author. Hypertext reader and writer are said to become co-learners or co-writers, as it were, fellow-travelers in the mapping and remapping of textual (and visual, kinetic and aural) components, not all of which are provided by what used to be called the author.

Though used at first primarily as a radically new teaching arena, by the mid–1980's hyperspace was drawing fiction writers into its intricate and infinitely expandable, infinitely alluring webs, its green-limned gardens of multiple forking paths, to allude to another author popular with hypertext buffs, Jorge Luis Borges.

Several systems support the configuring of this space for fiction writing. Some use simple randomized linking like the shuffling of cards, others (such as Guide and HyperCard) offer a kind of do-it-yourself basic tool set, and still others (more elaborate systems like Storyspace, which is currently the software of choice among fiction writers in this country, and Intermedia, developed at Brown University) provide a complete package of sophisticated structuring and navigational devices.

Although hypertext's champions often assail the arrogance of the novel, their own claims are hardly modest. You will often hear them proclaim, quite seriously, that there have been three great events in the history of literacy: the invention of writing, the invention of movable type and the invention of hypertext. As hyperspace-walker George P. Landow puts it in his recent book surveying the field, *Hypertext*: "Electronic text processing marks the next major shift in information technology after the development of the printed book. It promises (or threatens) to produce effects on our culture, particularly on our literature, education, criticism and scholarship, just as radical as those produced by Gutenberg's movable type."

Noting that the "movement from the tactile to the digital is the primary fact about the contemporary world," Mr. Landow observes that, whereas most writings of print-bound critics working in an exhausted technology are "models of scholarly solemnity, records of disillusionment and brave sacrifice of humanistic positions," writers in and on hypertext "are downright celebratory. . . . Most poststructuralists write from within the twilight of a wished-for coming day; most writers of hypertext write of many of the same things from within the dawn."

Dawn it is, to be sure. The granddaddy of full-length hypertext fictions is Michael Joyce's landmark "Afternoon," first released on floppy disk in 1987 and moved into a new Storyspace "reader," partly developed by Mr. Joyce himself, in 1990.

Mr. Joyce, who is also the author of a printed novel, *The War Outside Ireland: A History of the Doyles in North America with an Account of Their Migrations,* wrote in the on-line journal *Postmodern Culture* that hyperfiction "is the first instance of the true electronic text, what we will come to conceive as the natural form of multimodal, multisensual writing," but it is still so radically new it is hard to be certain just what it is. No fixed center, for starters—and no edges either, no ends or boundaries. The traditional narrative time line vanishes into a geographical landscape or exitless maze, with beginnings, middles and ends being no longer part of the immediate display. Instead: branching options, menus, link markers and mapped networks. There are no hierarchies in these topless (and bottomless) networks, as paragraphs, chapters and other conventional text divisions are replaced by evenly empowered and equally ephemeral window-sized blocks of text and graphics—soon to be supplemented with sound, animation and film.

As Carolyn Guyer and Martha Petry put it in the opening "directions" to their hypertext fiction "Izme Pass," which was published (if "published" is the word) on a disk included in the spring 1991 issue of the magazine *Writing on the Edge:*

> This is a new kind of fiction, and a new kind of reading. The form of the text is rhythmic, looping on itself in patterns and layers that gradually accrete meaning, just as the passage of time and events does in one's lifetime. Trying the textlinks embedded within the work will bring the narrative together in new configurations, fluid constellations formed by the path of your interest. The difference between reading hyperfiction and reading traditional printed fiction may be the difference between sailing the islands and standing on the dock watching the sea. One is not necessarily better than the other.

I must confess at this point that I am not myself an expert navigator of hyperspace, nor am I—as I am entering my seventh decade and thus rather committed, for better or for worse, to the obsolescent print technology—likely to engage in any major hypertext fictions of my own. But, interested as ever in the subversion of the traditional bourgeois novel and in fictions that challenge linearity, I felt that something was happening out (or in) there and that I ought to know what it was: if I were not going to sail the Guyer-Petry islands, I had at least better run to the shore with my field glasses. And what better way to learn than to teach a course in the subject?

Thus began the Brown University Hypertext Fiction Workshop, two spring semesters (and already as many software generations) old, a course devoted as much to the changing of reading habits as to the creation of new narratives.

Writing students are notoriously conservative creatures. They write stubbornly and hopefully within the tradition of what they have read. Getting them to try out alternative or innovative forms is harder than talking them into chastity as a life style. But confronted with hyperspace, they have no choice: all the comforting structures have been erased. It's improvise or go home. Some frantically rebuild those old structures, some just get lost and drift out of sight, most leap in fearlessly without even asking how deep it is (infinitely deep) and admit, even as they paddle for dear life, that this new arena is indeed an exciting, provocative if frequently frustrating medium for the creation of new narratives, a potentially revolutionary space, capable, exactly as advertised, of transforming the very art of fiction, even if it now remains somewhat at the fringe, remote still, in these very early days, from the mainstream.

With hypertext we focus, both as writers and as readers, on structure as much as on prose, for we are made aware suddenly of the shapes of narratives that are often hidden in print stories. The most radical new element that comes to the fore in hypertext is the system of multidirectional and often labyrinthine linkages we are invited or obliged to create. Indeed the creative imagination often becomes more preoccupied with linkage, routing and mapping than with statement or style, or with what we would call character or plot (two traditional narrative elements that are decidedly in jeopardy). We are always astonished to discover how much of the reading and writing experience occurs in the interstices and trajectories between text fragments. That is to say, the text fragments are like stepping stones, there for our safety, but the real current of the narratives runs between them.

"The great thing," as one young writer, Alvin Lu, put it in an on-line class essay, is "the degree to which narrative is completely destructed into its constituent bits. Bits of information convey knowledge, but the juxtaposition of bits creates narrative. The emphasis of a hypertext (narrative) should be the degree to which the reader is given power, not to read, but to organize the texts made available to her. Anyone can read, but not everyone has sophisticated methods of organization made available to them."

The fictions developed in the workshop, all of which are "still in progress," have ranged from geographically anchored narratives similar to "Our Town" and choose-your-own-adventure stories to parodies of the classics, nested narratives, spatial poems, interactive comedy, metamorphic dreams, irresolvable murder mysteries, moving comic books and Chinese sex manuals.

In hypertext, multivocalism is popular, graphic elements, both drawn and scanned, have been incorporated into the narratives, imaginative font changes have been employed to identify various voices or plot elements, and there has also been a very effective use of formal documents not typically used in fictions—statistical charts, song lyrics, newspaper articles, film scripts, doodles and photographs, baseball cards and box scores, dictionary entries, rock music album covers, astrological forecasts, board games and medical and police reports.

At our weekly workshops, selected writers display, on an overhead projector, their developing narrative structures, then face the usual critique of their writing, design, development of character, emotional impact, attention to detail and so on, as appropriate. But they also engage in continuous on-line dialogue with one other, exchanging criticism, enthusiasm, doubts, speculations, theorizing, wisecracks. So much fun is all of this, so compelling this "downright celebratory" experience, as Mr. Landow would have it, that the creative output, so far anyway, has been much greater than that of ordinary undergraduate writing workshops, and certainly of as high a quality.

In addition to the individual fictions, which are more or less protected from tampering in the old proprietary way, we in the workshop have also played freely and often quite anarchically in a group fiction space called "Hotel." Here, writers are free to check in, to open up new rooms, new corridors, new intrigues, to unlink texts or create new links, to intrude upon or subvert the texts of others, to alter plot trajectories, manipulate time and space, to engage in dialogue through invented characters, then kill off one another's characters or even to sabotage the hotel's plumbing. Thus one day we might find a man and woman encountering each other in the hotel bar, working up some kind of sexual liaison, only to return a few days later and discover that one or both had sex changes.

During one of my hypertext workshops, a certain reading tension was caused when we found that there was more than one bartender in our hotel: was this the same bar or not? One of the students—Alvin Lu again—responded by linking all the bartenders to Room 666, which he called the "Production Center," where some imprisoned alien monster was giving birth to full-grown bartenders on demand.

This space of essentially anonymous text fragments remains on line and each new set of workshop students is invited to check in there and continue the story of the Hypertext Hotel. I would like to see it stay open for a century or two.

However, as all of us have discovered even though the basic technology of hypertext may be with us for centuries to come, perhaps even as long as the technology of the book, its hardware and software seem to be fragile and short-lived; whole new generations of equipment and programs arrive before we can finish reading the instructions of the old. Even as I write, Brown University's highly sophisticated Intermedia system, on which we have been writing our hypertext fictions, is being phased out because it is too expensive to maintain and incompatible with Apple's new operating-system software, System 7.0. A good portion of our last semester was spent transporting our documents from Intermedia to Storyspace (which Brown is now adopting) and adjusting to the new environment.

This problem of operating-system standards is being urgently addressed and debated now by hypertext writers; if interaction is to be a hallmark of the new technology, all its players must have a common and consistent language and all must be equally empowered in its use. There are other problems too. Navigational procedures: how do you move around in infinity without getting lost? The structuring of the space can be so compelling and confusing as to utterly absorb and neutralize the narrator and to exhaust the reader. And there is the related problem of filtering. With an unstable text that can be intruded upon by other author-readers, how do you, caught in the maze, avoid the trivial? How do you duck the garbage? Venerable novelistic values like unity, integrity, coherence, vision, voice seem to be in danger. Eloquence is being redefined. "Text" has lost its canonical certainty. How does one judge, analyze, write about a work that never reads the same way twice?

And what of narrative flow? There is still movement, but in hyperspace's dimensionless infinity, it is more like endless expansion; it runs the risk of being so distended and slackly driven as to lose its centripetal force, to give way to a kind of static low-charged lyricism—that dreamy gravityless lost-in-space feeling of the early sci-fi fiims. How does one resolve the conflict between the reader's desire for coherence and closure and the text's desire for continuance, its fear of death? Indeed, what is closure in such an environment? If everything is middle, how do you know when you are done, either as reader or writer? If the author is free to take a story anywhere at any time and in as many directions as she or he wishes, does that not become the obligation to do so?

No doubt, this will be a major theme for narrative artists of the future, even those locked into the old print technologies. And that's nothing new. The problem of closure was a major theme—was it not?—of the "Epic of Gilgamesh" as it was chopped out in clay at the dawn of literacy, and of the Homeric rhapsodies as they were committed to papyrus by technologically innovative Greek literati some 26 centuries ago. There is continuity, after all, across the ages riven by shifting technologies.

Much of this I might have guessed—and in fact did guess—before entering hyperspace, before I ever picked up a mouse, and my thoughts have been tempered only slightly by on-line experience. What I had not clearly foreseen, however, was that this is a technology that both absorbs and totally displaces. Print documents may be read in hyperspace, but hypertext does not translate into print. It is not like film, which is really just the dead end of linear narrative, just as 12-tone music is the dead end of music by the stave.

Hypertext is truly a new and unique environment. Artists who work there must be read there. And they will probably be judged there as well: criticism, like fiction, is moving off the page and on line, and it is itself susceptible to continuous changes of mind and text. Fluidity, contingency, indeterminacy, plurality, discontinuity are the hypertext buzzwords of the day, and they seem to be fast becoming principles, in the same way that relativity not so long ago displaced the falling apple.

TOPICS FOR DISCUSSION AND WRITING

1. Describe hypertext.
2. Hypertext's existence is dependent on the computer, but what problems does the computer and its ever evolving technology present to the community of hypertext writers?
3. According to Coover, what problems does hypertext present?

4. Do you think hypertext will become a popular medium for story-telling? Why or why not?

5. In groups of four or five, choose a different well-known fairy tale to reinvent using the tools of hypertext. Read your collaborative effort to the class.

Never-Ending Saga

Michiko Kakutani

As an editor of *The New York Times Book Review,* Kakutani wields considerable influence in the literary world. She draws parallels between hypertext and current literary theories—deconstruction and also Marxist and feminist inspired criticism—and questions the impact of "multivocal" works on what she sees as the purpose of art.

Here is a glimpse of the electronic future, at least as some cyber-prophets see it: the 500-year-old Gutenberg revolution has come to an end, and the novel—that outmoded vestige of the bourgeoise industrial world—is a casualty of its own irrelevance. Indeed, the book itself is on the verge of extinction, and with it the colonial, patriarchal, hierarchical and authoritarian values its critics say it embodies. For that matter, distinctions are no longer made between writers and readers; there are only "co-learners," in the words of the experimental novelist Robert Coover, "fellow travelers in the mapping and remapping of textual (and visual, kinetic and aural) components. . . ."

In her new book, "Hamlet on the Holodeck," Janet H. Murray, an MIT research scientist, suggests that "the next Shakespeare of this world" may be "a great live-action role-playing GM"—computer game master—"who is also an expert computer scientist." And in "Hypertext," Prof. George P. Landow of Brown writes that electronic texts promise (or threaten) "to produce effects on our culture, particularly on our literature, education, criticism and scholarship, just as radical as those produced by Gutenberg's movable type."

That future may never arrive, but the innovations of computer technology have already begun to affect how some scholars and writers think about writing. Hypertext—nonsequential writing made up of text blocks that can be linked by the reader in multiple ways—has not only proved to be a remarkably useful research tool but has also spawned a growing body of "hyperfiction," available on disk and on the Web. Hyperfictions, typically, have no real beginnings, middles or ends; the reader can choose where to enter and exit the story and what the fates of its characters should be. Nothing is fixed; the same plot elements can be arranged and rearranged in myriad ways, the way children's Lego blocks can be used to build a log cabin, skyscraper or train. Hyperfiction might one day yield a truly inventive work of art, but for the time being it remains a self-conscious, gamelike diversion: something along the lines of Myst or Warcraft II as reimagined by Robbe Grillet. One well-known hyperfiction concerns a man who fears that his ex-wife and son have been killed in a car accident; another traces the adventures of a cyberpunk hero battling an evil kingdom.

Curiously enough, hypertext already stands as the living embodiment of theories promoted for several decades by radical post-structuralist critics. Like deconstruction, hypertext diminishes the author's role, even as it empowers readers by allowing them to connect the dots, decipher the clues and manufacture a meaning. Like Marxist, feminist and Foucault-inspired criticism, hypertext sees literature in terms of power; it announces itself as a highly egalitarian form, undermining what Coover has called the "domination by the author"—"that compulsory author-directed movement from the beginning of a sentence to its period, from the top of the page to the bottom, from the first page to the last."

The repudiation of linearity, of course, is nothing new. Laurence Sterne shattered the traditional narrative in "Tristram Shandy" back in the 18th century, and 20th-century novelists—from Faulkner and Eliot through Rushdie and DeLillo—have made fragmentation a cornerstone of their art. What's different about hypertext discontinuity is that it's not a choice made by the writer, it's a built-in fact of the form. In these respects, hypertext seems like a fitting genre for a generation brought up on channel-surfing and montage-driven action movies, a fitting genre for a world in which truth is relative and identity is an ongoing process. "There is no Final Word," Ted Nelson a hypertext pioneer, proclaims. "There can be no final version, no last thought. There is always a new view, a new idea, a reinterpretation."

Although hypertext may well turn out to be no more than an amusing detour in the history of the written word, its most ardent fans foresee a future in which traditional narratives would become obsolete, and discrete, self-contained books would also give way to vast interlinked electronic networks. Novels would come adorned with the electronic equivalent of gargantuan footnotes; they would be "contextualized" with literary, social and cultural commentary and speculation.

As lines between writers and readers blur, a group consciousness would prevail. In just the past few months, there have been two prominent works of "chain fiction": a short serial story written by five writers (beginning with Frank McCourt) in Esquire and a 46-installment story (beginning and ending with passages by John Updike) run as a contest by the on-line bookstore Amazon.com.

Like hypertext fictions, such "multivocal" works point to the obsolescence of the old idea of an author—a lone individual bent on expressing an idiosyncratic vision. They also reinforce the sort of self-absorption and egotism promoted by talk shows: everyone's an expert, anyone can be an artist and all opinions are equally valid, especially your own. The old notion of reading—immersing yourself in a stranger's world—vanishes, replaced by the solipsistic belief that other people's ideas are simply materials to be appropriated and manipulated for your own ends. As Landow writes, hypertext's absence of a center means "that anyone who uses hypertext makes his or her own interests the de facto organizing principle (or center) for the investigation at the moment."

In the end, one of the oddest arguments advanced by hypertext proponents is that hypertext is lifelike, that it captures the randomness, arbitrariness and repetitiousness of life. Do we really need a more lifelike art. Once upon a time, in the pre-hypertext past, art aspired not to imitate life but to shape it, intensify it, imprint it with a single person's vision. It represented an individual's attempt to find order in chaos, a pattern in the carpet. Hypertext smashes that old conception of art: the artist is dead, it suggests, and the rug is patternless—the reader alone is left to make sense of a senseless world.

TOPICS FOR DISCUSSION AND WRITING

1. In what ways is hyperfiction like current literary theory?
2. Why does Kakutani describe hyperfiction as "a highly egalitarian form"?
3. What does Kakutani imply is the purpose of art? What is hyperfiction's impact on that purpose?

www.claptrap.com

Laura Miller

We might expect Miller as a senior editor at the Internet magazine *Salon* to be a fan of hypertext, but her opinions are closer to Kakutani's than to Coover's. Like Kakutani, Miller sees hyperfiction as an electronic counterpart to current literary theories and an unwelcome alternative to traditional fiction.

Shortly after personal computers and word processing programs became commonplace tools for writers, a brave new future for fiction was trumpeted. In 1992, Robert Coover informed the readers of the Book Review that the novel, "as we know it, has comes to its end." Hypertext, "writing done in the nonlinear or nonsequential space made possible by the computer," would at last enable the reader to amble through a network of linked text blocks, or "lexias." Instead of following a linear story dictated by the author, the reader could now navigate at will through an "endless expansion" of words.

Proclamations about the death of the novel (or, as Coover's essay was titled, "The End of Books") can still get a rise out of a surprising number of people, even though, so far, they've all proved to be little more than empty, apocalyptic showboating. Six years after Coover's essay was published, and five years after a second article by him, this one recommending several "hyperfictions" for the curious reader, the market for hard cover books may be flat, but over a million people have nevertheless bought Charles Frazier's literary novel "Cold Mountain," and I've yet to encounter anyone who reads hypertext fiction. No one, that is, who isn't also a hypertext author or a journalist reporting on the trend.

Surely those readers, however few, must exist, but what's most remarkable about hyperfiction is that no one really *wants* to read it, not even out of idle curiosity. The most adventurous souls I know, people amenable to sampling cryptic performance art and even those most rare and exotic of creatures, readers of poetry who aren't poets themselves—all shudder at the thought, for it's the very concept of hypertext fiction that strikes readers as dreary and pointless. Yet Coover's announcement wasn't the last of its kind; recently Janet M. Murray examined the future of reader-controlled narratives at length in her book, "Hamlet on the Holodeck: The Future of Narrative in Cyberspace," and Mark Amerika started "Grammatron" (www.grammatron.com), a "novel-length hypertext work" on the World Wide Web. The promise that the fiction of the future will have no story, or a story of the reader's own devising, recalls a Lily Tomlin joke about the afterlife: it turns out that there is sex in heaven, you just can't feel it.

That Coover and hypertext authors and theorists like Michael Joyce, George P. Landow, Stuart Moulthrop and Mark Amerika apparently still believe in the eventual triumph of hyperfiction over the novel becomes less baffling when you understand that hypertext is a form of writing perfectly suited to contemporary literary theory. In his aptly titled book/Web site, "Hypertext: The Convergence of Contemporary Critical Theory and Technology" (www.stg.brown.edu/projects/hypertext/landow/ht/contents2.html), Landow observes that "using hypertext, critical theorists will have, or now already have, a laboratory with which to test their ideas." In fact, he says, hypertext is "an almost embarrassingly literal embodiment" of key post-structuralist notions. What the laboratory of hyperfiction demonstrates, though, is how alienated academic literary criticism is from actual readers and their desires.

The theory of hyperfiction insists that readers ought to be, and long to be, liberated from two mainstays of the traditional novel: linear narrative and the author. The reader, cruelly forced to read one word after another to reach the end of a sentence, one paragraph after another to reach the end of a scene, will rejoice to learn that, according to Coover, "true freedom from the tyranny of the line is perceived as only really possible now at last with the advent of hypertext." In reality, the common reader most likely will be surprised to be told that structured storytelling—from the most basic beginning-middle-end scheme of fairy tales to more elaborately constructed, nonchronological literary narratives and frolics like murder mysteries—is actually a form of oppression, rather than the source of delight it has always seemed in the past.

In Jostein Gaarder's novel "Sophie's World" (proof that a story can transform a seemingly uncommercial primer on philosophy into a popular book), a character describes a cat and a little girl in a room. If a ball rolls across the floor, the cat will chase it, but the little girl will look to see where the ball came from. Story—the idea that events happen in a specific, causal order—is both the way we see the world and what interests us most about it, and story is fiction's trump card. People who read for nothing else will read for plot, yet hyperfiction's advocates maintain that we find it "confining" and chafe against its "limitations."

A primary source for the peculiar notion that linear narratives "tyrannize" their readers and need to be broken is the French critic Roland Barthes, who in "S/Z," his book-length dissection of a Balzac story, champions an ideal that he calls "the writerly text": "It has no beginning; it is reversible; we gain access to it by several entrances, none of which can be authoritatively declared to be the main one." Barthes complains of "the pitiless divorce which the literary institution maintains between the producer of the text and its user, between its owner and its consumer, between its author and its reader," which prevents the reader from "gaining access to . . . the pleasure of writing."

That last point is true enough: reading doesn't offer the pleasure of writing. But it does offer the pleasure of *reading*, a practice much undervalued by literary critics and hyperfiction advocates. Meandering through the lexias of hypertext works like Michael Joyce's "Afternoon, a Story," Stuart Moulthrop's "Victory Garden" (both published on floppy disks by Eastgate Systems; www.eastgate.com) and even the floridly naughty "Grammatron" is a listless task, a matter of incessantly having to choose among alternatives, each of which, I'm assured, is no more important than any other. This process, according to Landow, makes me "a truly active reader," but the experience feels profoundly meaningless and dull. If any decision is as good as any other, why bother? Hypertext is sometimes said to mimic real life, with its myriad opportunities and surprising outcomes, but I already have a life, thank you very much, and it is hard enough putting that in order without the chore of organizing someone else's novel. Hyperfiction, Coover promises, will make me a "co-writer" by enabling me to rearrange its text blocks however I choose. Of course, I could just write my own book if writing is what I really want to do.

Readers like me stubbornly resist hyperfiction's efforts to free them from what Coover calls "domination by the author." Instead, I persist, like Lynne Sharon Schwartz, the author of "Ruined by Reading: A Life in Books," in perceiving my readerly enslavement as "a delectable exercise for the mind." Since Schwartz's anecdotal memoir could hardly be called plot-driven, why do I find following its aimless course so pleasant? The answer lies in the author herself, whom I experience as confiding, amusing and enlightening, not domineering. Like her, I consider a book to be "a solitary voice whispering in your ear," providing the possibility of an encounter with the author, whose theoretical "death" I neither long for nor believe in, however ingeniously Barthes and others may argue for it. Schwartz gracefully assumes the "authority" implicit in the profession of author. She knows what she thinks and she selects what she wishes to say, and in what order. She doesn't needlessly defer to me the option of rearranging her book. Yet at no point did I feel her boot on my throat.

I am not, however, an academic. The downtrodden reader depicted in hypertext manifestoes and post-structuralist literary theory is the creature of a world where books are assigned, not chosen. To the academic, a book is often a stony monument from which the relatively insignificant scholar must wring some drop of fresh commentary. As a result, the rhetoric of hyperfiction can be warlike, full of attacks launched against texts that can offer no "defense," prove "vulnerable" and ultimately "yield." Coover sees "readers who fall asleep on four or five books a year" and "surrender to novels as a way of going on holiday from themselves" as weaklings insufficiently girded for the glorious battle ahead.

That surrender, though, and the intimacy to be had in allowing a beloved author's voice into the sanctions of our minds, are what the common reader craves. We want to experience how someone as acerbic as Jane Austen, as morally passionate as Dostoyevsky, as psychologically astute as Henry James makes sense of the chaos of this world, and our passage through it, because making sense of it is humanity's great collective project. Is it merely a holiday or is it an expansion of ourselves when we issue this invitation to guests whose appeal lies precisely in their distinctive, unequivocal, undeniably authoritative voices? Hyperfiction's champions aren't the first self-styled revolutionaries threatening to liberate other people from their pleasures, but they make one of the weakest cases. The end of books will come only when readers abandon novels for the deconstructed stories of hypertext, and that exodus is strictly a fiction.

TOPICS FOR DISCUSSION AND WRITING

1. What reasons does Miller offer for her conclusion that hyperfiction will not supplant books? Do you agree with her conclusion?

2. According to Miller, how are hyperfiction and academic literary criticism out of touch with "actual readers and their desires"? What might an advocate of hypertext say in response to this criticism?

3. Visit one of the hypertext sites that Miller identifies for at least one hour. Then write a paper weighing the relative merits of hyperfiction and traditional fiction based on this experience. Feel free to include references to the Coover, Kakutani and Miller essays if it serves your purposes to do so.

Culture

There is probably no more accurate and complete a reflection of a culture than its language. A language emerges from the culture and also shapes the culture by offering certain choices to its speakers. Those choices will affect how one sees and evaluates the world. In the language of the Athapaskin Indians of Alaska, there is no word for "I"—only "we." What impact would the absence of a singular pronoun to refer to oneself have on an individual and his or her view of the world?

It is easier for us to see how language shapes and reflects culture and experience when that language is not our own. Because a foreign language is foreign, we don't take it for granted. We are more aware of its idiosyncracies and underlying assumptions. Such is the case in "Chinese Relations" by Nicholas Kristof. As an American journalist living in China he notes the paucity of words related to democracy and science and the abundance of words to denote family and relatives. Michael Specter, a reporter for the

New York Times, looks at Russian idioms to learn something about Russian culture in "The Rich Idioms of Russian: Verbal Soul Food of a Culture."

Any single culture is diverse, made up of many different racial, social, economic, geographic, and religious groups; in language this diversity may be reflected in a dialect, a form of speech that deviates from the standard language but is still intelligible to speakers of the language. In "Dialects," Margalit Fox questions the belief that some dialects are substandard. Tony Earley explores this phenomenon in "The Quare Gene," an essay about the dialect he and his family spoke in the Appalachian Mountains of North Carolina. In Earley's case, the dialect is the result of geography and history, but in Kirk Johnson's "Today's Kids Are, Like, Killing the English Language. Yeah, Right," the dialect is chosen by the young as a way to distinguish themselves from their parents, to establish their own identity and to assert their own view of the world. In "Languages Are Political Constructions," linguist Geoff Nunberg finds the terms "language" and "dialect" to be indefinite categories, subject to political events rather than linguistic precision.

Chinese Relations

Nicholas D. Kristof

In this essay, Beijing based *New York Times* writer Nicholas D. Kristof looks at the relationship between Chinese culture and language. As you read this essay, you might ask yourself what choices the language has made available to its speakers.

Arabic is a rich language. There are words for losing one's children, for a carriage taking a virgin into battle, for a disease striking camels in the head. But when I was sweltering in Cairo in the early 1980's, while studying Arabic, what struck me most was that there was only one word, *talg,* that refers, if somewhat hazily, to either ice or snow.

At the time I was yearning for good *talg*-fall in Cairo. I learned that the Eskimo language has several dozen words for "snow." Which makes perfect sense: the diversity in a language reflects the interests and obsessions of the society speaking it. As a continuing student of the Chinese language, I find that Chinese is especially rich in the specific areas one would expect, given the culture.

There are at least 19 words for silk, for example, and 8 for rice. Why? Well, *goo* refers to a tough, white silk; *qi* is a patterned silk; *qian* is a blue-red silk fabric; *kuang* is uncombed silk thread; *si* is regular silk thread; *chou* is another term for silk fabrics, and so on. As for rice, *fan* refers to the cooked product; *doo* to the rice when it is still in the paddy; *xian* to long-grained rice; *mi* to the husked kernels, and, in some dialects, *gu* means unhusked kernels.

Since the Chinese care even more for their families than they do for their rice or silk, there is a profusion of words for relations. For instance, Chinese has five words for "uncle." It depends on whether he is your father's older or younger brother, or your mother's brother, or your father's sister's husband, or your mother's sister's husband. In English, the word "cousin" is applied to males as well as females, older people as well as younger people, maternal as well as paternal relations. Not so in Chinese; the rules that apply to "uncle" also apply to "cousin."

When Americans hurl abuse at each other, they sometimes question each other's paternity or bring in each other's mothers. But the Chinese denounce uncles and grandfathers as well as parents, and one common insult calumniates the preceding 18 generations of the accursed one's family.

Chinese has about two dozen expressions for "wife," but in this case the richness of the language doesn't indicate any special esteem. On the contrary, most of the terms are unflattering: "the inside person," "the old woman," "the one on the bed," "the children's mother," "the cook." One reason for the many expressions may be that until early this century it wasn't unusual for peasant woman not to have given names. As they grew up, they were identified by numbers: second sister, fourth sister and so on.

"My mother didn't have a name, as far as I know," says an octogenarian friend who grew up in the country-side. I asked him what his father called his mother, and his brow furrowed. Then his face lighted up. "'Hey,'" he said triumphantly. "He called her 'Hey.'"

Where English is particularly rich, and Chinese poor, is in the areas of science and democracy—the two slogans that since 1919 have been a rallying cry for change. Indeed, "science" and "democracy" are sometimes known as *S Xiansheng* (Mr. S) and *D Xiansheng* (Mr. D), to signify that they are foreign guests who still have not taken up Chinese residency.

Although law, *fa,* is an ancient concept in China, it historically wasn't a champion of individual rights but a means of punishment. Indeed, the only area of the law in which the Chinese language distinguishes itself is in the designation of punishments. *Gua* refers to execution by slicing (a convict literally cut into pieces); *yi* refers to the cutting off of a felon's nose. (Both are mercifully no longer judicial sentences.)

Most of China's political vocabulary is relatively recent. Chinese expressions for "freedom," "politics," "democracy" and "economy" are all only about a century old. And words like "individualism" or "privacy" still have a negative connotation in Chinese, reflecting the traditional lack of concern for individual rights.

"This is a factional language, based on groups rather than individuals, and an inclusive language," says Geremie Barme, an Australian scholar whose mastery of the Chinese language gives other foreigners the "red eye disease" (one of the many expressions for "jealousy").

What's an inclusive language? In English, we tend to hold each other verbally at arm's length; it's the opposite in Chinese. Friends address each other as "Big Brother" or "Big Sister," as a sign of respect, and children are required to address adults who are friends or acquaintances of the family as "Auntie" or

"Uncle." This has to be done carefully, however. I once disconcerted a Chinese friend by calling her "Little Sister"—often a prelude to a pickup.

The two ways of saying "we" in Chinese help explain the usefulness of an inclusive expression. The first kind, *women* (pronounced waugh-mun), refers to the speaker and one or more other people but doesn't include the person being addressed. The second kind, *zamen,* includes the person being addressed. Thus, a young woman going out with her boyfriend might tell her parents that "*women* are leaving," but a group of boys flirting with some girls suggest that "*zamen* go to a movie." By comparison, English looks rather aloof and threadbare for lacking an inclusive "we." But never mind. *Zamen* have another area, besides science and democracy, where English triumphs: sex.

English seems to have far more words that are sex-related than contemporary Chinese. (Ancient Chinese pornography is another matter, but that rich vocabulary has been largely forgotten.) No one knows if this is because Americans are obsessed with sex or because the Chinese take lots of cold showers—hot-water heaters still being a rarity in China. A researcher of sexuality in Shanghai is stumped by the linguistic challenge of polling Chinese about their sexual practices. There are no common expressions for "foreplay" or "orgasm," and so surveys must resort to vaguer terms that people will at least understand. Instead of inquiring about the frequency of "a sexual high tide"—the technical term for "climax"—the surveys simply ask women how often they enjoy "a pleasant feeling."

It would be rash to draw conclusions on what this says about the Chinese, especially when there are more than 1.1 billion of them. Still, it's nice to know that English has the edge in a few areas. Science. Democracy. Sex. A language could do worse.

TOPICS FOR DISCUSSION AND WRITING

1. Choose a group you come in frequent contact with—family members, friends, teachers, students, fellow workers—and make a list of words or expressions they use often. After careful analysis of this list, write an essay about the group's language, speculating on the reasons for their frequent use of certain terms. What does their language reveal about their "culture," their values? (Refer to Writing Assignment 4 on page 42 for help with this assignment.)

2. Individually or as a group, choose an object or concept that you see as significant in American culture, and list all the words that refer to it. Note the subtle shades of meaning between the various words, the different connotations each term suggests, and write a paper about this vocabulary as if you were explaining these differences to a student for whom English was a new language.

The Rich Idioms of Russian: Verbal Soul Food of a Culture

Michael Specter

Specter, a journalist who has spent time in Russia, bases his inferences about Russian culture and values on that experience as well as a number of phrases he finds in a dictionary of Russian-English idioms—commonly used expressions whose meanings are not literal.

Of all the horrors confronting Russian society—political and economic instability, a lingering war, an average life expectancy for men so low it's hard to believe (57 years)—worrying about the current state of Russian conversational language might seem a little, well, petty.

But that would be taking the short view.

"There is nothing more important than language," said Sophia Lubensky , a professor of Slavic Language and Literature at the State University of New York at Albany. "Czars come and go. Presidents come and go. There are wars, there are famines. Language lives through it all."

Mrs. Lubensky, a Russian emigre has just produced the "Russian-English Dictionary of Idioms" (Random House) the first book in decades to try to translate the ideas of Russian idioms—and not just the words—into English. And while it is rich in the dark phrases of the 18th century, and not terribly up on the current slang one hears in the streets of Moscow, a careful tour of this volume can tell a reader as much about what matters to Russians as the results of any election or emergency meeting of the International Monetary Fund.

GOD, FOOD AND SOUL

The book is full of the language of God, food and the soul. Not surprising perhaps for a country that always seems to have something bad in its mouth (vodka is heavily linked to the soul in the Russian imagination; no doubt so are cigarettes, though there are no idioms here to prove it.)

For instance, a Russian could pretty much convey the entire range of human emotion with reference only to kasha, the grain dish. Nobody around here would argue with this notion, for example: "Kashu maslom ne isportish," which means literally you cannot spoil kasha with too much butter. What it really means, of course, is you can't have too much of a good thing—and in Russia a good thing is usually, well, food soaked in butter.

Then again, there are limits. If things go too well for too long a guy can simply "s zhiru besitsya," which means go mad from eating so much fat, or have it so cushy that he gets soft. "Bolno zhirno budet," sick with fat, painfully fat or it's a lot of fat, means, basically, who does this guy think he is? Is his diet so rich that he can treat everyone like a vassal? And if somebody does mess up pretty badly

(Boris Yeltsin in Chechnya for example) then the only thing to do is: "raskhly-obyvat kashu," which literally means eat up the kasha, but really means clean up his digusting mess.

Russians don't speak with marbles in their mouth, they speak with kasha in their mouth (kasha vo rtu). They're not green behind the ears; they have "malo kashi yel," which means they have eaten too little kasha in their lives to be worth much.

Even some of today's best-known idioms are food-based. When Prime Minister Viktor S. Chernomyrdin was being challenged not long ago about the war in Chechnya he erupted: "Veshat lapshu na ushi," which means don't try hanging noodles on my ears, buddy, or, as Americans might say it, that's a lot of bull. Mikhail S. Gorbachev spat the same phrase at a member of Parliament who was trying to explain why he participated in the 1991 coup.

Food matters, of course, but not as much as the Lord. Russians often express their most fundamental feelings with reference to God, even if God is nothing they actively believe in.

In addition to the many idioms that translate easily in English (God knows how much I have suffered; God knows what I have done; God be merciful) there are some phrases that mean far more to Russians than they do in America: "Radi boga" (for God's sake) is possibly the most commonly repeated phrase in the Russian language—except for a few profanities that translate quite well, but not in this newspaper. Instead of filling empty airspace with the all-purpose words well, um, and you know—all part of the America's national speech impediment—Russians are capable of repeating the phrase radi boga 20 times in five minutes.

God's name is invoked in every imaginable way. If somebody is a complete loser he is "ni bogu svechka ni chyortu kocherga"—neither a candle to God nor a rod to the devil, i.e., useless. If it's time to stand up and be a man then you say, "Ne bogi gorshki obzhigayut"—It's not God who bakes all the clay pots, or anybody can do this work if he really tries.

But not even God can compare with the soul. No word has more significance in the Russian language than dusha, or soul. A good human being has a "dusha naraspashku"—an unbuttoned soul, but really an open heart. But a bad guy—and this has been said of everyone from Dostoyevsky's Raskolnikov in "Crime and Punishment" to Gen. Dzhokhar Dudayev, the Chechen rebel leader—is a person who would "naplevat v dushu," or spit in your soul.

Russian souls are also always being engraved upon, trampled upon, put aside, unburdened and burdened. People worm their way into your soul, they rip their soul in two, and of couse, they are often caught selling the damn thing.

WINDOW ON CULTURE

"Without this type of idiomatic expression people simply could not communicate," said Yevgeny N. Shiryaev, deputy director of the Russian Academy of Sciences Institute of Russian Language and an expert on the development of common speech. "Words would not add up properly. And of course the type of idioms we often rely on—earthy, physical phrases—tell a lot about our culture."

That's no doubt because the Russian people are so practical. After all, "Snyavshi golovu, po volosam ne plachut"—or, once your head has been cut off, there's no use crying about your hair. Now doesn't that make "there's no use crying over spilt milk" seem a little pathetic?

TOPICS FOR DISCUSSION AND WRITING

1. Based on his reading of the *Russian-English Dictionary of Idioms*, Specter, finding a significant number of references to each, draws the conclusion that "God, food and the soul" are important values in Russian culture. Refer to a dictionary of English idioms, and gather a random sample of thirty or more idioms. After careful study of this list, what conclusions can you draw about American culture?

2. If you're bilingual, after completing the question above, refer to a dictionary of idioms from your other language, gather a random sample of thirty or more idioms, draw what conclusions you can about the culture and then compare them to the inferences you've made about American culture.

Dialects

Margalit Fox

Fox, an editor of *The New York Times Book Review* who writes frequently about language and linguistics, questions the belief that some English dialects are substandard.

Which of the following beliefs do you hold?

- There is a single standard variety of American English, distinguished by level Midwestern pronunciation, correct usage and logical grammatical agreement.

- Varieties of English that differ greatly from the standard are best considered substandard dialects.

- In the United States, as elsewhere, official encouragement of more than one language is an impediment to national unity.

All of these beliefs about language are widely accepted. They are advanced by educators, lawmakers and members of the news media. They inform public discourse and public policy, including the controversy over ebonics and successful attempts to curtail bilingual education.

And they are all myths, reflecting widespread popular misconceptions about how language works.

Nearly everyone has an opinion about language. In perhaps no other field, scholars who study social attitudes toward language say, is unscientific folk belief so consistently enshrined in high-level policy. It is as if, they say, the Federal Government seriously entertained a plan to harvest cheese from the moon. "People would never pontificate about a physics issue, because they would acknowledge that you need to consult an expert," says Donna Christian, the president of the Center for Applied Linguistics, in Washington, "But they wouldn't hesitate to pontificate about language."

In the past few years, a number of scholars have undertaken serious study of these grass-roots opinions, a discipline Dennis R. Preston, a linguist at Michigan State University, calls "folk linguistics." Examining what ordinary people believe to be true about language, they say, allows us to identify some of the deeper impulses beneath the public battles: among them, fear of the unfamiliar, insistence on language "standards" as a way of preserving the social status quo and the condemnation of "substandard" speech as a coded expression of prejudice against the speaker. "If we learn to appreciate diversity," Preston says, "then the way we talk has to be included."

Judged on purely linguistic grounds, all languages—and all dialects—have equal merit. All spring from the same human cognitive faculties; all have the same expressive potential and operate according to the same kinds of logical rule systems. Why, then, are some dialects considered substandard?

The answer is simple: judgments about relative worth—that Walter Cronkite speaks "better" English than, say, a black inner-city teen-ager—are socially determined. "I can't think of any situations in the United States where low-prestige groups have high-prestige language systems," says Walt Wolfram, a linguist at North Carolina State University who is an authority on American dialects.

Consider how the idea of socially stigmatized language played out in the ebonics debate, which began at the end of 1996 after the Oakland, Calif., School Board publicly affirmed the variety of English spoken by the district's black students—known as African-American vernacular English, or ebonics—and acknowledged its usefulness as a pedagogical tool in the teaching of mainstream English. The wording of the Oakland resolution was awkward in places, leaving it open to misinterpretation, but the linguistic recommendations at its core were sound. What's more, they were nothing new. Three decades before, the linguist William Labov demonstrated in seminal articles, including "The Logic of Nonstandard English," that African-American English, like all language varieties, displays its own, perfectly regular systems of grammatical concord; they are simply different from the ones most white speakers are accustomed to.

But the announcement from Oakland set off a firestorm. Commentators, including many African-Americans, excoriated ebonics as "broken" English. The Oakland board appeared to backpedal: a task force it appointed ultimately released a report in which the word "ebonics" never appeared.

To understand the level of outrage, it helps to tease out the two folk-linguistic beliefs at the heart of the debate: the myth of standard English and its corollary, the myth of substandard English.

Many Americans believe that there exists a single standard dialect—the one broadcasters use—kept free of regional and vernacular encroachments. But in reality, no one such creature exists. "If you said to anyone, 'Here's a room; put the hundred people in there you think speak the best English,' you'd get people that speak all different kinds of English," the linguist Rosina Lippi-Green says. "You'd get Dan Rather, who has a little bit of Texan; you'd get Peter Jennings, who's Canadian. They wouldn't be stigmatized varieties of English, but they wouldn't be the same variety of English."

But if we allow all these diverse Englishes into the pantheon, how can we keep out the ones that discomfort us like African-American vernacular or working-class Brooklynese? That is where language myth comes in.

One function of myth, as Lippi-Green points out in her book "English With an Accent" (Routledge, 1997), is to provide a rationale for preserving the existing social order. The myths of standard and substandard English do just that, permitting those in power to label others inferior on the basis of their "broken" language. "Nobody speaks 'nonstandard' or 'substandard' language," Preston explains, "unless they are regarded as nonstandard or substandard human beings."

But in matters of language, the myth of "good" versus "bad" is viscerally ingrained. That is why it seduced even black commentators, who would have instantly condemned racism in any other guise. "Even people who claim not to be prejudiced," Preston says, "believe in the linguistic part of this myth."

Similarly with the myth of national unity. This folk belief, linguists say, underpinned ballot initiatives like Proposition 227, which effectively ended bilingual education in California last year. (A drive to place a similar initiative on the ballot is under way in Arizona.) In reality, they say, there is no evidence that civic unity stems from sharing a single national language—look at Switzerland, whose three official languages don't seem to have done it any harm.

Why do language myths endure? They have, Lippi-Green says, a disturbing utility: "Right now, it's very hard for people to talk about race—they feel they can't say, 'I dont like black people; I don't like Asians.' But they are very comfortable saying, 'That person doesn't speak English to my satisfaction.' So it stands in for things we'd rather not talk about."

TOPICS FOR DISCUSSION AND WRITING

1. Why are some dialects considered substandard?

2. According to Fox, what are the commonly held beliefs about language? Why does she call them myths?

3. What reasons does Fox offer for the persistence of these myths?

4. Write an essay based on your own response to the three myths about language examined by Fox. Do you believe in these assertions? Why or why not? What impact, if any, has this article had on your thinking about language and dialects?

The Quare Gene

Tony Earley

A professor of English at Vanderbilt University, a novelist, and a short story writer, Tony Early grew up in the Appalachian Mountains of North Carolina where his family spoke a dialect of English, a fact which caused some elementary school classmates to correct his speech. No doubt, these classmates considered Earley's dialect substandard—a categorization Margalit Fox in the preceding essay, "Dialects," tells us shouldn't exist. As you read this essay, note the mixture of pride and embarrassment with which Earley describes his linguistic heritage.

I do not like, I have never liked, nor do I expect to like watermelon. For the record, I consider this a private, dietary preference, not a political choice, neither a sign of failing character nor a renunciation of Southern citizenship. I simply do not like watermelon. Nor, for that matter, do I like grits, blackberries, cantaloupe, buttermilk, okra, baked sweet potatoes, rhubarb, or collard greens. Particularly collard greens. I don't even like to look at collard greens. But, because I am a Southerner—a North Carolinian, of Appalachian, Scots-Irish descent, the offspring of farming families on both sides—my family finds my refusal to like the foods they like somehow distressing. When I eat at my grandmother's red-roofed, high-ceilinged Victorian barn of a house, in Polk County, North Carolina, my relatives earnestly strive to persuade me that I am making a big mistake by not sampling this or that, that I should just *try* the greens, have just a little *slice* of watermelon, a small *bite* of cantaloupe. They tell me that I will get used to the seeds in blackberries, the mealiness of grits, the swampy odor of greens boiled too long in a big pot. And when I passionately and steadfastly refuse, as I have done for the last thirty-seven years, they stare at me for a few seconds as if they didn't know me, their mouths set sadly, before looking down at their plates as if preparing to offer up a second grace. Then my grandmother pronounces, "Tony Earley, you're just quare."

According to my edition of the Shorter Oxford English Dictionary, "quare" is an Anglo-Irish adjective from the early nineteenth century meaning "queer, strange, eccentric." Most other dictionaries, if they list the word at all, will tell you that it is dialectical, archaic, or obsolete, an anachronism, a muted, aging participant in the clamoring riot of the English language. But when spoken around my grandmother's table, by my parents and aunts and uncles and cousins, "quare" is as current as the breath that produces it, as pointed as a sharpened stick. In my family's lexicon, "quare" packs a specificity of meaning which "queer," "strange," "eccentric," "odd," "unusual," "unconventional," and "suspicious" do not. The only adjective of synonymous texture would be "squir-relly," but we are a close bunch and would find the act of calling one another squirrelly impolite. So, in my grandmother's dining room when "quare" is the word we need, "quare" is the word we use.

Nor is "quare" the only word still hiding out in my grandmother's house which dictionaries assure us lost currency years ago. If I brought a quare person to Sunday dinner at Granny's and he ate something that disagreed with him, we might say that he looked a little peaked. Of course, we might decide that he was peaked not because he had eaten something that disagreed with him but be-cause he had eaten a bait of something he liked. We would say, Why, he was just too trifling to leave the table. He ate almost the whole mess by himself. And now we have this quare, peaked, trifling person on our hands. How do we get him to leave? Do we job him in the stomach? Do we hit him with a stob? No, we are kinder than that. We tell him, "Brother, you liked to have stayed too long." We put his desert in a poke and send him on his way.

When I was a child, I took these words for granted. They were part of the language I heard around me, and I breathed them in like air. Only when I began to venture away from the universe that revolved around my grandmother's table did I come to realize that the language of my family was not the language of the greater world. I was embarrassed and ashamed when my town-bred class-mates at Rutherfordton Elementary School corrected my speech, but by the time I entered college and signed up for an Appalachian-studies class I wasn't surprised to learn that my family spoke a dialect. I had begun to suspect as much, and was, by that time, bilingual: I spoke in the Appalachian vernacular when I was with my family and spoke standard English when I wasn't. This tai-loring of speech to audience, which still feels a shade ignoble to me, is not un-common among young people from my part of the world. In less generous re-gions of the greater American culture, the sound of Appalachian dialect has come to signify ignorance, backwardness, intransigence, and, in the most ex-treme examples, toothlessness, rank stupidity, and an alarming propensity for planting flowers in painted tractor tires.

This is not some sort of misguided, Caucasian appeal for ethnicity, nor is it a battle cry from the radical left against the patriarchal oppression of grammar, but the fact is that for me standard English has always been something of a sec-ond language. I have intuitively written it correctly from the time I started school, but speaking it still feels slightly unnatural, demands just enough con-scious thought on my part to make me question my fluency. When I am intro-duced to a stranger, when I meet a more showily educated colleague in the Eng-lish department at Vanderbilt, when I go to parties at which I feel unsure of my place in the evening's social pecking order, I catch myself proofreading sen-tences before I speak them—adding "g"s to the ends of participles, scanning clauses to make sure they ain't got no double negatives, clipping long vowels to affectless, Midwestern dimensions, and making sure I use "lay" and "lie" in a matter that would not embarrass my father-in-law, who is a schoolteacher from California. Occasionally, even my wife, whose Southern accent is significantly more patrician than my own, will smile and ask, "What did you just say?" And I'll realize that I have unwittingly slipped into the language of my people, that I have inadvertently become "colorful." I'll rewind my sentence in my head so that I can save it as an example of how not to speak to strangers. Only in the sanctity of Granny's house can I speak my mother tongue with anything resembling peace of mind.

In 1904, a librarian and writer named Horace Kephart, having recently left his wife and children and suffered a nervous breakdown, moved to the mountains around Bryson City, North Carolina. Although he travelled there initially to distance himself from human contact, he soon recovered enough to take an active interest in the world in which he found himself. An avid gatherer of information and a compulsive list-maker, Kephart spent the rest of his life compiling exhaustive journals and records detailing the geography, history, culture, and language of the southern Appalachians—a pursuit that resulted in countless magazine articles, a celebrated handbook, "Camping and Woodcraft," and two editions of a book entitled "Our Southern Highlanders."

Although Kephart had chosen the Appalachians over the deserts of the Southwest somewhat randomly, he arrived in Western North Carolina at a particularly fortuitous time for a man of his particular talents. In the roadless hollows of the Blue Ridge and the Smokies, Kephart found a people isolated by their hostile, vertical geography and living largely as their ancestors had, in the later half of the eighteenth century, when the great Scots-Irish migration out of Pennsylvania first filled the region with people of European descent.

"No one can understand the attitude of our highlanders toward the rest of the earth," Kephart wrote,

> until he realizes their amazing isolation from all that lies beyond the blue, hazy skyline of their mountains. Conceive a shipload of emigrants cast away on some unknown island, far from the regular track of vessels, and left there for five or six generations, unaided and untroubled by the growth of civilization. Among the descendants of such a company we would expect to find customs and ideas unaltered from the time of their forefathers. . . . The mountain folk still live in the eighteenth century. The progress of mankind from that age to this is no heritage of theirs.

Because the Scots-Irish settlers had spoken to and been influenced by so few outsiders, the language they brought with them from Scotland and Ireland, by way of Pennsylvania, had been preserved remarkably intact. And the English dialect that Kephart encountered in North Carolina was in many ways closer to the Elizabethan English of Shakespeare or the Middle English of Chaucer than to anything that had been spoken in England for centuries. Coincidentally, had Kephart come to these mountains a generation later, his research would have been less definitive. Within a few years after his death, in 1931, road-building initiatives, radio, and the Sears, Roebuck catalogue had begun to open even the darkest hollows of the Appalachians to twentieth-century America. In a very short time, the resulting cultural homogenization had turned the southern highlands into a vastly different world from the one that Kephart had originally discovered.

When I first read "Our Southern Highlanders," late last year, it held for me the power of revelation. It told me who I was—or at least where I came from—in a way that I had never fully understood before. All the words I had thought specific to my family had entries in a dictionary compiled from Kephart's research. And all of them—with the exception of "quare," which is a mere two hundred years old—were words of Middle English origin, which is to say anywhere from five hundred to eight hundred years old. Although most of the people I meet today wouldn't have any idea what it's like to eat a bait, Chaucer would have.

Of course, words of Middle English origin are mere babes compared with the words of Latin, Greek, and Hebrew etymology that constitute much of our language. The Latin and Greek roots of the words "agriculture" and "barbarian" were old long before the primitive tribes of the British Isles painted their faces blue and grunted in a dialect resembling English. So I am less taken by the age of the words of the Appalachian vernacular which found their way into my grandmother's house than I am by the specific history they hold.

The word "quare," for me, contains sea voyages and migrations. It speaks of families stopping after long journeys and saying, for any one of a thousand reasons, "This is far enough." It speaks to me of generations of farmers watching red dirt turn below plow blades, of young men stepping into furrows when old men step out. It speaks to me of girls fresh from their mothers' houses crawling into marriage beds and becoming mothers themselves. It bears witness to the line of history, most of it now unmappable, that led to my human waking beneath these particular mountains. If language is the mechanism through which we inherit history and culture, then each individual word functions as a type of gene, bearing with it a small piece of the specific information that makes us who we are, and tells us where we have been. My first cousin Greg and I came down with the same obscure bone disease in the same knee at the same age. For us, the word "quare" is no less a genetic signifier of the past than the odd, bone-eating chromosome carried down through history by one wonders how many limping Scots-Irish.

The last time I remember talking to my great-grandfather Womack, he was well into his nineties, and our whole family had gathered on the porch of the house he built as a young man, along Walnut Creek, in the Sunny View community of Polk County. When I tell this story, I choose to remember it as a spring day—although it may not have been—simply because I like to think that the daffodils in his yard were blooming. (My grandmother, who is eighty-three now, helped him plant them when she was a little girl.) At some point, everyone else got up and went inside, leaving Paw Womack and me alone on the porch. I was in high school, a freshman or sophomore, and was made self-conscious by his legendary age. He had been born in another century. His father had been wounded at Gettysburg. A preacher's son, he had never uttered a swear word or tasted alcohol. He had farmed with a mule until he was well into his eighties, and he had never got another car after one that he bought in 1926 wore out. He voted for Woodrow Wilson. He was *historical*. I felt that the family had somehow chosen me to sit with him; I felt that I needed to say something. I got out of my chair and approached him as one would a sacred relic. I sat down on the porch rail facing him. I remember his immense, knotted farmer's hands spread out on the arms of his rocker. We stared at each other for what seemed like a long time. Eventually, I blushed. I smiled at him and nodded. He smiled back and said, " Who *are* you?"

I said, "I'm Reba's boy. Clara Mae's grandson."

"Oh," he said. "Reba's boy."

If we ever spoke again, I don't remember it.

It seems significant to me now that when I told Paw Womack who I was I didn't give him my name. My position as an individual was secondary to my place in the lineage that had led to my sitting on his porch. I identified myself as a small part of a greater whole. *Who are you?* I'm Reba's boy. Clara Mae's grandson, Tom Womack's great-grandson. *Where are you from?* Over yonder. *Why don't you like watermelon?* I don't know. I guess I'm just quare.

Ironically, just as I have learned to appreciate the history contained in the word "quare," I have also had to accept the fact that it is passing out of my family with my generation. Neither I nor my cousins use it outside Granny's house unless we temper it first with irony—a sure sign of a word's practical death within a changing language. Of course, no language is a static property: the life cycles of words mirror the life cycles of the individuals who speak them. Every language, given enough time, will replace each of its words, just as the human body replaces each of its cells every seven years. The self-appointed guardians of English who protest that the word "celibate" means "unmarried," and not " abstaining from sexual intercourse," are wasting their time. "Sounds are too volatile and subtle for legal restraints," Samuel Johnson wrote in the 1755 Preface to his "Dictionary of the English Language"; "to enchain syllables, and to lash the wind, are equally the undertakings of pride."

I tell myself that the passing of Appalachian vernacular from my family's vocabulary is not a tragedy, or a sign of our being assimilated into a dominant culture, but simply the arrival of an inevitable end. "Tongues, like governments," Dr. Johnson wrote, "have a natural tendency to degeneration." I tell myself that it is a natural progression for my children to speak a language significantly different from that of my ancestors, but the fact that it has happened so suddenly, within the span of a single generation—my generation—makes me wonder if I have done something wrong, if I have failed the people who passed those words down. Sometimes the truest answer to the question "Who are you?" is "I don't know."

Words and blood are the double helix that connect us to our past. As a member of a transitional generation, I am losing those words and the connection they make. I am losing the small comfort of shared history. I compensate, in the stories I write, by sending people up mountains to look, as Horace Kephart did, for the answers to their questions, to look down from a high place and see what they can see. My characters, at least, can still say the words that bind them to the past without sounding queer, strange, eccentric, odd, unusual, unconventional, or suspicious. "Stories," says the writer Tim O'Brien, "can save us." I have put my faith in the idea that words, even new ones, possess that kind of redemptive power. Writers write about a place not because they belong there, but because they want to belong. It's a quare feeling.

TOPICS FOR DISCUSSION AND WRITING

1. What does Earley mean by "this tailoring of speech to audience?" Why does he think it is "a shade ignoble"? Is this something you ever do or observe others do?

2. How is the history of Earley's family reflected in their language?

3. Earley states that "no language is a static property" and gives as an example the word "celibate." Can you think of any words whose meanings have shifted? Why is it impossible for language to remain static?

4. Write an essay about the language of your family. Include as many generations as you can and reflect on your family's history as it is reflected in their language or languages.

Today's Kids Are, Like, Killing the English Language. Yeah, Right

Kirk Johnson

While Tony Earley's mountain dialect caused him some embarrassment as a child, young people often create a language or dialect of their own. Johnson, the father of two pre-teen sons, finds that the young have a language of their own, but rather than being annoyed by their slang, he finds it meaningful and appropriate.

As a father of two pre-teen boys, I have in the last year or so become a huge fan of the word "duh." This is a word much maligned by educators, linguistic brahmins and purists, but they are all quite wrong.

Duh has elegance. Duh has shades of meaning, even sophistication. Duh and its perfectly paired linguistic partner, "yeah right," are the ideal terms to usher in the millennium and the information age, and to highlight the differences from the stolid old 20th century.

Even my sons might stop me at this point and quash my hyperbole with a quickly dispensed, "Yeah, right, Dad." But hear me out: I have become convinced that duh and yeah right have arisen to fill a void in the language because the world has changed. Fewer questions these days can effectively be answered with yes or no, while at the same time, a tidal surge of hype and mindless blather threatens to overwhelm old-fashioned conversation. Duh and yeah right are the cure.

Good old yes and no were fine for their time—the archaic, black and white era of late industrialism that I was born into in the 1950's. The yes-or-no combo was hard and fast and most of all simple: It belonged to the Manichean red-or-dead mentality of the cold war, to manufacturing, to *Father Knows Best* and *It's a Wonderful Life.*

The information-age future that my 11-year-old twins own is more complicated than yes or no. It's more subtle and supple, more loaded with content and hype and media manipulation than my childhood—or any adult's, living or dead—ever was.

And duh, whatever else it may be, is drenched with content. Between them, duh and yeah-right are capable of dividing all language and thought into an exquisitely differentiated universe. Every statement and every question can be positioned on a gray scale of understatement or overstatement, stupidity or insightfulness, information saturation or yawning emptiness.

And in an era when plain speech has become endangered by the pressures of political correctness, duh and yeah right are matchless tools of savvy, winking sarcasm and skepticism: caustic without being confrontational, incisive without being quite specific.

With duh, you can convey a response, throw in a whole basket full of auxiliary commentary about the question or the statement you're responding to, and insult the speaker all at once! As in this hypothetical exchange:

> Parent: *"Good morning, son, it's a beautiful day."*
> Eleven-year-old boy: *"Duh."*

And there is a kind of esthetic balance as well. Yeah-right is the yin to duh's yang, the antithesis to duh's emphatic thesis. Where duh is assertive and edgy, a perfect tool for undercutting mindless understatement or insulting repetition, yeah right is laid back, a surfer's cool kind of response to anything overwrought or oversold.

New York, for example, is duh territory, while Los Angles is yeah-right. Television commercials can be rendered harmless and inert by simply saying, "yeah, right," upon their conclusion. Local television news reports are helped out with a sprinkling of well placed duhs, at moments of stunning obviousness. And almost any politician's speech cries out for heaping helpings of both at various moments.

Adolescent terms like "like," by contrast, scare me to death. While I have become convinced through observation and personal experimentation that just about any adult of even modest intelligence can figure out how to use duh and yeah right properly, like is different. Like is hard. Like is, like, dangerous.

Marcel Danesi, a professor of linguistics and semiotics at the University of Toronto who has studied the language of youth and who coined the term "pubilect" to describe the dialect of pubescence, said he believes like is in fact altering the structure of the English language, making it more fluid in construction, more like Italian or some other Romance language than good old hard-and-fast Anglo-Saxon. Insert like in the middle of a sentence, he said, and a statement can be turned into a question, a question into an exclamation, an exclamation into a quiet meditation.

Consider these hypothetical expressions: "If you're having broccoli for dinner, Mr. Johnson, I'm, like, out of here!" and "I was, like, no way!" and, perhaps most startlingly. "He was, like, duh!"

In the broccoli case, like softens the sentence. It's less harsh and confrontational than saying flatly that the serving of an unpalatable vegetable would require a fleeing of the premises.

In the second instance, like functions as a kind of a verbal quotation mark, an announcement that what follows, "no way," is to be heard differently. The quote itself can then be loaded up with any variety of intonation—irony, sarcasm, even self-deprecation—all depending on the delivery.

In the third example—"He was, like duh!"—like becomes a crucial helping verb for duh, a verbal springboard. (Try saying the sentence with out like and it becomes almost incomprensible.)

But like and duh and yeah right, aside from their purely linguistic virtues, are also in many ways the perfect words to convey the sense of reflected reality that is part of the age we live in. Image manipulation, superficiality, and shallow media culture are, for better or worse, the backdrop of adolescent life.

Adults of the yes-or-no era could perhaps grow up firm in their knowledge of what things "are," but in the Age of Duh, with images reflected back from every angle at every waking moment, kids swim in a sea of what things are "like." Distinguishing what is from what merely seems to be is a required skill of an 11-year-old today; like reflects modern life, and duh and yeah right are the tools with which such a life can be negotiated and mastered.

But there is a concealed paradox in the Age of Duh. The information overload on which it is based is built around the computer, and the computer is, of course, built around—that's right—the good old yes-or-no binary code: Billions of microcircuits all blinking on or off, black or white, current in or current out. Those computers were designed by minds schooled and steeped in the world of yes or no, and perhaps it is not too much of a stretch to imagine my sons' generation, shaped by the broader view of duh, finding another path: binary code with attitude. Besides, most computers I know already seem to have an attitude. Incorporating a little duh would at least give them a sense of humor.

TOPICS FOR DISCUSSION AND WRITING

1. What meanings do "duh" and "yeah, right" convey?

2. Why is the meaning and function of "like" difficult to determine?

3. Johnson uses "yeah, right" and "like" in his title. What does each word mean in this context?

4. How do the expressions "duh," "yeah, right" and "like" reflect the changes Johnson sees between the American culture of the 50s, when he was a boy, and his sons' America?

5. For one day, when you are on campus, list as many sentences as you can in which the speaker uses "duh," "yeah, right" or "like." (A tape recorder would be helpful.) Then write an analysis of their use. Do your findings confirm the conclusions of Johnson and linguistics professor Marcel Danesi? Based on your data, can you refine or add to their conclusions?

Languages Are Political Constructions

Geoff Nunberg

The previous four essays have illustrated that language reflects culture, and dialects reflect subcultures. What precisely is the difference between a language and a dialect? There is no precise distinction according to Geoff Nunberg, a linguist at Stanford University. Nunberg delivered this essay on the impact of politics on language on National Public Radio. He points out that war and political upheavals have changed the map of the world in recent years as new nations have formed and old ones have broken up and that these political changes are sometimes followed by linguistic changes, a pattern he reminds us that took place in this country when America won its independence from England.

Back when the Ebonics controversy was at its height about a year ago, linguists were getting a lot of calls asking them to sort out the question of whether black English was really a different language than standard English. To the disappointment of the press, they tended to duck the question.

You can't say whether two varieties belong to the same language just by looking at the words or constructions they use. There are cases where people identify distinct languages even when two varieties are grammatically similar and mutually intelligible like Danish and Norwegian, Czech and Slovak, or Dutch and Afrikaans.

And there are other cases where people perceive a single language even though its varieties are very far apart. The various dialects of Chinese for example, are far more different from one another than French, Italian, and Spanish. In the end, languages are political constructions; as linguists like to put the point, a language is just a dialect with an army.

There's a lot to this remark. In recent years a number of nations have felt that a declaration of political independence required a declaration of linguistic independence as well. Until a few years ago, for example, the central part of the region formerly known as Yugoslavia was filled with a jumble of very similar dialects that were considered a single language, Serbo-Croatian.

Apart from some differences in scholarly and philosophical vocabulary, the main thing that set the Serbs and Croats apart was that the Croats used the Latin alphabet, and the Serbs often use the Cyrillic alphabet. It was only when the country of Yugoslavia broke up that the separate nations felt the need to distinguish three languages: Serbian, Croatian, and Bosnian.

As one Sarajevo professor described the situation, "I used to think I was bad at languages, but I woke up one morning to find I was trilingual." At present the three languages are a lot closer than the English of New York, London, and Melbourne.

But the Serbs and Croats are doing all they can to change that; they've each got their academies working nights to devise distinctive vocabularies and new spellings, apparently with the ultimate aim of achieving complete incomprehensibility with their neighbors.

It may all seem a little alien to us, but we should bear in mind that we Americans went through a very similar experience 200 years ago; in the period following the American Revolution there were a lot of people who believed the American language would naturally go its separate way from English once it was free from what they like to describe as the feudal establishments of England.

As the patriot William Thornton told Americans in 1793, you have corrected the dangerous doctrines of European powers, correct now the languages you have imported. The American language will thus be as distinct as the government.

The idea of declaring American a separate language was enormously popular at the time. Its supporters included Adams, Jefferson, and most notably, the great lexicographer Noah Webster. To distinguish the American language symbolically from its English ancestor, Webster devised a number of new spellings.

He dropped the "U" in words like "honor" and "favor." Flipped the "R" and the "E" of "theater" and "meter," changed the "C" in "defense" to an "S," and so forth. Most of these are still with us, of course, a little token of national linguistic pride, though NASA seems to have lost track of this point when they spelled the name of the space shuttle Endeavour with a "U."

In the end, though, spelling differences are the only legacy of the episode. The idea of declaring American a separate language took a while to die out particularly among American writers who wanted to liberate our literature from what they regarded as an obsequious deference to British models.

As Walt Whitman proclaimed, the new world, the new times, the new peoples need a tongue accordingly. But by the middle of the 19th-century most Americans were willing to concede that they still spoke the same language that the English did. And the English, more or less, returned the favor.

Still, you have to wonder what would've happened if Webster's view had won the day and America and Britain had gone on to develop mutually incomprehensible languages the way the former Yugoslavians are doing now.

Probably, it would have been our loss in the end. After all, Alistair Cooke is a small price to pay for "absolutely fabulous" and Emma Peel.

TOPICS FOR DISCUSSION AND WRITING

1. Why did linguists avoid answering the question when asked "whether black English was really a different language than standard English"?

2. What does Nunberg mean when he says that "a language is just a dialect with an army"?

3. The Ebonics controversy which Nunberg refers to erupted in Oakland, California in 1997 when teachers there taught black English, or Ebonics, in the classroom. Many in the community and the country were incensed that this "dialect" was given the same status as standard English. Find at least four articles on this controversy, making sure that more than one point of view is represented, and write an essay in which you fully explain the controversy and the issues involved. Include the conclusions you have reached concerning Ebonics in the classroom. (Refer to Writing Assignment 11 on page 118 and How to Conduct Your Research in Chapter 9, for help with this assignment.)

Figurative Language

Metaphor, Simile, Personification

In Chapter 1 we asked you to identify metaphors in Richard Wilbur's poem *The Writer* and to create a metaphor that explains your own writing process. Metaphor is one example of figurative language—the use of language which ventures beyond the denotative limits of the dictionary. It does this primarily through comparison; one thing is compared to another to achieve a deeper meaning—to make language evocative, like rubbing two sticks together to create fire.

Figurative language is not exclusively reserved for the use of poets—playwrights, novelists, journalists, and politicians use it, and student writers are also allowed, or should we say encouraged, to use it in their writing as well. You will remember from our discussion in Chapter 1 that a *metaphor* is an implied comparison—

> Life's but a walking shadow, a poor player
> That struts and frets his hour upon the stage
> And then is heard no more.
> (from *Macbeth* by William Shakespeare)

A *simile* is a comparison made explicit by the use of the words "like" or "as"—

> I pause in the stairwell, hearing
> From her shut door a commotion of typewriter-keys
> *Like* a chain hauled over a gunwale.
> from *The Writer* by Richard Wilbur (See page 18 to read the entire poem.)

Personification is another device available to writers. With personification, an animal, object or abstraction is represented as a person—"Computers don't like to be yelled at."

We make the primary distinctions between these various categories, but in reality they sometimes overlap. (See Class Logic in Chapter 7 for a discussion of overlap between classes.) When this is the case, we may safely refer to the broader categories of metaphoric or figurative language. At the heart of all these uses of language is comparison. One thing suggests another, and words take on new and deeper meanings.

Simile

Rosanna Warren

Poet Rosanna Warren, perhaps ironically, titles her poem "simile," but as you read ask yourself what the actual subject of the poem is.

*As when her friend the crack Austrian skier, in the story
she often told us, had to face
his first Olympic ski jump and, from
the starting ramp over the chute that plunged
so vertiginously its bottom lip
disappeared from view, gazed
on a horizon of Alps that swam and dandled around him
like toy boats in a bathtub, and he could not
for all his iron determination,
training, and courage
ungrip his fingers from the railings of the starting gate, so that
his teammates had to join in prying
up, finger by finger, his hands
to free him, so*

*facing death, my
mother gripped the bed rails but still
stared straight ahead—and
who was it, finally,
who loosened
her hands?*

TOPICS FOR DISCUSSION AND WRITING

1. Is the poem a simile as the title implies? What is the comparison on which the poem is based?
2. What is the subject of the poem?

Concepts We Live By

....

George Lakoff and Mark Johnson

Aristotle believed that "the greatest thing by far is to be a master of metaphor. It is the one thing that cannot be learned from others; and it is also a sign of genius." We are not sure that George Lakoff, a professor of linguistics at the University of California at Berkeley, and Mark Johnson, head of the philosophy department at the University of Oregon, would completely agree with this statement. In their book *Metaphors We Live By,* they do not see metaphor-making as the exclusive province of geniuses or of professional writers, but as a fundamental activity of the human mind, fundamental to our thinking and our use of language. They have recently written a new book on the subject of metaphor, *The Embodied Mind and Its Challenge to Western Thought,* in which they state their belief that the foundation of our metaphorical thinking stems from our earliest physical reactions to our environment, reactions that create basic metaphors that connect the world and the body. Read the first chapter of their earlier book *Metaphors We Live By* excerpted below and see if you agree with their thesis that "metaphor is pervasive in everyday life, not just in language but in thought and action." The next essay, by Deborah Tannen, builds on the work of Lakoff and Johnson.

Metaphor is for most people a device of the poetic imagination and the rhetorical flourish—a matter of extraordinary rather than ordinary language. Moreover, metaphor is typically viewed as characteristic of language alone, a matter of words rather than thought or action. For this reason, most people think they can get along perfectly well without metaphor. We have found, on the contrary, that metaphor is pervasive in everyday life, not just in language but in thought and action. Our ordinary conceptual system, in terms of which we both think and act, is fundamentally metaphorical in nature.

The concepts that govern our thought are not just matters of the intellect. They also govern our everyday functioning, down to the most mundane details. Our concepts structure what we perceive, how we get around in the world, and how we relate to other people. Our conceptual system thus plays a central role in defining our everyday realities. If we are right in suggesting that our conceptual system is largely metaphorical, then the way we think, what we experience, and what we do everyday is very much a matter of metaphor.

But our conceptual system is not something we are normally aware of. In most of the little things we do everyday, we simply think and act more or less automatically along certain lines. Just what these lines are is by no means obvious. One way to find out is by looking at language. Since communication is based on the same conceptual system that we use in thinking and acting, language is an important source of evidence for what that system is like.

Primarily on the basis of linguistic evidence, we have found that most of our ordinary conceptual system is metaphorical in nature. And we have found a way to begin to identify in detail just what the metaphors are that structure how we perceive, how we think, and what we do.

To give some idea of what it could mean for a concept to be metaphorical and for such a concept to structure an everyday activity, let us start with the concept ARGUMENT and the conceptual metaphor ARGUMENT IS WAR. This metaphor is reflected in our everyday language by a wide variety of expressions:

ARGUMENT IS WAR

Your claims are *indefensible.*

He *attacked every weak point* in my argument.

His criticisms were *right on target.*

I *demolished* his argument.

I've never *won* an argument with him.

You disagree? Okay, *shoot!*

If you use that *strategy,* he'll *wipe you out.*

He *shot down* all of my arguments.

It is important to see that we don't just *talk* about arguments in terms of war. We can actually win or lose arguments. We see the person we are arguing with as an opponent. We attack his positions and we defend our own. We gain and lose ground. We plan and use strategies. If we find a position indefensible, we can abandon it and take a new line of attack. Many of the things we *do* in arguing are partially structured by the concept of war. Though there is no physical battle, there is a verbal battle, and the structure of an argument—attack, defense, counterattack, etc.—reflects this. It is in this sense that the ARGUMENT IS WAR metaphor is one that we live by in this culture; it structures the actions we perform in arguing.

Try to imagine a culture where arguments are not viewed in terms of war, where no one wins or loses, where there is no sense of attacking or defending, gaining or losing ground. Imagine a culture where an argument is viewed as a dance, the participants are seen as performers, and the goal is to perform in a balanced and aesthetically pleasing way. In such a culture, people would view arguments differently, experience them differently, carry them out differently, and talk about them differently. But *we* would probably not view them as arguing at all: they would simply be doing something different. It would seem strange even to call what they were doing "arguing." Perhaps the most neutral way of describing this difference between their culture and ours would be to say that we have a discourse form structured in terms of battle and they have one structured in terms of dance.

This is an example of what it means for a metaphorical concept, namely, ARGUMENT IS WAR, to structure (at least in part) what we do and how we understand what we are doing when we argue. *The essence of metaphor is understanding and experiencing one kind of thing in terms of another.* It is not that arguments are a subspecies of war. Arguments and wars are different kinds of things—verbal discourse and armed conflict—and the actions performed are different kinds of actions. But ARGUMENT is partially structured, understood, performed, and talked about in terms of WAR. The concept is metaphorically structured, the activity is metaphorically structured, and, consequently, the language is metaphorically structured.

Moreover, this is the *ordinary* way of having an argument and talking about one. The normal way for us to talk about attacking a position is to use the words "attack a position." Our conventional ways of talking about arguments presuppose a metaphor we are hardly ever conscious of. The metaphor is not merely in the words we use—it is in our very concept of an argument. The language of argument is not poetic, fanciful, or rhetorical; it is literal. We talk about arguments that way because we conceive of them that way—and we act according to the way we conceive of things.

The most important claim we have made so far is that metaphor is not just a matter of language, that is, of mere words. We shall argue that, on the contrary, human *thought processes* are largely metaphorical. This is what we mean when we say that the human conceptual system is metaphorically structured and defined. Metaphors as linguistic expression are possible precisely because there are metaphors in a person's conceptual system. . . .

Fighting for Our Lives

Deborah Tannen

Deborah Tannen, a professor of linguistics at Georgetown University, is best known for her book, *You Just Don't Understand,* about the differences in the way men and women communicate. Her next book, *Talking from 9 to 5,* focuses on communication in the workplace. Tannen believes, as Lakoff and Johnson do, that metaphor plays a central role in language, thought, and action. And like Lakoff and Johnson, she is concerned about the prevalence in our language of the "argument is war" metaphor. In her most recent book, *The Argument Culture,* she focuses on this metaphor, showing its impact on our culture and its institutions, an influence she finds harmful in the extreme.

METAPHORS: WE ARE WHAT WE SPEAK

Perhaps one reason suspicions of Robert Gallo were so zealously investigated is that the scenario of an ambitious scientist ready to do anything to defeat a rival appeals to our sense of story; it is the kind of narrative we are ready to believe.* Culture, in a sense, is an environment of narratives that we hear repeatedly until they seem to make self-evident sense in explaining human behavior. Thinking of human interactions as battles is a metaphorical frame through which we learn to regard the world and the people in it.

All language uses metaphors to express ideas; some metaphoric words and expressions are novel, made up for the occasion, but more are calcified in the language. They are simply the way we think it is natural to express ideas. We don't think of them as metaphors. Someone who says, "Be careful: You aren't a cat; you don't have nine lives," is explicitly comparing you to a cat, because the cat is named in words. But what if someone says, "Don't pussyfoot around; get

*Robert Gallo, an American scientist who co-discovered the AIDS virus, was suspected of having stolen his discovery from a French scientist who had independently identified the virus.

to the point"? There is no explicit comparison to a cat, but the comparison is there nonetheless, implied in the word "pussyfoot." This expression probably developed as a reference to the movements of a cat cautiously circling a suspicious object. I doubt that individuals using the word "pussyfoot" think consciously of cats. More often than not, we use expressions without thinking about their metaphoric implications. But that doesn't mean those implications are not influencing us.

At a meeting, a general discussion became so animated that a participant who wanted to comment prefaced his remark by saying, "I'd like to leap into the fray." Another participant called out, "Or share your thoughts." Everyone laughed. By suggesting a different phrasing, she called attention to what would probably have otherwise gone unnoticed: "Leap into the fray" characterized the lively discussion as a metaphorical battle.

Americans talk about almost everything as if it were a war. A book about the history of linguistics is called *The Linguistics Wars.* A magazine article about claims that science is not completely objective is titled "The Science Wars." One about breast cancer detection is "The Mammogram War"; about competition among caterers, "Party Wars"—and on and on in potentially endless list. Politics, of course, is a prime candidate. One of innumerable possible examples, the headline of a story reporting that the Democratic National Convention nominated Bill Clinton to run for a second term declares, "DEMOCRATS SEND CLINTON INTO BATTLE FOR A 2D TERM." But medicine is as frequent a candidate, as we talk about battling and conquering disease.

Headlines are intentionally devised to attract attention, but we all use military or attack imagery in everyday expressions without thinking about it: "Take a shot at it," "I don't want to be shot down," "He went off half cocked," "That's half the battle." Why does it matter that our public discourse is filled with military metaphors? Aren't they just words? Why not talk about something that matters—like actions?

Because words matter. When we think we are using language, language is using us. As linguist Dwight Bolinger put it (employing a military metaphor), language is like a loaded gun: It can be fired intentionally, but it can wound or kill just as surely when fired accidentally. The terms in which we talk about something shape the way we think about it—and even what we see.

The power of words to shape perception has been proven by researchers in controlled experiments. Psychologists Elizabeth Loftus and John Palmer, for example, found that the terms in which people are asked to recall something affect what they recall. The researchers showed subjects a film of two cars colliding, then asked how fast the cars were going; one week later, they asked whether there had been any broken glass. Some subjects were asked, "About how fast were the cars going when they bumped into each other?" Others were asked, "About how fast were the cars going when they smashed into each other?" Those who read the question with the verb "smashed" estimated that the cars were going faster. They were also more likely to "remember" having seen broken glass. (There wasn't any.)

This is how language works. It invisibly molds our way of thinking about people, actions, and the world around us. Military metaphors train us to think about—and see—everything in terms of fighting, conflict, and war. This perspective then limits our imaginations when we consider what we can do about situations we would like to understand or change.

Even in science, common metaphors that are taken for granted influence how researchers think about natural phenomena. Evelyn Fox Keller describes a case in which acceptance of a metaphor led scientists to see something that was not there. A mathematical biologist, Keller outlines the fascinating behavior of cellular slime mold. This unique mold can take two completely different forms: It can exist as single-cell organisms, or the separate cells can come together to form multicellular aggregates. The puzzle facing scientists was: What triggers aggregation? In other words, what makes the single cells join together? Scientists focused their investigations by asking what entity issued the order to start aggregating. They first called this bosslike entity a "founder cell," and later a "pacemaker cell," even though no one had seen any evidence for the existence of such a cell. Proceeding nonetheless from the assumption that such a cell must exist, they ignored noted evidence to the contrary: For example, when the center of the aggregate is removed, other centers form.

Scientists studying slime mold did not examine the interrelationship between the cells and their environment, nor the interrelationship between the functional systems within each cell, because they were busy looking for the pacemaker cell, which, as eventually became evident, did not exist. Instead, under conditions of nutritional deprivation, each individual cell begins to feel the urge to merge with others to form the conglomerate. It is a reaction of the cells to their environment, not to the orders of a boss. Keller recounts this tale to illustrate her insight that we tend to view nature through our understanding of human relations as hierarchical. In her words, "We risk imposing on nature the very stories we like to hear." In other words, the conceptual metaphor of hierarchical governance made scientists "see" something—a pacemaker cell—that wasn't there.

Among the stories many Americans most like to hear are war stories. According to historian Michael Sherry, the American war movie developed during World War II and has been with us ever since. He shows that movies not explicitly about war were also war movies at heart, such as westerns with their good guy–bad guy battles settled with guns. *High Noon,* for example, which became a model for later westerns, was in allegory of the Second World War: The happy ending hinges on the pacifist taking up arms. We can also see this story line in contemporary adventure films. Think of *Star Wars* with its stirring finale in which Han Solo, having professed no interest in or taste for battle, returns at the last moment to destroy the enemy and save the day. And precisely the same theme is found in a contemporary low-budget independent film, *Sling Blade,* in which a peace-loving retarded man becomes a hero at the end by murdering the man who has been tormenting the family he has come to love.

PUT UP YOUR DUKES

If war provides the metaphors through which we view the world and each other, we come to view others—and ourselves—as warriors in battle. Almost any human encounter can be framed as a fight between two opponents. Looking at it this way brings particular aspects of the event into focus and obscures others.

Framing interactions as fights affects not only the participants but also the viewers. At a performance, the audience, as well as the performers, can be transformed. This effect was noted by a reviewer in *The New York Times,* commenting on a musical event:

> *Showdown at Lincoln Center.* Jazz's ideological war of the last several years led to a pitched battle in August between John Lincoln Collier, the writer, and Wynton Marsalis, the trumpeter, in a debate at Lincoln Center. Mr. Marsalis demolished Mr. Collier, point after point after point, but what made the debate unpleasant was the crowd's blood lust; humiliation, not elucidation, was the desired end.

Military imagery pervades this account: the difference of opinions between Collier and Marsalis was an "ideological war," and the "debate" was a "pitched battle" in which Marsalis "demolished" Collier (not his arguments, but him). What the commentator regrets, however, is that the audience got swept up in the mood instigated by the way the debate was carried out: "the crowd's blood lust" for Collier's defeat.

This is one of the most dangerous aspects of regarding intellectual interchange as a fight. It contributes to an atmosphere of animosity that spreads like a fever. In a society that includes people who express their anger by shooting, the result of demonizing those with whom we disagree can be truly tragic.

But do audiences necessarily harbor within themselves a "blood lust," or is it stirred in them by the performances they are offered? Another arts event was set up as a debate between a playwright and a theater director. In this case, the metaphor through which the debate was viewed was not war but boxing—a sport that is in itself, like a debate, a metaphorical battle that pitches one side against the other in an all-out effort to win. A headline describing the event set the frame: "AND IN THIS CORNER . . . ," followed by the subhead "A Black Playwright and White Critic Duke It Out." The story then reports:

> the face-off between August Wilson, the most successful black playwright in the American theater, and Robert Brustein, longtime drama critic for The New Republic and artistic director of the American Repertory Theatre in Cambridge, Mass. These two heavyweights had been battling in print since last June. . . .
>
> Entering from opposite sides of the stage, the two men shook hands and came out fighting—or at least sparring.

Wilson, the article explains, had given a speech in which he opposed Black performers taking "white" roles in color-blind casting; Brustein had written a column disagreeing; and both followed up with further responses to each other.

According to the article, "The drama of the Wilson-Brustein confrontation lies in their mutual intransigence." No one would question that audiences crave drama. But is intransigence the most appealing source of drama? I happened to hear this debate broadcast on the radio. The line that triggered the loudest cheers from the audience was the final question put to the two men by the moderator, Anna Deavere Smith: "What did you each learn from the other in this debate?" The loud applause was evidence that the audience did not crave intransigence.

They wanted to see another kind of drama: the drama of change—change that comes from genuinely listening to someone with a different point of view, not the transitory drama of two intransigent positions in stalemate.

To encourage the staging of more dramas of change and fewer of intransigence, we need new metaphors to supplement and complement the pervasive war and boxing match metaphors through which we take it for granted issues and events are best talked about and viewed.

ALTERNATIVES TO WAR METAPHORS: THE BODY POLITIC

If the argument culture is seen in—and reinforced by—our tendency to talk about everything in terms of war, perhaps other cultures can suggest new metaphors and alternative ways of handling information and dealing with conflict. Kimberly Jones set out to learn how a culture that emphasizes harmony and discourages confrontation accomplishes conflict. She found that in some settings, such as among coworkers in offices, the Japanese tend to avoid open conflict, but in others, such as televised political debates, conflict is common. But it is carried out in ways that would strike most Americans, as "soft"; for example, opponents quickly reach consensus on minor issues so they can save their stronger rhetoric for more important ones. Also, the terms in which they express their opposition may be different from those we take for granted.

Listening to the ways other languages express ideas offers glimpses of how different a world of words can be. In American English we talk about so many matters in terms of war and sports metaphors that it is hard to think how else these ideas could be expressed. Whereas Americans frequently talk of illness as if the human body were a battleground, Japanese experts can speak of the economy as if it were a human body—the 'body politic."

For example, in a televised talk show analyzed by Japanese linguist Atsuko Honda, two guests differed in their assessment of Japan's economic situation: Suzuki was optimistic about the economy, and Takahashi was pessimistic. The moderator posed the medical metaphor; when asking Suzuki what had caused the recession, he used the word *yamu,* "ailing" (a verb meaning "to suffer from a disease") and asked for Suzuki's *shindan,* "diagnosis." Suzuki said he thought the problem was digestive: "Because of overeating and overdrinking, the digestive organs went wrong. So it needs to rest quietly for a while." This implies a condition no more serious than a little indigestion following a large meal. He elaborated: "It's not something constitutional, like internal organs such as the liver or kidney, where the patient is no good for a while and has to be in the hospital."

Takahashi accepted the overeating metaphor but used it to explain why the condition was more serious: "So the muscles have quite, so to speak, been exhausted. In other words, because the excess weight has been put on, its function has very much deteriorated." This describes a situation that warrants more concern and more strenuous efforts toward recovery. According to Takahashi, "the circulatory organs are afflicted." He continued the medical metaphor, using it to do something quite surprising for Americans in another way—to admit he does not have a solution: "As for what we should do so that we could invigorate business activities, we don't have a good prescription."

TOPICS FOR DISCUSSION AND WRITING

1. Look at the ad below and list all of the words which support the war metaphor. Then visit the Internet site noted at the bottom of the ad to see if the war metaphor is prevalent there as well. Finally, find an ad which is based on a metaphor, and analyze its effectiveness; in other words, why was this metaphor chosen to sell this product?

CANCER.

IT'S A WAR.

THAT'S WHY WE'RE DEVELOPING

316 NEW WEAPONS.

America's pharmaceutical companies are developing 316 new medicines to fight cancer—the second leading cause of death in the United States. Gene therapies, "magic bullet" antibodies, and light-activated medicines are all new weapons in the high-tech, high-stakes war against cancer. Pharmaceutical company researchers have already discovered medicines that are allowing more and more cancer survivors to say, "I won the battle." We hope one day we can all say, "We won the war."

America's Pharmaceutical Companies

Leading the way in the search for cures

www.searchforcures.org

2. Choose either the business or sports section of your local newspaper and read one or two pages. As you read, list all examples of metaphor. Now study your list. Are there any patterns? Can you pick out one or more dominant metaphors? If so, what cultural attitude toward business or sports do the metaphors reveal? How might these metaphors influence our actions in the arena of business or sports? Can you suggest an alternative metaphor that would produce different actions?

   For help with this assignment, refer to the "Argument is war" list in "Concepts We Live By" and to the following list taken from another section of Lakoff and Johnson's book.

TIME IS MONEY
You're *wasting* my time.
This gadget will *save* you hours.
I don't have time to *give* you.
How do you *spend* your time these days?
That flat tire *cost* me an hour.
I've *invested* a lot of time in her.
I don't *have enough* time to *spare* for that.
You're *running out* of time.
You need to *budget* your time.
Put aside some time for ping pong.
Is that *worth your while*?
Do you *have* much time *left*?
He's living on *borrowed* time.
You don't *use* your time *profitably*.
I *lost* a lot of time when I got sick.
Thank you for your time.

3. Deborah Tannen believes that: "Military metaphors train us to think about—and see—everything in terms of fighting, conflict, and war. This perspective then limits our imaginations when we consider what we can do about situations we would like to understand or change." Based on the readings and the work you've done on Topics 1 and 2 above, write a short paper in response to Tannen's statement.

Metaphor Monopoly

Steve Johnson

Thus far we have read that metaphor is central to thinking and to language. Now Steve Johnson, the editor of *Feed,* an on-line cultural magazine, describes the important role that metaphor plays in computer technology.

The Justice Department doesn't usually deal with existential matters—at least until last Monday, when Attorney General Janet Reno asked a Federal judge to impose a $1 million-a-day fine on Microsoft Corporation.

She alleged that the company was forcing computer makers to include its Internet browser with the Windows 95 operating system, a violation, she said, of the company's 1995 antitrust agreement with the Justice Department. The company vigorously denied any wrongdoing.

Whatever the outcome, however, this is the first major antitrust case to take place in the strange nether world of cyberspace, and as such it tells us how the computer has altered how we see the world.

Essentially, this whole fight is about the power of metaphor. Ms. Reno alleges that "Microsoft is unlawfully taking advantage of its Windows monopoly to protect and extend that monopoly and undermine consumer choice." But that monopoly lies less in technology than in the "interface," the pictures and symbols on the screen through which consumers interact with their computers.

The metaphor at the heart of the interface is that of the desktop, a personalized space where we keep our files and applications. We organize our documents by placing them into metaphoric folders; we discard files in a metaphoric trash can.

Look at it this way. Imagine that Microsoft controls the market for office desks, and it is also a major telephone maker. One day it announces that all its

BiZarRO   by Dan Piraro

desks will come with built-in phones—thereby putting all the other phone man-ufactures out of business.

The Internet browser is the phone here, and Microsoft, by building it in has effectively made itself into the de facto access provider to the Internet. This means, continuing in a metaphorical vein, that the 90 percent of the computer owners who use Windows software on their metaphorical desktop will now ride only metaphorical Microsoft rockets as they speed through metaphorical Inter-net universe.

These quandaries bring home how profoundly the computer has altered our world view, from one in which objects predominate the one in which "informa-tion," whatever that is, and the myriad shapes they can take are coming to dominate our lives. The most important antitrust issues no longer have to do with pricing, said Assistant Attorney General Joel I. Klein, they have to do with using innovation to gain an unfair competitive advantage. The Justice Depart-ment must now try to regulate a pure product of mind—thought itself.

We hear a great deal about the tremendous number-crunching power of the PC, but it is the symbolic capabilities of today's machines—all those visual metaphors and virtual desktops—that are altering our experience of the world.

The wizards at Microsoft have long understood how visual metaphors can be used to consolidate power while also making computers friendlier. Even if the Justice Department's latest crusade succeeds only in making explicit the mixed nature of this blessing, it will have done us a great service.

TOPICS FOR DISCUSSION AND WRITING

1. List the computer metaphors Johnson describes. Can you add to the list?

2. Why are these visual metaphors effective for computer users?

Analogy

An analogy is like a metaphor in that one thing is compared to another, but the comparison in an analogy is explicit while in a metaphor it is implicit. Analogies can be used in descriptions and exposition to explain something unfamiliar in terms of something familiar. An argument by analogy com-pares two or more things and suggests that because they are similar in cer-tain respects, it is reasonable to conclude that they are similar in other re-spects which we have not been able to observe directly.

Early in the last century, for example, it was known that the atmos-pheric conditions of the planet Mars are similar to those of Earth. From this similarity, some argued that Mars must be inhabited by living beings similar to those on Earth. This analogy has long since been proven false, but it illustrates how vivid and accessible reasoning by analogy can be.

Getting Off Easy in Tobacco Land

Barbara Ehrenreich

Writing in *Time* magazine, social critic Barbara Ehrenreich uses analogy as a weapon in her attack against the tobacco industry.

Three young people in Florida, barely out of their teens, have just been sentenced to 15 years each for removing a stop sign from an intersection. The defendants sobbed, and even the judge evinced regret, but everyone seems to agree that stealing stop signs is a particularly heinous prank. In this case, three other young people were killed when they drove through the signless intersection into an eight-ton Mack truck.

Now, suppose these three miscreants had done something else. Suppose that they had removed stop signs at not just one but 133,333 intersections annually, resulting in three deaths per intersection, or 400,000 dead drivers and passengers a year. Suppose further that they had not only removed the stop signs but also replaced them with Go signs or, better yet, billboards advertising how cool it is to zip heedlessly through intersections without being bothered by irritating, petty-minded, governmental instructions. In fact, make those very attractive billboards featuring yellow-slickered cowboys or a suave camel named Joe. Then what do you think the sentence would have been?

Well, if the kind judicial reasoning that applies to the tobacco companies also applied to the stop-sign cases, then the three witless young vandals would have faced a stiff fine and been forced to downsize the cowboy and put the camel out to pasture. But there would be no talk about prison terms; in fact, Congress would be considering legislation to bar any such vengefulness on the part of the courts. If the youths were fortunate enough to be a tobacco company, they might even find themselves rewarded for their crime with immunity from future class-action suits brought by the relatives of deceased drivers. They would be encouraged to take their act overseas and start focusing on signs saying *HALT* or *ARRET*.

You don't have to be a Floridian to find instructive contrasts to the proposed tobacco settlement. In Oklahoma earlier this year, a 38-year-old father of three was sentenced to 93 years for growing marijuana in his basement. (That's 70 years for possession alone.) Which suggests that the best strategy for legalizing marijuana might be to criminalize tobacco—and then just wait for the sentences for possession of smokable substances to drop, say, from 93 years in prison to 10 minutes of community service.

To be fair, there are some big differences between the stop-sign case and the tobacco settlement. Smokers know they're risking their life and their health; it says so on the cigarette pack, right near "tasteful/low tar" or some similarly enticing inscription. In contrast, the three teens killed at the intersection didn't have a clue about the missing sign. No one has ever declared a willingness to "walk a mile" to go through an unmarked intersection or congratulated herself for having "come a long way" when she got to one. But to continue in the vein of fairness, it is also true that the stop-sign thieves had throughout their young lives neglected to contribute to any major political campaign. Anyone contemplating a thoughtless act that might end up costing people their life should take a tip from the tobacco companies and start bankrolling politicians who might be sympathetic to their cause.

There is another way the three Florida vandals went wrong: they failed to incorporate before committing their dastardly act. According to a fateful 1886 Supreme Court decision, corporations or persons, entitled like anyone else to freedom of speech, even when they use it to promote the widespread consumption of a poisonous substance. They are not, however, persons who can be lethally injected or attached to a chain gang, no matter how wicked their crimes. In 1996, for example, Rockwell International was found guilty of causing an explosion that killed two company scientists. Pfizer manufactured a defective heart valve that caused 360 deaths worldwide. In all these cases, hefty fines were levied and stern statements were made, but no executive or plant manager spent so much as a night in the slammer.

The lesson from these cases, as well as from the tobacco settlement, is that that mysterious masked entity known as corporation is in fact an ingenious device for collectivizing responsibility. Even when a corporation is found guilty, no actual individual need to take the fall. But if the defense lawyer for a mere biological person attempts a similar diffusion of blame—by, for example, pointing out the defendant's history of abuse as a child, or the fact that several upstanding citizens had noticed the missing stop sign and failed to report it—said lawyer can expect these days to be laughed out of the court

So here's another tip for anyone contemplating the old stop-sign prank: don't do the sign removing yourself. Call yourself Superior Sign Relocation Inc., and hire others to do the manual labor so you can always point proudly to your contribution as a pillar of the economy and a creator of jobs. And if you wonder how you'll make the money to meet payroll, that's easy: you'll sell the purloined signs, of course, to the millions of homeowners who, like so many law-abiding, homeowning neighbors, favor them as decorations for their basement wet bars.

TOPICS FOR DISCUSSION AND WRITING

1. What is the conclusion of Ehrenreich's argument? (See Premises and Conclusions in Chapter 3.)

2. What is the central analogy in this argument? How rhetorically effective is it?

3. In Chapter 6 we discuss false analogies—two things are compared whose key features are different. Is Ehrenreich's analogy false? What criticisms does Ehrenreich make of her own analogy?

In Defense of Abortion

Judith Jarvis Thomson

In an excerpt from her essay "In Defense of Abortion," published in *Philosophy and Public Affairs* by Princeton University Press, Thomson, a philosophy professor, relies heavily on analogy to make her point that a woman must be allowed to decide whether or not she should have an abortion.

Most opposition to abortion relies on the premise that the fetus is a human being, a person from the moment of conception. The premise is argued for, but, as I think, not well. But I shall not discuss any of this. For it seems to me to be of great interest to ask what happens if, for the sake of argument, we allow the premise. How, precisely, are we supposed to get from there to the conclusion that abortion is morally impermissible? Opponents of abortion commonly spend most of their time establishing that the fetus is a person, and hardly any time explaining the step from there to the impermissibility of abortion. Perhaps they think the step too simple and obvious to require much comment. Or perhaps instead they are simply being economical in argument. Many of those who defend abortion rely on the premise that the fetus is not a person, but only a bit of tissue that will become a person at birth; and why pay out more arguments than you have to? Whatever the explanation, I suggest that the step they take is neither easy nor obvious, that it calls for closer examination than it is commonly given, and that when we do give it this closer examination we shall feel inclined to reject it.

I propose, then, that we grant that the fetus is a person from the moment of conception. How does the argument go from here? Something like this, I take it. Every person has a right to life. So the fetus has a right to life. No doubt the mother has a right to decide what shall happen in and to her body; everyone would grant that. But surely a person's right to life is stronger and more stringent than the mother's right to decide what happens in and to her body, and so outweighs it. So the fetus may not be killed; an abortion may not be performed.

It sounds plausible. But now let me ask you to imagine this. You wake up in the morning and find yourself back to back in bed with an unconscious violinist. A famous unconscious violinist. He has been found to have a fatal kidney ailment, and the Society of Music Lovers has canvassed all the available medical records and found that you alone have the right blood to help. They have therefore kidnapped you, and last night the violinist's circulatory system was plugged into yours, so that your kidneys can be used to extract poisons from his blood as well as your own. The director of the hospital now tells you, "Look, we're sorry the Society of Music Lovers did this to you—we would never have permitted it if we had known. But still, they did it, and the violinist now is plugged into you. To unplug you would be to kill him. But never mind, it's only for nine months. By then he will have recovered from his ailment, and can safely be unplugged from you." Is it morally incumbent on you to accede to this situation? No doubt it

would be very nice of you if you did, a great kindness. But do you have to accede to it? What if it were not nine months, but nine years? Or longer still? What
if the director of the hospital says, "Tough luck, I agree, but you've now got to
stay in bed, with the violinist plugged into you, for the rest of your life. Because
remember this. All persons have a right to life, and violinists are persons.
Granted you have a right to decide what happens in and to your body, but a
person's right to life outweighs your right to decide what happens in and to
your body. So you cannot be ever unplugged from him." I imagine you would
regard this as outrageous, which suggests that something really is wrong with
that plausible-sounding argument I mentioned a moment ago.

TOPICS FOR DISCUSSION AND WRITING

1. What is Thomson's analogy? In other words, what two things are being compared? In what ways are the two alike? In what ways are
   they different? Is the analogy effective? Explain your answer. (See
   False Analogy in Chapter 6.)
2. Create analogies for the following items:

   a computer
   the Internet
   a cell phone
   a pager
   a college degree

   Develop these analogies fully in a paragraph or two.
3. Much of Thomson's argument is based on deductive reasoning.
   Identify and complete the syllogisms she uses in her argument. (See
   Class Logic and the Deductive Syllogism in Chapter 7.)

Symbols

Figurative language also includes the use of symbols; *symbols* represent
something beyond themselves. They can be people, objects, situations or
actions which suggest other meanings. Virginia Woolf in her feminist essay,
A Room of One's Own (published in 1929), describes a meal she is served
at a women's college and a meal she receives at a men's college, one a
tasteless platter of beef and prunes, the other a feast of sole and partridge,
to symbolize the disparity between the education available to women and
the one offered to men. The two meals are actual, literal meals, described
in vivid detail, but they suggest something much larger and more significant than themselves. (For a discussion of the symbolic nature of language,
see Language: An Abstract System of Symbols in Chapter 5.)

Symbolism

....

David Lodge

A professor of literature at the University of Birmingham for twenty-seven years, British novelist and critic David Lodge has published nine novels, among them *Nice Work, Small World,* and *Changing Places.* This selection is taken from *The Art of Fiction,* a collection of newspaper columns on literature originally published in the *Washington Post* and the British paper, *Independent on Sunday.* Here Lodge explains symbolism using a passage from D. H. Lawrence's novel, *Women in Love.*

"The fool!" cried Ursula loudly. "Why doesn't he ride away till it's gone by?"

Gudrun was looking at him with black-dilated, spellbound eyes. But he sat glistening and obstinate, forcing the wheeling mare, which spun and swerved like a wind, and yet could not get out of the grasp of his will, nor escape from the mad clamour of terror that resounded through her, as the trucks thumped slowly, heavily, horrifying, one after the other, one pursuing the other, over the rails of the crossing.

The locomotive, as if wanting to see what could be done, put on the brakes, and back came the trucks rebounding on the iron buffers, striking like horrible cymbals, clashing nearer and nearer in frightful strident concussions. The mare opened her mouth and rose slowly, as if lifted up on a wind of terror. Then suddenly her fore-feet struck out, as she convulsed herself utterly away from the horror. Back she went, and the two girls clung to each other, feeling she must fall backwards on top of him. But he leaned forward, his face shining with fixed amusement, and at last he brought her down, sank her down, and was bearing her back to the mark. But as strong as the pressure of his compulsion was the repulsion of her utter terror, throwing her back away from the railway, so that she spun round and round on two legs, as if she were in the centre of some whirlwind. It made Gudrun faint with poignant dizziness, which seemed to penetrate to her heart.

Roughly speaking, anything that "stands for" something else is a symbol, but the process operates in many different ways. A cross may symbolize Christianity in one context, by association with the Crucifixion, and a road intersection in another, by diagrammatic resemblance. Literary symbolism is less easily decoded than these examples, because it tries to be original and tends towards a rich plurality, even ambiguity, of meaning (all qualities that would be undesirable in traffic signs and religious icons, especially the former). If a metaphor or simile consists of likening A to B, a literary symbol is a B that *suggests* an A, or a number of As. The poetic style known as Symbolism, which started in France in the late nineteenth century in the work of Baudelaire, Verlaine and Mallarmé, and exerted considerable influence on English writing in the twentieth, was characterized by a shimmering surface of suggested meanings without a denotative core.

Somebody once said, however, that the novelist should make his spade a spade before he makes it a symbol, and this would seem to be good advice for a writer who is aiming to create anything like the "illusion of life". If the spade is introduced all too obviously just for the sake of its symbolic meaning, it will tend to undermine the credibility of the narrative as human action. D. H. Lawrence was often prepared to take that risk to express a visionary insight—as when, in another episode of *Women in Love,* he has his hero rolling naked in the grass and throwing stones at the reflection of the moon. But in the passage quoted here he has kept a nice balance between realistic description and symbolic suggestion.

The "spade" in this case is a complex action: a man controlling a horse frightened by a colliery train passing at a level crossing, while being watched by two women. The man is Gerald Critch, the son of the local colliery owner, who manages the business and will eventually inherit it. The setting is the Nottinghamshire landscape in which Lawrence, a coalminer's son, was brought up: a pleasant countryside scarred and blackened in places by the pits and their railways. One might say that the train "symbolizes" the mining industry, which is a product of culture in the anthropological sense, and that the horse, a creature of Nature, symbolizes the countryside. Industry has been imposed on the countryside by the masculine power and will of capitalism, a process Gerald symbolically re-enacts by the way he dominates his mare, forcing the animal to accept the hideous mechanical noises of train.

The two women in the scene are sisters, Ursula and Gudrun Brangwen, the former a teacher, the latter an artist. They are out on a country walk when they wittness the scene at the level crossing. Both identify sympathetically with the terrified horse. Ursula is outraged by Gerald's behaviour, and speaks her mind. But the scene is described from Gudrun's point of view, and her response is more complex and ambivalent. There is sexual symbolism in the way Gerald controls his mount—"at last he brought her down, sank her down, and was bearing her back to the mark"—and there is certainly an element of macho exhibitionism in his display of strength in front of the two women. Whereas Ursula is simply disgusted by the spectacle, Gudrun is sexually aroused by it, almost in spite of herself. The mare "spun round and round on two legs, as if she were in the centre of some whirlwind. It made Gudrun faint with poignant dizziness, which seemed to penetrate to her heart." "Poignant" is a transferred epithet, which logically belongs to the suffering of the horse; its rather odd application to "dizziness" expresses the turmoil of Gudrun's emotions, and calls attention to the root meaning of *poignant*—pricking, piercing—which, with "penetrate" in the next clause, gives a powerfully phallic emphasis to the whole description. A couple of pages later Gudrun is described as "numbed in her mind by the sense of indomitable soft weight of the man bearing down into the living body of the horse: the strong, indomitable thighs of the blond man clenching the palpitating body of the mare into pure control." The whole scene is indeed prophetic of the passionate but mutually destructive sexual relationship that will develop later in the story between Gudrun and Gerald.

This rich brew of symbolic suggestion would, however, be much less effective if Lawrence did not at the same time allow us to picture the scene in vivid, sensuous detail. The ugly noise and motion of trucks as the train brakes is rendered in onomatopoeic syntax and diction ("clashing nearer and nearer in frightful strident concussions"), followed by an eloquent image of the horse, graceful even in panic: "The mare opened her mouth and rose slowly, as if lifted up on a wind of terror." Whatever you think of Lawrence's men and women, he was always brilliant when describing animals.

It is worth nothing that symbolism is generated in two different ways in this passage. The Nature/Culture symbolism is modelled on the rhetorical figures of speech known as metonymy and synecdoche. Metonymy substitutes cause for effect or vice versa (the locomotive stands for Industry because it is an effect of the Industrial Revolution) and synecdoche substitutes part for whole or vice versa (the horse stands for Nature because it is part of Nature). The sexual symbolism, on the other hand, is modelled on metaphor and simile, in which one thing is equated with another on the basis of some similarity between them: Gerald's domination of his mare is described in such a way as to suggest a human sexual act. This distinction, originally formulated by the Russian structuralist Roman Jakobson, operates on every level of a literary text, and indeed outside literature too, as my heroine Robyn Penrose demonstrated to a sceptical Vic Wilcox in *Nice Work,* by analysing cigarette advertisements. . . .

TOPICS FOR DISCUSSION AND WRITING

1. In Ernest Hemingway's short story "The Three-Day Blow," the protagonist, Nick Adams, and his friend, Bill, have a conversation about symbols:

   "Did you read the *Forest Lovers*?"
   "Yup. That's the one where they go to bed every night with the naked sword between them."
   "That's a good book, Wemedge."
   "It's a swell book. What I couldn't ever understand was what good the sword would do. It would have to stay edge up all the time because if it went over flat you could roll right over it and it wouldn't make any trouble."
   "It's a symbol," Bill said.
   "Sure," said Nick. "But it isn't practical."

   What does Hemingway imply about the use of symbols in literature that David Lodge would agree with?

2. Although Lodge defines the rhetorical terms "metonymy" and "synecdoche," if these are terms you are not familiar with, you may want to learn more. After finding the definitions of these terms in a dictionary, list two examples of each.

Symbolism in Advertising

As David Lodge notes at the conclusion of his essay on symbolism, its use is not limited to literature; advertising also frequently employs symbolism. Indeed, advertising has taken many of its tools from the poet. They both use rhyme and rhythm and depend on the connotative rather than the denotative meaning of words. Both poetry and advertising are brief in form and therefore rely on the expanded meanings that figurative language can supply to deliver their message. And we must be critically armed to defend ourselves against the sometimes manipulative messages that advertising delivers. (See Critical Thinking as Self-Defense in Chapter 1.) As the following ad for Mercedes Benz indicates, the advertising industry knows that visual symbols are a powerful means of communication.

The peace sign. The happy face. The four-leaf clover.

Glimpse at them for a split second, and you know exactly what they mean. Because right behind every powerful icon lies a powerful idea.

A little over a century ago, we set out with what we considered to be some pretty powerful ideas:

Build cars to be fast. (We set land speed records that would last for half a century.)

Safe. (Developments in crumple zones, antilock brakes, and restraint systems have helped make all cars safer.)

Innovative. (The pioneering spirit that drove Karl Benz to patent the first three-wheel motor carriage still guides everything we do today.)

And, just as important, beautiful. (Museums throughout the world have placed our cars in their permanent collections.)

Our symbol has stood for all of these things for over a hundred years.

We look forward to the next.

What makes a symbol endure?

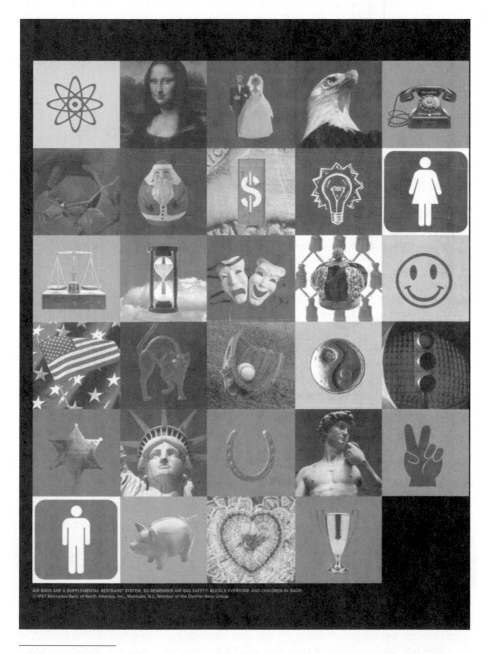

TOPIC FOR DISCUSSION AND WRITING

> As a class, identify each of the images, first in its literal sense and then in its symbolic sense. Next, as individuals choose the symbol that you find most evocative, the one that most powerfully represents something beyond itself, and write a paragraph or two about this image and what it represents.

Figurative Language in Fiction

Greasy Lake

T. Coraghessan Boyle

Novelist and short story writer T. Coraghessan Boyle did not read a book until he was eighteen. Since that time he has earned a Ph.D. and written three short story collections and five novels. His fiction is known for its outrageous and dark humor, its vigor and energy, and the richness and inventiveness of his language. We find an abundance of figurative language in his work. In "Greasy Lake" he uses similes in particular to reveal his themes as he tells the story of three young men looking for adventure.

There was a time when courtesy and winning ways went out of style, when it was good to be bad, when you cultivated decadence like a taste. We were all dangerous characters then. We wore torn-up leather jackets, slouched around with toothpicks in our mouths, sniffed glue and ether and what somebody claimed was cocaine. When we wheeled our parents' whining station wagons out onto the street we left a patch of rubber half a block long. We drank gin and grape juice, Tango, Thunderbird, and Bali Hai. We were nineteen. We were bad. We read André Gide and struck elaborate poses to show that we didn't give a shit about anything. At night, we went up to Greasy Lake.

Through the center of town, up the strip, past the housing developments and shopping malls, street lights giving way to the thin streaming illumination of the headlights, trees crowding the asphalt in its black unbroken wall: that was the way out to Greasy Lake. The Indians had called it Wakan, a reference to the clarity of its waters. Now it was fetid and murky, the mud banks glittering with broken glass and strewn with beer cans and the charred remains of bonfires. There was a single ravaged island a hundred yards from shore, so stripped of vegetation it looked as if the air force had strafed it. We went up to the lake because everyone went there, because we wanted to snuff the rich scent of possibility on the breeze, watch a girl take off her clothes and plunge into the festering murk, drink beer, smoke pot, howl at the stars, savor the incongruous full-throated roar of rock and roll against the primeval susurrus of frogs and crickets. This was nature.

I was there one night, late, in the company of two dangerous characters. Digby wore a gold star in his right ear and allowed his father to pay his tuition at Cornell; Jeff was thinking of quitting school to become a painter/musician/head-shop proprietor. They were both expert in the social graces, quick with a sneer, able to manage a Ford with lousy shocks over a rutted and gutted blacktop road at eighty-five while rolling a joint as compact as a Tootsie Roll Pop stick. They could lounge against a bank of booming speakers and trade "man"s with the best of them or roll out across the dance floor as if their joints worked on bearings. They were slick and quick and they wore their mirror shades at breakfast and dinner, in the shower, in closets and caves. In short, they were bad.

I drove. Digby pounded the dashboard and shouted along with Toots & the Maytals while Jeff hung his head out the window and streaked the side of my mother's Bel Air with vomit. It was early June, the air soft as a hand on your cheek, the third night of summer vacation. The first two nights we'd been out till dawn, looking for something we never found. On this, the third night, we'd cruised the strip sixty-seven times, been in and out of every bar and club we could think of in a twenty-mile radius, stopped twice for bucket chicken and forty-cent hamburgers, debated going to a party at the house of a girl Jeff's sister knew, and chucked two dozen raw eggs at mailboxes and hitchhikers. It was 2:00 A.M.; the bars were closing. There was nothing to do but take a bottle of lemon-flavored gin up to Greasy Lake.

The taillights of a single car winked at us as we swung into the dirt lot with its tufts of weed and washboard corrugations; '57 Chevy, mint, metallic blue. On the far side of the lot, like the exoskeleton of some gaunt chrome insect, a chopper leaned against its kickstand. And that was it for excitement: some junkie half-wit biker and a car freak pumping his girlfriend. Whatever it was we were looking for, we weren't about to find it at Greasy Lake. Not that night.

But then all a sudden Digby was fighting for the wheel. "Hey, that's Tony Lovett's car! Hey!" he shouted, while I stabbed at the brake pedal and the Bel Air nosed up to the gleaming bumper of the parked Chevy. Digby leaned on the horn, laughing, and instructed me to put my brights on. I flicked on the brights. This was hilarious. A joke. Tony would experience premature withdrawal and expect to be confronted by grim-looking state troopers with flashlights. We hit the horn, stopped the lights, and then jumped out of the car to press our witty faces to Tony's windows; for all we knew we might even catch a glimpse of some little fox's tit, and then we could slap backs with red-faced Tony, roughhouse a little, and go on to new heights of adventure and daring.

The first mistake, the one that opened the whole floodgate, was losing my grip on the keys. In the excitement, leaping from the car with the gin in one hand and a roach clip in the other, I spilled them in the grass—in the dark, rank, mysterious nighttime grass of Greasy Lake. This was a tactical error, as damaging and irreversible in its way as Westmoreland's decision to dig in at Khe Sanh. I felt it like a jab of intuition, and I stopped there by the open door, peering vaguely into the night that puddled up round my feet.

The second mistake—and this was inextricably bound up with the first—was identifying the car as Tony Lovett's. Even before the very bad character in greasy jeans and engineer boots ripped out of the driver's door, I began to realize that this chrome blue was much lighter than the robin's-egg of Tony's car, and that Tony's car didn't have rear-mounted speakers. Judging from their expressions,

Digby and Jeff were privately groping toward the same inevitable and unsettling conclusion as I was.

In any case, there was no reasoning with this bad greasy character—clearly he was a man of action. The first lusty Rockette kick of his steel-toed boot caught me under the chin, chipped my favorite tooth, and left me sprawled in the dirt. Like a fool, I'd gone down on one knee to comb the stiff hacked grass for the keys, my mind making connections in the most dragged-out, testudineous way, knowing that things had gone wrong, that I was in a lot of trouble, and that the lost ignition key was my grail and my salvation. The three or four succeeding blows were mainly absorbed by my right buttock and the tough piece of bone at the base of my spine.

Meanwhile, Digby vaulted the kissing bumpers and delivered a savage kung-fu blow to the greasy character's collarbone. Digby had just finished a course in martial arts for phys-ed credit and had spent the better part of the past two nights telling us apocryphal tales of Bruce Lee types and of the raw power invested in lightning blows shot from coiled wrists, ankles, and elbows. The greasy character was unimpressed. He merely backed off a step, his face like a Toltec mask, and laid Digby out with a single whistling roundhouse blow . . . but by now Jeff had got into the act, and I was beginning to extricate myself from the dirt, a tinny compound of shock, rage, and impotence wadded in my throat.

Jeff was on the guy's back, biting at his ear. Digby was on the ground, cursing. I went for the tire iron I kept under the driver's seat. I kept it there because bad characters always keep tire irons under the driver's seat, for just such an occasion as this. Never mind that I hadn't been involved in a fight since sixth grade, when a kid with a sleepy eye and two streams of mucus depending from his nostrils hit me in the knee with a Louisville slugger, never mind that I'd touched the tire iron exactly twice before, to change tires: it was there. And I went for it.

I was terrified. Blood was beating in my ears, my hands were shaking, my heart turning over like a dirtbike in the wrong gear. My antagonist was shirtless, and a single cord of muscle flashed across his chest as he bent forward to peel Jeff from his back like a wet overcoat. "Motherfucker," he spat, over and over, and I was aware in that instant that all four of us—Digby, Jeff, and myself included—were chanting "motherfucker, motherfucker," as if it were a battle cry. (What happened next? the detective asks the murderer from beneath the turned-down brim of his porkpie hat. I don't know, the murderer says, something came over me. Exactly.)

Digby poked the flat of his hand in the bad character's face and I came at him like a kamikaze, mindless, raging, stung with humiliation—the whole thing, from the initial boot in the chin to this murderous primal instant involving no more than sixty hyperventilating, gland-flooding seconds—I came at him and brought the tire iron down across his ear. The effect was instantaneous, astonishing. He was a stunt man and this was Hollywood, he was a big grimacing toothy balloon and I was a man with a straight pin. He collapsed. Wet his pants. Went loose in his boots.

A single second, big as a zeppelin, floated by. We were standing over him in a circle, gritting our teeth, jerking our necks, our limbs and hands and feet twitching with glandular discharges. No one said anything. We just stared down at the guy, the car freak, the lover, the bad greasy character laid low. Digby looked at me; so did Jeff. I was still holding the tire iron, a tuft of hair clinging to the crook like dandelion fluff, like down. Rattled, I dropped it in the dirt, already envisioning the headlines, the pitted faces of the police inquisitors, the gleam of handcuffs, clank of bars, the big black shadows rising from the back of the cell . . . when suddenly a raw torn shriek cut through me like all the juice in all the electric chairs in the country.

It was the fox. She was short, barefoot, dressed in panties and a man's shirt. "Animals!" she screamed, running at us with her fists clenched and wisps of blow-dried hair in her face. There was a silver chain round her ankle, and her toenails flashed in the glare of the headlights. I think it was the toenails that did it. Sure, the gin and the cannabis and even the Kentucky Fried may have had a hand in it, but it was the sight of those flaming toes that set us off—the toad emerging from the loaf in *Virgin Spring,* lipstick smeared on a child; she was already tainted. We were on her like Bergman's deranged brothers—see no evil, hear none, speak none—panting, wheezing, tearing at her clothes, grabbing for flesh. We were bad characters, and we were scared and hot and three steps over the line—anything could have happened.

It didn't.

Before we could pin her to the hood of the car, our eyes masked with lust and greed and the purest primal badness, a pair of headlights swung into the lot. There we were, dirty, bloody, guilty, dissociated from humanity and civilization, the first of the Ur-crimes behind us, the second in progress, shreds of nylon panty and spandex brassiere dangling from our fingers, our flies open, lips licked—there we were, caught in the spotlight. Nailed.

We bolted. First for the car, and then, realizing we had no way of starting at it, for the woods. I thought nothing. I thought escape. The headlights came at me like accusing fingers. I was gone.

Ram-bam-bam, across the parking lot, past the chopper and into the feculent undergrowth at the lake's edge, insects flying up in my face, weeds whipping, frogs and snakes and red-eyed turtles splashing off into the night: I was already ankle-deep in muck and tepid water and still going strong. Behind me, the girl's screams rose in intensity, disconsolate, incriminating, the screams of the Sabine women, the Christian martyrs, Anne Frank dragged from the garret. I kept going, pursued by those cries, imagining cops and bloodhounds. The water was up to my knees when I realized what I was doing: I was going to swim for it. Swim the breadth of Greasy Lake and hide myself in the thick clot of woods on the far side. They'd never find me there.

I was breathing in sobs, in gasps. The water lapped at my waist as I looked out over the moon-burnished ripples, the mats of algae that clung to the surface like scabs. Digby and Jeff had vanished. I paused. Listened. The girl was quieter now, screams tapering to sobs, but there were male voices, angry, excited, and the high-pitched ticking of the second car's engine. I waded deeper, stealthy, hunted, the ooze sucking at my sneakers. As I was about to take the plung—at the very instant I dropped my shoulder for the first slashing stroke—I blundered into something. Something uspeakable, obscene, something soft, wet, moss-grown. A patch of weed? A log? When I reached out to touch it, it gave like a rubber duck, it gave like flesh.

In one of those nasty little epiphanies for which we are prepared by films and TV and childhood visits to the funeral home to ponder the shrunken painted forms of dead grandparents, I understood what it was that bobbed there so inadmissably in the dark. Understood, and stumbled back in horror and revulsion, my mind yanked in six different directions (I was nineteen, a mere child, an infant, and here in the space of five minutes I'd struck down one greasy character and blundered into the waterlogged carcass of a second), thinking, The keys, the keys, why did I have to go and lose the keys? I stumbled back, but the muck took hold of my feet—a sneaker snagged, balance lost—and suddenly I was pitching face forward into the buoyant black mass, throwing out my hands in desperation while simulatneously conjuring the image of reeking frogs and muskrats revolving in slicks of their own deliquescing juices. AAAAArrrgh! I shot from the water like a torpedo, the dead man rotating to expose a mossy beard and eyes cold as the moon. I must have shouted out, thrashing around in the weeds, because the voices behind me suddenly became animated.

"What was that?"

"It's them, it's them: they tried to, tried to . . . *rape* me!" Sobs.

A man's voice, flat Midwestern accent. "You sons a bitches, we'll kill you!"

Frogs, crickets.

Then another voice, harsh, *r*-less, Lower East Side: "Motherfucker!" I recognized the verbal virtuosity of the bad greasy character in the engineer boots. Tooth chipped, sneakers gone, coated in mud and slime and worse, crouching breathless in the weeds waiting to have my ass thoroughly and definitively kicked and fresh from the hideous stinking embrace of a three-days-dead-corpse, I suddenly felt a rush of joy and vindication: the son of a bitch was alive! Just as quickly, my bowels turned to ice. "Come on out of there, you pansy mothers!" the bad greasy character was screaming. He shouted curses till he was out of breath.

The crickets started up again, then the frogs. I held my breath. All at once was a sound in the reeds, a swishing, a splash: thunk-a-thunk. They were throwing rocks. The frogs fell silent. I cradled my head. Swish, swish, thunk- a-thunk. A wedge of feldspar the size of a cue ball glanced off my knee. I bit my finger.

It was then that they turned to the car. I heard a door slam, a curse, and then the sound of the headlights shattering—almost a good-natured sound, celebratory, like corks popping from the necks of bottles. This was succeeded by the dull booming of the fenders, metal on metal, and then the icy crash of the windshield. I inched forward, elbows and knees, my belly pressed to the muck, thinking of guerrillas and commandos and *The Naked and the Dead*. I parted the weeds and squinted the length of the parking lot.

The second car—It was a Trans-Am—was still running, its high beams washing the scene, in a lurid stagy light. Tire iron flailing, the greasy bad character was laying into the side of my mother's Bel Air like an avenging demon, his shadow riding up the trunks of the trees. Whomp. Whomp. Whomp-whomp. The other two guys—blond types, in fraternity jackets—were helping out with tree branches and skull-sized boulders. One of them was gathering up bottles, rocks, muck, candy wrappers, used condoms, poptops, and other refuse and pitching it through the window on the driver's side. I could see the fox, a white bulb behind the windshield of the '57 Chevy. "Bobbie," she whined over the thumping, "come on." The greasy character paused a moment, took one good swipe at the left taillight, and then heaved the tire iron halfway across the lake. Then he fired up the '57 and was gone.

Blond head nodded at blond head. One said something to the other, too low for me to catch. They were no doubt thinking that in helping to annihilate my mother's car they'd committed a fairly rash act, and thinking too that there were three bad characters connected with that very car watching them from the woods. Perhaps other possibilities occurred to them as well—police, jail cells, justices of the peace, reparations, lawyers, irate parents, fraternal censure. Whatever they were thinking, they suddenly dropped branches, bottles, and rocks and sprang for their car in unison, as if they'd choreographed it. Five seconds. That's all it took. The engine shrieked, the tires squealed, a cloud of dust rose from the rutted lot and then settled back on darkness.

I don't know how long I lay there, the bad breath of decay all around me, my jacket heavy as a bear, the primordial ooze subtly reconstituting itself to accommodate my upper thighs and testicles. My jaws ached, my knee throbbed, my coccyx was on fire. I contemplated suicide, wondered if I'd need bridge-work, scraped the recesses of my brain for some sort of excuse to give my parents—a tree had fallen on the car, I was blinded by a bread truck, hit and run, vandals had got to it while we were playing chess at Digby's. Then I thought of the dead man. He was probably the only person on the planet worse off than I was. I thought about him, fog on the lake, insects chirring eerily, and felt the tug of fear, felt the darkness opening up inside me like a set of jaws. Who was he, I wondered, this victim of time and circumstance bobbing sorrowfully in the lake at my back? The owner of the chopper, no doubt, a bad older character come to this. Shot during a murky drug deal, drowned while drunkenly frolicking in the lake. Another headline. My car was wrecked; he was dead.

When the eastern half of the sky went from black to cobalt and the trees began to separate themselves from the shadows, I pushed myself up from the muck and stepped out into the open. By now the birds had begun to take over for the crickets, and dew lay slick on the leaves. There was a smell in the air, raw and sweet at the same time, the smell of the sun firing buds and opening blossoms. I contemplated the car. It lay there like a wreck along the highway, like a steel sculpture left over from a vanished civilization. Everything was still. This was nature.

I was circling the car, as dazed and bedraggled as the sole survivor of an army blitz, when Digby and Jeff emerged from the trees behind me. Digby's face was crosshatched with smears of dirt; Jeff's jacket was gone and his shirt was torn across the shoulder. They slouched across the lot, looking sheepish and silently came up beside me to gape at the ravaged automobile. No one said a word. After a while Jeff swung open the driver's door and began to scoop the broken glass and garbage off the seat. I looked at Digby. He shrugged. "At least they didn't slash the tires," he said.

It was true: the tires were intact. These was no windshield, the headlights were staved in, and the body looked as if it had been sledge-hammered for a quarter a shot at the county fair, but the tires were inflated to regulation pressure. The car was drivable. In silence, all three of us bent to scrape the mud and shattered glass from the interior. I said nothing about the biker. When we were finished I reached in my pocket for the keys, experienced a nasty stab of recollection, cursed myself, and turned to search the grass. I spotted them almost immediately, not more than five feet from the open door, glinting like jewels in the first taperish shaft of sunlight. There was no reason to get philosophical about it: I eased into the seat and turned the engine over.

It was at that precise moment that the silver Mustang with the flame decals rumbled into the lot. All three of us froze; then Digby and Jeff slid into the car and slammed the door. We watched as the Mustang rocked and bobbed across the ruts and finally jerked to a halt beside the forlorn chopper at the far end of the lot. "Let's go," Digby said. I hesitated, the Bel Air wheezing beneath me.

Two girls emerged from the Mustang. Tight jeans, stiletto heels, hair like frozen fur. They bent over the motorcycle, paced back and forth aimlessly, glanced once or twice at us, and then ambled over to where the reeds sprang up in a grey fence round the perimeter of the lake. One of them cupped her hands to her mouth: "Al," she called. "Hey, Al!"

"Come on," Digby hissed, "Let's get out of here."

But it was too late. The second girl was picking her way across the lot, unsteady on her heels, looking up at us and then away. She was older—twenty-five or six—and as she came closer we could see there was something wrong with her: she was stoned or drunk, lurching now and waving her arms for balance. I gripped the steering wheel as if it were the ejection lever of a flaming jet, and Digby spat out my name, twice, terse and impatient.

"Hi," the girl said.

We looked at her like zombies, like war veterans, like deaf-and-dumb pencil peddlers.

She smiled, her lips cracked and dry. "Listen," she said, bending from the waist to look in the window, "you guys seen Al?" Her pupils were pinpoints, her eyes glass. She jerked her neck. "That's his bike over there—Al's. You seen him?"

Al. I didn't know what to say. I wanted to get out of the car and retch, I wanted to go home to my parents' house and crawl into bed. Digby poked me in the ribs. "We haven't seen anybody," I said.

The girl seemed to consider this, reaching out a slim veiny arm to brace herself against the car. "No matter," she said, slurring the t's, "he'll turn up." And then, as if she'd just taken stock of the whole scene—the ravaged car and our battered faces, the desolation of the place—she said: "Hey, you guys look like some pretty bad characters—been fightin', huh?" We stared straight ahead, rigid as catatonics. She was fumbling in her pocket and muttering something. Finally she held out a handful of tablets in glassine wrappers: "Hey, you want to party, you want to do some of these with me and Sarah?"

I just looked at her. I thought I was going to cry. Digby broke the silence. "No, thanks," he said, leaning over me. "Some other time."

I put the car in gear and it inched forward with a groan, shaking off pellets of glass like an old dog shedding water after a bath, heaving over the ruts on its worn springs, creeping toward the highway. There was a sheen of sun on the lake. I looked back. The girl was still standing there, watching us, her shoulders slumped, hand outstretched.

TOPICS FOR DISCUSSION AND WRITING

1. Characterize the narrator and his two friends, Digby and Jeff. What kind of young men are they? Are they as "bad" as they think they are?

2. The phrase "This was nature" appears twice in the story, at the beginning and toward the end. How does the narrator's view of nature change? How do you account for the this change?

3. How does the young men's encounter with the two girls at the end of the story differ from their earlier encounter with the girl from the blue Chevy? How do you account for the difference?

4. Does the narrator change during the course of his evening at Greasy Lake? If so, what is the nature of the change and what causes it?

5. What role does the setting of Greasy Lake play in this story? Cite specific examples.

6. List as many examples of figurative language as you can find. (This might be fun to do as a class.) Then analyze them carefully. What patterns and categories do you find emerging from your list? How do they illuminate certain themes in the story?

7. Write an essay discussing how the figurative language reveals the theme of the story.

Language and Meaning—Concluding Topics

For the first of the concluding topics of this section, we ask you to read (or reread) David Mamet's *Oleanna* (see page 513) and to apply some of the themes covered in this chapter, *Language and Meaning* to the play.

1. You and your classmates will have different readings of *Oleanna*. In fact, as a contemporary playwright, Mamet intends for his audience to arrive at conflicting interpretations. Taking a page from hyperfiction, write a fourth act for *Oleanna* which illustrates your interpretation of the play. Reading these fourth acts aloud to the class would be a creative way to share your different interpretations of the play.

2. Choose a country in which the languages spoken are cause for political discontent—both Canada and the United States have had intensely debated ballot issues concerning language—and write a paper in which you fully explore the issue and form an opinion on how it might be resolved. (See Writing Assignment 11 on page 118 for help with this topic.)

TEXT CREDITS

Tom Abate, "Two Groups on Verge of Reading the Entire Human Gene Code," *San Francisco Chronicle,* April 28, 2000. Copyright © 2000. Reprinted by permission of Copyright Clearance Center.

Sharon Begley and Claudia Kalb, "Learning Right From Wrong," *Newsweek,* March 13, 2000. Copyright © 2000 Newsweek, Inc. All rights reserved. Reprinted by permission.

William Bennett, "Leave Marriage Alone," *Newsweek,* June 3, 1996. © 1996 Newsweek, Inc. All rights reserved. Reprinted by permission.

Sven Birkets, Chapter 6 from *The Gutenberg Elegies,* Farrar, Straus & Giroux. Copyright © 1994.

"Greasy Lake," from *Greasy Lake and Other Stories* by T. Coraghessan Boyle. Copyright © 1979, 1981, 1982, 1983, 1984, 1985 by T. Coraghessan Boyle. Used by permission of Viking Penguin, a division of Penguin Putnam, Inc.

Frank Browning, "Why Marry?" *The New York Times,* April 17, 1996. Copyright © 1996 by The New York Times Company. Reprinted by permission.

John Brunch, Letter To the Editor, response to "How Colleges Are Gouging You," *Time* magazine.

"Five Good Reasons to Oppose the Vouchers Initiative," California Teachers Association/NEA, Coalition to Educate Against Vouchers, Revised 29.VII.93.

Lowell Cohn, "Boxing, Doctors—Round Two" *San Francisco Chronicle,* July 24, 1988. © 1988. Reprinted by permission of Copyright Clearance Center.

Robert Coover, "The End of Books," *The New York Times,* June 21, 1992.

"Totleigh Riddles" by John Cotton from the *Times Literary Supplement,* July 24, 1981. Reprinted by permission of the author.

Meghan Daum, "Virtual Love" Reprinted by permission of International Creative Management. Copyright © 1997 Meghan Daum.

Excerpt from *Dialects.* From *The New York Times,* September 12, 1999. Copyright © 2000 The New York Times Company. Reprinted by permission.

"Dispute Over Claims of Ibuprofen Dangers." Copyright © 1990 by United Press International. Reprinted by permission of United Press International.

"Drawing Logical Inferences," Copyright © 1999 Time, Inc. Reprinted by permission.

Tony Early, "The Gene Quary," *The New Yorker,* September 21, 1998.

Barbara Ehrenreich, "Getting Off Easy in Tobacco Land," *Time,* July 14, 1997. © 1997 Time, Inc. Reprinted by permission.

"To Clone or Not to Clone" by Jean Bethke Elshtain. Copyright © 1998 by Jean Bethke Elshtain, from *Clones and Clones: Facts and Fantasies About Human Cloning* by Martha C. Nussbaum and Cass R. Sunstein. Used by permission of W.W. Norton & Company, Inc.

"What Are the Rules?" from *The Rules* by Ellen Fein and Sherrie Schneider. Copyright © 1995 by Ellen Fein and Sherrie Schneider. By permission of Warner Books.

INDEX